Handbook of Research on Artificial Intelligence Applications in Literary Works and Social Media

Pantea Keikhosrokiani
School of Computer Sciences, Universiti Sains Malaysia, Malaysia

Moussa Pourya Asl
School of Humanities, Universiti Sains Malaysia, Malaysia

A volume in the Advances in Computational
Intelligence and Robotics (ACIR) Book Series

Published in the United States of America by
 IGI Global
 Engineering Science Reference (an imprint of IGI Global)
 701 E. Chocolate Avenue
 Hershey PA, USA 17033
 Tel: 717-533-8845
 Fax: 717-533-8661
 E-mail: cust@igi-global.com
 Web site: http://www.igi-global.com

                        Library of Congress Cataloging-in-Publication Data

Names: Keikhosrokiani, Pantea, DATE- editor. | Pourya Asl, Moussa, DATE-
 editor.
Title: Handbook of research on artificial intelligence applications in literary
 works and social media / Pantea Keikhosrokiani, and Moussa Pourya Asl, editors.
Description: Hershey, PA : Engineering Science Reference, [2023] | Includes
 bibliographical references and index. | Summary: "This handbook presents
 contemporary developments in the adoption of artificial intelligence in
 textual analysis of literary works and social media, introducing current
 approaches, techniques, and practices in data science that are
 implemented to scrap and analyze text data"-- Provided by publisher.
Identifiers: LCCN 2022039793 (print) | LCCN 2022039794 (ebook) | ISBN
 9781668462423 (hardcover) | ISBN 9781668462447 (ebook)
Subjects: LCSH: Text processing (Computer science) | Content analysis
 (Communication)--Data processing. | Social media--Data processing. |
 Literature--Data processing. | Artificial intelligence. | Data mining. |
 Big data.
Classification: LCC QA76.9.T48 A78 2023 (print) | LCC QA76.9.T48 (ebook)
 | DDC 005.52--dc23/eng/20220915
LC record available at https://lccn.loc.gov/2022039793
LC ebook record available at https://lccn.loc.gov/2022039794

This book is published in the IGI Global book series Advances in Computational Intelligence and Robotics (ACIR) (ISSN:
2327-0411; eISSN: 2327-042X)

British Cataloguing in Publication Data
A Cataloguing in Publication record for this book is available from the British Library.

All work contributed to this book is new, previously-unpublished material. The views expressed in this book are those of the
authors, but not necessarily of the publisher.

For electronic access to this publication, please contact: eresources@igi-global.com.

Advances in Computational Intelligence and Robotics (ACIR) Book Series

Ivan Giannoccaro
University of Salento, Italy

ISSN:2327-0411
EISSN:2327-042X

MISSION

While intelligence is traditionally a term applied to humans and human cognition, technology has progressed in such a way to allow for the development of intelligent systems able to simulate many human traits. With this new era of simulated and artificial intelligence, much research is needed in order to continue to advance the field and also to evaluate the ethical and societal concerns of the existence of artificial life and machine learning.

The **Advances in Computational Intelligence and Robotics (ACIR) Book Series** encourages scholarly discourse on all topics pertaining to evolutionary computing, artificial life, computational intelligence, machine learning, and robotics. ACIR presents the latest research being conducted on diverse topics in intelligence technologies with the goal of advancing knowledge and applications in this rapidly evolving field.

COVERAGE

- Algorithmic Learning
- Intelligent Control
- Heuristics
- Agent technologies
- Cyborgs
- Robotics
- Fuzzy Systems
- Machine Learning
- Artificial Life
- Computational Logic

IGI Global is currently accepting manuscripts for publication within this series. To submit a proposal for a volume in this series, please contact our Acquisition Editors at Acquisitions@igi-global.com or visit: http://www.igi-global.com/publish/.

Titles in this Series

For a list of additional titles in this series, please visit: www.igi-global.com/book-series/advances-computational-intelligence-robotics/73674

Convergence of Deep Learning and Internet of Things Computing and Technology
T. Kavitha (New Horizon College of Engineering (Autonomous), India & Visvesvaraya Technological University, India) G. Senbagavalli (AMC Engineering College, Visvesvaraya Technological University, India) Deepika Koundal (University of Petroleum and Energy Studies, Dehradun, India) Yanhui Guo (University of Illinois, USA) and Deepak Jain (Chongqing University of Posts and Telecommunications, China)
Engineering Science Reference • © 2023 • 349pp • H/C (ISBN: 9781668462751) • US $270.00

Multi-Disciplinary Applications of Fog Computing Responsiveness in Real-Time
Debi Prasanna Acharjya (Vellore Institute of Technology, India) and P. Ahmed Kauser (Vellore Institute of Technology, India)
Engineering Science Reference • © 2023 • 300pp • H/C (ISBN: 9781668444665) • US $270.00

Deep Learning Research Applications for Natural Language Processing
L. Ashok Kumar (PSG College of Technology, India) Dhanaraj Karthika Renuka (PSG College of Technology, India) and S. Geetha (Vellore Institute of Technology, India)
Engineering Science Reference • © 2023 • 290pp • H/C (ISBN: 9781668460016) • US $270.00

Controlling Epidemics With Mathematical and Machine Learning Models
Abraham Varghese (University of Technology and Applied Sciences, Muscat, Oman) Eduardo M. Lacap, Jr. (University of Technology and Applied Sciences, Muscat, Oman) Ibrahim Sajath (University of Technology and Applied Sciences, Muscat, Oman) M. Kamal Kumar (University of Technology and Applied Sciences, Muscat, Oman) and Shajidmon Kolamban (University of Technology and Applied Sciences, Muscat, Oman)
Engineering Science Reference • © 2023 • 269pp • H/C (ISBN: 9781799883432) • US $270.00

Handbook of Research on Computer Vision and Image Processing in the Deep Learning Era
A. Srinivasan (SASTRA University (Deemed), India)
Engineering Science Reference • © 2023 • 440pp • H/C (ISBN: 9781799888925) • US $325.00

Multidisciplinary Applications of Deep Learning-Based Artificial Emotional Intelligence
Chiranji Lal Chowdhary (Vellore Institute of Technology, India)
Engineering Science Reference • © 2023 • 296pp • H/C (ISBN: 9781668456736) • US $270.00

701 East Chocolate Avenue, Hershey, PA 17033, USA
Tel: 717-533-8845 x100 • Fax: 717-533-8661
E-Mail: cust@igi-global.com • www.igi-global.com

List of Contributors

Table of Contents

Section 3
Artificial Intelligence for the Analytics of Social Media

Detailed Table of Contents

Section 1
Introduction

Pantea Keikhosrokiani, School of Computer Sciences, Universiti Sains Malaysia, Malaysia
Moussa Pourya Asl, School of Humanities, Universiti Sains Malaysia, Malaysia

Advancement of artificial intelligence has opened new horizons for the analytics of literary texts and social media. However, the current studies are very limited, and there is still need for further scholarships that use AI applications to analyze literary works and social media texts. After presenting a working definition of certain key terms in the background section of the study, this chapter offers a detailed review of related studies that have employed artificial intelligence in the analysis of texts. Next, the chapter delineates AI-narrative architecture as a proposed nine-phase method to demonstrate the steps for the analytics of literary texts and social media. Finally, the discussion focuses on the new applications and findings, which are presented in 13 different studies that are included in this volume.

Section 2
Artificial Intelligence for the Analytics of Literary Works

Nurul Najiha Jafery, Centre for Electrical Engineering Studies, Universiti Teknologi MARA, Malaysia
Pantea Keikhosrokiani, School of Computer Sciences, Universiti Sains Malaysia, Malaysia
Moussa Pourya Asl, School of Humanities, Universiti Sains Malaysia, Malaysia

Recently, the revolutionary transformations in social and political landscapes as well as the remarkable developments in artificial intelligence reinforced the importance of geography and spatial analyses in literary and cultural studies. This chapter proposes an analytical framework of topic modelling and sentiment analysis for exploring the connection between theme, place, and sentiment in 36 autobiographical narratives by or about women from the Middle East. In the proposed framework, a latent Dirichlet allocation and latent semantic analysis algorithm from topic modelling, TextBlob library for sentiment analysis are employed to detect the place names that come together and to point out the associated themes and emotions throughout the data source. The model gives a scoring of each topical clusters and reveals that the diasporic authors are more likely to write about their hometown than their current host land. The authors hope that the merging of topic modelling and sentiment analysis would be beneficial to literary critics in the analysis of long texts.

Abdikadir Hussein Elmi, School of Computer Sciences, Universiti Sains Malaysia, Malaysia
Pantea Keikhosrokiani, School of Computer Sciences, Universiti Sains Malaysia, Malaysia
Moussa Pourya Asl, School of Humanities, Universiti Sains Malaysia, Malaysia

Over the past two decades, literary works from Afghanistan have sought to depict the extensive and increasing level of violence directed against individuals and communities. This study aims to identify the different types of violence represented in selected literary works from the country. To this end, an artificial intelligence approach—comprised of opinion mining and hybrid machine learning models—is developed as a method of analysis. The Afghan American writer Khaled Hosseini's novels—The Kite Runner (2003), A Thousand Splendid Suns (2007), and And the Mountains Echoed (2017)—are used as primary data sources. As a theoretical framework, the study benefits from the Norwegian sociologist Johan Galtung's theory of conflict triangle—direct violence, structural violence, and cultural violence. To classify the sentiments related to types of violence in the selected novels, the study utilizes sentiment analysis and machine learning algorithms.

Pantea Keikhosrokiani, School of Computer Sciences, Universiti Sains Malaysia, Malaysia
Moussa Pourya Asl, School of Humanities, Universiti Sains Malaysia, Malaysia
Kah Em Chu, School of Computer Sciences, Universiti Sains Malaysia, Malaysia
Nur Ain Nasuha Anuar, School of Humanities, Universiti Sains Malaysia, Malaysia

In recent years, South-Asian literature in English has experienced a surge of newfound love and popularity both in the local and the global market. In this regard, Arundhati Roy's The God of Small Things (1997) has garnered an astounding mix of positive and negative reactions from readers across the globe. This chapter adopts an artificial intelligence approach to analyse netizen readers' feedback on the novel as documented in the book cataloguing website Goodreads. To this end, an opinion mining framework is proposed based on artificial intelligence techniques such as topic modelling and sentiment analysis. Latent semantic analysis (LSA) and latent Dirichlet allocation (LDA) are applied and compared to find the abstract "topics" that occur in a collection of reviews. Furthermore, lexicon-based sentiment analysis approaches such as Vader and Textblob algorithms are used and compared to find the review sentiment polarities.

Chapter 5

Artificial Intelligence Applications in Literary Works: Emotion Extraction and Classification of
Mohsin Hamid's *Moth Smoke*

Annuur Farahhim Zainol, School of Computer Sciences, Universiti Sains Malaysia, Malaysia
Pantea Keikhosrokiani, School of Computer Sciences, Universiti Sains Malaysia, Malaysia
Moussa Pourya Asl, School of Humanities, Universiti Sains Malaysia, Malaysia
Nur Ain Nasuha Anuar, School of Humanities, Universiti Sains Malaysia, Malaysia

The British Pakistani writer, Mohsin Hamid's debut novel, Moth Smoke (2000), has garnered conflicting responses from readers across the globe. Over the past few years and with the rapid advancements in social media platforms, readers around the world have publicly shared their opinions and feelings towards the text using online platforms such as Twitter, Goodreads, Facebook—among many others. The huge bulk of readers' reviews are useful data for publishers and booksellers in analyzing readers' interests to recommend similar texts to online readers. The analysis of sentiment and emotion attached to this data can help to determine the popularity or unpopularity of a literary text. Using reader-reviews of Hamid's novel from Goodreads as the main data source, this study a offers a data analytic approach: LSTM, LDA to detect and classify the dominant emotion existing within the readers' feedback. Understanding readers' emotions towards the novel can help in developing a recommendation system that can suggest readers stories of their interest.

Chapter 6

Artificial Intelligence and Human Rights Activism: A Case Study of Boochani's *No Friend But the Mountains* and His Tweets on Justice and Equality

Chun Keat Kng, School of Computer Sciences, Universiti Sains Malaysia, Malaysia
Pantea Keikhosrokiani, School of Computer Sciences, Universiti Sains Malaysia, Malaysia
Moussa Pourya Asl, School of Humanities, Universiti Sains Malaysia, Malaysia

Behrouz Boochani, the Kurdish-Iranian author of No Friends But the Mountains, has been using social media platforms such as Twitter to speak up against social injustice and human rights abuse against immigrants across the globe. This study proposes an artificial intelligence lifecycle for opinion mining of the dominant sentiments, topics, and emotions in Boochani's social media activism. Sentiment analysis (Vader and Textblob), topic modelling (LDA and NMF), and emotion detection are performed to extract hidden sentiments, topics, and emotions from the data that is collected from his tweets from 2017-2021. The results show Vader performs better than Textblob. LDA is considered the best algorithm. It extracted seven main topics as suicide, translator of book, publication of book, human rights, political, immigration, and detention. Finally, the main emotion detected from the tweets is sadness.

Chapter 7

Advanced Replicating Technology in Adventure Fiction: The Philosophical Implications of
Material Synthesizer in *The Orville*

Alexandria S. Zlatar, University of Glasgow, UK

In the adventure fiction and Sci-Fi TV show The Orville (2017), a material synthesizer is a machine that can create food, drink, clothing, and so much more. While the device in the show has a small role, the implications of unrestricted material access have vast effects on the cast and real-world implications on our identities as well. The framework of this chapter focuses on a qualitative and case study analysis of literary and film-based narrative to examine the implications of material synthesis in The Orville. It examines the plot element and expounds upon the impact on unrestricted indulgence, potential corruption, and the ability to create more freedom both for the characters and the show itself. Upon this analysis, the chapter concludes that while the device is incredibly far from a practical achievement, it does lead us to analyze how current food generators and 3D printers have the potential for unrestricted powers that need to be examined and better understood in order to prevent misuse and exploitation.

Section 3
Artificial Intelligence for the Analytics of Social Media

Chapter 8

This chapter aims at discussing how social media intelligence (SOCMINT) can be and has been applied to the field of criminal justice. SOCMINT is composed of a set of computer forensic techniques used for intelligence gathering on social media platforms. Through this chapter, readers will be able to better understand what SOCMINT is and how it may be helpful for criminal investigation and national security. Different aspects of SOCMINT are addressed, including application in criminal justice, intelligence gathering, monitoring, metadata, cyber profiling, social network analysis, tools, and privacy concerns. Further, the challenges and future research directions are discussed as well. This chapter is not meant to serve as a technical tutorial as the focus is on the concepts rather than the techniques.

Chapter 9

Of late, text and sentiment analysis have become essential parts of modern marketing. These play a vital role in the division of natural language processing (NLP). It mainly focuses on text classification to examine the intention of the processed text; it can be of positive or negative types. Sentiment analysis dealt with the computational treatment of sentiments, opinions, and subjectivity of text. This chapter tackles a comprehensive approach for the past research solutions that includes various algorithms, enhancements, and applications. This chapter primarily focuses on three aspects. Firstly, the authors present a systematic review of recent works done in the area of text and sentiment analysis; second, they emphasize major concepts, components, functionalities, and classification techniques of text and sentiment analysis. Finally, they provide a comparative study of text and sentiment analysis on the basis of trending research approaches. They conclude the chapter with future directions.

Chapter 10

Affective polarization is a phenomenon that has invaded the political arena empowered by social networks. In this chapter, the authors analyze the Capitol riot posts on Twitter. To achieve this, the authors use affective computing introducing the multi-emotional charge combined with statistical analysis based on the t-student test and Welch's t-test. The research questions guiding this study are: How do social media platforms' messages impact on inciting? Do social media platforms' messages with negative emotional charge affect legitimizing of the Capitol protest? Findings identify the significant influence of Donald Trump on Twitter during the Capitol riot. Moreover, data analysis identifies positive and negative emotions towards Donald Trump as well as similarities in the showed emotions of Trump and the audience.

Chapter 11

    Marilyn Minicucci Ibañez, National Institute for Space Research, Brazil
    Reinaldo Roberto Rosa, National Institute for Space Research, Brazil
    Lamartine Nogueira Frutuoso Guimarães, Technological Institute of Aeronautics, Brazil

The growing cases of armed conflicts over the past couple of decades have dramatically affected social landscapes and people's lives across the globe, urging everyone to find ways to minimize the negative consequences of the conflicts. Social media provides an inexhaustible data source that can be used in understanding the evolution of such conflicts. This chapter focuses on Syria-USA and Iran-USA relations to presents an approach to armed conflict analysis and examines the Russia-Ukraine conflicts by performing sentiment analysis on the text dataset as well as on a vocabulary data. All conflicts generate a social media news threat time series (TTS) that is used as input to the P-model algorithm to generate the endogenous time series. The following uses the TTS and endogenous time series for both conflicts as input to the deep-learning-LSTM neural network. Finally, this chapter compares the prediction result of the Russia-Ukraine TTS analysis with the Russia-Ukraine endogenous series using the P-model algorithm.

Chapter 12

    Syed Asif Ali, Department of Artificial Intelligence and Mathematical Sciences, Sindh
      Madressatul Islam University, Karachi, Pakistan

The special-needs individuals have their own literary system called Braille for printing, reading, and writing since 1824 that assist them in easily connecting with each other. Because of the isolated education system, formally called the heterogeneous education system, they faced a lot of problems and challenges from society. Artificial intelligence tools and techniques play a vital role in mitigating communication gap between blind/visually impaired individuals and non-blind people. Thus, this chapter focuses on reviewing artificial intelligence techniques to understand Braille for normal people associated with visual imperative individuals. It is found that natural language processing (NLP) helps in translating native language into Braille. Machine learning and artificial neural network algorithms help in translating by matching the equivalent pattern of Braille. The concept of finite automata is used with natural language processing to recognize and convert the Braille pattern equivalent to their native language pattern and vice versa.

Sylvia Shiau Ching Wong, School of Computer Sciences, Universiti Sains Malaysia,
Malaysia
Jing-Ru Tan, School of Computer Sciences, Universiti Sains Malaysia, Malaysia
Keng Hoon Gan, School of Computer Sciences, Universiti Sains Malaysia, Malaysia
Tien Ping Tan, School of Computer Sciences, Universiti Sains Malaysia, Malaysia

Widespread online misinformation that aims to convince vaccine-hesitant populations continues to threaten healthcare systems globally. Assessing features of online content including topics and sentiments against vaccines could help curb the spread of vaccine-related misinformation and allow stakeholders to draft better regulations and public policies. Using a public dataset extracted from Reddit, the authors performed text analytics including sentiment analysis, N-gram, and topic modeling to grasp the sentiments, the most popular phrases (N-grams), and topics of the subreddit. The sentiment analysis results revealed mostly positive sentiments in the subreddit's discussions. The N-gram analysis identified "cause autism" and "MMR cause autism" as the most frequent bigram and trigram. The NMF topic modeling results revealed five topics discussing different aspects of vaccines. These findings implied the significance of the ability to assess public confidence and sentiment from social media platforms to enable effective responses against the proliferation of vaccine misinformation.

Noman Islam, Karachi Institute of Economics and Technology, Pakistan
Muntaha Mehboob, NED University, Pakistan
Rimsha Javed, Mohammad Ali Jinnah University, Pakistan

Twitter is a leading social networking site when it comes down to topics such as politics, news, and trends around the globe. Another main reason for people to use Twitter is because they are able to share their emotions and feelings with others and form new relationships and views. With about 330 million users on Twitter (in 2020), it continues to rapidly grow, but at the same time, it is also losing users at a fast pace. In 2019, Twitter had 340 million users, but a year later, it lost 10 million of them. The goal of this chapter is to find the reasons of three questions. The first, to find the reason behind Twitter losing its users. The second, to see how a user changes behavior after usage of Twitter, and third, how a user's behavior changes when expanding his/her social circle on Twitter. For all of these questions, this chapter has designed a data set and executed experiments based on the authors' hypotheses. The results report the accuracies of each of these hypotheses.

Preface

INTRODUCTION

Scholars from various fields such as literary studies and social sciences have realized how crucial people's responses, feelings, and reactions are to commercial success or failure of an idea, a book, or a product. Previous research has indicated that publishers, bookstores, and sponsoring organizations are increasingly concerned about readers' emotions and reactions to literary works for marketing and award-giving purposes (Keikhosrokiani & Asl, 2022; Paremeswaran et al., 2022). The way books are published, distributed, purchased, read, and reviewed have been significantly altered by the fast expansion of the publishing industry as well as the introduction of online and social media platforms. On the one hand, the requirement for large publishing firms to serve as the intermediary between the author and the reader has been significantly reduced since the advent of the digital era in the closing decades of the twentieth century. For instance, the rise of internet-based self-publishing platforms has made it possible for both fiction and non-fiction writers to communicate with their readers and fans directly and share their books with them. Similarly, the proliferation of social media sites like Facebook, Twitter, and social cataloguing websites like Goodreads has given book lovers and readers throughout the world a special chance to interact with one another and express their opinions and sentiments about literary works.

Recent developments in artificial intelligence have emerged as intriguing alternatives to established methods of data gathering and processing. The long-standing problems of subjectivity in the studies of readers' responses to fictional stories and the analyses of literary works have been greatly reduced or removed as a result of the adoption and application of computerized analytical tools. Previous research has examined the topics, locations, characterizations, plot, reader responses, attitudes, and views using techniques like Opinion Mining and Text Analytics approaches like Topic Modelling and Sentiment Analysis (Asri et al., 2022; Fasha et al., 2022; Keikhosrokiani & Asl, 2022; Paremeswaran et al., 2022; Sofian et al., 2022; Suhendra et al., 2022). As more individuals and organizations learn about various usages, applications, and advantages of artificial intelligence, numerous sectors are employing artificial intelligence techniques. The application of artificial intelligence in literary works and social media analysis is a contemporary area of study that needs more attention as there is still a lot of room for advancement. As a result, developments in artificial intelligence are beneficial for many real-world applications, including those related to decision-making and customer service.

Figure 1. A multidisciplinary field initiated by this book

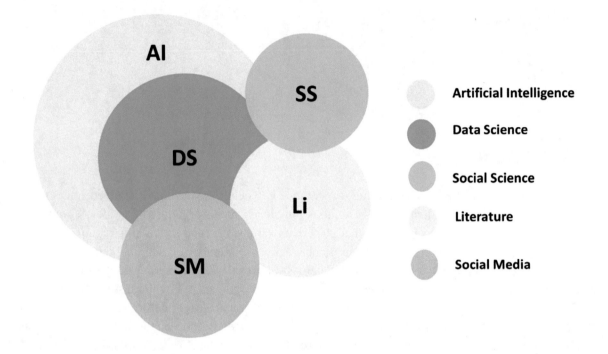

PURPOSE OF THE BOOK

This book initiates a new multidisciplinary field that combines artificial intelligence, data science, social science, literature, and social media study (Figure 1). The book contains chapters that cover a wide range of topics related to emergence, development, and applications of Artificial Intelligences (AI) techniques for text analytics. The chapters cover topics such as Opinion Mining and its use in literary studies (e.g., Topic Modelling, and Thematic analysis), the application of Machine Learning in the study of social media (e.g., Stance Detection, Classification of Emotions, and Sentiment Analysis), and data mining and processing techniques and applications.

ORGANIZATION OF THE BOOK

This book consists of three main sections, which focus on introduction and the use Artificial Intelligence (AI) techniques and applications on literary works and social media respectively. Chapter 1 introduces artificial intelligence for the analytics of literary works and social media. The main goal in this chapter is to present brief background information on the field of study and review the existing body of scholarship related to the central topic of the present volume. Chapter 2 proposes an AI-based model based on topic modelling and sentiment analysis approach for the analytics of theme and space in life writings of middle eastern women. Chapter 3 applies machine learning and sentiment analysis techniques to examine the analytics of representations of violence in Khaled Hosseini's novels. Chapter 4 develops an artificial intelligence framework for opinion mining of Netizen readers' reviews of Arundhati Roy's *The God of Small Things*. Chapter 5 applies AI techniques for the emotion extraction and classification of Mohsin Hamid's *Moth Smoke*. Chapter 6 proposes a data science life cycle for the analytics of Boochani's *No Friend But the Mountains* and his tweets on justice and equality. These chapters are important as the study of South Asian and Middle Eastern literature in English has gained increasing global attention in recent years (Pourya Asl, 2022, 2023). Chapter 7 discusses advanced replicating technology in adventure fiction and includes the philosophical implications of material synthesizer in *The Orville*. Chapter 8 deliberates on social media intelligence, specifically AI applications for criminal investigation and national security studies. Chapter 9 reviews artificial intelligence techniques in text and sentimental analysis. Chapter 10 proposes a model for affective polarization in the United States of America in which multi-emotional charge is analyzed through affective computing. Chapter 11 applies sentiment analysis techniques in social media data about threat of armed conflicts using two times series models. Chapter 12 reviews artificial intelligence techniques to understand the Braille literary for visually imperative individuals. Chapter 13 proposes a text analytics model for the analysis of Vaccine Myths on Reddit. Finally, Chapter 14 uses machine learning for the analytics of users' behaviors on Twitter.

Pantea Keikhosrokiani
School of Computer Sciences, Universiti Sains Malaysia, Malaysia

Moussa Pourya Asl
School of Humanities, Universiti Sains Malaysia, Malaysia

REFERENCES

Asri, M. A. Z. B. M., Keikhosrokiani, P., & Asl, M. P. (2022). *Opinion Mining Using Topic Modeling: A Case Study of Firoozeh Dumas's Funny in Farsi in Goodreads*. Advances on Intelligent Informatics and Computing.

Fasha, E. F. B. K., Keikhosrokiani, P., & Asl, M. P. (2022). Opinion Mining Using Sentiment Analysis: A Case Study of Readers' Response on Long Litt Woon's The Way Through the Woods in Goodreads. Advances on Intelligent Informatics and Computing.

Keikhosrokiani, P., & Asl, M. P. (Eds.). (2022). *Handbook of research on opinion mining and text analytics on literary works and social media*. IGI Global. doi:10.4018/978-1-7998-9594-7

Paremeswaran, P. p., Keikhosrokiani, P., & Asl, M. P. (2022). Opinion Mining of Readers' Responses to Literary Prize Nominees on Twitter: A Case Study of Public Reaction to the Booker Prize (2018–2020). Advances on Intelligent Informatics and Computing.

Pourya Asl, M. (Ed.). (2022). *Gender, place, and identity of South Asian women*. IGI Global. doi:10.4018/978-1-6684-3626-4

Pourya Asl, M. (Ed.). (2023). *Urban poetics and politics in contemporary South Asia and the Middle East*. IGI Global. doi:10.4018/978-1-6684-6650-6

Sofian, N. B., Keikhosrokiani, P., & Asl, M. P. (2022). Opinion mining and text analytics of reader reviews of Yoko Ogawa's The Housekeeper and the Professor in Goodreads. In P. Keikhosrokiani & M. Pourya Asl (Eds.), *Handbook of Research on Opinion Mining and Text Analytics on Literary Works and Social Media* (pp. 240–262). IGI Global. doi:10.4018/978-1-7998-9594-7.ch010

Suhendra, N. H. B., Keikhosrokiani, P., Asl, M. P., & Zhao, X. (2022). Opinion mining and text analytics of literary reader responses: A case study of reader responses to KL Noir volumes in Goodreads using sentiment analysis and topic. In P. Keikhosrokiani & M. Pourya Asl (Eds.), *Handbook of Research on Opinion Mining and Text Analytics on Literary Works and Social Media* (pp. 191–239). IGI Global. doi:10.4018/978-1-7998-9594-7.ch009

Section 1
Introduction

Chapter 1
Introduction to Artificial Intelligence for the Analytics of Literary Works and Social Media:
A Review

Pantea Keikhosrokiani
 https://orcid.org/0000-0003-4705-2732
School of Computer Sciences, Universiti Sains Malaysia, Malaysia

Moussa Pourya Asl
 https://orcid.org/0000-0002-8426-426X
School of Humanities, Universiti Sains Malaysia, Malaysia

ABSTRACT

Advancement of artificial intelligence has opened new horizons for the analytics of literary texts and social media. However, the current studies are very limited, and there is still need for further scholarships that use AI applications to analyze literary works and social media texts. After presenting a working definition of certain key terms in the background section of the study, this chapter offers a detailed review of related studies that have employed artificial intelligence in the analysis of texts. Next, the chapter delineates AI-narrative architecture as a proposed nine-phase method to demonstrate the steps for the analytics of literary texts and social media. Finally, the discussion focuses on the new applications and findings, which are presented in 13 different studies that are included in this volume.

INTRODUCTION

The rapid growth in the publishing industry and the emergence of internet and social media platforms have dramatically impacted the ways in which books are published, distributed, purchased, read, and reviewed. On the one hand, the onset of the digital age in the final decades of the twentieth century has greatly minimized the need for big publishing houses to be the linking chain between the writer and

DOI: 10.4018/978-1-6684-6242-3.ch001

the reader. The emergence of internet-based self-publishing platforms, for example, has allowed fiction and non-fiction writers to get their books directly into the hands of their fans and readers. Likewise, the surge of social media platforms such as Facebook and Twitter as well as social cataloging websites such as Goodreads have provided the fans and readers around the world with a unique opportunity to communicate with each other and share with the world their feedback and feelings about literary works (Keikhosrokiani & Asl, 2022). Readers' responses and feedback documented in these platforms are of great importance to companies and organizations whose benefits lie in comprehending the current trends. Previous studies have underlined the significance of readers' criticism and sentiments both in assigning meaning to a text and in its market success or failure (Al Mamun et al., 2022; Chu et al., 2022; Fasha et al., 2022; Sofian et al., 2022; Suhendra et al., 2022). On the other hand, the massive rise in the number of published materials and the huge number of opinions shared in the digital world have created a considerable amount of data that can no longer be handled with traditional ways of data analysis. For instance, the conventional method of manual text analysis proves to be inadequate and ineffective when it comes to the analysis of such big data. For a long time, the manual data analysis of literary narratives has been criticized for inaccuracy, bias, and prejudice. The inaccuracy seems to be particularly evident in the study of literary representations and readers' voicing of their sentiments with regards to the prevailing themes of a literary text.

Contemporary developments in Artificial Intelligence have appeared as promising substitutes to traditional ways of data collection and data analysis. The adoption and deployment of computerized analytical techniques have to a great extent eliminated or resolved the problems of inaccuracy and subjectivity in the analyses of literary works and the studies of readers' responses to fictional stories. Previous studies have used techniques such as Opinion Mining, and Text Analytics methods such Topic Modelling and Sentiment Analysis to examine the themes, settings, characterizations, storyline, readers' responses, sentiments, and opinions (Asri et al., 2022; Fasha et al., 2022; Keikhosrokiani & Asl, 2022; Paremeswaran et al., 2022; Sofian et al., 2022; Suhendra et al., 2022). Of the many studies, one can note the adoption of Artificial Intelligence in the study of the connection between theme, place, and sentiment in English narratives by writers from the Middle East and South Asia. The stories from these regions have been the subject matter of public and critical controversy, and the employment of computerized techniques in the analysis of those stories have proved highly beneficial for literary critics and scholars (Asl, 2022). In a similar way, studies have shown that book club judges, literary prize-givers, and publishing industries have benefited extremely in their decision makings from the application of Artificial Intelligence techniques in the study of literary fans and enthusiasts' sentiments and reactions to certain stories (Paremeswaran et al., 2022). In like manner, the developments in computer sciences and information technology have been useful to geographers and feminist geographers in the spatial mapping of certain events, characters, or themes in fictional worlds. An example of such a study is conducted by Jafery et al. (2022) where the authors explore a corpus of six life writings by or about Iraqi people to identify the connection between theme, place, and sentiment. In continuation of such studies, the present book aims to present contemporary developments in the adoption of artificial intelligence in textual analysis of literary works and social media, and hence to provide a multidisciplinary approach related to fields of computer science, data science, social sciences, and literary studies. Therefore, theories, approaches, techniques, models, and applications of artificial intelligence, which can be used to analyze data related to literary works and social media, will be introduced in this book.

The book contains chapters that cover a wide range of topics related to emergence, development, and applications of Text Analytics. The chapters cover topics such as Opinion Mining and its use in literary studies (e.g., Topic Modelling, and Thematic analysis), the application of Machine Learning in the study of social media (e.g., Stance Detection, Classification of Emotions, and Sentiment Analysis), and data mining and processing techniques and applications. In what follows, the study first presents a background definition of certain key terms together with a detailed review of the employment of artificial intelligence in the analysis of texts. After a thorough review of the existing body of works within the field, the chapter will delineate AI-Narrative Architecture as a proposed method. Finally, the discussion will focus on the new applications and findings presented throughout this volume.

BACKGROUND

Artificial Intelligence for Text Analytics

Social media has dragged increasing attention in recent years as people use it for different types of social engagement across multiple platforms. By using social opinion mining, it is now possible to translate natural language into the many opinion dimensions that individuals express. As a result, the advancements in the development of artificial intelligence benefit many real-world applications such as decision-making and customer service (Cortis & Davis, 2021). Opinion Mining has employed natural language processing, text analysis, computational linguistics, and biometrics to systematically identify, extract, quantify, and evaluate emotional states and subjective information (Keikhosrokiani, 2022b; Paremeswaran et al., 2022; Sofian et al., 2022; Suhendra et al., 2022; Ying, Keikhosrokiani, & Asl, 2022). Sentiment analysis and natural language processing (NLP) can assist researchers to find people's true feelings on a subject. NLP is considered as a subject of data science and artificial intelligence (AI) with origins in computational linguistics. NLP is strongly tied to AI and assists researchers to conduct automated translation studies (Hilborg & Nygaard, 2015). Computers can understand and alter natural language writings and speeches using NLP techniques to achieve useful outcomes (Chowdhary, 2020).

The study of opinion mining and sentiment analysis involves examining people's views, feelings, assessments, attitudes, and emotions in written language. It is one of the most common fields in natural language processing and is extensively investigated in data mining, web mining, and text mining. The rise of social media like reviews, forum conversations, blogs, microblogs, Twitter, and social networks parallels the rise in importance of sentiment analysis (Liu, 2012). We currently have access to a vast amount of subjective data that has been captured in digital form for analysis for the first time in human history. Because opinions are fundamental to practically all human activities and are significant determinants of our behavior, sentiment analysis tools are being employed in virtually every economic and social arena. Our decisions and our thoughts about the world are strongly influenced by other people's opinions and perspectives. Therefore, we frequently seek the advice of others when we need to make a decision not only for people but also for organizations (Keikhosrokiani, 2022a, 2022b; Liu, 2012).

Examples of Artificial Intelligence Applications on Literary Works and Social Media

Previous studies that have proposed Artificial Intelligence (AI) applications for the analytics of literary works and social media are listed in Table 1. For instance, our previous book titled *Handbook of Research on Opinion Mining and Text Analytics on Literary Works and Social Media*, which was published in 2022, is a comprehensive collection of AI applications for the analytics of literary texts such as novels, short stories, fictions, and social media data from twitter, product reviews, newspapers, etc. (Keikhosrokiani & Asl, 2022). In that volume, Valle-Cruz et al. (2022) offered a comprehensive review of application of lexicon-based political sentiment analysis in social media. Furthermore, Al Mamun et al. (2022) focused on the sentiment analysis of Harry Potter novel series using lexicon-based approach. Opinion mining, in particular topic modelling, was performed by Asri et al. (2022) to find users' points of view towards the novel Firoozeh Dumas's *Funny in Farsi in Goodreads*. Ibañez et al. (2022) used deep learning for the text analytics from newspaper and magazines in social media to find threat emotion considering armed conflicts as social extreme events. Sentiment analysis using VADER and TextBlob was performed by Fasha et al. (2022) on Goodreads Readers' Response for Long Litt Woon's *The Way Through the Woods*. Analytics of public reactions to the COVID-19 Vaccine on Twitter was done by Abadah et al. (2023) using sentiment analysis and topic modelling. Moreover, a study by Jafery et al. (2022) proposed a text analytics model to identify the connection between theme and sentiment in Iraqi life writings. Malik et al. (2021) also designed a text mining life cycle for a spatial reading of literary works such as Viet Thanh Nguyen's *The Refugees* (2017). Rosli and Keikhosrokiani (2022) developed a big medical data mining system (BigMed) for the detection and classification of COVID-19 misinformation which utilized machine learning. Similar to Asri et al. (2022), Fasha et al. (2022), Ying, Keikhosrokiani and Pourya Asl (2022), and Suhendra et al. (2022), Sofian et al. (2022) analyzed Goodreads review on literary works using opinion mining. Naing et al. (2022) focused on the analytics of 10 romance books using machine learning and topic modeling. A systematic review was conducted by Ravichandran and Keikhosrokiani (2022) for classification of COVID-19 misinformation on social media based on neuro-fuzzy and neural network. Similarly, John and Keikhosrokiani (2022) used topic modeling and clustering for the analytics of COVID-19 fake news from social media. Since booker prize is one of the world prestigious literary prize awarded each year for the best novel written in English, Paremeswaran et al. (2022) proposed a model for the opinion mining of readers' responses to literary prize nominees on Twitter. Chu et al. (2022) proposed a topic modeling and sentiment analysis model for detection and visualization of themes in literary texts. Küçük and Arıcı (2022) and García-Contreras et al. (2022) used various AI techniques such as machine learning and multimodal sentiment analysis for the social media analytics of COVID-19 vaccination and teleworker experiences in #COVID-19 respectively. Finally, (Noga-Hartmann & Kotzinos, 2022) used topic modelling and sentiment analysis for the analytics of articles from the traditional media.

After reviewing the existing studies in Table 1, this chapter proposed an AI taxonomy for the analytics of literary texts and social media as shown in Figure 1. This taxonomy includes some of the related AI techniques which are used for text analytics particularly from literary works and social media. However, some extra techniques are added for machine learning and deep learning. This taxonomy has room for improvement in future studies.

METHOD

The Proposed AI-Narratives Architecture

This chapter proposed a nine-phase Artificial Intelligence (AI)-based architecture called AI-Narratives for building and deploying analytical solutions to handle data related to literary works and social media

Table 1. Comparison of existing studies related to Artificial Intelligence Applications on Literary Works and Social Media

No.	Author & Year	Title	Category	Data	Technique	Details
1	(Keikhosrokiani & Asl, 2022)	Handbook of research on opinion mining and text analytics on literary works and social media.	Literary works & Social media	Novels, short stories social media reviews newspapers Product reviews	Machine learning Deep learning Sentiment analysis Topic modelling	- Linear models (Logistic Regression, Linear Discriminant Analysis) -Non-linear models (K-Nearest Neighbors, Decision Tree, Gaussian Naïve Bays, Support Vector Machine (SVM)) - Lexicon-Based - VADER - TextBlob - Latent Dirichlet Allocation (LDA) - Latent Semantic Analysis (LSA)
2	(Valle-Cruz et al., 2022)	Review on the Application of Lexicon-Based Political Sentiment Analysis in Social Media.	Social media	Political Sentiment	Sentiment analysis	Lexicon-Based
3	(Al Mamun et al., 2022)	Sentiment Analysis of the Harry Potter Series Using a Lexicon-Based Approach	Literary works	Harry Potter novel series	Sentiment analysis	Lexicon-Based
4	(Asri et al., 2022)	Opinion Mining Using Topic Modeling: A Case Study of Firoozeh Dumas's Funny in Farsi in Goodreads	Literary works & Social media	Goodreads reviews of the novel Firoozeh Dumas's Funny in Farsi	Topic modelling	- Latent Dirichlet Allocation (LDA) - Latent Semantic Analysis (LSA)
5	(Ibañez et al., 2022)	Threat Emotion Analysis in Social Media: Considering Armed Conflicts as Social Extreme Events.	Social media	Newspaper and Magazines in social media	- Sentiment analysis using Deep learning - Time series analysis	- Long Short-Term Memory (LSTM) - Detrended Fluctuation Analysis (DFA)
6	(Fasha et al., 2022)	Opinion Mining Using Sentiment Analysis: A Case Study of Readers' Response on Long Litt Woon's The Way Through the Woods in Goodreads.	Literary works & Social media	Readers' Response on Long Litt Woon's The Way Through the Woods in Goodreads	Sentiment analysis	- VADER - TextBlob
7	(Abadah et al., 2023)	Analytics of Public Reactions to the COVID-19 Vaccine on Twitter Using Sentiment Analysis and Topic Modelling	Social media	Public Reactions to the COVID-19 Vaccine on Twitter	- Sentiment Analysis - Topic Modelling	- lexicon-based approach using VADER - Latent Dirichlet Allocation (LDA)
8	(Jafery et al., 2022)	Text analytics model to identify the connection between theme and sentiment in literary works: A case study of Iraqi life writings.	Literary works	6 Iraqi Life Writings	Topic modelling Sentiment analysis	- Latent Dirichlet Allocation (LDA), Mallet model - Latent Dirichlet Allocation (LDA), Gensim model - lexicon-based approach using TextBlob
9	(Malik et al., 2021)	Text Mining Life Cycle for a Spatial Reading of Viet Thanh Nguyen's The Refugees (2017).	Literary works	Viet Thanh Nguyen's The Refugees (2017)	Sentiment analysis	lexicon-based approach
10	(Rosli & Keikhosrokiani, 2022)	Big medical data mining system (BigMed) for the detection and classification of COVID-19 misinformation	Social media	COVID-19 misinformation	Machine learning	Passive-aggressive classifier
11	(Sofian et al., 2022)	Opinion mining and text analytics of reader reviews of Yoko Ogawa's The Housekeeper and the Professor in Goodreads.	Literary works & Social media	Reader reviews of Yoko Ogawa's The Housekeeper and the Professor in Goodreads	-Topic modelling - Sentiment analysis	- Latent Dirichlet Allocation (LDA) - Latent Semantic Analysis (LSA) - VADER - TextBlob
12	(Naing et al., 2022)	What Is Love? Text Analytics on Romance Literature From the Perspective of Authors.	Literary works	10 romance books	- Machine learning - Topic modelling	- Linear models (Logistic Regression, Linear Discriminant Analysis) -Non-linear models (K-Nearest Neighbors, Decision Tree, Gaussian Naïve Bays, Support Vector Machine (SVM)) - Latent Dirichlet Allocation (LDA) - Latent Semantic Analysis (LSA)
13	(Suhendra et al., 2022)	Opinion mining and text analytics of literary reader responses: A case study of reader responses to KL Noir volumes in Goodreads using sentiment analysis and topic.	Literary works & Social media	Goodreads	- Sentiment analysis - Topic modelling	- Latent Dirichlet Allocation (LDA) - Latent Semantic Analysis (LSA)
14	(Ying, Keikhosrokiani, & Pourya Asl, 2022)	Opinion Mining on Viet Thanh Nguyen's The Sympathizer Using Topic Modelling and Sentiment Analysis.	Literary works	Viet Thanh Nguyen's The Sympathizer Novel	- Sentiment analysis - Topic modelling	- Latent Dirichlet Allocation (LDA) with Mallet and Gensim - Latent Semantic Analysis (LSA)
15	(Ravichandran & Keikhosrokiani, 2022)	Classification of Covid-19 misinformation on social media based on neuro-fuzzy and neural network: A systematic review.	Social media	Covid-19 misinformation on Twitter	Deep learning	- A hybrid model of neuro-fuzzy and neural network
16	(Paremeswaran et al., 2022)	Opinion Mining of Readers' Responses to Literary Prize Nominees on Twitter: A Case Study of Public Reaction to the Booker Prize.	Literary works & Social media	Readers' Responses to Literary Prize Nominees on Twitter	- Topic modelling - Sentiment classification using machine learning - Clustering	- Latent Dirichlet Allocation (LDA) with Mallet and Gensim - Naive Bayes and Logistic regression - K-means clustering
17	(John & Keikhosrokiani, 2022)	COVID-19 fake news analytics from social media using topic modeling and clustering.	Social media	Real and fake news related to COVID-19 from Twitter and Facebook	Topic modelling	- Latent Dirichlet Allocation (LDA)
18	(Chu et al., 2022)	A Topic Modeling and Sentiment Analysis Model for Detection and Visualization of Themes in Literary Texts	Literary works	28 books that cover contemporary life writings by the Iranian diaspora	- Topic modelling - Sentiment analysis	-Latent Dirichlet Allocation (LDA) - Latent Semantic Indexing (LSI) - Non-negative Matrix Factorization (NMF) - Hierarchical Dirichlet Process (HDP) - Vader - TextBlob
19	(Küçük & Arıcı, 2022)	Sentiment Analysis and Stance Detection in Turkish Tweets About COVID-19 Vaccination	Social Media	Turkish tweets about COVID-19 vaccination	Machine learning	Support Vector Machine (SVM) and Random Forest
20	(García-Contreras et al., 2022)	Teleworker Experiences in #COVID-19: Insights Through Sentiment Analysis in Social Media.	Social media	Public reactions on Twitter about telework during the pandemic period	Multimodal sentiment analysis	Lexicons- based
21	(Noga-Hartmann & Kotzinos, 2022)	Assessing Together the Trends in Newspaper Topics and User Opinions: A Co-Evolutionary Approach.	Traditional Media	Articles	- Topic Modelling - Opinion Mining (Sentiment analysis)	- Latent Dirichlet Allocation (LDA) - Lexicon-Based

Figure 1. AI Taxonomy for the Analytics of Literary Works and Social Media

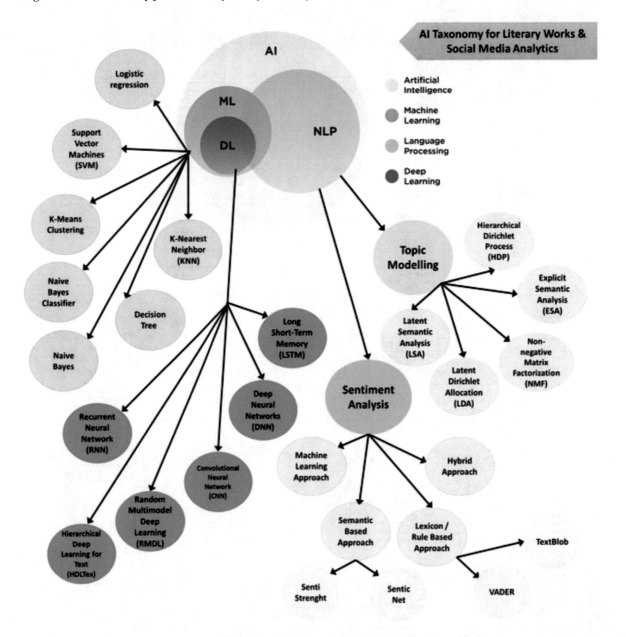

(Figure 2). The proposed AI-Narratives includes nine main phases: (1) data collection, (2) Data ingestion, (3) Data storage, (4) Data pre-processing, (5) Prebuilt API, (6) AI modelling, (7) Deployment, (8) Visualization, (9) Evaluation.

The first step of the proposed AI-Narratives model is data collection. The main textual data for the proposed AI-narratives are collected from literary works and social media. Literary works are considered as unstructured data which do not include a pre-defined data model, nor are they organized in a pre-defined manner. The literary data included in this book are normally short stories, novels, biographies and autobiographies, and life writings which are text-heavy but may contain data such as dates, numbers, and facts as well. On the other hand, data collected from social media such as tweets, newspaper articles, Facebook posts, magazines, and product reviews are semi-structured data. Semi-structured data (Buneman, 1997) is a type of structured data that does not adhere to the tabular structure of data models associated with relational databases or other types of data tables but still contains tags or other markers to separate semantic elements and enforce hierarchies of records and fields within the data. Semi-structured data is also known as a self-describing structure.

The next step of AI-Narratives focuses on data ingestion which is the process of acquiring and importing data for immediate use or storage in a database. In this step, data will be categorized and prepared for storing in databases. Data ingestion is considered as analytics architecture's backbone. Data can be transferred in real-time data streaming or ingested in batches. Setting priorities for the data sources is the first step in a successful data ingestion process. Data items must be directed to the appropriate destinations once each file has been approved individually. Auto-ingest streaming and event-driven data from Twitter can be done in this step using specific cloud-based tools. With the help of the Twitter API, live public Tweets can be streamed from the platform in realtime and shown along with some basic statistics about them (Abadah et al., 2023; Paremeswaran et al., 2022; Trupthi et al., 2017). In the case of AI-Narratives model, one pipeline can ingest data from literary works and the other pipeline ingest data from social media API such as twitter API.

Data storage is the third phase of AI-Narratives for storing and retrieving data when it is required. The use case of the data often commands how it is stored. For instance, a social networking platform must store data so that users may access it anytime they want. This data storage is called foreground copy. Some companies wish to keep their social media in bulk in order to analyze it and learn valuable information. This kind of data storage is called backdrop copy. Making smarter decisions requires using social media data, which includes indicators like shares, comments, retweets, referrals, and conversion rates. Furthermore, it offers crucial details about users' opinions. Therefore, for the successful decision making, it is required to use effective and secure social media data storage procedures.

After the smooth data collection, ingestion, and storage, data pre-processing is required before moving to data analytics using artificial intelligence. Data pre-processing can include data cleaning, removing unwanted words or symbols, lemmatization, stemming, splitting, and tokenization. Tokenization is the process of splitting longer string of text into smaller pieces, or tokens. Normalization refers to converting numbers to their equivalent words, removing punctuation, converting all text to the same case, lemmatization, and stemming. Stemming is related to removing affixes (suffixed, prefixes, infixes, infixes, circumfixes) whereas lemmatization captures canonical form based on a word's lemma.

After data pre-processing phase in AI-Narrative, prebuilt API can be used. Some examples of prebuilt API are Translate API and language services. Prebuilt APIs can be used to answer questions based on a passage of text using without needing to build projects or knowledge bases, keep up with question-and-answer pairings, or pay for underused infrastructure. The prebuilt API can provide the functionalities without a need to learn the details.

The next step of AI-Narratives is AI modelling phase which selects the proper techniques to propose the best text analytics method with higher accuracy. Some of the well-known artificial intelligence techniques which are used for text analytics are Natural Language Processing (NLP)—in particular, topic modelling and sentiment analysis—machine learning, and deep learning. A branch of linguistics, computer science, and artificial intelligence called "natural language processing", which studies how computers and human language interact, with a focus on how to design methods to process and analyse massive volumes of natural language data (Ahmad et al., 2022; Keikhosrokiani, 2022a, 2022b). A topic model is a form of statistical model used in statistics and natural language processing to identify the abstract "themes" that appear in a group of texts. A popular text-mining technique for locating latent semantic patterns in a text body is topic modelling (Asri et al., 2022; Chu et al., 2022; Vayansky & Kumar, 2020). On the other hand, sentiment analysis, often known as opinion mining, is a natural language processing (NLP) method for identifying the positivity, negativity, or neutrality of data (Al Mamun et al., 2022; Chu et al., 2022; Küçük & Arıcı, 2022). Machine learning is part of artificial intelligence. It is a topic of study devoted to comprehending and developing "learning" methods—methods that use data to increase performance on a certain set of tasks. Whereas a larger family of machine learning techniques built on artificial neural networks and representation learning is called deep learning. Deep learning can conduct unsupervised, semi-supervised, and supervised learning (Keikhosrokiani, 2022a; Wei et al., 2017).

After developing the text analytics method based on artificial intelligence techniques, the proposed method must be deployed. R and Python are the most famous programming languages which are used for natural language processing (NLP) and text analytics. Both R and Python are free and open source. R is used for procedural programming while Python is used for object-oriented programming types. The proper integrated development environment (IDE) for R programming is R Studio whereas Jupyter Notebook, VS Code, and Pycharm can be used as IDE for Python. Google Colab is a product from Google Research. Colab is particularly well suited to machine learning, data analysis, and teaching. It makes it possible to create and execute arbitrary Python code through the browser. Technically speaking, Colab is a hosted Jupyter notebook service that offers free access to computer resources, including GPUs, and requires no setup to use.

After deployment, the results need to be represented graphically for better interpretation. This step is called visualization which can be done using R, Python, and some tools such as Microsoft PowerBI, Tableau, etc. In order to improve human cognition, visual representations of abstract data. Both numerical and non-numerical data, such as text and geographic data, are included in the abstract data. From academic perspective, this data representation may be seen as a mapping between the original data, which is often numerical, and graphic elements. Text visualization will be used for AI-Narrative model as the data is mainly text. Text visualization is a method for presenting textual data visually by employing graphs, charts, or word clouds. This summarizes the content, identifies trends and patterns among documents, and gives rapid insight into the most essential terms inside a text.

Finally, the results need to be interpreted. In order to validate the results, the proposed AI methods need to be evaluated using different metrices. Based on the types of data analytics, different matrices will be used for evaluation. For instance, coherence score can be used to evaluate the topic modelling methods to measure how interpretable the topics are to humans. In addition, confusion matrix which includes precision, recall, F1 Score, and accuracy elements can be used for classification methods. Moreover, Root Mean Squared Error (RMSE) and Mean Squared Error (MSE) are both metrics for measuring the performance of regression machine learning models.

DISCUSSION

This book consists of three main sections that together are comprised of fourteen chapters. In Section One, an introductory chapter is included that offers a detailed overview of the volume. Section Two is comprised of six chapters—i.e., chapter one to chapter six—which focus on the adoption of Artificial

Figure 2. The Proposed AI-Narratives Architecture

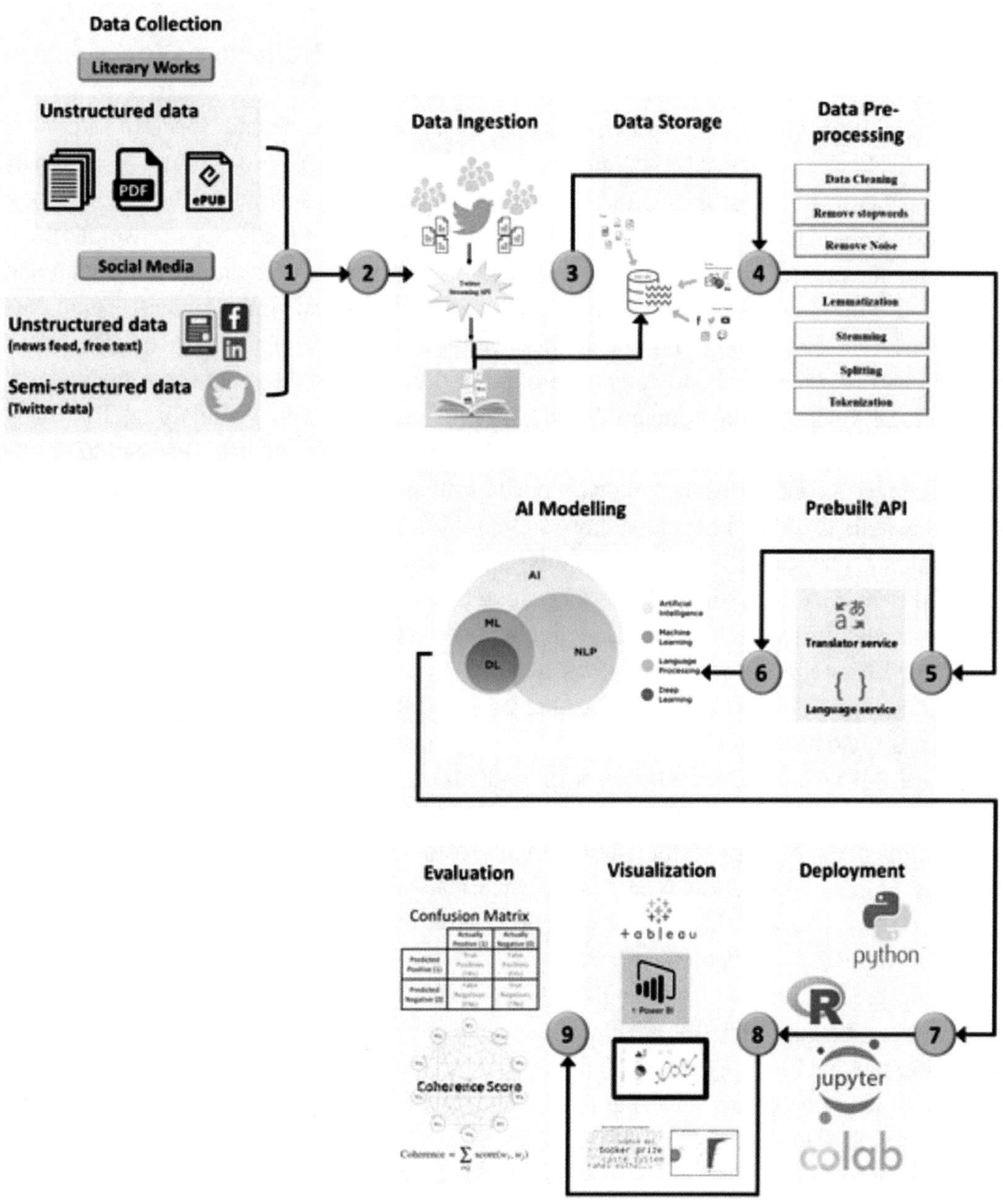

Intelligence in the analysis of fictional works. Section Three includes seven chapters—i.e., chapter seven to chapter thirteen—that explore Artificial Intelligence and social media.

Chapter one is titled "Introduction to Artificial Intelligence for the Analytics of Literary Works and Social Media: A Review". Written by Keikhosrokiani and Asl, this chapter presents a detailed review of previous studies within the filed followed by an overview of the critical works included in the volume.

The authors of the chapter also offer a delineation of AI-Narrative architecture as a proposed method of study in the present volume.

SECTION II: Artificial Intelligence for the Analytics of Literary Works

Chapter two is titled "An Artificial Intelligence Application of Theme and Space in Life Writings of Middle Eastern Women: A Topic Modelling and Sentiment Analysis Approach" and is written by Nurul Najiha Jafery, Pantea Keikhosrokiani, and Moussa Pourya Asl. The abstract of the chapter goes like:

Recently, the revolutionary transformations in social and political landscapes as well as the remarkable developments in artificial intelligence reinforced the importance of geography and spatial analyses in literary and cultural studies. This chapter proposes an analytical framework of Topic Modelling and Sentiment Analysis for exploring the connection between theme, place, and sentiment in 36 autobiographical narratives by or about women from the Middle East. In the proposed framework, a Latent Dirichlet Allocation and Latent Semantic Analysis algorithm from Topic Modelling, TextBlob library for Sentiment analysis are employed to detect the place names that come together and to point out the associated themes and emotions throughout the data source. The model gives a scoring of each topical clusters and reveals that the diasporic authors are more likely to write about their hometown than their current host land. The authors hope that the merging of topic modelling and sentiment analysis would be beneficial to literary critics in the analysis of long texts.

Chapter three is titled "A Machine Learning Approach to the Analytics of Representations of Violence in Khaled Hosseini's Novels" and is written by Abdikadir Hussein Elmi, Pantea Keikhosrokiani, and Moussa Pourya Asl. The abstract of the chapter goes like:

Over the past two decades, literary works from Afghanistan have sought to depict the extensive and increasing level of violence directed against individuals and communities. This study aims to identify the different types of violence represented in selected literary works from the country. To this end, an artificial intelligence approach—comprised of Opinion Mining and Hybrid Machine Learning Models—is developed as a method of analysis. The Afghan American writer Khaled Hosseini's novels— The Kite Runner (2003), A Thousand Splendid Suns (2007), And the Mountains Echoed (2017)—are used as primary data sources. As a theoretical framework, the study benefits from the Norwegian sociologist Johan Galtung's theory of Conflict Triangle—direct violence, structural violence, and cultural violence. To classify the sentiments related to types of violence in the selected novels, the study utilizes Sentiment Analysis and Machine Learning algorithms.

Chapter four is titled "Artificial Intelligence Framework for Opinion Mining of Netizen Readers' Reviews of Arundhati Roy's The God of Small Things" and is written by Pantea Keikhosrokiani, Moussa Pourya Asl, Kah Em Chu, Nur Ain Nasuha Anuar. The abstract of the chapter goes like:

In recent years, South-Asian literature in English has experienced a surge of newfound love and popularity both in the local and the global market. In this regard, Arundhati Roy's The God of Small Things (1997) has garnered an astounding mix of positive and negative reactions from readers across the globe. This chapter adopts an artificial intelligence approach to analyze netizen readers' feedback on the novel as documented in the book cataloguing website Goodreads. To this end, an opinion mining framework is proposed based on artificial intelligence techniques such as topic modelling and Sentiment Analysis. Latent Semantic Analysis (LSA) and Latent Dirichlet Allocation (LDA) are applied and compared to find the abstract "topics" that occur in a collection of reviews. Furthermore, lexicon-based sentiment analysis approaches such as Vader and Textblob algorithms are used and compared to find the reviews sentiments polarities.

Chapter five is titled "Artificial Intelligence Applications in Literary Works: Emotion Extraction and Classification of Mohsin Hamid's Moth Smoke" and is written by Annuur Farahhim Zainol, Pantea Keikhosrokiani, Moussa Pourya Asl, and Nur Ain Nasuha Anuar. The abstract of the chapter goes like:

The British Pakistani writer, Mohsin Hamid's debut novel Moth Smoke (2000) has garnered conflicting responses from readers across the globe. Over the past few years and with the rapid advancements in social media platforms, readers around the world have publicly shared their opinions and feelings towards the text using online platforms such as Twitter, Goodreads, Facebook—among many others. The huge bulk of readers' reviews are useful data for publishers and booksellers in analyzing readers' interests to recommend similar texts to online readers. The analysis of sentiment and emotion attached to this data can help to determine the popularity or unpopularity of a literary text. Using reader-reviews of Hamid's novel from Goodreads as the main data source, this study offers a data analytic approach: LSTM, LDA to detect and classify the dominant emotion existing within the readers' feedback. Understanding readers' emotion towards the novel can help in developing a recommendation system that can suggest readers stories of their interest.

Chapter six is titled "Artificial Intelligence and Human Rights Activism: A Case Study of Boochani's No Friend but the Mountains and His Tweets on Justice and Equality" and is written by Chun Keat Kng, Pantea Keikhosrokiani, and Moussa Pourya Asl. The abstract of the chapter goes like:

Behrouz Boochani, the Kurdish-Iranian author of No Friends but the Mountains, has been using social media platforms such as Twitter to speak up against social injustice and human rights abuse against immigrants across the globe. This study proposes an artificial intelligence lifecycle for opinion mining of the dominant sentiments, topics, and emotions in Boochani's social media activism. Sentiment analysis (Vader and Textblob), topic modelling (LDA and NMF), and emotion detection are performed to extract hidden sentiments, topics, and emotions from the data that is collected from his tweets from 2017 till 2021. The results show Vader performs better than Textblob. LDA is considered the best algorithm which extracted seven main topics as suicide, translator of book, publication of book, human rights, political, immigration and detention. Finally, the main emotion detected from the tweets is sadness.

Chapter seven is titled "Advanced Replicating Technology in Adventure Fiction: The Philosophical Implications of Material Synthesizer in The Orville" and is written by Alexandria S Zlatar. The abstract of the chapter goes like:

In the adventure fiction and Sci-Fi TV show titled *The Orville* (2017), a material synthesizer refers to a machine that can create food, drink, clothing and so on. While the device in the show has a small role, the implications of unrestricted material access have vast effects on the cast and real-world implications on our identities as well. The framework of this chapter focuses on a qualitative and case study analysis of literary and film-based narrative to examine the implications of material synthesis in *The Orville*. It examines the plot element and expounds upon the impact on unrestricted indulgence, potential corruption, and the ability to create more freedom both for the characters and the show itself. Upon this analysis the chapter concludes that while the device is incredibly far from a practical achievement, it does lead the viewers to analyze how current food generators and 3D Printers have the potential for unrestricted powers which need to be examined and better understood in order to prevent misuse and exploitation.

SECTION III: Artificial Intelligence for the Analytics of Social Media

Chapter eight is titled "Social Media Intelligence: AI Applications for Criminal Investigation and National Security" and is written by Szde Yu. The abstract of the chapter goes like:

This chapter aims at discussing how social media intelligence (SOCMINT) can be and has been applied to the field of criminal justice. SOCMINT is composed of a set of computer forensic techniques used for intelligence gathering on social media platforms. Through this chapter, readers will be able to better understand what SOCMINT is and how it may be helpful for criminal investigation and national security. Different aspects of SOCMINT are addressed, including application in criminal justice, intelligence gathering, monitoring, metadata, cyber profiling, social network analysis, tools, and privacy concerns. Further, the challenges and future research directions are discussed as well. This chapter is not meant to serve as a technical tutorial as the focus is on the concepts rather than the techniques.

Chapter nine is titled "Artificial Intelligence Techniques in Text and Sentimental Analysis" and is written by Muralidhara Rao, Anupama A, Stya keerthi G, Saraswathi Pedada. The abstract of the chapter goes like:

Text and Sentiment analysis have become essential part of modern marketing. Besides, they play a vital role in the division of Natural Language Processing (NLP), which mainly focuses on text classification to examine the intention of the processed text. The results can be of positive or negative types. Also, sentiment analysis deals with the computational treatment of sentiments, opinions, and subjectivity of text. This chapter tackles a comprehensive approach for the past research solutions that includes various algorithms, enhancements and applications. It primarily focuses on three aspects. First, the authors present systematic review of recent works done in the area of text and sentiment analysis; next, they emphasize major concepts, components, functionalities and classification techniques of text and sentiment analysis. Then, they provide a comparative study of text and sentiment analysis on the basis of trending research approaches. Finally, they conclude the chapter with future directions.

Chapter ten is titled "Affective polarization in the U.S.: Multi-emotional charge analyzed through affective computing" and is written by David Valle-Cruz, Rodrigo Sandoval-Almazán, and Asdrubal López-Chau. The abstract of the chapter goes like:

Affective polarization is a phenomenon that has invaded the political arena empowered by social networks. In this chapter, the authors seek to analyze the Capitol riot's post on Twitter. To achieve this, the authors use affective computing introducing the multi-emotional charge, combined with statistical analysis based on the t-Student test and Welch's t-test. The two research questions guiding this study are: How do social media platforms' messages impact on inciting? How do social media platforms' messages with negative emotional charge affect legitimizing of the Capitol protest? Findings of the study detect the significant influence of Donald Trump on Twitter during the Capitol riot. Moreover, data analysis identifies positive and negative emotions towards Donald Trump, as well as similarities in the showed emotions of Trump and his audience.

Chapter eleven is titled "Applying Sentiment Analysis Techniques in Social Media Data about Threat of Armed Conflicts using Two Times Series Models" and is written by Marilyn Minicucci Ibañez, Reinaldo Roberto Rosa, and Lamartine Nogueira Frutuoso Guimarães. The abstract of the chapter goes like:

Social media is an inexhaustible data source about varied subjects. One of the subjects that draws society's attention is extreme events such as the armed conflicts. Due to their great impact on human life and societies, the search for techniques that could facilitate the understanding of their evolution is of great importance to minimize the consequences of such events. This chapter presents an approach to armed conflict analysis by investigating the previous datasets about armed conflict Syria-USA and Iran-USA. It applies sentiment analysis on the text dataset as well as a vocabulary data about the conflict between Russia and Ukraine. All conflicts generate a social media news threat time series (TTS) that is used as input to the P-model algorithm to generate the endogenous time series. The study uses the TTS and endogenous time series for both conflicts, as input to the deep-learning-LSTM neural network. Finally, this chapter compares the prediction result of the Russia-Ukraine TTS analysis with the Russia-Ukraine endogenous series using the P-model algorithm.

Chapter twelve is titled "Artificial Intelligence Techniques to understand the Braille Literary: A Language for Visually Imperative Individuals" and is written by Syed Asif Ali. The abstract of the chapter goes like:

The special-needs individuals have their own literary system called Braille for printing, reading, and writing since 1824 which assists them in easily connecting with other each other. Because of the isolated education system, formally called the heterogeneous education system, those individuals have faced a lot of problems and challenges in their societies. Artificial intelligence tools and techniques play a vital role in mitigating the communication gap between blind and visually impaired individuals and non-blind people. Thus, this chapter focuses on reviewing artificial intelligence techniques to understand the Braille Literary for normal people associated with Visual Imperative Individuals. It is found that Natural Language Processing (NLP) helps in translating the native language into braille. Machine learning and artificial neural network algorithms help in translating by matching the equivalence pattern of braille. The concept of finite automata is used with natural language processing to recognize and convert the braille pattern equivalent to their native language pattern and vice versa.

Chapter thirteen is titled "Text Analytics of Vaccine Myths on Reddit" and is written by Sylvia Shiau Ching Wong, Jing-Ru Tan, Keng Hoon Gan, and Tien Ping Tan. The abstract of the chapter goes like:

Widespread online misinformation that aims to convince vaccine hesitant populations continues to threaten healthcare systems globally. Assessing features of online content including topics and sentiments against vaccines could help curb the spread of vaccine-related misinformation and allow stakeholders to draft better regulations and public policies. Using a public dataset extracted from Reddit, we performed text analytics including sentiment analysis, N-gram, and topic modeling to grasp the sentiments, the most popular phrases (N-grams), and topics of the subreddit. The sentiment analysis results revealed mostly positive sentiments in the subreddit's discussions. Our N-gram analysis identified "cause autism" and "MMR cause autism" as the most frequent bigram and trigram. The NMF topic modeling results revealed five topics discussing different aspects of vaccines. These findings implied the significance of the ability to assess public confidence and sentiment from social media platforms to enable effective responses against the proliferation of vaccine misinformation.

Chapter fourteen is titled "Analytics of users' behaviors on twitter using machine learning" and is written by Noman Islam, Muntaha Mehboob, and Rimsha Javed. The abstract of the chapter goes like:

Twitter is a leading social networking site when it comes down to topics such as politics, news and trends around the globe. Another main reason for people to use Twitter is because they are able to share their emotions and feelings with others and form new relationships and views. With about 330 million users in 2020, Twitter continues to rapidly grow. At the same time, however, it is also losing users at a fast pace. In 2019, Twitter had 340 million users but a year later, it lost 10 million of them. The goal of this chapter is to find the reasons for the following three questions: What is the reason behind Twitter losing its users? How does a user's behavior change after his or her using of Twitter? Finally, how does a user's behavior change when expanding his or her social circle on Twitter. To address these questions, the authors of this chapter have designed a data set and executed experiments based on their hypothesis. The results report the accuracies of each of those hypotheses.

CONCLUSION

Over the past few decades, artificial intelligence has been utilized in a diverse range of industries as more people and businesses discover its many uses, applications, and benefits. A current field of study that requires more attention, as there is much opportunity for improvement, is the use of artificial intelligence within literary works and social media analysis. The present book titled *Artificial Intelligence Applications in Literary Works and Social Media* presents contemporary developments in the adoption of artificial intelligence in textual analysis of literary works and social media and introduces current approaches, techniques, and practices in data science that are implemented to scrap and analyze text data. This book initiates a new multidisciplinary field that is the combination of artificial intelligence, data science, social science, literature, and social media study. The fourteen chapters in this volume cover key topics such as opinion mining, sentiment analysis, and machine learning.

REFERENCES

Abadah, M. S. K., Keikhosrokiani, P., & Zhao, X. (2023). Analytics of Public Reactions to the COVID-19 Vaccine on Twitter Using Sentiment Analysis and Topic Modelling. In D. Valle-Cruz, N. Plata-Cesar, & J. L. González-Ruíz (Eds.), *Handbook of Research on Applied Artificial Intelligence and Robotics for Government Processes* (pp. 156–188). IGI Global. doi:10.4018/978-1-6684-5624-8.ch008

Ahmad, H., Nasir, F., Faisal, C. M. N., & Ahmad, S. (2022). Depression Detection in Online Social Media Users Using Natural Language Processing Techniques. In P. Keikhosrokiani & M. Pourya Asl (Eds.), *Handbook of Research on Opinion Mining and Text Analytics on Literary Works and Social Media* (pp. 323–347). IGI Global. doi:10.4018/978-1-7998-9594-7.ch013

Al Mamun, M. H., Keikhosrokiani, P., Asl, M. P., Anuar, N. A. N., Hadi, N. H. A., & Humida, T. (2022). Sentiment Analysis of the Harry Potter Series Using a Lexicon-Based Approach. In P. Keikhosrokiani & M. Pourya Asl (Eds.), *Handbook of Research on Opinion Mining and Text Analytics on Literary Works and Social Media* (pp. 263–291). IGI Global. doi:10.4018/978-1-7998-9594-7.ch011

Asl, M. P. (Ed.). (2022). *Gender, Place, and Identity of South Asian Women*. IGI Global. doi:10.4018/978-1-6684-3626-4

Asri, M. A. Z. B. M., Keikhosrokiani, P., & Asl, M. P. (2022). Opinion Mining Using Topic Modeling: A Case Study of Firoozeh Dumas's Funny in Farsi in Goodreads. Advances on Intelligent Informatics and Computing. doi:10.1007/978-3-030-98741-1_19

Buneman, P. (1997). Semistructured data. In *PODS'97: Proceedings of the 16th ACM SIGACTSIGMOD-SIGART Symposium on Principles of Database Systems*. ACM Press. 10.1145/263661.263675

Chowdhary, K. R. (2020). Natural Language Processing. In K. R. Chowdhary (Ed.), *Fundamentals of Artificial Intelligence* (pp. 603–649). Springer India. doi:10.1007/978-81-322-3972-7_19

Chu, K. E., Keikhosrokiani, P., & Asl, M. P. (2022). A Topic Modeling and Sentiment Analysis Model for Detection and Visualization of Themes in Literary Texts. *Pertanika Journal of Science & Technology*, *30*(4), 2535–2561. doi:10.47836/pjst.30.4.14

Cortis, K., & Davis, B. (2021). Over a decade of social opinion mining: A systematic review. *Artificial Intelligence Review*, *54*(7), 4873–4965. doi:10.100710462-021-10030-2 PMID:34188346

Fasha, E. F. B. K., Keikhosrokiani, P., & Asl, M. P. (2022). Opinion Mining Using Sentiment Analysis: A Case Study of Readers' Response on Long Litt Woon's The Way Through the Woods in Goodreads. Advances on Intelligent Informatics and Computing. doi:10.1007/978-3-030-98741-1_20

García-Contreras, R., Muñoz-Chávez, J. P., Valle-Cruz, D., & López-Chau, A. (2022). Teleworker Experiences in #COVID-19: Insights Through Sentiment Analysis in Social Media. In P. Keikhosrokiani & M. Pourya Asl (Eds.), *Handbook of Research on Opinion Mining and Text Analytics on Literary Works and Social Media* (pp. 388–412). IGI Global. doi:10.4018/978-1-7998-9594-7.ch016

Hilborg, P. H., & Nygaard, E. B. (2015). *Viability of sentiment analysis in business*. The Copenhagen Business School. Retrieved from http://studenttheses. cbs. dk…

Ibañez, M. M., Rosa, R. R., & Guimarães, L. N. F. (2022). Threat Emotion Analysis in Social Media: Considering Armed Conflicts as Social Extreme Events. In P. Keikhosrokiani & M. Pourya Asl (Eds.), *Handbook of Research on Opinion Mining and Text Analytics on Literary Works and Social Media* (pp. 293–322). IGI Global. doi:10.4018/978-1-7998-9594-7.ch012

Jafery, N. N., Keikhosrokiani, P., & Asl, M. P. (2022). Text analytics model to identify the connection between theme and sentiment in literary works: A case study of Iraqi life writings. In P. Keikhosrokiani & M. P. Asl (Eds.), *Handbook of research on opinion mining and text analytics on literary works and social media* (pp. 173–190). IGI Global. doi:10.4018/978-1-7998-9594-7.ch008

John, S. A., & Keikhosrokiani, P. (2022). COVID-19 fake news analytics from social media using topic modeling and clustering. In P. Keikhosrokiani (Ed.), *Big Data Analytics for Healthcare* (pp. 221–232). Academic Press. doi:10.1016/B978-0-323-91907-4.00003-0

Keikhosrokiani, P. (Ed.). (2022a). *Big Data Analytics for Healthcare: Datasets, Techniques, Life Cycles, Management, and Applications*. Elsevier Science. doi:10.1016/C2021-0-00369-2

Keikhosrokiani, P. (Ed.). (2022b). *Handbook of Research on Consumer Behavior Change and Data Analytics in the Socio-Digital Era*. IGI Global. doi:10.4018/978-1-6684-4168-8

Keikhosrokiani, P., & Asl, M. P. (Eds.). (2022). *Handbook of research on opinion mining and text analytics on literary works and social media*. IGI Global. doi:10.4018/978-1-7998-9594-7

Küçük, D., & Arıcı, N. (2022). Sentiment Analysis and Stance Detection in Turkish Tweets About COVID-19 Vaccination. In P. Keikhosrokiani & M. Pourya Asl (Eds.), *Handbook of Research on Opinion Mining and Text Analytics on Literary Works and Social Media* (pp. 371–387). IGI Global. doi:10.4018/978-1-7998-9594-7.ch015

Liu, B. (2012). Sentiment analysis and opinion mining. *Synthesis Lectures on Human Language Technologies*, *5*(1), 1-167. doi: 1 doi:0.1007/978-3-031-02145-9

Malik, E. F., Keikhosrokiani, P., & Asl, M. P. (2021, 4-5 July 2021). Text mining life cycle for a spatial reading of Viet Thanh Nguyen's *The Refugees* (2017). *2021 International Congress of Advanced Technology and Engineering (ICOTEN)*. doi:10.1109/ICOTEN52080.2021.9493520

Naing, C. H., Zhao, X., Gan, K. H., & Samsudin, N.-H. (2022). What Is Love?: Text Analytics on Romance Literature From the Perspective of Authors. In P. Keikhosrokiani & M. Pourya Asl (Eds.), *Handbook of Research on Opinion Mining and Text Analytics on Literary Works and Social Media* (pp. 148–172). IGI Global., doi:10.4018/978-1-7998-9594-7.ch007

Noga-Hartmann, E., & Kotzinos, D. (2022). Assessing Together the Trends in Newspaper Topics and User Opinions: A Co-Evolutionary Approach. In P. Keikhosrokiani & M. Pourya Asl (Eds.), *Handbook of Research on Opinion Mining and Text Analytics on Literary Works and Social Media* (pp. 348–370). IGI Global. doi:10.4018/978-1-7998-9594-7.ch014

Paremeswaran, P. p., Keikhosrokiani, P., & Asl, M. P. (2022). Opinion Mining of Readers' Responses to Literary Prize Nominees on Twitter: A Case Study of Public Reaction to the Booker Prize (2018–2020). Advances on Intelligent Informatics and Computing. doi:10.1007/978-3-030-98741-1_21

Ravichandran, B. D., & Keikhosrokiani, P. (2022). Classification of Covid-19 misinformation on social media based on neuro-fuzzy and neural network: A systematic review. *Neural Computing & Applications*. Advance online publication. doi:10.100700521-022-07797-y PMID:36159189

Rosli, N. H. B., & Keikhosrokiani, P. (2022). Big medical data mining system (BigMed) for the detection and classification of COVID-19 misinformation. In P. Keikhosrokiani (Ed.), *Big Data Analytics for Healthcare* (pp. 233–244). Academic Press. doi:10.1016/B978-0-323-91907-4.00014-5

Sofian, N. B., Keikhosrokiani, P., & Asl, M. P. (2022). Opinion mining and text analytics of reader reviews of Yoko Ogawa's The Housekeeper and the Professor in Goodreads. In P. Keikhosrokiani & M. Pourya Asl (Eds.), *Handbook of Research on Opinion Mining and Text Analytics on Literary Works and Social Media* (pp. 240–262). IGI Global. doi:10.4018/978-1-7998-9594-7.ch010

Suhendra, N. H. B., Keikhosrokiani, P., Asl, M. P., & Zhao, X. (2022). Opinion mining and text analytics of literary reader responses: A case study of reader responses to KL Noir volumes in Goodreads using sentiment analysis and topic. In P. Keikhosrokiani & M. Pourya Asl (Eds.), *Handbook of Research on Opinion Mining and Text Analytics on Literary Works and Social Media* (pp. 191–239). IGI Global. doi:10.4018/978-1-7998-9594-7.ch009

Trupthi, M., Pabboju, S., & Narasimha, G. (2017). Sentiment analysis on twitter using streaming API. *2017 IEEE 7th International Advance Computing Conference (IACC)*.

Valle-Cruz, D., López-Chau, A., & Sandoval-Almazán, R. (2022). Review on the Application of Lexicon-Based Political Sentiment Analysis in Social Media. In P. Keikhosrokiani & M. Pourya Asl (Eds.), *Handbook of Research on Opinion Mining and Text Analytics on Literary Works and Social Media* (pp. 1–21). IGI Global., doi:10.4018/978-1-7998-9594-7.ch001

Vayansky, I., & Kumar, S. A. P. (2020). A review of topic modeling methods. *Information Systems, 94,* 101582. doi:10.1016/j.is.2020.101582

Wei, D., Wang, B., Lin, G., Liu, D., Dong, Z., Liu, H., & Liu, Y. (2017). Research on Unstructured Text Data Mining and Fault Classification Based on RNN-LSTM with Malfunction Inspection Report. *Energies*, *10*(3), 406. doi:10.3390/en10030406

Ying, S. Y., Keikhosrokiani, P., & Asl, M. P. (2022). Opinion Mining on Viet Thanh Nguyen's The Sympathizer Using Topic Modelling and Sentiment Analysis. *Journal of Information Technology Management, 14*, 163-183. doi: 10.22059/jitm.2022.84895

Ying, S. Y., Keikhosrokiani, P., & Pourya Asl, M. (2022). Opinion mining on Viet Thanh Nguyen's The Sympathizer using topic modelling and sentiment analysis. *Journal of Information Technology Management*, *14*, 163–183. doi:10.22059/jitm.2022.84895

Section 2
Artificial Intelligence for the Analytics of Literary Works

Chapter 2
An Artificial Intelligence Application of Theme and Space in Life Writings of Middle Eastern Women:
A Topic Modelling and Sentiment Analysis Approach

Nurul Najiha Jafery
Centre for Electrical Engineering Studies, Universiti Teknologi MARA, Malaysia

Pantea Keikhosrokiani
https://orcid.org/0000-0003-4705-2732
School of Computer Sciences, Universiti Sains Malaysia, Malaysia

Moussa Pourya Asl
https://orcid.org/0000-0002-8426-426X
School of Humanities, Universiti Sains Malaysia, Malaysia

ABSTRACT

Recently, the revolutionary transformations in social and political landscapes as well as the remarkable developments in artificial intelligence reinforced the importance of geography and spatial analyses in literary and cultural studies. This chapter proposes an analytical framework of topic modelling and sentiment analysis for exploring the connection between theme, place, and sentiment in 36 autobiographical narratives by or about women from the Middle East. In the proposed framework, a latent Dirichlet allocation and latent semantic analysis algorithm from topic modelling, TextBlob library for sentiment analysis are employed to detect the place names that come together and to point out the associated themes and emotions throughout the data source. The model gives a scoring of each topical clusters and reveals that the diasporic authors are more likely to write about their hometown than their current host land. The authors hope that the merging of topic modelling and sentiment analysis would be beneficial to literary critics in the analysis of long texts.

DOI: 10.4018/978-1-6684-6242-3.ch002

INTRODUCTION

The present century's fast sociopolitical upheavals have moved the issues of space and spatiality to the forefront of social, political, cultural, and literary studies (Tally Jr, 2017). In recent years, the explorations of auto-/biographical narratives by Middle Eastern writers have been marked with a growing focus on matters related to local and global migration, geographical displacement, and public opinion and sentiment (Asl, 2020). The contents of the diasporic women's life accounts are set in locations that evoke distinct emotions and reactions: misogynist dystopian spaces of the homeland (Anishchenkova, 2014); place as sites of discipline and punish (Asl, 2019; Pourya Asl, 2022); emancipatory utopia of the (Western) host land (Sassoon, 2016); heterotopic reality of the cyberspace; utopian longing for the homeland (Golley, 2007); transgressive sites of the third spaces (Asl, 2018), etc. The field of life writing by/about Middle Eastern women has remained significantly under-researched: First, the available volume of critical reviews does not complement the large quantity of fictional works written by Middle Eastern women over the past few decades. Secondly, existing reviews are often rejected for their biased and inauthentic views of the women's stories as presenting solely a subjective narrative of their country of birthplace. This particular problem emanates from the conventional data collection and analysis techniques that fail to provide accurate analysis, especially in relation to the analysis of spatial representations and emotion expressions in connection to dominant themes. Hence the significance of further investigation into the field with a computerized method, for analyzing literary works, remains a challenge more objectively with regard to the notions of theme, place and emotion. The intention of this study is to develop and adopt a computerized analytical method to explore contemporary auto-/biographical narratives by/about Middle Eastern women and examine the interconnection between the three aspects of content, space, and emotion. The goal is to identify the frequent spatial topics in the selected works and describe the common concerns as prevalent among those.

This study uses data science technique Natural Language Processing (NLP) to propose an analytical model of Topic Modelling and Sentiment Analysis for identifying theme and sentiment related to different spaces in a corpus of 36 auto-/biographical narratives. In the model, Latent Dirichlet Allocation (LDA), Latent Semantic Analysis (LSA) and Non-Negative Matrix Factorization (NMF) are us for Topic Modelling and results are compared in terms of accuracy. In order to detect the place names that come together and explain the existing connection between themes and sentiments as pointed out from the dataset, the TextBlob package for Sentiment analysis and Python are utilized as systematic techniques for analysis. Natural Language Processing is useful in parsing human language into structures that can be linked to other values.

This chapter starts with an introduction and a statement of the goal of study followed by literature review. Literature review focuses on text mining and opinion mining, topic modelling and sentiment analysis. After review of related literature, materials and methodology are stated which include the whole process of data science life cycle and techniques used to achieve the main goal of this study. Next, results and discussion are added and finally, paper concludes with remarks on implications of the study and future direction.

BACKGROUND

Text Mining and Opinion Mining

Emergence of big data has transformed the way artificial intelligence is utilized to analyze data (Binti Rosli & Keikhosrokiani, 2022; Keikhosrokiani & Kamaruddin, 2022). Big data analytical methods such as data mining, machine learning, deep learning, and NLP, etc., are required to handle, organize, and extract meaningful information from big data (Keikhosrokiani, 2022; Keikhosrokiani & Pourya Asl, 2022; Teoh Yi Zhe & Keikhosrokiani, 2021). The process of collecting relevant information and knowledge from unstructured text is referred to as text mining. Text mining is the combination of several techniques from information retrieval, information extraction and NLP, and it links all methodologies to algorithms and techniques of knowledge discovery in databases (KDD), data mining, machine learning and statistics. Usually, the aim of this analysis is to find and identify hidden patterns and the connection in these unstructured data. There are a lot of analysis techniques in text mining but the most common is opinion mining. Opinion mining, also known as sentiment analysis, is an active research area of NLP that analyses thoughts, sentiments, evaluations, attitudes, and emotions through computing subjectivity in text (Hutto & Gilbert, 2014).

Topic Modelling

Topic Modelling, which is considered as unsupervised machine learning, does not need to be trained by humans with tagged data. It can uncover underlying structures in sets or collections of texts or documents and is very helpful for clustering texts. It groups texts depending on how they are distributed to find latent topics (Asri et al., 2022; Keikhosrokiani & Pourya Asl, 2022; Sofian et al., 2022; Ying et al., 2022). This technique is founded upon the idea that every single document is comprised of a combination of topics, and that every topic is comprised of a certain number of words. In doing so, Topic Modelling can unravel the hidden message of the texts.

LSA Topic Modelling

Latent Semantic Analysis (LSA), also known as Latent Semantic Index (LSI), learns the latent topics by performing a matrix factorization on the document term matrix using Singular Value Decomposition (SVD). The model can be generated by using Gensim (Islam, 2019; Jafery et al., 2022; Keikhosrokiani & Pourya Asl, 2022). This algorithm is an effort to resolve issues like polysemy and synonymy in a document that is a mixture of words and corpus. LSA works by reducing an original term-by-document matrix representation of a corpus of documents into a filtered term-document matrix representation through a procedure called SVD. In comparing the smaller document representation of words in vector space to another vector of words, it is generally easier to compare two smaller vectors for similarity purposes (and thus facilitate the retrieval of document) than to compare two larger vectors. The input to LSA algorithm is generally a term-by-document matrix X and the output is a filtered term-by-document matrix $\bar{x}$.

SVD decomposes the original matrix into three matrixes: a document eigenvector matrix X is given by: $X = U\Sigma VT$. Where U is the t x r matrix of eigenvectors of the square symmetric matrix of term covariance XXT, V is the dx r matrix of eigenvectors of the square symmetric matrix of document covariance XTX and Σ is an r x r diagonal matrix containing the square roots of eigenvalues (singular values) of both XXT and XTX and r £ min (t,d) is the rank of matrix X.

LDA Topic Modelling

Latent Dirichlet Allocation (LDA) is a Bayesian used in natural language processing to discover latent topics in a collection of documents. It is an extension of the probabilistic latent semantic analysis (pLSA) method, and it is a model that was to be an improvement of LSA (Jafery et al., 2022; John & Keikhosrokiani, 2022; Suhendra et al., 2022; Ying et al., 2022). The basic idea for this model is that each topic is characterized by a distribution over word in a document that is represented by selecting a random mixture of topic distributions over words. Then a distribution of topic is included in a document. The main task of LDA is to estimate the parameters in the word and document topic distribution using Markov Chain Monte Carlo (MCMC) simulations. There are certain "plates" representing replicates in the LDA graphical model. The outer plate represents document, the inner plate represents the repeated choice of topics and words within a document. The parameters α is a probability on the per-document topic distribution and β is a probability on the per-word distribution, and it is assumed to be sampled once in the corpus level. Note that N is independent of all the other data generating variables (θ and z). A document is a sequence of N words denoted by w = (w1,w2,...,wN), where wn is the nth word in the sequence. A corpus is a collection of M documents denoted by D = {w1,w2,...,wM}. The variables θ are document-level variables that are sampled once per document. The variables zdn and wdn are word-level variables and are sampled once for each word in each document. LDA considers each document as a collection of topics in certain proportion and each topic as a collection of keywords topic (k-topics) or clusters of words. The LDA rearranges the topic distribution within the topics to obtain a good composition of k-topics or cluster of words.

NMF Topic Modelling

For the study of high-dimensional data, non-negative matrix factorization (NMF) is frequently employed since it will automatically extract sparse and useful features from a collection of non-negative data vectors. The matrices are constrained to be used by NMF method. Term frequency-inverse document- frequency (TF-IDF) will be applied to find important terms (Islam, 2019).

Sentiment Analysis

Sentiment analysis has two main approaches which are supervised learning approach and unsupervised learning approach. There are several classifiers in supervised learning like Naïve Bayes, Maximum Entropy and Support Vector Machine that are commonly used in supervised learning approach (Abadah et al., 2023; Jinjri et al., 2021). Unsupervised learning is used to classify the sentiment when there is training data, and it can solve the problem of domain dependency and the need to reduce the training data (Jagdale et al., 2016). There are two seeds such as poor and excellent to calculate the semantic orientation of the phrase. It calculates the average semantic orientation of all such phrases. There are three approaches as Lexicon based method, Dictionary based method and Corpus based method. A lexicon-based sentiment analysis is used to find words that convey ideas in the corpus and then analyze the opinions stated therein. This method involves counting the amount of positive and negative words in each text; the sentiment text will have a higher count. There are some lexical resources such as SentiWordNet, WordNet-Affect, MPQA, SenticNet, TextBlob, and Lexicon (Islam, 2019). TextBlob is the most popular library in Python for processing textual data, and it provides a simple API for diving into common natural language processing (NLP).

MATERIALS AND METHODOLOGY

In its handling the data science process, this study uses OSEMN framework which is described as a taxonomy of data science. There are several phases in this data science process which are Obtain(O), Scrub(S), Explore(E), Model(M) and iNterpret(N). Data science is a blend of the hackers' art especially in primary step "O" and "S". In addition, statistics and machine learning is used in phase "E" and "M". The last phase is "N" that is a main domain in this framework as it helps to understand the domain of data that has been generated to interpret the results (Hasan et al., 2018).

OSEMN Framework have become the main guideline of data science life cycle for this study. Started from collection of books as a dataset, data pre-processing, data analysis (text analytics using NLP) to extract the theme and space using the best algorithm of topic modelling, then proceed with sentiment analysis. All the findings will be interpreted and link to theories to conceive a conclusion (See Figure1).

Data Collection and Dataset

There are two parts of analysis in this study which are Topic modelling and Sentiment analysis. A corpus of 36 life essays by diasporic women from the Middle East were utilized as the data for this research. The writings all offer autobiographical and nonfictional information on women's lives in the area as many of the writers depict their experiences of urban life (Pourya Asl, 2023). The data used in this article is unstructured and is available in EPUB and PDF formats. Table 1 provides information about the 36 books that are selected as datasets for this study.

Data Pre-processing

The main task in data pre-processing stage is to clean and filter to ensure data can be used easily when using the selected analytical tool. The analytical tool that is used in this project is python because python due to its multiple functions that makes data retrieval a lot easier. This stage is very critical because unfiltered and unclean data will give inaccurate and meaningless results for the analysis (Asri et al., 2022; Jafery et al., 2022). The cleaning process is to throw out and replace the missing values when it is necessary. The filtering process is processed to select and include only necessary data or texts that are meaningful and related to the objectives of this study.

The data have two formats which are EPUB and PDF. There are three steps for a simple data pre-processing which is convert, merge and store. Firstly, all the e-books that are in EPUB format are converted into PDF format, and then the converted books are merged into a PDF format. Then, the PDF file is converted into text file using python. The entire text is then divided into sentences, any extra spaces are eliminated, and the text and sentences are then saved in a data frame. There are 359 303 sentences in the 36 books. The number of sentences in the data frame increases to 178 447 after all the sentences with a single word are eliminated.

Figure 1. The proposed analytical framework

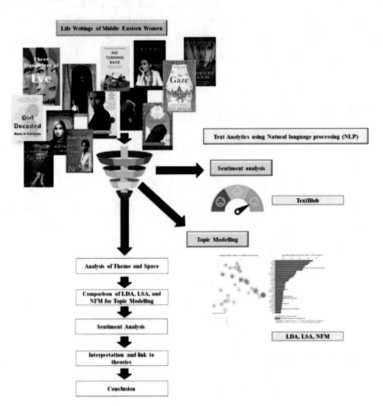

Data Analysis

In this stage, the study examines the patterns and data structure to gain ideas for building a model. Before creating the classification model, the data structure is checked to avoid any complications. Three steps of topic modelling, TextBlob sentiment analysis, and Visualization and Interpretation are used which are briefly explained in this section.

The steps of topic modelling are including the required packages, data pre-processing steps, and building the model. Before conducting LDA, LSA and NMF in Python, several packages are installed in command prompt. The stopwords from NLTK and spacy's en_core_web_sm model have been installed and imported for text pre-processing. All the packages are imported before building Topic modelling. This is necessary for data handling, visualization and recording the time to build a model. In data pre-processing step for LDA, LSA and NMF, irrelevant data such as stop words, which are commonly used in a language and do not bring important meaning to Search Queries, are removed. Removing all the stop words, new line characters, extra space and single quotes in the text are done to save the memory space of the machine and reduce the processing time (Ying et al., 2022). Following that, sentences are tokenized into a list of words, and unnecessary punctuation and characters are eliminated using Gensim's straightforward _preprocess. The deacc=True command is used to remove all punctuation from the phrases. N-grams are groups of words that regularly appear together in writing. Gensim's Phrases model's min count and threshold inputs may be adjusted to create bigrams, trigrams, and n-grams. After bigrams and trigrams model are built, the stop words are removed, and n-grams is built. To find the locations

Table 1. Description of dataset (A corpus of 36 life essays by diasporic women from the Middle East)

No	Title	Author, Year
1	Diary of a Teenage Girl in Iraq	(Ross, 2009)
2	No Turning Back: Life, Loss and Hope in Wartime Syria	(Abouzeid, 2018)
3	In the Land of Invisible Women: A Female Doctor's Journey in the Saudi Kingdom	(Ahmed, 2008)
4	Betrayed: A terrifying true story of a young woman dragged back to Iraq	(Shears & Shears, 2009)
5	Daring to Drive: A Saudi Woman's Awakening	(Al-Sharif, 2017)
6	The Woman from Tantoura: A Palestinian Novel	(Ashour, 2014)
7	Infidel	(Ali, 2008)
8	Nomad: From Islam to America: A personal journey through the clash of civilizations	(Ali, 2011)
9	The caged virgin: an emancipation proclamation for women and Islam	(Ali, 2006)
10	Things I've Been Silent About: Memories of a Prodigal Daughter	(Nafisi, 2010)
11	Rain over Baghdad: A novel of Iraq	(El Badry, 2014)
12	Balcony on the Moon_ Coming of Age in Palestine	(Barakat, 2016)
13	Born with Wings: The spiritual Journey of a Modern Muslim Woman – Spiegel & Grau	(Khan, 2018)
14	Brownies and Kalashnikovs: A Saudi Woman's Memoir of American Arabia and Wartime Beirut	(Basrawi, 2009)
15	This is what America Looks Like: My Journey from Refugee to Congresswoman	(Omar, 2020)
16	American Chick in Saudi Arabia: A Memoir	(Sasson, 2012)
17	For the Love of a Son: One Afghan Woman's Quest for her Stolen Child	(Sasson, 2010)
18	Mayada: Daughter of Iraq- Dutton Adult	(Sasson, 2003)
19	Princess: A True Story of Life Behind the Veil in Saudi	(Sasson, 1992)
20	The Boy on the Beach: My Family's Escape from Syria and Our Hope for a New Home	(Kurdi, 2018)
21	The Shadow of the Crescent Moon	(Bhutto, 2016)
22	The Beekeeper: Rescuing the Stolen Women of Iraq	(Mikhail, 2018)
23	One Girl's Journey from War: Torn Syria in a Wheelchair	(Mustafa & Lamb, 2016)
24	The last girl: My story of captivity, and my fight against the Islamic State	(Murad & Krajeski, 2017)
25	Laughing All the Way to the Mosque: The Misadventures of a Muslim Woman	(Nawaz, 2016)
26	Osama's Wife and Son Take Us Inside Their Secret World	(Bin Laden et al., 2009)
27	Girl Decoded: A Scientist's Quest to Reclaim Our Humanity by Bringing Emotional Intelligence to Technology- Crown	(El Kaliouby & Colman, 2020)
28	Threading My Prayer Rug: One Woman's Journey from Pakistani Muslim to American Muslim	(Rehman, 2016)
29	The Wrong End of the Table: A mostly Comic Memoir of a Muslim Arab American Woman Just Trying to fit in	(Salman, 2019)
30	Yasmeena's Choice: A true Story of War, Rape, Courage and Survival	(Sasson, 2013)
31	The Gaze	(Shafak, 2015)
32	Three Daughters of Eve	(Shafak, 2017)
33	Ghosts of Revolution_ Rekindled Memories of Imprisonment in Iran	(Talebi, 2011)
34	A God Who Hates: The Courageous Woman Who Inflamed the Muslim World Speaks Out Against the Evils of Islam	(Sultan, 2011)
35	A Woman in the Crossfire_ Diaries of the Syrian Revolution	(Yazbek, 2012)
36	Between Two Worlds: Escape from Tyranny: Growing Up in the Shadow of Saddam	(Salbi & Becklund, 2006)

and major themes that arise in the corpus is the main goal of applying LDA in this project. The model's produced keyword aids in identifying the locations and the topics that correspond. The construction of the lexicon and corpus comes last before constructing the Gensim model. (Ying et al., 2022).

Before starting to perform sentiment analysis by using Textblob, several packages are installed in Command Prompt and Python Jupyter notebook 3 such as U textblob, m textblob.download_corpora and wordcloud. In the data pre-processing step, there are several text files for different themes, all of which are imported. The data is then stored in a data frame. Before dropping the irrelevant data there, the text type is changed to string. After that, the text is changed into lowercase. Lowercasing all the text can help to deal with sparsity issues. For example, searching the documents for the term "arab" showed no results because "arab" was labelled as "Arab". Lowercasing can be generally helpful to detect the identical terms. The punctuation and stop words are removed before calculating the polarity for the sentences. By removing punctuation and stop words, the focus can be directed on important words as punctuation and stop words do not hold any information. Lastly, the model is built, and the polarity is calculated and recorded in the same data frame (Keikhosrokiani & Pourya Asl, 2022; Ying et al., 2022).

The last phase in data science cycle is to visualize and interpret the results. Interpreting the results refers to how to present and deliver the data and results to solve problem and answer the research question of the study. Choosing the number of topics is crucial for topic modelling. The number of topics is currently fixed at 36. The Mallet model is then constructed using the Gensim wrapper and implemented within Gensim. Classification using clustering does not require training data to group the observation based on the similar characteristics because algorithms define the output based on the theory. The tools used to understand the results of topic modelling with Gensim and LDA with Mallet include the amount of time the model took to develop, the weighted keywords, the coherence score, and an intertopic distance map. The mean of the polarity score is generated in the context of sentiment analysis to categorise the spatial representation as either positive or negative.

RESULTS AND DISCUSSION

This section will explain the way optimal number of topics are decided as well as which algorithm will be used for extracting the place name and theme and will explain the sentiment score for each theme that is extracted using topic modelling.

To find the optimal number of topics, many LDA, LSA and NMF models with different values numbers of topics are built, and the model that gives the highest coherence score is chosen. To make it easier in deciding the number of topics "compute_coherence_values" has helped us to trains multiple LDA and LSA models and provide the models and corresponding coherence score. Figure 2 shows a graph of topic number against the coherence score. For LDA, gensim's coherence model and mallet's coherence score are used to calculate topic coherence score. For LSA, only gensim's coherence model is used to calculate the topic coherence. For NMF, topic coherence measure called TC-W2V is used for gensim implementation (Islam, 2019; Mikolov et al., 2013). Based on Table 2 and Figure 2, the highest coherence score = 0.4346 is achieved when the number of topics is 38 for LDA. For LSA, the highest coherence score = 0.1298 is achieved when the number of topics is 20; and for NMF, the highest coherence score = 0.3970 is achieved when the number of topics is 2. The results show that more informative and meaningful topics can be obtained by using LDA model than LSA and NMF models. Because the LSA decomposed matrix is a relatively dense matrix and it is challenging to index specific dimensions,

Table 2. Number of topics with coherence score for LDA and LSA

Number of topics	2	8	14	20	26	32	38
LDA	0.3944	0.2753	0.3326	0.3861	0.4006	0.4139	0.4346
LSA	0.1290	0.1210	0.1290	0.1298	0.1290	0.1200	0.1205
NMF	0.3970	0.1853	0.1916	0.2115	0.2378	0.2512	0.2670

LSA is unable to capture the numerous meanings of words and has lesser accuracy than LDA (Islam, 2019). This study uses LDA for further analysis because it has the highest coherence score.

After doing topic modelling by LDA, LSA and NMF, LDA is used for further analysis. For LDA, Gensim and mallet can be used to calculate the topic coherence. Here, two models are built to decide which model can be used in this analysis. Table 3 shows the results from LDA algorithm using Gensim and mallet that provide the time taken to build the LDA model and the coherence score. Mallet took 118.8928 seconds and Gensim 654.2989 seconds to generate the LDA model, respectively. The size of the dataset used in the model makes both approaches time-consuming. LDA using Gensim requires more time to construct than LDA with a mallet does. Mallet has a coherence score of 0.4436, whereas

Figure 2. The Graph of optimal Number of Topics vs Coherence Score. Number of Topics (k) are selected based on the highest coherence score

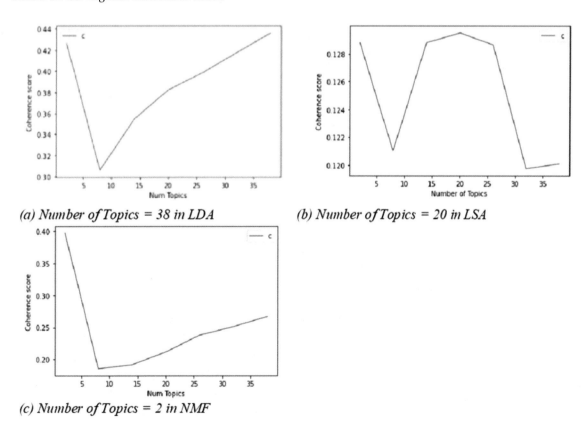

(a) Number of Topics = 38 in LDA   *(b) Number of Topics = 20 in LSA*

(c) Number of Topics = 2 in NMF

Table 3. Result from LDA model

Performance	LDA With Gensim	LDA With Mallet
Time Taken to Build Model	654.2989 seconds	118.8928 seconds
Coherence Score	0.3700	0.4346

Gensim's is 0.3700. The LDA model is constructed using the model with the best coherence score. The LDA with mallet outcome is chosen as it has the greatest coherence rating.

The result shows that LDA with Mallet contains a higher coherence score and the number of topics is set to 36. Next, a web-based interactive visualization of topics which is pyLDAvis library used to visualize the topics and the associated keywords which is shown in Figure 3.

The left side contains 36 bubbles that represent 36 topics or clusters, and the larger the bubble the more prevalent that topic is. But as illustrated in the Figure 3(a), all the bubbles have a same size. A good model should have a fairly big and non-overlapping bubbles scattered throughout the map instead of being in same region. The model that contains too many topics will have many overlapping topics. The right-hand side shows the top 30 salient keywords and when the cursor moves over one bubble, the words and bars are updated. Since the bubbles on the left are scattered throughout the model and they do not overlap between them in the Figure 3 then it shows that LDA with Mallet algorithm has success-fully built a good topic model. In Figure 3(b), when the cursor is moved over one of the bubbles (topic 2), the words and bars on the right-hand side are updated and the top 30 salient keywords for selected and their term frequency are shown. It is clear that topic 2 contains the keywords "Arab", "America", "state", "Power", "Political", "Support" as top 30 salient keywords. It can be concluded that authors are likely to discuss the political issues in the Arab world and the United States of America. The results clearly show a noticeable association of geographical terms and themes.

Table 4 shows that only 15 topics are selected to be included to achieve the goal of representing interconnection between the three aspects of content, space, and emotion. The theme is decided based on the top 30 salient words. Besides, polarities are generated from Sentiment Analysis in which polarity scores as calculated by TextBlob are divided into three positive (P>0), neutral (P=0) and negative(P<0).

Table 4 is the summary of results from two natural language processing techniques. There are 15 topics that are selected from 36 topics that have been drawn. LDA with mallet has helped us to list down the places that have been mentioned by all the writers as well as the 15 themes that have been discussed by the women writers. Based on the polarity score, Topic 2 has the highest polarity score and the places that have been mentioned are Saudi Arabia, America, United States, Europe and Middle East that are accompanied with the major theme of political. This means that places that have been mentioned in this topic are associated with the same political theme, and the sentiment is positive. The lowest score is Topic 22 and the writers have shown negative sentiment when they write about Osama's Family, and the places that are related to this theme are Afghanistan and Pakistan. This result shows that these places are mostly related to topics related to Osama's Family and the sentiment is negative. By looking at the places that are mentioned by the writers, it becomes clear that the writers like to mention their home-town compared to their current places. Having analyzed the data about sentiment alongside the data on theme and geography, the study examines the common grounds where certain places are associated with certain themes and/or emotions. For example, the themes most closely associated with Saudi Arabia are those of political, economy, woman's right, and violence. Unexpectedly, the polarity score or sentiment

Figure 3. Intertopic distance map of LDA with Mallet model using pyLDAVis

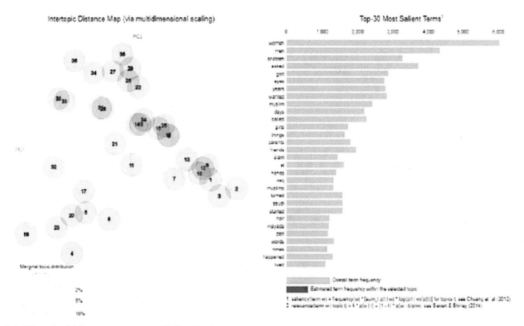

(a) Blue bubble represents all the topic

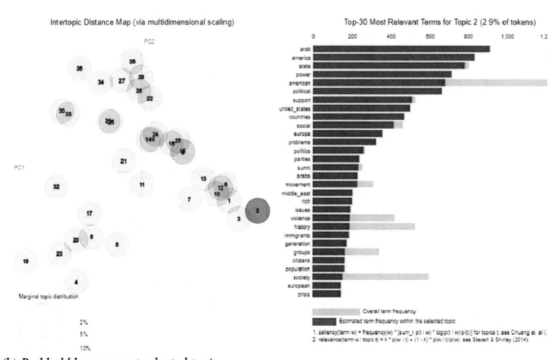

(b) Red bubble represent selected topic

Table 4. List of the name of places, themes, and polarity score

	LDA with Mallet		TextBlob	
	Places	**Themes**	**Polarity Score**	**Sentiment Score**
Topic 2	Saudi Arabia, America, United States, Europe, Middle East	Political	0.4140	Positive
Topic 3	Saudi Arabia, Dhahran, Riyadh	Economy	0.0498	Positive
Topic 5	'Mir Ali' a city in Pakistan	Food Struggling due to economic issues	0.0095	Positive
Topic 6	Iraq, Iran, Mosul, British, Kuwait, Tehran	Saddam Hussien's Regime	0.0603	Positive
Topic 7	Damascus, Syria	Syrian Civil War	0.0647	Positive
Topic 9	Baghdad, Egypt, Cairo	Medium Media	0.0369	Positive
Topic 10	Saudi Arabia	Women's Rights	0.0427	Positive
Topic 11	Mahad, Beirut, Somalia, Palestine, Sidon, Israel	Refugees	0.0468	Positive
Topic 12	Syria, Turkey, Germany, Aleppo	Terrorist/activist	0.0223	Positive
Topic 15	Mecca	Knowledge	0.0299	Positive
Topic 20	Saudi Arabia	Violence	0.0321	Positive
Topic 22	Afghanistan, Pakistan	Osama's Family	-0.0164	Negative
Topic 25	Holland	School's Issues	0.0471	Positive
Topic 28	Jeddah, York	Memories of Family	0.0414	Positive
Topic 32	Samarra	Prison	0.0457	Positive

for this particular theme is more than 0 and is positive. The themes that are related to Syria are Syrian Civil War, terrorism and activism. With regards to countries like Iran and Iraq, the related themes are oppressions of Saddam Hussien's regime, terrorist activities and prison life. Almost all the topics have lowest polarity score and are given positive sentiment. From a human perspective, however, the themes and places are expected to be associated with a negative sentiment.

According to result from other studies (Anaya, 2011), LDA and LSA have the same accuracy rate at a high level of abstraction which is 84%. But at a lower level of abstraction, the accuracy rate for LDA is 64%, and is 67% for LSA. But here when a real experiment is conducted it shows that LDA has a high accuracy compared to LSA. For NMF, even though the accuracy for LDA and NMF are similar (Islam, 2019), LDA is more consistent. This is agreeable because the results show that LDA and NMF have almost the same result, but LDA has a high coherence score compared to NMF. Even though this method is not very efficient in identifying themes, geography and sentiment, this method is still helpful in giving a sense to discover the dominant topics, places and sentiment score for each topic in a corpus as a whole (Jockers, 2016). In previous studies, this method has been applied on social media (twitter) and movie review dataset, but here it is applied on a number of auto-/biographical narratives that comprise a long text.

CONCLUSION

Analyzing a large corpus data based on textual reading is very challenging as this traditional method has generated fierce debate in literary studies with regard to the accuracy of representations and truth-telling in creative writings. The present study aimed at proposing a computerized model to explore themes and sentiments related to different spaces in Middle Eastern auto-/biographical narratives, a subject area that has drawn equally controversial attention over the past two decades (Asl, 2019, 2020). For the proposed model, topic modelling (i.e. LDA, LSA, NMF), sentiment analysis (TextBlob library) and Python are used as analytical tools to discover collocated place names and to determine the overall impression of the corpus's linked themes and sentiments. After using LDA, LSA, NMF for topic modelling, the highest coherence score = 0.4346 is achieved for LDA when the number of topics is 38, the highest coherence score = 0.1298 is obtained for LSA when the number of topics is 20, and the highest coherence score = 0.3970 is achieved for NMF when the number of topics is 2. The results indicate that more informative and meaningful topics are attained by using LDA model than LSA and NMF models. Having employed different topic modelling algorithms, the study discovered interesting association between theme, geography and sentiment in this dataset. For the topic modelling part, LDA is successfully found as the best analytical model of topic modelling that can handle the dataset in the present project. For the sentiment analysis part, the polarity score is obtained by using TextBlob. With limited resources, the association between theme, geography and/or sentiment is established. In doing so, this study becomes important within the discipline of literary studies as the proposed methodology can work as a reference for future research on analyzing huge literary textual data. To address these sentiment analysis issues and take an initiative to next level, this study recommends applying supervised techniques and using other dictionaries to reveal the pattern and context of these books in future research. Another interesting direction to extend this study is to design and improve topic interpretability to implement Local Interpretable model-agnostic Explanation (LIME).

ACKNOWLEDGMENT

The authors would like to thank School of Computer Sciences and School of Humanities for the unlimited support.

REFERENCES

Abadah, M. S. K., Keikhosrokiani, P., & Zhao, X. (2023). Analytics of Public Reactions to the COVID-19 Vaccine on Twitter Using Sentiment Analysis and Topic Modelling. In D. Valle-Cruz, N. Plata-Cesar, & J. L. González-Ruíz (Eds.), *Handbook of Research on Applied Artificial Intelligence and Robotics for Government Processes* (pp. 156–188). IGI Global. doi:10.4018/978-1-6684-5624-8.ch008

Abouzeid, R. (2018). *No turning back: Life, loss, and hope in wartime Syria*. WW Norton & Company.

Ahmed, Q. (2008). *In the land of invisible women: A female doctor's journey in the Saudi Kingdom* (1st ed.). Sourcebooks, Inc.

Al-Sharif, M. (2017). *Daring to drive: A Saudi woman's awakening* (1st ed.). Simon and Schuster.

Ali, A. H. (2006). *The caged virgin: An emancipation proclamation for women and Islam.* Simon and Schuster.

Ali, A. H. (2008). *Infidel.* Simon and Schuster.

Ali, A. H. (2011). *Nomad: From Islam to America: A personal journey through the clash of civilizations.* Simon and Schuster.

Anishchenkova, V. (2014). *Autobiographical identities in contemporary Arab culture.* Edinburgh University Press.

Ashour, R. (2014). *The woman from Tantoura: A Palestinian novel* (1st ed.). Oxford University Press.

Asl, M. P. (2018). Practices of counter-conduct as a mode of resistance in Middle East women's life writings. *3L: Language, Linguistics, Literature®, 24*(2), 195-205. doi:10.17576/3L-2018-2402-15

Asl, M. P. (2019). Foucauldian rituals of justice and conduct in Zainab Salbi's Between Two Worlds. *Journal of Contemporary Iraq & the Arab World, 13*(2-3), 227–242. doi:10.1386/jciaw_00010_1

Asl, M. P. (2020). Spaces of change: Arab women's reconfigurations of selfhood through heterotopias in Manal al-Sharif's Daring to Drive. *KEMANUSIAAN the Asian Journal of Humanities, 27*(2), 123–143. doi:10.21315/kajh2020.27.2.7

Asri, M. A. Z. B. M., Keikhosrokiani, P., & Asl, M. P. (2022). Opinion Mining Using Topic Modeling: A Case Study of Firoozeh Dumas's Funny in Farsi in Goodreads. Advances on Intelligent Informatics and Computing. doi:10.1007/978-3-030-98741-1_19

Barakat, I. (2016). *Balcony on the moon: Coming of age in Palestine.* Farrar, Straus and Giroux (BYR).

Basrawi, F. (2009). *Brownies and kalashnikovs: A Saudi moman's memoir of American Arabia and wartime Beirut.* South Street Press Reading.

Bhutto, F. (2016). *The shadow of the crescent moon.* Penguin Books.

Bin Laden, N., bin Laden, O., & Sasson, J. (2009). Growing up Bin Laden: Osama's wife and son take us inside their secret world (1st ed.). St. Martin's Press.

Binti Rosli, N. H., & Keikhosrokiani, P. (2022). Big medical data mining system (BigMed) for the detection and classification of COVID-19 misinformation. In P. Keikhosrokiani (Ed.), *Big Data Analytics for Healthcare* (pp. 233–244). Academic Press. doi:10.1016/B978-0-323-91907-4.00014-5

El Badry, H. (2014). Rain Over Baghdad: An Egyptian Novel (1st ed.). The American University in Cairo Press.

El Kaliouby, R., & Colman, C. (2020). *Girl decoded: A scientist's quest to reclaim our humanity by bringing emotional intelligence to technology.* Currency.

Golley, N. A.-H. (2007). *Arab women's lives retold: Exploring identity through writing.* Syracuse University Press.

Hasan, A., Moin, S., Karim, A., & Shamshirband, S. (2018). Machine learning-based sentiment analysis for twitter accounts. *Mathematical and Computational Applications*, *23*(1), 11. doi:10.3390/mca23010011

Hutto, C., & Gilbert, E. (2014). Vader: A parsimonious rule-based model for sentiment analysis of social media text. *Proceedings of the International AAAI Conference on Web and Social Media*.

Islam, T. (2019). Yoga-veganism: Correlation mining of twitter health data. *8th KDD Workshop on Issues of Sentiment Discovery and Opinion Mining (WISDOM)*. doi:10.1609/icwsm.v8i1.14550

Jafery, N. N., Keikhosrokiani, P., & Asl, M. P. (2022). Text analytics model to identify the connection between theme and sentiment in literary works: A case study of Iraqi life writings. In P. Keikhosrokiani & M. Pourya Asl (Eds.), *Handbook of Research on Opinion Mining and Text Analytics on Literary Works and Social Media* (pp. 173–190). IGI Global. doi:10.4018/978-1-7998-9594-7.ch008

Jagdale, R. S., Shirsat, V. S., & Deshmukh, S. N. (2016). Sentiment analysis of events from Twitter using open source tool. *IJCSMC*, *5*(4), 475–485.

Jinjri, W. M., Keikhosrokiani, P., & Abdullah, N. L. (2021). Machine Learning Algorithms for The Classification of Cardiovascular Disease-A Comparative Study. *2021 International Conference on Information Technology (ICIT)*. doi:10.1109/ICIT52682.2021.9491677

John, S. A., & Keikhosrokiani, P. (2022). COVID-19 fake news analytics from social media using topic modeling and clustering. In P. Keikhosrokiani (Ed.), Big Data Analytics for Healthcare (pp. 221–232). Academic Press. doi:10.1016/B978-0-323-91907-4.00003-0

Keikhosrokiani, P. (2022). *Handbook of Research on Consumer Behavior Change and Data Analytics in the Socio-Digital Era*. IGI Global. doi:10.4018/978-1-6684-4168-8

Keikhosrokiani, P., & Kamaruddin, N. S. A. B. (2022). IoT-Based In-Hospital-In-Home Heart Disease Remote Monitoring System with Machine Learning Features for Decision Making. In S. Mishra, A. González-Briones, A. K. Bhoi, P. K. Mallick, & J. M. Corchado (Eds.), *Connected e-Health: Integrated IoT and Cloud Computing* (pp. 349–369). Springer International Publishing. doi:10.1007/978-3-030-97929-4_16

Keikhosrokiani, P., & Pourya Asl, M. (Eds.). (2022). *Handbook of Research on Opinion Mining and Text Analytics on Literary Works and Social Media*. IGI Global. doi:10.4018/978-1-7998-9594-7

Khan, D. (2018). *Born with wings: The Spiritual Journey of a modern muslim woman*. Random House.

Kurdi, T. (2018). *The boy on the beach: My family's escape from Syria and our hope for a new home*. Simon and Schuster.

Mikhail, D. (2018). *The beekeeper: Rescuing the stolen women of Iraq* (1st ed.). New Directions Publishing.

Murad, N., & Krajeski, J. (2017). *The last girl: My story of captivity, and my fight against the Islamic State*. Tim Duggan Books.

Mustafa, N., & Lamb, C. (2016). *Nujeen: One girl's incredible journey from war-torn Syria in a wheelchair*. Harper Wave.

Nafisi, A. (2010). *Things I've been silent about: Memories of a prodigal daughter*. Random House Incorporated.

Nawaz, Z. (2016). *Laughing all the way to the mosque: The misadventures of a Muslim woman*. Virago.

Omar, I. (2020). *This is what America looks like: My Journey from refugee to congresswoman*. C. Hurst (Publishers) Limited.

Pourya Asl, M. (Ed.). (2022). *Gender, place, and identity of South Asian women*. IGI Global. doi:10.4018/978-1-6684-3626-4

Pourya Asl, M. (Ed.). (2023). *Urban poetics and politics in contemporary South Asia and the Middle East*. IGI Global. doi:10.4018/978-1-6684-6650-6

Rehman, S. (2016). Threading my prayer rug: One woman's journey from Pakistani Muslim to American Muslim. Audible Studios on Brilliance Audio.

Ross, J. (2009). *IraqiGirl: Diary of a teenage girl in Iraq*. Haymarket Books.

Salbi, Z., & Becklund, L. (2006). *Between two worlds: Escape from tyranny: Growing up in the shadow of Saddam*. Penguin.

Salman, A. (2019). *The wrong end of the table: A mostly comic memoir of a muslim Arab American woman just trying to fit in*. Skyhorse.

Sasson, J. (1992). *Princess: A true story of life behind the veil in Saudi* (1st ed.). Windsor-Brooke Books.

Sasson, J. (2003). *Mayada, daughter of Iraq* (1st ed.). Dutton Adult.

Sasson, J. (2010). *For the love of a son: One Afghan woman's quest for her stolen child*. Liza Dawson Associates.

Sasson, J. (2012). *American chick in Saudi Arabia*. Liza Dawson Associates.

Sasson, J. (2013). *Yasmeena's choice: A true story of war, rape, courage and survival*. LDA.

Sassoon, J. (2016). *Anatomy of authoritarianism in the Arab republics*. Cambridge University Press. doi:10.1017/CBO9781107337893

Shafak, E. (2015). *The gaze*. Penguin Books

Shafak, E. (2017). *Three daughters of eve*. Bloomsbury Publishing USA.

Shears, L. A., & Shears, R. (2009). Betrayed: A terrifying true story of a young woman dragged back to Iraq (1st ed.). Academic Press.

Sofian, N. B., Keikhosrokiani, P., & Asl, M. P. (2022). Opinion mining and text analytics of reader reviews of Yoko Ogawa's The Housekeeper and the Professor in Goodreads. In P. Keikhosrokiani & M. Pourya Asl (Eds.), *Handbook of Research on Opinion Mining and Text Analytics on Literary Works and Social Media* (pp. 240–262). IGI Global. doi:10.4018/978-1-7998-9594-7.ch010

Suhendra, N. H. B., Keikhosrokiani, P., Asl, M. P., & Zhao, X. (2022). Opinion mining and text analytics of literary reader responses: A case study of reader responses to KL Noir volumes in Goodreads using sentiment analysis and topic. In P. Keikhosrokiani & M. Pourya Asl (Eds.), *Handbook of Research on Opinion Mining and Text Analytics on Literary Works and Social Media* (pp. 191–239). IGI Global. doi:10.4018/978-1-7998-9594-7.ch009

Sultan, W. (2011). *A god who hates: The courageous woman who inflamed the muslim world speaks out against the evils of Islam.* St. Martin's Press.

Talebi, S. (2011). *Ghosts of revolution: Rekindled memories of imprisonment in Iran* (1st ed.). Stanford University Press. doi:10.1515/9780804775816

Tally, R. T. Jr. (2017). *The Routledge handbook of literature and space.* Taylor & Francis. doi:10.4324/9781315745978

Teoh Yi Zhe, I., & Keikhosrokiani, P. (2021). Knowledge workers mental workload prediction using optimised ELANFIS. *Applied Intelligence, 51*(4), 2406–2430. doi:10.100710489-020-01928-5

Yazbek, S. (2012). *A woman in the crossfire: Diaries of the Syrian revolution.* Haus Publishing. doi:10.2307/j.ctt1zxsm7p

Ying, S. Y., Keikhosrokiani, P., & Asl, M. P. (2022). Opinion Mining on Viet Thanh Nguyen's The Sympathizer Using Topic Modelling and Sentiment Analysis. *Journal of Information Technology Management, 14*, 163-183. 10.22059/jitm.2022.84895

Chapter 3
A Machine Learning Approach to the Analytics of Representations of Violence in Khaled Hosseini's Novels

Abdikadir Hussein Elmi
School of Computer Sciences, Universiti Sains Malaysia, Malaysia

Pantea Keikhosrokiani
ⓘ https://orcid.org/0000-0003-4705-2732
School of Computer Sciences, Universiti Sains Malaysia, Malaysia

Moussa Pourya Asl
ⓘ https://orcid.org/0000-0002-8426-426X
School of Humanities, Universiti Sains Malaysia, Malaysia

ABSTRACT

Over the past two decades, literary works from Afghanistan have sought to depict the extensive and increasing level of violence directed against individuals and communities. This study aims to identify the different types of violence represented in selected literary works from the country. To this end, an artificial intelligence approach—comprised of opinion mining and hybrid machine learning models—is developed as a method of analysis. The Afghan American writer Khaled Hosseini's novels—The Kite Runner (2003), A Thousand Splendid Suns (2007), and And the Mountains Echoed (2017)—are used as primary data sources. As a theoretical framework, the study benefits from the Norwegian sociologist Johan Galtung's theory of conflict triangle—direct violence, structural violence, and cultural violence. To classify the sentiments related to types of violence in the selected novels, the study utilizes sentiment analysis and machine learning algorithms.

DOI: 10.4018/978-1-6684-6242-3.ch003

INTRODUCTION

Over the past two decades, literary works from Afghanistan have sought to depict the extensive and increasing level of violence directed against individuals and communities. Since the invasion of the country by US-led forces in late 2001, Afghanistan has become a locus of uncertain political and religious tensions, fear, conflict, and violence. The high levels of violence in the country are often portrayed by literary writers through fictional narratives (Asl, 2019). The novelist Khaled Hosseini is among the forerunners of Afghan writers whose works are replete with instances of violence prevalent in the country. His three novels *The Kite Runner* (2003), *A Thousand Splendid Suns* (2007), and *And the Mountains Echoed* (2017) provide illuminating insights about the daily experiences of conflict and violence in contemporary Afghanistan. This study aims to analyze the three novels to identify the different types of violence represented in the stories in light of the Norwegian sociologist Johan Galtung's theory of Conflict Triangle—direct violence, structural violence, and cultural violence.

To achieve this goal, an artificial intelligence approach—comprised of Opinion Mining and Hybrid Machine Learning Models—is developed as a method of data mining and data analysis. More specifically, the study utilizes Opinion Mining, Sentiment Analysis, and Machine Learning algorithms to identify and classify the sentiments related to the various types of violence as depicted in the selected novels. Opinion Mining or Sentiment Analysis are useful in analyzing NLP applications. With the development of applications like network public opinion analysis, the demand for sentiment analysis and opinion mining has been growing. OM is one of the most interesting applications of Natural Language Processing (NLP) used in social media applications whose goal is the evaluation and classification of text with emotionally charged language which expresses or implies positive, negative, and neutral sentiments. Sentiment analysis in a broad sense is a way to know a user's emotion (sentiment) using his features (Oramas Bustillos et al., 2019). Positive emotion can be happy or liking something while negative emotions include anger, unhappiness, etc. Neutral emotions are when a person shows no expression (Asri et al., 2022a; Fasha et al., 2022a; Sofian et al., 2022a; Suhendra et al., 2022a)

The main objective of this chapter is to identify the different types of violence in selected literary books based on Johan Galtung's framework. In addition, this chapter attempt to classify the sentiments in the selected novels using sentiment analysis. Finally, this chapter aims to classify sentiments related to the types of violence as detected in objective one using machine learning.

Other sections of this chapter are structured as follows. Section 2 presents a review of literature, while Section 3 discusses the methodology of the study. Section 4 is the analysis and results, and section 5 provides the discussions. Finally, the conclusions and future works are discussed in sections 6.

LITERATURE REVIEW

Human life is filled with emotions and opinions. We cannot imagine the world without them. Emotions and opinions play a vital role in nearly all human actions. They lead the human life by influencing the way we think, what we do and how we act. (*View of Study of Learning Classifiers Over Review Text Dataset for Aspect Level Sentiment Analysis.Pdf*, n.d.) Having access to large quantities of data through internet and its transformation into a social web is no longer an issue, as there are terabytes of new information produced on the web every day that are available to any individual (Tsapatsoulis & Djouvas, 2019). Even more importantly, it has changed the way we share information. The receivers of the information do not only consume the available content on web, but in turn, actively annotate this content and generate new pieces of information (Demidova, 2021). Today people not only comment on the existing information, bookmark pages, and provide ratings but they also share their ideas, news, and knowledge with the community at large. In this way, the entire community becomes a writer, in addition to being a reader (Demidova, 2021). Sentiment analysis, also referred to as opinion mining, is an approach to natural language processing (NLP) that identifies the emotional tone behind a body of text (Abadah et al., 2023; al Mamun et al., 2022; Chu et al., 2022; García-Contreras et al., 2022; Yousaf et al., 2021). This is a popular way for organizations to determine and categorize opinions about a product, service, or idea. It involves the use of data mining, machine learning (ML) and artificial intelligence (AI) to mine text for sentiment and subjective information. Sentiment analysis systems help organizations gather insights from unorganized and unstructured text that comes from online sources such as emails, blog posts, support tickets, web chats, social media channels, forums, and comments. Algorithms replace manual data processing by implementing rule-based, automatic or hybrid methods (Demidova, 2021). Rule-based systems perform sentiment analysis based on predefined, lexicon-based rules while automatic systems learn from data with machine learning techniques. A hybrid sentiment analysis combines both approaches. The existing mediums like Blogs, Wikis, Forums and Social Networks where users can post information, give opinions, and get feedback from other users on different topics, ranging from politics and health to product reviews and travelling (Ingole et al., 2018). The increasing popularity of personal publishing services of different kinds suggests that opinionated information will become an important aspect of the textual data on the web. Recently, many researchers have focused on this area. They are trying to fetch opinion information to analyze and summarize the opinions expressed automatically with computers (Li et al., 2019). This new research domain is usually called Opinion Mining and Sentiment Analysis. Until now, researchers have evolved several techniques to the solution of the problem. Current-day Opinion Mining and Sentiment Analysis is a field of study at the crossroad of Information Retrieval (IR) and Natural Language Processing (NLP) and share some characteristics with other disciplines such as text mining and Information Extraction (Keyvanpour et al., 2020). Text analysis typically takes place in the following order: document collection, analysis and filtering, structuring, frequency analysis and similarity analysis. Word clouds, word networks, topic modelling, document classification and semantic analysis are all ways to display the results of the analysis (Ingole et al., 2018; Jafery et al., 2022; Keikhosrokiani, 2022; Keikhosrokiani & Asl, 2022; Suhendra et al., 2022b). Text analysis can be used on any text data available on the Web and in any mother tongue, such as Japanese, Chinese, English or Hindi. Web data may also include photos, audios, and videos in addition to text, which makes data completely unstructured (Khalifa et al., 2022). Text analytics' task is to extract text from retrieved actual information from the web and use text mining to visualize the text data only. Text analytics and text mining are both used alternately, however there is a fine line between the two (Khalifa et al., 2022). Text mining is defined as the process of extracting information from data. However, text analytics techniques can also be used to extract information from data. Text analytics only utilizes a bag of words, word frequencies, and used for summarization, document clustering, and document topic classification (Rameshbhai & Paulose, 2019).

Opinion Mining

Opinions are subjective statements that reflect people's sentiments or perceptions about the entities and events. Much of the existing research on text information processing has been (almost exclusively) focused on mining and retrieval of information, e.g., information retrieval, Web search, and many other text mining and natural language processing tasks. Little work has been done on the processing of opinions until only recently. Yet, opinions are so important that whenever one needs to decide one wants to hear others' opinions. This is not only true for individuals but also true for organizations (Asri et al., 2022a, 2022b; Fasha et al., 2022b; Keikhosrokiani & Asl, 2022; Sofian et al., 2022a, 2022b; Suhendra et al., 2022b; Yousaf et al., 2021; Yun Ying et al., 2022).

Sentiment Analysis

Sentiment analysis is the field of study that analyzes people's opinions, sentiments, evaluations, attitudes, and emotions from written language. It is one of the most active research areas in natural language processing and is also widely studied in data mining, Web mining, and text mining. The growing importance of sentiment analysis coincides with the growth of social media such as reviews, forum discussions, blogs, micro-blogs, Twitter, and social networks. For the first time in human history, we now have a huge volume of opinionated data recorded in digital form for analysis. Sentiment analysis systems are being applied in almost every business and social domain because opinions are central to almost all human activities and are key influencers of our behaviors. Our beliefs and perceptions of reality, and the choices we make, are largely conditioned by how others see and evaluate the world. The computational study of people's opinions, appraisals, attitudes, and emotions toward entities, individuals, issues, events, topics, and their attributes is known as sentiment analysis or opinion mining.

There are three approaches available for sentiment analysis such as machine learning, lexicon-based approach, and rule-based approach, as shown in Table 1 (Devika et al., 2016)

Table 1. Comparison of three approaches for sentiment analysis

Criteria	Machine Learning Approach	Lexicon-Based Approach	Rule-Based Approach
Classification	Supervised Learning Unsupervised Learning	Unsupervised Learning	Supervised Learning Unsupervised Learning
Advantages	- Does not need Dictionary - Demonstrate the hight accuracy of classification.	- Labelled data and the procedure of learning is not required	- Sentence level sentiment classification performs better than the word level.
Disadvantages	- Classifier trained are domain based - Required time to train	- Requires powerful linguistic resource which is difficult resource	- Finite number of words - Efficiency and accuracy depend on the defining rules.
Algorithms	Support Vector Machine Naïve Bayes Neural Networks	VADER (Valence Aware Dictionary and sEntimentReasoner) SentiWordNet	Textblob VADER

Summary of Related Works

Table 2 summarizes the data source used, methodology and the accuracy obtained presented from 11 studies (Wan et al., 2012).

Table 2. Summary of related works

No.	Title (author, year)	Dataset	Methodology	Accuracy
1	Sentiment Analysis of Twitter Data Using Machine Learning Approaches and Semantic Analysis (Gaba & Verma, 2022)	Twitter	Naive Bayes Maximum Entropy Support Vector Machine Semantic Analysis (WordNet)	88.2 83.8 85.5 89.9
2	Detection and Classification of mental illnesses on social media using RoBERTa. (Murarka et al., 2020)	Reddit	Long short-term memory (LSTM), BERT, RoBERTa	72.0 82.0 86.0
3	A deep learning model for detecting mental illness from user content on social media (Kim et al., 2020)	Pushshif API	A Convolutional Neural Network (ConvNet/CNN), XGBoost	75.13 71.69
4	Sentiment Analysis and Opinion Mining using Machine Learning Techniques (Sari & Kalender, 2021)	IMDB movie reviews	Random Forest, Naïve Bayes, Support Vector Machine (SVM)	88.0 89.0 87.0
5	Characterisation of mental health conditions in social media using Informed Deep Learning (Gkotsis et al., 2017)	Reddit	Feed Forward, CNN, SVM	90.78 91.08 85.87
6	Deep Learning for Depression Detection of Twitter Users (Sisk, 1975)	Twitter	CNN Recurrent Neural Network (RNN)	87.96 78.12
7	Machine Learning, text classification and mental health (Nabil M Abbas, 2016)	Text files	SVM	92.0
8	A Novel Co-Training-Based Approach for the Classification of Mental Illnesses Using Social Media Posts (Tariq et al., 2019)	Reddit	Random Forest, SVM, Naïve Bayes	83.0 84.0 83.0
9	Behavioral Modeling for Mental Health using Machine Learning Algorithms (Srividya et al., 2018)	Questionnaire	SVM, Decision Trees, Naïve Bayes, K-nearest Neighbor, Logistic Regression	89.0 81.0 73.0 89.0 84.0
10	Using Machine Learning and Thematic Analysis Methods to Evaluate Mental Health Apps Based on User Reviews (Oyebode et al., 2020)	Mental health apps	SVM, Multinomial, Naïve Bayes, Stochastic Gradient Descent (SGD), Logistic Regression, Random Forest	89.4 89.1 89.4 89.4 87.7
11	Detecting and Characterizing Mental Health Related SelfDisclosure in Social Media (Gkotsis et al., 2017)	Reddit	Decision trees, k-Nearest Neighbor, Naive Bayes, Perceptron	58.8 60.7 62.5 78.4

METHODOLOGY

Figure 1 describes the overall framework of this study. First, data was collected from the three novels (Table 3) which was followed by data preprocessing. The data was divided into two parts namely Training set (80%) and Testing Set (20%). Then, data processing was carried out. This was followed by Sentiment Analysis using the two algorithms Vader and Textblob, and Sentiment Classification which was performed using three types of violence (1) Direct, (2) Structural, and (3) Cultural. Next, three different machine learning algorithms namely Naïve Bayes (NB), Support Vector Machine (SVM), and K-Nearest Neighbors (KNN) were used for violence classification to evaluate the results based on F1Score, preci-

Figure 1. Overall research framework

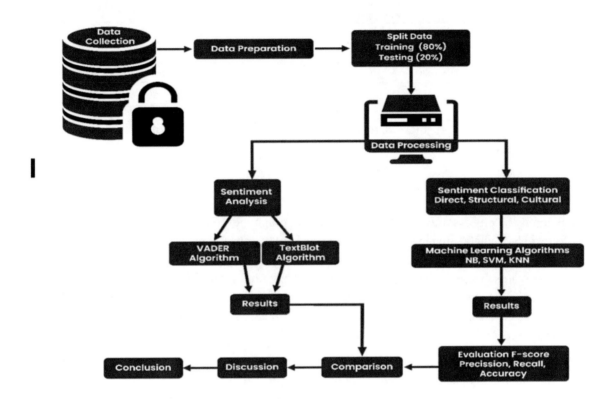

sion, recall, and accuracy. Then, the result of machine learning algorithms and the result of Sentiment analysis were compared in the discussion.

Three novels by Khaled Hosseini are used in this study as listed in Table 3. The novels are selected as they portray the daily hardships faced by Afghan people living in the country and in diaspora. Over the past two decades, diasporic stories from South Asia and Middle East have garnered global attention to the condition of human rights in the region as well the everyday experiences of violence, oppression, and conflict (Asl, 2020). While some of these narratives have been applauded for their truthful representation of the daily life in the (Pourgharib et al., 2022; Pourgharib & Asl, 2022), others have been criticized for their Orientalist depictions (Asl, 2018, 2019; Hadi & Asl, 2022). Khaled Hosseini is among the writers who has attracted much of the positive criticism. As stated in the table above, all the three books are in PDF format which were converted to text format for text processing.

Text Processing

Tokenization and normalization are the two main phases of text processing in this study. The text from extracted from the book cannot be directly used as a text analytics model input. Since the original text is lengthy, putting it directly into the model will greatly lengthen the time it takes to run. Moreover, there are many terms in the discourse that have no value, such as conjunction words like 'and' and determi-

Table 3. List of the selected literary books

No	Book Name	Reference	Page No
1	Hosseini, Khaled - A Thousand Splendid Suns.pdf	(Hosseini, 2009)	382
2	Hosseini, Khaled - And the mountains Echoed.pdf	(Hosseini, 2013)	410
3	Hosseini, Khaled - Kite Runner.pdf	(Hosseini, 2003)	242

nants like 'the.' There are also numbers, punctuation, and possibly symbols in the text. Text processing is required to assure the model's accuracy and efficiency.

Tokenization

Tokenization is the process of breaking down a text paragraph into smaller parts such as words or sentences. A token is a single thing that serves as the basis for a sentence or paragraph. For instance, a document could be divided into paragraphs or sentences into words. It helps to divide the textual information into separate words. Word Tokenize, WordPunctTokenizer, and RegexpTokenizer are three common word tokenizers for Python that break large texts into a list of words or tokens. The Sent Tokenize is a sentence tokenizer that divides a paragraph into a list of sentences. Table 4 shows the number of tokens or sentences discovered after tokenizing.

Table 4. The number of tokens or sentences discovered after tokenizing

Tokenizer	Output
word_tokenize	416848 tokens were found
WordPunctTokenizer	423571 tokens were found
RegexpTokenizer	404235 tokens were found
sent_tokenize	27452 sentences were found

When comparing word tokenizers, WordPunctTokenizer separates text and punctuation better than word tokenizer and has a simpler method than RegexpTokenizer. In the tokenize form of the words with "'s ", the difference between word tokenizer and word punctuation tokenizer can be seen. "Live's" will be tokenized as "live" and "'s" in the work tokenizer, and "live," "'," and "s" in the word punctuation tokenizer. RegexpTokenizer tokenizes texts based on regular words or values such as time, which is useful when tokens such as price and date are needed. WordPunctTokenizer separates the punctuation from the words, which makes the text processing process easier.

Normalization

Normalization is the process for converting a list of words into a more consistent sequence, which is beneficial when preparing text for further processing. It also involves converting to standard word, removing punctuation, convert the text into the same case, lemmatization and stemming. In this study, the following normalization step were performed: (1) change the character to lowercase, remove all white space, punctuation, and default stop words. (2) stemming -the method of reducing a word to its word stem which affixes to suffixes and prefixes or to the roots of words. (3) lemmatization -the method for grouping words with various inflected forms into the root form, which has the same meaning.

Since the corpus is so large, irrelevant values are removed before stemming or lemmatizing it to speed up the process. Punctuations, special symbols, and integers are among the values removed since they are not alphabetical. The tokens with two or fewer characters, or consonants exclusively, will then be removed from the corpus. The next step is to remove stop words from the corpus. The Python NLTK Library contains the stop words for English. There are few stop words added, the words are ""could", "though", "would", "also", "us", "many", and "much" which does not give any meaning. The list of stop words which are removed are as follows:

['i', 'me', 'my', 'myself', 'we', 'our', 'ours', 'ourselves', 'you', "you're", "you've", "you'll", "you'd", 'your', 'yours', 'yourself', 'yourselves', 'he', 'him', 'his', 'himself', 'she', "she's", 'her', 'hers', 'herself', 'it', "it's", 'its', 'itself', 'they', 'them', 'their', 'theirs', 'themselves', 'what', 'which', 'who', 'whom', 'this', 'that', "that'll", 'these', 'those', 'am', 'is', 'are', 'was', 'were', 'be', 'been', 'being', 'have', 'has', 'had', 'having', 'do', 'does', 'did', 'doing', 'a', 'an', 'the', 'and', 'but', 'if', 'or', 'because', 'as', 'until', 'while', 'of', 'at', 'by', 'for', 'with', 'about', 'against', 'between', 'into', 'through', 'during', 'before', 'after', 'above', 'below', 'to', 'from', 'up', 'down', 'in', 'out', 'on', 'off', 'over', 'under', 'again', 'further', 'then', 'once', 'here', 'there', 'when', 'where', 'why', 'how', 'all', 'any', 'both', 'each', 'few', 'more', 'most', 'other', 'some', 'such', 'no', 'nor', 'not', 'only', 'own', 'same', 'so', 'than', 'too', 'very', 's', 't', 'can', 'will', 'just', 'don', "don't", 'should', "should've", 'now', 'd', 'll', 'm', 'o', 're', 've', 'y', 'ain', 'aren', "aren't", 'couldn', "couldn't", 'didn', "didn't", 'doesn', "doesn't", 'hadn', "hadn't", 'hasn', "hasn't", 'haven', "haven't", 'isn', "isn't", 'ma', 'mightn', "mightn't", 'mustn', "mustn't", 'needn', "needn't", 'shan', "shan't", 'shouldn', "shouldn't", 'wasn', "wasn't", 'weren', "weren't", 'won', "won't", 'wouldn', "wouldn't", 'could', 'though', 'would', 'also', 'us', 'many', 'much']

The next step is Part-of-Speech (POS) tagging which is the process of selecting a word in a text that correlates to a part of speech. While tag set is a list of part-of-speech tags which each token in a text corpus has labels that specify the part of speech and other grammatical categories. The POS tagging is done before stemming or lemmatize process, after lemmatizing and stemming process because stemming process will change the tag of word.

With POS Tagging, only nouns and adjectives are left for the next step, as other word tags such as pronoun and determiner are meaningless. The NLTK POS Tagger and Spacy POS Tagger libraries are two common POS Tagging libraries. The NLTK POS Tagger was used in this study because it provides a more accurate tagset. The tokenized words will be duplicated twice after POS Tagging, with one tagset being lemmatized, another being stemmed, and the last tagset remaining constant. Based on the POS Tag, lemmatization returns the word to its base form. Porter, Lancaster, and Snowball are three stemming techniques used on the tokens. By comparing the output, Porter and Snowball are both moderate, with most words accurately returning to their base form, however Lancaster is the strictest technique, hence Snowball will be utilized in this study. Figure 2 shows the differences between the three stemming methods.

The affixes 'ed', 'ity', and 's' can be removed using all three stemming techniques. However, the Lancaster technique is very strict, and after removing the affixes, it is unable to return the proper word. For example, after stemming with the Lancaster technique, the uncles became unc. There are three set of

Figure 2. The results of Porter, Lancaster, and Snowball Stemming

INPUT WORD	PORTER	LANCASTER	SNOWBALL
bestsei	bestsei	bestse	bestsei
ling	ling	ling	ling
author	author	auth	author
hile	hile	hil	hile
unncr	unncr	unncr	unncr
sea	sea	sea	sea
prayer	prayer	pray	prayer
khaled	khale	khal	khale
hosseini	hosseini	hossein	hosseini
dear	dear	dear	dear
marwan	marwan	marw	marwan
long	long	long	long
summers	summer	sum	summer
childhood	childhood	child	childhood
boy	boy	boy	boy
age	age	ag	age
uncles	uncl	unc	uncl
spread	spread	spread	spread
mattress	mattress	mattress	mattress
roof	roof	roof	roof
grandfathers	grandfath	grandfath	grandfath
farmhouse	farmhous	farmh	farmhous
outside	outsid	outsid	outsid
homs	hom	hom	hom
woke	woke	wok	woke

tagset: (1) Tagset 1: Before stemming and not lemmatize, (2) Tagset 2: Before stemming but lemmatized, and (3) Tagset 3: After stemmed (not lemmatizing because its already in root form).

Text Exploration

The three tagsets containing nouns and adjectives were created from the previous step. The tagset will be visualized in this section using WordCloud to recognize the differences between the tagset and to get a general overview of the corpus. Next, the sentences containing the keywords related to depression will be extracted. The extracted sentences will be subjected to additional text processing stages before being visualized with WordCloud and a bar chart to acquire a better understanding of the corpus before being used to build a model.

Text Exploration Using Unigram

Figure 3 to Figure 8 show the WordCloud obtained with the tagset from previous section which the tagset has been separated into nouns and adjectives.

The differences between stemming and lemmatizing are shown in these figures (Figure 3-8). The word 'hous' in Figure 8 shows how stemming changes the POS Tag of a word, the word might be 'housing,'

Figure 3. WordCloud of Noun (Tagset 1)

Figure 4. WordCloud of Adjective (Tagset 1)

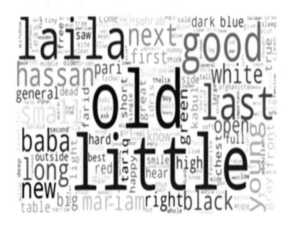

Figure 5. WordCloud of Noun (Tagset 2)

Figure 6. WordCloud of Adjective (Tagset 1)

Figure 7. WordCloud for Noun (Tagset 3)

Figure 8. WordCloud for Adjective (Tagset3)

Figure 9. WordCloud of Noun (Extracted)

'house,' or 'houses,' but not an adjective. The most common nouns and adjectives might help to understand the key topics discussed in the corpus. The main topic is related to body parts, as 'hand', 'face' and 'eye' appear frequently in the WordCloud of nouns, as well as time, as 'year', 'day', and 'life' are all related to time. The sentiment is more neutral in the WordCloud of adjectives, because 'new' and 'good' are positive adjectives, whereas other adjectives appear to be neutral. A hypothesis may be developed based on the frequently appearing nouns and adjectives, which is that the corpus major discussions are humans have suffered physical injury because of events that have caused them to seek a new and good life, which has resulted in depression.

Since the original text contained a wide range of topics, sentences containing any of the 140 keywords will be extracted to focus the study on violence. There are 350 out of 26259 sentences extracted from the corpus. After extracting the sentences, the data cleaning process is repeated on the extracted text, which includes tokenization, removal stop words and irrelevant values, POS Tagging, and lemmatization. Figure 9 and 10 shows the WordCloud of nouns and adjectives from extracted text.

Figure 10. WordCloud of Adjective (Extracted)

Figure 11. Top 10 Most Common Words in Extracted Text

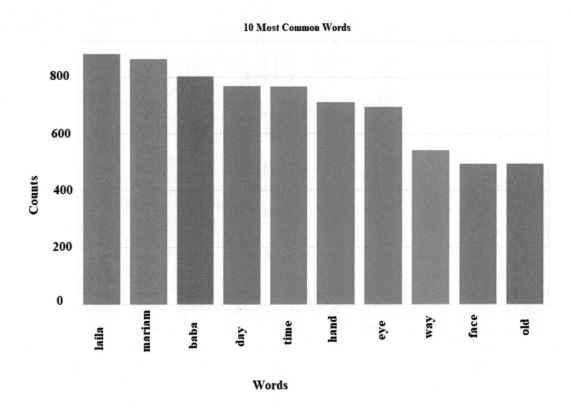

The body part and time are still the main topics of discussion in the corpus, but there are also new frequently used terms, such as sorry and pain, and the adjectives are neutral with a hint of negative. The top ten most common words in the corpus are depicted in Figure 11.

Sentiment Classification Using Machine Learning

In this step, the sentiments in the literary texts from Afghanistan writers are classified based on three types of violence. For this reason, the different types of violence in selected literary books based on Johan Galtung's framework are identified first. The term "violence" originates from the Latin language where we can find a differentiation between positive and negative violence which is preserved in the English language: *potestas – power* and *violence–violence*. The phenomenon of violence appears in many ways in every society all over the world and is mostly defined as "intentional physically aggressive behavior against another person" and respectively as "the use of physical force to apply a state to others contrary to their wishes" (Volavka, 1999, p. 117), as well as a way of manipulation. This common definition illustrates violence as (aggressively) the physical influencing of another human being – which is very far from reality. For the classification of different forms of violence, we will therefore follow the definition of the Norwegian sociologist Johan Galtung who was also the founder of the discipline of Peace and Conflict Research, which divides violence into three main groups: direct, structural, and cultural violence. In this point we will discuss three types of violence: (1) Direct, (2) structural, and (3) cultural Violence.

Figure 12. Sub types of direct violence

Direct violence

Personal	Interpersonal	Community/Society
Suicide Drug Abuse Self-harming behavior	Gender-based violence: intimate partner violence, rape, sexual violence, forced marriage, etc. Child abuse & neglect Emotional & verbal abuse; coercion & threats of individuals Psychological abuse & manipulation Bullying and intimidation Murder or physical attack Isolation, exclusion & neglect	War & armed conflict Sexual violence in war & conflict Mob violence & communal violence Coercion & threats of groups Violent crime, gang violence, etc. Active shooter, terror attack, etc. Pogroms & genocide Torture Violence by law enforcement & other state sponsored violence

Direct Violence

Direct violence is visible, it occurs physically or verbally, and the victim and the offender can be clearly pointed out. Direct violence is highly interdependent with structural and cultural violence: cultural and structural violence cause direct violence which on the other hand reinforces the former ones, in Figure 12 we discussed the sub types of Direct violence.

Structural Violence

Along with the direct use of violence between persons or groups, structural violence should also be mentioned as a prevalent form of violence. The concept of structural violence refers to institutionalized forms of discrimination and exclusion and therefore it reflects unequal levels of power. Structural violence "is not carried out by individuals but is hidden, to a greater or lesser extent, in structures" – it is "built into the social system and expresses itself in the unequal distribution of power and, as a result, unequal opportunities" (Obagbinoko, 2018, p. 161). It occurs when "some groups, classes, genders, nationalities, etc. are assumed to have, and in fact do have, more access to goods, resources and opportunities, than other groups, classes, genders, nationalities, etc., and this unequal advantage is built into the very social, political, and economic systems that govern societies, states, and the world" (Obagbinoko, 2018, pp. 160-161). Therefore, structural violence includes all forms of exclusion or inequality in distribution of income, education opportunities, participation in social/cultural life, medical care etc. In Table 5, we discuss the sub types of structural violence and the way they may spread.

Cultural Violence

Cultural Violence includes all facets of culture that can be employed to justify or legitimate the utilization of direct or structural violence (Galtung, 1990). It is the sum of attitudes and beliefs we have been taught since early childhood, as well as beliefs that surround us in today's everyday life about the necessity of violence. This form of violence does not include killing or affect people's lives directly, but it justifies structural or direct violence. Table 6 shows the sub types of cultural violence and the way it may spread.

Table 5. Sub type of structural violence

Outcomes Violence	Operational Violence	Policies and Practices Violence	
Economic, Provery and Income inequality. Lower-level educational attainment for some groups over others. Unequal distribution of power, privileges and opportunities. Unequal life chances some groups over others.	Unbalanced representations in structure and institutions. Lack of transparency, Accountability, corruptions.	Permit heightened use of violence by policy and security personal. Protect military and policy from criminal prosecution. Overfund police while neglecting community needs. Block or pose barriers for some populations to access credit or get loans. Produce mass incarceration. Replicate neo-colonial patterns and practices. Deny access to goods and services to specific population.	**Structural Violence May Spread.** Governments. International Polices. Institutions.

Table 6. Sub types of Cultural Violence

Narratives that justify war or violence.	Narratives that promote injustice or inequality.	Ideologies	
● Amplify threats. ● Create Enemies. ● Distort facts to build case for war. ● Promote the lie that winning the war will be easy and will be result peace.	● Obscure the legacy of historic injustice. ● Conceal the suffering of marginalized persons. ● Reject perspectives and contributions of minority groups. ● Stoke nationalism and patriotism. ● Communicate hate speech	● Fundamentalism, extremism and other ideologies that promote intolerance. ● Nationalism, patriotism. ● White supremacy.	**Narratives that cultural violence may be spread:** ● Media Organizations. ● Political leaders. ● Community Leaders. ● Social media Influencers. ● Formal and Informal Associations.

Supervised Machine Learning Algorithms for Sentiment Classification

Next, the dataset is split into training and test where 70% of the data for training and 30% for testing. Then, the sentiment classification is started using k-Nearest Neighbor (KNN) algorithm. Before that, an appropriate k value needs to be selected by running the algorithm with different k value and then plotting a graph to determine the optimal k value. Lastly, the training data is used to train the algorithm and testing data is utilized to predict the class label. Parameter tuning and at least 5-fold cross-validation are performed to obtain the optimal accuracy. Moving on to the Support Vector Machine (SVM) algorithm, the same test and train ratio will be used. Some parameter tuning techniques are also performed to obtain optimal accuracy. The same repeated step will be performed for Naïve Bayes classifier and Decision Tree algorithms as well.

Table 7. Class distribution of labeled data based on three violence types

Label	Class	Count
1	Direct	198
2	Structural	129
3	Cultural	125
	Total	452

Evaluation

The performance of the selected classification algorithms is compared based on accuracy, precision, recall, and F1-score. It is important to evaluate and review the model again in terms of business perspective and find out whether it solves the problem and achieves the objective before proceeding to the final deployment of the model. At the end of this stage, a decision should be made on the use of the outcomes of data mining.

Sentiment Analysis

Unsupervised sentiment analysis was performed using Vader and TextBlob algorithms to classify the polarity of the sentences to positive, neutral, and negative in the selected literary books. The analyzer in Vader library calculates the score of the sentences for positivity, neutrality, and negativity, and generates the compound score based on those three scores. The analyzer calculates the polarity and subjectivity of the sentences in Text blob. Both compound score and polarity have a range of -1.0 to +1.0, while subjectivity has a range of 0 to 1, with 0 representing a very objective sentence and 1 representing a very subjective sentence. Sentiment Analysis, like Topic Modeling, uses only the extracted text. Since the text data for this study is merely retrieved from the dialogue, there is no label for each sentence's polarity. A sample is taken from the model's output to evaluate the accuracy of the polarity computed by the models. To ensure that the model operates as expected, the polarity of each piece of text in the sample will be manually identified.

ANALYSIS AND RESULTS

The results for sentiment classification using machine learning and sentiment analysis are presented in this section.

Class Distribution

As mentioned in the methodology section, this study aims to classify violence into three classes of class (1) direct, (2) structural, and (3) cultural. Therefore, the data was labeled based on these three classes. The class distribution of type of violence in the selected literary books is shown in Table 7 and Figure 13.

As shown in Figure 13, the most sentiment in the selected literary books belongs to direct violence followed by structural and cultural. The challenge of working with imbalanced datasets is that most

Figure 13. Class distribution of Labeled Violence data

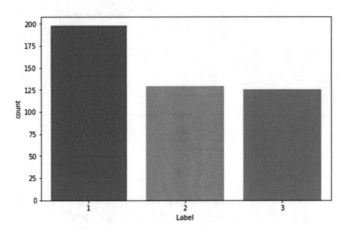

machine learning techniques will ignore, and in turn have poor performance on, the minority class, although typically it is performance on the minority class that is most important. Thus, one approach to addressing imbalanced datasets is to oversample the minority class. The simplest approach involves duplicating examples in the minority class, although these examples do not add any new information to the model. Instead, new examples can be synthesized from the existing examples. Therefore, since the classes are imbalanced, SMOTE which is an oversampling technique, is used before performing machine learning techniques.

Violence Sentiments Classification Using Machine Learning Algorithms

Data is split into two parts where 70% of the data is used to train by the machine learning algorithm while 30% of the data is used to predict the class of violence. Then the performance results is evaluated based on some indices such as accuracy, precision, recall and f1-score.

Support Vector Machine (SVM)

Three types of support vector machine are used in this study which are linear kernel, polynomial kernel, and radial basis function kernel. Table 8 shows that all of the support vector machine algorithm yields pretty good result in classifying violence labeled data. Support vector machine using linear kernel accuracy is 60% while support vector machine using polynomial kernel accuracy is 61.7%. Whereas support vector machine using radial basis function kernel accuracy is 65%. Support vector machine with radial basis function kernel achieved the highest accuracy followed by polynomial kernel and linear kernel. In summary, support vector machine with radial basis function kernel performs the best in classifying violence labeled data.

K-Nearest Neighbor (KNN)

Before modelling K-Nearest Neighbor (KNN), the suitable k value must be determined to obtain the optimal result. Therefore, we decided to plot a graph of accuracy against k value to determine which

Table 8. Performance of support vector machine algorithms

Algorithm	Class	Precision	Recall	F1-score	Accuracy
SVM (linear)	Direct	0.54	0.57	0.55	60%
	Structural	0.68	0.74	0.71	
	Cultural	0.55	0.63	0.48	
SVM (polynomial)	Direct	0.56	0.61	0.58	61.7%
	Structural	0.68	0.74	0.71	
	Cultural	0.60	0.63	0.50	
SVM (radial basis function)	Direct	0.58	0.65	0.61	65%
	Structural	0.74	0.74	0.74	
	Cultural	0.64	0.50	0.56	

k value has the optimal result. Figure 14 shows that when k value increases, accuracy decreases. As a result, the optimal k value is 1. At this stage, we plot a K-nearest Neighbor classifier using Euclidian distance with k value of 1 to determine the class of Label data about the violence. Then, a 10-fold cross validation is performed to compare which classifier has the optimal result.

Figure 14. Graph of accuracy against k value

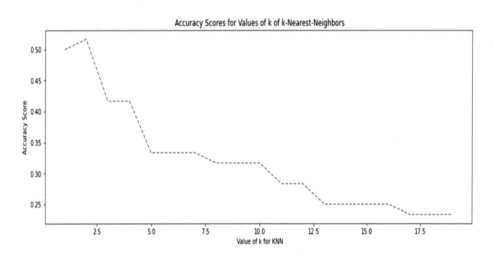

The overall performance of K-nearest Neighbor algorithm is shown in Table 9 which reveals KNN achieve 51.7% accuracy. In addition, Table 9 shows that K-nearest Neighbor with 10-fold cross validation was unable to obtain the confusion matrix, precision, recall and f1-score for each class because each cross validation yields one result. Hence, 10-fold cross validation yields 10 results. Therefore, it is much complicated to concatenate the 10 results together into one confusion matrix. Since our aim is to compare all the supervised machine learning algorithms using these aspects, K-nearest Neighbor without cross validation proves to be the most suitable algorithm.

Table 9. Performance of K-nearest neighbor algorithm

Algorithm	Class	Precision	Recall	F1-score	Accuracy
KNN	Direct	0.50	0.13	0.21	51.7%
	Structural	0.88	0.65	0.75	
	Cultural	0.35	0.93	0.51	
KNN with cv	NIL				50.9%

Naïve Bayes

Two types of Naïve Bayes are performed in this study, which are Gaussian Naïve Bayes and Bernoulli Naïve Bayes. Because Multinomial Naïve Bayes does not accept negative input, we decided to skip this algorithm. The overall performance of Naïve Bayes classifier is shown in Table 10. Gaussian Naïve Bayes accuracy is 71.7%. However, Bernoulli Naïve Bayes accuracy is 56.6%. Bernoulli Naïve Bayes does not perform well for the dataset used in this study because it is only suitable for classification of binary class. Gaussian Naïve Bayes is the most suitable for Naïve Bayes classifier.

Table 10. Performance of Naïve Bayes algorithm

Algorithm	Class	Precision	Recall	F1-score	Accuracy
Gaussian Naïve Bayes	Direct	0.70	0.61	0.65	71.7%
	Structural	0.77	0.87	0.82	
	Cultural	0.64	0.64	0.64	
Bernoulli Naïve Bayes	Direct	0.57	0.17	0.27	56.6%
	Structural	0.78	0.78	0.78	
	Cultural	0.40	0.86	0.55	

Comparing the Performance of Machine Learning Algorithms for Violence Classification

The performance of the selected machine learning algorithms for the classification of violence are compared in Table 11 and Figure 15. By looking at accuracy scores, we can see that the K-Nearest Neighbor model produces only 51.7%, the Support Vector Machine obtains 65%, while the Naive Bayes model classification is 71.7% accurate. This shows that the NB model can perform better in terms of accuracy than the other models. So, in terms of accuracy, NB model produces better classification compared to other models which makes it as acceptable to be used. Next is to recognize the misclassified observations and to consider those observations within our evaluation of the model. We considered the precision F1-score and recall evaluation. Table 11 shows that the precision of the NB model is 77% which means that, of all the true predictions that our model made, 77% of them are true in actual cases. This mean the text that our model predicts to structural, 87% them are Structural class while another 17% of the predicted do not belong to Structural class. The recall score of the NB model is 87%, which means that the text

Table 11. Performance of supervised machine learning

Algorithm	Class	Precision	Recall	F1-score	Accuracy
Naïve Bayes	Direct	0.70	0.61	0.65	71.7%
	Structural	0.77	0.87	0.82	
	Cultural	0.64	0.64	0.64	
KNN	Direct	0.50	0.13	0.21	51.7%
	Structural	0.88	0.65	0.75	
	Cultural	0.35	0.93	0.51	
SVM	Direct	0.58	0.65	0.61	65%
	Structural	0.74	0.74	0.74	
	Cultural	0.64	0.50	0.56	

is Structural. The model labelled 87% of them correctly, and another 10% are labelled wrongly. Lastly, the F1 score represents the harmonic mean for the combination of both evaluations. So, in this case, the model F1 score is 82% for structural class, 65% for Direct class and 64% in labelling the Cultural class.

It is clear that the accuracy of the NB model is 71.7% which means that the model is able to perform an accurate classification. For example, if we would like to predict 10 instances, we would be confident that nearly 7 of them are classified correctly. The F1 macro and F1 weighted show good results which means that the model is not affected by Type I and Type II error severely. These indicators strengthen our conclusion that the model is good at classifying the violence. Then, to compare the model performances that we used, the scores of accuracies, F1 macro and F1 weighted scores can be compared. Those scores provide insights about different aspects that can help in understanding more about the performance of models. Based on the F1 macro and weighted scores, we can see that NB models have 70% score and 71% score respectively. This means that when we look at the model in general and consider individual class contributions, we can say that the model bears a medium level of Type I and Type II error. While SVM performance is 64% for F1 macro and 65% for F1 weighted score. KNN model has 49% and F1 macro and F1 weighted score also have 49%. All the model scores show that the Naïve Bayes model bears a low level of Type I and Type II errors. By comparing the model, we can see that the Naïve Bayes model excels as the model classifies inputs with lower error. So, in the context of F1 score, the Naïve Bayes model also performs better than the other models. In a nutshell, the Naïve Bayes model has higher performance compared to others. Therefore, the Naïve Bayes model produces more accurate classification with lower Type I and Type II error. Therefore, the Naïve Bayes model can be selected to be the model that we will use in the deployment phase in future work.

Sentiment Analysis

Sentiment analysis is used to analyze the emotion of the text. In other words, it is the process of detecting a positive, neutral, or negative emotion of a text. As mentioned before, Vader and TextBlot algorithms are used for sentiment analysis for each type of violence (direct, structural, and cultural) in this study. The comparison between the positive, neutral, and negative sentiments for each type of violence are shown in Figure 16. As shown in the figure, neutral and negative sentiments are mostly related to direct

Figure 15. Performance of supervisor machine learning Algorithm

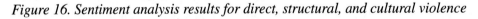

Figure 16. Sentiment analysis results for direct, structural, and cultural violence

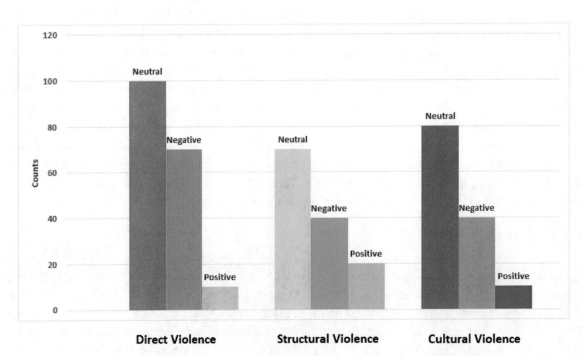

violence whereas positive sentiments are more related to structural violence. The number of negative sentiments for structural and cultural violence are almost the same. The top ten positive and negative sentiments are compared for Vader and Textblob algorithms in Figure 17 to Figure 27 in APPENDIX.

CONCLUSION AND FUTURE WORKS

The opinion mining for literary works based on selected novels by Khaled Hosseini can be done through processing the textual data into a machine friendly input. The data quality then needs to be enhanced using lemmatization, stop word removal and so forth. In this study, we used two algorithms of Vader and TextBlob for sentiment analysis to see the polarity of the sentences as positive, neutral, or negative. The raw data needed to be labelled first before using it in classification model. Hence, we labelled it into 3 classes, 1 for Direct, 2 for Structural and 3 Cultural types of violence based on the sociologist Johan Galtung's theories. Then, the data is used as inputs into multiple classification model. The best performing model proves to be the Naïve Bayes with accuracy of 71%. Moreover, the details show that the model can predict well for all classes as the dataset is balanced. Further works need to be done to include more layers of analysis in the process of labeling the dataset. This could include few models in extracting possible topics that lie within the corpus, thus the label generated is more carefully assigned to increase the quality of the dataset. In future works, the available techniques for the problem shall be revised, and these algorithms can be implemented and compared with the results in this study. The different algorithm also might provide a different insight on the same data. Hence the classifier will be able to perform better with higher quality of data.

The machine learning algorithm proposed in this study are the most popular and common algorithms. There are many more machine learning algorithms such as random forest classifier, artificial neural network, etc. that can be used in classification and prediction of violence. Also, the more machine learning algorithms we can apply, the more selection and comparison we can have to determine which algorithm is the most suitable for this topic.

REFERENCES

Abadah, M. S. K., Keikhosrokiani, P., & Zhao, X. (2023). Analytics of Public Reactions to the COVID-19 Vaccine on Twitter Using Sentiment Analysis and Topic Modelling. In D. Valle-Cruz, N. Plata-Cesar, & J. L. González-Ruíz (Eds.), *Handbook of Research on Applied Artificial Intelligence and Robotics for Government Processes* (pp. 156–188). IGI Global. doi:10.4018/978-1-6684-5624-8.ch008

Abbas. (2016). *Machine Learning and Mental Health.* Academic Press.

al Mamun, M. H., Keikhosrokiani, P., Asl, M. P., Anuar, N. A. N., Hadi, N. H. A., & Humida, T. (2022). Sentiment Analysis of the Harry Potter Series Using a Lexicon-Based Approach. In P. Keikhosrokiani & M. Pourya Asl (Eds.), *Handbook of Research on Opinion Mining and Text Analytics on Literary Works and Social Media* (pp. 263–291). IGI Global. doi:10.4018/978-1-7998-9594-7.ch011

Asl, M. P. (2018). Fabrication of a desired truth: The oblivion of a Naxalite woman in Jhumpa Lahiri's The Lowland. *Asian Ethnicity*, *19*(3), 383–401. doi:10.1080/14631369.2018.1429892

Asl, M. P. (2019). Foucauldian rituals of justice and conduct in Zainab Salbi's Between Two Worlds. *Journal of Contemporary Iraq & the Arab World, 13*(2–3), 227–242. doi:10.1386/jciaw_00010_1

Asl, M. P. (2020). Micro-Physics of discipline: Spaces of the self in Middle Eastern women life writings. *International Journal of Arabic-English Studies, 20*(2). Advance online publication. doi:10.33806/ijaes2000.20.2.12

Asri, M. A. Z. B. M., Keikhosrokiani, P., & Asl, M. P. (2022a). Opinion Mining Using Topic Modeling: A Case Study of Firoozeh Dumas's Funny in Farsi in Goodreads. In F. Saeed, F. Mohammed, & F. Ghaleb (Eds.), *Advances on Intelligent Informatics and Computing* (pp. 219–230). Springer International Publishing. doi:10.1007/978-3-030-98741-1_19

Asri, M. A. Z. B. M., Keikhosrokiani, P., & Asl, M. P. (2022b). Opinion Mining Using Topic Modeling: A Case Study of Firoozeh Dumas's Funny in Farsi in Goodreads. In F. Saeed, F. Mohammed, & F. Ghaleb (Eds.), *Advances on Intelligent Informatics and Computing* (pp. 219–230). Springer International Publishing. doi:10.1007/978-3-030-98741-1_19

Chu, K. E., Keikhosrokiani, P., & Asl, M. P. (2022). A Topic Modeling and Sentiment Analysis Model for Detection and Visualization of Themes in Literary Texts. *Pertanika Journal of Science & Technology, 30*(4), 2535–2561. doi:10.47836/pjst.30.4.14

Demidova, L. A. (2021). Two-stage hybrid data classifiers based on svm and knn algorithms. *Symmetry, 13*(4), 615. Advance online publication. doi:10.3390ym13040615

Devika, M. D., Sunitha, C., & Ganesh, A. (2016). Sentiment Analysis: A Comparative Study on Different Approaches. *Procedia Computer Science, 87*, 44–49. doi:10.1016/j.procs.2016.05.124

Fasha, E. F. B. K., Keikhosrokiani, P., & Asl, M. P. (2022a). Opinion Mining Using Sentiment Analysis: A Case Study of Readers' Response on Long Litt Woon's The Way Through the Woods in Goodreads. In F. Saeed, F. Mohammed, & F. Ghaleb (Eds.), *Advances on Intelligent Informatics and Computing* (pp. 231–242). Springer International Publishing. doi:10.1007/978-3-030-98741-1_20

Fasha, E. F. B. K., Keikhosrokiani, P., & Asl, M. P. (2022b). Opinion Mining Using Sentiment Analysis: A Case Study of Readers' Response on Long Litt Woon's The Way Through the Woods in Goodreads. In F. Saeed, F. Mohammed, & F. Ghaleb (Eds.), *Advances on Intelligent Informatics and Computing* (pp. 231–242). Springer International Publishing. doi:10.1007/978-3-030-98741-1_20

Gaba, V., & Verma, V. (2022). Sentiment Analysis of Twitter Data Using Machine Learning Approaches. *Communications in Computer and Information Science, 1572 CCIS*, 140–152. doi: 1 doi:0.1007/978-3-031-05767-0_12

Galtung, J. (1990). Cultural Violence. *Journal of Peace Research, 27*(3), 291–305. doi:10.1177/0022343390027003005

García-Contreras, R., Muñoz-Chávez, J. P., Valle-Cruz, D., & López-Chau, A. (2022). Teleworker Experiences in #COVID-19: Insights Through Sentiment Analysis in Social Media. In P. Keikhosrokiani & M. Pourya Asl (Eds.), *Handbook of Research on Opinion Mining and Text Analytics on Literary Works and Social Media* (pp. 388–412). IGI Global. doi:10.4018/978-1-7998-9594-7.ch016

Gkotsis, G., Oellrich, A., Velupillai, S., Liakata, M., Hubbard, T. J. P., Dobson, R. J. B., & Dutta, R. (2017). Characterisation of mental health conditions in social media using Informed Deep Learning. *Scientific Reports*, *7*(1), 1–11. doi:10.1038rep45141 PMID:28327593

Hadi, N. H. A., & Asl, M. P. (2022). The Real, the Imaginary, and the Symbolic: A Lacanian Reading of Ramita Navai's City of Lies. *GEMA Online® Journal of Language Studies, 22*(1), 145–158. doi: 1 doi:0.17576/gema-2022-2201-08

Hosseini, K. (2003). *The kite runner*. Penguin.

Hosseini, K. (2009). *A thousand splendid suns*. Bloomsbury Publishing.

Ingole, P., Bhoir, S., & Vidhate, A. V. (2018). Hybrid Model for Text Classification. *Proceedings of the 2nd International Conference on Electronics, Communication and Aerospace Technology, ICECA 2018, Iceca*, 7–15. doi: 10.1109/ICECA.2018.8474738

Jafery, N. N., Keikhosrokiani, P., & Asl, M. P. (2022). Text analytics model to identify the connection between theme and sentiment in literary works: A case study of Iraqi life writings. In P. Keikhosrokiani & M. Pourya Asl (Eds.), *Handbook of Research on Opinion Mining and Text Analytics on Literary Works and Social Media* (pp. 173–190). IGI Global. doi:10.4018/978-1-7998-9594-7.ch008

Keikhosrokiani, P. (2022). *Handbook of Research on Consumer Behavior Change and Data Analytics in the Socio-Digital Era*. IGI Global. doi:10.4018/978-1-6684-4168-8

Keikhosrokiani, P., & Asl, M. P. (2022). *Handbook of research on opinion mining and text analytics on literary works and social media*. IGI Global. doi:10.4018/978-1-7998-9594-7

Keyvanpour, M., Karimi Zandian, Z., & Heidarypanah, M. (2020). OMLML: A helpful opinion mining method based on lexicon and machine learning in social networks. *Social Network Analysis and Mining*, *10*(1), 10. Advance online publication. doi:10.100713278-019-0622-6

Khalifa, S. M., Marie, M. I., & El-Defrawi, M. M. (2022). Aspects Detection Model for Users' Reviews Using Machine Learning Techniques. *Journal of Theoretical and Applied Information Technology*, *100*(19), 5776–5786.

Kim, J., Lee, J., Park, E., & Han, J. (2020). A deep learning model for detecting mental illness from user content on social media. *Scientific Reports*, *10*(1), 1–6. doi:10.103841598-020-68764-y PMID:32678250

Li, Z., Fan, Y., Jiang, B., Lei, T., & Liu, W. (2019). A survey on sentiment analysis and opinion mining for social multimedia. *Multimedia Tools and Applications*, *78*(6), 6939–6967. doi:10.100711042-018-6445-z

Murarka, A., Radhakrishnan, B., & Ravichandran, S. (2020). *Detection and Classification of mental illnesses on social media using RoBERTa*. Academic Press.

Obagbinoko, C. O. (2018). State Response to Violent Conflicts: An Assessment of the Nigerian State and the Indigenous People of Biafra (Ipob) Separatist Movement. *AfSol*, *2*, 157.

Oramas Bustillos, R., Zatarain Cabada, R., Barrón Estrada, M. L., & Hernández Pérez, Y. (2019). Opinion mining and emotion recognition in an intelligent learning environment. *Computer Applications in Engineering Education*, *27*(1), 90–101. doi:10.1002/cae.22059

Oyebode, O., Alqahtani, F., & Orji, R. (2020). Using Machine Learning and Thematic Analysis Methods to Evaluate Mental Health Apps Based on User Reviews. *IEEE Access: Practical Innovations, Open Solutions*, *8*, 111141–111158. doi:10.1109/ACCESS.2020.3002176

Pourgharib, B., & Asl, M. P. (2022). Cultural Translation, Hybrid Identity, and Third Space in Jhumpa Lahiri's Interpreter of Maladies. *Pertanika Journal of Social Science & Humanities*, *30*(4). Advance online publication. doi:10.47836/pjssh.30.4.10

Pourgharib, B., Hamkhiyal, S., & Asl, M. P. (2022). A Non-Orientalist Representation of Pakistan in Contemporary Western Travelogues. *GEMA Online Journal of Language Studies*, *22*(3), 103–118. doi:10.17576/gema-2022-2203-06

Rameshbhai, C. J., & Paulose, J. (2019). Opinion mining on newspaper headlines using SVM and NLP. *Iranian Journal of Electrical and Computer Engineering*, *9*(3), 2152–2163. doi:10.11591/ijece.v9i3.pp2152-2163

Sari, S., & Kalender, M. (2021). Sentiment Analysis and Opinion Mining Using Deep Learning for the Reviews on Google Play. *Lecture Notes in Networks and Systems*, *183*(July), 126–137. doi:10.1007/978-3-030-66840-2_10

Sisk, D. (1975). Simulation: Learning by doing revisited. *Gifted Child Quarterly*, *19*(2), 175–180. doi:10.1177/001698627501900225

Sofian, N. B., Keikhosrokiani, P., & Asl, M. P. (2022a). Opinion Mining and Text Analytics of Reader Reviews of Yoko Ogawa's The Housekeeper and the Professor in Goodreads. In P. Keikhosrokiani & M. Pourya Asl (Eds.), *Handbook of Research on Opinion Mining and Text Analytics on Literary Works and Social Media* (pp. 240–262). IGI Global. doi:10.4018/978-1-7998-9594-7.ch010

Sofian, N. B., Keikhosrokiani, P., & Asl, M. P. (2022b). Opinion mining and text analytics of reader reviews of Yoko Ogawa's The Housekeeper and the Professor in Goodreads. In P. Keikhosrokiani & M. Pourya Asl (Eds.), *Handbook of Research on Opinion Mining and Text Analytics on Literary Works and Social Media* (pp. 240–262). IGI Global. doi:10.4018/978-1-7998-9594-7.ch010

Srividya, M., Mohanavalli, S., & Bhalaji, N. (2018). Behavioral Modeling for Mental Health using Machine Learning Algorithms. *Journal of Medical Systems*, *42*(5), 88. Advance online publication. doi:10.100710916-018-0934-5 PMID:29610979

Suhendra, N. H. B., Keikhosrokiani, P., Asl, M. P., & Zhao, X. (2022a). Opinion Mining and Text Analytics of Literary Reader Responses: A Case Study of Reader Responses to KL Noir Volumes in Goodreads Using Sentiment Analysis and Topic. In P. Keikhosrokiani & M. Pourya Asl (Eds.), *Handbook of Research on Opinion Mining and Text Analytics on Literary Works and Social Media* (pp. 191–239). IGI Global. doi:10.4018/978-1-7998-9594-7.ch009

Suhendra, N. H. B., Keikhosrokiani, P., Asl, M. P., & Zhao, X. (2022b). Opinion mining and text analytics of literary reader responses: A case study of reader responses to KL Noir volumes in Goodreads using sentiment analysis and topic. In P. Keikhosrokiani & M. Pourya Asl (Eds.), *Handbook of Research on Opinion Mining and Text Analytics on Literary Works and Social Media* (pp. 191–239). IGI Global. doi:10.4018/978-1-7998-9594-7.ch009

Tariq, S., Akhtar, N., Afzal, H., Khalid, S., Mufti, M. R., Hussain, S., Habib, A., & Ahmad, G. (2019). A Novel Co-Training-Based Approach for the Classification of Mental Illnesses Using Social Media Posts. *IEEE Access: Practical Innovations, Open Solutions, 7*, 166165–166172. doi:10.1109/ACCESS.2019.2953087

Tsapatsoulis, N., & Djouvas, C. (2019). Opinion mining from social media short texts: Does collective intelligence beat deep learning? *Frontiers in Robotics and AI, 6*(JAN), 1–14. doi:10.3389/frobt.2018.00138 PMID:33501016

Volavka, J. (1999). The Neurobiology of Violence. *The Journal of Neuropsychiatry and Clinical Neurosciences, 11*(3), 307–314. doi:10.1176/jnp.11.3.307 PMID:10440006

Wan, C. H., Lee, L. H., Rajkumar, R., & Isa, D. (2012). A hybrid text classification approach with low dependency on parameter by integrating K-nearest neighbor and support vector machine. *Expert Systems with Applications, 39*(15), 11880–11888. doi:10.1016/j.eswa.2012.02.068

Ying, Y. S., Keikhosrokiani, P., & Pourya Asl, M. (2022). Opinion Mining on Viet Thanh Nguyen's The Sympathizer Using Topic Modelling and Sentiment Analysis. *Journal of Information Technology Management, 14*, 163–183. doi: 10.22059/jitm.2022.84895

Yousaf, A., Umer, M., Sadiq, S., Ullah, S., Mirjalili, S., Rupapara, V., & Nappi, M. (2021). Emotion Recognition by Textual Tweets Classification Using Voting Classifier (LR-SGD). *IEEE Access: Practical Innovations, Open Solutions, 9*, 6286–6295. doi:10.1109/ACCESS.2020.3047831

APPENDIX

Figure 17. Top 10 positive sentences using for direct violence using Vader algorithm

```
The top 10 positive sentences are:     Score Compound  Score Negative  Score Neutral  Score Positive  \
57         0.8290        0.000            0.785           0.215
191        0.8126        0.000            0.693           0.307
95         0.8074        0.000            0.771           0.229
126        0.7783        0.000            0.685           0.315
21         0.7579        0.000            0.552           0.448
175        0.7569        0.083            0.814           0.103
157        0.7351        0.036            0.726           0.237
82         0.7184        0.000            0.739           0.261
11         0.7003        0.000            0.691           0.309
201        0.6908        0.000            0.551           0.449

                                                         Sentence
57     They laughed like this at each others reflecti...
191    ÃâÃ erica stared then she started to laughÃââa...
95     Laila thinks of her own life and all that has ...
126    My heart sank and I almost blurted out the tru...
21      My heart sank and I almost blurted out the truth
175    but part of her still resisted the idea of mov...
157    He was the sort of fellow who started a lot of...
82     Rasheed muttered He half smiled and it  seemed...
11     a day to celebrate how  the prophet Ibrahim al...
201                      âæBut Iâd like to be your friend
```

Figure 18. Top 10 negative sentences using for direct violence using Vader algorithm

```
---            ------ --- ----- -- -- ---- ------
The top 10 negative sentences are:     Score Compound  Score Negative  Score Neutral  Score Positive  \
178       -0.9875        0.120            0.810           0.070
114       -0.9538        0.504            0.408           0.088
172       -0.9460        0.362            0.638           0.000
182       -0.9460        0.505            0.495           0.000
187       -0.9186        0.387            0.613           0.000
257       -0.9151        0.541            0.459           0.000
122       -0.9081        0.189            0.811           0.000
137       -0.9052        0.207            0.793           0.000
169       -0.8885        0.269            0.731           0.000
251       -0.8808        0.230            0.713           0.057

                                                         Sentence
178    militants from saeed and nadiaÃââs country had...
114    but the thief stabbed him in the throat killin...
172    i had uncharitable thoughts of prison inmates ...
182    he killed because his nature is to kill becaus...
187    but when i told ozi i was leaving when i saw h...
257    But I cannot help but be disturbed by the brut...
122    But no one woke up and in the silence that fol...
137    Babaâs dead and now I have to bury him but the...
169    she had hung up knowing that for the rest of h...
251    It wasnt easy tolerating him talking this way ...
```

Figure 19. Top 10 positive sentences using for direct violence using Textblob algorithm

In [10]: `top_10_pos`

Out[10]:

	Score Compound	Score Negative	Score Neutral	Score Positive	Sentence
57	0.8290	0.000	0.785	0.215	They laughed like this at each others reflecti...
191	0.8126	0.000	0.693	0.307	ÃâÃ erica stared then she started to laughÃâãa ...
95	0.8074	0.000	0.771	0.229	Laila thinks of her own life and all that has ...
126	0.7783	0.000	0.685	0.315	My heart sank and I almost blurted out the tru...
21	0.7579	0.000	0.552	0.448	My heart sank and I almost blurted out the truth
175	0.7569	0.083	0.814	0.103	but part of her still resisted the idea of mov...
157	0.7351	0.036	0.726	0.237	He was the sort of fellow who started a lot of...
82	0.7184	0.000	0.739	0.261	Rasheed muttered He half smiled and it seemed...
11	0.7003	0.000	0.691	0.309	a day to celebrate how the prophet Ibrahim al...
201	0.6908	0.000	0.551	0.449	âœBut Iâd like to be your friend

Figure 20. Top 10 negative sentences using for direct violence using Textblob algorithm

In [11]: `top_10_neg`

Out[11]:

	Score Compound	Score Negative	Score Neutral	Score Positive	Sentence
178	-0.9875	0.120	0.810	0.070	militants from saeed and nadiaÃâãs country had...
114	-0.9538	0.504	0.408	0.088	but the thief stabbed him in the throat killin...
172	-0.9460	0.362	0.638	0.000	i had uncharitable thoughts of prison inmates ...
182	-0.9460	0.505	0.495	0.000	he killed because his nature is to kill becaus...
187	-0.9186	0.387	0.613	0.000	but when i told ozi i was leaving when i saw h...
257	-0.9151	0.541	0.459	0.000	But I cannot help but be disturbed by the brut...
122	-0.9081	0.189	0.811	0.000	But no one woke up and in the silence that fol...
137	-0.9052	0.207	0.793	0.000	Babaâs dead and now I have to bury him but the...
169	-0.8885	0.269	0.731	0.000	she had hung up knowing that for the rest of h...
251	-0.8808	0.230	0.713	0.057	It wasnt easy tolerating him talking this way ...

Figure 21. Top 10 positive sentences using for structural violence using Vader algorithm

	The top 10 positive sentences are:		Score Compound	Score Negative	Score Neutral	Score Positive \
100	0.9593	0.026	0.703	0.271		
0	0.8720	0.053	0.731	0.216		
84	0.8465	0.000	0.746	0.254		
3	0.8306	0.000	0.556	0.444		
134	0.7814	0.046	0.713	0.241		
107	0.7351	0.138	0.608	0.254		
95	0.6806	0.000	0.699	0.301		
110	0.6486	0.000	0.773	0.227		
23	0.6369	0.000	0.724	0.276		
104	0.6249	0.160	0.619	0.222		

	Sentence
100	and so irrespective of the reason decency on t...
0	hey fell from the sky like shooting stars with...
84	But not to worry the plastics guys sewed it ba...
3	the good looks dont hurt eitherÃâ âthe muscular...
134	Mariam thought of Jalil of the emphatic jovial...
107	but now new york was starting to feel empty a ...
95	it never endsÃâ âthe misery the apologies the p...
110	i now play sitting down and i try to be unpred...
23	Mariam fixed her eyes on Jalil her heart somer...
104	Ãâ â i try to fight it but iÃâ âm laughing too h...

Figure 22. Top 10 negative sentences using for structural violence using Vader algorithm

	The top 10 negative sentences are:		Score Compound	Score Negative	Score Neutral	Score Positive \
41	-0.9517	0.333	0.667	0.0		
118	-0.9460	0.362	0.638	0.0		
18	-0.9274	0.274	0.726	0.0		
24	-0.9118	0.235	0.765	0.0		
158	-0.9001	0.208	0.792	0.0		
151	-0.8957	0.518	0.482	0.0		
17	-0.8885	0.697	0.303	0.0		
138	-0.8720	0.273	0.727	0.0		
25	-0.8689	0.450	0.550	0.0		
35	-0.8689	0.521	0.479	0.0		

	Sentence
41	There was something imposing and rather forbid...
118	i had uncharitable thoughts of prison inmates ...
18	But mainly tears of a deep deep shame at how f...
24	She was being sent away because she was the wa...
158	When she turns the key and lets them in she fi...
151	When the Taliban take over life becomes a desp...
17	They were tears of grief of anger of disillusi...
138	Homes that lay in roofless ruins of brick and ...
25	an empire had been defeated old wars had ended...
35	They collapsed buildings destroyed one of the ...

Figure 23. Top 10 positive sentences using for structural violence using Textblob algorithm

In [9]: top_10_pos

Out[9]:

	Score Compound	Score Negative	Score Neutral	Score Positive	Sentence
100	0.9593	0.026	0.703	0.271	and so irrespective of the reason decency on t...
0	0.8720	0.053	0.731	0.216	hey fell from the sky like shooting stars with...
84	0.8465	0.000	0.746	0.254	But not to worry the plastics guys sewed it ba...
3	0.8306	0.000	0.556	0.444	the good looks dont hurt eitherÄââthe muscular...
134	0.7814	0.046	0.713	0.241	Mariam thought of Jalil of the emphatic jovial...
107	0.7351	0.138	0.608	0.254	but now new york was starting to feel empty a ...
95	0.6806	0.000	0.699	0.301	it never endsÄââthe misery the apologies the p...
110	0.6486	0.000	0.773	0.227	i now play sitting down and i try to be unpred...
23	0.6369	0.000	0.724	0.276	Mariam fixed her eyes on Jalil her heart somer...
104	0.6249	0.160	0.619	0.222	Äââ i try to fight it but iÄââm laughing too h...

Figure 24. Top 10 positive sentences using for cultural violence using Vader algorithm

```
The top 10 positive sentences are:   Score Compound  Score Negative  Score Neutral  Score Positive  \
79              0.8733          0.032          0.813          0.155
92              0.8306          0.000          0.556          0.444
51              0.7184          0.000          0.684          0.316
68              0.7096          0.057          0.731          0.211
67              0.7003          0.047          0.859          0.094
158             0.6369          0.000          0.819          0.181
103             0.6348          0.000          0.698          0.302
32              0.5410          0.108          0.628          0.264
5               0.5267          0.032          0.880          0.088
34              0.4939          0.000          0.686          0.314

                                                Sentence
79      I hope you dont think this excuses you from ch...
92      the good looks dont hurt eitherÄââthe muscular...
51      The mullah gave a few blessings said a few wor...
68      A worried look crossed his  face On the surfac...
67      Ahmad had epilepsy and always wore a wool vest...
158     She became intensely aware of her heart thumpi...
103     no violence no profanity suitable for viewing ...
32      She could hear so clearly now the insincerity ...
5       Black leather coat red scarf faded jeans excep...
34          Mullah Faizullah put his hand on her knee
```

Figure 25. Top 10 negative sentences using for cultural violence using Vader algorithm

```
The top 10 negative sentences are:       Score Compound  Score Negative  Score Neutral  Score Positive \
99          -0.9257       0.226          0.731           0.043
107         -0.9209       0.242          0.707           0.051
17          -0.9062       0.386          0.614           0.000
16          -0.8720       0.447          0.553           0.000
64          -0.8720       0.212          0.788           0.000
93          -0.8658       0.300          0.700           0.000
94          -0.8625       0.658          0.342           0.000
126         -0.8625       0.395          0.523           0.082
46          -0.8591       0.368          0.632           0.000
27          -0.7958       0.278          0.722           0.000

                                                        Sentence
99   saeed desperately wanted to leave his city in ...
107  but i had come to suspect that hers were not m...
17   When you kill a man you steal a life that not ...
16   But theft was the one unforgivable sin the com...
64   But we were kids who had learned to crawl toge...
93   they ran for the yard out of panic and despera...
94                            worst comes to worst ill pay for it
126  The children wept with terror and also sorrow ...
46   She thought of her entry into this world the h...
27   he had been the most stoic man i had ever know...
```

Figure 26. Top 10 positive sentences using for cultural violence using Textblob algorithm

In [9]: top_10_pos

Out[9]:

	Score Compound	Score Negative	Score Neutral	Score Positive	Sentence
79	0.8733	0.032	0.813	0.155	I hope you dont think this excuses you from ch...
92	0.8306	0.000	0.556	0.444	the good looks dont hurt eitherÂâãthe muscular...
51	0.7184	0.000	0.684	0.316	The mullah gave a few blessings said a few wor...
68	0.7096	0.057	0.731	0.211	A worried look crossed his face On the surfac...
67	0.7003	0.047	0.859	0.094	Ahmad had epilepsy and always wore a wool vest...
158	0.6369	0.000	0.819	0.181	She became intensely aware of her heart thumpi...
103	0.6348	0.000	0.698	0.302	no violence no profanity suitable for viewing ...
32	0.5410	0.108	0.628	0.264	She could hear so clearly now the insincerity ...
5	0.5267	0.032	0.880	0.088	Black leather coat red scarf faded jeans excep...
34	0.4939	0.000	0.686	0.314	Mullah Faizullah put his hand on her knee

Figure 27. Top 10 negative sentences using for cultural violence using Textblob algorithm

In [10]: top_10_neg

Out[10]:

	Score Compound	Score Negative	Score Neutral	Score Positive	Sentence
99	-0.9257	0.226	0.731	0.043	saeed desperately wanted to leave his city in ...
107	-0.9209	0.242	0.707	0.051	but i had come to suspect that hers were not m...
17	-0.9062	0.386	0.614	0.000	When you kill a man you steal a life that not ...
16	-0.8720	0.447	0.553	0.000	But theft was the one unforgivable sin the com...
64	-0.8720	0.212	0.788	0.000	But we were kids who had learned to crawl toge...
93	-0.8658	0.300	0.700	0.000	they ran for the yard out of panic and despera...
94	-0.8625	0.658	0.342	0.000	worst comes to worst ill pay for it
126	-0.8625	0.395	0.523	0.082	The children wept with terror and also sorrow ...
46	-0.8591	0.368	0.632	0.000	She thought of her entry into this world the h...
27	-0.7958	0.278	0.722	0.000	he had been the most stoic man i had ever know...

Chapter 4
Artificial Intelligence Framework for Opinion Mining of Netizen Readers' Reviews of Arundhati Roy's *The God of Small Things*

Pantea Keikhosrokiani

 https://orcid.org/0000-0003-4705-2732

School of Computer Sciences, Universiti Sains Malaysia, Malaysia

Moussa Pourya Asl

 https://orcid.org/0000-0002-8426-426X

School of Humanities, Universiti Sains Malaysia, Malaysia

Kah Em Chu

School of Computer Sciences, Universiti Sains Malaysia, Malaysia

Nur Ain Nasuha Anuar

School of Humanities, Universiti Sains Malaysia, Malaysia

ABSTRACT

In recent years, South-Asian literature in English has experienced a surge of newfound love and popularity both in the local and the global market. In this regard, Arundhati Roy's The God of Small Things (1997) has garnered an astounding mix of positive and negative reactions from readers across the globe. This chapter adopts an artificial intelligence approach to analyse netizen readers' feedback on the novel as documented in the book cataloguing website Goodreads. To this end, an opinion mining framework is proposed based on artificial intelligence techniques such as topic modelling and sentiment analysis. Latent semantic analysis (LSA) and latent Dirichlet allocation (LDA) are applied and compared to find the abstract "topics" that occur in a collection of reviews. Furthermore, lexicon-based sentiment analysis approaches such as Vader and Textblob algorithms are used and compared to find the review sentiment polarities.

DOI: 10.4018/978-1-6684-6242-3.ch004

INTRODUCTION

South-Asian Literature in English (SLE hereafter) refers to a broad collection of literary works written in English encompassing the people and the topics of South-Asian countries such as Pakistan, Bangladesh, Sri Lanka, and India. Over the past few decades, there has been a surge of newfound love and popularity for SLE both in the local and the global market (Asl, 2022; Dwivedi & Lau, 2014). The recent development of SLE is a result of "a new kind of social experience, born out of South Asia's accelerated economic and demographic growth, its global reach and its complex internal and regional politics" that has permeated the lives of many, and is demanding fictional representation suited to represent these changes (Tickell, 2016, p. 2). In other words, SLE is seen as a colossal body of literary works continuously reforming and adapting to reflect present issues that shape reality and social fabrics of South-Asian communities. 'Colossal', in particular, is used to describe SLE for its inclusion of literary works not only by home-based writers but also by diaspora writers.

Among the woman writers of SLE, Arundhati Roy is a name widely known for being a prolific home-based Indian woman writer writing about gender issues and politics. She has published two novels relating to these subjects—*The God of Small Things* in 1997 and *The Ministry of Utmost Happiness* in 2017. *The God of Small Things* (1997)—TGST hereafter—tells a story about family and social obligation, Indian politics and society and class, and love and sexuality. Since its publication, TGST has garnered attention from critics and readers alike. In 1997, it has won the Booker Prize award. Expectedly, the reception of Roy's debut novel is an astounding mix of positive and negative reactions. Nevertheless, it has been noted by critics that the responses are so extreme and polarized that it is difficult to believe that they are reading the same work (Anuar & Asl, 2021). Tickell (2007) provides that the two opposing groups would either love the novel deeply or dislike it with passion:

admiring readers describe [an] almost mystical attachment to her fiction and regard the novel as 'magical', 'breathtakingly beautiful' and 'close to perfection'. Many also note the book's emotional impact and its lingering 'imprint' on the reader, and others talk perceptively about the fantastic, interlocking musical patterns of Roy's writing, its descriptive originality and the way key words and phrases evoke specific moods and events. In the opposite camp, Roy's less appreciative readers repeatedly attack the novel's unwarranted 'hype', its 'tediously' overwritten or needlessly embellished style and the difficulty of following the plot through its fragmented time scheme. (p. xiii)

In other words, the audience of TGST are so divided in their opinions regarding the work that the same elements which make the novel 'beautiful' are also seen as 'tedious' by different critics and readers.

With the advancement of technology and the emergence of book cataloguing websites such as Goodreads, literary readers and enthusiasts across the world have found a unique platform to share their reviews of literary works. For instance, when one opens the homepage of the book in Goodreads, one can see 16,904 reviews and 276,016 ratings (as of 15 November 2022) documented for the book. Apparently, the amount of data in such websites created every day is enormous since internet-based platforms now allow millions of people to exchange information. The issue is how this enormous amount of data that includes conflicting views can be processed. Here is where text mining is revealed which aims to extract useful information for a specific purpose by analyzing the text (Keikhosrokiani & Asl, 2022; Suhendra et al., 2022). This type of analysis is often carried out manually by literary critics and readers which poses certain methodological difficulties (Chu et al., 2022; Malik et al., 2021; Yun Ying et al., 2022).

This chapter attempts to develop an artificial intelligence approach to analyse netizen readers' reviews of the novel in Goodreads platform to ascertain the dominant views in their feedback regarding Arundhati Roy's *The God of Small Things* (1997). For this reason, an opinion mining framework is proposed based on artificial intelligence techniques such as topic modelling and sentiment analysis. The Goodreads reviews towards the family drama novel, *The God of Small Things* are used as the main datasets for opinion mining. Latent Semantic Analysis (LSA) and Latent Dirichlet Allocation (LDA) are applied and compared to find the abstract "topics" that occur in a collection of reviews. Furthermore, lexicon-based sentiment analysis approaches such as Vader and Textblob algorithms are used and compared to find the reviews sentiments polarities. The following sections are comprised of literature review, methodology, results, and discussion. Finally, this chapter is wrapped up with conclusion.

LITERATURE REVIEW

The God of Small Things

Tickell (2016) and Dwivedi and Lau (2014) have noted that SLE acknowledges South-Asian writers who live in the subcontinents and overseas, although diaspora writers are often more internationally recognized for their works than home-based writers. Regardless, SLE is undeniably a flourishing ground where social concerns are encapsulated in the form of fictional writing. One of the contributing elements that has led to massive attention in SLE is the portrayal of gender issues by woman writers underlying the construction of their stories and their characters (Anuar & Asl, 2022b; Laxmiprasad, 2020). According to Anuar and Asl (2022a), gender issues of South-Asian women are primary elements in literary works by South-Asian woman writers, where "the heterogeneity and constant metamorphosis of identities" are explored in the novels' narratives (p. 1204). Some established names of South-Asian woman writers include Arundhati Roy, Anita Desai, Jhumpa Lahiri, Taslima Nasrin, and Monica Ali (Asl, 2018).

Suzanna Arundhati Roy was born in north-eastern Indian state of Assam on 24 November 1961. Following the divorce of her parents, Roy's mother brought her and her brother back to the family home in Ayemenem where she spent most of her childhood. Her mother is a teacher and activist who is an influential figure in Roy's youth. The early exposure to her mother's feminism and social activism leads to Roy's "political awareness and sensitivity to social injustice" (Tickell, 2007, p. 12) that become apparent in her novels. The unique approach to language and style of writing that Roy employs in her novels may be traced back to her childhood and her education. According to Roy, her "childhood's greatest gift was a lack of indoctrination", and that with such an upbringing, she has become somebody remarkable not "because [she has] learned to think outside the box" but because "that the box was never imposed on [her]" (Tickell, 2007, p. 13). Roy admits that she has been given a considerable amount of freedom growing up, and this has resulted in her rebellious tendency towards authority. The unconventional education Roy had received is reflected in her writing, becoming the foundation of her stylistic approach. Tickell asserts that "Roy's use of language, with its ability to disconcert, convey subtle tonal change and challenge received ideas, is an unmistakable characteristic of her fiction" (p. 7). This characteristic can be observed in her two published novel, particular in her debut novel *The God of Small Things*.

The God of Small Things (1997) spans from the late 1960 to early 1990 Kerala centralizing on a Syrian-Christian family, specifically on a woman named Ammu and her twin children, Estha and Rahel. It pivots around a forbidden cross-caste relationship between Ammu and Velutha, an 'untouchable', as it relates the small insignificant things in life to bigger things that ultimately shape the characters' fates. TGST highlights seemingly small events that persistently take place within the background of the novel, unfurling slowly but surely leading to inevitable tragedies befallen the characters. Much of the narrative of TGST is presented from the perspective of the twin children, following their life from childhood into adulthood. Although the novel has a chronological order to the events unfolding, Roy has strategically divided it in such a way that the time scheme seems fragmented—with the 'ending' of the novel telling an event that has supposedly happened in the middle of the story timeline. In addition, Roy's use of language is distinctively lush and rich with "non-standard spellings, reversed words, neologisms, repetitions and emphatic capitalizations" (Tickell (2007), p. 7). This deliberation in Roy's style of writing has been questioned and studied by many scholars, and although there is no conclusive answer, her experimentation with language is suggested to have been a stylistic choice with underlying postcolonial concerns (Tickell, 2020). Hence, Roy's TGST is considered to be challenging and redefining the English language—making it a reflective, poignant, and subversive piece.

Artificial Intelligence and Opinion Mining

People are increasingly adopting social media for various forms of social contact across many platforms, which has increased social media's relevance and appeal. Natural language may be interpreted in terms of the many opinion dimensions that people express via the use of social opinion mining. This advances the development of artificial intelligence, which in turn advances a number of practical use cases including decision-making and customer service (Cortis & Davis, 2021). Natural language processing, text analysis, computational linguistics, and biometrics are all used in opinion mining to systematically identify, extract, quantify, and evaluate emotional states and subjective information (Keikhosrokiani & Asl, 2022; Paremeswaran et al., 2022; Sofian et al., 2022; Suhendra et al., 2022; Yun Ying et al., 2022). Finding out what people's true feelings are on a subject may be done via sentiment analysis and natural language processing (NLP).

A subject of data science and artificial intelligence (AI) with origins in computational linguistics is known as natural language processing (NLP). The area is strongly tied to AI and helped with automated translation projects in the 1950s (Hilborg & Nygaard, 2015). With the use of NLP approaches, computers can comprehend and modify natural language writings and speeches to produce meaningful results (Chowdhary, 2020).

Opinion mining can be done using supervised or unsupervised learning. One of the unsupervised methods used to do text clustering in massive document sets is topic modelling. It is a statistical model that aids in searching a text for a set of keywords or subjects. It is based on the premise that each document is composed of a set of subjects or keywords. Every topic or keyword in the text is made up of a group of words. It is a type of opinion mining that may discover word trends in textual documents (Chu et al., 2022; Kumar et al., 2019).

One of the most modern methods for extracting and analysing emotive and sentimental remarks in a text is sentiment analysis (SA) (Bakshi et al., 2016; Keikhosrokiani & Asl, 2022; Li & Wu, 2010; Ravi & Ravi, 2015). Since it is used to identify sentiments and categorise them according to their polarity, it may also be referred to as a "emotional polarity computation." It is possible to use positive, neutral, or negative polarities. When the data is la-belled, conventional machine learning algorithms on n-grams, parts of speech, and other bag of words characteristics may be employed. Another technique for leveraging tagged data is the knowledge-based strategy, which was first presented by (Andreevskaia & Bergler, 2007; Fasha et al., 2022; Keikhosrokiani & Asl, 2022).

Topic Modelling

One of the powerful techniques in text mining for latent data discovery and finding relationship among data and text document is Topic Modelling which helps in discovering hidden semantic structures in a body of text. In simple word, given that a document is about a particular topic, it would be expected that certain topics would appear in the document more or less frequently. Topics identified by this technique are clusters of similar words that reveal, discover and annotate thematic structure in collection of documents (Asri et al., 2022; Jafery et al., 2022; Kherwa & Bansal, 2020; Suhendra et al., 2022).

The weighting of a desired subject throughout the entire corpus is referred to as topic modelling. It may be used to determine the proportion of nation names that are mentioned in a text. There are many different visualisations for topic modelling, including line charts, bar charts, pie charts, word clouds, and heat maps. Words for a collection of texts are grouped using topic modelling. Unsupervised learning is the term used to describe the automated categorization of words without the use of a predetermined list of labels. A group of terms will emerge after feeding the data model, from which the main topic may be inferred. However, only by looking at a mix of words and figures, it is complex and difficult to comprehend the correct issue (Chu et al., 2022).

A term in a document is assigned a weight, depending on the number of appearances of the term in a document. It is a bit special as those frequently occurring will be given less weight as compared to those unexpected ones. The most famous way to formalize the idea for term document matrices is (term frequency * inverse document frequency) [TF*IDF] (Keikhosrokiani & Asl, 2022; Mutanga & Abayomi, 2022). This involves a mathematical framework by examining a set of documents, based on the statistics of the words used in each document, and concluding what topics might be and what each document's balance of topics is. The most frequently used and most famous topic modelling methods that are included in this study are Latent Semantic Analysis (LSA) and Latent Dirichlet Allocation (LDA).

SVD matrix can be used to find the similar topics and documents using the cosine similarity method. LSA always finds low dimension representation of documents and words by applying SVD, so it works well in the task of dimensionality reduction. Those terms with similar meaning will occur very closer in their contextual usage as this is distributional hypotheses for LSA. LSA uses vector representation of text to compute how likely it is for to discover similar words in text as all the semantic relations between texts are inferred directly from given corpus text. LSA addresses the issues of meaning and usage of words as word may have multiple senses and multiple usage in different contexts which are defined as polysemy. Different words which may have a similar meaning in certain contexts denote the same concept defined as synonyms by mapping high-dimensional count vectors to a lower dimensional representation in a so-called latent semantic space that provides information well beyond the lexical level and revels semantical relations between the entities of interest. The fundamental idea of LDA is that documents are represented as random mixtures over latent topics, where a topic is characterized by a distribution over words. LDA is a form of dimension reduction that uses a probabilistic model to find the co-occurrence patterns of terms that correspond to semantics topics in a collection of documents (Jafery et al., 2022; Keikhosrokiani & Asl, 2022). Based on definition theorem to capture significant inter and intra document statistical structure via mixing distributional assumes that document arise from multiple topics, a topic is defined as distribution over a vocabulary. Corpus is associated with predefined number of topics

Table 1. Comparison between different approaches for topic modelling

Method Criteria	Latent Semantic Analysis (LSA)	Latent Dirichlet Allocation (LDA)
Characteristics	- Create vector-based representation for texts' to make semantic content and compute the similarity between text's to pick the heist efficient related words. - Not robust statistical background as it uses Singular Value Decomposition. - LSA can get from the topic if there are any synonym words	- Generative model does not consider order of words in producing documents and purely based on bag of words (BOW) approach. - Create a randomly assigned document-topic and word-topic distribution and iterate over words in each document, the distributions are updated according to probability that a document or a word belongs to a certain topic. - To increase the performance of model as user need manually remove stop words.
Advantages	- Single Value Decomposition does not need grammar, semantics and other basic knowledge of natural languages processing as SVD in LSA only executes mathematical treatment to the matrix. - SVD in LSA will reduce the data sparseness problem as a word only appears in a few documents that many element values of the matrix will be zero by making the space dimension reduced significantly	- Supply more semantically interpretable data and performs well where there is no time constraint. - LDA able to enhance transitive relations between topics and obtain high-order co-occurrence in small documents like in paragraphs and sentences text.
Limitations	- It is hard to label a topic in some cases and to establish a number of topics. - It is difficult to decide what is the value of K in the SVD algorithm. Normally, the value of K is usually determined by empirical equations via comparing possible choices one by one.	- Not able to form relations among topics that help to understand deep structures of documents. - It is difficult to decide number of topics (T) as too large of T will cause topic overlapping with another whereas T too small will cause the topics to become general.

k, and each document in corpus contain these topics with different proportion. Topic modelling aims to learn these topics form data or corpus.

Summary of characteristics, advantages, and limitations of four most well-known modelling approaches as described by (Deerwester et al., 1990; Hofmann, 1999, 2001; Torkkola, 2004) are shown in Table 1.

Sentiment Analysis

Sentiment analysis, a type of opinion mining, is frequently carried out on user comments about an item or a topic to ascertain its sentiment orientation, or if the remarks of a chosen topic are positive, negative, or neutral (Abadah et al., 2023; Al Mamun et al., 2022; Fasha et al., 2022; Keikhosrokiani & Asl, 2022; Malik et al., 2021). Attribute level, phrase level, and document level are the three levels at which sentiment analysis may be done. Machine learning and semantic orientation are the two basic methods that may be used for sentiment analysis. Orientation to meaning is uncontrolled. Therefore, training the data beforehand is not required. But when we talk about machine learning, we're talking about both supervised and unsupervised learning. Data that has already been trained is crucial for supervised machine learning. There is also a lot of use of a mixed semantic/machine learning approach (Chu et al., 2022).

Sentiment analysis is a subtopic under Natural Language Processing (NLP) which are apply to determine the subjectivity and opinion in text (Lodin & Balani, 2017). Sentiment analysis can be used to study the reviews to obtain information, which can be either objective or subjective. Objective reviews

Table 2. Comparison of Two Main Approaches of Sentiment Analysis

Criteria	Machine Learning Approach	Lexicon-Based Approach
Classification	· Supervised Learning · Unsupervised Learning	· Unsupervised Learning
Advantages	· Unlike Lexicon-based approach that required dictionary for sentiment analysis, ML does not need dictionary. · ML approach has the ability to adapt can create trained models for specific purposes and contexts. · Demonstrate the hight accuracy of classification.	· Unlike ML based approach that labelled data and the procedure of learning is not required. · Domain independent as it suitable to diverse of domains as it performs sentiment analysis based on dictionary.
Limitations	· Low applicability on new data due to it is a domain-based application, model trained on texts in most case not appropriate to another domain.	· Finite number of words in the lexicon and the assignation of a fixed sentiment orientation. · Requires a sold linguistics resources which those resources are scarce.
Algorithms	· Linear Classifiers (SVM, Neural Network) · Decision Tree Classifier · Probabilistics Classifier (Naïve Bayes, Bayesian Network)	· Senti WordNet · SenticNet · NTLK (Natural Language Toolkit) · TextBlob · VADER (Valence Aware Dictionary and sEntimentReasoner)

are factual, it contain evidences while subjective reviews are opinionated, its more about the feelings and own belief and judgement (Alaei et al., 2019).

Sentiment analysis includes two main approaches of (1) Machine Learning (ML) Approach and (2) Lexicon-Based Approach which are comparted in Table 2. Each approach has its own limitation and advantages, primary key to decide the success of machine learning approach are the quantity and quality of training data as it will generate better result in sentiment analysis if there is more data to be trained whereas a Lexicon-Based approach more suitable for variety of domains as it is unsupervised approach and domain independent, thus it has a more robust performance across domains as compared to ML approach (Hogenboom et al., 2014).

METHODOLOGY

This study proposed an opinion mining framework as shown in Figure 1. The proposed framework consists of nine main phases: (1) data collection, (2) text extraction, (3) data exploration, (4) text normalization, (5) text visualization, (6) topic modelling, (7) sentiment analysis, (8) deployment, and (9) evaluation.

The details for different phases of the proposed opinion mining framework are added as follows:

Data Collection

The data for this study was collected from Goodreads reviews for Arundhati Roy's *The God of Small Things*. This family drama novel was written by an Indian author Arundhati Roy. In her first book, Roy tells the tale of fraternal twins whose lives are ruined by the "Love Laws" that were in place in Kerala,

Figure 1. The proposed opinion mining framework based on artificial intelligence techniques

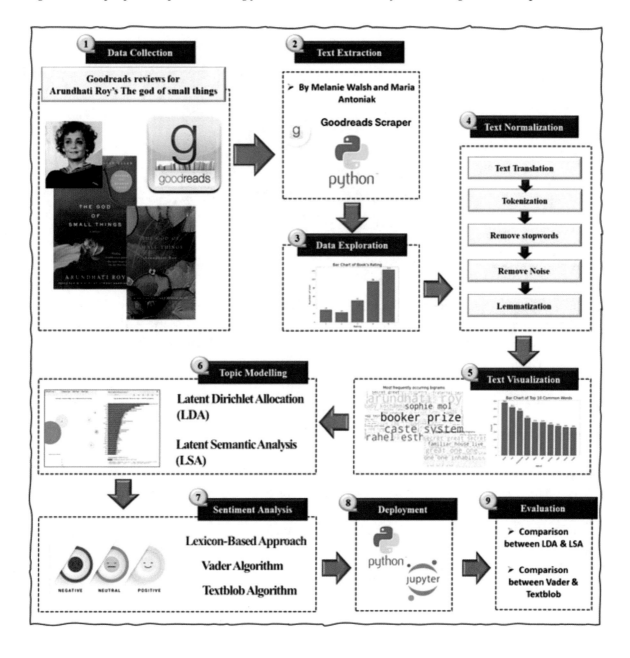

India, in the 1960s. The story examines how seemingly unimportant, little things may have a big impact on how individuals act and live. The narrative also examines casteism's enduring impact in India. It was awarded the 1997 Booker Prize. The novel is worthy of attention as it has left an imprint—being listed among 10 all-time greatest Asian novels by *The Telegraph* in 2014 and recognized as one of the 12 best Indian novels by *The Independent*. Furthermore, reviews from major newspapers like *The New York Times, Los Angeles Times, Toronto Star,* and *Time* have been positive—marking and cementing TGST as one of the defining pieces of SLE to date.

Figure 2. Bar chart of rating of the book

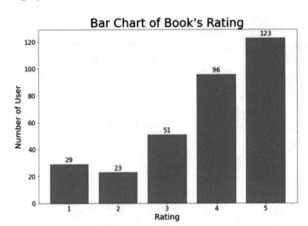

Text Extraction

In this phase, the main process is to collect the reviews of the novel from Goodreads website. The Goodreads Scraper wad adopted from the codes by Melanie Walsh and Maria Antoniak. Goodreads only show 300 reviews for each sorting mode, which are 'Default', 'Oldest' and 'Newest'. For 'Default' mode, only 270 reviews manage were taken, while 300 reviews have been scraped for the other two modes. Hence, the total number of 870 reviews have been scraped in total. After removing the duplicated reviews, only 332 unique reviews remained as the datasets included in this study.

Data Exploration

The reviews section not only contain the reviews written by the reader, also their ratings toward the books. Figure 2 shows the distribution of the readers' ratings toward the novel *The God of Small Things*. Based on the figure out of the 332 collected reviews, 123 readers or 37.05% of the readers have given the novel the highest rating of 5, followed by 28.91% rating of 4.

TEXT NORMALIZATION

The general ways of text exploration are presenting the frequent words by Bar Chart and WordCloud. In order to produce the accurate figure, the text need to be normalized. The standard process of text normalisation includes the process of (1) tokenization, (2) noise removal, (3) stopwords removal, (4) and lemmatization. In this study, other than tokenization, noise removal, stopwords removal, and lemmatization, text translation is also performed beforehand as the reviews collected are not all in English.

1. Text Translation

The review contains various languages. As python was not able to translate all the review into English accurately, some of the reviews in foreign language are translated manually. This limitation is due to some

Figure 3. Example of reviews in different languages

> Mungkin karena Estha sudah kehilangan "suara"nya? Entah lah..."Things can change in a day."

of the reviews contain two languages. For example, Bahasa Malaya and English as shown in Figure 3. The sentence shown in Figure 3 is extracted from reviews 187th (Translation: Maybe it's because Estha lost her voice? I don't know..."Things can be changed in a day."). After translating every review into English (Figure 4), the text normalization process can be performed.

Figure 4. Example of reviews in English languages

	Review Translated
review_count	
0	Okay, first things first. The God Of Small Thi...
1	That\'s what careless words do. They make peo...
2	Lush, gorgeous prose: reading The God of Small...
3	Please excuse me while I go sit in this corner...
4	This review is going to be a short one because...
...	...
327	"The God of Small Things" is Complex, Cryptic,...
328	It\'s quite difficult to put the reading exper...
329	It's hard to characterize the plot of this tal...
330	5/5 Stars This is not a novel for the average ...
331	In a little village-town called Eminem Ayemene...

332 rows × 1 columns

2. Tokenization

In this step, the long texts are split into sentences and sentences into words for the analytics process.

3. Remove Stopwords

Repetitive words in the reviews such as 'book', 'story', 'novel' and other words that does not carry much insight, like 'would', 'should' and 'could' has been removed in this step.

4. Remove Noise

Remove the nonalphabetical character like numbers and symbols.

Figure 5. Bar chart of top 10 common words

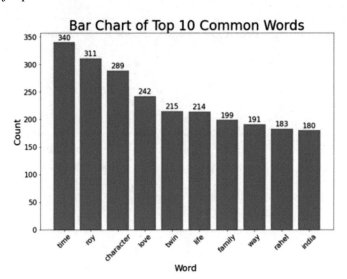

5.   Lemmatization

In this step, the words were returned into their root form and the words which are not in the category of adjectives and nouns were removed.

Text Visualization

The text normalization process is crucial for text visualization. When the words are returned into their root words, the words like 'time' and 'times' are categorized together as 'time'. As shown in Figure 5, in the review, the readers often discuss about the author Roy, the location of the novel, India and the characters in the novel like the twin, Rahel and the family.

The bigram wordcloud illustrated in Figure 6, the Booker Prize won by the author and the caste system are the most frequent words mentioned by the readers. Furthermore, the readers are discussing about the author Arundhati Roy frequently, and the main characters like Rahel Estha and Sophie Mol.

The trigram wordcloud shown in Figure 7 depicts the frequent phases that can help us understand the readers feelings about the book is a positive. In addition, readers feel the book have a deceive thrill ending. From both wordclouds (Figure 6 and 7), the reviews are positive towards the books.

Topic Modelling

For **topic modelling**, two famous algorithms which are Latent Semantic Analysis (LSA) and Latent Dirichlet Allocation (LDA) are applied to find the abstract "topics" that occur in a collection of reviews. As both of the algorithms require to predetermine the number of topics to generate the keywords, both algorithms are tested for the topics from number 1 to 9 to find the best performance for each algorithm. Then performance results from two algorithm are compared and evaluated to finalize the better model.

Figure 6. WordCloud of Most Frequently Occuring Bigrams

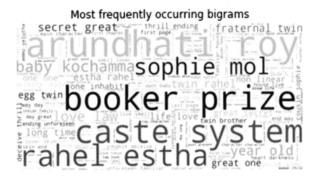

Sentiment Analysis

For sentiment analysis, the model required no parameter tuning, hence only two selected algorithms of VADER and Textblob done are applied and compared.

Deployment

The topic modelling model and sentiment analysis model are deployed using Python Programming Language as it includes uncountable packages to perform various functions. Moreover, Python is best known for its fast-to-built. Python has ready to use package for both topic modelling and sentiment analysis, hence, this study focused on tuning the parameters and comparing Python Packages for the models' performance.

Figure 7. WordCloud of Most Frequently Occuring Trigrams

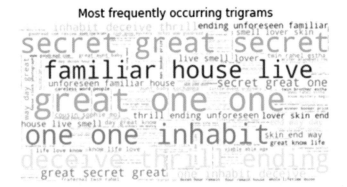

Figure 8. Line Chart of LDA model performance

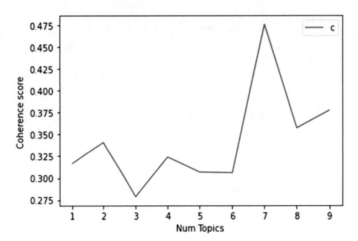

Evaluation

In this step LDA and LSI are compared based on with coherence score to find the best model for topic modelling. Furthermore, VADER and Textblob are compared based on the count of polarities for positive, neutral, and negative opinions.

RESULTS AND DISCUSSION

Topic Modelling

The purpose of applying topic modelling in this study is to find the major topics discussed by the Goodread users in relation to the book. The topic modelling output is multiple keyword list, where each keyword list belongs to a topic. In order to ensure the topics assigned are correct, the original reviews are assigned to the relevant keyword list. By studying the group of reviews of each keyword list, the topics can be assigned easily and accurately. After that, the topics could be grouped into themes if applicable. Figure 8 and 9 show the performance of LDA and LSA model for the number of topics from 1 to 9. As shown in Figure 8 (a) and (b), the optimal number of topics is 7 with coherence score of 0.47591748 for LDA while the optimal number of topics is 7 with coherence score of 0.39390974 for LSA.

Table 3 shows the keywords and related topics for each topic generated from topic modelling model. The main topics extracted from the reviews are related to childhood of Rahel, fountain referring to the hair and some event, readers' discussion about the shocking plot and enjoyment reading the book, readers' comments about the book, the main story of the book, unfortunate event faced by the characters, characters in the book, and characters' family of in the novel.

Figure 10 shows the bubble map created using Python Libraries "pyLDAvis". The red bubble on the left side shows the Topic Number of the keywords on the right side. The red bar refers to the estimated term frequency within the selected topics while the blue bars refer to the overall term frequency or the total frequency of the words in all reviews. The top 30 words in Figure 9 are Roy, character, word, fam-

Figure 9. Line Chart of LSA model performance

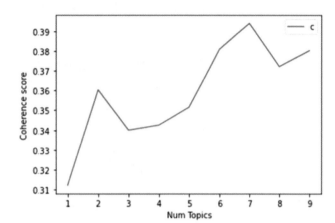

ily, love, time, life, way, Kerala, twin, language, little, end, chapter, child, India, history, good, poetic, reader, certain, village, beautiful, plot, narrative, style, Rahel, Indian, and event. The rest of the bubble models for topic 2 to 7 are added in Appendix.

Based on the reviews listed in Table 4, these 30 words and the keywords can be divided into few groups. As shown in group 1, one of the biggest discussions by the readers is the story in the books, they discussed about such as: (1) characters like Rahel and Kerala and their character design, such as twin, family, Indian, and child, (2) the background of the story, like the location India, where the story

Table 3. Keywords and relevant topics

No	Keyword	Topic
1	0.027*"tokyo" + 0.025*"fountain" + 0.019*"black" + 0.017*"hair" + 0.017*"naxalite" + 0.014*"fire" + 0.011*"malevolence" + 0.010*"blame" + 0.008*"silence" + 0.007*"child"	Childhood of Rahel, fountain referring to the hair and some event
2	0.046*"shocking" + 0.007*"month" + 0.005*"value" + 0.004*"foot" + 0.003*"enjoyment" + 0.003*"count" + 0.002*"basic" + 0.002*"accessible" + 0.002*"shot" + 0.002*"roy"	Reader discusses about the shocking plot and enjoyment reading the book
3	0.006*"depth" + 0.006*"left" + 0.006*"five_star" + 0.006*"category" + 0.006*"turn" + 0.005*"well" + 0.005*"church" + 0.004*"com" + 0.004*"humanity" + 0.004*"spot"	Readers comments about the book
4	0.021*"family" + 0.021*"twin" + 0.017*"child" + 0.015*"parent" + 0.014*"love" + 0.014*"man" + 0.013*"roy" + 0.013*"india" + 0.012*"ammu" + 0.012*"childhood"	The main story of the book
5	0.024*"regard" + 0.020*"gossip" + 0.013*"skin" + 0.011*"roy" + 0.010*"sorry" + 0.007*"soft" + 0.007*"blame" + 0.006*"window" + 0.006*"war" + 0.005*"floor"	Unfortunate event faced by the characters
6	0.024*"salman" + 0.021*"jewel" + 0.016*"poetry" + 0.011*"dancer" + 0.009*"slow" + 0.008*"average" + 0.008*"search" + 0.008*"curious" + 0.007*"sex" + 0.007*"need"	Characters in the book
7	0.029*"roy" + 0.022*"character" + 0.019*"word" + 0.016*"family" + 0.015*"love" + 0.012*"time" + 0.011*"life" + 0.011*"way" + 0.010*"kerala" + 0.010*"lot"	Characters' family of in the novel

Figure 10. Term frequency of topic 1

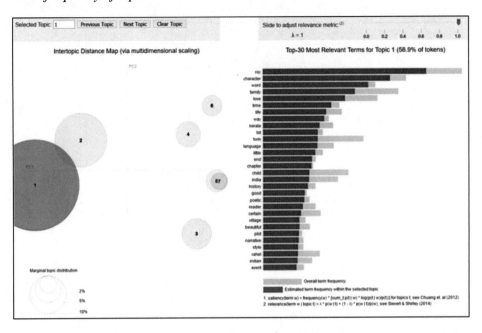

based on, and the village, (3) the event in the books, like their life, way and time. Group 2 shows another popular discussion by the readers which is about the writing style of the author (Roy). In addition, most of the readers praise the author for using the beautiful words in the book, how the author able to write the story according to the history, the narrative style, and the humanity is shown in the book. Finally, group 3 shows that the last chapter or ending chapter is one of the most frequent discuss topic. Readers discussed about the emotional shocking ending and most of the readers felt the ending is the best part in the book.

Sentiment Analysis using Vader Algorithm

Figure 11 shows the count of review polarities generated from Vader algorithm. Based on the results, most of the reader have positive sentiments towards the book.

The model does not determine the novel is good or bad according based the review of readers, but it classifies the reviews into positive, neutral, and negative according to their sentiment in the review. A positive review is mostly referring that readers like the novel and like the author. The negative reviews are not necessarily shows that the readers do not like the book, but just describing how they feel the melancholy in the novel. Overall, most of the reviews are positive and most of the readers gave high rating to this book.

By going thru the positive and negative reviews in Table 5 to 8, most positive reviews are praising the structure of the novel, how the author connect all the small things, the ending, and author style of writing. While the negative reviews are mostly pointing that the novel is bored and the plot. Table 5 and 6 show the results generated by Vader algorithm which listed the top 10 positive and negative sentences respectively, whereas Table 7 and 8 listed the top 10 positive and negative sentences generated by Textblob algorithm. Vader is better in classifying formal reviews with nice grammar while Textblob is able

Table 4. Keywords from bubble plot

Group	Keywords
1	Character, family, love, time, life, way, kerala, twin, india, village, rahel, indian, child, event
	0.027*"tokyo" + 0.025*"fountain" + 0.019*"black" + 0.017*"hair" + 0.017*"naxalite" + 0.014*"fire" + 0.011*"malevolence" + 0.010*"blame" + 0.008*"silence" + 0.007*"child"
	0.021*"family" + 0.021*"twin" + 0.017*"child" + 0.015*"parent" + 0.014*"love" + 0.014*"man" + 0.013*"roy" + 0.013*"india" + 0.012*"ammu" + 0.012*"childhood"
	0.024*"regard" + 0.020*"gossip" + 0.013*"skin" + 0.011*"roy" + 0.010*"sorry" + 0.007*"soft" + 0.007*"blame" + 0.006*"window" + 0.006*"war" + 0.005*"floor"
	0.024*"salman" + 0.021*"jewel" + 0.016*"poetry" + 0.011*"dancer" + 0.009*"slow" + 0.008*"average" + 0.008*"search" + 0.008*"curious" + 0.007*"sex" + 0.007*"need"
2	Word, poetic, language, history, good, plot, beautiful, narrative, style. little, lot, reader, roy
	0.046*"shocking" + 0.007*"month" + 0.005*"value" + 0.004*"foot" + 0.003*"enjoyment" + 0.003*"count" + 0.002*"basic" + 0.002*"accessible" + 0.002*"shot" + 0.002*"roy"
	0.006*"depth" + 0.006*"left" + 0.006*"five_star" + 0.006*"category" + 0.006*"turn" + 0.005*"well" + 0.005*"church" + 0.004*"com" + 0.004*"humanity" + 0.004*"spot"
3	End, chapter

to classify the reviews with Internet slang based on the output of both models (Chu et al., 2022). As most of the review collected are formal English, Vader algorithm is more suitable for further analysis.

CONCLUSION

This study aimed to propose an opinion mining framework based on artificial intelligence techniques such as topic modelling and sentiment analysis. The netizens' reviews of Arundhati Roy's *The God of Small Things* on Goodreads served as the source of the data for this study. After some data pre-processing steps, topic modelling was applied using Latent Semantic Analysis (LSA) and Latent Dirichlet Allocation (LDA). The results of LSA and LDA were compared based on coherence score which the optimal number of topics is 7 with coherence score of 0.47591748 for LDA while the optimal number of topics

Figure 11. Bar chart of review polarity

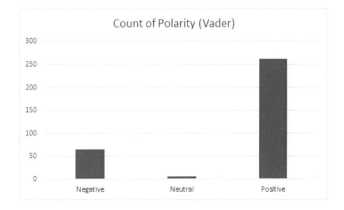

Table 5. The top 10 positive sentences using Vader

The top 10 positive sentences	Sentence	Score Compound	Score Negative	Score Neutral	Score Positive
141	The God of Small Things 1997 Once in awhile a...	0.9996	0.074	0.778	0.148
40	There is a lot of interesting material in here...	0.9989	0.040	0.863	0.097
70	Arundhati Roys amazing 1st novel The God of Sm...	0.9989	0.073	0.782	0.144
184	I have always believed that the right book com...	0.9988	0.008	0.760	0.232
264	And there it was again Another religion turned...	0.9987	0.069	0.761	0.170
319	You can find my review in Swedish further down...	0.9987	0.039	0.794	0.167
326	Winner of the Book Award in 1997 a prestigious...	0.9987	0.028	0.766	0.206
328	Its quite difficult to put the reading experie...	0.9986	0.050	0.836	0.113
22	There was no reasoning with this book It caugh...	0.9985	0.065	0.763	0.172
61	pretentious adjective1 Attempting to impress b...	0.9984	0.067	0.767	0.166

is 7 with coherence score of 0.39390974 for LSA. Furthermore, sentiment analysis was used using Vader and Textblob. Going through both positive and negative reviews, it becomes clear that the majority of positive reviews praise the novel's structure, the way the author weaves together all the small things, the resolution, and the author's writing style. While the majority of the negative reviews mentioned how boring the book and the narrative are. Based on the output of both models, Vader performs better at categorising reviews with formal language and good grammar than Textblob does at classifying reviews with Internet slang. Finally, it can be concluded that Vader algorithm is more suited for future examination. For the future works, deep learning techniques can be considered to detect and classify the emotions of the reviews towards Arundhati Roy's *The God of Small Things*.

Table 6. The top 10 negative sentences using Vader

The top 10 negative sentences	Sentences	Score Compound	Score Negative	Score Neutral	Score Positive
259	Well That was completely disappointing While i...	-0.9967	0.108	0.820	0.072
272	Up there with Sunshine Learners when the ballo...	-0.9943	0.151	0.775	0.074
66	This book has literally no chill None Zero Zil...	-0.9941	0.174	0.741	0.085
186	Basically this book doesnt offer anything but ...	-0.9933	0.203	0.704	0.093
93	Haunting Roys story focuses on Rahel and Estha...	-0.9883	0.146	0.841	0.014
271	Roy weaves a beautiful story The story which i...	-0.9873	0.166	0.784	0.050
100	Its about India one of my favorite reading sub...	-0.9832	0.165	0.741	0.094
205	I did not enjoy this book AT ALLI constantly q...	-0.9820	0.199	0.722	0.079
180	I have never seen a better way of sorrow and t...	-0.9816	0.184	0.713	0.103
84	July 2017 review So funny I just finished my t...	-0.9658	0.122	0.790	0.088

Table 7. The top 10 positive sentences using Textblob

The top 10 positive sentences	Sentences	Polarity	Subjectivity
79	Wonderful book	1.000000	1.000000
305	The Best Novel I Have Ever Read	1.000000	0.300000
163	A masterpiece Great literature has an impact o...	0.766667	0.766667
211	Wonderful Cant wait to read more of Arundhati ...	0.750000	0.750000
162	Brilliantly written though on a sordid topic L...	0.700000	0.875000
239	Everything can change in one day A timeless b...	0.700000	0.600000
280	WHAT A BEAUTIFUL BOOK THIS IS OMG my words hav...	0.588281	0.728125
165	OMG I wish this wasnt set in Kerala I wish I c...	0.587500	0.925000
38	One of the best contemporary novels Ive read T...	0.583333	0.233333
69	THE BEST BOOK I EVER READ DEFINITELY THE STRUC...	0.566667	0.533333

Table 8. The top 10 negative sentences using Textblob

The top 10 negative sentences	Sentences	Polarity	Subjectivity
122	One word BORING	-1.000000	1.000000
237	Baby fcking Kochamma	-0.600000	0.800000
111	Never before has a book touched me as deeply a...	-0.331061	0.688333
258	Cant sleep Then try Arundhati Roys cure for in...	-0.295833	0.600000
307	I added an extra star due to the excellency of...	-0.281250	0.618750
164	Thank GodI did finish itno small featVery word...	-0.250000	0.400000
302	I started reading the book last night but foun...	-0.165278	0.397222
196	I tried reading this and forced myself to go o...	-0.144444	0.574074
262	I think Im burnt out on the similemetaphor hea...	-0.143878	0.550510
310	I was very close to abandon this book it bored...	-0.129437	0.470184

REFERENCES

Abadah, M. S. K., Keikhosrokiani, P., & Zhao, X. (2023). Analytics of Public Reactions to the COVID-19 Vaccine on Twitter Using Sentiment Analysis and Topic Modelling. In D. Valle-Cruz, N. Plata-Cesar, & J. L. González-Ruíz (Eds.), *Handbook of Research on Applied Artificial Intelligence and Robotics for Government Processes* (pp. 156–188). IGI Global. doi:10.4018/978-1-6684-5624-8.ch008

Al Mamun, M. H., Keikhosrokiani, P., Asl, M. P., Anuar, N. A. N., Hadi, N. H. A., & Humida, T. (2022). Sentiment Analysis of the Harry Potter Series Using a Lexicon-Based Approach. In P. Keikhosrokiani & M. Pourya Asl (Eds.), *Handbook of Research on Opinion Mining and Text Analytics on Literary Works and Social Media* (pp. 263–291). IGI Global. doi:10.4018/978-1-7998-9594-7.ch011

Alaei, A. R., Becken, S., & Stantic, B. (2019). Sentiment Analysis in Tourism: Capitalizing on Big Data. *Journal of Travel Research*, *58*(2), 175–191. doi:10.1177/0047287517747753

Andreevskaia, A., & Bergler, S. (2007). CLaC and CLaC-NB: Knowledge-based and corpus-based approaches to sentiment tagging. *Proceedings of the Fourth International Workshop on Semantic Evaluations (SemEval-2007)*.

Anuar, N. A. N., & Asl, M. P. (2022). Gender, Resistance, and Identity: Women's Rewriting of the Self in Chitra Banerjee Divakaruni's Before We Visit the Goddess. *Pertanika Journal of Social Science & Humanities*, *30*(3). Advance online publication. doi:10.47836/pjssh.30.3.15

Anuar, N. A. N., & Asl, M. P. (2022). Rewriting of Gender and Sexuality in Tanwi Nandini Islam's Bright Lines: A Cixousian Approach. In M. Pourya Asl (Ed.), *Gender, Place, and Identity of South Asian Women* (pp. 131–151). IGI Global. doi:10.4018/978-1-6684-3626-4.ch007

Anuar, N. A. N. B., & Asl, M. P. (2021). Gender and Sexual Identity in Arundhati Roy's The Ministry of Utmost Happiness: A Cixousian Analysis of Hijra's Resistance and Remaking of the Self. *Pertanika Journal of Social Science & Humanities*, *29*(4), 2335–2352. Advance online publication. doi:10.47836/pjssh.29.4.13

Asl, M. P. (2018). Fabrication of a desired truth: The oblivion of a Naxalite woman in Jhumpa Lahiri's The Lowland. *Asian Ethnicity*, *19*(3), 383–401. doi:10.1080/14631369.2018.1429892

Asl, M. P. (Ed.). (2022). *Gender, place, and identity of South Asian women*. IGI Global., doi:10.4018/978-1-6684-3626-4

Asri, M. A. Z. B. M., Keikhosrokiani, P., & Asl, M. P. (2022). Opinion Mining Using Topic Modeling: A Case Study of Firoozeh Dumas's Funny in Farsi in Goodreads. Advances on Intelligent Informatics and Computing. doi:10.1007/978-3-030-98741-1_19

Bakshi, R. K., Kaur, N., Kaur, R., & Kaur, G. (2016). Opinion mining and sentiment analysis. *2016 3rd International Conference on Computing for Sustainable Global Development (INDIACom)*.

Chowdhary, K. R. (2020). Natural Language Processing. In K. R. Chowdhary (Ed.), *Fundamentals of Artificial Intelligence* (pp. 603–649). Springer India., doi:10.1007/978-81-322-3972-7_19

Chu, K. E., Keikhosrokiani, P., & Asl, M. P. (2022). A Topic Modeling and Sentiment Analysis Model for Detection and Visualization of Themes in Literary Texts. *Pertanika Journal of Science & Technology*, *30*(4), 2535–2561. doi:10.47836/pjst.30.4.14

Cortis, K., & Davis, B. (2021). Over a decade of social opinion mining: A systematic review. *Artificial Intelligence Review*, *54*(7), 4873–4965. doi:10.100710462-021-10030-2 PMID:34188346

Deerwester, S., Dumais, S. T., Furnas, G. W., Landauer, T. K., & Harshman, R. (1990). Indexing by latent semantic analysis. *Journal of the American Society for Information Science, 41*(6), 391-407.

Dwivedi, O., & Lau, L. (2014). *Indian Writing in English and the Global Literary Market*. Springer. doi:10.1057/9781137437716

Fasha, E. F. B. K., Keikhosrokiani, P., & Asl, M. P. (2022). Opinion Mining Using Sentiment Analysis: A Case Study of Readers' Response on Long Litt Woon's The Way Through the Woods in Goodreads. Advances on Intelligent Informatics and Computing. doi:10.1007/978-3-030-98741-1_20

Hilborg, P. H., & Nygaard, E. B. (2015). *Viability of sentiment analysis in business*. The Copenhagen Business School. Retrieved from http://studenttheses. cbs. dk…

Hofmann, T. (1999). Probabilistic latent semantic indexing. *Proceedings of the 22nd Annual International ACM SIGIR Conference on Research and Development in Information Retrieval*.

Hofmann, T. (2001). Unsupervised Learning by Probabilistic Latent Semantic Analysis. *Machine Learning*, *42*(1), 177–196. doi:10.1023/A:1007617005950

Hogenboom, A., Heerschop, B., Frasincar, F., Kaymak, U., & de Jong, F. (2014). Multi-lingual support for lexicon-based sentiment analysis guided by semantics. *Decision Support Systems*, *62*, 43–53. doi:10.1016/j.dss.2014.03.004

Jafery, N. N., Keikhosrokiani, P., & Asl, M. P. (2022). Text analytics model to identify the connection between theme and sentiment in literary works: A case study of Iraqi life writings. In P. Keikhosrokiani & M. Pourya Asl (Eds.), *Handbook of Research on Opinion Mining and Text Analytics on Literary Works and Social Media* (pp. 173–190). IGI Global. doi:10.4018/978-1-7998-9594-7.ch008

Keikhosrokiani, P., & Asl, M. P. (Eds.). (2022). *Handbook of research on opinion mining and text analytics on literary works and social media*. IGI Global. doi:10.4018/978-1-7998-9594-7

Kherwa, P., & Bansal, P. (2020). Topic modeling: a comprehensive review. *EAI Endorsed Transactions on Scalable Information Systems, 7*(24).

Kumar, S. A., Vijayalakshmi, M., Divya, T., & Subramanya, K. (2019). Computational Intelligence for Data Analytics. In *Recent Advances in Computational Intelligence* (pp. 27–43). Springer. doi:10.1007/978-3-030-12500-4_2

Laxmiprasad, P. (2020). Diasporic literature—An overview. *Journal of English Language and Literature, 7*(3), 98–106. doi:10.33329/joell.7.3.20.98

Li, N., & Wu, D. D. (2010). Using text mining and sentiment analysis for online forums hotspot detection and forecast. *Decision Support Systems, 48*(2), 354–368. doi:10.1016/j.dss.2009.09.003

Lodin, H., & Balani, P. (2017). Rich Semantic Sentiment Analysis using Lexicon Based Approach *ICTACT JOURNAL ON. Soft Computing, 07*(04), 1486–1491.

Malik, E. F., Keikhosrokiani, P., & Asl, M. P. (2021, July 4-5). Text Mining Life Cycle for a Spatial Reading of Viet Thanh Nguyen's *The Refugees* (2017). *2021 International Congress of Advanced Technology and Engineering (ICOTEN)*. doi:10.1109/ICOTEN52080.2021.9493520

Mutanga, M. B., & Abayomi, A. (2022). Tweeting on COVID-19 pandemic in South Africa: LDA-based topic modelling approach. *African Journal of Science, Technology, Innovation and Development, 14*(1), 163–172. doi:10.1080/20421338.2020.1817262

Paremeswaran, P. p., Keikhosrokiani, P., & Asl, M. P. (2022). Opinion Mining of Readers' Responses to Literary Prize Nominees on Twitter: A Case Study of Public Reaction to the Booker Prize (2018–2020). Advances on Intelligent Informatics and Computing. doi:10.1007/978-3-030-98741-1_21

Ravi, K., & Ravi, V. (2015). A survey on opinion mining and sentiment analysis: Tasks, approaches and applications. *Knowledge-Based Systems, 89*, 14–46. doi:10.1016/j.knosys.2015.06.015

Sofian, N. B., Keikhosrokiani, P., & Asl, M. P. (2022). Opinion mining and text analytics of reader reviews of Yoko Ogawa's The Housekeeper and the Professor in Goodreads. In P. Keikhosrokiani & M. Pourya Asl (Eds.), *Handbook of Research on Opinion Mining and Text Analytics on Literary Works and Social Media* (pp. 240–262). IGI Global. doi:10.4018/978-1-7998-9594-7.ch010

Suhendra, N. H. B., Keikhosrokiani, P., Asl, M. P., & Zhao, X. (2022). Opinion mining and text analytics of literary reader responses: A case study of reader responses to KL Noir volumes in Goodreads using sentiment analysis and topic. In P. Keikhosrokiani & M. Pourya Asl (Eds.), *Handbook of Research on Opinion Mining and Text Analytics on Literary Works and Social Media* (pp. 191–239). IGI Global. doi:10.4018/978-1-7998-9594-7.ch009

Tickell, A. (2007). *Arundhati Roy's the god of small things: A Routledge study guide* (1st ed.). Routledge. doi:10.4324/9780203004593

Tickell, A. (2016). *South-Asian Fiction in English: Contemporary Transformations*. Springer. doi:10.1057/978-1-137-40354-4

Tickell, A. (2020). Postcolonial Fiction and the Question of Influence: Arundhati Roy, The God of Small Things and Rumer Godden. *Postcolonial Text*, *15*(1), 1–20.

Torkkola, K. (2004). Discriminative features for textdocument classification. *Formal Pattern Analysis &Applications*, *6*(4), 301–308. doi:10.100710044-003-0196-8

Ying, Y. S., Keikhosrokiani, P., & Pourya Asl, M. (2022). Opinion Mining on Viet Thanh Nguyen's The Sympathizer Using Topic Modelling and Sentiment Analysis. *Journal of Information Technology Management, 14*, 163-183. doi: 10.22059/jitm.2022.84895

APPENDIX

Figure 12. Term Frequency of Topic 2

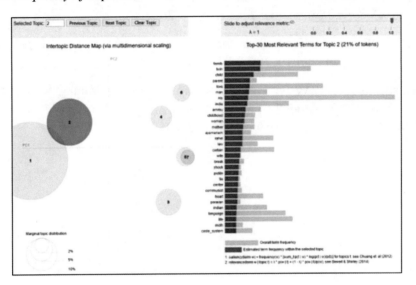

Figure 13. Term Frequency of Topic 3

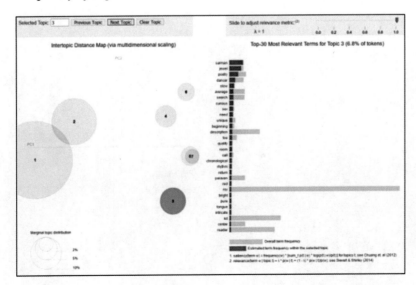

Figure 14. Term Frequency of Topic 4

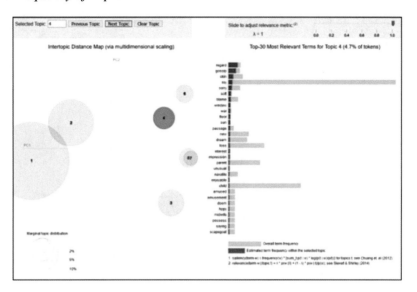

Figure 15. Term Frequency of Topic 5

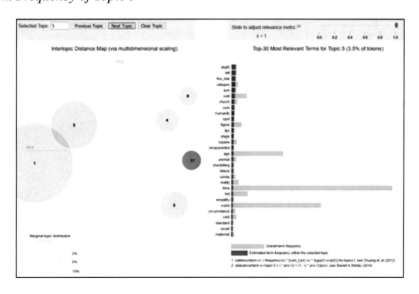

Figure 16. Term Frequency of Topic 6

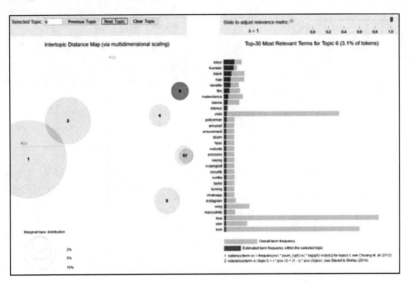

Figure 17. Term Frequency of Topic 7

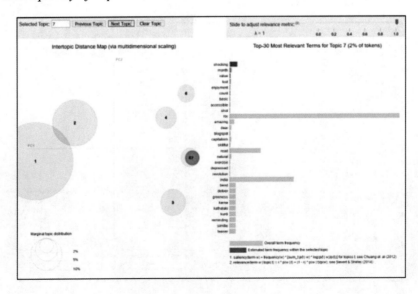

Chapter 5
Artificial Intelligence Applications in Literary Works:
Emotion Extraction and Classification of Mohsin Hamid's *Moth Smoke*

Annuur Farahhim Zainol
School of Computer Sciences, Universiti Sains Malaysia, Malaysia

Pantea Keikhosrokiani
https://orcid.org/0000-0003-4705-2732
School of Computer Sciences, Universiti Sains Malaysia, Malaysia

Moussa Pourya Asl
https://orcid.org/0000-0002-8426-426X
School of Humanities, Universiti Sains Malaysia, Malaysia

Nur Ain Nasuha Anuar
School of Humanities, Universiti Sains Malaysia, Malaysia

ABSTRACT

The British Pakistani writer, Mohsin Hamid's debut novel, Moth Smoke (2000), has garnered conflicting responses from readers across the globe. Over the past few years and with the rapid advancements in social media platforms, readers around the world have publicly shared their opinions and feelings towards the text using online platforms such as Twitter, Goodreads, Facebook—among many others. The huge bulk of readers' reviews are useful data for publishers and booksellers in analyzing readers' interests to recommend similar texts to online readers. The analysis of sentiment and emotion attached to this data can help to determine the popularity or unpopularity of a literary text. Using reader-reviews of Hamid's novel from Goodreads as the main data source, this study a offers a data analytic approach: LSTM, LDA to detect and classify the dominant emotion existing within the readers' feedback. Understanding readers' emotions towards the novel can help in developing a recommendation system that can suggest readers stories of their interest.

DOI: 10.4018/978-1-6684-6242-3.ch005

INTRODUCTION

The British Pakistani writer, Mohsin Hamid's debut novel *Moth Smoke* (2000) has garnered conflicting responses from readers across the globe. The novel tells the story of a young man named Darashikoh Shezad or Daru who plunges into a life of drugs and crime. While some have acclaimed the novel for depicting a more vivid and disturbing portrait of Pakistan than the exoticized and stereotypical images of South Asia known to most Western readers, others have criticized it for promoting a negative image of the country (Asl, 2022; Dagamsheh & Downing, 2016; Perner, 2010). Over the past few years and with the rapid advancements in social media platforms, readers around the world have used online platforms such as Twitter, Goodreads, Facebook—among many others—to share their opinions and feelings towards literary texts (Keikhosrokiani & Asl, 2022). When one explores the landing page of the novel in Goodreads—which includes rating details, number of ratings and number of reviews—it becomes evident that the story has provoked differing responses from readers. The emotional categories of readers' responses can be classified into three basic types of positive, negative, and neutral as in sentiment feedback. This study aims to analyze the reviews of Mohsin Hamid's debut novel *Moth Smoke* (2000) in Goodreads to detect the dominant emotion existing within the readers' feedback. Understanding readers' emotion towards the novel can help in developing a recommendation system that can suggest readers stories of their interest. The next section of this chapter focusses on the background of the study followed by the proposed method. Then results and discussion are added. Finally, the chapter is wrapped up with a conclusion.

BACKGROUND

Mohsin Hamid and The *Moth Smoke*

In the late twentieth century and early twenty-first century, literary works by South-Asian writers have begun to permeate the global market where such works have taken to representing South-Asian politics, communities, and cultures and traditions (Anuar & Asl, 2021; Anuar & Asl, 2022a; Anuar & Asl, 2022b). Mohsin Hamid is a prolific South-Asian writer—specifically a British Pakistani writer, of Punjabi and Kashmiri descent. He was born in 1971 in Lahore, Pakistan where he spent most of his childhood. When he was eighteen, he attended and received his higher education at Princeton University and Harvard Law School in the United States. For several years, Hamid worked in Management Consultancy in New York before he pursued a writing career as a freelance journalist in Lahore. He had acquired dual citizenship of the United Kingdom in 2006 and had lived and worked in London. Currently, Hamid lives in between Lahore, New York, and London following the birth of his daughter in 2009. He has written and published several notable works such as *Moth Smoke* (2000), *The Reluctant Fundamentalist* (2007), *How to Get Filthy Rich in Rising Asia* (2013) and *Exit West* (2017). The themes of his works are most commonly "globalization, economy, neoliberalism, politics, multiculturalism, [and] identity" (Madiou, 2021). Hamid's works have obtained local and international recognition—seen through his record of million-copy sales, multiple book awards, and licensed translation of his works to more than twenty different languages.

Hamid's debut novel, *Moth Smoke*, tells a story of falling from grace—about a banker in Lahore who loses his job, and following this, spirals downward by having an affair with his best friend's wife and descending into the world of drug and crime. It has become the winner of the Betty Trask Award, shortlisted for Hemingway Foundation/PEN Award, and selected as *The New York Times* Notable Book of the Year. As a debut novel, it has received attention and made a place for Hamid as a writer in the global market. Anita Desai, an illustrious Indian woman writer, comments in her review about the book in *The New York Review*:

One could not really continue to write, or read about, the slow seasonal changes, the rural backwaters, gossipy courtyards, and traditional families in a world taken over by gun-running, drug-trafficking, large-scale industrialism, commercial entrepreneurship, tourism, new money, nightclubs, boutiques... Where was the Huxley, the Orwell, the Scott Fitzgerald, or even the Tom Wolfe, Jay McInerney, or Brett Easton Ellis to record this new world? Mohsin Hamid's novel Moth Smoke, set in Lahore, is one of the first pictures we have of that world.

In this sense, Hamid has painted a vivid picture of Lahore as never before—of what the place offers—its backgrounds, its people, its traditions, and its culture. Desai highlights that *Moth Smoke* is the first that gives access to the reality and the distinctiveness of Lahore captured within the setting of the novel.

His second novel that was published seven years later, *The Reluctant Fundamentalist,* follows a similar and an even bigger success. It is arguably Hamid's best and most famous work to date. It has become the winner of several different book awards such as Ambassador Book Award of the English-Speaking Union, Anisfield-Wolf Book Award, Asian American Literary Award, and South Bank Show Annual Award for Literature. It has also been shortlisted for renowned book awards like Booker Prize and Commonwealth Writers Prize. In 2012, it is adapted for screening and premiered in Venice Film Festival. *The Reluctant Fundamentalist* has solidified and cemented Hamid's name and status as a writer of Pakistani Anglophone fiction. The novel uses frame story technique that tells a story within a story. It begins in Lahore, where a Pakistani man approaches and invites a stranger—who seems to be an American—for tea. In the span of the evening, the Pakistani man, Changez, unwinds a long story about his life to the stranger—about the declined of his respectable family, the education he receives from Princeton University that indoctrinates a pro-American mindset into him, the woman he falls in love with named Erica, and the increasing racism and discrimination he experiences in New York City following the 9/11 incident. Due to the subject matter in the novel, *The Reluctant Fundamentalist* has been dubbed a political novel. In addition to representation of real event and its aftermath, the frame narrative employed "works to create a textual uncertainty, even paranoia, that allegorically represents the global fear of terrorism in the post-9/11 era" (White, 2017). The novel becomes a million-copy international best-seller and has been assigned as a study material in universities such as Tulane University, Washington University in St. Louis, Drake University, Lehigh University, and Bucknell University.

Based on the first two published novels by Hamid, his interests lie in bringing to life the colors of Lahore, Pakistan—that of which becomes an important setting in both novels. When asked in an interview with Amina Yaqin in 2008 about the significant presence of Lahore in two of his earliest novels—*Moth Smoke* and *The Reluctant Fundamentalist*—Hamid states that he has "a very strange emotional attachment" to Lahore despite having lived more than half of his life abroad. This has become the reason he turns the narratives of his works to Lahore, Pakistan, where the accumulation of his childhood memories creates "a really strong sense of storytelling" (p. 44). Hamid also states that in *Moth Smoke*, he intends to encapsulate the kind of urban reality he experiences from an insider perspective, although he admits that it may have been rather exclusive to a small group of people in Lahore. In contrast, *The Reluctant*

Fundamentalist can be viewed as a reverse of *Moth Smoke*, through which Hamid attempts to divert his gaze to America but with "still stubbornly Pakistani eyes" (p. 45) that reflects the place he comes from. In Hamid's words, *The Reluctant Fundamentalist* is written by "looking at a culture that [he] has lived in with a perspective which is somewhat formed by that other culture" (p. 45). Nevertheless, although the two books are very different, they contain fundamentally essential components of Lahore that Hamid implements in his works.

How to Get Filthy Rich in Rising Asia, Hamid's third novel, takes a different approach to its voice and narrative than the previous two. It employs a second-person point of view, where the protagonist is not named but simply referred to as 'you'. The setting of the novel also takes place in an unnamed place resembling Pakistan, detailing the journey of the protagonist in his conquest for love and attaining wealth through business. *How to Get Filthy Rich in Rising Asia* is read like a meditation—as if someone is "reading out or talking to you, to the reader as all the names are erased. Place names, identity, and it's all created in the story, in the reader's mind" (Hamid & Veyret, 2022, p. 7). Hence, it is known as a self-reflection or self-help novel that uses personal voice to bring readers to contemplate about self-improvement, education, and class. According to Naydan (2016), the novel demonstrates the inescapable reality of "economic globalization's failures and in turn illustrates the violence that it produces", but also provides "opportunities for reading creatively [to] counter its detriments" (p. 1). In 2013, the same year of its publication, the novel becomes the winner of Tiziano Terzani International Literary Prize. It is also shortlisted for DSC Prize for South Asian Literature in 2013 and International Literature Award in 2014.

Hamid's latest published novel, *Exit West*, tells the story of Saeed and Nadia—two individuals who fall in love with each other before the breakout of a civil war. In their attempt to escape the situation, they discover the existence of magic doors that can lead them to other places. Saeed and Nadia decide to leave and travel through the doors, first transporting them to Mykonos, then to London and California. The story continues to unfold their journey of moving from one place to another, meeting other refugees, and the ups and downs of their relationship. The plot of the novel is a representation of contemporary mobilities, in which Hamid seeks to "humanise refugees" and illustrates "evocation of a world in which human beings – like capital, images, and (mis)information – have gained access to largely ungovernable networks of instantaneous travel across vast distances" (Perfect, 2019). In other words, the magical realism aspect of the novel is set up to reflect this sense of rapid modernization that allows traveling across long distance in a short time—through a mere action of opening a door. Like his other works, *Exit West* receives recognition and has won book awards such as *Los Angeles Times* Book Prize for Fiction in 2017 and Aspen Words Literary Prize in 2018. It has been selected under the categories of Booklist Editors' Choice: Adult Books and ALA Notable Books: Fiction and shortlisted for Booker Prize and International Dublin Literary Award.

Among the two latest novels, *Exit West* has gained fascination over its exploration of the issues of migration and being a migrant. In an interview with Saba Karim Khan in 2021 (Khan, 2021), Hamid emphasizes that through *Exit West*, he wants to capture this experience in what he terms as the "universality of migration". Hamid states the following:

I became interested in exploring the notion of the universality of migration [...] set up against an increasingly powerful dynamic of migrants being vilified, treated as the enemy, the 'other', something to be resisted. And so, the notion that there's a universal human experience of being a migrant, juxtaposed against a rapidly contagious anti-migrant discourse, was something I was keen to explore (p. 15).

His interest in bringing forward this notion allows him to slightly deviate from an entirely realistic approach to the plot element, namely with the existence of the magic doors in *Exit West*. According to Hamid, some form of 'unrealness' has always permeated his works. He has taken the liberty to slight bend what is called reality as "it is useful to slightly skew reality in order to approach more closely something that feels true" (p. 17).

In the same interview, Hamid is asked about the possibility of his works being adapted for screening. Hamid replies that *Exit West* has a project currently underway, where a few drafts of the screenplay and various conversations in terms of director and actors have been considered. As for *How to Get Filthy Rich in Rising Asia*, it is presently at the stage of adapting the novel into a screenplay by a Swedish director of partly Egyptian origin, Tarik Saleh. With *Moth Smoke*, Hamid states that there are always conversations, although it has been adapted into a Pakistani television series many years ago. All of Hamid's published novels—*Moth Smoke, The Reluctant Fundamentalist, How to Get Filthy Rich in Rising Asia*, and *Exit West*—are impactful and influential in their own ways. His works have given entry to the vivid and reclusive world of Pakistan, and along the way, paved a path for Pakistani Anglophone fiction to thrive on international scale.

Text Mining Techniques

Text extraction is also known as the extraction of keywords that is based on machine learning. Text mining is a process to discover useful information from a collection of unstructured text data. By using appropriate text mining techniques, quality information and knowledge can be obtained with less human effort for optimal decisions (Dang & Ahmad, 2014; Jafery et al., 2022; Keikhosrokiani & Asl, 2022; Ravichandran & Keikhosrokiani, 2022; Keikhosrokiani, 2022). It is an application that allows the system to automatically learn and improve its experience.

Sentiment Analysis

Sentiment analysis is a natural language processing technique to determine if the data obtained from those reviews is neutral, positive, or negative. It is often used in business to help have better understanding regarding the customer needs. It usually aims to detect emotions such as happiness, anger, satisfaction, sadness, and many others. Sentiment analysis can be categorized into two—machine learning and lexicon-based approach. Sentiment Classification is considered as a simple task as compared to text auto categorization (Al Mamun et al., 2022; Fasha et al., 2022).

The feature selection techniques treat documents as a bag of words, or as a string which retains the sequence of words in the document. There are a lot of reviews given on *Goodreads* that consist of various sentiments expressed by the readers to show how a particular book satisfies them or otherwise. It would take time for the author to go through the review section and read the reviews one by one to identify if his book benefits others or not (Sofian et al., 2022; Suhendra et al., 2022).

Thus, this study is conducted to perform sentiment analysis and detect the type of emotions expressed. Book reviews always come in different length of sentences which are hard to classify manually, and it requires a significant model to automate the review analysis and necessary classification using data science approach. According to new research, there are various methods that have been applied to detect correct emotion from the text (Sailunaz & Alhajj, 2019).

The main purpose of this study is to identify and classify the positive, negative, and neutral and be able to visualize the results by using a significant model. This study may provide advantages to authors as it reduces a lot of time to know what customers want and not about the book they write. In this study, it is important because it may help authors or publishers become aware of the overall opinions about books. In such cases, they can come up with better improvements to meet the customers' needs.

Topic Modelling

Topic modelling is a popular methodology used in text mining. It is an information technology approach that extracts "topical" information from a text document. It is a method for unsupervised classification of documents in which the concept is like clustering on numeric data. Based on the study that is conducted by Tang in 2019, it provides methods for automatically discovering the hidden themes in a large collection of documents. In short, topic modelling can handle text categorization, extraction of keywords, and search in similarities.

Choi and Joo (2020) conduct a study that presents the preliminary results on topic detection of online book reviews. Topic modelling using Latent Dirichlet Allocation (LDA) generates several topic terms from online reviews, and these researchers categorize those topic terms into eleven categories. Later, the sentiment analysis is applied to examine the emotional aspects of the reviews. They examine sentiment words which have a powerful effect on polarity values to determine whether those sentiment words appear as topic words extracted by the LDA topic modelling. Their study manages to have a significant implication in understanding user behavior for online book reviews.

Ostrowski (2015) conducts a study that uses Latent Dirichlet Allocation (LDA) for topic modelling in twitter. He explores topic modelling by considering LDA which is a generative probabilistic model for a collection of discrete data. He then evaluates the techniques to classify topics as it is applied to Twitter messages that have been filtered. Based on the results, he concludes that the method is quite effective for the identification of sub-topics. According to his study as well, it is important to have better understanding about the topics circulating through Social Networks as they give more advantages towards Customer Relationship Management.

South African government has declared COVID-19 a national disaster and implemented a nationwide lockdown with regulations. In a study conducted by Mutanga Murimo and Abayomi (2022), they aim to discover the main topic issues related to the pandemic. By using Twitter, they analyze the discussion topics related to COVID-19 using the data harvested based on that social media and opinion mining platform. Hence, the Latent Dirichlet Allocation (LDA) algorithm is applied for the extraction of noteworthy topics.

Many customers usually share their experience on social media about the products and services that they consume. Detecting issues reported by customers is significant for providing solutions to their existing problems. Topic modelling algorithms is a branch of machine learning that allows extraction of relevant insights from customer's posts by identifying hidden words and patterns (Rashmi & Batra, 2021). They conducted a comparative study between LDA against GSDMM topic.

In summary, these previous studies focus on using LDA as topic modelling (Asri et al., 2022; Choi & Joo, 2020; Mutanga Murimo & Abayomi, 2022; Ostrowski, 2015; Paremeswaran et al., 2022; John & Keikhosrokiani, 2022). LDA can be said to relay the most important and reliable topics relating to the sentiment of the customers and end users. In this study, the LDA approach is used as it can achieve a well-performed analysis of related works—particularly in opinion mining platform to extract latent topics related to customer or end users' reviews and their reactions towards it. Table 1 summarizes sentiment analysis and topic modelling approaches applied based on the related works.

Table 1. Comparison of Sentiment Analysis topic modelling techniques

Work	Dataset	Approach	Techniques
(Nahar et al., 2019)	Social Network Services	Machine learning approach and Lexicon-based approach	Support Vector Machines Classifiers (SVM), Natural language process (NLP)
(Shirbhate & Deshmukh, 2016)	Twitter	Machine Learning	Naïve Bayes
(Sailunaz & Alhajj, 2019)	Twitter	Machine Learning	(i) Including replies to tweets in the dataset and measurements, (ii) Introducing agreement score, sentiment score and emotion score of replies in influence score calculation, (iii) Generating general and personalized recommendation containing list of users who agreed on the same topic and expressed similar emotions and sentiments towards that particular topic.
(Choi & Joo, 2020)	Online Book Reviews	LDA	Examined that sentiment words which have a powerful effect on polarity values to determine whether those sentiment words appear as topic words extracted by the LDA topic modelling.
(Ostrowski, 2015)	Twitter	LDA	Classification as well as identification of noteworthy topics as it is applied to a filtered collection of Twitter messages.
(Mutanga Murimo & Abayomi, 2022)	Twitter	LDA	The pre-processed tweets were converted into a corpus of text, and a word cloud was used to verify that there were no unwanted data within the corpus. The word cloud also served as a way of verifying the output from the pre-processing stage. The bag of words feature representation technique was used to represent the corpus. Consequently, the Latent Dirichlet Allocation (LDA) topic modelling technique was implemented on the bag of words created from a text corpus.

Data Science and Analytic Techniques - Natural Language Processing

This section describes data science and analytics techniques that will be used in this study. Natural Language Processing (NLP) is complex research in the field of computer science especially in knowledge management, semantic mining, and empowering computers to derive meaning from the processing of human text-document. Text classification is a method of categorizing a text into text's context. It is often used in a variety of applications such as sentiment analysis, topic modelling and emotion analysis.

Sentiment Analysis

Sentiment analysis refers to the identification of the sentiment in each text—whether it is positive, negative, or neutral. There is a lot of research conducted regarding the sentiment analysis field. It can be divided into levels of words, phrases, sentences, documents and multi documents depending on the granularity of analysis (Al Mamun et al., 2022; Asri et al., 2022). According to research conducted by

Gupta and Yang (2018), CrystalFeel is used for English messages, and it is first presented at SemEval 2018 that uses a combination of lexicons, part of speech, N-grams, number of words and words embedded into SVM classifier. This method is with the intention to identify different emotions.

Sentiment analysis or so-called SA has also been used by political candidates and administrative to monitor the public opinions about policy changes and campaigns. This can fine-tune their approach towards the public and voters. This study focuses more on text, and not voice or speech.

Tokenization

Tokenization is a process of separating a text into trivial pieces. In other words, tokenization splits the text strings into a list of tokens. Later, the tokens assist in knowing the context or developing the model for the NLP. Tokenization can help in interpreting the meaning of the text by analyzing the sequence of the words. The function applied to carry out this process is called a tokenizer. There are two types of tokenizers: word tokenizer and sentence tokenizer. The word tokenizer tokenizes the sentence into words while the sentence tokenizer can tokenize the paragraph into sentences. Various tokenization techniques can be applied based on the language and the purpose of modelling (Keikhosrokiani & Asl, 2022).

Emotion Analytics

According to (Hakak et al., 2017), emotions form a very important and specific aspect in our lives. Emotional analysis is formed based on affective computing. "Affect" means emotion. The emotions can be expressed as sadness, love, hatred, joy, etc. Identifying and analyzing the complete range of human emotions, including mood, attitude, and emotional personality, is the focus of the emerging area known as "Emotions Analytics."

The improvement of emotion depiction in digital media is made possible by the development of sentiment analysis (Chung & Zeng, 2020). As a result of the crucial role that emotions play in human-machine interaction, approaches for identifying and categorizing emotions from text have become quite popular. Machines can produce more suitable replies or value-added services by recognizing and categorizing human emotions. Characterization is a popular method for modelling and analyzing emotions such as anger, contempt, fear, pleasure, sorrow, and surprise as the primary emotions.

RESEARCH METHODOLOGY

Text Analytical Framework

This study proposed a text analytical framework as shown in Figure 1. This framework consists of five main steps: (1) data collection, (2) data cleaning, (3) text exploration, (4) sentiment analysis, and (5) emotion classification.

In the first step, the *Goodreads* reviews for *Moth Smokes* (2000) are scrapped using Goodreads scrapper. The total number of reviews is more than 800 and the total ratings given by the readers is about 10,405. The overall community review for *Moth Smokes* (2000) is 3.85 stars. The data of readers' reviews obtained from the latest 10-pages of the online reviews are shown in Figure 2.

Figure 1. The proposed text analytical framework

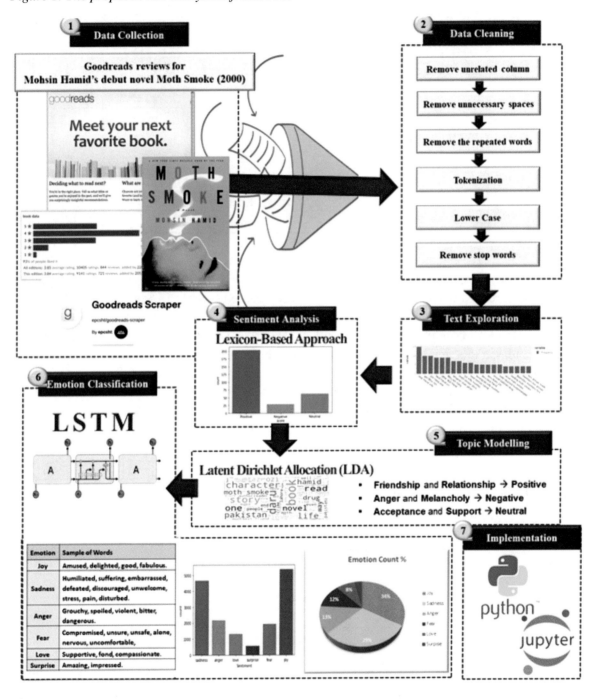

Once the raw data is collected, the next stage focuses on preparing and cleaning the data. This step includes selecting the right data, cleaning dataset, and dealing with missing values. It is one of the most time-consuming processes based on the total project duration time. Text pre-processing or cleaning is an important task in Natural Language Processing (NLP) to transform text data into a form that is ana-

Figure 2. Screenshot of raw data from Goodreads

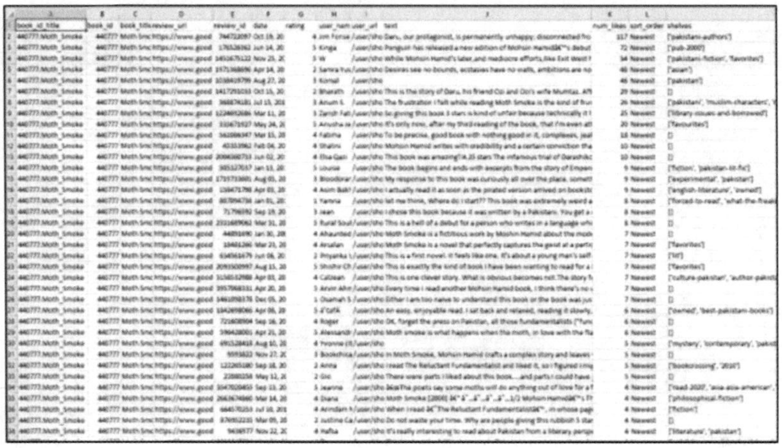

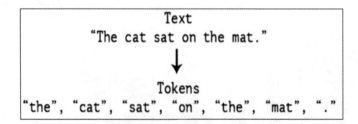

lyzable because raw text data usually contains a lot of noises. The steps of data cleaning are as follows: (1) Remove unrelated column: based on what we have learned from Data Science, it is necessary to remove column unrelated to our study during this stage. This is because we must prioritize the data that has potential to lead us to the results and solutions that are aimed for. (2) Remove unnecessary white spaces: the reason this step is performed is to remove the noise as this study is focusing on analyzing text, which is the reviews drop by the readers. White spaces are considered as noises in text analytics, and it is crucial to minimize noise. (3) Remove the repeated words: repeated words characters are unnecessary in the data which are removed in this step. (4) Tokenization Process: tokenization is a process of converting text into tokens before transforming them into vectors. In this study, we are focusing on tokenizing reviews into words as shown in Figure 3.

Figure 3. Example of tokenization process

Text

"The cat sat on the mat."

↓

Tokens

"the", "cat", "sat", "on", "the", "mat", "."

(5) Lower Case: one of the common text pre-processing techniques is lower casing which is meant to convert the input text into same casing format—so that "good", "Good", "gOoD" and "GOOD" are treated the same way in this data pre-processing stage. (6) Remove stop words: stop words are the English words that do not add much meaning to a sentence. They can be ignored without changing the actual meaning of the sentence. The most common stop words are "a", "an", "the", and others.

It is important to summarize the clean data to allow us to identify the data's structure, outliers, anomalies, and trends. Thus, in text exploration step, data exploration was done using unigram, bigram, and trigram frequency analysis as well as creating wordclouds. Data modelling is the process of analyzing data attributes and their relationship between those attributes. This step is also considered as conceptual design. The goal of the data modelling process is to obtain high-quality and high-accuracy data, not to mention to achieve consistent results. Therefore, sentiment analysis was done using a lexicon-based approach. The sentiments were classified based on three classes of positive, neutral, and negative.

After sentiment analysis, topic modelling was performed using Latent Dirichlet Allocation (LDA) to find the topics related to the positive, negative, and neutral sentiments. Wordclouds were generated to show the frequent words of each related topic.

In the next step, Long Short-Term Memory (LSTM) is used for emotion classification in this study. An artificial neural network called Long Short-Term Memory (LSTM) is used in deep learning and artificial intelligence. LSTM features feedback connections as opposed to typical feedforward neural networks. Such a recurrent neural network (RNN) may analyze whole data sequences in addition to single data points (such as photos) (such as speech or video) (Hochreiter & Schmidhuber, 1997; Schmidhuber, 2015). LSTM works when RNN output from previous step is fed as input in the current step. It can provide higher prediction accuracy based on recent information which is able to handle the problem of long-term dependencies on RNN.

The structure of LSTM has a chain structure which consists of 4 NN and cells that have different memory blocks. The information is retained by the cells meanwhile the memory manipulation is done by the gates. There are three gates as shown in Table 2: (1) forget, (2) input, and (3) output.

Table 2. LSTM Gates type

Forget Gate	Input Gate	Output Gate
✓ Removing the information that is no longer useful in cell. ✓ Binary output; 0 - Forgotten, 1- Future use	✓ The addition of useful information ✓ Output; -1 to 1	Extracting useful information from the current cell state; as output

LSTM is an improvement over RNN as RNN can only remember things for a short duration of time, but when a lot of words are fed, the information gets lost. LSTM works smartly so that it can selectively remember or forget the information. LSTM architecture is illustrated in Figure 4. LSTM has a structure that resembles a chain, but the repeating module is structured differently. There are four neural network layers instead of just one, and they interact in a unique way. The difference between the architectures of RNN and LSTM refers to the hidden layer of a gated unit or a gated cell. RNN only has a single neural layer, tanh. Meanwhile LSTM consists of three sigmoid gates and only 1 layer of tanh. Gates are applied to limit the information that is passing through the cell, which enables them to determine if the information is needed for the next cell or otherwise.

Table 3 shows the classes for emotion classification along with their sample keywords. Emotion classification in this study focuses on words such as joy, sadness, anger, fear, love, and surprise as different classes.

Finally, the proposed method is implemented using python as programming language and Jupyter Notebook as tool or platform for implementation.

Figure 4. LSTM Architecture (Olah, 2015; Hochreiter & Schmidhuber, 1997)

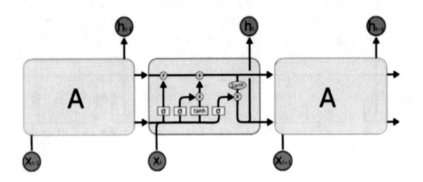

RESULTS AND DISCUSSION

This section discusses the results according to the objectives of the study. The present section includes the results of four main text analytics done by this study: (1) text exploration, (2) sentiment analysis, (3) topic modelling, and (4) emotion analysis.

Word Frequency Analysis (Unigram, Bigram, & Trigram)

Figure 5 shows the top 20 one-word frequencies that are often used in *Moth Smokes* (2000). The most common words used in the reviews are the words 'book', 'daru', 'story' and 'Hamid', by which each word records above 200 times frequency value. It proves that people are referring to the book while writing what they think of the book.

Meanwhile Figure 6 shows the top 20 two-word frequencies being used in the reviews by the book's readers. The top two listed in the two-word frequency value are "Moth Smoke" and "Mohsin Hamid". As shown in the bi-gram, the other two words that are mostly picked by the reviewers are referring to the different parts of the book content that they are interested in to give their point of views. Some of these two-words which occur less than 30 to 40 times are "loses job", "filthy rich", "shah Jahan", "middle class" and so on.

Table 3. Emotion-word classes

Emotion	Sample of Keywords
Joy	Amused, delighted, good, fabulous.
Sadness	Humiliated, suffering, embarrassed, defeated, discouraged, unwelcome, stress, pain, disturbed.
Anger	Grouchy, spoiled, violent, bitter, dangerous.
Fear	Compromised, unsure, unsafe, alone, nervous, uncomfortable,
Love	Supportive, fond, compassionate.
Surprise	Amazing, impressed.

Figure 5. The Results of Word Frequency Analysis (Unigram)

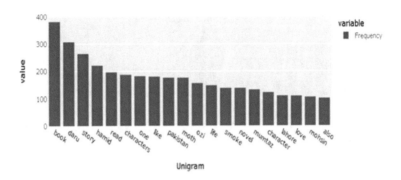

This variation in the result may have been because the readers are focusing on the different characters' issues which include losing job and the struggles of belonging in the middle class. The characters in the book manage to catch the readers' attention for them to comment and review about the characters' lifestyle. Characters play a huge part in connecting to readers, and they can be the reasons for readers to have taken a liking to a particular book and otherwise.

Figure 6. The Results of Word Frequency Analysis (Bigram)

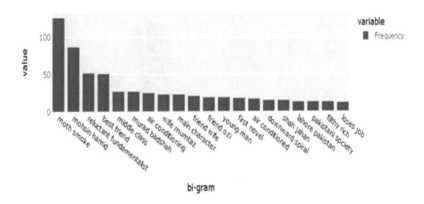

Figure 7 shows a trigram of the top 20 three-word frequency. The most frequently occurring three-word is "best friend wife" followed by "get filthy rich", and others. With this, it shows that the readers have their own interests, their own reasons, and their own perspectives about *Moth Smoke* (2000). The frequency obtained from this N-Gram also defines that readers are in sync at some point and are sharing the same thoughts about the book—leading to repetitive selection of words.

Figure 7. The Results of Word Frequency Analysis (Trigram)

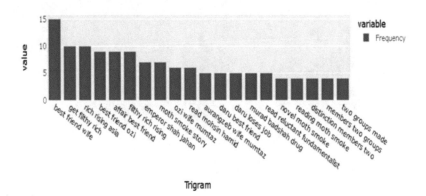

Sentiment Analysis

Figure 8 shows the number of ratings by the readers of the novel. Based on the chart above, the majority of the rating is 4.0 followed by 5.0 in the second place. This shows that the readers love the book they read. Rating 4.0 and 5.0 are higher in comparison to 3 and below ratings.

Figure 8. Number of Ratings

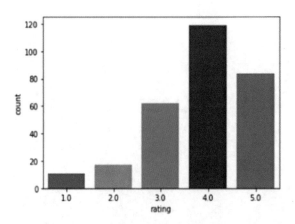

Figure 9 shows the sentiment classification based on the readers' responses to the book. Based on the chart above, positive sentiment is higher compared to negative and neutral. Hence, readers generally feel positive reading it although a few readers feel negative or neutral reading it.

Topic Modelling (Wordcloud)

As shown in Figure 10, some of the most used positive words in the reviews are about the book; "read", "life", "real", "love", and "best friend". Despite the book being about a man losing his job, taking a

Figure 9. The Sentiment Classification

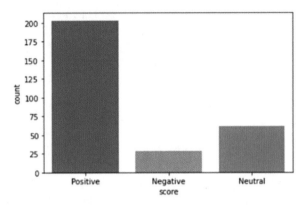

wrong path and other bad decisions, readers are showing optimism towards what they feel about the book. It may be due to readers having not finished the whole story yet, that the matters of friendship and relationship introduced are assumed by the readers to be long lasting.

Figure 10. Wordcloud related to the Topic - Friendship and Relationship for Positive Themes

Figure 11 shows some of the most used negative words expressed in the reviews about the book: "enough", "bad", "end", and "protagonist". Because the main character of the book chooses to cheat with his best friend's wife over their friendship, readers are sharing and writing their reviews relating to this topic. They probably feel sad and angry with the way the whole story turns out, regardless of it having a bad or a good ending. Readers may have felt like that because they think the story could have turned out better by considering other story options. They are also possibly expecting the character to be a wise man who chooses the right path in his life.

Figure 12 depicts some of the most used neutral words in the reviews about the book; 'life', 'society', 'feel', 'even', 'good', 'better', 'well', 'work', 'rather', and 'give'. The review topics are neutral which indicate that readers do not display a particularly strong positive or negative reactions. The readers discuss the topics of acceptance and support without having any objection or unsatisfaction regarding the parts within the book.

Figure 11. Wordcloud related to the Topic - Anger and Melancholy for Negative Themes

Figure 12. Wordcloud related to the Topic - Acceptance and Support for Neutral Themes

Emotion Analysis

The sample of the *train.txt* text use for the emotion classification in this study is shown in Table 5.

Table 6 listed emotion descriptions for each emotion class (sadness, joy, fear, anger, surprise, and love) used in this study.

Based on *train.txt* and *test.txt* computation, analysis manage to obtain the data as shown in Figure 13. There are different types of emotion such as sadness, anger, love, surprise, fear, and joy. The emotion of surprise is the least portrayed by the readers. Despite the bad things that happen within the story, readers

Table 5.Train.txt sample for emotion classification

Sample Text	Emotion
I can go from feeling so hopeless to so damned hopeful just from being around someone who cares and is awake.	Sadness
I feel very happy and excited since I learned so many things.	Joy
I will be able to lay on my bed in the dark and not feel terrified at least for a while.	Fear
I could claim to redeem the genre, but it didn't t leave me feeling as entirely frustrated to the point of beating my head against a wall either.	Anger
I was feeling an act of God at work in my life and it was an amazing feeling.	Surprise

Table 6. Emotion Descriptions

Type of Emotion	Descriptions
Sadness	The condition or quality of being sad.
Joy	The emotion of great delight and happiness.
Fear	A distressing emotion aroused by danger, evil and etc.
Anger	A strong displeasure feeling that is aroused.
Surprise	A sudden feeling of wonder or astonishment.
Love	Passionate affection towards another person or situation.

still feel enjoyment after reading the book. Referring to the number of ratings given by the readers, it can be observed that the ratings 4.0 and 5.0 are higher in comparison to ratings 1.0, 2.0, and 3.0. Logically, ratings 1.0 and 2.0 are low or bad, meanwhile rating 3.0 is medium or average. Normally, people will rate 4.0 for "good" and 5.0 for "excellent".

Figure 13. Emotion Data Obtained

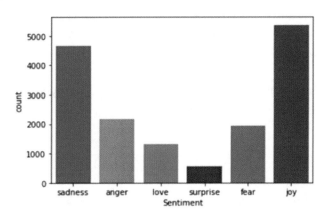

As shown in Figure 14, which is the pie chart of percentage of emotion analysis breakdown, the book has a high percentage of the emotion "joy" compared to the other emotions; "love", "surprise", "sadness", "anger", and "fear". However, there is only a slight, 5% difference between "sadness" and "joy". From here it can be concluded that a lot of readers either experience joy or sadness when reading this book. Meanwhile between fear and anger, there is just a slight 1% difference.

Some reviews are selected as an example to show the results of this study. For example, the following is a selected review written by Arvin Ahmadi:

"Every time I read another Mohsin Hamid book, I think there's no way he can one-up the last one. Absolutely no way. And then I'm wrong. I LOVED Reluctant Fundamentalist, Exit West, and How to Get Filthy Rich in Rising Asia (oh what a title) ... but Moth Smoke might just be my favorite."

Figure 14. Percentage of Emotion Analysis Breakdown

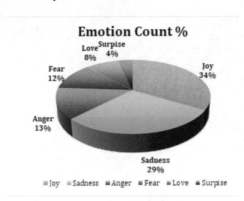

In this example, "favorite" is a positive emotion, which belongs to the amusement category as one of the sub-categories of "joy". Another example is the selected review written by Robert Hyman:

"I had never heard of Mohsin Hamid, until one day I heard an interview with him on NPR. I was intrigued enough to get hold of three of his books. If the others are as good as Moth Smoke I have a treat in store for me. He is funny; informative about life in Pakistan, and critical of both Pakistani society and those who criticise Pakistani society. His technique of telling the story through multiple points of view adds spice. Very highly recommended!".

In this example, "recommend" is a positive emotion and it will happen when the reader enjoy reading the book. Therefore, this review is also categorized under "joy" class.

CONCLUSION

The primary objective of the study has been to analyze literary readers' sentiment to classify book reviews into sentiment classes which includes the sentiments of emotions portrayed through the reviews presented in online platforms. This project is meant to ease the process of selecting the right book for readers to read based on sentiment analysis and topic determination. The sentiment analysis of a selected novel, Hamid's *Moth Smoke* (2000), revealed that readers are generally satisfied with the story. It is recommended to readers who do not feel the necessity for a book to limit its potential by needing to have a morally good story and characters, or a happy ending. Readers can also learn more deeply about Pakistan cultures by reading the book. In short, it is a book that is worth reading and buying. Based on the work completed in this project, there are many improvements that can be made in the future. The first improvement that can be considered is using multiple books from the same author or using another online book website such as Amazon. Besides, the usage of Vader approach or any other updated deep learning methods may also be considered since modernization does not have limitations and continues to evolve each day especially in technology adaptation and application. In the future, a tool or website engine can be developed that is able to do sentiment and emotion analysis after adding the book title.

REFERENCES

Al Mamun, M. H., Keikhosrokiani, P., Asl, M. P., Anuar, N. A. N., Hadi, N. H. A., & Humida, T. (2022). Sentiment Analysis of the Harry Potter Series Using a Lexicon-Based Approach. In P. Keikhosrokiani & M. Pourya Asl (Eds.), *Handbook of Research on Opinion Mining and Text Analytics on Literary Works and Social Media* (pp. 263–291). IGI Global. doi:10.4018/978-1-7998-9594-7.ch011

Anuar, N. A. N. B., & Asl, M. P. (2022a). Rewriting of gender and sexuality in Tanwi Nandini Islam's *Bright Lines*: A Cixousian approach. In M. P. Asl (Ed.), *Gender, place, and identity of South Asian women* (pp. 131–151). IGI Global. doi:10.4018/978-1-6684-3626-4.ch007

Anuar, N. A. N. B. A., & Asl, M. P. (2021). Gender and sexual identity in Arundhati Roy's *The Ministry of Utmost Happiness*: A Cixousian analysis of Hijra's resistance and remaking of the self. *Pertanika Journal of Social Science & Humanities*, 29(4), 2335–2352. doi:10.47836/pjssh.29.4.13

Anuar, N. A. N. B. A., & Asl, M. P. (2022b). Gender, Resistance, and Identity: Women's Rewriting of the Self in Chitra Banerjee Divakaruni's *Before We Visit the Goddess*. *Pertanika Journal of Social Science & Humanities*, 30(3), 1201–1221. doi:10.47836/pjssh.30.3.15

Asl, M. P. (Ed.). (2022). *Gender, place, and identity of South Asian women*. IGI Global. doi:10.4018/978-1-6684-3626-4

Asri, M. A. Z. B. M., Keikhosrokiani, P., & Asl, M. P. (2022). Opinion Mining Using Topic Modeling: A Case Study of Firoozeh Dumas's Funny in Farsi in Goodreads. Advances on Intelligent Informatics and Computing. doi:10.1007/978-3-030-98741-1_19

Choi, Y., & Joo, S. (2020). Identifying facets of reader-generated online reviews of children's books based on a textual analysis approach. *The Library Quarterly*, 90(3), 349–363. doi:10.1086/708962

Chung, W., & Zeng, D. (2020). Dissecting emotion and user influence in social media communities: An interaction modeling approach. *Information & Management*, 57(1), 103108. doi:10.1016/j.im.2018.09.008

Dagamsheh, A. M., & Downing, D. (2016). *Neoliberal Economy: Violence of Economic Deregulation in Mohsin Hamid's* Moth Smoke. Retrieved 9 20, 2022, from https://journals.ju.edu.jo/dirasathum/article/view/14174

Dang, S., & Ahmad, P. H. (2014). Text mining: Techniques and its application. *International Journal of Engineering & Technology Innovations*, 1(4), 22–25.

Fasha, E. F. B. K., Keikhosrokiani, P., & Asl, M. P. (2022). Opinion Mining Using Sentiment Analysis: A Case Study of Readers' Response on Long Litt Woon's The Way Through the Woods in Goodreads. Advances on Intelligent Informatics and Computing. doi:10.1007/978-3-030-98741-1_20

Gupta, R. K., & Yang, Y. (2018). Crystalfeel at semeval-2018 task 1: Understanding and detecting emotion intensity using affective lexicons. *Proceedings of the 12th International Workshop on Semantic Evaluation*.

Hakak, N. M., Mohd, M., Kirmani, M., & Mohd, M. (2017). Emotion analysis: A survey. *2017 International Conference on Computer, Communications and Electronics (Comptelix)*.

Hamid, M., & Veyret, P. (2022). "The glint of catastrophe": An Interview with Mohsin Hamid. *Angles. New Perspectives on the Anglophone World*, (14). doi:10.4000/angles.5349

Hochreiter, S., & Schmidhuber, J. (1997). Long Short-Term Memory. *Neural Computation*, *9*(8), 1735–1780. doi:10.1162/neco.1997.9.8.1735 PMID:9377276

Jafery, N. N., Keikhosrokiani, P., & Asl, M. P. (2022). Text analytics model to identify the connection between theme and sentiment in literary works: A case study of Iraqi life writings. In P. Keikhosrokiani & M. Pourya Asl (Eds.), *Handbook of Research on Opinion Mining and Text Analytics on Literary Works and Social Media* (pp. 173–190). IGI Global. doi:10.4018/978-1-7998-9594-7.ch008

John, S. A., & Keikhosrokiani, P. (2022). COVID-19 fake news analytics from social media using topic modeling and clustering. In P. Keikhosrokiani (Ed.), *Big Data Analytics for Healthcare* (pp. 221–232). Academic Press. doi:10.1016/B978-0-323-91907-4.00003-0

Keikhosrokiani, P. (Ed.). (2022). *Handbook of Research on Consumer Behavior Change and Data Analytics in the Socio-Digital Era*. IGI Global. doi:10.4018/978-1-6684-4168-8

Keikhosrokiani, P., & Asl, M. P. (Eds.). (2022). *Handbook of research on opinion mining and text analytics on literary works and social media*. IGI Global. doi:10.4018/978-1-7998-9594-7

Khan, S. K. (2021). 'Anxious Citizens of the Attention Economy': In Conversation with Mohsin Hamid. *Wasafiri*, *36*(1), 14–19. doi:10.1080/02690055.2021.1838796

Kherwa, P., & Bansal, P. (2020). Topic modeling: a comprehensive review. *EAI Endorsed Transactions on Scalable Information Systems, 7*(24).

Madiou, M. S.-E. (2021). The Truth Will Out: Mohsin Hamid Speaks His Name in The Reluctant Fundamentalist. *Arab Studies Quarterly*, *43*(4), 304–319. doi:10.13169/arabstudquar.43.4.0304

Mutanga Murimo, B., & Abayomi, A. (2022). Tweeting on COVID-19 pandemic in South Africa: LDA-based topic modelling approach. *African Journal of Science, Technology, Innovation and Development*, *14*(1), 163–172. doi:10.1080/20421338.2020.1817262

Nahar, L., Sultana, Z., Iqbal, N., & Chowdhury, A. (2019). Sentiment Analysis and Emotion Extraction: A Review of Research Paradigm. *2019 1st International Conference on Advances in Science, Engineering and Robotics Technology (ICASERT)*.

Naydan, L. M. (2016). Beyond economic globalization in Mohsin Hamid's How to Get Filthy Rich in Rising Asia: The false promise of self-help and possibilities through reading with a creative mind. *Journal of Commonwealth Literature*, *53*(1), 92–108. doi:10.1177/0021989416632565

Olah, C. (2015). Understanding LSTM Networks. *Colah's blog*. http://colah.github.io/posts/2015-08-Understanding-LSTMs/

Ostrowski, D. A. (2015). Using latent Dirichlet allocation for topic modelling in twitter. *Proceedings of the 2015 IEEE 9th International Conference on Semantic Computing (IEEE ICSC 2015)*.

Paremeswaran, P. p., Keikhosrokiani, P., & Asl, M. P. (2022). Opinion Mining of Readers' Responses to Literary Prize Nominees on Twitter: A Case Study of Public Reaction to the Booker Prize (2018–2020). *Advances on Intelligent Informatics and Computing*. doi:10.1007/978-3-030-98741-1_21

Perfect, M. (2019). 'Black holes in the fabric of the nation': Refugees in Mohsin Hamid's Exit West. *Journal for Cultural Research*, *23*(2), 187–201. doi:10.1080/14797585.2019.1665896

Perner, C. (2010). Tracing the Fundamentalist in Mohsin Hamid's Moth Smoke and The Reluctant Fundamentalist. *Ariel-a Review of International English Literature, 41*(3), 23-31. Retrieved 9 20, 2022, from https://questia.com/library/journal/1g1-266467176/tracing-the-fundamentalist-in-mohsin-hamid-s-moth

Ravichandran, B. D., & Keikhosrokiani, P. (2022). Classification of Covid-19 misinformation on social media based on neuro-fuzzy and neural network: A systematic review. *Neural Computing & Applications*. Advance online publication. doi:10.100700521-022-07797-y PMID:36159189

Sailunaz, K., & Alhajj, R. (2019). Emotion and sentiment analysis from Twitter text. *Journal of Computational Science*, *36*, 101003. doi:10.1016/j.jocs.2019.05.009

Schmidhuber, J. (2015). Deep learning in neural networks: An overview. *Neural Networks*, *61*, 85–117. doi:10.1016/j.neunet.2014.09.003 PMID:25462637

Shirbhate, A. G., & Deshmukh, S. N. (2016). *Feature Extraction for Sentiment Classification on Twitter Data*. Academic Press.

Sofian, N. B., Keikhosrokiani, P., & Asl, M. P. (2022). Opinion mining and text analytics of reader reviews of Yoko Ogawa's The Housekeeper and the Professor in Goodreads. In P. Keikhosrokiani & M. Pourya Asl (Eds.), *Handbook of Research on Opinion Mining and Text Analytics on Literary Works and Social Media* (pp. 240–262). IGI Global. doi:10.4018/978-1-7998-9594-7.ch010

Suhendra, N. H. B., Keikhosrokiani, P., Asl, M. P., & Zhao, X. (2022). Opinion mining and text analytics of literary reader responses: A case study of reader responses to KL Noir volumes in Goodreads using sentiment analysis and topic. In P. Keikhosrokiani & M. Pourya Asl (Eds.), *Handbook of Research on Opinion Mining and Text Analytics on Literary Works and Social Media* (pp. 191–239). IGI Global. doi:10.4018/978-1-7998-9594-7.ch009

White, M. (2017). Framing travel and terrorism: Allegory in The Reluctant Fundamentalist. *Journal of Commonwealth Literature*, *54*(3), 444–459. doi:10.1177/0021989417738125

Chapter 6
Artificial Intelligence and Human Rights Activism:
A Case Study of Boochani's *No Friend But the Mountains* and His Tweets on Justice and Equality

Chun Keat Kng
School of Computer Sciences, Universiti Sains Malaysia, Malaysia

Pantea Keikhosrokiani
iD https://orcid.org/0000-0003-4705-2732
School of Computer Sciences, Universiti Sains Malaysia, Malaysia

Moussa Pourya Asl
iD https://orcid.org/0000-0002-8426-426X
School of Humanities, Universiti Sains Malaysia, Malaysia

ABSTRACT

Behrouz Boochani, the Kurdish-Iranian author of No Friends But the Mountains, has been using social media platforms such as Twitter to speak up against social injustice and human rights abuse against immigrants across the globe. This study proposes an artificial intelligence lifecycle for opinion mining of the dominant sentiments, topics, and emotions in Boochani's social media activism. Sentiment analysis (Vader and Textblob), topic modelling (LDA and NMF), and emotion detection are performed to extract hidden sentiments, topics, and emotions from the data that is collected from his tweets from 2017-2021. The results show Vader performs better than Textblob. LDA is considered the best algorithm. It extracted seven main topics as suicide, translator of book, publication of book, human rights, political, immigration, and detention. Finally, the main emotion detected from the tweets is sadness.

DOI: 10.4018/978-1-6684-6242-3.ch006

INTRODUCTION

Over the past two decades, social media has played a key role in progressive social, political, and cultural changes in the world. As a platform that allows the creation and exchange of User Generated Content, social media is now widely used by human rights activists to report on discriminations and coordinate individual and collective campaigns and actions. One prime example is the literary writer, journalist, and human rights defender, Behrouz Boochani. Aa an asylum-seeker from the Middle East, who was detained by Australia in Manus Island for six years from 2013 until its closure in 2017, Boochani used smartphone and WhatsApp text-messaging application to document and share his experience as a refugee in what became an award-winning book, *No Friend But the Mountains* (2018). Since fleeing Australia's detention island, Boochani has actively used social media platforms such as Twitter to distribute information on a vast number of topics related to human rights and social justice. His tweets have been followed closely by those monitoring developments in matters related to refugees and life in the Middle East. In this study, we argue that Boochani's activism in Twitter is a perfect example of how social media has expanded access to evidence of human rights abuses beyond that which is presented by the mainstream media and non-government organizations (NGOs). In this regard, a content analysis of his tweets would be helpful in shedding light on matters that are often overlooked or shrouded by mainstream media.

This study aims to use Opinion Mining techniques to identify the dominant topics in Boochani's social media activism. The data for this study is collected from his tweets from the beginning of 2017 to the end of 2021. To achieve the main objective of the study, sentiment analysis techniques of TextBlob and VADER rule-based approach are used to study the underlying sentiments. Moreover, Topic Modelling is performed to extract hidden topics by using Latent Dirichlet Allocation (LDA) and Non-negative Matrix Factorization (NMF). The inputs are then processed based on grammatical rules, linguistic habits, and standard algorithms to produce computer-based natural language. Natural language processing (NLP) uses machine learning (ML) systems to ingest and learn words and syntax (Al Mamun et al., 2022; Asri et al., 2022; Fasha et al., 2022; Keikhosrokiani & Asl, 2022; Malik et al., 2021; Paremeswaran et al., 2022; Sofian et al., 2022). Lastly, the dominant emotion is detected from such tweets using LSTM which helps to detect the user's emotion.

This chapter is organized as follows: It begins with an introduction and a statement of the overall aim of the study. Next is Literature Review that explores sentiment analysis, topic modelling, Latent Semantic Analysis (LSA) and Latent Dirichlet Allocation (LDA), and Non-Negative Matrix Factorization (NMF), Probabilistic Latent Semantic Analysis (PLSA), deep learning and emotion detection including Recurrent neural network (RNN), Long Short-Term Memory Units (LSTM), and Recurrent Neural Network- Long Short Term Memory network (RNN-LSTM) Model. After literature review, materials and methodology are presented. Next, results and findings are discussed, and finally, the study is ended with a conclusion that includes recommendations for future studies.

BACKGROUND

Sentiment Analysis

The emergence of big data has changed how artificial intelligence is used to data analysis (Binti Rosli & Keikhosrokiani, 2022; Keikhosrokiani, 2022a; Keikhosrokiani & Kamaruddin, 2022). To manage, organize, and extract useful information from large data, big data analytical approaches like data mining, machine learning, deep learning, and NLP, among others, are needed (Keikhosrokiani, 2022b; Keikhosrokiani & Pourya Asl, 2022; Teoh Yi Zhe & Keikhosrokiani, 2021). Sentiment Analysis (SA) is a field that examines people's opinions, appraisal, attitudes, sentiments, and emotions towards entities such as organizations, products, services, issues, topics, events or individuals and their attributes expressed in written text. A methodology provided by sentiment analysis is to computationally process unstructured data (Fasha et al., 2022; Keikhosrokiani & Asl, 2022). Unstructured data in refers to unstructured text not limited to an entire document but also part of sentence, with or without embedded metadata. Sentiment analysis normally involves texts that are pre-processed through tokenization, stemming, lemmatization, part of speech tagging, entity extraction and relation extraction and polarity detection, which usually categorizes sentiment-based scale of rating (Al Mamun et al., 2022; Chu et al., 2022; Fasha et al., 2022; Jacobs, 2019; Sofian et al., 2022; Suhendra et al., 2022). There are two approaches that perform sentiment analysis, lexicon-based approaches, and machine learning approaches. The word lexicon renders insight about a picture as it requires a priori construction of a suitable lexicon to classify text into positive phrases or negative phrases. First, sentiment lexicon will be created by researchers through compiling sentiment word list to determine the degree of subjectivity of a text unit based on positive or negative indicators identified by the lexicon (Pang & Lee, 2004). There is no limited domain restriction on using lexicon-approaches to perform sentiment analysis as it is domain independence and it is prone to be improved and extended when error occurs, one can correct some existing rules or add new rule to system's rule base. Unfortunately, text is often considered as a collection of words without considering and relations between individual words as limited to identify semantic or comparative sentiment. Nevertheless, much time and efforts will be consumed to build the initial knowledge based of lexicon, pattern and rules (Liu, 2012). Machine learning approaches automatically perform classification. However, they need training data sets. Algorithms are constructed, and model is built by selecting features and by learning from labelled training datasets (Pang et al., 2002). Through optimization, learning algorithm can automatically adapt and learn from all kinds of features for classification (Liu, 2012). Machine learning can be categorized as supervised machine-learning and unsupervised machine-learning. The ways on how both machine-learning approaches used to learn about data will make significant differences. Prior information about real value of outputs needed for supervised machine-learning before algorithm was used to approximate the mapping function from the input to the output. Once the algorithm learned about the dataset on what input or output is, and new input is inserted, the model can make prediction on what the output will be. Well-known methods include the support vector machine (SVM), Naïve Bayes, and the N-grams model which are used for sentiment classification (Ye et al., 2009). Unsupervised machine-learning requires no prior information as it uses clustering concept to cluster sentiment based on the hidden structure from the given input. Most researchers adopt supervised machine-learning as compared to unsupervised machine-learning. However, supervised machine-learning technique requires manual annotation of sufficient and representative training data, which is often very costly and time consuming. Moreover, as it relies on training data, a sentiment classifier trained from the labelled data in one domain often does not work in another domain (Liu, 2012). Regardless of machine learning approaches or lexicon-based approaches, sentiment analysis can be conducted at three levels of document level, sentence level and aspect level.

Document-level

Document-level sentiment analysis is applied on document level to determine overall positive or negative sentiments of a text. Normally, it is used in forum discussions, question-answering systems, online reviews, or blogs to identify and classify sentiment orientations or polarities within a whole opinion document (Pang & Lee, 2004).

Aspect-level

Aspect-level sentiment analysis is used in the case of availability of attributes inside post, entity, or input text. Instead of relying on language constructs such as paragraphs, sentences, documents, aspect level analysis directly concentrate at opinion that aims to identify sentiment targets and assign sentiments to the targets (Hu & Liu, 2004). For example, a review on a tablet has the attribute of battery life, screen light, camera, and other attributes where each attribute has a different sentiment. The review is: "My tablet is really nice with high camera pixel and vivid screen but non lasting battery". The aspect in this example is the tablet while the attributes are battery, camera where sentiment detection lead following results (screen, positive), (battery, negative) and (camera, positive).

Sentence-level

Only sentences are analyzed to determine sentiment polarities. Subjective classification is the main focus of sentence-level analysis which distinguishes sentences (i.e., objective sentences) that express factual information from sentences that express subjective views and opinions (i.e., subjective sentences) (Liu, 2012). Unlike document-level analysis that often neglects the neutral sentiment, the neutral sentiment cannot be ignored in sentence-level classification because a document may contain many sentences that express neither positive nor negative sentiments.

Topic Modelling

One of the powerful techniques in text mining for latent data discovery and finding relationship between data and text document is Topic Modelling which helps in discovering hidden semantic structures in a body of text. In simple words, given that a document is about a particular topic, it would be expected that certain topics would appear in the document more or less frequently. Topics identified by this technique are clusters of similar words that reveal, discover, and annotate thematic structure in a collection of documents (Jafery et al., 2022; John & Keikhosrokiani, 2022; Kherwa & Bansal, 2020; Suhendra et al., 2022).

A term in a document is assigned a weight, depending on the number of appearances of the term in a document. It is a bit special as those frequently occurring will be given less weight as compared to those unexpected ones. The most famous way to formalize the idea for term document matrices is (term frequency * inverse document frequency) [TF*IDF] (Keikhosrokiani & Asl, 2022; Mutanga & Abayomi, 2022). This involves a mathematical framework by examining a set of documents, based on the statistics of the words used in each document, and concluding what topics might be and what each document's balance of topics is. The most frequently used and most famous topic modelling methods are Latent Semantic Analysis (LSA), Latent Dirichlet Allocation (LDA), Non-Negative Matrix Factorization (NNMF) and Probabilistic Latent Semantic Analysis (PLSA). LSA is an algebraic method based on Single Value Decomposition (SVD) and presenting the semantic space of documents in which more semantic relationship, contextual usage come closer. For example, a collection of 'm' text documents with a total of 'n' unique words for each document. The TF-IDF for matrix m*n contains the TF-IDF score for each word in the document. Matrix will be reduced to 'k' dimensions as 'k' is defined as desired number of topics through using SVD.

Latent Semantic Analysis (LSA) and Latent Dirichlet Allocation (LDA)

SVD matrix can be used to find similar topics and documents using the cosine similarity method. LSA always finds low dimension representation of documents and words by applying SVD, so it works well in the task of dimensionality reduction. Those terms with similar meaning will occur very closer in their contextual usage as this is distributional hypotheses for LSA. LSA uses vector representation of text to compute how likely it is to discover similar words in a text as all the semantic relations between texts are inferred directly from given corpus text. LSA addresses the issues of meaning and usage of words as words may have multiple senses and multiple usage in different contexts which are defined as polysemy. Different words which may have a similar meaning in certain contexts denote the same concept defined as synonyms by mapping high-dimensional count vectors to a lower dimensional representation in a so-called latent semantic space that provides information well beyond the lexical level and revels semantical relations between the entities of interest. The fundamental idea of LDA is that documents are represented as random mixtures over latent topics, where a topic is characterized by a distribution over words. LDA is a form of dimension reduction that uses a probabilistic model to find the co-occurrence patterns of terms that correspond to semantics topics in a collection of documents (Abadah et al., 2023; Asri et al., 2022; Chu et al., 2022; Jafery et al., 2022; Keikhosrokiani & Asl, 2022; Kherwa & Bansal, 2020). Based on De Finetti's theorem, capturing significant inter and intra document statistical structure via mixing distributional assumes that document arise from multiple topics, and a topic is defined as distribution over a vocabulary. Corpus is associated with predefined number of topics k, and each document in corpus contains these topics with different proportions. Topic modelling aims to learn these topics from data or corpus.

Non-Negative Matrix Factorization (NNMF) and Probabilistic Latent Semantic Analysis (PLSA)

NNMF is also a statistical method to reduce the dimension of input corpora, by providing much less weightage to the words with less coherence through factor analysis. For example, a dataset consisting of reviews of superhero movies, using document term matrix (input matrix), the rows of matrix represented by documents and the column of matrix represented by word. In case, the reviews consist of texts like Tony Stark, Ironman, Mark 48. It would probably be grouped under the topic Ironman. Each word will be assigned weightage based on the semantic relationship between words and the highest weight is considered topic for a set of words. The main point of NNMF is that it can address the issues of negative number present in dataset by placing non-negativity constraint on the data model. PLSA was released as substitute of LSA to fix limitations discovered in LSA. PLSA not only can improve LSA but also it can automate document indexing which is based on a statistical latent class model for factor analysis of count data. One of the characteristics of PLSA is to distinguish and identify different contexts of word usage without recourse to a dictionary or thesaurus. It permits to disambiguate polysemy (words with multiple meanings) and discloses typical similarities by organizing words that share a common context (Hofmann, 2001). It is accepted that "PLSA is based on a statistical model that is referred to as an aspect model. An aspect model is a latent variable model for co-occurrence data, which associates unobserved class variables with each observation" (Tuomo et al., 2008).

Deep Learning and Emotion Detection

RNN-Model

RNN is a type of Neural Network where the output from the previous step is fed as the input of the current step. It is a generalization of feed forward neural network which has an internal memory. This model is designed to identify the sequential characteristics of the data and use patterns to predict the next scenario. It is assumed that inputs and outputs are independent from each other in a neural network. On the other hand, RNN model is not suitable for many cases like predicting the next word in the text. In the model, it will be better to know which word came before it. RNN is making use of sequential information. This information is called recurrent because they perform the same process for every element of a sequence. Output depends on the previous computations, and they have a memory that captures information about what has been calculated. RNN uses its internal memory to process sequence of inputs.

RNN is one of the model deep learning models that is used for emotion detection (Sapiński et al., 2019; Savva et al., 2012). Some study experiment was based on temporal characteristics including body segment rotation, angular velocity, angular frequency, orientation, angular acceleration, body directionality, and quantity of movement (Savva et al., 2012). Recurrent neural network (RNN) results are equivalent to human observer standards, with an average recognition rate of 58.4%.

Long Short-Term Memory Units (LSTM)

RNN faces a problem with short-term memory. If a sequence is long, RNN has difficulty in carrying information from previous time steps to next ones. If trying to process a paragraph of text for prediction, RNN can leave out important parts from the beginning. For this reason, this problem causes the need for Long Short-Term Memory, a kind of RNN. LSTM remembers the information for a long time. A common LSTM is composed of a cell, input gate, forget gate, and output gate. The challenge of capturing long-term memory in RNNs led to the development of long short-term memory (LSTM) networks in (Hochreiter & Schmidhuber, 1997; Wei et al., 2017).

The main component of the LSTM is the memory cell. The cell remembers values over time intervals and consists of cell state vector and gating units. Gating units regulate the data flow into and out of the memory. Cell state vector represents the memory of the LSTM. Forget gate controls the information to throw away from the memory. Input or update gate controls the new data is added to cell state from current input. Output gate decides what to output from the memory. The RNN-LSTM is continually updated and enhanced in the publications mentioned above as deep learning is applied to natural language processing. RNN-LSTM is now used in numerous NLP applications, however, it has not been used to analyze the grid's unstructured data (Wei et al., 2017).

RNN-LSTM Model

In many artificial intelligences (AI) based applications, automatic emotion identification has grown in importance and has been extensively studied in recent years. The majority of automated emotion recognition research is focused on speech or facial expressions. Even though it is evident that emotional state affects how a person moves, automated analysis still undervalues this source of expression. An RNN extension called the Long Short Term Memory network (RNN-LSTM) performs significantly better than the original RNN for emotion detection (Sapiński et al., 2019). Neural networks have been known and developed for decades and been widely used for emotion detection as well as industries not only for time series applications, but also in many other applications such as object recognitions, natural language processing, fraud detections, recommender systems and more (Sapiński et al., 2019; Selvin et al., 2017). Neural network is widely used in the world nowadays because of its capability to explore, recognize, or identify the hidden or underlying relationships, patterns or interactions of the data through a process called self-learning process that can also be known as deep learning (Selvin et al., 2017). Over the decades, many different types of neural networks have been developed by researchers along with different algorithms for time series analysis such as Recurrent Neural Network (RNN), Long Short-Term Memory (LSTM), Convolutional Neural Network (CNN) and many more. All these types of neural networks are in fact developed from the same basic neural network which is Artificial Neural Network (ANN) (Siami-Namini et al., 2018).

METHODOLOGY

This study proposed an artificial intelligence lifecycle for opinion mining as shown in Figure 1. The proposed lifecycle consists of six main steps: (1) data collection, (2) text exploration, (3) text preprocessing, (4) modelling, (5) deployment, and (6) evaluation. For modelling steps, sentiment analysis, topic modelling, and emotion detection are used. Sentiment analysis is done using Vader and textblob algorithm whereas topic modelling used some common techniques such as Latent Dirichlet Allocation (LDA) and Non-Negative Matrix Factorization (NNMF). Deep learning techniques such as Recurrent Neural Network- Long Short Term Memory network (RNN-LSTM) are used for emotion detection. Then, the proposed models are deployed using python programming language and Jupiter notebook platform.

Data Collection

The data is collected from Behrouz Boochani's online tweets. Behrouz Boochani is a Kurdish-Iranian social and political activist who is the author of the book *No Friend but the Mountains: Writing from Manus Prison* (2018). In his tweets, Boochani mainly seeks to speak for the marginalized, to raise awareness about injustices, and to protest against racial, gender, and ethnic inequalities. The rise of social media platforms such as Twitter, Facebook, and so forth have provided a unique opportunity for activities like Boochani not only to document their life stories (Asl, 2020, 2022) but also to interact with a global audience. To extract the tweets of Boochani, Twitter API is used. By using Twitter API, the total number of 2925 tweets were downloaded from 2017-01-01 until 2021-04-25 as shown in Figure 2.

Figure 1. The proposed artificial intelligence lifecycle for opinion mining

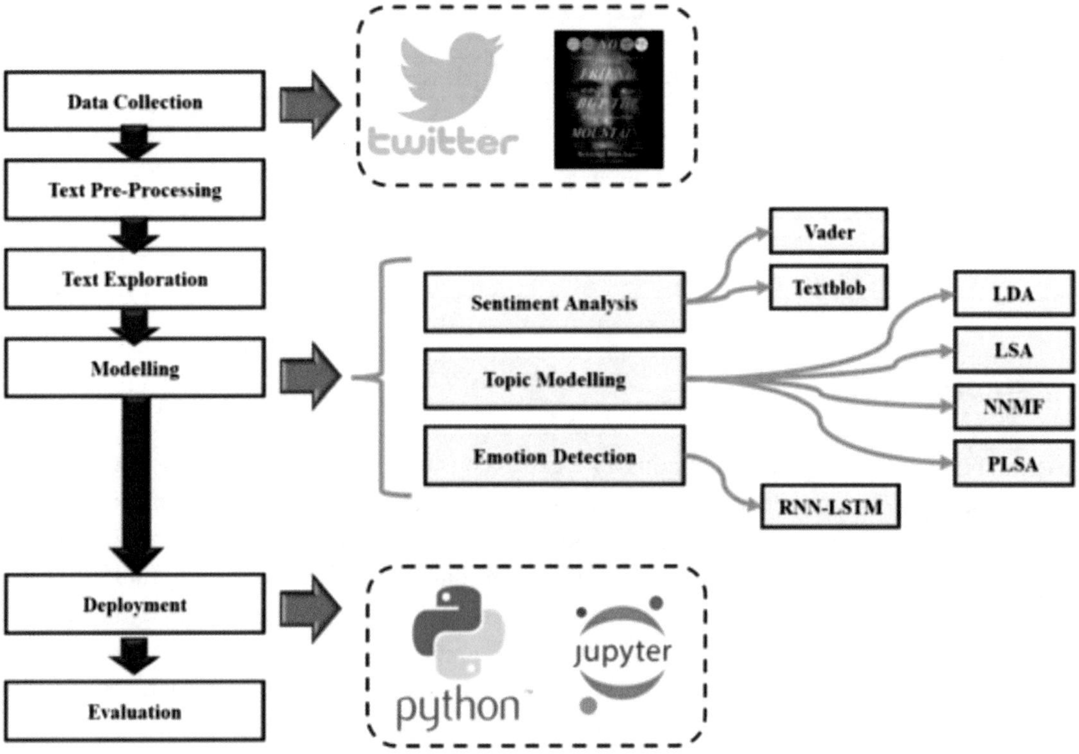

Figure 2. Collected data from twitter for this study

	Tweets	Length	Date	Source	Favourites	Retweets
0	RT @KavehGhoreishi: I'm discussing on No Frien...	140	2021-04-25 11:20:12	Twitter for Android	0	11
1	5) Australian government is legally responsibl...	140	2021-04-22 08:20:01	Twitter for Android	346	153
2	4) One of the resident resisted and gangs assa...	140	2021-04-22 08:18:49	Twitter for Android	173	69
3	3) After that, invaders or criminals broken in...	140	2021-04-22 08:18:13	Twitter for Android	164	81
4	2) Incident taken in place when around 8 armed...	140	2021-04-22 08:17:29	Twitter for Android	163	79
...	...	...	...	...	...	...
2920	Today will be court for those two refugees tha...	137	2017-01-03 21:48:14	Twitter for Android	43	31
2921	The main question in Manus prison is that who ...	121	2017-01-03 11:17:41	Twitter for Android	10	47
2922	mmigration came to us and said if you would li...	131	2017-01-03 04:44:34	Twitter for Android	10	26
2923	@pontuna2run Just some context. https://t.co/X...	55	2017-01-02 12:46:17	Twitter for Android	10	17
2924	Death is not a normal occurrence on Manus and ...	86	2017-01-01 20:46:49	Twitter Web App	15	21

2925 rows × 6 columns

Table 1. List of cleaning tasks

No.	Step
1)	Ensuring the code is non-case sensitive, all tweets have been set to lower case.
2)	Removing twitter username where the username starts with "@[username]".
3)	Removing all punctuations.
4)	Removing *"RT"* words.
5)	Removing URL.
6)	Replacing *"\n"* with an empty string.
7)	Replacing open and close quotation with an empty string.

Text Preprocessing

The textual data used for analysis contains a lot extraneous and unnecessary tokens and characters that should be removed before performing any further operations like tokenization or normalization techniques. Before performing sentiment analysis on the user's tweets, the ones that cannot be used directly or are non-essential need to be removed. Cleaning steps have been listed clearly in Table 1.

After cleaning the textual data, we proceed to clean non-English tweets as this study focuses on English textual data only by using detect function from "langdetect" library from python. Langdetect library does not allow texts to contain empty string (NaN), null value, whitespace, number, special character such as emojis and URL; thus, those tweets are dropped from the data frame.

Text Exploration

Because the maximum length for each tweet is restricted to 140 words, those tweets will not be separated into a variety of tagsets, and all words in tweet will be used after text preprocessing. Word cloud is used to depict keywords that are most frequently mentioned in tweets. Terms such as "manu", "refugee", "australian", "imgration" depicted explicitly experiences encountered by Behrouz Boochani in Papua New Guinea as shown in Figure 3. The purpose of having a visualization on most frequents words used is just to have a visual and a general idea of what kind of topic author concerns the most, word cloud does not help in predicting sentiment of the authors even separate keywords into noun or adjectives.

Based on 4, few assumptions of the topics can be made:

1. Refugees: The user is still concerned about the lives of refugees by voicing out through social media platforms.
2. Human rights: The user might be demanding fair treatment for those who seek asylum from other countries as he did initially.
3. Government: The user might be demanding government of Australia to take responsibility for the death of detainees happened in Papua New Guinea.

Because this study performs sentiment analysis and topic modelling on user's tweets from Twitter, hashtag words are extracted to identify which core keywords used might help in topic modeling and

Figure 3. Frequent keywords used

validate general ideas mentioned above. Figure 4 and Table 2 show the top ten frequently used hashtags in the bar chart.

Modelling

Three models are developed in modelling steps which are (1) sentiment analysis, (2) topic modelling, and (3) emotion detection. The sentiment analysis model is used to analyze whether the whole story as depicted in his book by the user has any impact on him after released from prison. This study uses Textblob sentiment analyzer and VADER sentiment analyzer on user's historical tweets by comparing results from both analyzers. Next, under the same textual data, topic models are created using Latent

Figure 4. Top 10 Frequently used hashtag (Bar Chart)

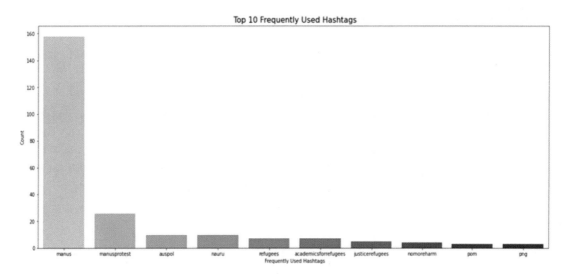

Table 2. Top 10 Frequently used hashtag (Table)

No.	Bigram	Count
1	manus	158
2	manusprotest	26
3	asupol	10
4	nauru	10
5	refugees	7
6	academicsforrefugees	7
7	justicefugees	5
8	nomoreharm	4
9	pom	3
10	Png	3

Dirichlet Allocation (LDA) and Non-negative Matrix Factorization (NMF). Finally, emotion detection is performed using Recurrent Neural Network- Long Short Term Memory network (RNN-LSTM) model.

Sentiment Analysis

The steps of sentiment analysis are illustrated in Figure 5. After pre-processing the textual tweets, each sentiment analyzer (Textblob & VADER) is used to calculate the score of Polarity directly on textual data tweets and it is worth mentioning that tokenization, lemmatization, or stemming are not necessary. VADER is a lexicon and rule-based sentiment analysis tool that is specifically attuned to sentiments expressed in social media. It provides sentiment scores based on words used (for instance, "completely" boosts a score, while "slightly" reduces it), on capitalization and punctuation ("GREAT!!!" is stronger than "great.") and negations (words like "isn't" and "doesn't" affect the outcome). In VADER libraries, the analyzer calculates the score of negative, neutral, and positive textual data whereas TextBlob is a Python library for processing textual data that provides a simple API for diving into common NLP tasks such as part-of-speech tagging, noun phrase extraction, sentiment analysis, classification, translation, and more. Textblob sentiment analyzer returns two properties for a given input sentence:

- Polarity is a float that lies between [-1,1], -1 indicates negative sentiment and +1 indicates positive sentiments.
- Subjectivity is also a float which lies in the range of [0,1]. Subjective sentences generally refer to opinion, emotion, or judgment.

There is a slight modification on the calculation score using Textblob analyzer to make alignment with VADER libraries return positive, neutral, and negative. Thus, if score below zero, returns Negative, else if score equals 0 returns Neutral and score > 0 returns Positive.

Figure 5. Process of Sentiment Analysis

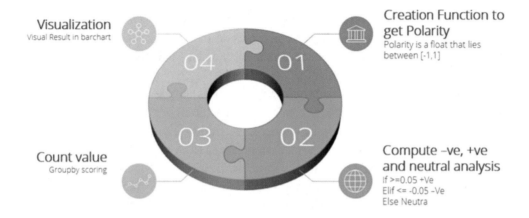

Topic Modelling

Figure 6 shows how the process of Topic Modelling is developed. Step 1 is data cleaning, which performed some tasks such as: Ensuring the code is non-case sensitive; all tweets have been set to lower case; removing twitter username where the username starts with "@[username]"; removing all punctuations; removing *"RT"* words; removing URL; replacing *"\n"* with an empty string; and replacing open and close quotation with an empty string. Because lexicon-based sentiment analyzer does not need to tokenize, lemmatize, and remove stop-words (topic modelling needs), extra cleaning steps are performed before moving forward on the textual tweet data. Three additional cleaning steps are tokenizing tweets, removing stop-words, and lemmatizing all words. Lemmatizing is preferred instead of steaming because coherent words are needed, and not just random words. Step 2 is using K-means to familiarize with the

Figure 6. The Proposed data science lifecycle based on CRISP-DM method

information contained in the textual data as this is a good way to understand what kind of topics should be expected.

Step 3 is building topic modeling using Latent Dirichlet Allocation (LDA) and Non-negative Matrix Factorization (NMF). Both models require several topics defined to build the model. The topics can be obtained from coherence measures. Coherence is a set of statements or facts which are said to be coherent if they support each other. Thus, a coherent fact set can be interpreted in a context that covers all or most of the facts. An example of a coherent fact set is "the game is a team sport", "the game is played with a ball", "the game demands great physical efforts". There are different coherence measures, this project uses c_umass which is based on document cooccurrence counts, a one-preceding segmentation and a logarithmic conditional probability as confirmation measure. LDA or NMF begin using text in Coherence Model algorithm, and the number of topics started with 15 topics which is the middle range topics identified by k-means in step 2. Fifteen topics provide insight about the number of keywords generated from the model. Those lists contain a lot of nouns or adjectives in the clusters that are used to describe different topics as those terms do not give any information about what tweets are about. Those nouns or adjectives that are much repeated will be added into the stop-words list in Step 4. For topic modelling, the model (LDA & NMF) with the least coherence score is considered a better model.

Emotion Detection

Emotion Detection is one of the most popular applications of Natural Language Processing. The key idea of emotion detection is to analyze a text to understand the opinion that is expressed in the user's tweets and his book. The text is usually expressed via a person who has moods, emotions, and feelings. Emotion Detection is generally used in social media analysis (to launch better products). Emotion Detection is an analysis of sentences. In the dataset, text gives an opinion about the sentence. In the project, a model is implemented that inputs a sentence and finds the most appropriate emotion to be used in the sentence.

In this assignment, the topic is how to apply deep learning techniques to emotion analysis. Emotion analysis determines if the sentence's emotional tone is positive or negative with the emotions called joy, sadness, anger, fear, love, and surprise. This project contains some topics such as word vectors, recurrent neural networks- long short-term memory units (RNN-LSTM). Figure 7 shows the steps on how to apply deep learning techniques on tweets and Goodreads reviews.

Step 1 is importing data from nlp package (this project extracted those data into flat files) by split data into training (15999 rows), validation (2000 rows) and test set (2000 rows then initialize tokenizer with more than 10k seq length and replace out of vocabulary with token UNK (unknown).

Step 2 is padding and truncating sequences. Some of the tweets are either short or long. Thus, by fixed max lengths of tweets or reviews within 80 vocabularies, those tweets with more than 80 characters will be truncated after 81 vocabularies.

Step 3 is preparing the labels by converting string labels into integers to be used in the model. Those labels in training, validation and text set are converted into vector after converted string label (joy':0, 'anger':1, 'love':2, 'sadness':3, 'fear':4, 'surprise':5}).

Step 4 is creating and evaluating the models using sequential models. Adding embedding layer and dropout to model to prevent overfitting and add bidirectional LSTM later with return sequences on first LSTM layer, lastly, add softmax layer as model to predict multiclass. Once the model is created, it is evaluated on a test set.

Figure 7. Process of emotion detection

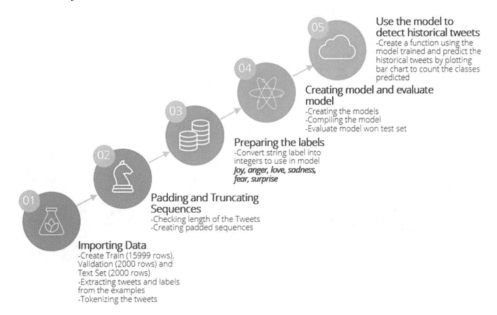

05 Use the model to detect historical tweets
-Create a function using the model trained and predict the historical tweets by plotting bar chart to count the classes predicted

Creating model and evaluate model
-Creating the models
-Compiling the model
-Evaluate model won test set

Preparing the labels
-Convert string label into integers to use in model
Joy, anger, love, sadness, fear, surprise

Padding and Truncating Sequences
-Checking length of the Tweets
-Creating padded sequences

Importing Data
-Create Train (15999 rows), Validation (2000 rows) and Text Set (2000 rows)
-Extracting tweets and labels from the examples
-Tokenizing the tweets

Step 5 is to create a function to take the sentences and yield the predicted emotions. Next is plotting bar chart to count the predicted classes

Deployment

Python is the most popular programming technique. It has the most powerful libraries for math, statistics, artificial intelligence, and machine learning. Python provides many libraries for text preprocessing such as NLTK, spaCy, Gensim, polyglot, CoreNLP, scikit-learn and Pattern. Each of them can be integrated to compensate for the disadvantages of each other. Besides, python has a lot of extension and incredible community support, simple and easy to understand as python uses the concept of object-oriented language whereas R is created as a statistical language and is more functional which is more suitable to perform data mining and time series analysis. Moreover, different integrated development environment available for Python such as Pycharm, Visual Studio Code, Intellij IDEA, Jupyter Notebook, different IDEs equipped with deployment function and can integrated many other tools whereas R are limited to R studio only. Thus, this study utilized python programming language in Jupyter Notebook.

Evaluation

To perform sentiment analysis, Textblob and VADER algorithms are used because they are simple library which support complex analysis and operations on textual data that does not need any trained models to classify negative and positive words as there are available pre-defined dictionaries. In evaluation step, the results of Textblob and VADER modeling are compared. In addition, LDA and NMF are used in topic modelling to extract the hidden topics from the selected tweets, regardless of whether those topics are similar to what is depicted in his book. LDA is used because it allows ranking terms for a given topic in terms of both the frequency of the term under that topic as well as the term's exclusivity to the

Figure 8. Sentiments Count by using TextBlob library

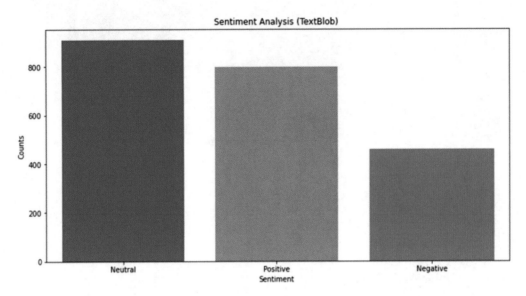

topics, which accounts for the degree to which it appears in that topic to the exclusion of others. NMF gives semantically meaningful results that is easily interpretable in clustering application, NMF has been widely used as a clustering method especially for document data and as a topic modelling method. Besides both actively support by community as compared to other methods, if researcher encountered any difficulties, answer can easily be found in community. The results of LDA and NMF are compared based on Coherence Score.

ANALYSIS AND RESULTS

Sentiment Analysis

As mentioned in chapter 3, the study focuses on two NLP python libraries which are TextBlob and VADER to analysis the sentiment of the selected tweets. Both libraries render two different results on the same dataset. Under TextBlob library, out of the 2164 tweets (different when execute the algorithm as it will retrieve the latest tweets), there are 908 tweets categorized under neutral sentiment, which is almost 42%, following by 798 tweets under positive sentiments (37%) and 458 tweets under negative sentiment (21%) as shown in Figure 8. It can be inferred that most of the tweets are between positive and neutral even though words such as suffering, death, detention etc. appear in WordCloud as can be seen in Figure 9.

On the other hand, under VADER library, out of the 2164 tweets (different when execute the algorithm as it will retrieve the latest tweets), there are only 393 tweets categorized under neutral sentiment, which is 18% out of overall, followed by 649 tweets with positive sentiments (30%), and the rest of 1122 tweets with negative sentiment (52%) as shown in Figure 10.

Figure 9. Words frequently used over the tweets

It is surprising that both libraries yield completely different results as TextBlob library categorized more on neutral sentiment and positive sentiment which aggregate both 908 tweets and 798 tweets of total 1706 tweets. Whereas under VADER library, results are dominated by negative sentiment of 1122 tweets, as mathematical comparison, 1122 tweets divided by 1706 tweets, almost 60% distributed solely on negative sentiment under VADER. Furthermore, to validate both results, only sample tweets with

Figure 10. Sentiments Count by using VADER library

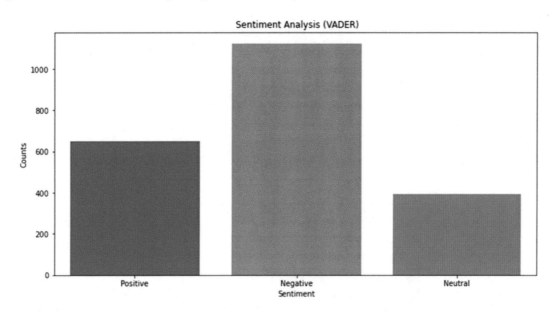

Table 3. Comparison of Top 10 Favorites Positive Tweets analyzed by TextBlob and VADER

Tweets	Favourites	TextBlob_Analysis	Vader_Analysis
i just arrived in new zealand. so exciting to get freedom after more than six years. i have been invited by word feâ€¦	21368	Positive	Positive
since last night that australian story was broadcasted, many supporters been calling for my freedom. while i trulyâ€¦	6130	Positive	Positive
i â€¯m in a third country now and dont need you. if you are honest, do something for others who are suffering in pngâ€¦	4965	Positive	Positive
take it easy, it was only an egg that did not even huyou. so far 12 people have been killed under your care in mâ€¦	4203	Positive	Positive
its a historical moment for all of the refugees on manus and nauru. many people are happy now because they will finâ€¦	3947	Positive	Positive
iâ€™ve just been released. they **hancuffed** me for more than two hours in a place behind the prison camp. the police coâ€¦	3875	Positive	**Negative**
imran mohammad, the young rohingya who was a refugee in manus & accepted last yr by america today graduated from hâ€¦	3718	Positive	Positive
2 gaining asylum in new zealand is an important milestone in my life. my journey and work are about the marginaliâ€¦	3621	Positive	Positive
the kids rally for climate change and what the egg boy did proves that young people are keenly involved in politicsâ€¦	3573	Positive	Positive
what kind of liberal democracy australia claims that after two weeks of **moral crisis** in the heaof its parliamentâ€¦	3263	Positive	**Negative**

more than 2000 favorites will be taken to make comparison. Comparison of top 10 favorites positive, neutral, and negative Tweets analyzed by TextBlob and VADER are shown in Table 3 to 5 respectively.

Table 3 shows there is not much difference between the results of top 10 positive tweets by TextBlob and VADER except two parts which VADER categorized as negative sentiment, but TextBlob categorized as positive sentiment. After reading the sentences, VADER is more accurate as the word 'hancuffed' and 'moral crisis' words used in sentences, it has no reason to categorize as positive sentiment.

Table 4 shows the comparison of the top 10 Favorites Neutral Tweets analyzed by TextBlob and VADER. There are seven differences in the results in which TextBlob categorized as Neutral sentiment whereas VADER categorized as three positives and four negatives sentiment. Three out of four negative sentiments and one out three positives sentiments seem more reasonable as words such as 'congratulation' (Positive), 'why'(Negative), 'begging'(Negative), 'condemnation'(Negative) are used.

Table 5 shows the top 10 Favorites Negative Tweets analyzed by VADER as compared with TextBlob in which there are six main differences. While VADER categorized the sentiments as Negative, TextBlob categorized the sentiments as three positives and three neutral. The results shows that the categorized negative sentiments by VADER are more reasonable. For instance, words like 'shooting', 'torture', 'violence', 'shame', 'rejected', and 'execute' are more related to negative sentiment while TextBlob categorized them as neutral. In conclusion, the user is concerned about refugees' issues after he was freed from detention as he tries to voice out topics related to refugees such as government policies that affect those seeking asylum. The user's sentiment is mostly negative as most of the words used are in the negative category and VADER library performed quite accurately compared with TextBlob after validating the samples.

Table 4. Comparison of Top 10 Favorites Neutral Tweets analyzed by TextBlob and VADER

Tweets	Favourites	TextBlob_Analysis	Vader_Analysis
such a rediclilius and unacceptable statement by labor party. you exiled me to manus and you have supported this exâ€¦	8822	Neutral	**Positive**
twenty six refugees who were locked up in the park prison have got their bridging visa today. **congratulation** to allâ€¦	5536	Neutral	**Positive**
four pms changed since we were sent to manus and nauru in 2013. nothingâ€™s changed for us, we are still are here. itâ€¦	4208	Neutral	Neutral
we havenâ€™t seen any service provided by paladin on manus, only 500 locals employed to walk around here and watch whâ€¦	2711	Neutral	Neutral
the question is not **why** the gov didnâ€™t let senator visit biolla family in christmas island prison camp.â€¦	2698	Neutral	**Negative**
as a witness to six years of torture & violence by the aus gov on manus, iâ€™m **begging** the people who still believe iâ€¦	2493	Neutral	**Negative**
the **condemnation** of senator fraser anning by scott morrison shouldnâ€™t let us forget that he and peter dutton and maâ€¦	2476	Neutral	**Negative**
political parties in australia are running their election campaigns these days. people on manus and nauru are non eâ€¦	2376	Neutral	**Positive**
this man has practiced dictatorship in manus and nauru for years and now is running australia as a camp state. i wiâ€¦	1815	Neutral	Neutral
as a person who has been **excluded from australian politics** i fully suppomarriage equality in australia. from manus prison camp i vote yes	1805	Neutral	**Negative**

Table 5. Comparison of Top 10 Favorites Negative Tweets analyzed by TextBlob and VADER

Tweets	Favourites	TextBlob_Analysis	Vader_Analysis
people of australia are frustrated by the politicians these days but remember that you can kick them all out of parâ€¦	2064	Negative	Negative
many people still cannot believe that scott morison made a comment about **shooting** at protesters, but he already didâ€¦	1558	**Positive**	Negative
north korea reviewed australia's rights record at the un today and recommended they cease cruel, inhumane or degradâ€¦	1244	Negative	Negative
the question is not **why** the gov didnâ€™t let senator visit biolla family in christmas island prison camp.â€¦	2698	**Neutral**	Negative
as a witness to six years of **torture** & **violence** by the aus gov on manus, iâ€™m begging the people who still believe iâ€¦	2493	**Neutral**	Negative
dear, if you take dangerous political rhetoric seriously, why you dont suspend dictators like khamenâ€¦	1267	Negative	Negative
the condemnation of senator fraser anning by scott morrison shouldnâ€™t let us forget that he and peter dutton and maâ€¦	2476	**Neutral**	Negative
what a **shame** that uk is listening to a politician who has been completely rejected in australia. tonny abbot failedâ€¦	1348	**Positive**	Negative
the iranian regime is going to **execute five** young protesters. once again the people of iran are demanding suppoâ€¦	1196	**Positive**	Negative
1 i salute the people of new zealand for rejecting the politics of hate & division. australiaâ€™s asylum policies arâ€¦	10968	Negative	Negative

Figure 11. Line Chart of Coherence Score for LDA Model. (Coherence Score: -15.47, Number of Topics: 19)

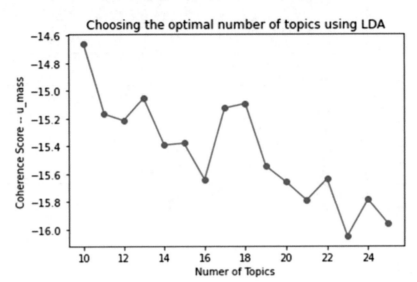

Topic Modelling

To gain the number of topics which yield the optimal coherence score, the model is iterated from 10 topics to 25 topics with 5 intervals in each, for example, 10 topics, 15 topics, 20 topics up to 25 topics. Once each model (LDA & NMF) goes through all the iterations, umass-graph is used to identify the number of topics with the highest coherence score, and generated topics are saved for analysis in a later section. Comparison of coherence score of the models from 10 topics to 30 topics are shown in Figure 11 and 12.

Figure 11 shows the line chart of LDA model's coherence score: as the number of topics increases, the performance keeps increasing but slowing down in proportion. In total, 19 topics are emerged based on the analysis of LDA model. Whereas Figure 12 shows the line chart of NMF model's coherence score in increasing trend. The best number of topics for NMF is 10 topics. Last is Step 5: after keywords are obtained from the topics in the list, the most relevant theme is assigned for each list to make hypothesis what is the most relevant topics related to the list.

As shown in Figure 11 and 12, LDA is the best model for topic modelling as the coherence score is -15.47. There are different coherence scores. In this project, the coherence score is calculated based on c_umass which is based on document (tweet) cooccurrence counts, a one-preceding segmentation and a logarithmic conditional probability as confirmation measure that is why coherence score is negative.

A total of 19 topics are identified with least repeated topics after parameter of cluster tuning from 10 to 25 topics. Table 6 shows the keywords or terms generated by LDA model. As those keywords are important to one topic, they might be important to other topics as well. Thus, such words do not help us in differentiating the topics from one another. For example, under Topic 16, using keywords such a 'manus', 'detention', 'song', 'melbourne', it is difficult to infer what related topics are because Topic Modelling is an unstructured technique. With those keywords highlighted, grouping keywords by referring the original tweets would help to better understand what those topics are about.

Figure 12. Line Chart of Coherence Score for NMF Model. (Coherence Score: -14.50, Number of Topics: 10)

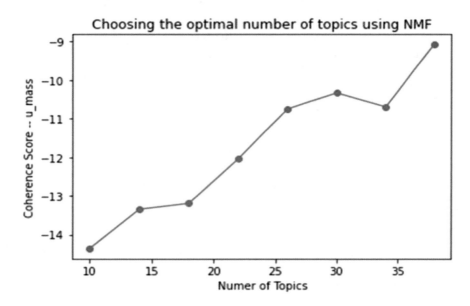

By using keywords generated from LDA model and relating them to original tweets, 7 main topics have been derived which are (1) Suicide, (2) Translator of Book, (3) Human Rights, (4) Political, (5) Publication of Book, (6) Immigration and (7) Detention. Table 7 shows the original tweets for suicide topic.

LDA model takes unigrams in process of model building and bi-grams to render a clear pair of words. As original tweets shown in Table 7, user keeps mentioning the harsh conditions of detention center at Manus Prison that cause refugees attempt suicide. Based on the tweets, those who stayed there have gone through a lot of emotional and psychological pressure. Hence, authorities refuse to replace razors for men as they think prisoners will be more inclined to commit suicide or self-haram.

There are interconnections between topics of Translator of Book and Publication of Book as shown in Table 8 and Table 9, respectively. Translator Omid Tofighian is a lecturer, researcher and community advocate. He is a translator of Behrouz Boochani's book *No Friend but the Mountains: Writing from Manus Prison*. The book originally was not written in English version and was written on a mobile phone using WhatsApp which was smuggled out of Manus Island as PDF files. It was translated from Persian into English by Omid Tofighian, and it was finally published by Picador in late 2018.

Boochani condemned Australia for breaching human rights by exiling thousands of innocent people to Manus Island as prisoners and detaining them with the worst condition ever. Table 10 shows the original tweets for human rights topic.

In like manner, Boochani condemned the Australian government's refugee policies that led to imprisoning innocent people without charge, without conviction, and without sentence. Table 11 shows original tweets for political topics.

Author deemed himself become a political hostage by the Australian fascist government on Manus and Nauru as he experienced almost six years of detention. He condemned that what is happening in Manus and Nauru is a human disaster and should be solved above political point scoring.

Table 6. Keywords generated with LDA model

Topics	Keywords
0	0.041*"manus" + 0.017*"island" + 0.017*"manus island" + 0.014*"suicide" + 0.013*"pomoresby" + 0.011*"immigration" + 0.009*"attempted" + 0.008*"**attempted suicide**" + 0.007*"police" + 0.006*"morning"
1	0.016*"**omid tofighian**" + 0.016*"tofighian" + 0.016*"omid" + 0.012*"manus" + 0.006*"mountains" + 0.006*"article" + 0.006*"critical" + 0.005*"ihms" + 0.005*"innocent" + 0.005*"png"
2	0.038*"human" + 0.029*"rights" + 0.027*"**human rights**" + 0.018*"manus" + 0.006*"story" + 0.005*"media" + 0.005*"hate" + 0.005*"news" + 0.004*"aus" + 0.004*"island"
3	0.022*"manus" + 0.006*"reading" + 0.005*"gov" + 0.005*"movie" + 0.005*"preventing" + 0.005*"detention" + 0.005*"medical" + 0.005*"immigration" + 0.004*"**academicsforrefugees**" + 0.004*"offshore detention"
4	0.012*"manus" + 0.011*"interview" + 0.007*"long" + 0.006*"abc" + 0.005*"gov" + 0.005*"**death**" + 0.005*"asylum" + 0.005*"interview abc" + 0.004*"situation" + 0.004*"**suicide**"
5	0.012*"manus" + 0.009*"system" + 0.008*"medical" + 0.008*"sick" + 0.007*"innocent" + 0.007*"pouf" + 0.005*"pomoresby" + 0.005*"innocent manus" + 0.004*"**politics**" + 0.004*"life"
6	0.034*"manus" + 0.008*"police" + 0.008*"immigration" + 0.006*"election" + 0.005*"thing" + 0.005*"history" + 0.004*"auspol" + 0.004*"situation" + 0.004*"**political**" + 0.004*"move"
7	0.014*"manus" + 0.010*"time" + 0.009*"haus" + 0.009*"camps" + 0.009*"west" + 0.009*"food" + 0.009*"west haus" + 0.008*"**chauka time**" + 0.007*"chauka" + 0.007*"water"
8	0.032*"dutton" + 0.026*"peter" + 0.026*"**peter dutton**" + 0.013*"morrison" + 0.011*"manus" + 0.009*"scott morrison" + 0.009*"scott" + 0.008*"article" + 0.007*"women" + 0.006*"don"
9	0.019*"manus" + 0.011*"work" + 0.010*"gov" + 0.009*"aus" + 0.008*"png" + 0.008*"paof" + 0.007*"**aus gov**" + 0.006*"remain" + 0.006*"number" + 0.006*"work manus"
10	0.007*"manus" + 0.007*"situation" + 0.006*"provide" + 0.006*"water" + 0.006*"story" + 0.005*"kurdish" + 0.005*"critical" + 0.005*"mother" + 0.004*"article" + 0.004*"**detention**"
11	0.008*"png" + 0.007*"wrote" + 0.007*"days" + 0.007*"story" + 0.006*"manus" + 0.006*"**png governments**" + 0.006*"governments" + 0.006*"life" + 0.005*"kazem" + 0.005*"work"
12	0.010*"manus" + 0.006*"iranian" + 0.006*"**government**" + 0.006*"iran" + 0.005*"groups" + 0.004*"letter" + 0.004*"wonderful" + 0.004*"medical" + 0.004*"human" + 0.003*"pomoresby"
13	0.021*"manus" + 0.009*"**killed**" + 0.007*"kurdish" + 0.007*"young" + 0.006*"island" + 0.006*"reza" + 0.006*"death" + 0.005*"png" + 0.005*"iran" + 0.005*"government"
14	0.016*"manus" + 0.008*"policy" + 0.006*"camps" + 0.005*"iran" + 0.005*"arrested" + 0.005*"exile" + 0.005*"barbaric" + 0.005*"close" + 0.005*"**political**" + 0.005*"detention"
15	0.017*"manus" + 0.011*"time" + 0.010*"**government**" + 0.006*"event" + 0.006*"great" + 0.006*"call" + 0.006*"ihms" + 0.005*"three" + 0.005*"film" + 0.005*"living"
16	0.015*"manus" + 0.010*"**detention**" + 0.008*"song" + 0.006*"melbourne" + 0.006*"indefinite" + 0.006*"kurdish" + 0.005*"media" + 0.005*"hope" + 0.005*"bill" + 0.005*"beautiful"
17	0.045*"mountains" + 0.035*"manus" + 0.025*"writing" + 0.016*"read" + 0.015*"**mountains writing**" + 0.013*"writing manus" + 0.011*"mountains writing manus" + 0.010*"launch" + 0.007*"launch mountains" + 0.006*"story"
18	0.017*"manus" + 0.010*"hear" + 0.006*"working" + 0.005*"medical" + 0.005*"detention" + 0.005*"men" + 0.005*"gov" + 0.005*"pm" + 0.004*"**immigration**" + 0.004*"bill"

Australian government announced a new radical migration policy which denied settlement to all asylum seekers arriving illegally by boat. Author was deported to Australia's new offshore so-called processing centers on Manus Island, Papua New Guinea (PNG) soon after his arrival. The author relates all these that involve big corruption scandal as billions of dollars paid as claimed on onshore detention with only 1/10 real cost. Boochani is convinced that the public have yet to grasp the horrors of systematic

Table 7. Original tweets for suicide topic

Tweets	Topic
6. Over the past few days some of these men ***attempted suicide*** or self harm because of the harsh conditions. Some now transferred to PIH hospital in Port Moresby. Most were already extremely sick because of 6yrs living in indefinite detention.	**Suicide**
While the Australian major parties are attacking each other two more people ***attempted suicide*** here and have been transferred to hospital. One in Manus and another one in Port Moresby.#auspol	
Since yesterday at least three people have attempted suicide or self harm. Two today in Granville Motel in Port Moresby, and one in Manus. I can't say how they ***attempted suicide***. Many people cannot eat in Manus, there are high numbers with deep depression here.#auspol	

Table 8. Original tweets for translator topic

Tweets	Topic
My response to Anne Surma published recently in Continuum (translated by ***Omid Tofighian***): Manus prison poetics/our voice: revisiting 'A Letter From Manus Island', a reply to Anne Surma	**Translator of Book**
plz join us at this event with ***Omid Tofighian*** & @ShazzShams. we will have a conversation about poetry & prison literature Omid Tofighian, @Moones_M and other translators have had a great role in exposing crimes of Australian govt in indefinite detention	
Omid Tofighian's translation of No Friend but the Mountains has been shortlisted for the 2020 Medal for Excellence in Translation (Australian Academy of the Humanities).	

torture which is integral to the detention system as all have been described in topic of immigration and

Table 9. Original tweets for publication of book topic

Tweets	Topic
For our friends in Canada and America, The book No Friend But the Mountains: ***Writing* from Manus Prison** is now released in North America by @HouseofAnansi publisher. Here is the first interview with CBC in Canada.#auspol #WorldRefugeeDay	**Publication of Book**
I had a wonderful night with the people of Byron Bay and discussed my book" No Friend But the Mountains: ***writing* from Manus prison**", and also the Australian exile policy portrayed through literature. Thank you to all the beautiful people who made this happen#Manus	
Excellent review by Brigid Delaney of No Friend but the Mountains: ***Writing From Manus Prison***	

Table 10. Original tweets for human rights topic

Tweets	Topic
1: The Australian ***Human Rights*** Commission says that Australia has breached the human rights for their immoral treatment of only four families. This is a shameful statement, denying the suffering of thousands throughout the past six years of the exile policy.	**Human Rights**
2: Australia has breached ***human rights*** not only for what they did to four families but to more than 2000 innocent people who sought asylum in Australia and are guilty of no crime. What Aus has done is crime against humanity. Twelve people were killed by this gov in Manus & Nauru.	
In solidarity with the people of West Papua who are protesting for respect of their ***human rights***. Up to seven dead in West Papua as protest turns violent	

detention in Table 12 and Table 13 respectively.

Table 11. Original tweets for political topic

Tweets	Topic
The major threat in this period is the governmental terrorism. These ***political*** structures feed from spreading hatred and manufacturing fear. A gov that justifies the right to torture people outside the boundaries of its nation, can easily apply that strategy to its own people too	
This story shows how Peter Dutton has used innocent people on Manus and Nauru to his personal ***political*** benefit. His power has increased day by day over the past few years. Labor is only allowing him to get more power by withdrawing from his threat.#Manus	**Political**
Liberal party has ***political*** benefits from keeping people in prison. They are showing how cruel this government is and it's unacceptable. How long do you want to keep people in an indefinite situation? How long till your sadistic desire is satisfied?#Manus	

Table 12. Original tweets for immigration topic

Tweets	Topic
This is a notice by the ***Immigration*** on Manus island, ordering that the refugees are not allowed to leave their camps after 6pm. This is against the PNG court order.#Manus	
Wish Royal Commission would investigate how ***immigration*** spent $10billion in Manus & Nauru. Big corruption under secrecy and exile, companies like IHMS need to be investigated.#Manus	**Immigration**
Deporting ppl from Manus after 5yrs is unacceptable.Australian ***immigration*** processed ppl under too much pressure & many were too ill to be assessed fairly. Some refused to give their cases because believed it would put them in danger & are now punished with negative status.#Manus	

Emotion Detection

Emotion detection model detected that most of the author's tweets are categorized as sad followed by joy category as second highest. It is so surprising as the emotion detected on the tweets are identical with the emotion detected on reviews from Goodreads. Most of the reviews felt sad after the incident happened to author as described on the book as shown on Figure 13 and Figure 14 respectively.

Table 13. Original tweets for political topic

Tweets	Topic
All of the Paladin workers left Hillside Haus in Lorengau. Hillside is one of three ***detention*** centres where we're refusing to go	
Just now the Navy & immigration prevented a boat from coming close to ***detention*** centre. They're stopping food entering into the prison camp.	**Detention**
Why does Australian gov deny independent journalists access to ***detention*** centre? Why only allowing Murdoch press in?	

Figure 13. Count of emotion by category (Tweets)

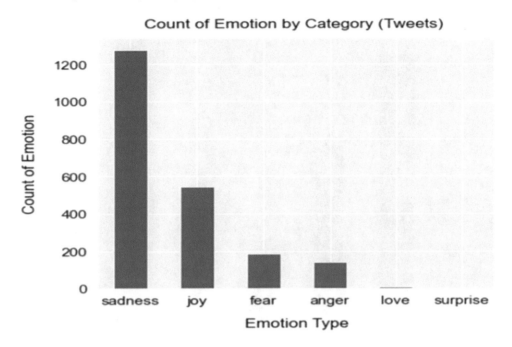

To identify whether words used in author's book are mostly negative or positive, function using VADER packages to identify polarity_score, most of the words used in the book as negative such as "sad", "fearful", "angry" and "sad"

CONCLUSION

This study aimed to propose an artificial intelligence lifecycle for the opinion mining of Boochani's tweets. For this reason, three main modelling steps were performed consisting of sentiment analysis, topic modelling, and emotion detection. After performing sentiment analysis using two techniques of TextBlob and VADER, the empirical results depict that VADER is the tool specifically created for working with messy social media textual data. VADER belongs to a type of sentiment analysis that is based on lexicons of sentiment-related words, each word in the lexicon is rated as to whether it is positive or negative and, in many cases, how positive and how negative. The comparison results between TextBlob and VADER shows VADER correctly identifies sentiment of the author which are more towards negative based on his tweets. It can be inferred that Boochani is unable to forget six years of detention on Manus Island as most of the words used in his tweets are categorized as negative and related to horrors of human rights abuse.

Based on the topic modelling results, there are seven main topics detected from keywords generated by LDA Topic Modelling. All seven topics are interrelated as they depict the situation of how the author ran away from the political oppression in his own country to Indonesia, only to be imprisoned by the Australian government. His intention has been to show the Australian public what the government was doing to detainees on the Manus Island and to speak of the mental torture caused by being deprived of

Figure 14. Count of Emotion by Category (Goodread Review)

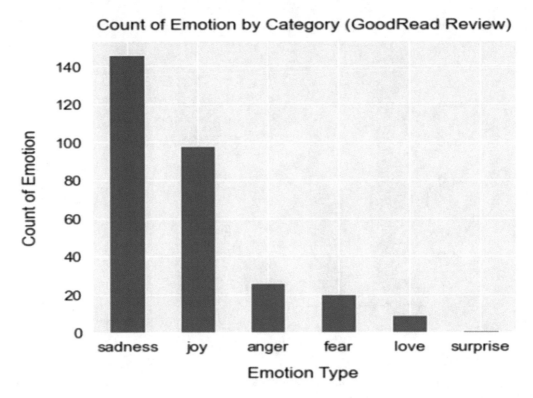

hope. From the detected topics of Suicide, Translator of Book, Human Rights, Political, Publication of Book, Immigration, and Detention, the different emotions that can be retrieved are a sense of weakness, helplessness, misery, and frustration. Also, the tension that develops among prisoners often causes many of them to attempt suicide which means that the horrible conditions have not only affected prisoners' physical conditions but also their psychological well-being. Throughout the analysis, LDA model performed well in uncovering themes in tweets as all critical keywords were revealed correctly. To understand exactly what the topics described, those keywords need to be manually related to original tweets.

After experiment with both LDA and NMF for topic modelling, performances of the two models were not much different as coherence score from LDA was slightly higher and considered the best algorithms that was able to extract seven main hidden topics which are 'Suicide', 'Translator of Book', 'Publication of Book', 'Human Rights', 'Political', 'Immigration' and 'Detention'. Emotion Detection model successfully categorized author's tweets mostly to sadness which is like the reviews on his book from Goodreads platform. Deep learning techniques performed better than machine learning approach and lexicon-based approach. For the future direction, Bidirectional Encoder Representations from Transformers (BERT) and other Transformer encoder architectures can be used as they are wildly successful on a variety of tasks in NLP (natural language processing). They compute vector-space representations of natural language that are suitable for use in deep learning models. The BERT family models use the Transformer encoder architecture to process each token of input text in the full context of all tokens before and after, hence the name: Bidirectional Encoder Representations from Transformers. BERT models are usually pre-trained on a large corpus of text, then fine-tuned for specific tasks. Thereby, learning how BERT will help in sentiment analysis.

REFERENCES

Abadah, M. S. K., Keikhosrokiani, P., & Zhao, X. (2023). Analytics of Public Reactions to the COVID-19 Vaccine on Twitter Using Sentiment Analysis and Topic Modelling. In D. Valle-Cruz, N. Plata-Cesar, & J. L. González-Ruíz (Eds.), *Handbook of Research on Applied Artificial Intelligence and Robotics for Government Processes* (pp. 156–188). IGI Global. doi:10.4018/978-1-6684-5624-8.ch008

Al Mamun, M. H., Keikhosrokiani, P., Asl, M. P., Anuar, N. A. N., Hadi, N. H. A., & Humida, T. (2022). Sentiment Analysis of the Harry Potter Series Using a Lexicon-Based Approach. In P. Keikhosrokiani & M. Pourya Asl (Eds.), *Handbook of Research on Opinion Mining and Text Analytics on Literary Works and Social Media* (pp. 263–291). IGI Global. doi:10.4018/978-1-7998-9594-7.ch011

Asri, M. A. Z. B. M., Keikhosrokiani, P., & Asl, M. P. (2022). Opinion Mining Using Topic Modeling: A Case Study of Firoozeh Dumas's Funny in Farsi in Goodreads. Advances on Intelligent Informatics and Computing. doi:10.1007/978-3-030-98741-1_19

Binti Rosli, N. H., & Keikhosrokiani, P. (2022). Big medical data mining system (BigMed) for the detection and classification of COVID-19 misinformation. In P. Keikhosrokiani (Ed.), *Big Data Analytics for Healthcare* (pp. 233–244). Academic Press. doi:10.1016/B978-0-323-91907-4.00014-5

Chu, K. E., Keikhosrokiani, P., & Asl, M. P. (2022). A Topic Modeling and Sentiment Analysis Model for Detection and Visualization of Themes in Literary Texts. *Pertanika Journal of Science & Technology*, *30*(4), 2535–2561. doi:10.47836/pjst.30.4.14

Fasha, E. F. B. K., Keikhosrokiani, P., & Asl, M. P. (2022). Opinion Mining Using Sentiment Analysis: A Case Study of Readers' Response on Long Litt Woon's The Way Through the Woods in Goodreads. Advances on Intelligent Informatics and Computing. doi:10.1007/978-3-030-98741-1_20

Hochreiter, S., & Schmidhuber, J. (1997). Long Short-Term Memory. *Neural Computation*, *9*(8), 1735–1780. doi:10.1162/neco.1997.9.8.1735 PMID:9377276

Hofmann, T. (2001). Unsupervised Learning by Probabilistic Latent Semantic Analysis. *Machine Learning*, *42*(1), 177–196. doi:10.1023/A:1007617005950

Hu, M., & Liu, B. (2004). *Mining opinion features in customer reviews*. American Association for Artificial Intelligence.

Jacobs, A. M. (2019). Sentiment Analysis for Words and Fiction Characters From the Perspective of Computational (Neuro-)Poetics. *Frontiers in Robotics and AI*, *6*. Advance online publication. doi:10.3389/frobt.2019.00053

Jafery, N. N., Keikhosrokiani, P., & Asl, M. P. (2022). Text analytics model to identify the connection between theme and sentiment in literary works: A case study of Iraqi life writings. In P. Keikhosrokiani & M. Pourya Asl (Eds.), *Handbook of Research on Opinion Mining and Text Analytics on Literary Works and Social Media* (pp. 173–190). IGI Global. doi:10.4018/978-1-7998-9594-7.ch008

John, S. A., & Keikhosrokiani, P. (2022). COVID-19 fake news analytics from social media using topic modeling and clustering. In P. Keikhosrokiani (Ed.), *Big Data Analytics for Healthcare* (pp. 221–232). Academic Press. doi:10.1016/B978-0-323-91907-4.00003-0

Keikhosrokiani, P. (Ed.). (2022a). *Handbook of Research on Consumer Behavior Change and Data Analytics in the Socio-Digital Era*. IGI Global. doi:10.4018/978-1-6684-4168-8

Keikhosrokiani, P. (2022b). *Handbook of Research on Consumer Behavior Change and Data Analytics in the Socio-Digital Era*. IGI Global. doi:10.4018/978-1-6684-4168-8

Keikhosrokiani, P., & Asl, M. P. (Eds.). (2022). *Handbook of research on opinion mining and text analytics on literary works and social media*. IGI Global. doi:10.4018/978-1-7998-9594-7

Keikhosrokiani, P., & Kamaruddin, N. S. A. B. (2022). IoT-Based In-Hospital-In-Home Heart Disease Remote Monitoring System with Machine Learning Features for Decision Making. In S. Mishra, A. González-Briones, A. K. Bhoi, P. K. Mallick, & J. M. Corchado (Eds.), *Connected e-Health: Integrated IoT and Cloud Computing* (pp. 349–369). Springer International Publishing. doi:10.1007/978-3-030-97929-4_16

Keikhosrokiani, P., & Pourya Asl, M. (Eds.). (2022). *Handbook of Research on Opinion Mining and Text Analytics on Literary Works and Social Media*. IGI Global. doi:10.4018/978-1-7998-9594-7

Kherwa, P., & Bansal, P. (2020). Topic modeling: A comprehensive review. *EAI Endorsed Transactions on Scalable Information Systems, 7*(24).

Liu, B. (2012). Sentiment analysis and opinion mining. *Synthesis Lectures on Human Language Technologies, 5*(1), 1-167. doi: 1 doi:0.1007/978-3-031-02145-9

Malik, E. F., Keikhosrokiani, P., & Asl, M. P. (2021, July 4-5). Text Mining Life Cycle for a Spatial Reading of Viet Thanh Nguyen's *The Refugees* (2017). *2021 International Congress of Advanced Technology and Engineering (ICOTEN)*. doi:10.1109/ICOTEN52080.2021.9493520

Mutanga, M. B., & Abayomi, A. (2022). Tweeting on COVID-19 pandemic in South Africa: LDA-based topic modelling approach. *African Journal of Science, Technology, Innovation and Development, 14*(1), 163–172. doi:10.1080/20421338.2020.1817262

Pang, B., & Lee, L. (2004). *A sentimental education: Sentiment analysis using subjectivity summarization based on minimum cuts*. doi:10.48550/arXiv.cs/0409058

Pang, B., Lee, L., & Vaithyanathan, S. (2002). *Thumbs up? Sentiment classification using machine learning techniques*. doi:10.48550/arXiv.cs/0205070

Paremeswaran, P. p., Keikhosrokiani, P., & Asl, M. P. (2022). Opinion Mining of Readers' Responses to Literary Prize Nominees on Twitter: A Case Study of Public Reaction to the Booker Prize (2018–2020). *Advances on Intelligent Informatics and Computing*. doi:10.1007/978-3-030-98741-1_21

Sapiński, T., Kamińska, D., Pelikant, A., & Anbarjafari, G. (2019). Emotion Recognition from Skeletal Movements. *Entropy (Basel, Switzerland), 21*(7), 646. doi:10.3390/e21070646 PMID:33267360

Savva, N., Scarinzi, A., & Bianchi-Berthouze, N. (2012). Continuous Recognition of Player's Affective Body Expression as Dynamic Quality of Aesthetic Experience. *IEEE Transactions on Computational Intelligence and AI in Games*, *4*(3), 199–212. doi:10.1109/TCIAIG.2012.2202663

Selvin, S., Vinayakumar, R., Gopalakrishnan, E. A., Menon, V. K., & Soman, K. P. (2017). Stock price prediction using LSTM, RNN and CNN-sliding window model. *2017 International Conference on Advances in Computing, Communications and Informatics (ICACCI)*.

Siami-Namini, S., Tavakoli, N., & Namin, A. S. (2018). A Comparison of ARIMA and LSTM in Forecasting Time Series. *2018 17th IEEE International Conference on Machine Learning and Applications (ICMLA)*.

Sofian, N. B., Keikhosrokiani, P., & Asl, M. P. (2022). Opinion mining and text analytics of reader reviews of Yoko Ogawa's The Housekeeper and the Professor in Goodreads. In P. Keikhosrokiani & M. Pourya Asl (Eds.), *Handbook of Research on Opinion Mining and Text Analytics on Literary Works and Social Media* (pp. 240–262). IGI Global., doi:10.4018/978-1-7998-9594-7.ch010

Suhendra, N. H. B., Keikhosrokiani, P., Asl, M. P., & Zhao, X. (2022). Opinion mining and text analytics of literary reader responses: A case study of reader responses to KL Noir volumes in Goodreads using sentiment analysis and topic. In P. Keikhosrokiani & M. Pourya Asl (Eds.), *Handbook of Research on Opinion Mining and Text Analytics on Literary Works and Social Media* (pp. 191–239). IGI Global. doi:10.4018/978-1-7998-9594-7.ch009

Teoh Yi Zhe, I., & Keikhosrokiani, P. (2021). Knowledge workers mental workload prediction using optimised ELANFIS. *Applied Intelligence*, *51*(4), 2406–2430. doi:10.100710489-020-01928-5

Tuomo, K., Niko, M., Erkki, S., & Jari, T. (2008). Comparison of Dimension Reduction Methods for Automated Essay Grading. *Journal of Educational Technology & Society*, *11*(3), 275–288. https://www.jstor.org/stable/jeductechsoci.11.3.275

Wei, D., Wang, B., Lin, G., Liu, D., Dong, Z., Liu, H., & Liu, Y. (2017). Research on Unstructured Text Data Mining and Fault Classification Based on RNN-LSTM with Malfunction Inspection Report. *Energies*, *10*(3), 406. doi:10.3390/en10030406

Ye, Q., Zhang, Z., & Law, R. (2009). Sentiment classification of online reviews to travel destinations by supervised machine learning approaches. *Expert Systems with Applications*, *36*(3, Part 2), 6527–6535. doi:10.1016/j.eswa.2008.07.035

Chapter 7

Advanced Replicating Technology in Adventure Fiction:
The Philosophical Implications of Material Synthesizer in *The Orville*

Alexandria S. Zlatar

(iD) https://orcid.org/0000-0002-9860-478X

University of Glasgow, UK

ABSTRACT

In the adventure fiction and Sci-Fi TV show The Orville (2017), a material synthesizer is a machine that can create food, drink, clothing, and so much more. While the device in the show has a small role, the implications of unrestricted material access have vast effects on the cast and real-world implications on our identities as well. The framework of this chapter focuses on a qualitative and case study analysis of literary and film-based narrative to examine the implications of material synthesis in The Orville. It examines the plot element and expounds upon the impact on unrestricted indulgence, potential corruption, and the ability to create more freedom both for the characters and the show itself. Upon this analysis, the chapter concludes that while the device is incredibly far from a practical achievement, it does lead us to analyze how current food generators and 3D printers have the potential for unrestricted powers that need to be examined and better understood in order to prevent misuse and exploitation.

"I don't want my last meal to be a twinkie"
- The Orville - 2x14 *"The Road Not Taken"*

DOI: 10.4018/978-1-6684-6242-3.ch007

INTRODUCTION

With the rise of Sci-Fi TV shows such as *The Orville* and *Star Trek: The Next Generation* (2017), innovative ideas in robotics, transportation and technology are being explored. One of these concepts is the creation of food and material synthesizers. However, there has been extraordinarily little discourse about the potential impacts this could have if we examined the concept. Companies such as Nestlé were working on technology comparable to synthesizers, with the goal of providing food tailored to an individual's nutritional requirements (Hudson, 2014). Imperial College London physicists have discovered how to create matter from light and BeeHex has been working with NASA to develop spaceflight food 3D printing technology (Pike, O., Mackenroth, F., Hill, E. et al., 2014; Imperial College London, 2014; Rutland Bauer, 2016). They, alongside several other key players, are now building food printing robots aimed at public use (Rutland Bauer, 2016.) With the realization of the potential direction toward this concept becoming a reality there is a need to understand the implications of this notion. Kelly Grayson stated to John LaMarr in the show: "Lieutenant, have you ever studied the history of money?... It became obsolete with the invention of matter synthesis."[1] Both the importance of the concept, and 'the real world' application of the synthesizer on *The Orville* provides unique insights into how a world which has control of material synthetization would function. This chapter, therefore, aims to explore the key differences of life with this unlimited material access, how it can potentially impact individuals, and the possible philosophical analyses of the approach to this concept.

LITERATURE REVIEW

The Orville is not the only series nor the only sci-fi work in which the possibilities offered by the advent of advanced replicating technology are portrayed. Robert A. Heinlein's *Future History* (1973) employed a 'Universal Pantograph' that could scan and duplicate any object, alongside Will McCarthy's *The Queendom of Sol* (2001) that featured fax machines which could print copies of inanimate objects. Perhaps most famously, food replicator devices were depicted in the *Star Trek* franchise whilst in deep space (Bell, 2005). Living in a universe where there is no want, and no material need is easier said than done. Most of these portrayals of matter synthesis are inventive and fit into their narratives. Film Theorists Carmen Tu and Steven Brown (2020) examined how plot is the abstract and overarching structure which is often external to the protagonist and their actions are determined by the thematic goals of the plot. In accordance, plot devices are both physical and abstract concepts that move the plot forward (Ryan, 200). Furthermore, Ryan highlights how plot devices are employed when conflict arises between the character and the author's objectives (2020). Material synthesis is often utilized as a "cheap plot trick" that is a hackneyed device that is used to fix plot holes. There is a lack of considerable thought and attention to the potential socio-and economic impacts of this adaptive technology (Hollow, 2013).

THEORY AND METHOD

The framework of this chapter focuses on a qualitative and case study analysis of literary and film-based works to examine the implications of material synthesis in *The Orville*. Through cross-universe investigation into Star Trek, Venus Equilateral alongside other fictional pieces will provide contextual grounding and diversity of experiences with material synthesis technology. In accordance these fictional narratives are supported by philosophical analysis to expand upon the theoretical premises. Theis will include a diversity of Philosophers ranging from German Philosopher Martin Heidegger and contemporary thinkers such as Fiona Ellis and Cara Fabre. Finally, these conceptual examinations are analyzed through several real-world notions primarily through the closest technology currently available of 3D Printing technology. This will aid to reaffirm the validity of the application to our society. The findings discuss some of these key themes including unrestricted indulgence, exploitation, personal development and systemic/galatic impacts hopes of shining light on the depths of material synthesis and the potential powers and harms of this plot device.

FINDINGS AND DISCUSSION

If we think about how material synthesizers can be abused despite living in a so-called society that does not have capitalism or material need. In 'Episode 2x11: Lasting Impressions', Bortus uses his Food Synthesizer to produce cigarettes. When he and his partner Klyden first try them, they become quickly addicted:

"[Bortus and Klyden smoking cigarettes]
Bortus: *I have never experienced such a flavor.*
Klyden: *I feel as if I have been standing my entire life, and I just sat down.*
Klyden: *The tingles. Do you feel them?*
Bortus: *I do.*
Klyden: *We must have more.*
Bortus: [Presses Material Synthesizer Button] *500 cigarettes.*" (*The Orville*, S2, Ep .11)

In the show overconsumption is not just an overly long gag throughout the program but illustrates both Bortus and Klyden struggles to overcome their addiction. 'Compressed Vice' is a tv trope that focuses a plot line on a character developing an addiction (when no previous indications were present) to setup for some sort of gag, Aesop, or character development (García-Ortega et al., 2020). Drawing upon *Futurama,* in one episode Bender develops an obsession with being remembered that was heightened to the extreme of becoming a tyrannical pharaoh and subsides by the end of the episode when they reaffirm that he will be remembered for the terror he caused (Season 3 Episode 17).[2] Similarly, children's tv shows such as *Lizzie McGuire* had an episode where one of the main cast members named Miranda became anorexic and then 'got over' it within the course of a week (Season 2 Episode 16). In the same series, Gordo developed an addiction to gaming and his friends conducted aversion therapy to help cure him (Season 1, Episode 27).[3] While these portrayals of addictions are highly problematic for many reasons, they outline a key trope in film studies and that is a reductive understanding of the lived-in experiences of mental illness (Lissauer, 2014). Literature Scholar Cara Fabre iterates "Dominant representations of addiction are most often expressed in tones of warning about "the terrible consequences of drug and alcohol addiction," such as "crime, loss of earnings and productivity, and social damage" (p. 26). Reconsidering *The Orville's* characters, the audience saw how difficult it was for the pair to quit. Several scenes showed the pair fighting while trying to quit and even Bortus hiding cigarettes throughout his quarters. Kosovski and Smith (2011) further explore this notion by looking at the portrayal of those who have addictions: "the narrative presented by the addict is often framed as clouded and distorted by drug and alcohol abuse," while "the narrative presented by friends and family is coded as authoritative and honest" (p.853). The addicted individual is persistently framed as unreliable and unable to resolve their own difficulties or obtain critical insight into addiction. In *The Orville this* trope is reaffirmed as near the end of the episode Doctor Claire Finn formulates a medical treatment to their tobacco dependency. Within popular representations and even within the Sci-Fi genre addictions are still following problematic narratives. This example illustrates that regardless of cultural and technological advancements, the same struggles with the potency of addiction, material goods and substances will always stand.

It should also be noted that several other times throughout the series the crew indulge in and abuse behaviors such as with alcohol. Chief of Security Alara Kitan uses a Food Synthesizer located in *The Orville's* halls to produce a shot of Xelayan tequila to calm her nerves.[4] Gordon Malloy uses the Food Synthesizer to produce a glass of whiskey and Xelayan rum for himself and Chief of Security Talla Keyali.[5] It is quickly realized that humans are still flawed beings, and the temptation of food, alcohol and other 'worldly' substances could remain with us, which could lead to abuse of material synthesizers.

Despite the described difficulties, the U.S.S Orville crew appears to mostly have a healthy relationship with food and material goods. However, this ease of access could cultivate eating disorders, alcohol and drug addictions, alongside other mental health issues if used irresponsibly. Desire is often unescapable as writer C.S Lewis stated "Creatures are not born with desires unless satisfaction for those desires exists. A baby feels hunger: well, there is such a thing as food" (Ellis, 2013, p. 1). To the Orville team's merits, they rarely exploit the powers of material synthesis. The rooms are very minimal with Ed's office only having some small personal belongings including a Kermit doll and a model plane. The crew partakes in occasional shopping trips such as when Chief Engineer John LaMarr created a stylish jacket for Helmsman Gordon Malloy.[6] Nonetheless, with unlimited access to material goods and worldly delights comes the potential of a world of hedonism. One could argue that hedonism has always existed for the ruling classes and wealthy elite overtly and aggressively (Probst, 2010). As the middle classes are rising and the affordability of goods increasing, more people are developing hedonistic behavior (ibid.). Despite the characters on *The Orville* choosing to live simplistically with minimalist rooms and the occasional outfit splurges, the potential of a world filled with over-indulgence and material delights could occur, along with profound consequences.

The viewers are introduced to this established world where material synthesizers are fully integrated into society. No less common than a mobile phone today. While the history and development of material synthesis is not clearly explained in the show, there might have been a transitional period before *Orville*-Universe achieved their current relationship with matter synthesis. In another Sci-Fi series George Smith's *Venus Equilateral* (1975) explores the problems with authenticity and intellectual property with printing technology. The plot featured stories of 3D printed money and personal items such as priceless diamonds being replicated (Smith, 1975). In contrast, most Sci-Fi series do not examine the socio-economic impacts or potential collapses of the supply-and-demand chain due to narrative flow. *Venus Equilateral* highlights the potential exploitation of matter duplicators in terms of the potential reduction in the value of current goods and services. It is just as easy to produce the queen's crown jewels as it would be a ham and cheese sandwich which poses puzzling questions for axiology theorists.

With the unlimited potential of matter synthesizers and the complex psychology and emotional states of humans, it could lead to disasters. Drawing upon a real-world example in May 2013, a video was released of a man firing a single shot from a gun. This went viral because this gun was fully produced in a 3D printer (Van Vugt, 2015). The digital designs of the gun were released online and downloaded over 100,000 times before the authorities shut it down (ibid.). With the rise of 3D printer technology, it can lead to mass exploitation and potentially manufacture deadly weapons outside of regulated industrial channels (Biggs, 2011). Idealistically, the hope is that people would be able to have better judgment than to exploit material synthesis. However as shown in the series, two adolescents; James Duncan and Marcus Finn hacked into a Food Synthesizer to create a bottle of vodka.[7] Not all people have the ethical standards and morality to be responsible for their behavior. As Fioridi outlined, moral responsibility is highly subjective, and the allocation of responsibility can be dependent upon numerous factors of distributed moral actions. He further argues that it is very difficult to separate autonomous actions from larger systematic structures for accountability and very few can understand the network of inter-related factors and what their individual impact is (Fioridi, 2016). To elaborate, corporate negligence is a prime example of the difficulties entailed in taking accountability for autonomous acts within the larger systemic systems. and not use material synthesis for self-destructive or harmful practices (Soares, 2003). Even within *The Orville,* when the boys hack the device, it is a clear example of how easily someone could exploit it. When Commander Grayson synthesizes hash brownies in the shuttle and eats it when she is trapped in the zoo, it exemplifies that although humans have come so far with their relationship with matter synthesis, there is still room for poor moral judgement, and that can be deadly. As easy as it was for any of these characters to order drugs, alcohol, cigarettes, or a slice of cake they could have just as easily created poisons, harmful substances or an assault rifle without proper governance and restrictions in place. German philosopher Martin Heidegger stressed that humanity is not in charge of technology, but that technology shapes humanity through forming our world view (Heidegger, 1977; Keikhosrokiani & Asl, 2022; Seubold, 1986). When applying this philosophy to the show, the essence of technology is to frame the world and to make it quantifiable, rationalized and destructively instrumental. The material synthesizer co-existed with humans, but with temperamentality and the impaired judgement of humans, material synthesis can become an agent of chaos.

More than any other device the material synthesizers helped form the foundation of the show. The social reality of the series was able to develop major plot points, because of the ease and accessibility of goods. Seth MacFarlane supported this idea when he stated in an interview that:

"With a show like this, there are certain concessions you have to make. I don't entirely agree with that. I think the replicator was one of the greatest inventions because the replicator, more than any other device, allowed the philosophy of that show to exist. How is there no money? Of course, you wouldn't need any money because you have f—king replicators." [8]

These objects helped negate situations where story points could be written around limitations of what a crew could have brought along to the final frontier. In late 2419, Klyden orders a bowl of ice cream from his quarters' Food Synthesizer to remedy his depression.[9] Just the concept of finding a meal has been the core focus of several cinema plots including 2004 comedy *Harold & Kumar Go to White Castle* and *How I Met Your Mother's* episode where Ted and Marshall try for years to find Gazzola's Pizza.[10] In a material synthesized world, this device has a potentially positive impact on freedom. Drawing briefly on Marxism, in class— exploitative societies:

"Personal freedom has existed only for the individuals who developed under the conditions of the ruling class;" but under the "real community" of communism, "individuals obtain their freedom in and through their association". [11]

Instead of opportunities for individual development being obtained they are exerted at the expense of others. Marx further argues that in the future of these non-class-based societies "community" will provide "each individual [with] the means of cultivating his gifts in all directions; hence personal freedom becomes possible".[12] Similarly in the show, the plot does not linger too long on the material needs of the characters but allows the shows story lines to focus on more philosophically challenging concepts such as personal fulfillment, belonging, and even Artificial Intelligence love (Innes, 2021). In short, material synthesis provides individuals with one of the most desired tools, a device that allows more freedom to focus on their development as an individual and gives them unrestricted scope to explore their passions and talents.

As examined, material synthesis as a speculative technology can be applied to wider applications in science fiction and we can see how this technology fits into several aspects of the genre. One key element of this analysis thus far has been the human element of the application of this tool. Harvey (2020) iterates how humans repeatedly throughout history have had insatiable desires. Everything is simply not enough. Our current domination and envelopment of consumer culture and industrialized capitalism has led to our "commodity canopy" (Harvey, 2020). While contemporary humans and humans in *The Orville* appear to have a lack of control around this device, could other species thrive with it? Noticeably in the show's canon, there is discussion of how Bortus; a Moclan Second Officer and Lieutenant Commander also fell victim to the powers of unprecedented abundance with his cigarette addiction. Similarly, Alara Kitan, a Xelayan Lieutenant and former Chief of Security aboard the USS Orville also was shown several times with an alcohol addiction (Season 1, Episode 2).

In accordance, the *Star Trek* cinematic universe featured particle synthesizerrs and their crew had a dissimilar experience. Within *Star Trek* this plot device was limited in its application and made appearances briefly such as in *Star Trek: Enterprise*. Particle synthesis was small scale with a "protein sequencer" that could only replicate certain foods for chefs on board. Additionally, that ship had a "biomatter sequencer" to recycle waste products into usable material (Star Trek: Enterprise: "Breaking the Ice", 2001). While not all creatures would have the same responses to material synthesis such as AI's or species without pleasure sensors, what this key point solidifies is that humans are not exclusively the only species to be prone to abusing material synthesis technology. Perhaps, with government moderation or regulations limiting our advancements we could maximize the benefits of material synthesis. Hollow (2013) explored how we could potentially incorporate mass 3D printing technology into a wider socio-economic framework through these pratical restrictions. He reaffirmed that it would require mass revision and measures put in place as there is a long way to go to fit material synthesis into our economic models. Primarily because as they are based on this postulated mode of production, there are still potential aid and cultural transformations that could unfold because of the emergence of mass replicating technology (Hollow, 2013).

Material synthesis can be a problematic device across the galaxy. In *The Dark Forest* a science fiction novel written by Liu Cixin, the characters struggle with an impending war for Earth's resources with the Trisolaris species. Liu iterates that there is life in every part of the universe and by each civilization's exponential growth and limited resources, the incentive is very high for each galactic nation to preemptively destroy others to carry their one forward (Liu, 2008). The Fermi Paradox expands upon this notion and states that the roadblock from doing this is the lack of knowledge of other civilizations locations (Landis, 1998). Limited resources at any scale is stopping civilizations from growing. It is evident within *The Orville* with theKaylons (AI species) and the Krill (alien species) both competing with the Union for domination of the galaxy. Material synthesis at a small scale can create food, tools and medical aid to keep civilizations going. At a large scale, material synthesis could render spaceships, new bodies, and even mass weaponary technology. Only the potential user decides on how to utilize synthesis technology and the potential impacts of material synthesis both in the show and in our world is immensely dangerous.

CONCLUSION

The material synthesizer, although a minute aspect of the show, has proven to have a substantial impact both on the crew, and provides a depth of insight into the real world implications. Although a device such as this could be used simply for ordering a vegetable wrap or chicken nuggets, it comes down to analyzing how the user intends to use it. There is hope that a society with this power and unrestricted freedom from capitalism restraints can live peacefully with material synthesis. The aim is for people to use time, space, and access to resources for personal development, and yet so often it is not the case. Both those in the show, and real-world similar cases illustrate how people are not always rational and could utilize such a device to cater to their desires. Whether it be a weed-infused chocolate cake, copious pints of alcohol, or a weapon. Furthermore, limited materials are some of the only restricting factors for space exploration and with material synthesis this could be highly impactful on the progression of a civilization. If a device such comes into being, there would have to be further research and precautionary measures put into place to prevent exploitation and corruption or else pandemonium could ensue. What myself and many other fans of the show enjoyed about the material synthesizer was the countless remarkable things it could create, and that is what it remains, a device of unlimited possibilities and unlimited outcomes.

REFERENCES

Bell, J. (2005, February 23). *Transporters, replicators and phasing FAQ*. Star Trek. https://www.calor-men.com/Star_Trek/FAQs/transport-faq.htm

Biggs, J. (2011, September 21). *Is printing a gun the same as buying a gun?* Tech Crunch. https://techcrunch.com/2011/09/20/is-printing-a-gun-the-same-as-buying-a-gun/

Ellis, F. (2013). Insatiable Desire. *Philosophy (London, England)*, *88*(02), 243–265. doi:10.1017/S0031819113000041

Fabre, C. (2016). 1. Ideological Tropes of Contemporary Addiction Narratives. In *Challenging Addiction in Canadian Literature and Classrooms* (pp. 25–49). University of Toronto Press. doi:10.3138/9781442624443-004

Floridi, L. (2016). Faultless responsibility: On the nature and allocation of moral responsibility for distributed moral actions. *Philosophical Transactions - Royal Society. Mathematical, Physical, and Engineering Sciences*, *374*(2083), 20160112. doi:10.1098/rsta.2016.0112 PMID:28336791

García-Ortega, R. H., García-Sánchez, P., & Merelo-Guervós, J. J. (2020). StarTroper, a film trope rating optimizer using machine learning and evolutionary algorithms. *Expert Systems: International Journal of Knowledge Engineering and Neural Networks*, *6*(37), 1–15. doi:10.1111/exsy.12525

Harvey, C. (2020). *Insatiable: Why everything is not enough*. Philosophy in the Contemporary.

Heidegger, M. (1977). *The question concerning technology and other essays* (W. Lovitt, Trans.). Garland Publishing. (Original work published 1954)

Hollow, M. (2013). *Confronting a new era of duplication? 3D printing, replicating technology and the search for authenticity in George O. Smith's Venus Equilateral Series*. SSRN Electronic Journal. doi:10.2139srn.2333496

Hudson, A. (2014, June 24). *Nestle plans to create a 'Star Trek-like food replicator'*. BBC News. https://www.bbc.co.uk/news/newsbeat-27996163

Imperial College London. (2014, May 18). *Scientists discover how to turn light into matter after 80 years quest*. Phys.org. https://phys.org/news/2014-05-scientists-year-quest.html

Innes, C. M. (2021). Thinking about bad taste in a funny way. In D. K. Johnson & M. R. Berry (Eds.), *Exploring the Orville: Essays on Seth MacFarlane's space adventure* (p. 245). McFarland & Company.

Keikhosrokiani, P., & Asl, M. P. (Eds.). (2022). *Handbook of research on opinion mining and text analytics on literary works and social media*. IGI Global., doi:10.4018/978-1-7998-9594-7

Kosovski, J. R., & Douglas, C. S. (2011). Everybody hurts: Addiction, drama, and the family in the reality television show Intervention. *Substance Use & Misuse*, *7*(46), 852–858. doi:10.3109/10826084.2011.570610 PMID:21599500

Landis, G. A. (1998). The Fermi paradox: An approach based on percolation theory. *JBIS. Journal of the British Interplanetary Society*, *5*(51), 163–166.

Lissauer, G. (2014). *The Tropes of Fantasy Fiction*. McFarland.

Liu, C. (2015). *The Dark Forest* (K. Liu & J. Martinsen, Trans.). Tor Books. (Original work published 2008)

Marx, K. (1967). Capital, Vols. I—III. International Publishers.

Marx, K. (1967). *Value, Price, and Profit*. International Publishers.

Pascale, A. (2017, September 4). *Interview: Seth MacFarlane talks mission of 'The Orville' and defends Star Trek: TNG's replicators*. TrekMovie.com. https://trekmovie.com/2017/09/04/interview-seth-macfarlane-talks-mission-of-the-orville-and-defends-star-trek-tngs-replicators/

Pike, O. J., Mackenroth, F., Hill, E. G., & Rose, S. J. (2014). A photon–photon collider in a vacuum hohlraum. *Nature Photonics*, *8*(6), 434–436. doi:10.1038/nphoton.2014.95

Probst, E. (2010). *Exploring hedonistic consumption from an identity perspective: an interpretative study*. [Doctoral dissertation, Nottingham Trent University]. IRep. https://irep.ntu.ac.uk/id/eprint/207

Rutland, M. (2016, August 10). *NASA's 3D food printer will make pizza at amusement parks*. Vice. https://www.vice.com/en/article/aekjnb/nasas-3dfood-printer-will-make-pizza-at-amusement-parks

Ryan, M. L. (2009). Cheap plot tricks, plot holes, and narrative design. *Narrative, 1*(17), 56–75.

Seubold, G. (1986). *Heideggers Analyse der neuzeitlichen Technik*. Alber.

Smith, G. O. (1975). *Venus Equilateral: Volume One*. Futura Publications Ltd.

Soares, C. (2003). Corporate versus individual moral responsibility. *Journal of Business Ethics, 2*(46), 143–150. doi:10.1023/A:1025061632660

Tu, C., & Brown, S. (2020). Character mediation of plot structure: Toward an embodied model of narrative. *Frontiers of Narrative Studies, 6*(1), 77–112. doi:10.1515/fns-2020-0007

Van Vugt, G. (2016). The killer idea: How some gunslinging anarchists held freedom of speech at Gunpoint. In B. V. D. Berg, S. V. D. Hof & E. Kosta. (Eds.), 3D Printing: Information Technology and Law Series (pp. 117-134). Asser Press. doi: 1 doi:0.1007/978-94-6265-096-1_7

ENDNOTES

[1] New Dimensions

[2] This could be a recurring character trait tied to his ego and budding megalomania, but this episode exemplified compressed vice at the time of first airing.

[3] Some portrayals of compressed vice have plots that may suggest characters have always had or been prone to this problem, even though previous episodes show otherwise. Especially when it comes to substance addiction such as cigarettes, alcohol, or other vices these are developed over a long period of time and are often not convincing due to the one-episode explanation and portrayal.

[4] Episode 1x02: Command Performance

[5] Episode 1x02: Command Performance, Episode 2x10: Blood of Patriots

[6] Episode 2x01: Ja'loja

[7] Episode 2x01: Ja'loja

[8] https://trekmovie.com/2017/09/04/interview-seth-macfarlane-talks-mission-of-the-orville-and-defends-star-trek-tngs-replicators/

[9] Episode 1x04: If the Stars Should Appear

[10] Episodes 5x05 and 9x05

[11] Page 87

[12] Page 86

Section 3
Artificial Intelligence for the Analytics of Social Media

Chapter 8
Social Media Intelligence:
AI Applications for Criminal Investigation and National Security

Szde Yu
Wichita State University, USA

ABSTRACT

This chapter aims at discussing how social media intelligence (SOCMINT) can be and has been applied to the field of criminal justice. SOCMINT is composed of a set of computer forensic techniques used for intelligence gathering on social media platforms. Through this chapter, readers will be able to better understand what SOCMINT is and how it may be helpful for criminal investigation and national security. Different aspects of SOCMINT are addressed, including application in criminal justice, intelligence gathering, monitoring, metadata, cyber profiling, social network analysis, tools, and privacy concerns. Further, the challenges and future research directions are discussed as well. This chapter is not meant to serve as a technical tutorial as the focus is on the concepts rather than the techniques.

INTRODUCTION

Traditionally, common forms of intelligence include imagery intelligence (IMINT), signals intelligence (SIGINT), and human intelligence (HUMINT). These forms of intelligence rely on collection of imagery (e.g. satellite images), interception of signals, or interpersonal contact. There are also measurement and signature intelligence (MASINT) and financial intelligence gathered from the analysis of monetary transactions (FININT), among others. In modern days, the intelligence community started to value social media as an important and reliable source of intelligence because of so much human activity on these platforms that generates abundant information in every second and so much interrelation between people's everyday life and their online presence. Therefore, social media intelligence (SOCMINT) has been gradually accepted as a form of intelligence during the past decade (Omand, et al., 2012).

SOCMINT typically involves two types of sources, open source (i.e., public information) and private data that requires privileged access (Dover, 2020; Lombardi et al., 2015). In terms of purposes,

DOI: 10.4018/978-1-6684-6242-3.ch008

SOCMINT can be intended for data collection (i.e., after the fact) or monitoring (i.e., as it happens). As for analysis, it may focus on data points, including user-generated content and metadata, but it may also focus on cyber profiling in an attempt to extract implicit information that is not directly revealed in the data collected. SOCMINT can also be aimed at performing one or more subjects' social network analysis in order to uncover any connections among several subjects of interest or the connections among seemingly unrelated events. All these SOCMINT applications can conceivably play a helpful role in criminal investigation and national security, two of the most important domains in the field of criminal justice. This chapter introduces and explains how SOCMINT has been and can be utilized in the field of criminal justice. However, as helpful as it may be, SOCMINT is not without controversy. In particular, privacy issues have been the center of scrutiny both in social media and in criminal justice. Accordingly, this chapter discusses such issues from different perspectives to offer a comprehensive understanding.

SOCIAL MEDIA INTELLIGENCE (SOCMINT)

Applications in Criminal Justice

Currently SOCMINT is mainly used for detecting potential threats to national security. Most notably, National Security Agency is believed to have partnered with social media companies to access their users' data and allegedly turned some platforms into a surveillance tool (Weber, 2022). It is sometimes also used in criminal investigations as a supplementary method to gather more information about a suspect, a victim, or other persons of interest. Some agencies may spend resources on monitoring groups, such as domestic terrorists or pedophiles that use social media as a platform to exchange resources and recruit new members (Dean & Bell, 2012; Asongu et al., 2019). In addition to the well-known social media platforms, such as Facebook, Twitter, YouTube, and TikTok, the dark web and some online forums that emphasize anonymity are believed to particularly attract criminal-minded people and organizations to look for tools, ideas, associates, and illegal services. Gathering SOCMINT from these sources potentially can reveal a great deal of criminal activities or the sign of future crimes. For example, after the tragic shooting incidents in the Robb Elementary School in Texas, in which 19 children and 2 adults were killed, and in a grocery store in Baffalo, in which 10 people were killed by a 19-year-old, some have called for surveillance on school social media surveillance hoping to spot potential threats from SOCMINT (Levinson-Waldman, 2022).

Other than the usual applications, SOCMINT may also be helpful in locating missing persons and solving cold cases (Jeanis, 2020; Gray & Benning, 2019). Some human trafficking rings are using social media as a hunting ground (Yu, 2015), which leads to victims going missing. A systematic analysis on SOCMINT might shed light on such operations. Some missing persons, including abductees and runaways might face drastic changes in their circumstances as time goes by, and SOCMINT could help reconnect them with their family through a social network analysis (Gray & Benning, 2019). In terms of cold cases, some cases were unsolved due to insufficient information at the time of investigation, but new information could surface after a few years or even decades. In this regard, SOCMINT could help keep track of those who are involved in the case until a better timing arrives, and it could also help keep an eye on any new leads that might be uncovered as better analytic methods are being developed. Of course, there are many ethical, legal, and practical factors to consider in each case, but at least the potential of SOCMINT deserves to be recognized. In the following sections, the most prominent aspects of SOCMINT are discussed while acknowledging there is always a gap between theory and practice.

In USA, the federal government has dedicated units to deal with applying artificial intelligence for criminal justice purposes, which includes the collection of SOCMINT (Rigano, 2019; US Department of Justice, 2020). National Institute of Justice (NIJ) has been partnering with researchers from academia to explore the use of AI in the criminal justice domain, such as facial recognition and predictive profiling in court proceedings (Rigano, 2019). While AI application is not limited to SOCMINT, the use of SOCMINT is certainly being explored as well (US Department of Justice, 2020). The Cybersecurity Unit under the US Department of Justice provides guidance regarding how to legally access online intelligence, including SOCMINT. Normally agents need to use fabricated identities online to access sources, such as forums and social media. Such fake identities should not be illegal representing an actual person without authorization, and the collection of information needs to comply with the law. The specific laws regulating such practices are beyond the scope of this chapter, and the specific operations are unsuitable to be disclosed. Nevertheless, it is important to note that criminal justice agencies typically would seek information from all sources. Social media is only one of them but it is an important one because of its ubiquity and relatively easy access.

Intelligence Gathering

Intuitively, the main purpose of SOCMINT is to gather intelligence from social media. Intelligence requires interpretation of information and it is often predictive in nature because if intelligence is not capable of shedding some light on future events or offering guidance for future action, then it has very little value and therefore is usually not worth the effort of intelligence gathering. Hence, the first step of intelligence gathering is to identify good sources of information. In this regard, social media contains abundant information and serves as a good source. The next step is to determine what information is of interest, since it is unlikely all information on social media is relevant. The purpose of intelligence gathering usually determines what kinds of information are being targeted. Mostly, information about a person of interest (e.g. a suspect, a victim, a witness, an associate, etc.), or an event (e.g. a crime or an incident) is sought after in SOCMINT, and such information typically consists of data that could be generated by users (e.g. comments, posts, memes, likes, photos, messages, etc.) or generated by the system (e.g. metadata). Sometimes, it is the social trend or social climate being looked for in SOCMINT, especially in social research.

If the purpose is criminal investigation on a specific case, the subject (e.g. suspects) of investigation needs to be clearly identified first. Subsequently, information related to the subject is to be collected. In the past, investigators typically would only focus on what they deemed relevant to the case. However, with today's artificial intelligence application, all information related to the subject can be and should be collected to the extent possible, even if it seems irrelevant at first glance. This is because today's computer technology has made it easier to collect a large quantity of data without time-consuming manual work, and AI applications, such as machine learning and other analytic methods, can potentially identify hidden connections that tend to be overlooked by a human eye. Such hidden connections might make what seems irrelevant become relevant or even crucial after all.

If the purpose of intelligence gathering is to prevent attacks in terms of national security, information would be first collected in the sense of general population rather than specific subjects. If there are specific suspects in mind already, then it is essentially a criminal investigation as mentioned above.

Oftentimes, SOCMINT in national security is meant to prevent possible attacks that may or may not have become an actual threat. In this scenario, intelligence gathering aims at all human activities and interactions manifested on social media. All information available is seen as relevant. However, without a specific subject in mind, information can be highly disorganized and inevitably there will be many false positives as well as false negatives. For example, in 2013 after Edward Snowden disclosed the US National Security Agency (NSA) had been spying on US citizens in general (as opposed to targeting any specific citizens) by soliciting user data from various Internet companies, such as Yahoo, Apple, and Facebook, it was reported that NSA was looking for a 51% confidence rating (Kelion, 2013). This means when NSA determined someone as a foreign threat, there could be a 49% chance of being wrong. It appears to be very unreliable, but it is not unusual to see in this type of aggregate intelligence gathering. In contrast, individual-specific intelligence gathering normally would aim at a higher confidence rating as in this type of intelligence gathering more individualized context is usually available to help draw a conclusion. Ideally, aggregate intelligence and individual-specific intelligence gathering should be implemented as a two-step procedure, by which aggregate data generates red flags on certain subjects and a closer interpretation of these subjects' individual data should ensue.

As mentioned, intelligence required interpretation of information (aka. analysis). Artificial intelligence has been widely used in this aspect so as to make any prediction more reliable based on in-depth and accurate interpretation. Machine learning is probably the most popular AI application by far. Machine learning is meant to build computer algorithms that can improve automatically through experience (Jordan & Mitchell, 2015; Keikhosrokiani & Asl, 2022). SOCMINT can benefit from machine learning but what is supposed to be learned needs to be defined. With supervised machine leaning, computers can be trained to predict a pre-defined outcome (y) in response to an input (x). Thus, SOCMINT needs to clearly define what (y) is and what (x) is. For example, (y) can be a terrorist threat while (x) can be a list of risk factors. Although it is easy to understand and implement, there is a high possibility that some other risk factors are overlooked and thus left out of the machine learning process. The idea of using SOCMINT in criminal justice is predicated on the assumption that crime can be a result of many different reasons. If the mindset is still confined to the traditional belief that only so-called criminogenic factors (e.g. anti-social personality, poverty, prior criminal behavior, etc.) are related to crime, then it somewhat defeats the innovation of SOCMINT application in criminal justice. This is not to say criminogenic factors have no merit in predicting criminality. Rather, today's society is much more complicated than what it was when criminology first emerged as an academic discipline. The cause of crime could manifest in very unconventional ways, especially in terms of cybercrimes.

Unsupervised machine learning, on the other hand, involves the analysis of unlabeled data (Jordan & Mitchell, 2015). This method might be better suited for SOCMINT since it could help reduce dimensions and create clusters or categories in a large disorganized dataset, which makes analysis on social media information easier without assuming causal relationships arbitrarily. Simply put, the analysis of SOCMINT should allow data to reveal association by itself instead of forcing computers to confirm a relationship pre-defined by humans, which is known as "tunnel vision" in criminal investigation (Yu, 2020b). This can effectively reduce the chance of false positives and false negatives. Certainly, there are other methods of machine learning. This chapter does not intend to discuss machine learning in detail since other chapters have covered this topic in this book.

Social media provides data in many different formats. Among them, text, photos, and videos are the most common types. While AI can be applied to analyze all these types of data, sometimes they need to be interpreted simply by human intelligence. For example, if a video has recorded a criminal act, then this video alone is sufficient to serve as forensic evidence without the need for AI. That said, AI could still be useful in a case like this as there might be more digital evidence that leads to other crimes committed by the same subject. This could be overlooked if the investigators only focus on this one video. Through AI analysis, such as facial recognition, connections could be found among other videos or other types of data. Further, most social media platforms do not offer a direct way to download photos and videos in bulk, and some platforms also make it hard to download textual data. As such, to collect social media data for analysis manually can be extremely time-consuming. With proper AI algorithms, this task could be performed more efficiently.

In sum, AI application in SOCMINT is useful in both collecting information and transforming information into intelligence. When the purpose is criminal investigation or national security, traditionally investigators would tend to look for crime-related information and does not usually feel there is a need to seek help from AI application. Nonetheless, this mentality can be inadequate even though it is not necessarily wrong. Crime does not occur in a different universe that is isolated from non-criminal activities. It is one aspect of our daily life, closely connected to other aspects. SOCMINT allows investigators to understand more aspects of a suspect's life and see how crime can be associated with or even caused by non-criminal activities. The diversity and volume of social media data can be overwhelming but utilizing AI methods can make intelligence gathering more practicable, given the limited human resources faced in most criminal justice agencies.

Monitoring

As mentioned in the previous section, one of main purposes of SOCMINT is intelligence gathering. To gather useful intelligence, very often SOCMINT requires monitoring a certain platform or a user over a period of time. Thus, data is being collected in real time as behaviors or events are taking place. SOCMINT monitoring can be done either covertly or overtly. When it is done overtly, it is usually considered a form of open source intelligence (OSINT). OSINT is different from other intelligence sources in that open source information is available to the public without the need to infringe on copyrights, patents, or privacy laws (Hribar et al., 2014; Glassman & Kang, 2012). As so many people are openly sharing personal information on social media, SOCMINT has become a dominant variant of OSINT. The data of interest in SOCMINT monitoring usually involves published content, messages, images, comments, videos, and interactions among users or groups. Moreover, social media identities and their associated data are also the focal concern in terms of monitoring because it is not always easy to determine who is behind a social media identity as one user could own multiple accounts and one account could be accessed by more than one user. Other than monitoring an entire social media platform (which usually results in aggregate data), monitoring can be done in an individual-specific manner or it can be event-specific. The main difference is that in individual-specific monitoring, it starts with a subject and every activity and every individual associated with this subject is subsequently monitored, whereas in event-specific monitoring, it starts by defining the perimeters of an event and then the monitoring expands to cover every individual related to this event.

Conceivably, in the criminal justice field, the subject of monitoring is very likely to be a criminal or a crime. Since crime is essentially a private matter, the investigators cannot always count on open source information. Even if there is open source information available, criminal investigations typically still need to dig deeper into more private information to collect more evidence. In this case, covert SOCMINT monitoring is needed. Covert monitoring inevitably has to invade privacy to some extent, ideally with legal justification. It might involve hacking into a user's social media account to access data or installing spyware to keep track of the user's activity and interaction on a platform or even across platforms. Actually, covert monitoring has been conducted by almost every Internet company. These companies, such as Google, Facebook, and Amazon are adept at using AI algorithms to keep track of their users' online activities in order to understand every user's shopping interests and other inclinations, which in turn helps them create customized advertising. Therefore, after you search for something on a search engine, in a few hours you probably will start to see some products related to your search being advertised to you on your social media page or you might start receiving emails from online shopping sites promoting similar items. While companies engage in this practice for commercial reasons for the most part, law enforcement or national security agencies could also use similar AI technologies to collect information and turn such information into useable intelligence. In fact, it has been revealed that NSA had or still has partnership with many Internet companies to gain access to their user data (Greenwald & MacAskill, 2013; Greenwald et al., 2013; Rosenbach et al., 2013). Ethical issues aside, this at least proves how valuable SOCMINT is in the eye of government agencies and corporations alike.

Metadata Analysis

While data collection is important, intelligence requires effective analysis of data. Data collected from social media can be in many forms. In this section, the focus is on metadata, such as personal identifiable data (PID), geo-location information, time stamps, and so on. As mentioned in the previous section, social media identities and their associated information are part of intelligence gathering. Metadata is one crucial component in the information associated with social media identities. This is especially true in criminal investigation and national security. Criminal investigation mostly aims at acquiring forensic evidence that can prove one specific person is responsible for a criminal act. Therefore, it is particularly important to link SOCMINT to the correct person by accurately identifying this person's social media identity. Without accurate identification, SOCMINT lacks forensic value. Simply put, you cannot convict a social media account no matter what crime this account is associated with unless you can prove who is responsible for this account's activity. In this regard, metadata is more reliable since user-generated data could be modified or manipulated by the user while metadata is less likely to be altered willingly. Metadata basically is data that offers information about other data. Most of it is generated and documented by the platform system, which most users do not have authorization to access. Investigators should look for metadata not only on social media platforms, but also on the artifacts found on social media, such as photos and documents, because when these files are created on an electronic device there is metadata attached to them as well. This by no means suggests metadata is always trustworthy. Some software can erase metadata on a file and some counter-forensic methods could render metadata misleading, such as using VPN to disguise IP addresses. However, metadata still plays an integral role in every digital forensic investigation (Buchholz & Spafford, 2004; Alanazi & Jones, 2015). In every criminal investigation, it is always important to confirm timeline and location before legal liability can be assigned, and in terms of computer forensics this mostly relies on metadata to establish.

A thorough analysis of metadata usually can help investigators answer questions regarding "where", "what", and "when", which in turn might reveal "who" as well. Metadata analysis also can help link identities cross-platforms, which oftentimes is very helpful in consolidating SOCMINT from various platforms related to one particular subject under investigation. More and more social media platforms and websites now allow users to log in with the same credentials. For example, you can sign in Twitter with a Google account or Apple account. This provides users convenience and it also makes SOCMINT easier to be linked across multiple platforms. Metadata may also be used to establish proof of collaboration among a group of people (Alanazi & Jones, 2015), which can reveal a suspect's social network. Why is the revelation of one's social network important in criminal investigation? It is discussed in the following section.

Social Network Analysis

Although most people probably think of social media when it comes to social networking, social network analysis actually has been adopted in social sciences for a long time, long before social networking websites were invented (Wasserman & Faust, 2019; Scott, 1988). Nonetheless, the emergence of social media has indeed made social network analysis easier to perform with more public data available and documented online, and computer software has been developed to aid in social network data collection and analysis, such as UCINET (Knoke & Yang, 2019). In more recent years, law enforcement has started to utilize social network analysis as part of crime analysis (Johnson & Reitzel, 2011; Bailey et al., 2020; Fox et al., 2021).

In criminal investigation, one important component is to outline a subject's social network. The most common subject of social network analysis is a suspect or a victim. Since crime is a social event committed by humans, a good understanding on the interpersonal relationships among those who are involved in such an event can help clarify motive, opportunity, and criminal association (Yu, 2020b). What is being looked for in a social network analysis typically include network members (e.g. numbers and backgrounds), connectedness within networks, outreach to other networks, reciprocity (e.g. information flow directions), clusters within networks (e.g. sub-groups), degree of centralization or decentralization, sustainability (e.g. member attrition), common interests, and so on. For instance, when the police try to turn criminals into an informant, a full understanding on their social networks provides confidence in what information they are most likely to have access to and what can be used as leverage to ensure cooperation.

A thorough social network analysis may also lead to key witnesses and forensic evidence (Yu, 2020b).

The role SOCMINT plays in social network analysis should be quite intuitive. Data from SOCMINT, such as photos, videos, text messages, and other forms of online interaction can reveal who-knows-who rather obviously. The more active a person is on social media, the more likely he or she will either intentionally or subconsciously reveal social connections. Moreover, A deeper analysis may reveal secondary association as well. For example, two spy operatives may not necessarily have direct interaction but they could be working for the same organization, thereby forming indirect association in their respective social network. In counter-terrorism investigations or organized crime investigations, these covert overlaps among social networks are often of great significance. While most social network analysis software relies on quantitative metrics to draw conclusions, social network analysis can also be conducted qualitatively. In fact, SOCMINT data might require some qualitative review to be reliable. For instance, photos and videos shared on social media probably are still better suited for qualitative analysis to identify appearances, even with facial recognition technologies. At least for now, qualitative analysis is still more reliable in interpreting the nature of interaction between two persons in a video, for example. Qualitative analysis is traditionally considered more time-consuming and arbitrary. However, in the future artificial intelligence might offer a solution to shorten the time needed for qualitative analysis and add more objectivity to the interpretation.

Cyber Profiling

Intelligence requires analysis because not all data being collected is organized and informative in a way to readily provide conclusions or answers. Common methods for SOCMINT analysis include text analytics and visual analytics, considering text, images, and videos are the most popular forms of data found on social media. Text analytics may look for text sentiment, writing patterns, time sensitivity, event detection, semantic knowledge, text classification, theme extraction, text visualization, and social tagging (Anandarajan et al., 2019; Hu & Liu, 2012). Visual analytics may involve facial recognition, action/event detection, audio processing, image enhancement, movement tracking, authentication, device determination, scene measurement, and so on. These methods essentially are aimed at content analysis as they mainly analyze the information being presented. With adequate analysis, the content of social media artifacts combined with metadata analysis can provide good intelligence already. Nevertheless, content analysis can only tell you what the content presents, but intelligence is not always visible in the information being presented. It could be latent or implied in a subtle manner, in which case content analysis alone is not sufficient and profiling becomes another crucial method to effectively extract intelligence. In other words, content analysis reads the lines and tell you what is being said, whereas profiling is meant to read between the lines and predict what is not being said.

As mentioned above, intelligence essentially is predictive in nature. It is supposed to help predict something that is unknown based on the known information at hand. Using the known to predict the unknown is the basis of profiling (Yu, 2020b). Profiling is widely utilized for commercial purposes, as merchants and advertisers strive to predict where potential buyers are and what products are most appealing to these buyers. Profiling is also commonly adopted by dating services to predict a good match. Even though the actual method can be somewhat different (e.g. deductive v. inductive), the underlying rationale is the same, that is, they are using what they know about you to predict what might interest you, which they do not really know (i.e., the unknown). With AI, such practices have become more prevalent online, because AI makes collecting data (i.e., the known) more efficient, which theoretically should improve the accuracy rate in predicting the unknown. AI also makes prediction more objectively methodical rather than rely on human profilers' subjective opinions, although being more objective does not necessarily mean it will be more accurate. It depends on the quality of the AI algorithms.

In criminal justice, profiling is also used to help with criminal investigation. Despite the notoriety associated with racial profiling, in which race is the only or predominant factor in prediction, criminal profiling is often glorified in fictions and TV dramas, in part thanks to the fame of Sherlock Holmes and some successful TV shows, such as Criminal Minds. Moreover, there have been some famous real-life profilers, such as John Douglas and Robert Ressler to inspire more and more people to be interested in profiling. One may even find a job in US federal agencies, such as the FBI and ATF to work as a criminal profiler (ATF, 2022). While criminal profiling is by no means a new investigative technique, relying on SOCMINT to perform profiling is relatively new in the criminal justice field (Rogers, 2003; Yu, 2020a). When profiling is based on electronic data only, it is called cyber profiling (Yu, 2021). Cyber profiling is not necessarily about criminal investigation since it can also be used for other purposes such as online advertising, whereas electronic data does not have to be SOCMINT since data can be collected from sources other than social media. Nonetheless, SOCMINT-based cyber profiling in criminal justice is a promising field of study. Social network analysis, discussed in the previous section, is basically a form of cyber profiling.

The idea of SOCMINT-based cyber profiling is not hard to understand. The challenge is how to perform it methodically so that it can be deemed reliable. So far, criminal profiling is still mostly performed by human profilers. It is seen as an educated guess at best, as criminal profiling has never really gained much scientific support for its reliability and validity (Snook et al., 2007; Muller, 2000). However, the incorporation of SOCMINT and AI in profiling might change that. Companies, like Facebook and Google, have been using machine learning and other AI methods to perform cyber profiling for years. The fact that they have gained massive profit from doing so as their main revenue stream seems to attest to the success of this practice. However, there is one crucial difference between what they do and what criminal justice agencies need. Internet commerce and online advertising can afford to be less accurate in the sense that the consequences of their being wrong in prediction does not generally result in too much harm. On the other hand, when criminal justice agencies want to charge someone with a crime, they need to be much more certain about their prediction, because a wrongful accusation or even a wrongful conviction can practically ruin an innocent person's life. Agencies also do not want to spend their limited resources on intelligence that has a very high chance of being wrong.

Research is still largely lacking in terms of how reliable cyber profiling is, but some evidence has shown promise. A study has proven that using OSINT data collected form Facebook, it is possible to correctly predict a person's personality with regard to self-control (Yu, 2013), and another study has shown that using machine learning can help predict an author's gender with accuracy rates up to 100% while analyzing only the author's electronic discourse (Yu, 2020a). All in all, preliminary evidence seems to suggest performing cyber profiling on SOCMINT can reveal more than the explicit information displayed on social media as it also predicts implicit information with good confidence, and applying AI to the analysis may further improve accuracy.

To perform cyber profiling, first the subject of profiling needs to be determined. The subject's online identity then needs to be identified. There could be multiple online identities associated with one subject and these identities may not always come from social media. For example, online banking requires online identities, but banks are not considered social media. However, if the profiler is able to link the same person's identities on social media to the identities used for other online services, it will greatly expand the availability of data for analysis. The data sought after in cyber profiling is usually in the form of digital footprints. Digital footprints are the data trail left behind in online activities by a user, either intentionally or unknowingly. Cyber profiling collects such data and then converts it into online behavioral evidence (Yu, 2020b). Behavioral evidence is normally the key ingredient in criminal profiling, as the profiler tries to analyze an unknown subject's behavioral patterns in order to identify this subject. In cyber profiling, the subject's real-world identity may or may not be known beforehand. Either way, studying online behavioral evidence helps understand this subject better. It helps connect online identities to real-world identities, and it helps perceive the subject as a person rather than just an ID.

There are three major components to look for in behavioral evidence. First, the content of the behavior is obviously important. An online behavior could be posting a comment, hitting the like button, retweeting a meme, and so on. What is manifested in such a behavior needs attention, which has been discussed in previous sections. Second, the rationale behind such a behavior needs analysis. In addition to the manifest behavior, the underlying rationale is valuable behavioral evidence as well. Everything happens for a reason. Although this old saying might be disputable, it has merit in profiling since the basic assumption of profiling is that a person's intention and psychology can be understood through analyzing their behavior. Therefore, why a person engages in a certain online behavior is important to study in cyber profiling. Third, the dynamics of behavior should be noted. Human behavior is rarely an isolated event. Usually one thing leads to another and there are consequences of everything that has happened. An online behavior may be continuing or repeating after being observed. Hence, the ways, the frequencies, the patterns, and any pattern shifts in online behavior could all be indicative of a subject's mentality, personality, motive, opportunity, and means (including knowledge and skills). They could also suggest changes in the circumstances surrounding the subject.

The effectiveness of cyber profiling is predicated on the quality of online behavioral evidence. SOCMINT offers large amounts of diverse digital footprints for this purpose, and therefore cyber profiling is one of the most suitable methods for SOCMINT analysis. Besides good data, the profiler's skill also determines effectiveness. Cyber profilers may utilize AI to collect digital footprints and AI may assist in analyzing online behavior as well. However, AI is only as good as how it is trained. To train AI or humans alike for the purpose of cyber profiling, there are three aspects to note. First, the context matters. Any behavior needs to be interpreted with the context in mind, because the same behavior in a different context could carry a totally different meaning. Likewise, cyber profiling needs to take into consideration the cyber-context in which the online behavior is observed. For instance, different social media platforms and websites tend to have different restrictions on what a user can or cannot do, such as Twitter has a word count limit and Facebook's background color is always blue. Profiling without context is nothing but a judgmental conjecture. Second, victimology offers perspectives. Victimology assumes there are some factors or characteristics contributed by the victim that could have facilitated or even caused the victimization to occur. This is not to accuse the victim of being responsible for the crime. Rather, from an investigative perspective, the victim and the offender must have had their paths crossed at some point, and for victimization to happen, there must be an opportunity being created by or presented to the offender. Victimology aims at understanding how the victim might have contributed to such an opportunity and in turn it helps narrow down who could have perceived this opportunity. Third, forensics should be minded during the process. Eventually profiling is meant to help convict the offender in court and conviction requires solid forensic evidence. Profiling itself is rarely seen as adequate evidence because it is possible for innocent people to fit a profile perfectly. Hence, cyber profiling needs to be accompanied by computer forensics to the extent possible. In fact, much online behavioral evidence used for profiling is potentially forensic evidence in its own right. Thus, cyber profiling and computer forensics are actually a very good match (Roger, 2003; Colombini & Colella, 2011).

Privacy Concerns

Privacy has always been a controversial issue related to social media (Smith et al., 2012; Ellison et al., 2011). On the one hand, social media users seem to voluntarily upload personal information to the platform, thereby not in a good position to argue their privacy is invaded. On the other hand, the platform administrators seem to often secretly use the data provided by users for undisclosed purposes without explicit consent. For example, some platforms allegedly could be selling user information to a third party for profit, or they could be conducting experiments on users without acknowledging it, or they could be trying to promote certain political views by brainwashing users with filtered news information. While some allegations are unconfirmed yet, what is certain is that almost all social media platforms are tracking their users' activities and compiling so-called big data (Mantelero & Vaciago, 2015; Jain et al., 2016). Such big data is then fed to AI algorithms for analysis, which is expected to help companies make commercial decisions and enact business strategies. Even if users generally have to agree to it when they sign up for the platform, users do not usually know what their information is actually used for, whom their information is shared with, and whether these social media companies are capable of protecting user data from cyberattacks. To say the least, there are legitimate reasons to be concerned about privacy on social media. The willingness to participating in social networking online does not mean one has to give up all expectation of privacy.

From the perspective of SOCMINT, it is inconvenient if all data on social media is kept private. The idea of SOCMINT is based on the assumption that there is much public information to be gathered on social media. From the perspective of criminal investigation, privacy invasion to some degree is almost inevitable since crime is a private matter for the most part. Although some criminals do indeed show off their criminal involvement on social media publicly (Christie, 2015), most criminals tend to hide it. It is often imperative for criminal investigators to invade the suspect's privacy before being able to find sufficient evidence. At times, it might even be necessary to invade a victim's privacy in order to gain useful clues. As a result, privacy issues also have always been the center of dispute in the criminal justice field. Concepts, like search warrants, the poisonous tree doctrine, the good faith exception, and the exclusionary rule are all a response to privacy-related controversies. In the era of information technology, it remains arguable regarding how far law enforcement can go to collect cell phone data from civilians without a warrant (Gershowitz, 2015; Daniel, 2017). Likewise, how much private information on social media investigators can access in the name of criminal investigation or national security is also disputable, especially when these people are not officially a suspect.

The Fourth Amendment to the US Constitution prohibits unreasonable searches and seizures. However, what is considered unreasonable is very open to interpretation as even high courts in USA did not always have a consensus in their rulings. SOCMINT is a relatively new area for criminal justice, so it remains to be seen how the application of SOCMINT might lead to legal disputes in the future. It is also not yet clear how much evidence derived from SOCMINT will be admissible in court. For example, on April 12, 2022, Frank Robert James fired a handgun 33 times and threw smoke grenades on the New York City Subway, resulting in 29 people injured (Lim, 2022). During the investigation, it was easy to find lots of violent content on Frank Robert James' social media accounts as he had been sharing and posting such information that clearly indicates his extreme political views and violent propensity. From hindsight, it seems this man probably could have been monitored if SOCMINT was gathered and analyzed in time. However, before he actually took action, how much could really be done from the legal point of view without violating his constitutional rights? Would the police have been allowed to take a deeper look into this man's privacy based on the violent content on his social media before a crime was committed? Can threats detected by SOCMINT justify search warrants, surveillance, or even an arrest? Laws like the Patriot Act have made the idea of privacy further blurry especially in the name of national security. There will never be a perfect answer to satisfy everyone concerned about this issue. When emphasizing the suspect's rights, it is equally important to consider the potential harm that the suspect's action, if unchecked, could cause; when advocating for the authorities' need to protect the society by any means necessary, it is also imperative to be mindful of the consequences of possible mistakes and abuse of power.

SOCMINT Challenges

Privacy issues aside, the implementation of SOCMINT itself is often faced with a few challenges. For SOCMINT to be comprehensive, the data should be diverse and ideally should be collected from multiple sources. Identifying sources and consolidating data related to the same subject is time consuming enough. Collecting data, such as downloading photos and text messages also requires laborious work.

Furthermore, there is analysis to be performed. If all these procedures are to be carried out manually, it will greatly limit the use of SOCMINT in criminal investigation because of how much time it requires for one case. Although AI-powered software is now available to shorten the time needed, such software is quite expensive. It thus presents a dilemma for criminal justice agencies to choose between time and money. Some agencies end up choosing a third option, that is, they avoid using SOCMINT as part of their investigation.

Further, how to accurately identify ownership of social media accounts is not an easy task. While most social media now require user verification for registration or login through a phone number or email address, it is circumstantial at best to prove who is actually using the social media accounts in question because theoretically a phone number or email address could be borrowed from someone else and it is not illegal to do so. Besides, the phones and email accounts themselves could be registered without authentic owner information to begin with. The possibility that multiple people could have access to one account makes it more complicated as far as legal accountability is concerned. Tracking IP addresses used to be and still are the primary way to associate an online ID with a physical location, but technologies like VPNs are not exactly hard to use if hiding IP addresses is desired. Even if identification is not a problem, an investigation is very likely to encounter jurisdictional issues given the borderless nature of the Internet. Jurisdictional issues are usually accompanied by different privacy-related rules and legislations, which can present many hurdles for investigators to overcome before they can legally gather information from social media.

The above-mentioned challenges should be of no surprise to experienced criminal investigators because they face similar problems in most investigations with or without SOCMINT. Nevertheless, even seasoned investigators sometimes overlook some other factors that could affect the reliability of SOCMINT. As discussed in cyber profiling, online behavior needs to be interpreted with the cyber-context in mind, because some cyber-context restricts or alters the true intent of the user. For example, more and more social media platforms are imposing censorship of some sort to regulate user-generated content on account of either legal or political concerns. This means when data are collected from social media, they could be missing some crucial pieces that have been removed against the creator's initial intent. Conceivably, content forcibly removed or forbidden by a social media platform is likely to be controversial in nature, but such controversial content might have been the best indicator of a person's propensity and personality. In other words, what the investigator would have seen could be the most valuable from the perspective of cyber profiling, but the investigator is unable to see it because of censorship, which can be misleading in the analysis of SOCMINT. In addition, the rapid evolvement of Internet cultures and languages could perplex investigators if they fail to catch up. To be fair, it can be hard to catch up with all the new phrases and acronyms being used on social media.

Besides, SOCMINT could be gathered from aggregate data, and applying conclusions drawn from aggregate patterns to a particular individual might be inappropriate. This has something to do with the difference between inductive profiling and deductive profiling. Inductive profiling tends to rely on aggregate data to look for generalizable patterns. For instance, after studying serial arsonists caught in the past, the FBI concluded 95% of serial arsonists are male. Therefore, next time in another serial arson case, profilers tend to predict the offender is a male since historical statistics suggest such likelihood (Yu, 2020b). In contrast, deductive profiling focuses on behavioral evidence manifested in one specific case and deduces conclusions from facts in this one case, which avoids generalizations and stereotypes. Normally aggregate data is easier to obtain considering all the statistics available, and inductive analysis certainly has merit especially in the absence of enough deductive data. Despite this, mistakes are likely if investigators blindly apply generalizations to every case without considering the idiosyncrasy in each case and every person.

In sum, the major challenges regarding incorporating SOCMINT into criminal investigation mainly involve time, money, and precision. It takes time to gather ample data that are suitable for analysis, and the analysis of such data itself requires time. Money can help reduce time spent, but funding has always been an issue for most criminal justice agencies and SOCMINT might not be seen as a priority in the allocation of limited resources. Current methods for data collection and analytics are mostly developed with commercial purposes in mind and therefore tend to focus on aggregate trends and patterns derived from big data, whereas criminal investigation calls for a more micro focus on specific individuals.

SOCMINT Tools

Some online tools are available for gathering SOCMINT as OSINT. Google has always been a good start when looking for information online, but it fails to search data on the dark web. In this regard, some other search engines can be more useful, such as (https://intelx.io/). Websites like (https://lookup-id.com/) can help look up Facebook IDs or search for various artifacts (https://sowsearch.info/), and (https://www.whoxy.com/) offers WHOIS lookup. There are also websites that search public records on personal information, such as (https://www.truepeoplesearch.com/). Webpage archives can also become helpful when some people intend to alter their previous digital footprints (https://archive.org/). Other web tools include EXIF information examination, which is good for analyzing the metadata associated with digital photos, and company data search (https://opencorporates.com/). Image reverse searches are also handy in some cases. Some tools are dedicated to a specific platform. For example, to collect data from Twitter, there are quite a few websites to consider, such as (https://tweetbeaver.com/), (https://developer.twitter.com/en/docs/twitter-api/v1/rules-and-filtering/search-operators), (https://spoonbill.io/), and (https://www.trendsmap.com/).

These free tools and services may require more manual searches or require more advanced coding skills to conduct automated searches and collections. To save time and hassles, corporate software products are available, such as (https://www.page-vault.com/), (https://www.spiderfoot.net/), (https://www.shodan.io/), (https://www.maltego.com/), and (https://www.x1.com/). The convenience of these AI-powered data mining tools is not free, however. To look for free alternatives, Github is one place to consider as open source tools like (https://github.com/lanmaster53/recon-ng) could meet the need just fine, but open source tools are mostly less user-friendly.

FUTURE RESEARCH DIRECTIONS

The use of SOCMINT in criminal investigation or national security has merit, since many people including criminal-minded ones are constantly expressing themselves on social media through various online activities, such as posting comments, sharing photos, creating videos, and interacting with other like-minded entities. Unless they are carefully disguising themselves all the time while online, which is unlikely in most cases, social media is usually a place where people are prone to manifest their true colors either knowingly or subconsciously. Future research in this area should be aimed at three main aspects.

First, the accuracy of any conclusions drawn from SOCMINT should be improved. While solving crime and protecting national security are important tasks and sometimes require special measures, it is crucial to reduce errors and mistakes, because when criminal justice agencies make a mistake the consequences are usually quite severe and can be detrimental to the people who are wrongfully accused. On the other hand, some tragedies might have been preventable if red flags on social media had been taken seriously sooner. For now, SOCMINT is not very reliable yet. When it is analyzed manually, the human bias and oversight are hard to avoid. When it is analyzed by AI methods, it lacks precision on the individual level, in part due to immature algorithms that cannot fully emulate human decision making and in part due to the wide variation in personal idiosyncrasy that does not fit into any patterns suggested by big data. To improve this, more emphasis on deductive cyber profiling is called for. Deductive cyber profiling examines not only the patterns outlined by big data but also the unique storylines in each case.

Second, better tools designed for criminal justice agencies are needed. These tools should be user-friendly and cost-effective. Most criminal justice agents are not particularly computer savvy, so any high-tech tools need to be made easy to use and the tools should be budget friendly as well. This does not seem to be the case currently as open source tools tend to entail a steep learning curve whereas commercial products tend to have paywalls blocking full functions. Since money is usually the major driving force behind new software development, it is understandable why most SOCMINT tools are costly. However, it can be frustrating that after paying high fees, agencies still find the tools fail to deliver desired results. Tools need to be developed by people who are not only knowledgeable about machine learning but also familiar with the actual needs of criminal justice practitioners.

Third, although it is trendy to rely on AI or machine learning to gather data and run analysis, SOCMINT should by no means exclude human intelligence. Although human errors are undesirable, potential errors should not be the reason to dismiss human judgement altogether, especially in criminal investigation. As stressed, criminal investigation requires much more precision in its decisions and this level of precision currently cannot rely on AI to deliver. Simply put, predicting who is factually guilty of a crime is not quite the same thing as predicting who scores the highest percentage on the suspect list. Moreover, in criminal investigation, at times some clues can hardly be converted into data as they exist only as a hunch, an off-the-record understanding, or an informal observation guided by experience, not to mention some data although existent could be unattainable. Such clues may not provide data readable by machines, but they may help form judgement that can still be highly valuable. Future research should look to incorporate such judgement into SOCMINT analysis. AI should be directed to help reduce human errors while human judgement should be taken into consideration as a variable in AI algorithms.

CONCLUSION

This chapter discusses social media intelligence and its application for the purpose of criminal investigation or national security. Criminal investigation needs information and social media platforms typically garner abundant information, and therefore it makes sense for investigators to be seeking information on social media. However, information on social media is not often readily useable for criminal justice agencies and needs to be converted into useful intelligence through proper analysis. Hence, SOCMINT is much more than just reading through some people's Facebook pages or tweets to see if they have said something directly implicating a crime. SOCMINT usually requires a significant amount of data to be collected and analyzed, and sometimes this process takes place over a longer period of time as a way of monitoring or surveillance on social media. SOCMINT data mainly include metadata and user-generated data. Data could be in many different formats, which adds difficulty to data collection and analysis. Text analytics, visual analytics (e.g. videos and images), cyber profiling, social network analysis, timeline confirmation, geospatial analysis, and other forensic analysis could all be necessary before data can be effectively turned into intelligence. Apparently SOCMINT calls for certain specialties to serve its full purpose but these specialties may not be commonly available in a criminal justice agency. As a result, some might claim they are adopting SOCMINT but the way it is adopted might not be proven helpful. The lack of specialties and money are the two main hurdles preventing SOCMINT from being trusted whether the purpose is criminal investigation or national security. In turn, the lack of trust may prevent resources from being allocated to develop SOCMINT. Regardless, SOCMINT is valuable in modern day investigation. If the Internet moves from Web 2.0 to Web 3.0 as some have predicted, there will be new dynamics on social media and SOCMINT will become even more important from the perspective of intelligence gathering because Wen 3.0 renders the Internet users more initiative and control in terms of content, connectivity, decentralization, and collaboration. In short, under Web 3.0 SOCMINT will reveal more about the user and less about the platform, although theoretically Web 3.0 should also provide users with more privacy.

Certainly, SOCMINT itself as an investigative method is not without flaws. This chapter also discusses the challenges SOCMINT is facing and what directions future research should look into. SOCMINT tools are currently available but improvement on precision and cost-effectiveness should be expected. Finally, whenever a new technology is discussed, ethics should always be part of the discussion. This is especially imperative in the context of criminal justice. In particular, privacy has always been a big concern centered around social media and it happens to be a controversial topic surrounding criminal justice as well. This chapter is not capable of offering a perfect solution, but it is suggested that perhaps emphasizing awareness and accountability is a good start.

REFERENCES

Alanazi, F., & Jones, A. (2015). The value of metadata in digital forensics. *2015 European Intelligence and Security Informatics Conference*. 10.1109/EISIC.2015.26

Anandarajan, M., Hill, C., & Nolan, T. (2019). *Practical text analytics*. Advances in Analytics and Data Science. doi:10.1007/978-3-319-95663-3

Asongu, S. A., Orim, S.-M. I., & Nting, R. T. (2019). Terrorism and social media: Global evidence. *Journal of Global Information Technology Management, 22*(3), 208–228. doi:10.1080/1097198X.2019.1642023

ATF. (2022, September 8). *Criminal profilers*. https://www.atf.gov/careers/criminal-profilers

Bailey, L., Harinam, V., & Ariel, B. (2020). Victims, offenders and victim-offender overlaps of Knife Crime: A Social network analysis approach using Police Records. *PLoS One, 15*(12), e0242621. Advance online publication. doi:10.1371/journal.pone.0242621 PMID:33306696

Buchholz, F., & Spafford, E. (2004). On the role of file system metadata in digital forensics. *Digital Investigation, 1*(4), 298–309. doi:10.1016/j.diin.2004.10.002

Christie, J. (2015, September 8). *Are these the dumbest thieves ever?* Dailymail. https://www.dailymail.co.uk/news/article-3248275/Are-dumbest-thieves-Cocky-bank-robbing-couple-arrested-posing-Facebook-photos-thousands-dollars-cash-stole.html

Colombini, C., & Colella, A. (2011). Digital profiling: A computer forensics approach. In *International Conference on Availability, Reliability, and Security* (pp. 330-343). Springer.

Daniel, L. (2017). *Cell Phone Location Evidence for Legal Professionals: Understanding Cell Phone Location Evidence from the Warrant to the Courtroom.* Academic Press.

Dean, G., & Bell, P. (2012). The dark side of social media: Review of online terrorism. *Pakistan Journal of Criminology*, *3*(4), 191–210.

Dover, R. (2020). SOCMINT: A shifting balance of opportunity. *Intelligence and National Security*, *35*(2), 216–232. doi:10.1080/02684527.2019.1694132

Ellison, N. B., Vitak, J., Steinfield, C., Gray, R., & Lampe, C. (2011). Negotiating privacy concerns and social capital needs in a social media environment. In *Privacy online* (pp. 19–32). Springer. doi:10.1007/978-3-642-21521-6_3

Fox, A. M., Novak, K. J., Van Camp, T., & James, C. (2021). Predicting violent victimization using social network analysis from Police Data. *Violence and Victims*, *36*(3), 436–454. doi:10.1891/VV-D-19-00037 PMID:34103416

Gershowitz, A. M. (2015). The post-riley search warrant: Search protocols and particularity in cell phone searches. SSRN *Electronic Journal.* doi:10.2139/ssrn.2634473

Glassman, M., & Kang, M. J. (2012). Intelligence in the internet age: The emergence and evolution of Open Source Intelligence (OSINT). *Computers in Human Behavior*, *28*(2), 673–682. doi:10.1016/j.chb.2011.11.014

Gray, G., & Benning, B. (2019). Crowdsourcing criminology: Social Media and citizen policing in missing person cases. *SAGE Open*, *9*(4), 215824401989370. doi:10.1177/2158244019893700

Greenwald, G., & MacAskill, E. (2013). *NSA Prism program taps into user data of Apple, Google and others.* https://www.pulitzer.org/files/2014/public-service/guardianus/02guardianus2014.pdf

Greenwald, G., MacAskill, E., Poitras, L., Ackerman, S., & Rushe, D. (2013, September 8). Revealed: How Microsoft handed the NSA access to encrypted *messages. The Guardian.* http://shorturl.at/ajmR8

Hribar, G., Podbregar, I., & Ivanuša, T. (2014). OSINT: A "grey zone"? *International Journal of Intelligence and CounterIntelligence*, *27*(3), 529–549. doi:10.1080/08850607.2014.900295

Hu, X., & Liu, H. (2012). Text analytics in social media. In *Mining text data* (pp. 385–414). Springer. doi:10.1007/978-1-4614-3223-4_12

Jain, P., Gyanchandani, M., & Khare, N. (2016). Big data privacy: A technological perspective and review. *Journal of Big Data*, *3*(1), 1–25. doi:10.118640537-016-0059-y

Jeanis, M. N. (2020). Missing Persons and Runaway Youth: The Role of Social Media as an Alert System and Crime Control Tool. In *Science Informed Policing* (pp. 181–193). Springer. doi:10.1007/978-3-030-41287-6_9

Johnson, J. A., & Reitzel, J. D. (2011, September 8). *Social network analysis in an operational environment: Defining the utility of a network approach for crime analysis using the Richmond City Police Department as a case study.* Researchgate. http://shorturl.at/dIKRU

Jordan, M. I., & Mitchell, T. M. (2015). Machine learning: Trends, perspectives, and prospects. *Science*, *349*(6245), 255–260. doi:10.1126cience.aaa8415 PMID:26185243

Keikhosrokiani, P., & Asl, M. P. (Eds.). (2022). *Handbook of research on opinion mining and text analytics on literary works and social media.* IGI Global., doi:10.4018/978-1-7998-9594-7

Kelion, L. (2013, September 8). *Q&A: NSA's Prism internet surveillance scheme.* BBC. https://www.bbc.com/news/technology-23051248

Knoke, D., & Yang, S. (2019). *Social network analysis.* SAGE Publications.

Levinson-Waldman, R. (2022, September 8). *School social media monitoring won't stop the next mass shooting.* Brenna Center. https://www.brennancenter.org/our-work/analysis-opinion/school-social-media-monitoring-wont-stop-next-mass-shooting

Lim, C. (2022, September 8). *Police have arrested 62-year-old Frank James, the Brooklyn Subway shooting suspect.* MSN. https://www.msn.com/en-us/news/crime/police-have-arrested-62-year-old-frank-james-the-brooklyn-subway-shooting-suspect/ar-AAWbTfB?ocid=BingNewsSearch

Lombardi, M., Rosenblum, T., & Burato, A. (2015, September 8). *From SOCMINT to digital humint: Re-frame the use of social media within the intelligence cycle.* Academia. http://shorturl.at/fqtz2

Mantelero, A., & Vaciago, G. (2015). Data protection in a big data society. Ideas for a future regulation. *Digital Investigation*, *15*, 104–109. doi:10.1016/j.diin.2015.09.006

Muller, D. A. (2000). Criminal profiling: Real science or just wishful thinking? *Homicide Studies*, *4*(3), 234–264. doi:10.1177/1088767900004003003

Omand, D., Bartlett, J., & Miller, C. (2012). Introducing social media intelligence (SOCMINT). *Intelligence and National Security*, *27*(6), 801–823. doi:10.1080/02684527.2012.716965

Rigano, C. (2021, September 8). *Using artificial intelligence to address criminal justice needs.* Office of Justice Programs. https://www.ojp.gov/pdffiles1/nij/252038.pdf

Rogers, M. (2003). The role of criminal profiling in the computer forensics process. *Computers & Security*, *22*(4), 292–298. doi:10.1016/S0167-4048(03)00405-X

Rosenbach, M., Poitras, L., & Stark, H. (2013). How the NSA accesses smartphone data. *Spiegel Online, 9*.

Scott, J. (1988). Social network analysis. *Sociology*, *22*(1), 109–127. doi:10.1177/0038038588022001007

Smith, M., Szongott, C., Henne, B., & von Voigt, G. (2012). Big Data Privacy Issues in public social media. *2012 6th IEEE International Conference on Digital Ecosystems and Technologies (DEST)*. 10.1109/DEST.2012.6227909

Snook, B., Eastwood, J., Gendreau, P., Goggin, C., & Cullen, R. M. (2007). Taking stock of criminal profiling. *Criminal Justice and Behavior, 34*(4), 437–453. doi:10.1177/0093854806296925

US Department of Justice. (2020, September 8). *Legal considerations when gathering online cyber threat intelligence and purchasing data from illicit sources.* DOJ. https://www.justice.gov/criminal-ccips/page/file/1252341/download

Wasserman, S., & Faust, K. (2019). *Social network analysis: Methods and applications.* Cambridge University Press.

Weber, H. (2022, September 8). *How the NSA and FBI made Facebook the perfect mass surveillance tool.* https://venturebeat.com/business/how-the-nsa-fbi-made-facebook-the-perfect-mass-surveillance-tool/

Yu, S. (2013). Behavioral Evidence Analysis on Facebook: A Test of cyber-profiling. *Defendologija, 16*(33), 19–30. doi:10.5570/dfnd.en.1333.02

Yu, S. (2015). *Human trafficking and the internet. In Combating Human Trafficking: A multidisciplinary approach.* CRC Press.

Yu, S. (2020a). Predicting the writer's gender based on electronic discourse. *International Journal of Cyber Research and Education, 2*(1), 17–31. doi:10.4018/IJCRE.2020010102

Yu, S. (2020b). *The art of criminal investigation.* Kindle Publishing.

Yu, S. (2021). Cyber profiling in criminal investigation. In *Encyclopedia of Information Science and Technology* (5th ed., pp. 333–343). IGI Global. doi:10.4018/978-1-7998-3479-3.ch024

ADDITIONAL READING

Dover, R. (2020). SOCMINT: A shifting balance of opportunity. *Intelligence and National Security, 35*(2), 216–232. doi:10.1080/02684527.2019.1694132

Hu, X., & Liu, H. (2012). Text analytics in social media. In *Mining text data* (pp. 385–414). Springer. doi:10.1007/978-1-4614-3223-4_12

Knoke, D., & Yang, S. (2019). *Social network analysis.* SAGE Publications.

Omand, D., Bartlett, J., & Miller, C. (2012). Introducing social media intelligence (SOCMINT). *Intelligence and National Security, 27*(6), 801–823. doi:10.1080/02684527.2012.716965

Rigano, C. (2019). Using artificial intelligence to address criminal justice needs. *National Institute of Justice Journal, 280*, 1–10.

Rønn, K. V., & Søe, S. O. (2019). Is social media intelligence private? Privacy in public and the nature of social media intelligence. *Intelligence and National Security, 34*(3), 362–378. doi:10.1080/02684527.2019.1553701

Yu, S. (2021). Cyber Profiling in Criminal Investigation. In *Encyclopedia of Information Science and Technology* (5th ed., pp. 333–343). IGI Global. doi:10.4018/978-1-7998-3479-3.ch024

Yu, S. (2022). *Digital investigation: The essentials.* Kindle Publishing.

KEY TERMS AND DEFINITIONS

Criminal Investigation: The process and methods that are aimed at solving crime and determine culpability.

Cyber Profiling: An investigative method that relies predominantly on electronic data to predict the unknown based on the known information about a subject whose identity may or may not have been recognized.

National Security: A broad domain that includes all studies, precautions, and investigations regarding any security threats to a sovereign state or nation.

OSINT: Open source intelligence as a practice about analyzing data legally gathered from free, public sources without violating copyrights, patents, and privacy laws.

Privacy: The reasonable expectation of being free from being observed and disturbed.

Social Media: Digital platforms that allow users to create self-expressive content and interact with other users.

SOCMINT: Social media intelligence as a practice about analyzing data gathered from social media platforms, typically with the purpose to gain understanding on specific persons or social trends among a group of people.

Chapter 9
Artificial Intelligence Techniques in Text and Sentiment Analysis

Muralidhara Rao Patruni

https://orcid.org/0000-0001-6651-3501

Vellore Institute of Technology, India

Anupama Angadi

Anil Neerukonda Institute of Technology and Sciences, India

Satya Keerthi Gorripati

Gayatri Vidya Parishad College of Engineering, India

Pedada Saraswathi

GITAM School of Technology, Visakhapatnam, India

ABSTRACT

Of late, text and sentiment analysis have become essential parts of modern marketing. These play a vital role in the division of natural language processing (NLP). It mainly focuses on text classification to examine the intention of the processed text; it can be of positive or negative types. Sentiment analysis dealt with the computational treatment of sentiments, opinions, and subjectivity of text. This chapter tackles a comprehensive approach for the past research solutions that includes various algorithms, enhancements, and applications. This chapter primarily focuses on three aspects. Firstly, the authors present a systematic review of recent works done in the area of text and sentiment analysis; second, they emphasize major concepts, components, functionalities, and classification techniques of text and sentiment analysis. Finally, they provide a comparative study of text and sentiment analysis on the basis of trending research approaches. They conclude the chapter with future directions.

DOI: 10.4018/978-1-6684-6242-3.ch009

INTRODUCTION

Introduction to Artificial Intelligence and Machine Learning

Machine Learning (ML) is a buzzword for many years, the motive for this might be the massive data generated by applications, and to increase computation power for better algorithms. ML is used to automate ordinary tasks to offer intelligent insights; businesses in each domain try to benefit from it. Customers may be by now using such devices. For example, to keep track of users' fitness apps like GoodFit, Leap Fitness Step Counter, MyFitnessPal, or home automation like Google Home. Still, there are many more examples of ML are in use like image recognition, speech recognition, prediction, medical diagnoses, and financial trading.

Artificial Intelligence (AI) is all over us, "search by voice" in Google Chrome or "automotive navigation system" in cars. Even E-commerce sites like Amazon, Snapdeal, Flipkart, and Jabong suggestions are based on AI. Interacting with Alex, Siri, and Google Assistant is also a practice of AI. AI is a wide area of Computer Science; it marks machines act like human brains. AI is not just obeying instructions about instructions to drive a car. But an AI should work more effectively and independently like a human to make a decision.

Sentiment Analysis (SA) or Opinion Analysis (OA) composed of ML & AI algorithms is an influential tool to boost businesses' brand value and profit from popular customer experiences. SA is an ML tool that analyses texts for polarity, from negative to positive. By preparing ML tools with textual instances of emotions, machines automatically acquire knowledge of detecting a sentiment without human involvement. To make it simple, ML permits machines to learn new tasks without being programmed. Therefore, this chapter aims to review artificial intelligence techniques in text and sentimental analysis. The rest of the chapter focuses on background

Introduction to Sentiment Analysis

Customer requirement often dominates businesses' spare time to carry out effective marketing strategy, from the reviews and opponents' strategy to items' release in the markets. As we live in a 'Digital Age', companies are transforming their strategies such as new product launches and opinion gathering on social platforms (Zucco et al.2020). Microblogging and Social media web sources are the best sources for potential advertising to reach more groups. The rapid adoption of these groups in social media promotes new launches effectively. On other hand, monitoring and analyzing reviews of all the chats taking place on open forums and social platforms about a new launch was each company's dream. Hence, these chats can be used as a valuable source for knowing the public pulse.

Using (OA), companies can discover the opinions' conveyed by customers and evaluate customer reviews found in tweets and forums (Khan & Qamar, 2014). From outsiders' terminology, it evaluates every text and recognizes if the opinion or sentiment is positive, negative, or neutral. For companies who want to know what the customers' perception is and how they feel, sentiment analysis delivers strategic use from the extraction of online comments and interactions. Eventually, that's massive unstructured data to process. To keep an eye on what customers, comment on new arrivals, we need to undertake AI sentiment analysis, which helps in the automatic recognition of emotion in review text and obtaining quick, actual intuition from huge customer data.

The occasion to provide sense to unstructured data using Natural Language Processing (NLP) will allow AI optimizes OA. Cognitive technology (CT) is a field of AI, which is very prominent to understand social language and the routines that customers convey themselves on online forums. Social language is an informal language that uses slang terms (like 2day, B4, ABT), acronyms (like BF, TY, PLZ), abbreviations (like RT, PM, LI), etc. Customers can also express emotions, needs, and preferences using symbolic gestures. Due to the advancement in CT, the underlying tasks enable machines to simulate humans. As AI becomes better-found at human conveying, businesses slowly adopting this technology where CT would be influential.

Preliminary Concepts

OA is a suitable way to extract subjective information from social language, and serve businesses to understand the feeling (or sentiments) of their endeavours while keeping track of online exchanges. However, analyzing this huge social data is practically impossible, therefore a smart and effective approach is required that can analyze and produce the polarity of a review. Many tools and methods are accessible for automating this polarity classification for social data. Mostly, two techniques are used for this purpose NLP and ML approaches.

ML approaches are successful and reliable for OA and polarity classification. Many options and additions of ML approaches give us to explore its significance as well as boosts interest in research. NLP converts conversations into something that machines can recognize. Syntactic and Semantic techniques are applied to detect the structure and meaning of textual data. Some of these techniques include parse trees, tokenization, lemmatization, and parts-of-speech. As soon as the text is prepared with NLP methods, it is ready for ML classification. ML methods acknowledge patterns and produce predictions.

ML approaches learn by themselves without relying on instructions written in the programming language. To build an ML model that classifies review text by sentiment, we need to train the model with corpus. Every sample text in a corpus is labelled with the matching category. To increase the accuracy of the ML model, we will need a descriptive amount of samples of every label. Since ML methods progress through learning, OA models will become intelligent as they cross new labelled data. We can use OA with AI to label huge datasets all at once and in real time.

The basic step in evolving any model is collecting training data. There exist standard datasets as benchmarks, but novel datasets are also being deployed every day to become accessible. The following standard datasets available for research are mentioned in Table 1.

THEORETICAL BACKGROUND

ML model resembles the human brain. This model was generated in 1949 by Donald Hebb. His concepts define the association between neurons. This association strengthens if neurons are activated simultaneously, if neurons are activated differently this association becomes weakens. This association is described as weight which can be either positive or negative. In 1950, Arthur Samuel developed the checkers game. Later, he initiated alpha-beta, Minmax, and rote learning strategies. In 1952, Arthur Samuel came up with the phrase "Machine Learning". In 1957 Frank Rosenblatt, Hebb, and merged Samuel's models to create the perceptron. Initially, perceptron was designed as a machine, later it is programmed as a program that has been used for many ML applications.

Table 1. Standard Datasets

Dataset	Description	Size
Amazon Product Reviews Dataset (Haque et al., 2018)	Holds amazon product reviews. Like rating, productid, description, price, and so on.	5 million
IMDB Movie Reviews (Topal & Ozsoyoglu 2016)	Holds movie reviews	50,000
Sentiment140	Holds social platform posts and informal textual data	1.6 million
476 Million Twitter Tweets	Holds all public tweets	June 1st and December 31st of 2009 Tweets
Stanford Sentiment Treebank	Holds movie reviews	6920 sequences

In the 1960s, a multilayer neural network was discovered which uses two or more layers in the perceptron model. In 1967, the Nearest Neighbor algorithm was proposed, and it was the initiation of pattern recognition. This was used as a solution for a traveling salesperson's problem. In the 1970s, the backpropagation algorithm was proposed and used in Artificial Neural Networks. In the mid-1970s and 1980s, AI was introduced and focused on knowledge-based approaches.

OA is a significant research field of a vast number of daily tweets, posts and videos shared on social media (Bagheri & Islam,2017). The application of SA is to extract people's feedback. Social media platforms like Twitter, Facebook, and Instagram currently have millions of accounts and are rich resources to know about peoples' pulse (Saif et al., 2016). Let us explore the areas where SA essentially works. Table 2 shows the taxonomy of major SA adopting ML approaches.

Social Media

People express their feedback by writing textual messages. SA is typically considered for languages with a distinct form, such as English. Meanwhile, SA requires textual analysis in numerous languages. Computational understanding of these languages is a vital problem. A summary of major SA adopting ML approaches was shown in Table 3.

Academics

Institutes gather feedback from students to know their sentiments towards infrastructure, academics, and hostel amenities. SA plays a major role in this analysis to process these comments for betterment.

TEXT ANALYSIS

Components

SA components can be grouped into two major clusters: one is Opinion Mining (OM) and Emotion Mining (EM). The source for these components is tokens, sentences, phrases, and entities from a review text. The task of OM is separated into a sequence of steps: Subjectivity Detection, Opinion polarity

Table 2. Taxonomy of major SA adopting ML approaches

Ref.	Dataset	Size	Pre-processing Scheme	ML technique	Libraries	Language
(Saif et al., 2016).	Twitter	300 tweets	NLTK	--	Tweepy Textblob	English
(Alomari, et al., 2017)	Twitter	1800 tweets	N-gram TF-IDF	Support Vector Machine (SVM) Naïve Bayes (NB).	--	Arabic
(Shabaz & Kumar, 2018)	Twitter		Topic Modelling	Binary Classifier	R programming	English
(Krishnaveni et al., 2017)	Translated	10000	Tokenization	LSTM	TensorFlow	Malayalam
(Jamal et al., 2019)	Kaggle	1,600,000 tweets	Tokenization	Principal Component Analysis	TensorFlow	English
(Kim et al. 2019)	News Articles from 'bigkinds'	67,968 articles	morphological analyzer	Positive Indexing	--	Korean
(Sharma & Ghose, 2020)	Twitter	Tweets from Jan 2019 To March 2019	AYLIEN	Lexicon Based Approach	tweetR ggplot wordcloud sentimentr Tidytext twitteR	English
(Shrestha et al., 2020)	Social Media Feeds	--	Tokenization NLTK	NB Decision Tree Classifier	--	Hindi
(Naresh, & Venkata Krishna, 2021).	Twitter	1000 tweets	--	SVM Decision Tree	--	English
Suryawati et al., 2018)	Social Media	178,736 words	POS Tagging	Word Embedding	TweetNLP, TwitterNLP,and TwitIE	Indonesian

Table 3. Processing techniques

Reference	Dataset	Size	Pre-processing Scheme	ML technique	Libraries	Language
(Dsouza et al., 2019).	Students feedback using Excel	--	TF-IDF	SVM NB	Valence Aware Dictionary and Sentiment Reasoner (VADER)	English
Thomas, & Latha,. (2020).	Web repos Using APIs	--	NLTK	NB	Splitter	English

Figure 1. Popular types of classifiers, extracted features, datasets, and evaluation

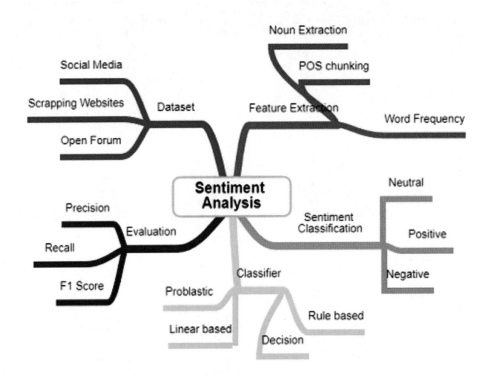

classification, etc. The task of SM is separated into a sequence of steps Emotion Detection, Emotion Polarity Classification, and Emotion Cause Detection

OM is a notion, estimation, and belief conclusion that any single or a group of persons hold for a particular product, idea, or topic which can have polarity such as positive, negative, or neutral. Opinion can be objective or subjective and have two portions: Opinion target is an entity that can be an item, organization, or a topic, and Opinion polarity.

EM is the science of finding, studying, and estimating customers' emotions toward products and brands. EM can be separated into three groups based on the purpose of emotions mining. The first kind focuses on extracting text and signifying its associated polarity. The second kind targets finding the subjectivity of the text. The third kind targets identifying emotion and its strength.

Architecture

OM process mainly discovers the opinion or the sentiment in the text, it mainly aims at identifying the customers' outlook towards an item or a post. The SA method is described in Figure 1 where every component does some precise tasks as mentioned below.

In Figure 2 most popular types of classifiers, extracted features, datasets, and evaluation metrics were listed. Figure 2 shows various approaches to ML while Figure 3 listed various pre-processing methods.

Figure 2. various approaches to ML

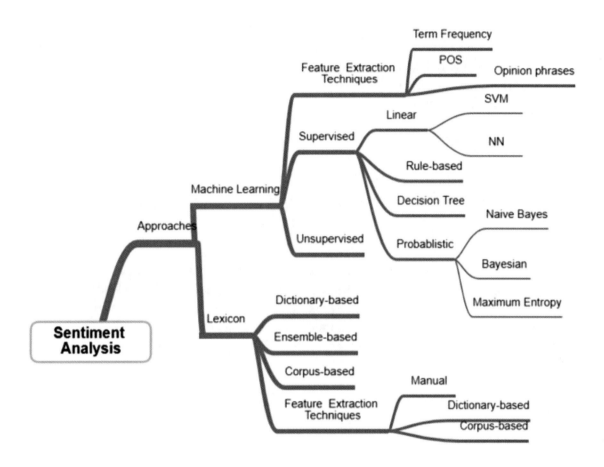

Figure 3. Pre-processing Methods

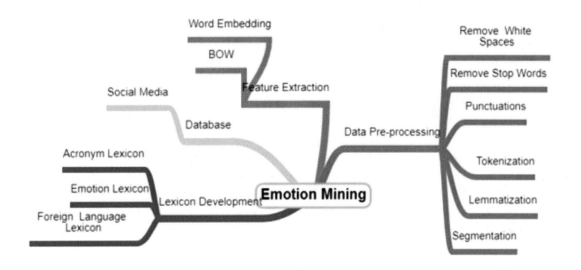

Taxonomy of Supervised Classification Techniques

The acceptance of fast-growing social and electronic media-based societies has inclined researchers to follow their work on sentiment analysis. These societies distribute their data handily and easily on the web. People share their views and emotions on the open forums. The businesses hire researchers to examine the hidden facts about their products and amenities. It became vital to recognize the types of SA which fits the business research.

Fine-Grained Sentiment

This study provides an understanding of the opinion received from customers. The accurate results are conveyed in terms of the polarity. However, the process is harder and costlier.

Emotion Detection Sentiment Analysis

This is a popular way to detect the sentiment in a tweet. Lexicons and ML algorithms are used to identify this sentiment. Lexicons bag-of-words that are positive, negative, or neutral. This method separates these words according to their sentiment. The benefit of this method is that a business can recognize what a customer feels about their brand. This algorithm is complex to understand.

Aspect-Based

This approach is based on one aspect of an item or service. For instance, if an organization that sells mobiles leverages SA, it would focus on only one aspect of mobiles—like memory size, pixels, etc. So they can realize how customers feel about particular features of the item.

Intent Analysis

This method provides a deep understanding of the purpose of the customer. For instance, an organization can predict if a customer plans to buy an item or not. This means that the purpose of a specific customer can be tracked, forming a pattern, and then used as marketing.

Automatic detection of sentiment from text is the major task of businesses. The AI methods made this possible by improving accuracy and advancing the automation of sentiments. The exhibiting of four methods is concisely conferred below.

Naïve Bayes

The polarity of sentiments is normally decided by the mind-set of the people towards a product. Naïve Bayes (NB) is a classifier, that provides a way to express feelings in three groups: positive, negative, and neutral. NB uses conditional probability to classify words into their corresponding groups. The advantage of NB it requires smaller datasets for the training phase of the model. The input data goes through processing, removal of stop words, and special words yielding the set of words. Tagging words with labels requires manual entry by human professionals. This processing produces words with label pairs and assumes no relationship among features.

Consider an unlabelled term 'y' from the test phase and a window of n-terms $(x_1, x_2, \ldots\ldots x_n)$ from a review text. The probability of giving a term 'y' to be in the group of n-terms from the training phase is specified by: $P(xi/y)$. NB method identifies the probabilities of groups given to terms by using joint probability of terms and groups. NB can be tuned moderately fast compared to existing ML models. The algorithmic process of NB is shown below:

Input: Corpus of reviews holds positive and negative tweets
Output: Model evaluation by Accuracy, Precision, and Recall
Notations: C corpus, T term, S sentence, B Constant
For each S€C:
For each T€S:
do NT ¬ CountTerms(S)
do NS ¬ CountSentences(C)
do P(t) ¬ T+1/å(T+1)
do probability ¬ T+1/å(T)+B
return probabliity

Support Vector Machine

SA is the NLP method that performs analysis of customers' views on any data i.e., politics, business, social platforms, etc., SA is the job of NLP which is a field of AI that benefits machines to handle translations. Support Vector Machine (SVM) is an ML technique that can be cast off both classification and regression. SVM implements classification by identifying the hyper-plane that separates the vectors that fit into a specified group and vectors not belong to the group. Hence it can be functional on any vectors which transform any data. This means to influence the control of text classification, textual data has to transform into vectors. Vectors are set of numerals that denote a set of coordinates in n-dimensional space.

SVM draws this hyperplane by converting data into mathematical functions named "kernels". Many types of kernels exist called linear, sigmoid, polynomial, and RBF. The RBF kernel is an all-purpose kernel used when there is no previous knowledge exists and the linear kernel is named as a separable problem. The algorithmic process of SVM is shown below:

Input: Online Reviews
Output: Models' Evaluation score by F1 score
for the trained data set
create feature vectors for the given input
create a linear SVM model to train and predict the data
test the model classifier on new data
return labelled output

Multi-Layer Perceptron

Multi-Layer Perceptron (MLP) is a network comprised of multiple perceptron. MLP comprises multiple fully connected layers (FC). FC has an input, hidden layer, and output layer. MLP is normally used in regression techniques. The algorithmic process of MLP is shown below:

Input: Reviews from open forums
Output: Models evaluation
for the review text
create review text in digital form
divide the corpus into training and testing sets
feed the training text into the classifier
test the models' accuracy
return labelled output

Text Classifier- Building Blocks

The continuous disposal of data on the web produces a demand for sentiment tools that process review information. Furthermore, it's extremely significant that this textual analysis can provide solutions for NLP tasks such as the polarity of the sentences or finding patterns. Each sentence is a continuous order of words from a given Corpus. Until now we have taken words as separate units and measured their relationship to sentiments. Moreover, numerous fascinating analyses depend on the word correspondences, while inspecting which words tend to co-occur or follow within a sentence. These words in NLP are referred to as N-grams, where N refers to a number of words. The following forms of N-grams are commonly notable:

Tokenization: It is the procedure of slicing a sentence into smaller pieces (tokens or words). This segmentation can be prepared with decision trees, which hold data to correctly solve the problems we might face.

Unigram: An N-gram holds a single string (for example token, or string)

2-gram or Bigram: A mixture of two strings in a statement. (for example Machine Learning, Artificial Intelligence). We can use bigrams to afford context in a review text. Context really matters for finding polarity. For instance, a sentence with the words "love", "like" and "happy" is a positive sentiment. In a statement like "I am happy to hear this song", where data is sequenced into bigrams, it's easy to tell the occurrence of a positive word (Tripathy et al., 2016).

Text analysis assumes a strong correlation between the positions of every word in a sentence, computing the occurrence of the subsequent word with respect to the former one. In another instance, N-grams can be used to detect plagiarism.

For mathematical modelling, preparing data for ML algorithms is to turn data into vectors. Vectors capture word correspondences to predict the sentiment observations on the textual context in which the words seem. In machine words transforming the data into vectors is termed a feature (Devi et al., 2016,). Since text only is not skilled of being changed and compelled into mathematical space without being converted into numerals for the machine to learn. The following are a few techniques to change text into vectors:

Bag-of-Words (BoW)

The BoW is the simplest model in NLP. It is a method to find exclusive words (unigrams) i.e., corpus from the list of sentences. Parse each sentence from the corpus, if the word is not present assign '0'else '1'. These words have been normalized and tokenized and assigned a subjective score, to prepare a simple

BoW model. This can be later castoff as features for classifiers. The drawback is it accepts all documents of the same size. We use this vocabulary for the new sentence vectorization.

CountVectorizer (CV)

It is a method to tokenize the group of articles and create a vocabulary with it and consider this to encode new articles. We acquire this approach from a python package called sci-kit learn. It by default removes special symbols and lowers the articles. This method turns every vector into a sparse matrix. It verifies every word is existing and if it exists it displays the total occurrences of the word in the vocabulary.

TF-IDF Vectorizer

BoW and CV are very basic. Though the stop words have repeated with this word the technique can't conclude any meaning. These words can repeat many times in an article and word count arrange the words by their occurrences. From CV, we lose the exciting words and assign more priority to insignificant words.

TF-IDF is a general technique. It is a word frequency technique that tries to focus on the most important word e.g., a frequently occurring word in an article but not across articles.

TF-IDF is a great vectorization technique among BoW, and CV methods because it prioritizes important words in an article. IDF value for the stop word "the" is less since it exists in many articles. However, the other two methods assign a higher value for stop words. The BoW model can implement topic classification well, but it shows inaccuracy in SA.

Word Vectors

Each sentence denotes a vector of numbers that considers both the words' arrivals and the semantic structure (Liu, H., 2017). This approach is known as an n-feature vector, where n represents the size of the vocabulary, and every word is denoted by an index vector. For instance, if a vector size is 10,000, it denotes the presence of the jth word with a 1 in the jth position and 0 elsewhere. To figure out this we incorporate a hidden layer of neurons that convert larger vectors to shorter ones. These vectors are taken as an input of a CNN and train the model as a whole, so that these trained vectors are fit to the sentiment model, and capture adequate data on the words to predict the sentences 'sentiment.

Word vectors (WV) (Fauzi, 2019), sentences (SR), and document representations (DR) not only take words and also their organizations. The comfortable way to denote an SR is to enclose WV and fabricate a matrix that denotes the sentence (Joshi & Vekariya, 2017). In DR, the entire document is to be untagged to produce distributed vector of words using these documents as features. These features are abstract associations, like the context and their order of occurrences (supposing words with the same contexts must have the same meanings). This is beneficial when the particular order of the essential features which bond the words is unknown.

Pre-Trained Vectors

There are various pre-trained vectors available such as Spacy, FastText, Glove, Flair, and Elmo. The benefit of these pre-trained is that they consider the word's context while producing vector notation (El-Din, 2016). Another key benefit is that this can precisely capture the context in which the word is used.

Figure 4. Step-by-step process of text classifier

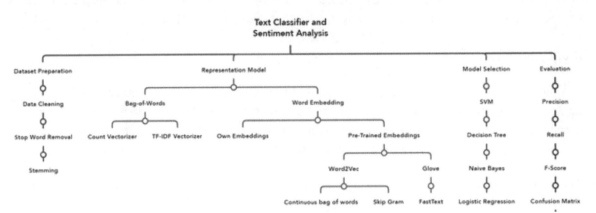

These are trained on a massive corpus with millions of instances and words. However, for a 10k model training with a huge corpus will be ineffective. A required word's embedding needs to be selected. For Google's word2vec pre-trained model, there exist two ways: Continuous bag of words (CBoW) and Skip-Gram (SG). Both of these processes use a NN with one hidden layer to produce the embedding Rezaeinia et al., 2019)

For the CBoW, the context is given as input to the NN i.e., the preceding and the succeeding words, and the model predicts the word. But, for the SG, the words are fed and the model has to predict the context. In both algorithms, the feature vectors are given to the input. The output has an activation function with nodes equivalent to the size of the vocabulary, which provides the predictions' proportion for every word. This complete guide of text classifier is shown in Figure 4.

Visualizing SA

To visualize the outcomes of SA, authors use various methods, such as histograms, graphs, and confusion matrices. Due to multiple data sources and responsibilities, visualization methods such as wordcloud, maps, scattertext, and style plots are also very standard. Visualizing either structured or unstructured data is a vital task to gain insights. Figure 5 shows the 9 best tools available for visualization.

In general, the text does not afford us with complete information. However, to represent a language model and associations (word frequency, word sequences, etc.) visualizations answer the following queries such as: what are the frequent words in the dataset, and how many hashtags are linked to corona?

Contextual Semantic Search Technique

Contextual Semantics (CS) has been usually used in various areas of computer science, like NLP and AI. The basic principle behind the concept of CS is that it suggests co-occurred words in a given message based on context. To develop actionable visions, it is significant to recognize what phase of the product (or brand) a customer is conversing about. For instance: Flipkart would need to separate text messages that belong to item reviews, billing matters, customer queries, etc. On the other side, Uber organization

Figure 5. Best visualization tools for SA

wants to give incentives by classifying messages based on staff behavior and feedback, etc. But how the system can filter these?

An intellectual smart search technique called CS takes hundreds of messages related to a concept as input and filters textual messages that match closely with the target concept. Traditional methods search for a message "review" on the web and filter closely associated words like (audit, assess, and explore). This web content is organized and optimized with keyword structures. So, the outcome of the keyword search is extremely relevant and obliges the purpose of the customer. This approach is not very efficient as it is practically unachievable to think of all the associated keywords and their options that signify a specific context. Now, business search is greatly different from web content, because this data is raw, unorganized, and unstructured. Perhaps CS accepts the keyword "reviews" and filters all the associated words mentioned like (inquiry, exploration, and notice) based on context.

The methodology of CS described as it's a smart AI method to transfer every word into a particular point in the n-dimensional space where the distance between every two points is used to detect the contextual similarity of the words which we have explored. This benefits the customer discover the mostly associated data and marks the process as fast and efficient.

The required parameters used in CS are Geographical location, Search History, and Attributes of the current customer. Firstly, the outcome of the customers' query varies with the location of the customer. The CS analyses the given query based on the vocabulary of the Geographical location where the customer is, and delivers efficient results. Secondly, the search history of the customer gives a clue to the system about customers' preferences. A CS engine makes a customer's personalized profile and considers this in order to sort out appropriate results. Finally, each customer is dissimilar, and in addition to the customers' manners, what the CS includes are the customers' attributes. Demographic data like the age of the customer and qualified background can affect the results of the query.

Customers practice personalized search experiences using CS. But, is all this conceivable with the help of technologies, are listed below: Semantic Technology: It is a text mining technique that grabs the semantics of a query to get the appropriate results. Conversely, CS enables us to include not only results along with synonyms. This extends the outcome as well as ensures appropriate results.

Artificial Intelligence: It is a technology that aids to keep track of the search history of every customer and pull accurate inferences about what they are exactly looking for. AI technology makes the CS engine smart and intelligent to analyze numerous customers' attributes to fetch appropriate results.

NLP: CS uses NLP to permit users to search using colloquial language and still get accurate results. With NLP, customers can query in their native language.

SENTIMENT ANALYSIS

Methods

SA is relative to opinions, and sentiments about customers' textual conversation on social platforms. The sentiment is a six tuple (entity, feature, opinion, customer, shipping, and time) where: An entity may be a product, a film, or an article, the feature is an aspect, opinion is a triple holds type, polarity and its intensity or belief of the customer towards an entity, customer represents details of who has conveyed the opinion, shipping represents overall customer details and time denotes when the sentiment is conveyed (Keikhosrokiani & Asl, 2022).

Each type of SA requires these five parameters depending on their study. Fine-grained sentiment requires opinion and customer, Emotion detection SA requires entity, opinion, and customer, Aspect-based SA requires feature, opinion, and shipping whereas Intent analysis requires entity, opinion, and customer.

The major goal of SA is to classify a review text into contents. The general task of SA is to classify the polarity: Given an input I, by its context, conclude its polarity by classifying it as either positive (P) or negative (N), fall into binary classification. If the neutral polarity is also considered then it falls into multiclass classification. For instance, in the review statement "The movie was awesome", has a polarity of 1.0 and subjectivity of 0.75. In this case, the target variable ranges between [-N, N], where a positive value denotes a positive polarity and a negative value denotes a negative polarity.

In accumulation to polarity detection, an additional task is to identify emotion in a context. Emotion is the customer's feeling that describes his mindset, like happiness, fear, love, and so on. The emotion is a quintuple (entity, feature, type, customer, time). In this framework, the type can be denoted as a triple (feeling, polarity, subjectivity), in which feeling signifies the type of feeling, polarity denotes positive or negative and subjectivity is the same as polarity subjectivity.

Tools

Businesses use SA to analyze customers' sentiments in the form of reviews on social network platforms. This analysis is an admirable source of input and affords customers insight that can identify brand success, improve customers' involvement, finds future endorsements, and advance marketing schemes. Using inefficient tools analysis data can show disastrous. Therefore, selecting the correct tool is crucial. These tools imitate customers' brains, to a larger or smaller extent, allowing tools to monitor the emotion behind the online conversation. SA tools are listed in Table 4.

Sentiment Classification

Using ML, the system can classify sentiment correctly. There are two methods, supervised and unsupervised. In supervised, trained ML algorithms conclude sentiment as positive, negative, or neutral. This involves libraries or manual labelling of NLP models. In unsupervised, presumes data, and the AI has to study the design-build a model on its own.

There are numerous supervised algorithms exist used to train systems to implement SA (Zou et al., 2015). Few are listed in previous sections, where the system has to train with a large corpus of tagged text for training. The following are the phases involved in developing the classifier:

Table 4. Sentiment Analysis tools

Tool	Availability	Analysis type	Choice of Views	Language	User-Friendly
Quick Search	Free	Analyses news sites, open forums, and blogs	ggplot2 visualization against competitors	English	Yes
Sentiment Viz	Free	Tweets	Sentiment, Topic, and Heatmap	English	Yes
RapidMiner	30 days for Free	Online conversations, posts	Charts, Plots, SOM	English	Yes
MeaningCloud	Free	Aspect based	Plots	English, Spanish, French, Italian, Catalan, and Portuguese	
Social Mention	Free	Tweets	Charts, TagClouds		Yes
SentimentAnalyzer	Free			English, German, French	
SentiStrength	Free	Short social Web text	Reports binary and ternary single scale results	Finnish, German, Russian, French, Arabic, English	Yes
Sentigem	Free with an organization mail	Social test	Displays overall sentiment on the dashboard	English	Yes
Social searcher	14-day free trial	Direct access to social media	Dashboard	English, German, French, Italian, Portuguese, Russian, Dutch, Spanish	Yes
OpenText	Free	News articles	Dashboard	English, German French, Spanish, and Portuguese.	Yes

Phase 1: Clean Data: This phase removes misplaced texts, an uppercase letter, HTML links, brand words, punctuations, and stop words.

Phase 2: Data Preparation: In this phase data gets separates into training and testing folders. This means once the model is built; it can predict new review text. Later, we Load the cleaned data and analyze the corpus. During the analysis it randomizes the data and explores relevant relationships to avoid an unbalanced corpus, usually, it arises when there are extra samples of some classes than others.

Phase 3: Feature Selection: For this task, many models exist to purge features and choose the best one. The fundamental idea is to traverse through all the tokens that occur a few times and to identify an existing token with high similarity.

Phase 4: Train the Model: During this phase, the system predicts accurately as often as possible. For instance, the Linear Regression algorithm requires W, x, and b values for learning. Each iteration is equivalent to a step-in training.

Phase 5: Evaluate the Model: This phase utilizes some metrics to measure the performance of the model. Usually, the data will have an unbalanced issue as customers probably turn towards neutral or positive than negative reviews in most circumstances. These unseen reviews are destined to be meant

Table 5. Required Functions and Libraries for the phases

Phases	Required Functions and Libraries		Description
Phase-1	decode() lower()	re nltk Spacy	Open-source libraries for NLP processing.
Phase-3	Counter() Similarity()	Counter Spacy	The counter is a collection that holds the count of every element
Phase-4	Numpy SciPy PyTorch Scikit-learn		
Phase-5	sklearn		

to be representative of both for organization and the model. Thus, to keep an eye out on this model use f1-score, precision, and recall. Table 5 shows the list of required functions and libraries for each phase.

Unsupervised methods to SA can resolve the difficulty of domain dependency and decrease the requirement for labeling training data. The task behind unsupervised learning is that it doesn't presume about the input and outcome of the data. It is extremely suitable where there is no tagging and structure of data.

Subjective Classification

Based on the category of data, there are three classification types: topic, intent, and sentiment classifiers exist. A topic analysis is an NLP method that permits us to obtain the meaning of texts by finding themes. The intent analysis classifies email replies automatically to marketing promotions as, between others, Fascinated, Not Fascinated, Bounce, etc. SA classifies text by polarity. Another significant task is to identify the subjectivity of the text.

A subjective text articulates someone's attitude concerning a subject it is defined as: Given an input text T, identify if T holds a feeling or not, if it holds T is termed as subjective otherwise it is termed as objective. It can be expected that the input for SA must be a subjective text. SA applies a combination of statistics, NLP, and ML to find and extract subjective text from the input. This analysis is also called OA.

Subjective Classification is a little more complicated than finding polarity as numerous types of text such as articles, news, blogs, and videos need the identification of both the theme and the feeling of the customer. Therefore, for classification, the algorithms must identify conversational language and differentiate it from the objective text. However, ML is effective, and the lexicon-based method is also used.

Deep Learning and Machine Learning-Based Methods

Deep Learning (DL) is a sub-field of ML which practices deep neural nets. Recently, DL algorithms were applied for SA. Several methods have been explored for SA using a neural network (NN) with a convolutional layer, and many dense layers with an activation function. A convolutional layer is the method developed for visual imagery and increases the accuracy of image classification models.

The idea behind convolution is to apply a set of filters and to yield new images to provide as inputs to the next layers. Several filters exist such as vertical, horizontal, and Sobel to capture the edges or sharpen images. Training these filters helps the model to construct features to forward the succeeding layers. These features it trains will be local-invariant. It will convolve the shape as the original image, which is the key for not only computer vision but for SA also.

For NLP tasks like SA, and OA, the model uses word vectors and convolves the image constructed by comparing these vectors to build significant features. Usually, these filters will permit us to focus on positive or negative words. It will allow us to recognize the relationships among words and negations to understand what follows the current word. It learns specific words or n-grams that abide by sentiment information. The model takes images as input, an array of 2-D numbers and hence we need to identify features in this matrix. A convolutional layer comprises "maps" known as the "feature map". Each map has two modules: A linear map and an activation function.

Like images, the text also represents as an array of word vectors (each token is mapped to a particular vector in n-dimensional space that comprises the vocabulary) that can be managed with the support of a CNN (Severyn & Moschitti, 2015). The Design of CNN architecture for sentence classification is shown in Figure 6. Here we use a 1D filter of sizes: 3, 4, and 5, each of which has a single filter. Each filter implements convolution on the sentence matrix and produces feature maps. Then max pool operation is performed on the output of every filter over the sentence (i.e., size=4 (sentence length - filter size + 2 * padding)/ stride +1) picking a maximum number out of four values). Thus a feature vector is produced from all feature maps, and these 4 features are merged. The last layer accepts this feature vector as input and utilizes a binary classifier and therefore represents two possible outputs. Textual data is processed sequentially as 1-D convolutions, but the claim and notion remain the same. Figure 6 shows the steps for workflow.

1.   Imports the required data and pre-process it in a suitable format
2.   Use pre-trained word embedding (with Glove, BERT)
3.   Train data on a CNN and evaluate the accuracy of the validation set

Hybrid Approaches

The mixture of ML methods to address SA is known as a Hybrid (Appel et al., 2016). For instance, a classification scheme is hybrid if it is a combination of multiple methods like emoticons, BoW, and sentiment weight. Emoticons are regular expressions that classify a statement into either positive or negative by identifying the existence of an "emotion icon". These are domain and language-dependent. To avoid this, BoW uses the classified list of positive (or negative) words. Each word has been assigned the same weight in the list which results in an incorrect outcome. Whereas, in sentiment weight approach assigns different weights to words depending on their usage in the sentence (i.e., using Part-of-Speech tagging). The hybrid approach is achieved by using different pre-processing approaches as follows. Each step results in a list of features as mentioned:

1.   Run tagging & tokenization process.
2.   Parts Of Speech tagging, mis-spelling process applied on the output of step 1.
3.   Applying semantic rules, managing distinct particles, and handling sentences' negotiations through smart parsing. If these particles negated this step would infer varying the polarity of a sentence.
4.   Take it out the crucial particles that carry opinion.
5.   Go through each sentence, and substitute lexicon with associated words. An output list is produced for those words which are not in the lexicon.

6.   Lexicons are labelled as (POS, and NEG) and the computations are implemented to disclose the semantic orientation of a sentence.

Figure 6. Workflow

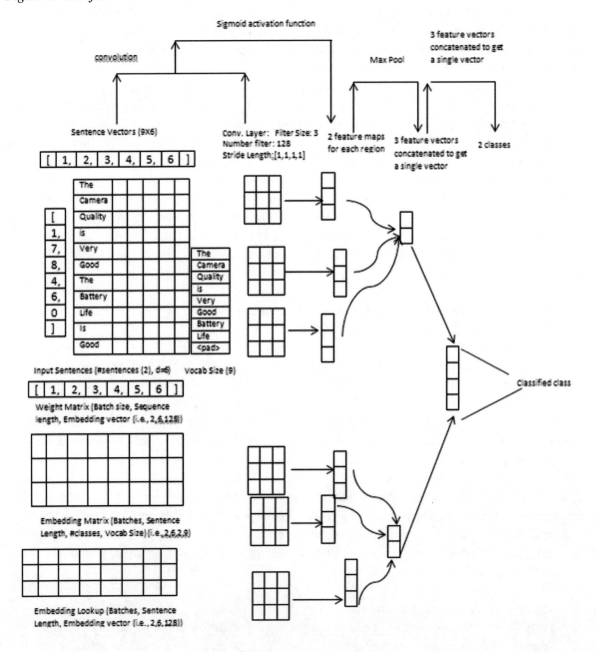

CONCLUSION

The study of text and sentiment has become an important aspect of modern marketing. Apart from that, it is crucial in the division of Natural Language Processing (NLP). It primarily focuses on text classification in order to determine the processing text's intent, which might be positive or negative. Sentiment analysis was also concerned with the computational treatment of sentiments, views, and text subjectivity. This chapter takes a holistic view of prior research solutions, taking into account diverse algorithms, methods, and applications. It provides a comprehensive assessment of recent work in the field of text and sentiment analysis, and then we focus on the major principles, components, functions, and classification algorithms of text and sentiment analysis. We have explored datasets, the supervised classifier models, and required libraries for pre-processing and visualization of the results. We have presented a CNN-based deep learning model and BoW using emoticons. However, SA will delve deeper in the future using XLNet, LSTM, BiLSTM, and RNN to achieve more accuracy.

REFERENCES

Alomari, K. M., ElSherif, H. M., & Shaalan, K. (2017). Arabic tweets sentimental analysis using machine learning. *Advances in Artificial Intelligence: From Theory to Practice*, 602–610. doi: 1 doi:0.1007/978-3-319-60042-0_66

Appel, O., Chiclana, F., Carter, J., & Fujita, H. (2016). A hybrid approach to sentiment analysis. *2016 IEEE Congress on Evolutionary Computation (CEC)*, 4950-4957. 10.1109/CEC.2016.7744425

Bagheri, H., & Islam, M. J. (2017). *Sentiment analysis of twitter data.* arXiv preprint arXiv:1711.10377. doi: 1 doi:0.48550/arXiv.1711.10377

Devi, D. N., Kumar, C. K., & Prasad, S. (2016). A feature based approach for sentiment analysis by using support vector machine. *2016 IEEE 6th International Conference on Advanced Computing (IACC)*, 3-8. doi: 10.1109/IACC.2016.11

Dsouza, D. D., Deepika, D. P. N., Machado, E. J., & Adesh, N. D. (2019). Sentimental analysis of student feedback using machine learning techniques. *International Journal of Recent Technology and Engineering (IJRTE)*, 8(1S4), 986-991.

El-Din, D. M. (2016). Enhancement bag-of-words model for solving the challenges of sentiment analysis. *International Journal of Advanced Computer Science and Applications*, 7(1), 244–252. doi:10.14569/IJACSA.2016.070134

Fauzi, M. A. (2019). Word2Vec model for sentiment analysis of product reviews in Indonesian language. *Iranian Journal of Electrical and Computer Engineering*, 9(1), 525–530. doi:10.11591/ijece.v9i1.pp525-530

Haque, T. U., Saber, N. N., & Shah, F. M. (2018). Sentiment analysis on large scale Amazon product reviews. *2018 IEEE international conference on innovative research and development (ICIRD)*, 1-6. doi: 1. doi:0.1109/ICIRD.2018.8376299

Jamal, N., Xianqiao, C., & Aldabbas, H. (2019). Deep learning-based sentimental analysis for large-scale imbalanced twitter data. *Future Internet*, *11*(9), 190. doi:10.3390/fi11090190

Joshi, V. C., & Vekariya, V. M. (2017). An approach to sentiment analysis on Gujarati tweets. *Advances in Computational Sciences and Technology*, *10*(5), 1487–1493.

Keikhosrokiani, P., & Asl, M. P. (Eds.). (2022). *Handbook of research on opinion mining and text analytics on literary works and social media*. IGI Global. doi:10.4018/978-1-7998-9594-7

Khan, F. H., Bashir, S., & Qamar, U. (2014). TOM: Twitter opinion mining framework using hybrid classification scheme. *Decision Support Systems*, *57*, 245–257. doi:10.1016/j.dss.2013.09.004

Kim, J., Seo, J., Lee, M., & Seok, J. (2019). Stock price prediction through the sentimental analysis of news articles. *2019 Eleventh International Conference on Ubiquitous and Future Networks (ICUFN)*, 700-702. 10.1109/ICUFN.2019.8806182

Krishnaveni, K. S., Pai, R. R., & Iyer, V. (2017). Faculty rating system based on student feedbacks using sentimental analysis. *2017 International Conference on Advances in Computing, Communications and Informatics (ICACCI)*, 1648-1653. 10.1109/ICACCI.2017.8126079

Liu, H. (2017). *Sentiment analysis of citations using word2vec*. doi: 1 doi:0.48550/arXiv.1704.00177

Naresh, A., & Venkata Krishna, P. (2021). An efficient approach for sentiment analysis using machine learning algorithm. *Evolutionary Intelligence*, *14*(2), 725–731. doi:10.100712065-020-00429-1

Rezaeinia, S. M., Rahmani, R., Ghodsi, A., & Veisi, H. (2019). Sentiment analysis based on improved pre-trained word embeddings. *Expert Systems with Applications*, *117*, 139–147. doi:10.1016/j.eswa.2018.08.044

Saif, H., He, Y., Fernandez, M., & Alani, H. (2016). Contextual semantics for sentiment analysis of Twitter. *Information Processing & Management*, *52*(1), 5–19. doi:10.1016/j.ipm.2015.01.005

Severyn, A., & Moschitti, A. (2015, August). Twitter sentiment analysis with deep convolutional neural networks. *SIGIR '15: Proceedings of the 38th International ACM SIGIR Conference on Research and Development in Information Retrieval*, 959–962. 10.1145/2766462.2767830

Shabaz, M., & Kumar, A. (2018). AS: A novel sentimental analysis approach. *International Journal of Engineering and Technology*, *7*(2.27), 46-49. https://doi/org/1 doi:0.14419/ijet.v7i2.27.11679

Sharma, A., & Ghose, U. (2020). Sentimental analysis of twitter data with respect to general elections in India. *Procedia Computer Science*, *173*, 325–334. doi:10.1016/j.procs.2020.06.038

Shrestha, H., Dhasarathan, C., Munisamy, S., & Jayavel, A. (2020). Natural Language Processing Based Sentimental Analysis of Hindi (SAH) Script an Optimization Approach. *International Journal of Speech Technology*, *23*(4), 757–766. doi:10.100710772-020-09730-x

Suryawati, E., Munandar, D., Riswantini, D., Abka, A. F., & Arisal, A. (2018). POS-Tagging for informal language (study in Indonesian tweets). *Journal of Physics: Conference Series*, *971*(1), 012055. doi:10.1088/1742-6596/971/1/012055

Thomas, M., & Latha, C. A. (2020). Sentimental analysis of transliterated text in Malayalam using recurrent neural networks. *Journal of Ambient Intelligence and Humanized Computing*, *12*(6), 6773–6780. doi:10.100712652-020-02305-3

Topal, K., & Ozsoyoglu, G. (2016). Movie review analysis: Emotion analysis of IMDb movie reviews. *2016 IEEE/ACM International Conference on Advances in Social Networks Analysis and Mining (ASONAM)*, 1170-1176. 10.1109/ASONAM.2016.7752387

Tripathy, A., Agrawal, A., & Rath, S. K. (2016). Classification of sentiment reviews using n-gram machine learning approach. *Expert Systems with Applications*, *57*, 117–126. doi:10.1016/j.eswa.2016.03.028

Zou, H., Tang, X., Xie, B., & Liu, B. (2015). Sentiment classification using machine learning techniques with syntax features. *2015 International Conference on Computational Science and Computational Intelligence (CSCI)*, 175-179. 10.1109/CSCI.2015.44

Zucco, C., Calabrese, B., Agapito, G., Guzzi, P. H., & Cannataro, M. (2020). Sentiment analysis for mining texts and social networks data: Methods and tools. *Wiley Interdisciplinary Reviews. Data Mining and Knowledge Discovery*, *10*(3), e1333. doi:10.1002/widm.1333

Chapter 10
Affective Polarization in the U.S.
Multi-Emotional Charge Analyzed Through Affective Computing

David Valle-Cruz

iD https://orcid.org/0000-0002-5204-8095

Universidad Autónoma del Estado de México, Mexico

Rodrigo Sandoval-Almazán

iD https://orcid.org/0000-0002-7864-6464

Universidad Autónoma del Estado de México, Mexico

Asdrubal López-Chau

iD https://orcid.org/0000-0001-5254-0939

Universidad Autónoma del Estado de México, Mexico

ABSTRACT

Affective polarization is a phenomenon that has invaded the political arena empowered by social networks. In this chapter, the authors analyze the Capitol riot posts on Twitter. To achieve this, the authors use affective computing introducing the multi-emotional charge combined with statistical analysis based on the t-student test and Welch's t-test. The research questions guiding this study are: How do social media platforms' messages impact on inciting? Do social media platforms' messages with negative emotional charge affect legitimizing of the Capitol protest? Findings identify the significant influence of Donald Trump on Twitter during the Capitol riot. Moreover, data analysis identifies positive and negative emotions towards Donald Trump as well as similarities in the showed emotions of Trump and the audience.

INTRODUCTION

The takeover of the Capitol in January 2021 by supporters of Donald Trump is an unprecedented event that is attributed to the communication by social media platforms - especially Parler - that organized the far-right groups: QAnon, Patriots, ProudBoys, and many others around the disturbances and the inva-

DOI: 10.4018/978-1-6684-6242-3.ch010

sion of the iconic facilities of American democracy (Prabhu et al., 2021). However, this event is one of many generated in social media, showing polarization and ideological discrepancies. These phenomena sometimes get out of control, inciting the public to carry out real mobilizations or opposing actions between groups to legitimize their ideologies (Munn, 2021).

In this regard, some leaders and groups have generated virtual political and ideological movements, which exacerbate emotions and increase society's polarization, from political campaigns to vaccination measures for the pandemic caused by COVID-19 (Kerr et al., 2021). All this polarization, boosted by social media, has generated a large amount of data that can be analyzed algorithmically, with the support of artificial intelligence techniques. Particularly, in the academic field, the exploitation and understanding of data generated in social media have mostly focused on unimodal sentiment analysis, based on polarity measurement only (Keikhosrokiani & Asl, 2022; Hand & Ching, 2020; Terán & Mancera, 2019). Nevertheless, there is the possibility to perform multimodal sentiment analysis based on different emotional scales, not only on polarity (Poria et al., 2017; Valle-Cruz et al., 2021, 2022), which can be helpful in areas such as marketing, business, and the public sector.

Studies in the political arena have focused on polarity analysis. However, a multi-emotional analysis could provide a richer explanatory quality of the social media audience's emotions, thoughts, and sentiments (López-Chau et al., 2020, 2021). Social media platforms such as Facebook and Twitter have been used to communicate with citizens and the government since their emergence. Social Media platform advantages are synchronous, immediate, low-cost, but above all, viral communication allows for almost instantaneous dissemination of bi-directional government information. This is a double-edged sword for governments; on the one hand, they need to receive feedback from citizens to encourage cooperation and participation. On the other hand, it has exposed governmental errors, bad practices, uncomfortable data, and exposed acts of corruption that were previously hidden.

This governmental communication through social media platforms has changed the way citizens relate to politics. In its beginnings, we saw it when the German pirate party tried to influence the elections (Jungherr et al., 2012). Later, the Arab Spring took off through Facebook and other social media platforms (Arafa & Armstrong, 2016; Passini, 2012). Other cases followed, such as #OccupyWallStreet (Tan et al., 2013) and #Yosoy132 (Treré, 2015), and the gender revolution with #BlackLivesMatter (Ince et al., 2017) and others. More recently, Hong Kong independence fighters and the umbrella revolution (Shen et al., 2020) have used social media, instant messaging, and even gaming applications such as Pokemon Go to organize and communicate their protest worldwide (Vincent, 2019) expressing emotions in a virtual world.

The importance of the study of emotions plays a relevant role in decision-making and a better understanding of social phenomena, as well as political events. Some AI techniques (e.g. convolutional neural, networks and natural language processing) can help advance in this direction (Criado et al., 2021; Valle-Cruz, Criado, et al., 2020). AI techniques have developed different kinds of machines capable of recognizing, expressing, modeling, communicating, and responding to emotional information: this area of knowledge is called "affective computing" (Picard, 2003; Turing, 1950).

The Capitol riot can be analyzed with the Preparatory Media Model, developed by Munn (2021), in three phases: mobilization, incitement, and legitimization:

"Mobilizing occurs through digitally native mechanisms, the same features we use to communicate, to share with others, and to stay informed of events. Digital affordances allow these calls to circulate widely, winning adherents and building inertia. Participants no longer need to commit to being a card-carrying member of a far-right organization but can instead be drawn into a tighter affiliation with radical right elements over time. Inciting seeks to energize these converts, escalating anger until it reaches a critical threshold and erupts into violence. This incitement is not limited to the hushed voices of splinter cells but takes place openly on the free speech havens of Alt-tech platforms like Gab, Parler, and others. Inciting media uses these spaces as testbeds, experimenting with different scenarios, eroding ethical boundaries, and anticipating a range of future activities, legitimizing aims to rationalize future violence as moral, ethical, or even spiritual. These justifications are often based on longstanding tropes: nationalist renewal or religious warfare. However, digital affordances allow this material to be repackaged, spliced into new configurations, and presented in the vernacular of the Web."

This chapter is threefold: 1) Aims to explore the Twitter messages during the Capitol riot. 2) Understands the emotions in Tweets related to the Capitol riot, and 3) addresses if affective polarization (in terms of social identity) is one of the leading causes of the mob using affective computing and statistical analysis. To achieve this, the authors use affective computing with multi-emotional charge1, combined with statistical analysis based on the t-Student test and Welch's t-test. The research questions guiding this study are: Social media platforms' messages impact on inciting? Social media platforms' messages with negative emotional charge affect legitimizing the Capitol riot? The authors analyze the multi-emotional charge of Biden, Trump, and the audience (based on eight emotional levels), as well as the potential relationship of emotions detected with the multi-emotional charge (Terán & Mancera, 2019).

The document consists of six sections. The first one is this introduction. The second section presents the literature review on affective computing and affective polarization and the Hourglass of Emotions Model towards the calculation of the multi-emotional charge. The third section presents the methods based on the multi-emotional charge detected on Twitter data and the statistical analysis. The fourth section shows the results. The fifth section systematically discusses the findings. Finally, the last section shows the conclusions, limitations, and future research paths in affective computing and affective polarization.

AFFECTIVE POLARIZATION AND AFFECTIVE COMPUTING

While new concepts are emerging in the public sphere, new techniques or methods are being implemented in artificial intelligence for the public sector. In this regard, two concepts guide this chapter. The first concept refers to affective polarization, based on Manichean and simplistic views of political adversaries (us versus them), who are presented and perceived as enemies to be eliminated and denied the legitimacy of their existence (Iyengar et al., 2019). The second, purely computational, is affective computing, which refers to an AI area, which has the potential to take advantage of human-machine interaction, information extraction, and multimodal signal processing to detect different people's sentiments from the data generated daily in social media (Chatterjee et al., 2019; López-Chau et al., 2020). In this regard, this section is threefold. The first subsection explains what affective polarization is; the second presents the research on affective computing, and the third shows the Hourglass of Emotions framework.

Affective Polarization

Abramowitz (2015) is one of the pioneer scholars to propose the change of affective polarization in the American electorate. According to Iyengar et al. (2012), affective polarization implies an identity-based sorting of people belonging to either an emotionally favored in-group (us) or an emotionally disfavored out-group. Another concept comes from Druckman and Levendusky (2019). Affective polarization is commonly defined as a growing dislike and distrust of political out-groups such as certain parties and their supporters. As such, affective polarization is related to but conceptually different from ideological polarization based on left or right attitudes on specific policy domains and social polarization along, for example, socio-economic or racial lines (Iyengar et al., 2019).

According to Webster and Abramowitz (2017), the literature says that affective polarization in the electorate is not reflected in the ideological differences between the two parties. Accordingly, Republican and Democratic elites are divided. The authors show a connection between ideology and affective polarization, based on survey data, showing that ideological distance influences feelings toward opposing candidates and the party as a whole.

Several scholars recently focused on affective polarization; Rogowski and Sutherland (2016) found that ideological differences between political figures increasingly polarized affective evaluations; ideology seems to be an essential component of affective polarization. Druckman and Levendusky (2019) focused on measuring the phenomenon in American politics, voters, prejudiced attitudes, and the different types of items to understand affective polarization. Harel et al.'s (2020) research on echo chambers political-ideological group: right-wing Israeli Jews demonstrate that affective polarization and dehumanization manifest through threat, distortion, and collusion statements. Researchers studied a Facebook webpage (The Shadow) until 2019.

Affective polarization research on political party systems and elections is an essential subfield of research—Wagner's (2021) research on two-party systems. Hernandez et al. (2021) studied 99 post-electoral surveys conducted in 42 countries between 1996 and 2016 to understand the origins of affective polarization. Hobolt et al. (2021) analyzes the Brexit vote in light of affective polarization of social identities through different evaluative biases such as partisanship, stereotyping, and prejudice. Lelkes (2021) attempts to explain affective polarization origins between social identity and a reaction to increasingly extreme political actors, which is more related to ideology.

Research on affective polarization and social media is incipient. Norbrandt's (2021) research supports that social media platforms impulse polarization in society. She studied Dutch citizens with secondary data and found that non-users or moderate users in the previous wave attained more polarized attitudes, elevating their subsequent usage of Facebook. Törnberg et al. (2021) developed a model to understand affective polarization based on "echo chambers" they found that information technology catalyzed affective polarization by lowering search and interaction costs. However, moderate Twitter users reduced their subsequent usage and gained more polarized attitudes. This finding reinforces the idea that affective polarization supports social identity from Iyengar et al. (2012).

Yarchi et al. (2021) is the closest research to this one. These scholars analyze Israel's Facebook, Twitter, and WhatsApp over 16 months. They assume that social media has other cross-platform differences. They found three aspects for political polarization (1) interactional polarization, (2) positional polarization, and (3) affective polarization.

Affective Computing

Artificial intelligence (AI) is an area of science that is bio-inspired and psychologically motivated (Floreano & Mattiussi, 2008). Several AI methods, which are in vogue, were created years ago, but their potential was not exploited due to computational limitations. Today, the public sphere and governments worldwide are beginning to automate at unimaginable levels in the last century. In this regard, AI has now been applied to different public administration sectors, from data analysis to predictive analytics applied to policing, the fight against the COVID-19 pandemic, and political election campaigns (Campion et al., 2020; Valle-Cruz, Criado, et al., 2020; Wirtz et al., 2019). In the same way, some government services have been automated, democracy and politics have also been digitized, expressing themselves in new forms of communication based on social media, and the emotions generated in the virtual public sphere towards political mobilization.

According to Calvo et al. (2015, p. 3), affective computing is a scientific and engineering endeavor that draws on theories from different related areas, such as psychology, neuroscience, computer science, and linguistics. It has the potential to be applied to different contexts or problems. In this regard, speech is the hallmark of human-to-human communication, and it is widely recognized that how something is said is as important as what is said. Facial expressions are perhaps the most natural way in which humans express emotions. Social media has become a means of communication between people regarding this idea. Texts generated on social networks are impregnated with emotions, reacting to certain events, or responding to different users.

Affective computing is a nascent area that refers to the study of emotions. Understanding emotions is one of the most important aspects of personal development and growth and, as such, is a key part of emulating human intelligence (Picard, 2000). Affective computing is an emerging interdisciplinary research field bringing together researchers and practitioners from different fields of knowledge, ranging from artificial intelligence and natural language processing to cognitive and social sciences (Poria et al., 2017). Additionally, it is significant to the advancement of AI, and emotion processing is also essential to the closely related task of polarity detection. The ability to automatically capture public emotions about social events, political movements, marketing campaigns, and product preferences has sparked a growing interest in the scientific community because of the exciting challenges. Also, in the business world, because of the remarkable implications for marketing and financial market prediction (Cambria et al., 2017). We could also include the political arena, which is not far behind.

Nowadays, there is a boom in research on AI in the public sector and the political context (Aoki, 2020; Desouza et al., 2020). However, there is a gap in the research related to the AI application in this field. Some studies have analyzed polarity based on sentiment analysis (Ansari et al., 2020; Chauhan et al., 2020; Sandoval-Almazan & Valle-Cruz, 2020) that can be expanded using a broader spectrum of emotional categories through multidimensional sentiment analysis with affective computing techniques (Barron-Estrada et al., 2019; Cambria et al., 2017; Kiritchenko et al., 2014).

Affective computing is an AI area that allows identifying and modeling emotions and interpreting moods, opinions, and trends in texts, images, videos, facial expressions, and body language. Affective computing focuses on technologies and theories that advance understanding of human behavior, considering emotion and cognition in the design of related technologies to fulfill human needs, which gains substantial attention from researchers all over the world (Guo et al., 2020).

Affective computing techniques study and develop systems and devices that recognize, interpret, process, and simulate human emotions in a multidisciplinary approach between the fields of neuroscience and computational cognitive science (Picard, 2003). Affective computing conceptualizes the user's emotional state. It allows adjusting the system to the user's state of mind, having a potential application in different areas of knowledge such as psychology, economy, business, politics, and finance by understanding user-profiles and segmenting customers, besides having application in the analysis of political campaigns (Akhtar et al., 2020; Cambria et al., 2017; Valle-Cruz, Fernandez-Cortez, et al., 2020). Affective computing has also been used to understand the personality and individuals' affective profiles, as well as the generation of affective agents that allow the simulation of the cognitive behavior of human beings (Becker-Asano & Wachsmuth, 2010; Santos, 2016; Vinciarelli & Mohammadi, 2014).

Social media is an essential source of information for data extraction to detect emotional patterns through affective computing and natural language processing techniques (Liu, 2012). Social media analytics have proven valuable in numerous research areas as a pragmatic tool for public opinion mining and analysis. Sentiment analysis addresses the dynamics of complex socio-affective applications that permeate intelligence and decision-making in the sentient and solution-savvy social Web (Wang et al., 2020). With the proliferation of diverse information posted online for product reviews, movie reviews, political views, and more, affective computing research has increasingly evolved from conventional unimodal analysis to more complex forms of multimodal emotion recognition (Poria et al., 2017).

There are two main approaches for applying sentiment analysis on texts. The first one uses machine-learning techniques on features extracted from documents. The second is a lexicon-based approach. Sentiment lexicons are lists of words (and phrases) with prior associations to positive and negative sentiments. Some lexicons can additionally provide a sentiment score for a term to indicate its evaluative intensity strength. Higher scores indicate greater intensity or charge. For example, an entry "great" (positive, 1.2) states that the word "great" has a positive polarity with the sentiment score of 1.2. An entry "acceptable" (positive, 0.1) specifies that the word "acceptable" has a positive polarity, and its intensity is lower than that of the word "great" (Keshavarz & Abadeh, 2017; Kiritchenko et al., 2014). An example of the AI use in political contexts is for voting advice applications to recommend parties and candidates that are close to a citizen's political preferences and require the construction of candidate and party profiles (Terán & Mancera, 2019).

In this regard, some rare attempts to study affective polarization with affective computation have to do with the research of Sandoval-Almazán and Valle-Cruz (2020). In this chapter, the authors analyze voters' emotions in political campaigns, classifying the Facebook emojis (like, love, haha, wow, sad, angry) into positive and negative, and applying a sentiment index to propose a measurement of the emotions generated on Facebook users. Besides, Valle-Cruz, López-Chau, and Sandoval-Almazán (2020) studied tweets generated by the 2017 earthquake in Mexico, proposing a multidimensional perspective of impressions for analyzing emotions in disaster situations. Wang (2020) leverage the reaction emojis delivered from users to media fan pages on Facebook to investigate how users react to media organizations and the implications of selective exposure. The outcomes suggest that the report genres and topics are key factors to categorize media groups through reaction emojis from the online audience. Finally, Valle-Cruz et al. (2021) propose the multi-emotional charge to analyze 2020 U. S. political elections.

The Hourglass of Emotions: A Multimodal Sentiment Analysis Framework

The Hourglass of Emotions is a biologically inspired and psychologically motivated emotion categorization model (Figure 1). In this model, there are four affective dimensions – sensitivity, aptitude, pleasantness, and attention – which measure the strength of a specific emotion in the particular dimension, giving rise to a set of 24 basic emotions, divided into three levels: low, medium, and high (Wang et al., 2020).

To carry out this study, we selected the medium emotional levels of the Hourglass Model that correspond to the categories of 1) disgust, 2) sadness, 3) anger, 4) fear, 5) eagerness, 6) calmness, 7) joy and 8) pleasantness, considering that low levels of the analyzed emotions are equivalent to the emotions with lower levels of activation (dislike, melancholy, annoyance, anxiety, responsiveness, serenity, contentment,

Figure 1. The Hourglass of Emotions
Source: Extracted from https://sentic.net/about/

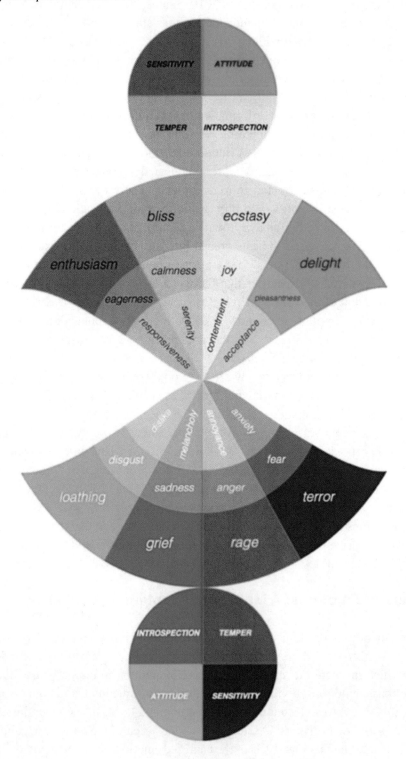

and acceptance). Besides, high levels in the thresholds of the emotions correspond to the highest levels of activation (loathing, grief, rage, terror, enthusiasm, bliss, ecstasy, and delight).

The procedure to extract the emotional content of each document (tweet) is as follows:

- Process a document. The classic text cleaning procedure is performed. This is the one commonly used in the natural language area.
- Separate the document into tokens. The text is separated into tokens, and then each token is looked up in the SenticNet lexicon.
- Emotion recognition. If the token exists in the lexicon, then its emotional charge is retrieved. Because in the used model (Hourglass of Emotions), there are several sentiments, a vector of emotional charges is created, containing all the accumulated emotions.
- Once all tweets have been processed as stated above, we have a matrix composed of all vectors of emotional charges. These vectors are averaged along each dimension (or emotional charge), then we end up with a vector that summarizes all the emotional charges, i.e., a vector of multi-emotional charges.
- The vectors of multi-emotional charges summarize the emotional content of each group of analyzed tweets. Significance tests were applied to identify a statistically significant difference in the emotional charge in each group. Great care was taken to apply the correct statistical test, taking as a criterion the difference or similarity between the variances of each group.

METHOD

The first stage describes the data collected during the Capitol riot. This section shows the data analysis method, based on affective computing techniques, specifically with a sentiment lexicon approach and the Hourglass of Emotions Model towards the multi-emotional charge calculation. The second section explains the emotional charge calculation. The third section shows some examples of the analyzed tweets with their calculated multi-emotional charge and predominant emotions. The fourth section presents the statistical test for comparing the multi-emotional charge of candidates and the audience based on the t-Student test and Welch's t-test.

Data Description

For organizations that monitor the activities of radical and extreme right-wing groups on the Internet, the events did not come as a surprise. On January 6, 2021, hundreds of Donald Trump supporters stormed the Capitol after attending a march in which the former president himself encouraged them to contest the election result. Groups such as the Coalition for a Safer Internet, Advance Democracy, and Alethea also warned, before the 6th, about the conversations taking place online in the run-up to the march in Washington DC. The exchange of messages took place on platforms frequented by Trump supporters, such as TheDonald.win or Parler and on more widely used networks such as Facebook or Twitter, where tags such as #StormTheCapitol or #StopTheSteal encouraged mobilization (Redacción, 2021). As a result of this event, Facebook, Twitter, and Instagram blocked Donald Trump's social media accounts. In addition to removing content that was in serious and repeated violation of the digital platforms' civic integrity policies, his social networks' accounts were permanently suspended.

When news related to the Capitol riot was reported in the mass media, the researchers downloaded all possible Twitter data about this unprecedented event. For this reason, the analyzed data consists of existing tweets downloaded on January 6, 2021. Data correspond to the tweets published by Donald Trump and Joe Biden during the Capitol riot, including trending topics that emerged because of the affective polarization generated. The data sets analyzed are organized as follows: Tweets published by Donald Trump (@realDonaldTrump = 12 tweets) and Joe Biden (@JoeBiden = 15 tweets); trending topics that emerged represented by the Twitter trends due to the Capitol riot, where Twitter audience' emotions were exacerbated. Some trends emerged as a hashtag or by repeating some phrase or words on Twitter (Table 1).

Table 1. Analyzed trending topics

Trending topics	Tweets	Trending topics	Tweets
#Amerikkka	10000	Invoke the 25th	10000
#democracy	10000	Kanye	10000
#ImpeachTrumpNow	10000	Law and Order	10000
#MUNMCI	10000	MAGA	10000
#StormTheCapitol	10000	Maguire	10000
#StopTheSteal	10000	Nancy Pelosi	10000
#ToqueDeQueda	10000	National Guard	10000
#URGENTE	10000	Patriots	10000
#WashingtonDC	10000	PEACEFUL	10000
#Whiteprivilege	10000	Pedri	10000
25th Amendment	10000	Pence	10000
America	10000	Portland	10000
Antifa	10000	Putin	10000
Area 51	10000	Republicans	10000
Biden	10000	Resign	10000
Black Lives Matter	10000	Salvio	10000
Capitol	10000	Soteldo	10000
Capitol Riot	82309	The US	10000
Capitolio	10000	THUGS	10000
Congress	10000	Trump	10000
Estados Unidos	10000	Trumps Legacy	56571
George Floyd	10000	Venezuela	10000
Golpe de Estado	10000	White House	10000
Total		**578880**	

Source: Authors' elaboration

Multi-Emotional Charge Calculation

The processing of emotions is by a lexicon-based approach using the Hourglass of Emotions Model, specifically the SenticNet lexicon (that detects medium emotional levels) (Cambria et al., 2020). For this reason, each tweet detected the emotions according to the following classification: disgust, sadness, anger, fear, eagerness, calmness, joy, and pleasantness. The emotion analysis process based on sentiment lexicons begins with the 1) extraction of posts from Twitter related to the study phenomenon. 2) The publications were classified into two types of data sets: a) Donald Trump's posts, b) Joe Biden's posts, and c) Twitter's audience: posts found in the trending topics that emerged during the Capitol riot. 3) Each post was analyzed using a sentiment lexicon approach to determine the emotions presented only in the texts, omitting hashtags, usernames, emojis, URLs, images, and videos. 4) The mean of the multi-emotional charge was calculated, based on the results of the sentiment lexicons and classified into three main categories: a) Donald Trump, b) Joe Biden, and c) Audience. 5) We generated figures to visualize and compare, in a descriptive way, the mean of the multi-emotional charge during the Capitol riot. 6) Finally, a statistical comparison of the mean of multi-emotional charge was developed, based on the t-Student test and Welch's t-test, to obtain an inference analysis (Figure 2). The following section shows examples of publications calculating their emotional charge and a dominant emotion.

Figure 2. Multi-emotional charge analysis
Source: Authors' elaboration

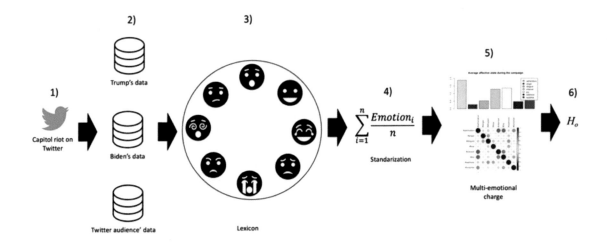

Examples of Emotional Charge with a Highly Predominant Emotion

We calculated the emotional charge with the sentiment lexicon approach. The calculated emotional charge represents the emotions expressed in each Tweet towards the study phenomenon. Since our model detects emotions in a multimodal way, some words contain different emotional values, and therefore, each post on Twitter has different emotional levels. In this manner, we obtained the values of the multi-emotional charge of each post as the sum of the multimodal values of each of the words in the analyzed text.

Table 2 shows some examples of publications that were generated in reaction to the Capitol riot. Each of these publications expresses different emotions towards the event, which makes up the multi-emotional charge. Each post contains a highly predominant emotion towards the Capitol riot event, but with emotional values in different dimensions.

Table 2. Examples of emotional charge with a highly predominant emotion

Tweet	Dominant emotion	anger	calmness	disgust	eagerness	fear	joy	pleasantness	sadness
Stop saying the president needs to call it off stop giving him power he doesn't have only in racist America can armed white people calmly amp comfortably stage a coup storm the United States capitol breaking windows clowning on the house floor without fear of reprisal	Anger	6	2	1	2	2	3	3	3
My suggested motto for a real infrastructure week "infrastructure you can touch" trump failed over and over on infrastructure and some prior infrastructure was just let's spend some money, let's build roads bridges schools mass transit real infrastructure real jobs.	Calmness	1	11	0	4	0	8	1	1
You have really destroyed America Donald Trump from day 1 you have undermined America's reputation in the world you go around talking nonsense inciting violence implement awful policies including racist travel ban Muslim ban diving opinions it is getting out of hands now	Disgust	0	1	9	1	3	3	2	5
There was no reason to force Americans to buy oil from Saudi Arabia at a cost of 20 million jobs when we had just as much oil in Texas, Trump brought oil production back to America it is why gas costs 200 per gallon instead of deep state 450 it would be much higher by now	Eagerness	1	3	0	14	0	5	0	1
Impeached and loser trump has done nothing in his 74 years, except lie cheat, steal, file bankruptcy 6 times, stiff his contractors, tax fraud. Ruin our economy, sexually assault dozens of women, inc minors, & kill 360000 Americans. Trump is a sociopathic amp seditious traitor	Fear	4	0	3	1	9	1	2	8
Just remember to maintain your perspective, my Fintwit friends, Clinton record stock market, Bush record stock market for a while, Obama record stock market, Trump record stock market, Biden likely record stock market	Joy	0	1	0	6	0	11	0	0
According to recorded testimony from our whistle blower, Rosenstein together with Pence's knowledge and consent went on to help engineer the entire coup attempt against President Trump in an attempt to oust trump and promote Pence to the presidency	Pleasantness	2	2	1	5	0	5	6	2
Trump is the first president in 90 years, since Herbert Hoover, to have a net loss of jobs during his term, 4 million jobs lost, an exploding deficit, a failed trade war, a bungled pandemic response and the destruction of our economy, a historically bad one term failed presidency	Sadness	3	0	3	0	5	2	3	12

Source: Authors' elaboration

Comparison of Multi-Emotional Charge

Significance tests are among the most used clinical, pharmaceutical, and psychology studies. It is applied to assess some claims about the population/mean from which the sample has been drawn.

Among the different significance tests, an unpaired t-test (t-student test) is applied to test if there is a significant difference between the means of the two groups. The null hypothesis H0 of this test states that there is no significant difference between the means of the two groups. H0 is accepted if the p-value is greater than the limit chosen by statistical significance (usually 0.05). Otherwise, the alternative hypothesis H1 is accepted, which establishes a significant difference between the means of the two groups. The number of samples in the two groups does not need to be in the same test.

Some assumptions that must be met to apply the unpaired t-test:

- The observations are sampled independently from the population.
- The dependent variable is continuous.
- The dependent variable is normally distributed.
- The data variance is the same between groups, i.e., they have the same standard deviation.

Levene's test for equality of variances can be used to verify the last of these assumptions.

In some data, the standard deviations between groups are significantly different; in these cases, Welch's t-test can be used to obtain reliable results instead of t-student's test. Welch's t-test for comparing means of groups does not rely on the assumption of the same variances between groups.

This chapter uses significance tests to compare the means of multi-emotional charge identified in the tweets. One of the groups is formed by the texts of each candidate, and the other group is formed by the tweets of the audience. Whether the standard deviations are the same between the two groups, then the t-student test is used; otherwise, Welch's t-test is applied. The use of significance tests for the multi-emotional charge between groups enables the analysis of agreement between the emotions detected in the tweets posted by Trump, Biden, and the audience.

RESULTS

In the analyzed Twitter post in the trending topics, a significant proportion referred to or mentioned Donald Trump (19.58%), only 3.68% mentioned Joe Biden. Figure 3 shows that the most important topics identified in the audience were related to Trump, the Capitol riot, the COVID-19 pandemic, vaccination, and mask's use, among other terms (Figure 3).

We were able to gather Donald Trump's last posts on Twitter before his account was shut down regarding the election result. Donald Trump's central theme referred to the voter fraud, and hours later, there was also a call to calm tempers before the Capitol riot (Figure 4).

Joe Biden's speech had three main strands: First, Georgia, an important state in the presidential race, where Biden won by a narrow margin by leveraging an effective campaign to get citizens out to vote. Second, a call for unity, respect, and calm because of the Capitol riot. Third, he mentioned Donald Trump in his speech (Figure 5).

Based on the results of the multi-emotional charge for each data set, we calculated the mean of the multi-emotional charge for the audience of Donald Trump and Joe Biden. Consequently, the mean of the multi-emotional charge shows the emotions of the audience's posts during the election, the emotions of Donald Trump's posts, the emotions of Joe Biden's posts, the mean of the multi-emotional charge of the audience towards Donald Trump and Joe Biden, and the mean of the multi-emotional charge of Donald Trump to Joe Biden and vice versa.

This section is divided into four stages. The first stage shows the general results of the data analysis and the mean of the multi-emotional charge of users. The second stage presents the mean of the multi-emotional charge of Donald Trump. The third stage shows the mean of the multi-emotional charge of Joe

Figure 3. The twitter word cloud from the audience in the capitol riot
Source: Authors' elaboration

Figure 4. Donald trump's twitter word cloud on the capitol riot
Source: Authors' elaboration

Figure 5. Joe Biden's twitter word cloud on the capitol riot
Source: Authors' elaboration

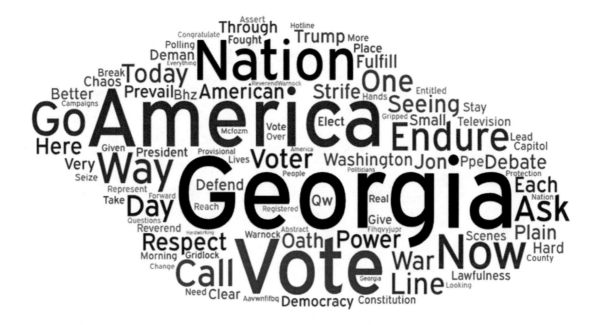

Biden. The fourth section presents the mean results of the comparison of the multi-emotional charges with the t-Student test and Welch's t-test.

General Results and the Average Emotional Charge of the Audience

The emotions generated by the Capitol riot on Twitter were classified into eight groups due to the lexicon approach. The calculation of the mean of the multi-emotional charge resulted in the range of 0.08 to 1.47. In this regard, the most predominated emotions were joy, eagerness, and sadness, because these emotions reached the highest levels. According to the Hourglass of Emotions, this means that there were high levels of ecstasy, enthusiasm, and grief. The low-leveled emotions were anger and pleasantness. Also, according to the Hourglass of Emotions, these types of emotions manifest low levels of annoyance and acceptance. On January 6, 2021, there was an atmosphere of anger and conflict, our analysis of the downloaded data capture this with detected emotions related to sadness, fear, and eagerness.

In brief, the importance of emotions in the Capitol riot placed joy in the first place, followed by impatience and sadness. Joy is explained by the type of data downloaded on Twitter, and the social media like content entertainment including, jokes, pranks, trolling, and fake news. Secondly, impatience was noted by the uncertainty caused by the polarized environment of the election impeachment and the Capitol riot, where an atmosphere of polarization permeated the scenario. On one side by the Trump supporters, and the other by those who disapproved it. The third, sadness arose from disappointment in what was happening, and the perception of an undemocratic and impeachable process not seen in decades in the U. S.

The emotions that predominated in the audience were eagerness, joy, and sadness, like the mean of the multi-emotional charge towards Trump and Biden. The audience showed a medium correlation between joy and eagerness (0.63), disgust and sadness (0.56), and fear and sadness (0.45). However,

Figure 6. Mean of the Multi-emotional Charge Shown by the Audience

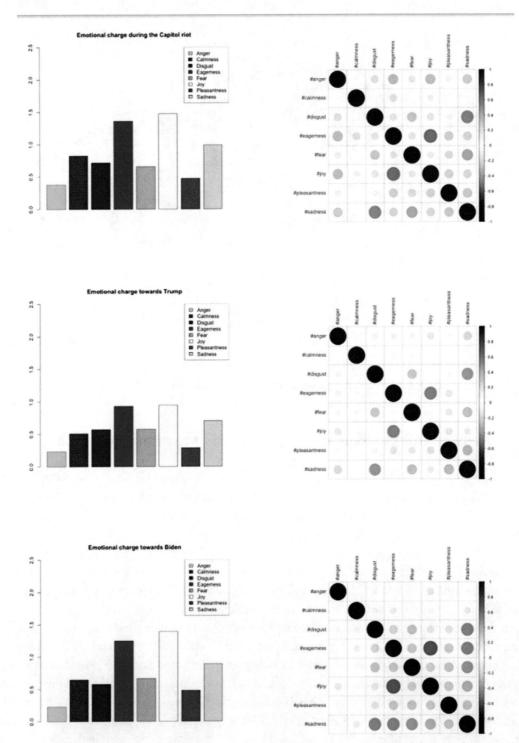

there are similarities in the audience's multi-emotional charge toward Trump and Biden. A greater multi-emotional charge toward Biden is noted, especially in joy and eagerness. Practically, the other emotions have similar levels (See Figure 6).

Donald Trump's Multi-Emotional Charge Mean

According to our multi-emotional sentiment analysis, an important feature of Donald Trump's Twitter posts was steeped in joy and eagerness. The remaining emotions had low levels, especially disgust, anger, pleasantness, and calmness (Figure 7). None of Donald Trump's posts, in this chapter, mentioned or referenced Joe Biden.

Figure 7. Mean of the Multi-emotional Charge Shown by Donald Trump

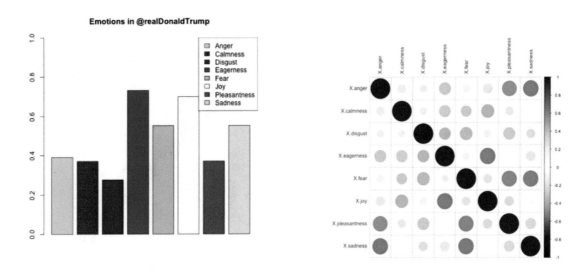

Joe Biden's Multi-Emotional Charge Mean

The predominant emotions in Joe Biden's publications were eagerness and joy. But with a higher level than Donald Trump's posts. The remaining emotions had low levels, especially anger, fear, disgust, and sadness (Figure 8). Joe Biden's predominant emotions toward Trump were eagerness, joy, and disgust. In this regard, the emotions with the least intensity were anger, pleasantness, and fear.

Comparison of Emotional Charges in Tweets

In this section, we present statistical tests to compare the mean of the multi-emotional charge between candidates and the multi-emotional charge of the audience towards candidates. We applied t-student tests to the data related to emotions calculated with SenticNet. A hypothesis test is a rule that specifies whether a statement about a population/mean can be accepted or rejected depending on the evidence provided by a sample of data.

Figure 8. Average Emotional Charge Shown by Joe Biden

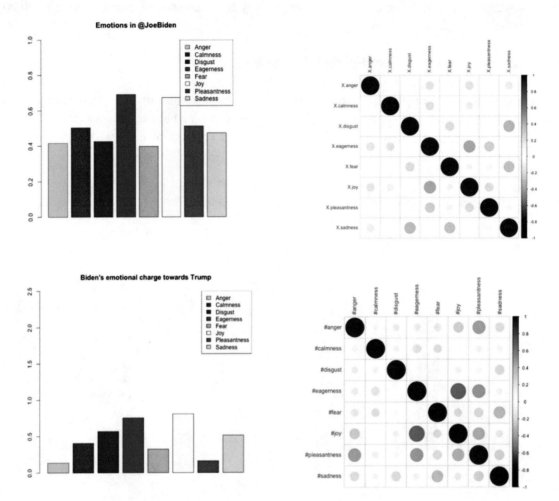

A hypothesis test examines two opposing hypotheses about a population/mean: the null hypothesis (H0) and the alternative hypothesis (H1). The null hypothesis is the statement to be tested. Usually, the null hypothesis is a statement that "there is no effect" or "there is no difference." The alternative hypothesis is the statement that you want to be able to conclude is true according to the evidence provided by the sample data (Anderson et al., 2016). Table 3 shows the mean and standard deviation of the multi-emotional charge of Biden and Trump's tweets and the audience.

An independent-samples test was conducted to compare the mean of the multi-emotional charge of presidential candidates and the audience. The type of test applied, statistics, and the test result are included when the mean of the emotional charges is statistically similar to H0 (Table 4).

According to the analysis results of the multi-emotional charge on Twitter, combined with the comparison of means based on Levenes' test and Welch's t-test, we identified that the mean of the multi-emotional charge between Joe Biden and Donald Trump were similar during the Capitol riot. Similarly, the mean of the multi-emotional charge between Donald Trump and the audience is similar, except for

Table 3. Mean and Standard Deviation of the Multi-emotional Charge

Dataset	Emotion	Mean	SD
Audience	anger	0.38	0.73
	calmness	0.82	1.26
	disgust	0.71	1.01
	eagerness	1.36	1.63
	fear	0.66	0.95
	joy	1.47	1.81
	pleasantness	0.47	0.80
	sadness	0.99	1.25
Trump	anger	0.17	0.39
	calmness	0.25	0.62
	disgust	0.08	0.29
	eagerness	0.58	0.51
	fear	0.33	0.49
	joy	0.67	0.65
	pleasantness	0.25	0.62
	sadness	0.33	0.49
Biden	anger	0.24	0.52
	calmness	0.48	0.82
	disgust	0.34	0.71
	eagerness	1.14	1.19
	fear	0.24	0.56
	joy	1.13	1.24
	pleasantness	0.36	0.60
	sadness	0.34	0.64
Audience toward Trump	anger	0.23	0.55
	calmness	0.51	0.96
	disgust	0.57	0.87
	eagerness	0.93	1.09
	fear	0.58	0.84
	joy	0.95	1.12
	pleasantness	0.29	0.63
	sadness	0.70	1.05
Audience toward Biden	anger	0.22	0.54
	calmness	0.65	1.07
	disgust	0.58	0.90
	eagerness	1.24	1.73
	fear	0.66	0.91
	joy	1.39	1.78
	pleasantness	0.48	0.69
	sadness	0.89	1.23

Source: Authors' elaboration

eagerness (the same is true between Joe Biden and Donald Trump). Finally, the only common emotion expressed by Joe Biden and the audience during the Capitol riot was "disgust." In the next section, we will discuss the findings of the study.

Table 4. Comparison of the Multi-emotional Charge of Trump, Biden, and the Audience

Comparison of the multi-emotional charge		Anger	Calmness	Disgust	Eagerness	Fear	Joy	Pleasantness	Sadness
Joe Biden vs Donald Trump[1]	p-value Levenes' test	0.226	0.642	0.120	0.000	0.034	0.068	0.373	0.013
	t-student / Welch's t-test p-value	0.586	0.994	0.999	0.0222	0.354	0.0591	0.340	0.311
	H_0	Accepted	Accepted	Accepted	Rejected	Accepted	Accepted	Accepted	Accepted
Donald Trump vs Audience[2]	Levenes' test p-value	0.063	0.569	0.238	0.004	0.012	0.018	0.806	0.028
	t-student / Welch's t-test p-value	0.424	0.629	0.999	0.049	0.217	0.086	0.881	0.193
	H_0	Accepted	Accepted	Accepted	Rejected	Accepted	Accepted	Accepted	Accepted
Joe Biden vs Audience[3]	Levenes' test p-value	0.000	0.002	0.077	0.000	0.000	0.000	0.000	0.000
	t-student / Welch's t-test p-value	0.003	0.000	0.314	0.001	0.005	0.000	0.001	0.000
	H_0	Rejected	Rejected	Accepted	Rejected	Rejected	Rejected	Rejected	Rejected

Source: Authors' elaboration

[1]H_0: There is no difference in the mean of the multi-emotional charge in Biden and Trump's posts.

H_1: There is difference in the mean of the multi-emotional charge in Biden and Trump's posts.

[2]H_0: There is no difference in the mean of the multi-emotional charge in Trump and Audience's posts.

H_1: There is difference in the mean of the multi-emotional charge in Trump and Audience's posts.

[3]H_0: There is no difference in the mean of the multi-emotional charge in Biden and Audience's posts.

H_1: There is difference in the mean of the multi-emotional charge in Biden and Audience's posts.

DISCUSSION

Affective polarization is a growing phenomenon in our modern society. The case of the Capitol riot is one of many events that have been generated worldwide. Other important recent events are Brexit and the COVID-19 pandemic. In our analysis, we identified emotions (both positive and negative) towards Donald Trump, perhaps one of the most polarizing presidents in contemporary history, which exacerbated the temperament between Republicans and Democrats (Webster & Abramowitz, 2017). Harel et al. (2020) argue that affective polarization and dehumanization manifest through threat, distortion, and collusion statements. In this regard, in previous days, and even in his social networks, Donald Trump tried to discredit the electoral results. He even held a meeting before the Capitol riot.

This chapter found a high impact of Donald Trump's posrts on the audience; at least we detected that 19.58% of 578,880 talked about him. The emotional multi-charge was aligned and mimicked the emotions he provoked on Twitter. This makes sense from the idea that affective polarization implies an identity-based classification of people as belonging to an emotionally favored in-group or an emotionally disadvantaged out-group (Iyengar et al., 2012). In this sense, Rogowski & Sutherland (2016) argued that ideological differences between political figures increasingly polarized affective evaluations. Before the Capitol riot, ideological differences could be identified in the multi-emotional charge. The most important one was that Donald Trump and his followers claimed electoral fraud. Those on the opposite side celebrated Joe Biden's triumph in an atmosphere of uncertainty and chaos. Another relevant topic was how to handle the pandemic caused by COVID-19.

In several messages directed towards Donald Trump, there is a strong criticism towards him (see some examples in Table 2), coinciding with the idea that affective polarization manifests as a growing partisan aversion and distrust (Iyengar et al., 2019). On the one hand, there are negative emotions (anger, fear, disgust, and sadness) akin to those displayed by Donald Trump, and positive emotions such as joy, calmness, and pleasantness. This means that Donald Trump was fervently supported by his followers but also hated by his detractors.

After all, what happened on January 6, 2021, was that Donald Trump's social network accounts were shut down, generating another controversy between the thin line between what can and cannot be published on social networks and freedom of expression. What is certain is that Donald Trump had a great influence with every Tweet he published, generating affective polarization since his first electoral campaign (Abramowitz & McCoy, 2019). In addition to this, Trump and Biden showed different approaches to address America's challenges. The central issues were the response to the coronavirus pandemic, the solution to the economic crisis and unemployment, the fight against climate change and immigration policy, highly polarizing issues, adding to this a series of false information related to issues of the U. S. election campaign (Arciniegas, 2020).

According to our findings, the average multi-emotional charge had a more remarkable similarity between Donald Trump and the audience than between Joe Biden and the audience. This is inferentially supported by our statistical hypothesis testing, based on the t-Student test and Welch's t-test. This can be understood by two main causes: 1). Twitter was permeated with Donald Trump's supporters who were contaminated by Donald Trump's emotions. 2) His detractors reacted the same way he did.

The multi-emotional charge produced by the tweets during the Capitol riot could be interpreted as:

- Donald Trump's supporters on Twitter replicate and expand the emotions generated by his discourse to increase followers and support its claims.
- Supporters of Biden cannot neutralize the discourse and the emotions with their tweets.
- Before and during the Capitol riot, Trump's speech was magnified by tweets.

According to Munn (2021), inciting energizes these converts and escalates anger into violence. Our analysis of multi-emotional charge provides evidence that supports this argument. Despite this, the emotional multi-charge between Donald Trump and Joe Biden was very similar, perhaps because they pose a purely political discourse on Twitter. Joe Biden may have reacted to Donald Trump's provocations and polarization strategies. This may be possible, as there are some Tweets where Biden mentions Trump, but in the analyzed tweets from the Capitol riot, there are no tweets from Donald Trump mentioning Joe Biden. On the other hand, the multi-emotional charge has no similarities between Joe Biden and the audience. This may result from the change in government and the impact that the attempted storming of the Capitol and contesting of the election results had. Alternatively, almost all the information revolved around Donald Trump because of the event.

According to our descriptive analysis, the most prevalent emotions during the Capitol riot were joy, eagerness, and sadness. This makes sense because the data analyzed is from Twitter and social media is full of jokes and memes. In addition, because this was an unprecedented event for the democratic process in the U. S., eagerness arose from the uncertainty that the Capitol riot caused. Sadness was generated among Twitter users because of their perceived disappointment with what was happening at the Capitol. These emotions also predominate in Donald Trump and Joe Biden's emotional charge.

Regarding our first research question: do posts on social media platforms affect incitement? This may be possible. A significant portion of the conversation on Twitter revolved around Donald Trump, which may have led the audience to mimic Trump's emotions. In this regard, Donald Trump's multi-emotional charge was reflected in the audience. According to our hypothesis testing, there was a difference in the mean of the multi-emotional charge in Trump and audience posts, only in the "eagerness" emotion. For all other emotions, it was found that there was no difference in the means of the multi-emotional charge, which may mean that Donald Trump exacerbated and transferred his emotions in the audience in the face of alleged electoral fraud. For this reason, his social media accounts had to be permanently deleted so that he would not continue to generate influence.

Related to our second research question: do posts on social media platforms with negative emotional charges affect the legitimization of the Capitol riot? There may also be evidence, as the emotional charge on dimensions such as anger, fear, disgust, and sadness were similar between Donald Trump and the audience. However, one of our findings is that also positive emotional charge has an influence, as emotions such as calmness, joy, and pleasantness were similar between Donald Trump and the audience. This may be possible because of the mimicry effect or echo bubble between the influencer and his followers. The positive emotions could be explained as social identity (affective polarization) to its leader, but the claims - #democracy and #ImpeachTrumpNow – are polarized among the two groups; our data shows this difference. The negative emotions emerged in the affective polarization exacerbated by the emotions of his detractors. In the final section, we present our conclusions, limitations, and future research regarding affective polarization and affective computing.

CONCLUSIONS, LIMITATIONS, AND FUTURE RESEARCH

In this chapter, we proposed seminal research to examine the potential of affective computing in a climate of affective polarization. We suggested a multi-emotional charge-based analysis model to explore the emotions of the audience, Donald Trump, and Joe Biden at the Capitol riot, to accomplish this objective. According to the Emotion Hourglass framework, the predominant emotions during the political campaign were joy, eagerness, and sadness. This is explained because the data analysis was based on Twitter posts, where jokes, banter, and memes pervade the content.

The results showed that the emotions of Donald Trump and Joe Biden were similar, except for eagerness, as Joe Biden had a higher level of eagerness in his Twitter content. Given this unprecedented fact in modern U.S. democracy, we found a similarity of Donald Trump's positive and negative emotions with the audience. Moreover, much of the Twitter content from both the audience and Joe Biden revolved around Donald Trump. This is contrary to Joe Biden, as the only similar emotion between Joe Biden and the audience was "disgust". This type of research can provide a broader analysis of political events on Twitter to learn about affinity or repulsion towards certain political figures or events that generate affective polarization. Also, this type of analysis can provide a better understanding of the virtual profile of political actors.

Our limitations in this chapter are related to the data collected; it is not possible to know the particular behavior of each type of political ideology, political wing, or political party to identify the voter's reactions who are for or against a candidate. Nor is it possible to gather all the information that happens at an event like the Capitol riot and much information becomes obsolete in a matter of minutes (volatility). These limitations are inherent in the study type because it was conducted with Twitter posts. However, a large part of the posts shows writing errors and misspellings, which may indicate the socio-economic level of a portion of those who participated in the Twitter discussion. Also, there are opportunities for improvement in identifying specific characteristics such as ideological polarization based on left- or right-wing attitudes and social polarization along socio-economic or racial lines.

One limitations of the study led us to reflect on our future work on this research problem. The content of social networks presented certain levels of sarcasm and irony that we did not analyze. However, their study may lead us to a better understanding of the effect of affective polarization on Twitter. Another limitation is that several Twitter accounts, including Donald Trump's, and several tweets within the trending topics were deleted, making post-Capitol riot analysis with Twitter data difficult. Future work will explore these types of techniques to perform analyses that will lead us to obtain better results in the analysis of affective polarization, political campaigns, profiling, and election prediction, through different types of data and artificial intelligence techniques.

Our findings show the impact of emotions on the different tweets and actors. Trump's tweets manipulated emotions like joy, eagerness, and sadness. Also, Biden's tweets did not affect public opinion. Our data does not explain the Capitol riot, organization, or incitation. It explains the multi-emotional charge of the messages that strongly relate to social behavior.

Our main contribution is that using affective computing techniques, multi-emotional charge helps explain affective polarization. The Capitol riot is an example of Twitter datasets to expand the unimodal understanding to a broader explanation of the emotions and motivation of the audience. Another contribution of our research is that it contributes to linking the impacts among Twitter, political polarization, ideology, and beliefs. It is a tool to broadcast and make viral positions with enough repetition to become truth. Finally, our research tests Munn's (2021) framework to understand the Capitol riot's event. Further research is needed to expand this model.

REFERENCES

Abramowitz, A., & McCoy, J. (2019). United States: Racial resentment, negative partisanship, and polarization in Trump's America. *The Annals of the American Academy of Political and Social Science*, *681*(1), 137–156. doi:10.1177/0002716218811309

Abramowitz, A. I. (2015). The new American electorate. American Gridlock. *The Sources, Character, and Impact of Political Polarization*, *19*, 408–446.

Akhtar, M. S., Ekbal, A., & Cambria, E. (2020). How intense are you? predicting intensities of emotions and sentiments using stacked ensemble. *IEEE Computational Intelligence Magazine*, *15*(1), 64–75. doi:10.1109/MCI.2019.2954667

Anderson, D. R., Sweeney, D. J., Williams, T. A., Camm, J. D., & Cochran, J. J. (2016). *Statistics for Business & Economics*. Cengage Learning.

Ansari, M. Z., Aziz, M. B., Siddiqui, M. O., Mehra, H., & Singh, K. P. (2020). Analysis of political sentiment orientations on twitter. *Procedia Computer Science*, *167*, 1821–1828. doi:10.1016/j.procs.2020.03.201

Aoki, N. (2020). An experimental study of public trust in AI chatbots in the public sector. *Government Information Quarterly*, *37*(4), 101490. doi:10.1016/j.giq.2020.101490

Arafa, M., & Armstrong, C. (2016). Facebook to Mobilize, Twitter to Coordinate Protests, and YouTube to Tell the World": New Media, Cyberactivism, and the Arab Spring. *Journal of Global Initiatives: Policy, Pedagogy, Perspective*, *10*(1), 6.

Arafa, M., & Armstrong, C. (2016). Facebook to Mobilize, Twitter to Coordinate Protests, and YouTube to Tell the World": New Media, Cyberactivism, and the Arab Spring. *Journal of Global Initiatives: Policy, Pedagogy, Perspective*, *10*(1), 6.

Arciniegas, Y. (2020). *Trump vs. Biden: las promesas de los candidatos en cinco temas cruciales*. France 24. https://www.france24.com/es/ee-uu-y-canadá/20201030-eeuu-propuestas-campaña-trump-biden-pandemia-salud-economia

Barron-Estrada, M. L., Zatarain-Cabada, R., & Oramas-Bustillos, R. (2019). Emotion Recognition for Education using Sentiment Analysis. *Research in Computing Science*, *148*(5), 71–80. doi:10.13053/rcs-148-5-8

Becker-Asano, C., & Wachsmuth, I. (2010). Affective computing with primary and secondary emotions in a virtual human. *Autonomous Agents and Multi-Agent Systems*, *20*(1), 32–49. doi:10.100710458-009-9094-9

Calvo, R. A., D'Mello, S., Gratch, J. M., & Kappas, A. (2015). *The Oxford handbook of affective computing*. Oxford Library of Psychology. doi:10.1093/oxfordhb/9780199942237.001.0001

Cambria, E., Das, D., Bandyopadhyay, S., & Feraco, A. (2017). Affective computing and sentiment analysis. In *A practical guide to sentiment analysis* (pp. 1–10). Springer. doi:10.1007/978-3-319-55394-8_1

Cambria, E., Li, Y., Xing, F. Z., Poria, S., & Kwok, K. (2020). SenticNet 6: Ensemble application of symbolic and subsymbolic AI for sentiment analysis. *Proceedings of the 29th ACM International Conference on Information & Knowledge Management*, 105–114. 10.1145/3340531.3412003

Campion, A., Hernandez, M.-G., Jankin, S. M., & Esteve, M. (2020). Managing Artificial Intelligence Deployment in the Public Sector. *Computer*, *53*(10), 28–37. doi:10.1109/MC.2020.2995644

Chatterjee, A., Gupta, U., Chinnakotla, M. K., Srikanth, R., Galley, M., & Agrawal, P. (2019). Understanding emotions in text using deep learning and big data. *Computers in Human Behavior*, *93*, 309–317. doi:10.1016/j.chb.2018.12.029

Chauhan, P., Sharma, N., & Sikka, G. (2020). The emergence of social media data and sentiment analysis in election prediction. *Journal of Ambient Intelligence and Humanized Computing*, 1–27.

Criado, J. I., Sandoval-Almazan, R., Valle-Cruz, D., & Ruvalcaba-Gómez, E. A. (2021). Chief information officers' perceptions about artificial intelligence. *First Monday*.

Desouza, K. C., Dawson, G. S., & Chenok, D. (2020). Designing, developing, and deploying artificial intelligence systems: Lessons from and for the public sector. *Business Horizons*, *63*(2), 205–213. doi:10.1016/j.bushor.2019.11.004

Druckman, J. N., & Levendusky, M. S. (2019). What do we measure when we measure affective polarization? *Public Opinion Quarterly*, *83*(1), 114–122. doi:10.1093/poq/nfz003

Floreano, D., & Mattiussi, C. (2008). *Bio-inspired artificial intelligence: theories, methods, and technologies*. MIT Press.

Guo, F., Li, F., Lv, W., Liu, L., & Duffy, V. G. (2020). Bibliometric Analysis of Affective Computing Researches during 1999~ 2018. *International Journal of Human-Computer Interaction*, *36*(9), 801–814. doi:10.1080/10447318.2019.1688985

Hand, L. C., & Ching, B. D. (2020). Maintaining neutrality: A sentiment analysis of police agency Facebook pages before and after a fatal officer-involved shooting of a citizen. *Government Information Quarterly*, *37*(1), 101420. doi:10.1016/j.giq.2019.101420

Harel, T. O., Jameson, J. K., & Maoz, I. (2020). The normalization of hatred: Identity, affective polarization, and dehumanization on Facebook in the context of intractable political conflict. *Social Media+ Society, 6*(2).

Hernandez, E., Anduiza, E., & Rico, G. (2021). Affective polarization and the salience of elections. *Electoral Studies*, *69*, 102203. doi:10.1016/j.electstud.2020.102203

Hobolt, S. B., Leeper, T. J., & Tilley, J. (2021). Divided by the vote: Affective polarization in the wake of the Brexit referendum. *British Journal of Political Science*, *51*(4), 1476–1493. doi:10.1017/S0007123420000125

Ince, J., Rojas, F., & Davis, C. A. (2017). The social media response to Black Lives Matter: How Twitter users interact with Black Lives Matter through hashtag use. *Ethnic and Racial Studies*, *40*(11), 1814–1830. doi:10.1080/01419870.2017.1334931

Iyengar, S., Lelkes, Y., Levendusky, M., Malhotra, N., & Westwood, S. J. (2019). The origins and consequences of affective polarization in the United States. *Annual Review of Political Science*, *22*(1), 129–146. doi:10.1146/annurev-polisci-051117-073034

Iyengar, S., Sood, G., & Lelkes, Y. (2012). Affect, not ideologya social identity perspective on polarization. *Public Opinion Quarterly*, *76*(3), 405–431. doi:10.1093/poq/nfs038

Jungherr, A., Jürgens, P., & Schoen, H. (2012). Why the pirate party won the german election of 2009 or the trouble with predictions: A response to tumasjan, a., sprenger, to, sander, pg, & welpe, im "predicting elections with twitter: What 140 characters reveal about political sentiment." *Social Science Computer Review*, *30*(2), 229–234. doi:10.1177/0894439311404119

Keikhosrokiani, P., & Asl, M. P. (Eds.). (2022). *Handbook of research on opinion mining and text analytics on literary works and social media*. IGI Global. doi:10.4018/978-1-7998-9594-7

Kerr, J., Panagopoulos, C., & van der Linden, S. (2021). Political polarization on COVID-19 pandemic response in the United States. *Personality and Individual Differences*, *179*, 110892. doi:10.1016/j.paid.2021.110892 PMID:34866723

Keshavarz, H., & Abadeh, M. S. (2017). ALGA: Adaptive lexicon learning using genetic algorithm for sentiment analysis of microblogs. *Knowledge-Based Systems*, *122*, 1–16. doi:10.1016/j.knosys.2017.01.028

Kiritchenko, S., Zhu, X., & Mohammad, S. M. (2014). Sentiment analysis of short informal texts. *Journal of Artificial Intelligence Research*, *50*, 723–762. doi:10.1613/jair.4272

Lelkes, Y. (2021). Policy over party: Comparing the effects of candidate ideology and party on affective polarization. *Political Science Research and Methods*, *9*(1), 189–196. doi:10.1017/psrm.2019.18

Liu, B. (2012). Sentiment analysis and opinion mining. *Synthesis Lectures on Human Language Technologies*, *5*(1), 1–167. https://www.cs.uic.edu/~liub/FBS/liub-SA-and-OM-book.pdf

López-Chau, A., Valle-Cruz, D., & Sandoval-Almazán, R. (2020). Sentiment Analysis of Twitter Data Through Machine Learning Techniques. In Software Engineering in the Era of Cloud Computing (pp. 185–209). Springer. doi:10.1007/978-3-030-33624-0_8

López-Chau, A., Valle-Cruz, D., & Sandoval-Almazán, R. (2021). Sentiment Analysis in Crisis Situations for Better Connected Government: Case of Mexico Earthquake in 2017. In Web 2.0 and Cloud Technologies for Implementing Connected Government (pp. 162–181). IGI Global. doi: 10.4018/978-1-6684-6303-1.ch006

Munn, L. (2021). More than a mob: Parler as preparatory media for the US Capitol storming. *First Monday*. Advance online publication. doi:10.5210/fm.v26i3.11574

Nordbrandt, M. (2021). Affective polarization in the digital age: Testing the direction of the relationship between social media and users' feelings for out-group parties. *New Media & Society*.

Passini, S. (2012). The Facebook and Twitter revolutions: Active participation in the 21st century. *Human Affairs*, *22*(3), 301–312. doi:10.247813374-012-0025-0

Picard, R. W. (2000). *Affective computing*. MIT Press. doi:10.7551/mitpress/1140.001.0001

Picard, R. W. (2003). Affective computing: Challenges. *International Journal of Human-Computer Studies*, *59*(1–2), 55–64. doi:10.1016/S1071-5819(03)00052-1

Poria, S., Cambria, E., Bajpai, R., & Hussain, A. (2017). A review of affective computing: From unimodal analysis to multimodal fusion. *Information Fusion*, *37*, 98–125. doi:10.1016/j.inffus.2017.02.003

Prabhu, A., Guhathakurta, D., Subramanian, M., Reddy, M., Sehgal, S., Karandikar, T., Gulati, A., Arora, U., Shah, R. R., Kumaraguru, P., & Associates. (2021). *Capitol (Pat) riots: A comparative study of Twitter and Parler*. ArXiv Preprint ArXiv:2101.06914.

Redacción. (2021). *Asalto al Capitolio: las pistas sobre cómo el ataque no fue tan espontáneo (y las sospechas de que hubo ayuda desde dentro)*. BBC News Mundo. https://www.bbc.com/mundo/noticias-internacional-55671725

Rogowski, J. C., & Sutherland, J. L. (2016). How ideology fuels affective polarization. *Political Behavior*, *38*(2), 485–508. doi:10.100711109-015-9323-7

Sandoval-Almazan, R., & Valle-Cruz, D. (2020). Sentiment Analysis of Facebook Users Reacting to Political Campaign Posts. *Digital Government: Research and Practice*, *1*(2), 1–13. doi:10.1145/3382735

Santos, O. C. (2016). Emotions and personality in adaptive e-learning systems: an affective computing perspective. In *Emotions and personality in personalized services* (pp. 263–285). Springer. doi:10.1007/978-3-319-31413-6_13

Shen, F., Xia, C., & Skoric, M. (2020). Examining the roles of social media and alternative media in social movement participation: A study of Hong Kong's Umbrella Movement. *Telematics and Informatics*, *47*, 101303. doi:10.1016/j.tele.2019.101303

Terán, L., & Mancera, J. (2019). Dynamic profiles using sentiment analysis and twitter data for voting advice applications. *Government Information Quarterly*, *36*(3), 520–535. doi:10.1016/j.giq.2019.03.003

Törnberg, P., Andersson, C., Lindgren, K., & Banisch, S. (2021). Modeling the emergence of affective polarization in the social media society. *PLoS One*, *16*(10), e0258259. doi:10.1371/journal.pone.0258259 PMID:34634056

Turing, I. B. A. (1950). Computing machinery and intelligence-AM Turing. *Mind*, *59*(236), 433–460. doi:10.1093/mind/LIX.236.433

Valle-Cruz, D., Criado, J. I., Sandoval-Almazán, R., & Ruvalcaba-Gomez, E. A. (2020). Assessing the public policy-cycle framework in the age of artificial intelligence: From agenda-setting to policy evaluation. *Government Information Quarterly*, *37*(4), 101509. doi:10.1016/j.giq.2020.101509

Valle-Cruz, D., Fernandez-Cortez, V., López-Chau, A., & Sandoval-Almazan, R. (2020). *Does Twitter affect Stock Market Decisions? Financial Sentiment Analysis in Pandemic Seasons: A Comparative Study of H1N1 and COVID-19*. Academic Press.

Valle-Cruz, D., López-Chau, A., & Sandoval-Almazán, R. (2020). Impression analysis of trending topics in Twitter with classification algorithms. *Proceedings of the 13th International Conference on Theory and Practice of Electronic Governance*, 430–441. 10.1145/3428502.3428570

Valle-Cruz, D., Lopez-Chau, A., & Sandoval-Almazan, R. (2021). How much do Twitter posts affect voters? Analysis of the multi-emotional charge with affective computing in political campaigns. *DG. O2021: The 22nd Annual International Conference on Digital Government Research*, 1–14.

Valle-Cruz, D., López-Chau, A., & Sandoval-Almazán, R. (2022). Review on the Application of Lexicon-Based Political Sentiment Analysis in Social Media. In Handbook of Research on Opinion Mining and Text Analytics on Literary Works and Social Media (pp. 1-21). IGI Global. doi:10.4018/978-1-7998-9594-7.ch001

Vincent, D. (2019). *Hong Kong protesters turn to Uber and Pokemon*. BBC News, Hong Kong. Https://Www. Bbc. Com/News/Technology-49280726

Vinciarelli, A., & Mohammadi, G. (2014). A survey of personality computing. *IEEE Transactions on Affective Computing*, *5*(3), 273–291. doi:10.1109/TAFFC.2014.2330816

Wagner, M. (2021). Affective polarization in multiparty systems. *Electoral Studies*, *69*, 102199. doi:10.1016/j.electstud.2020.102199

Wang, M.-H. (2020). Positioning and Categorizing Mass Media Using Reaction Emojis on Facebook. *The Computer Journal*.

Wang, Z., Ho, S.-B., & Cambria, E. (2020). A review of emotion sensing: Categorization models and algorithms. *Multimedia Tools and Applications*, *79*(47-48), 1–30. doi:10.100711042-019-08328-z

Webster, S. W., & Abramowitz, A. I. (2017). The ideological foundations of affective polarization in the US electorate. *American Politics Research*, *45*(4), 621–647. doi:10.1177/1532673X17703132

Wirtz, B. W., Weyerer, J. C., & Geyer, C. (2019). Artificial intelligence and the public sector—Applications and challenges. *International Journal of Public Administration*, *42*(7), 596–615. doi:10.1080/01900692.2018.1498103

Yarchi, M., Baden, C., & Kligler-Vilenchik, N. (2021). Political polarization on the digital sphere: A cross-platform, over-time analysis of interactional, positional, and affective polarization on social media. *Political Communication*, *38*(1–2), 98–139. doi:10.1080/10584609.2020.1785067

Yarchi, M., Baden, C., & Kligler-Vilenchik, N. (2021). Political polarization on the digital sphere: A cross-platform, over-time analysis of interactional, positional, and affective polarization on social media. *Political Communication*, *38*(1-2), 98–139. doi:10.1080/10584609.2020.1785067

KEY TERMS AND DEFINITIONS

Affective Computing: It is also called emotional intelligence, being the one whose purpose is the development of artificial affective systems (capable of measuring, interpreting and simulating emotions) based on the design and development of techniques.

Affective Polarization: The emotional distance between the affection aroused by those who sympathize with our same political ideas as opposed to the rejection of those who have different opinions.

Artificial Intelligence: Science and technique that aims to develop systems or machines that imitate human intelligence using various techniques to perform specific tasks.

Capitol Riot: The event took place on January 6, 2021, when supporters of former U.S. President Donald Trump stormed the congressional headquarters violating security and occupying parts of the building for several hours.

Multi-Emotional Charge: Multiple emotional or sentiment levels provoked by an event in terms of anger, sadness, joy, anxiety, etc.

Sentiment Analysis: Artificial intelligence technique that allows to perform data analysis collected from various sources and understand people's opinions, attitudes, and emotions. The tools dedicated to sentiment analysis use technologies such as natural language processing, text analysis, among others.

ENDNOTE

[1]   According to the APA Dictionary of Psychology, the emotional charge is a "strong emotion, such as anger, conceived as being bottled up under pressure and ready to explode. The concept also involves the idea that emotions are negatively or positively charged."

Chapter 11
Applying Sentiment Analysis Techniques in Social Media Data About Threat of Armed Conflicts Using Two Times Series Models

Marilyn Minicucci Ibañez
National Institute for Space Research, Brazil

Reinaldo Roberto Rosa
National Institute for Space Research, Brazil

Lamartine Nogueira Frutuoso Guimarães
Technological Institute of Aeronautics, Brazil

ABSTRACT

The growing cases of armed conflicts over the past couple of decades have dramatically affected social landscapes and people's lives across the globe, urging everyone to find ways to minimize the negative consequences of the conflicts. Social media provides an inexhaustible data source that can be used in understanding the evolution of such conflicts. This chapter focuses on Syria-USA and Iran-USA relations to presents an approach to armed conflict analysis and examines the Russia-Ukraine conflicts by performing sentiment analysis on the text dataset as well as on a vocabulary data. All conflicts generate a social media news threat time series (TTS) that is used as input to the P-model algorithm to generate the endogenous time series. The following uses the TTS and endogenous time series for both conflicts as input to the deep-learning-LSTM neural network. Finally, this chapter compares the prediction result of the Russia-Ukraine TTS analysis with the Russia-Ukraine endogenous series using the P-model algorithm.

DOI: 10.4018/978-1-6684-6242-3.ch011

INTRODUCTION

The evolution of the internet has enabled the advent of the social media as one of the main means of circulation of personal, political, and public information. As such, there is a need for the use of modern techniques such as machine learning and sentiment analysis to assist in accurate verification of specific information among these enormous volumes of data. One such areas of the society that calls for a more profound analysis of its causes and consequences is social extreme events, such as armed conflicts. An extreme event is a sequence of small events generated by human emotions or some reactions of nature that can evolve into a major event and even a catastrophic event. Armed conflicts are social extreme events that are part of the history of the human development (Sornette, 2006). Armed conflicts, within this context, are sequences of threats followed by attacks until they reach their climax with an armed conflict or war. All the problems generated by armed conflicts, call the attention to a solution that helps in the analysis, prediction, and possible alert of the population for a reduction of the damages that such events usually cause (Ibañez, et al., 2022). In this project three models of armed conflicts are used as case studies of social extreme events: the armed conflict between Syria and the USA, the armed conflict between Iran and the USA, and the armed conflict between Russia and Ukraine.

The study of the dynamics of the process of triggering an armed conflict is an area that has been analyzed for decades in many ways. One of the great scholars in this area, Lewis Richardson, has several approaches to the analysis of armed conflicts that cover different models: game-theoretic models, evolutionary games and agent-based models (ABMs), differential equations (DEQ) models, and statistical analyses of time-structured data (Richardson, 1960; Gleditsch, 2020). Thus, this chapter applies an approach using the concepts of sentiment analysis and machine learning to perform an analysis that considers the emotions contained in social media texts as a possible source of the beginning of armed conflicts. In this case, it analyzes more specifically the emotion of threat between heads of states involved in the conflicts addressed.

For information collection, the web search engine Google (Google LLC, 1998) and a chatbot (Lateral GmbH, 2019) are used to performs a search for news related to the topics addressed in this study, which are social and political threats. Each news is collected, stored, and grouped in ascending order according to its publication date.

As for the context, development to an approach of analysis and prediction of threat variation of endogenous social extreme events will be using information collected from news website and social media, such as (Reuters, 2019) (CNN, 2020) (The Guardian, 2020). In processing the news collected from social media, the technique of sentiment analysis is employed to enable the identification of human emotions present in the texts. Sentiment analysis makes it possible to identify similarities of a text to its given context by using a base text with words or vocabularies referring to and representing a domain (Bird et al., 2009). In this case, the domain is the threat of these extreme events (Ibañez, Rosa, & Guimarães, Sentiment Analysis Applied to Analyze Society's Emotion in Two Different Context of Social Media Data, 2020). Thus, each news piece is collected, analyzed, and identified for the percentage of threat existing in its text (Ibañez et al., 2022).

The result of this collection is a portfolio of threats with time series TTS, with the threat level referring to these extreme events. The time series TTS data is applied as input to a P-model algorithm (Meneveau & Sreenivasan, 1987) to generate a time series with endogenous characteristics (Ibañez et al., 2022). This model of time series is considered as the only elements that exert some internal influence on the domain under (Sornette, 2006). The TTS and endogenous series generated are used as input for a system developed with machine learning, more specifically deep learning, to create a model for predicting social extreme events. The social media data allows the application of deep learning technique due to its properties that automatically extracts features and nonlinear correlations existing in the data (Goodfellow et al., 2016). By applying the concepts of deep learning, the study can develop a recursive neural network, Long Short-Term Memory — LSTM, in a system that uses deep learning API TensorFlow Kera's (Chollet, 2015). LSTMs are suitable for classifying, processing, and predicting time series due to the unknown length delays of some series (Hochreiter & Schmidhuber, 1997).

In this chapter, a methodology that uses the technique of sentiment analysis to identify the degree of threat emotion in each news item collected is presented. After this collection, two models of time series—TTS and endogenous series—are generated. Following this, the results generated by the two models are compared to forecast future threat variation of these social extreme events, thus enabling the identification of possible future occurrence of these phenomena. The result of the comparison finds that collecting social media news is better than generating interpolated data to forecast the threats' emotion variation. In this way, the methodology created can be applied to data from the most diverse areas and presents a new approach to analyzing social media information that is of great interest for public utility.

This chapter applies sentiment analysis techniques in social media data about threat of armed conflicts using two times series models. The remaining of this chapter includes background related to sentiment analysis, extreme events of armed conflict, predicting the times series using deep learning, proposed solution to the issue raised in the chapter, discussion, conclusion, and future direction.

BACKGROUND

This section presents the studies related to sentiment analysis and prediction of extreme social events that is armed conflict to show the state of the art of these areas.

Papers Related with Sentiment Analysis

The article, entitled *A Model for Sentiment Analysis Based on Ontology and Cases* (Ceci et al., 2016), presents a work using Case-Based Reasoning technique with the use of ontology to assist in the classification process in sentiment analysis. The model proposes that the stores to reasoning are already developed to be used in future classification. The project uses Amazon's information about cameras and movies as a database, and the ratings posted by users as star rating. The paper presents a result that comprises the comparison of the developed model with Naive Bayes (NB) and Support Vector Machine (SVM) techniques. For the movie domain, the model has an accuracy of 85.0% while the NB and SVM techniques have 78.7% and 78.6%, respectively. For the camera domain, the model has an accuracy of 91.0%, while both the NB and SVM techniques have 84.5%.

Google has released an API of the JAVA language (Google LLC, 2016) about natural language in the cloud. This new service offers developers access to Google's sentiment, entity recognition, and syntax analysis from Google. The part of the sentiment analysis of the API shows the following functionalities:

1. Checking the structure and meaning of text, offering powerful machine learning models that are easy to use.

2. Extracting information about people, places, events and more that are mentioned in text documents, news articles or blog post.
3. Understanding the sentiment about products in social media or analyzing the intent of conversations with customers in a call center or a messaging application.
4. Analyzing the text sent in a request or integration with Google Cloud Storage.

The book *Sentiment Analysis in Social Networks* (Pozzi et al., 2016) reviews published works in sentiment analysis. In each chapter, a topic related to the theme of sentiment analysis is discussed and, at the end, it presents the articles used for the elaboration of the theme in question. Chapter 6 discusses the theme of *Sentiment Analysis in Social Network: A Machine Learning Perspective*, which presents research done using supervised and unsupervised machine learning with biased and supervised machine learning with polarized and non-polarized classification.

The article *Social Media Sentiment Analysis: lexicon versus machine learning* (Dhaoui et al., 2017) compares a lexical analysis-based approach and a machine learning approach to address three research questions:

1. Are there two existing sentiment analysis techniques appropriate for the analysis of social media conversations?
2. To what extent do the results of the two approaches differ when used in social network conversations?
3. Does a combined approach improve the overall accuracy of the classification of sentiment of social media conversations?

To answer these questions, the study uses:

- Data from the social network Facebook,
- The RTextTools, which is a machine learning package in R for automatic text classification,
- The LIWC2015 text mining tool, which is used to conduct a sentiment analysis based on lexical analysis of the data sample.

Results reveal that both approaches achieve higher accuracy in classifying positive sentiment than negative sentiment.

The article *Understanding #worldenvironmentday User Opinions on Twitter: A Topic Based in the Approach of Sentiment Analysis* (Reyes-Menendez et al., 2018) identifies the social, economic, environmental, and cultural factors related to sustainable care for the environment and public health that concern most Twitter users. To identify the factors related to sustainable care for the environment and public health, n = 5.873 tweet that used the hashtag #WorldEnvironmentDay on the respective day are downloaded. A neural network Support Vector Machine (SVM) is used for sentiment classification, and NVivo Pro tool is used to classify the sentiments into positive, neutral, and negative. As for the result, they manage to identify the main factors that concern the global population regarding the planet's sustainable development of public health and environment. The importance and relevance of these results are determined by the analysis of public opinions in social networks about environment.

The article named *Topic Modeling and Sentiment Analysis of Global Climate Change Tweets* (Dahal et al., 2019) addresses the use of social network data for the verification of climate change in different locations. In this study, they use the data from social network Twitter with geotags that make possible the identification of location, date, and time of the messages. To perform the data classification, they use Natural Language Processing techniques such as sentiment analysis and Latent Dirichlet Allocation (LDA). The result of the study shows that general discussion is negative, especially when users are reacting to extreme political or weather events. The discussions on climate change are diverse, but some topics are more prevalent than others.

Papers Related with Extreme Events – Armed Conflict

Muchlinski et al. (2016) take to comparing random forest with logistic regression for predicting class-imbalanced civil war onset data. This paper shows a comparison of the performance of the Random Forest technique with three versions of logistic regression (classical logistic regression, rare event logistic regression, and L1 regularized L1). This comparison finds that the algorithmic approach provides significantly more accurate predictions of the onset of the civil war on sample data than any of the logistic regression models. The paper further discusses these results and the ways in which algorithmic statistical methods such as Random Forest may be useful for a more accurate prediction of rare events in conflict data.

The study entitled *Predicting Armed Conflict: Time to Adjust our Expectations?* (Cederman & Weidmann, 2017) presents a review of several papers on prediction of armed conflict. The review shows the use of simple neural network techniques and the problems each have, mainly related to obtaining realistic information about the social and realistic information of the social and political conditions of the region in conflict. Finally, the author suggests the use of more current machine learning techniques for the analysis and prediction of armed conflicts due to the diverse characteristics of its data.

Project Views: A Political Violence Early Warning System (Hegre, et al., 2019) presents an early warning system on political violence that seeks to be maximally transparent, publicly available, and uniformly covered. O project describes the methodological innovations needed to achieve these goals. ViEWS still produces national and subnational monthly forecasts for 36 months into the future and all three types of violence organized by UCDP: state-based conflict, non-state conflict, and unilateral violence in Africa. The project uses data from UCDP and ACLED, as well as logit modeling (a generalized linear model), dynamic simulation, and Random Forest technique.

Subsequently, the project *Improving Armed Conflict Prediction Using Machine Learning: Views+* (Helle et al., 2018) expands the functional age of the software Violew Early Warning System (ViEWS), which uses numerous variables to perform forecasting. The goal of the project is to perform variable selection automatically, and thus improving the efficiency, speed, and accuracy of forecasts compared to the previous version of the tool. This project uses the techniques of Random Forest and the Python Scikit-learn API.

Paper Trends and Fluctuations in the Severity of Interstate Wars (Clauset, 2018) presents a data-based analysis of the general evidence for trends in the sizes and years between interstate wars around the world. It also shows the use of the resulting models to characterize the plausibility of a trend toward peace since the end of World War II. The underlying variability in these data is captured using an ensemble approach that specifies a stationary process to distinguish trends from fluctuations in the time of onset of war, the severity of wars, and the joint attacks and severity distribution.

The chapter *Modeling Social and Geopolitical Disasters as Extreme Events: A Case Study Considering the Complex Dynamics of International Armed Conflicts* (Rosa et al., 2019) from the book *Towards Mathematics, Computers, and Environment: A Disasters Perspective*, presents how the turbulent dynamics of international armed conflicts are related to the framework of complex multiagent systems.

The analysis explicitly considers the properties of the inhomogeneous multiplicative cascade, where endogeny and exogeny are key points in the phenomenon mathematical model. The result of the study presents a prototype cellular automaton that allows characterizing regimes of extreme armed conflicts, such as the September terrorist attacks and the great world wars.

The article *The Global Conflict Risk Index: A Quantitative Tool for Policy Support on Conflict Prevention* (Halkia et al., 2020) presents, validates, and discusses the Global Conflict Risk Index (GCRI), which is the quantitative starting point of the Global Conflict Early Warning European Union's System. Using logistic regression, the GCRI calculates the probability of national and sub-national conflict risks. Despite its standard and simple methodology, the model predicts better than the other six published quantitative conflict early warning systems for ten out of twelve reported performance metrics. As such, the paper aims to contribute to a cross-fertilization of academic and governmental efforts in quantitative conflict risk modeling.

The article *Characterizing the 2022 Russo-Ukrainian Conflict Through the Lenses of Aspect-Based Sentiment Analysis: Dataset, Methodology, and Preliminary Findings* (Caprolu et al., 2022) studies the 2022 Russo-Ukrainian conflict on the social media platform Twitter. This study quantitatively and qualitatively analyzes a dataset of more than 5.5+ million tweets related to the subject, generated by 1.8+ million unique users. Quantitative analysis and qualitative analysis are applied on the collected data using a statistical analysis technique and an advanced Natural Language processing (NLP) technique called Aspect-Based Sentiment Analysis (ABSA). ABSA allows the extraction of aspects (feature, entity, or topic that is being discussed) and associates a sentiment to them (positive, negative, neutral). The results identify several anomalies in users' behavior and sentiment trends for some subjects that call for further research in the field. In particular, Twitter accounts with a low Friend Ratio (FR) tweet more frequently, with a sentiment trend for some keywords that diverge from other users.

Papers Related the Predicting of Times Series using Deep Learning

The article *A Survey on Deep Learning for Time-Series Forecasting* (Mahmoud & Mohammed, 2021) presents the overview of the most common Deep Learning types for time series forecasting and explains the relationships between deep learning models and classical approaches to time series forecasting. The study presents a brief background on the challenges in time-series data and the most common deep learning techniques that are used for time series forecasting. Previous studies that apply deep learning to time series are reviewed.

The article *Time-series Forecasting with Deep Learning: A Survey* (Lim & Zohren, 2021) presents a review of several papers that center around data modeling using time series that applied topics such as climate modeling, life sciences, medicine, business decisions, and finance. The study also presents a review of how deep learning technique perform to the prediction of these series. In this prediction, machine learning concepts such as nonlinear layers, convolutional neural network (CNN), recurrent neural network (RNN) with LSTM – Long Short-Term Memory, probabilistic hybrid models, non-probabilistic hybrid models, multivariate hybrid models are applied. As a conclusion, the study shows that despite the various models used to learn how to predict time series, there are still some limitations such as data sets with random intervals and improved performance in multivariate models.

The article *DeepAR: Probabilistic Forecasting with Autoregressive Recurrent Networks* (Salinas et al., 2018) proposes a methodology for producing accurate probabilistic forecasts based on the usage of autoregressive recurrent network model on numerous related time series. The DeepAR shows numerous key advantages compared to classical approaches and other global methods:

1. As the model learns seasonal behaviors and dependencies on given covariates across time series, minimal manual feature engineering is needed to capture complex, group-dependent behaviors.
2. DeepAR makes probabilistic forecasts in the form of Monte Carlo samples that can be used to compute consistent quantile estimates for all sub-ranges in the prediction horizon.
3. By learning from similar items, the proposed method can provide forecasts for items with little or no history at all, a case where traditional single-item forecasting method has failed.
4. The proposed approach does not assume Gaussian noise but can incorporate a wide range of likelihood functions, allowing the user to choose one that is appropriate for the statistical properties of the data.

The result of the study shows an extensive empirical evaluation on several real-world forecasting data sets with accuracy improvement of around 15% compared to state-of-the-art methods.

The article *Deep State Space Models for Time Series Forecasting* (Rangapuram, et al., 2018) presents a novel approach to probabilistic time series forecasting that combines State Space Models (SSM) with deep learning. The method scales gracefully from systems where little training data is available to systems where data from a large collection of time series can be leveraged to learn accurate models. In this study, the researchers propose to bridge the gap between these two approaches by fusing SSMs with deep (recurrent) neural networks. The researchers also present a forecasting method that parametrizes a particular linear SSM using a recurrent neural network (RNN). The study concludes that under systems of limited data, the method clearly outperforms other methods by using explicitly modeling seasonal structure.

The literature review provided about topics and techniques addressed in the chapter demonstrates the innovation of the multidisciplinary methodology used. This methodology applies the techniques of sentiment analysis, time series, endogenous time series and deep learning with LSTM networks with data model on an extreme social event that is armed conflicts.

PROPOSED SOLUTION AS THE MAIN FOCUS OF THE CHAPTER

Newspaper and Magazines as Source Information on Social Media

The concept of social media emerged in the mid-1979s with the development of an on-line posting system known as Usenet by Tom Truscott and Jim Ellis of the Duke University in North Carolina, USA. For many years, the concept was used for any means of communication such as magazines, newspapers, and radios. This media model had the characteristic of single-handed means of communication, in which there is little interaction with the user. With the emergence of the social networks such as blogs, wikis, and sharing sites, the concept of social media has also started to include user interaction applications. Today, social media is defined as a set of applications that are based on the Internet and founded on the ideological and technological advances of Web 2.0, allowing the creation and exchange of user-generated content (Moyer & Kaplan, 2020). The following shows a resume of the concepts of social media used in this chapter:

1. Social Media in the beginning of 1979: Single-handed means of communication with little iteration with the user (magazines, newspapers, radio).
2. Social Media currently: Set of applications based on Web 2.0 that allow for creation and exchange of content by the user (magazines, newspapers, radios, wikis, blogs, social networks).
3. Social Media in this chapter: Single-handed means of communication (magazines and newspapers),

This chapter applies the concept of social media as a single-handed means of communication through newspapers and magazines.

Armed Conflict as Social Extreme Events

According to (Department of Peace and Conflict Research at Uppsala University, 1980), armed conflict is characterized by a disagreement between governments and territories. In this disagreement, there is the use of armed force by one of the governments of the states involved. To be characterized as armed conflict, an extreme event needs to generate at least 25 battle-related deaths in a calendar year.

According to (Clauset, 2018), an extreme event involves a human or natural action that can even lead to a catastrophe. Thus, Sornette (2006) argues that extreme events are part of evolution of society, and can designate social, political, and natural events in an endogenous system due to their self-organizing characteristics. So, armed conflict can be considered as a social extreme event—an endogenous system characterizes by events that suffer action only inside its domain (Sornette, 2006).

For the analysis of endogenous social extreme event—the armed conflicts—data is collected from newspapers and magazines with large global circulation ((CNN, 2020), (Reuters, 2019), (The Guardian, 2020), etc. Moreover, the data is considered to have relation with some form of verbal threats or offenses between heads of states or countries that might suggest an outbreak of an armed conflict. For this analysis, the case study considers the news about three different conflicts models as follows:

1. Syrian and USA in the period from January 1, 2016, to April 5, 2017. The end date of this conflict coincides with the day before the launch of Tomahawk missiles—considered medium-range and invisible to radars—by two USA ships in the Mediterranean Sea to the air base of Bashar Al-Assad's regime (UOL, 2017).
2. Iran and USA in the period from January 16, 2019, to January 7, 2020. The end date of the Iran and USA conflict coincides with the attack by jihadist group on the USA base in Iraq.
3. Russia and Ukraine in the period from February 24, 2021, to February 23, 2022. The end date of this conflict coincides with the day before Russia invades Ukraine.

To carry out this research, data is initially collected from news sites that present evidence of threats related to the analyzed extreme event. Next, these threats are verified to recognize potential lead to a sequence of minor events that may finally lead to an endogenous extreme event. Figure 1 illustrates the reflection of this process.

The process that leads to armed conflict shown in Figure 1 are characterized by different forms as presented in Table 1 below.

In newsgathering about armed conflict, internet search and automated search with chatbots (Lateral GmbH, 2019) are used to recognize a list of associated words like the ones presented in Table 2.

Figure 1. Reflection for social media news gathering

Table 1. Characterization of the terms threat, event, and extreme event for social extreme events

Concept	Characterization
Threat	any form of verbal offense
Event	attack occasioned by threat
Extreme Event	armed conflict generated by verbal offense and attack

Table 2. Sample of some words about armed conflicts used in the news collect by search internet and by the chatbot

arms	attack	Force
threat	weapons	Tanks
conflict	armed	War

For each news piece, the date and the URL information are retrieved and stored in a .csv file. The collected news pieces are presented as shown in Table 3.

Table 3. Example of the organization of news about extreme social events stored in the ".csv" file

Data	URL
03/06/17	cnn.com/trump-travel-ban
03/07/17	cnn.com/save-the-children
03/09/17	cnn.com/jon-huntsman
03/10/17	cnn.com/russia-turk
03/10/17	cnn.com/syria-aleppo

Sentiment Analysis on Social Media Mining Datasets

Data Science is an orderly study of data and information pertinent to business and all the inferences that may involve a given topic. It is a science that studies information, its process of capture, transformation, generation and, later, data analysis. Data science involves several disciplines: computing, statistics, mathematics, and business knowledge (Zafarani et al., 2014). Figure 2 illustrates this concept of data science.

Figure 2. Illustration of the data mining concept
Source: *(Zafarani et al., 2014)*

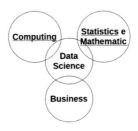

Figure 3. Usage of basic phases of the KDD
Source: *(Zafarani et al., 2014)*

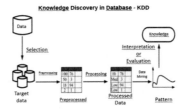

Data science is applied in this research using the concept of social media mining. This concept is an emerging discipline that performs the process of representation, analysis, and extraction of actionable patterns from social media data (Zafarani et al., 2014).

In discovering the patterns of collected data from social media, the process called Knowledge Discovery in Database (KDD) is applied. The usage of basic phases of the KDD in this research is shown in Figure 3.

Figure 4. Application of the basic phase of KDD in this study

Knowledge Discovery in Database (KDD) in this Study

Date	URL
03/10/17	cnn.com/syria-aleppo
03/09/17	cnn.com/jon-huntsman
03/07/17	cnn.com/save-the-children
03/10/17	cnn.com/russia-turk
03/06/17	cnn.com/trump-travel-ban

Date	URL
03/06/17	cnn.com/trump-travel-ban
03/07/17	cnn.com/save-the-children
03/09/17	cnn.com/jon-huntsman
03/10/17	cnn.com/russia-turk
03/10/17	cnn.com/syria-aleppo

Social Media

Selection

Armed Conflict — Preprocessing

Target data

Preprocessed

Processing

Processed Data

Knowlegde or Threat Emotion

Sentiment Analysis

Figure 4 shows a sample of the application of KDD process on social media data collected from the research. In this chapter, KDD is applied to organize data in terms of date.

Natural Language Processing on News Reading in Real Time

After the KDD process, the phase of treatment and analysis of the collected news texts is started. The reading of these news texts is performed in real time, directly from the source of information on the Internet. This process allows the extraction of the texts contained between the tags *<p> </p>* in the .html file of each of the news. Natural Language Processing (NLP) concepts are applied in analyzing the news. NLP is a subfield of artificial intelligence that enables development of systems that allow the interaction between computer and human (Jackson & Mouliner, 2002; Keikhosrokiani & Asl, 2022) using natural human language either by text or by speech (Oliveira, 1990). Second (Jackson & Mouliner, 2002), NLP can be divided into phases. Each phase of NLP is presented as follows:

1. **Text:** News from social media.
2. **Tokenization:** In this research, characters with no meaning for the text such as the symbols !, ?, #, @, http,::, etc are eliminated. In this way, the tokenization process will consider the approach of Languages Delimited by spaces – like the European languages that only indicate word boundaries by the insertion of blank spaces.
3. **Lexical Analysis:** Text analysis at the level of words is performed. In this analysis of natural language, logical analysis dismantles the words in a sentence in terms of their grammatical components (noun, adjective, pronoun, etc.).
4. **Syntactic Analysis:** It is the task of recognizing a sentence and assigning it a syntactic structure. The syntactic structures are attributed by Context-Free Grammar (CFG) that generates representation in the form of tree structure. These trees analyze an important intermediate state of representation for semantic analysis.
5. **Semantic Analysis:** These representations of intermediate meanings to phrases are attributed based on the knowledge acquired with logical and grammatical phases. Thus, this type of analysis is used in understanding the meaning of a sentence. It is also widely used for elimination of ambiguities.
6. **Pragmatic Analysis:** In this phase, the meaning based on contextual knowledge and logical form is elaborated. Moreover, this type of analysis is used to validate semantic analysis. In this analysis, those words are considered to be associated by meanings (water, swimming) or subject proximity (water, well).
7. **Text Knowledge:** In this research, the emotions associated with threat are obtained as knowledge of text.

In this work, the tokenization phase of NLP process is used to eliminate symbols and characters, !, ?, $, &, etc., that have no meaning or representation for analysis. The tokenization is applied using the NLTK – Natural Language toolkit (Bird, Klein, & Loper, 2009) in the Python and Embedded Language of Keras TensorFlow APIs (Chollet, 2015).

Table 4. Sentiment analysis tasks classification

Classification	Definition
Subjectivity	Deals with the identification of parts of the texts that demonstrate a feeling of subjectivity.
Polarity	Classifies to the texts into positive or negative feelings.
Intensity	Works with the emotional intensity expressed in the text. This approach divides to into the classes: strongly positive, positive, strongly negative or neutral.
Sentiment analysis based on topics or features	model of analysis basis to on the verification of existing characteristics related to feelings about the subject.
Sentiment Mining	Retrievals information from a query. Thus, it is possible to query a specific topic and classify it into a certain category.

Table 5. Excerpt from the base text for the theme armed conflict between Syria and USA

> The jihadist organization Jabhat al-Nusra, involved in Síria civil war since 2012, announced in a video that it is formally detaching itself from al-Qaeda. The move, which had been negotiated for well over a year, was confirmed on July 28. Renamed as Jabhat Fatah al-Sham, Nusra will try to bring other rebel factions into a unified body, liberating their lands, giving victory to their faith and upholding their testimony of faith. Some US-based observers quickly reacted with suspicion and derision. Thomas Joscelyn in the Long War Journal dismissed the statement as propaganda with no substance: Even if Joulani did say that his group had really split from al-Qaeda. White House spokesman Josh Earnest commented: There continues to be increasing concern about Nusra Fronts growing capacity for external operations that could threaten both the United States and Europe.

Sentiment Analysis for Times Series generation by Extraction Threats Emotion

The area of Sentiment Analysis refers to the tasks of analyzing, identifying, and classifying all information that is characterized as emotionally, subjectively or opinion-generating, whether the information is in the format of text, image, or sound (Cuadrado & Gómez-Navarro, 2011). In order to perform these tasks of sentiment characterization, the techniques of Natural Language Processing, statistics, and machine learning methods are usually used. According to (Cuadrado & Gómez-Navarro, 2011), these tasks can be divided as shown in the Table 4.

In this work, the task classification of the sentiment analysis based on topics or features is used to analysis the texts collected from social media. In this phase of news analysis, the concepts of sentiment analysis are applied using SpaCy (Industrial-Strength Natural Language) library (SpaCy, 2019). SpaCy is a free, open-source library for advanced natural language processing in Python. SpaCy is designed specifically for production use and helps in creating applications that process and understand large volumes of text. It can be used to build systems for information extraction or natural language under-

Table 6. Excerpt from the base text for the theme armed conflict between Iran and USA

> The United States Army has released a bleak assessment of its 2003 invasion of Iraq and subsequent attempts to defeat a Sunni Muslim insurgency until a 2011 withdrawal claiming that neighboring Iran was the only true winner of the operation the decision to attack was a preemptive response to accusations that Iraqi President Saddam Hussein possessed weapons of mass destruction and offered tacit support to the AlQaeda militant group that conducted the attacks of 2001 US President Donald Trump's view that a conflict with Iran would be a short war was an illusion and that his threat of obliteration amounted to threatening genocide Citing a number of troubling and escalatory indications from Iran Bolton said the US was deploying warships to the Middle East to send a clear and unmistakable message that it would meet any Iranian attacks on US interests with unrelenting force United Kingdom Russia France China Germany and the European Union failed to protect Iran oil and banking industries from US sanctions

Table 7. Vocabulary Words sample that represent armed conflict between Russia and Ukraine

Aggression	combat	Invasion	sanction
Armed	conflict	Kremlin	strike
Army	crisis	Military	tank
Attack	cyber	Missile	threat
Battle	dispute	Putin	violence
Battle	drill	Russia	war
Battle	elimination	Ukraine	weapon
Battle	fight	Weapon	Zelensky

standing, or to pre-process text for deep learning. This process is carried out in two different ways: the first is by using a base text for the armed conflicts between Syria and the USA and between Iran and the USA, and the second way is by using a vocabulary of words referring to the armed conflict between Russia and Ukraine.

In the knowledge extraction process using base text, the concept of threat emotion is defined empirically, considering the knowledge of the people in this study on the subject. Thus, the base text represents 100% the threat emotion. Table 5 shows excerpt from the base text for the armed conflict between Syria and USA, and Table 6 shows excerpts from the base text for the armed conflict between Iran and USA.

The process uses a set of vocabulary of 100 selected words that make reference to armed conflict between Russia and Ukraine. In each news collected, the number of words from the set of vocabulary are verified in the news analyzed to identify the similarity percentage that represents threat similarity degree (TSD) relating to the extreme event in Russia and Ukraine. Table 7 shows the examples of words presented in the vocabulary.

After that, the generated base text and vocabulary are identified with the similarity percentage of the news by processing it with the base text through the SpaCy library. The result of this process is the degree of threat similarity (DTS) that each news item represents relating to the extreme event analyzed. This threat degree for each news story is stored in the DTS field of the .csv file.

Figure 5. Steps following in this study for application of the concepts of the sentiment analysis

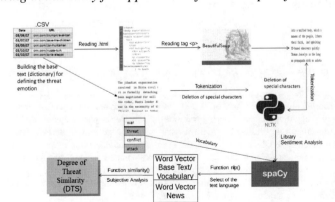

Table 8. Excerpt from the threats' portfolio of the armed conflict of the Syrian and USA

Date	URL	Degree of Threats Similarity (DTS)
12/01/2016	https://time.com/4180526/what-obama-gets-wrong-about-conflic t-in-the-middle-east/	0.941640414401327
29/02/2016	https://qz.com/625389/us-backed-rebel-groups-are-ready-to-tu rn-on-each-other-in-syria/	0.895609868593785
04/05/2016	https://mepc.org/commentary/who-blame-syria	0.946603316792111
03/06/2016	https://www.washingtonpost.com/graphics/national/obama-legac y/intervention-libya-and-syrian-crisis.html	0.952931143190229
07/10/2016	https://www.euractiv.com/section/global-europe/interview/mid dle-east-expert-syrian-war-is-only-going-to-get-bloodier-no- end-in-sight/	0.869353843401692
16/11/2016	https://www.dw.com/en/donald-trumps-vision-for-syria/a-36412 242	0.939145174720283
21/12/2016	https://time.com/4611414/donald-trump-middle-east-policy/	0.947719027093682
25/01/2017	https://blog.cei.iscte-iul.pt/obamas-military-legacy-iii-the -wars-in-libya-and-syria/	0.956159081557196
21/02/2017	https://www.forbes.com/sites/dougbandow/2017/02/21/u-s-troop s-dont-belong-in-syria-america-should-stay-out-of-another-mi ddle-eastern-ground-war/?sh=11c11aaf40c8	0.939912987021703
14/03/2017	https://www.thelancet.com/journals/lancet/article/PIIS0140-6 736(17)30758-4/fulltext	0.750967102048839
05/04/2017	https://www.vox.com/world/2017/4/5/15189820/trump-response-a trocity-syria-blame-obama	0.935767353592602

The processing of the information contained in the texts collected from social media is performed using the concepts of natural language processing by applying the tokenization step. After the base text and the vocabulary creation, the similarity percentage of the next news is identified by processing it with the base text or vocabulary using the SpaCy library. The result of this process is the degree of threat similarity (DTS) that each news item represents relating to the extreme event analyzed. Figure 5 presents a representative scheme of the steps described for the application of sentiment analysis.

In this chapter, DTS values are applied to generate the time series (TTS) that represent the variation of threat in the period analyzed.

Time Series to Representation of the Threat Variation

In generating the time series of the threats, date of DTS values is organized in ascending order. The time series calculation process generates a result of a threat portfolio that contains the information on date, URL, threat degree, and threat for each event model analyzed. Table 8 presents the excerpt from the threats' portfolio of the armed conflict of between Syria and USA.

The date and URL information from the threats' portfolio allow for generation of a threats' time series with 47 elements, as seen in the Figure 6.

Figure 6. Threat´s time series of armed conflict between Syrian and USA

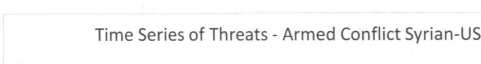

Table 9. Excerpt from the threats' portfolio of the armed conflict of the Iran and USA

Date	URL	Degree of Threats Similarity (DTS)
15/01/2019	https://smallwarsjournal.com/jrnl/art/americas-strategic-options-middle-east	0.929298929
21/01/2019	https://www.jpost.com/arab-israeli-conflict/defense-site-iran-has-a-stronger-military-than-israel-578131	0.71554728
29/01/2019	https://iranprimer.usip.org/blog/2019/jan/29/us-intelligence-community-iran	0.961092571
04/02/2019	https://edition.cnn.com/interactive/2019/02/middleeast/yemen-lost-us-arms/	0.95993139
04/02/2019	https://www.aljazeera.com/news/2019/2/4/us-needs-military-base-in-iraq-to-watch-iran-trump-says	0.942323328
05/02/2019	https://www.trtworld.com/opinion/iraq-is-more-than-just-a-watchtower-for-the-us-over-iran-23897	0.970754268
05/01/2019	https://qz.com/1779727/attack-on-irans-soleimani-fits-a-long-history-of-us-military-actions/	0.941168922
05/01/2020	https://www.reuters.com/article/us-iraq-security-iran-usa/u-s-lacks-courage-for-military-confrontation-with-iran-iran-army-chief-idUSKBN1Z407W	0.781198346
06/01/2020	https://edition.cnn.com/2020/01/05/opinions/us-iran-history-ware-intl/index.html	0.789359923
06/01/2020	https://www.marketwatch.com/story/what-stock-market-investors-need-to-know-about-intensifying-us-iran-tensions-2020-01-04	0.948445074
07/01/2020	https://www.reuters.com/article/us-iraq-security/trump-softens-rhetoric-after-iranian-missile-attacks-says-tehran-appears-to-be-standing-down-idUSKBN1Z60NL	0.852567888

Figure 7. Threats time series of armed conflict between Iran and USA

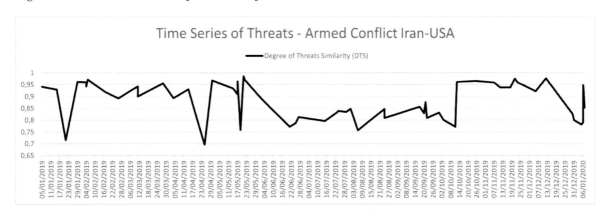

Table 10. Excerpt from the threats' portfolio of the armed conflict between Russia and Ukraine

Date	URL	Degree of Threats Similarity (DTS)
02/03/2021	https://www.stratagem.no/russian-cyber-strategy-implications-for-the-west/	0.9620171591275499
02/03/2021	https://www.themoscowtimes.com/2021/03/02/eu-says-bloc-will-not-lift-sanctions-on-russia-over-ukraine-a73127	0.9601405924515877
01/03/2021	https://www.ft.com/content/bf26bf68-e2a7-4b89-9f28-f66a92c945b4	0.956394508070634
01/03/2021	https://www.atlanticcouncil.org/blogs/ukrainealert/getting-ukraines-security-service-reform-right/	0.971228110560096
28/02/2021	https://tass.com/russia/1261143	0.96659686832207496
27/02/2021	https://www.rferl.org/a/ukraine-slaps-sanctions-on-ex-yanukovych-officials-/31124029.html	0.9683289378954442
27/02/2021	https://khpg.org/en/1608808855	0.969938133312595
27/02/2021	https://www.whitehouse.gov/briefing-room/statements-releases/2021/02/26/statement-by-president-biden-on-the-anniversary-of-russias-illegal-invasion-of-ukraine/	0.9634371697027805
26/02/2021	https://rsf.org/en/ukraine-escalates-information-war-banning-three-pro-kremlin-media	0.9650705446040381
26/02/2021	https://www.atlanticcouncil.org/blogs/ukrainealert/why-ukraine-sanctioned-putins-ally-medvedchuk/	0.9702329832841633

Figure 8. Threats time series of armed conflict between Russia and Ukraine with 1024 elements

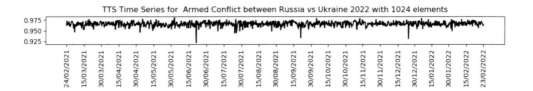

Figure 9. Threats time series of armed conflict between Russia and Ukraine with 2048 elements

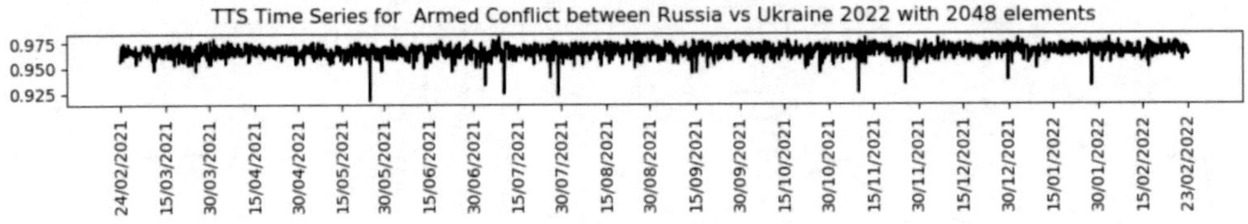

TTS Time Series for Armed Conflict between Russia vs Ukraine 2022 with 2048 elements

For the case study of Iran-US armed conflict, the same process is applied for the creation of the portfolio and the consequent time series. Table 9 shows an excerpt from the threats' portfolio of armed conflict of the Iran and USA.

The threats' portfolio information of armed conflict between Iran and USA generates a time series of threats with 58 elements. The representation of this time series can be visualized in the Figure 7.

For the case study of Russia-Ukraine armed conflict, the same process is applied for the creation of the portfolio and the consequent time series. Table 10 shows an excerpt from the threats' portfolio of armed conflict between Russia and Ukraine.

The threats' portfolio information of armed conflict between Russia and Ukraine generates a time series of threats with two different sizes. The first time series shown in Figure 8 contains 1024 elements and the second time series shown in Figure 9 contains 2048 elements.

Figure 10. Multiplicative cascade for armed conflict. (a) Scale hierarchy for armed conflict; (b) Respective density expected of energy spectrum pattern showing the transition from the inertial range to extreme event, response to high dissipative regime

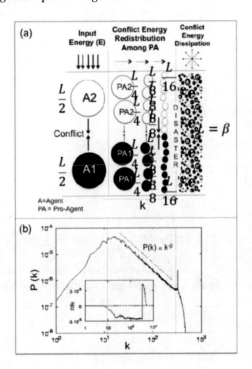

The threats' time series data is applied in the generation of endogenous threats' time series, as presented in the next section.

Endogenous Characteristics in the Threats' Time Series

In the time series creation with endogenous characteristics, the P-Model algorithm is applied (Meneveau & Sreenivasan, 1987; Halsey et al., 1987). In Rosa et al. (2019), this algorithm creates a non-homogeneous cascade compatible with the fluctuations observed in the stochastic time series. According to (Rosa et al., 2019), this non-homogeneous cascade is compatible with the energy dissipated by extreme events up to the moment of their apex, where one has the maximum energy dissipation. Figure 10 presents an example of this energy dissipation for extreme events referring to armed conflicts.

The multiplicative cascade of the P-Model is represented by Equation 1, and is defined in (Halsey et al., 1987).

Equation 1: Equations to represent multiplicative cascade of the P-Model

$$\alpha = \frac{log_2 p_1 + (w-1) log_2 p_2}{log_2 l_1 + (w-1) log_2 l_2}$$

$$f(\alpha) = \frac{(w-1) log_2 (w-1) - w log_2 w}{log_2 l_1 + (w-1) log_2 l_2}$$

where,

α- singularity strength
p_i - probability that some event occurs in the i-th fraction, for i = 1, 2
w - multiplication weight given by 1 - (1 - 2p)
l_i - i - ith fraction of an eddy of size L, for i = 1, 2
f() - describes how densely distributed the singularities are

In Rosa et al. (2019), the generalized form of P-Model presents a classical view of the eddy cascade before the inertial interval of a fully developed turbulence, in which the energy flux (EK), as presented in Figure 8 (a), dissipates over the Kolmogorov scale length (Keylock, 2017) into eddies of size *L*. Subsequently, each eddy of size *L* is divided into two equal parts, being represented as $\frac{L}{2}$, l_1 and l_2. In this way, it is distributed at each step of the cascade, the energy flows as a probability, unequally in fraction of p_1 and p_2 $1-p_1$, where $p_1+p_2=1$. This process is iterated over fixed p_1 until each eddy reaches the Kolmogorov scale (Keylock, 2017). Starting with a non-homogeneous energy distribution, a fraction $f(\alpha)$ of the multifractal mass is transferred from one half to the other in the randomly chosen direction. This is equivalent to multiplying the originally uniform density field on both sides by factors. The same

Figure 11. Two typical time series shaved from the PModel algorithm by fixing p=0.25 and varying the value of β. (a) Pattern XEendo of β=0.39. (b) XEexo pattern of β=0.72. Figures (c) and (d) show the respective cumulative energy, endogeny (log) and exogeny (exp)

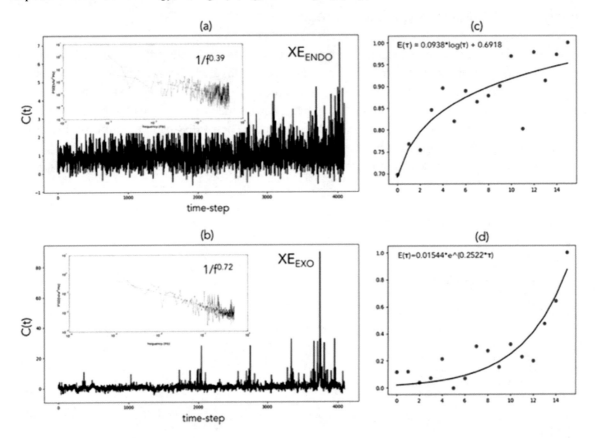

procedure is repeated M times, recursively at smaller and smaller scales, using fractions varying from in segments of length L2$_n$, in which the multiplicative weight w is parameterized as 1−(1−2p), resulting in the discrete matrix C(m) where m counts as time steps. This procedure of P-Model algorithm given by Venema (Bonn, 2019) can produce time series in which the variance is finite if their power spectrum is extrapolated to infinitely large scales (Rosa et al., 2019).

The time series, $C(m=\tau)$, with M=211, representing the extreme inhomogeneous, is generated according to the turbulent event using Venema's algorithm (Bonn, 2019), in which the inputs are: the size of the time series in number of points (M), the power spectrum $PSD(\beta PS_{D}$, and the value of p, with the cascading fractional energy distribution being similar to inhomogeneous turbulence (Rosa et al., 2019). The homogeneous dissipative process is recovered near thermodynamic equilibrium when

$$\left(\beta_{PSD}, p\right) = \frac{-5}{3}, 0.5.$$ Deviations from the homogeneous cascade are exacerbated by abrupt changes in the frequency and magnitude of social conflict. These changes are called extreme events (XE), and their cause may be due to internal rather than external factors. When the level of conflict increases significantly due to internal interactions, the extreme event is called endogenous (XEendo). When external energy transfer or abrupt dissipation is the main cause of XE, it is called an exogenous extreme event

Figure 12. Schematic representation of the application P-Model algorithm to generate the threat´s endogenous time series

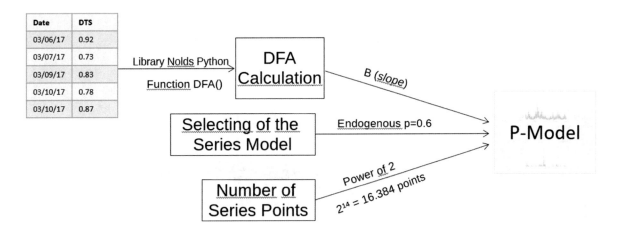

(XEexo). In the power law domain, XEendo and XEexo events belong to different universality classes (Rosa et al., 2019). The typical endogenous and exogenous processes combine P-Model and SDGA (Sornette-Deschtres-Gilbert-Ageo) algorithm (Sornette, 2006) to obtain ($\beta PS_{D\approx}$ –0.4, p=0.25) and ($\beta PSD_{\approx}$ 0.7, p=0.25), respectively. Figure 11 shows the XE time series for different combinations of p and PSD. The cumulative energy of the process is defined in the time domain as normalized mean $\beta_{PSD} \langle C(\tau) \rangle \beta_{PSD}$ where there is a chosen window time interval along the signal. According to Rosa et al. (2019), typical cumulative energy trends are nonlinear—being logarithmic for XEendo (Figure 11 (c)) and exponential for XEexo (Figure 11 (d)).

In this chapter, endogenous series and the following parameters are used as input to the P-Model algorithm

1. $M = 2^{14} = 16384$ points: amount of data of the endogenous series with better representation, according to Ibañez, Rosa, & Guimarães (2021)
2. p=0.60 (Rosa et al., 2019): parameter for the definition of endogenous series
3. β: spectral index, named *slope* and calculated using the concept of DFA (Detrended Fluctuation Analysis) (University of Harvard, 2019). In this chapter, the calculation of DFA using the function

Table 10. Input values used in the P-Model algorithm for the creation of the endogenous time series of the armed conflicts between Syria and USA, Iran and USA, and Russia and Ukraine

Armed Conflict	Amount of Data of the Endogenous Series (M)	p	β (slope)
Syria and USA	2^{14}=16384	-0.60	0.5606194965951611
Iran and USA	2^{14}=16384	-0.60	0.9132939832232201
Russia and Ukraine	2^{10}=1024	-0.60	0.7494743783803075
Russia and Ukraine	2^{11}=2048	-0.60	0.842808975417272

Figure 13. Endogenous threat's time series of the Syria-USA armed conflict

Figure 14. Endogenous threat's time series of the Iran-USA armed conflict

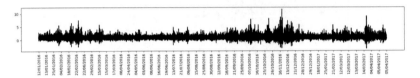

DFA is performed from the nops library of the programming language Python 3.7. The input of the function is the threat's series, generated by applying the technique of sentiment analysis on the data collected from social media.

Figure 12 shows a schematic representation of the use of P-Model in the generation of endogenous threat's time series.

Table 10 shows the data input of P-Model algorithm for each armed conflict analyzed in this study.

Figure 13 shows the endogenous time series generated, with values from Table 10, for armed conflict between Syrian and USA. Whereas, Figure 14 shows the endogenous time series generated, with values from Table 10, for armed conflict between Iran and USA.

Figure 15. Endogenous threat's time series of the Russia-Ukraine armed conflict with 1024 elements

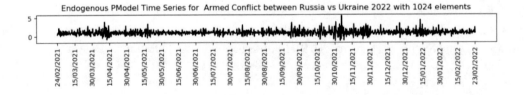

Figure 16. Endogenous threat's time series of the Russia-Ukraine armed conflict with 2048 elements

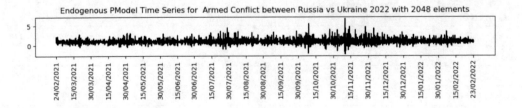

Figure 17. LSTM neural network architecture representation

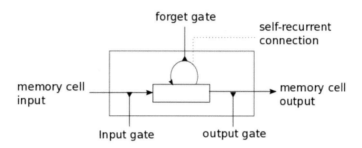

Figure 15 shows the endogenous time series generated, with values from Table 10, for armed conflict between Russia and Ukraine with 1024 elements. Figure 16 shows the endogenous time series generated, with values from Table 10, for armed conflict between Russia and Ukraine with 2048 elements.

Forecasting Endogenous Time Series with Deep Learning-LSTM

Deep Learning is a subarea of artificial intelligence that enables the creation of neural network models with large dimensions that can be taught to make decisions with high accuracy based on data characteristics (Goodfellow et al., 2016). This technique performs well in extracting features from large volumes of data (Emmert-Strib et al., 2018). Various network architectures can be used to build these models. A recursive neural network known as Long Short-Term Memory – LSTM is used in this chapter.

Long Short-Term Memory networks are a recurrent neural network model capable of learning order dependence in sequence prediction problems (Brownlee, 2017). The LSTM consists of a cell, an input gate, an output gate, and a forget gate. The cell remembers values for arbitrary time intervals, and the three gates regulate the flow of information in and out of the cell. The gates control the interactions between neighboring memory cells and the memory cell itself. The input gate adds useful information to the current state of the cell. On the other hand, the output gate extracts useful information from the current state of the cell to pass to the next cell. In addition, the forget gate deletes information that does

Figure 18. Architecture of the neural network deep learning - LSTM built with API Keras

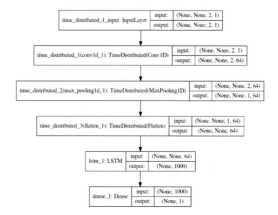

Figure 19. Original endogenous time series in black color and prediction time series with 3276 points in gray color, referring to the armed conflict between Syria and USA

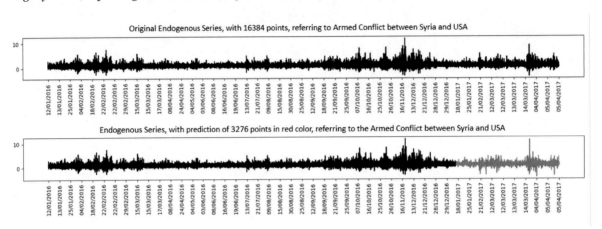

not contribute to the current state of the cell (Bao et al., 2017). Figure 17 shows an example of this network architecture.

For elaboration of Deep Learning-LSTM model, the deep learning Keras (Chollet, 2015) is used from the language Python 3.7. This architecture that uses LSTM network is applied to perform the prediction of social extreme events (armed conflicts) with analysis using the technique of sentiment analysis. The representation of each layer of the neural network architecture built with deep learning API Keras is shown in Figure 18.

The main objective of this chapter is to predict the threat variation of social extreme events, using the data of armed conflicts stored in threat portfolios. The prediction of the endogenous time series uses 20% fraction of the endogenous data for comparison with the remaining data in the series, and the prediction of the future of that series, which generates new data of threat variation. The 20% fraction is selected based on the suggested split of training, validation, and testing data of 60%, 20%, 20%, as suggested in (Haykin, 2008). This prediction is divided into three phases, as shown below:

- First phase: performs the prediction of a fraction of the endogenous time series.
- Second phase: performs the prediction of the future of the analyzed threat data.

Figure 20. Original endogenous time series in black color and prediction time series with 3276 points in gray color, referring to the armed conflict between Iran and USA

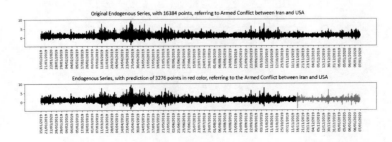

Figure 21. Overlap of the prediction with the original part of the series together with similarity value for armed conflict between Syria and USA

- Third phase: performs the prediction of the threats about Russia and Ukraine armed conflict and the comparison between the TTS time series prediction and the endogenous time series.

First Phase: Prediction of a Fraction of the Endogenous Time Series

After the creation of the endogenous time series of threats, we perform the application of deep learning architecture with LSTM neural to predict a fraction of this endogenous time series for the application of the developed methodology. Figure 15 and Figure 16 show two endogenous time series for armed conflicts between Syria-USA and Iran-USA, respectively: the first is the original P-Model's time series, which is all in black, and the second is the series with prediction of 3276 points in gray, of the original time series.

To verify the accuracy of the result presented in Figure 19 and Figure 20, an overlay plot of the predicted data is generated with the original series data. In addition to this overlap, the similarity between the two series is calculated using Dynamic Time Warping – DTW concept. DTW is used to calculate the dissimilarity between two time series of the same dimension (Giusti & Batista, 2013) that represents the degree of difference between the two parts of the series. In this chapter, DTW is used through the package of tslearn.metrics.dtw (Tavenard et al., 2020) in Python 3.7. Equation 2 presents the math representation of Dynamic Time Warping concept.

Equation 2: Mathematic representation of the DTW concept

$$DTW\left(x, y\right) = \sqrt{\sum\nolimits_{i, j \in \pi} \left(X_i - Y_j\right)^2}$$

where,

X and Y — represent the series to be compared
i and j — represent the positions i, j in a matrix of each element of the series
π — represents the set of paths between the series

The graph in Figure 21, with the overlapping of the time series for the armed conflict Syria-USA, shows the DTW value subtracted from 100 to obtain the value of similarity between the excerpts of the analyzed series.

Figure 21 presents a similarity of about 66.54% between the parts of the analyzed time series. This similarity value also represents the prediction accuracy of this endogenous series by using the deep learning architecture with LSTM network developed in the methodology. This value also demonstrates a good performance for the developed prediction model.

The same concepts of DTW employed for the armed conflict between Syria and the USA is also employed in the graph in Figure 22 that shows the overlapping of the time's series for the armed conflict of Iran-USA. This graph shows the subtraction of DTW value from 100 to obtain the value of similarity between the excerpts of the analyzed series.

Figure 22. Overlap of the prediction with the original part of the series together with similarity value for the armed conflict between Iran and USA

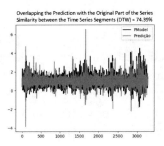

Figure 22 observes that the similarity between the parts of the analyzed time series is 74.39%. Again, this value of similarity demonstrates a good performance of the developed prediction model.

Second Phase: Prediction of the Future of the Analyzed Threat Data

In the second phase, the prediction of the future of the time series of threats of armed conflicts between Syria and the USA and armed conflict between Iran and USA is performed. In this prediction phase, the same deep learning architecture is used in the prediction of the endogenous series fraction of the prediction in the first phase. The difference consists in the application of a repetition structure that, for each new set of predicted values, feeds back the network. This process is repeated until the prediction of 3276 elements represents 20% of the total number of data points of the input series. This number of

Figure 23. Prediction of the future of 3 months of the threats of the armed conflict between Syria and USA in gray color

Figure 24. Prediction of the future of 3 months of the threats of the armed conflict between Iran and USA in gray color

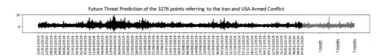

points represents an approximate period of 3 months. Figure 23 shows the result of the prediction of the future of about 3 months for armed conflict of Syria-USA in gray color.

Figure 23 shows that the variations of future threats continue at the same in the same intensity over the predicted period. Considering that the armed conflict between Syria and the USA had a continuity in threats (Dejevsky, 2017), which lasts until now, the result suggests that the architecture of deep learning makes a good representation of the future of this conflict.

For the armed conflict between Iran and USA, the same technique used in the results of the Figure 23 is applied. These results are visualized in Figure 24.

Figure 24 observes that the variations of future threats continue in the same intensity over the predicted period. Whereas the threats between the heads of state of these countries continued after the analyzed period (Marcus, 2020) there is a good response of the methodology and architecture for predicting the future of this conflict.

Third Phase: Prediction of the threat's variations about Russia and Ukraine armed conflict and the comparison between the TTS time series and endogenous time series prediction

In the third phase, the prediction of the future of the time series of threats of armed conflicts between Russia and Ukraine is performed. In this prediction phase, the same deep learning architecture is used in the prediction of the endogenous series fraction of the prediction in the first phase and the same idea and repetition structure used in the second phase. The difference in this phase consists in the comparison between TTS prediction result and the endogenous prediction result.

The objective of this phase is to demonstrate that a larger amount of news used in the application of sentiment analysis and deep learning techniques will result in a more reliable representative of data. The same amount of news also obtains a prediction with a similarity percentage that is very close to the data interpolation performed by the P-Model algorithm. To perform this verification, a series with

Figure 25. Prediction of the future of 3 months using TTS time series, in the gray color, of the threats of the armed conflict between Russia and Ukraine with 1024 elements

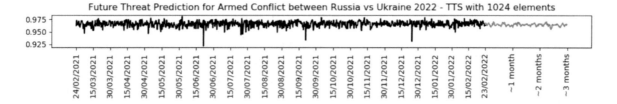

Figure 26. Prediction of the future of 3 months using endogenous time series, in the gray color, of the threats of the armed conflict between Russia and Ukraine with 1024 elements

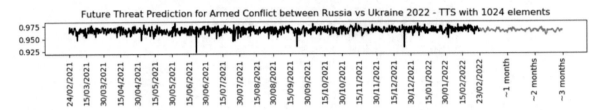

Figure 27. Prediction of the future of 3 months using TTS time series, in the gray color, of the threats of the armed conflict between Russia and Ukraine with 2048 elements

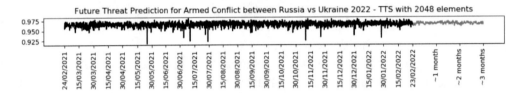

1024 elements considering the news about the armed conflict between Russia and Ukraine is built to perform a prediction of the future 3 months for the threats. This prediction is performed both for the original series defined as TTS and for the endogenous series generated by the P-Model algorithm, as shown in Figure 25 and Figure 26. The same methodology is applied for a series of 2048 elements, as shown in Figure 27 and Figure 28.

Figure 28. Prediction of the future of 3 months using endogenous time series, in the gray color, of the threats of the armed conflict between Russia and Ukraine with 2048 elements

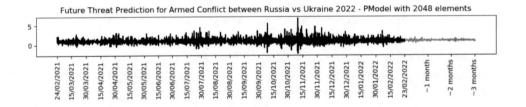

As observed in both figures, the variations of future threats maintain the variation intensity over the predicted period. Whereas the threats between the heads of state of these countries continue after the analyzed period (Marcus, 2020). This result presents that methodology and architecture for predicting the future of this conflict have a good response using another data set.

As observed, the TTS time series has the same accuracy as the endogenous P-Model time series, and TTS time series maintain the original values of the degree of the threat similarity to shows the time series. The endogenous time series presents a lot of values in comparing the degree of the threat similarity.

Figure 29. Overlap of the prediction of the TTS time series and endogenous time series with similarity value for armed conflict between Russia and Ukraine with 1024 elementsd

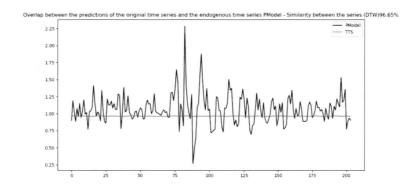

The next step in this phase is identifying the overlapping of prediction stretch of the time series TTS and prediction stretch of the endogenous time series for the armed conflict of Russia-Ukraine using 1024 elements. The result of this overlapping is presented in the Figure 29, together with DTW value subtracted from 100. The DTW value obtain similarity percent between the stretches of the analyzed series.

As observed in Figure 29, the similarity between the parts of the analyzed time series is 96.65%. This value of similarity demonstrates that prediction using TTS times series is very similar to the result using endogenous time series.

The graph in Figure 30 shows the overlapping of the prediction of the time series TTS and the prediction of the endogenous time series for the armed conflict of Russia-Ukraine. This overlapping uses 408 elements and shows the DTW value subtracted from 100 to obtain the value of similarity between the excerpts of the analyzed series.

As observed in Figure 30, the similarity between the parts of the analyzed time series is 96.30%. This value of similarity demonstrates that prediction using TTS times series increases the value of similarity, in comparison with the result using endogenous time series.

Figure 30. Overlap of the prediction of the TTS time series and endogenous time series with similarity value for armed conflict between Russia and Ukraine with 2048 elements

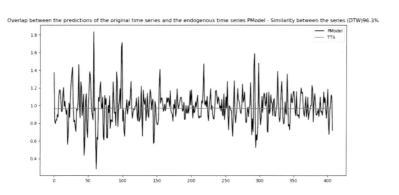

The result shown in Figures 27, 28, 29 and 30 demonstrate that a larger database is better in representing information and generating the same prediction value as interpolating the data with the P-Model algorithm.

CONCLUSION

In this chapter, analysis of data collected from globally circulating social media ((CNN, 2020), (Reuters, 2019), (The Guardian, 2020)), etc. is performed. The information about extreme social events is taken from three samples of armed conflicts: between Syria and USA in the period from January 2016 to April 2017, between Iran and USA in the period from January 2019 to January 2020, and between Russia and Ukraine in the period from February 2021 to February 2022.

The processing of this information uses the techniques of natural language processing and sentiment analysis. This processing creates a threat portfolio, from which the information is used to generate endogenous time series and predict future threats of these conflicts by applying Deep Learning and LSTM neural network techniques. The results find that with the application of the neural network model developed, an accuracy of 65.12% for the conflict of Syria and USA and 74.39% for the conflict between Iran and USA is reached. So, these results indicate that the prediction of future threats of this extreme event using the methodology of this study shows a good representation of the continuity of this event.

The results using the data set about armed conflict in Russia and Ukraine demonstrate that interpolating values are not necessary if more news are increased in the database. The comparison of prediction between the TTS series and endogenous series (interpolating data) results in the similarity of 96.65% to 1024 elements and of 96.30% to 2048 elements.

FUTURE RESEARCH DIRECTIONS

In the study, the use of sentiment analysis in relation to the identification of emotions in the most diverse form of information is an area that has a lot of potential to grow. Thus, as a continuation of this study, some suggestions for future research directions are: 1) increase the database to analyze texts, and 2) consider using other extreme events, and improve the analysis through the identification of emotions such as sarcasm and irony, and the use of image data.

ACKNOWLEDGMENT

I would like to thank the Federal Institute for Education, Science, and Technology of São Paulo - IFSP campus São José dos Campos, for the qualification license granted for the development of the studies.

REFERENCES

Bao, W., Yue, J., & Rao, Y. (2017). A deep learning framework for financial time series using stacked autoencoders and long-short term memory. *PLoS One*, *12*(7), e0180944. doi:10.1371/journal.pone.0180944 PMID:28708865

Bird, S., Klein, E., & Loper, E. (2009). *Natural language processing with python: Analysing text with the natural language toolkit*. O'Reilly Media.

Bonn, U. (2019). *Venema P-Model algorithm*. https://www2.meteo.uni-bonn.de/staff/venema/themes/surrogates/

Brownlee, J. (2017, May 24). *A Gentle introduction to long short-term memory networks by the experts*. Machine Learning Mastery. https://machinelearningmastery.com/gentle-introduction-long-short-term-memory-networks-experts/

Caprolu, M., Sadighian, A., & Di Pietro, R. (2022). *Characterizing the 2022 Russo-Ukrainian conflict through the lenses of aspect-based sentiment analysis: Dataset, methodology, and preliminary findings*. doi:10.48550/arXiv.2208.04903

Ceci, F., Gonçalves, A. L., & Webe, R. (2016). A model for sentiment analysis based on ontology and cases. *IEEE Latin America Transactions*, *14*(11), 4560–4566. doi:10.1109/TLA.2016.7795829

Cederman, L., & Weidmann, N. (2017). Predicting armed conflict: Time to adjust our expectations? *Science*, *355*(6324), 474–476. doi:10.1126cience.aal4483 PMID:28154047

Chollet, F. (2015). *Keras: The Python deep learning library*. Keras. https://keras.io/

Clauset, A. (2018). Trends and fluctuations in the severity of interstate wars. *Science Advances*, *4*(2), 1–10. doi:10.1126ciadv.aao3580 PMID:29507877

CNN. (2020). *CNN - breaking news, latest news and videos*. CNN. https://edition.cnn.com

Cuadrado, J. C., & Gómez-Navarro, D. P. (2011). *Un modelo lingüístico-semántico basado en emociones para la clasificación de textos según su polaridad e intensidad*. [Doctoral Thesis]. Complutense University of Madrid. http://nil.fdi.ucm.es/sites/default/files/Thesis_Jorge_Carrillo_De_Albornoz.pdf

Dejevsky, M. (2017, June 21). As Syria's war enters its endgame, the risk of a US-Russia conflict escalates. *The Guardian*. https://www.theguardian.com/commentisfree/2017/jun/21/syria-war-endgame-us-russia-conflict-washington-moscow-accidental-war

Department of Peace and Conflict Research at Uppsala University. (1980). *Uppsala Conflict Data*. Uppsala Conflict Data Program – UCDP. https://ucdp.uu.se/

Dhaoui, C., Webster, C. M., & Tan, L. P. (2017). Social media sentiment analysis: Lexicon versus machine learning. *Journal of Consumer Marketing*, *34*(6), 480–488. doi:10.1108/JCM-03-2017-2141

Emmert-Strib, F., Yang, Z., Feng, H., Tripathi, S., & Dehmer, M. (2018). An introductory review of deep learning for prediction models with big data. *Frontiers in Artificial Intelligence - Deep Learning in Computational Social Science, 27,* 16-32. doi:10.3389/frai.2020.00004

Giusti, R., & Batista, G. E. (2013). An empirical comparison of dissimilarity measures for time series classification. *Brazilian Conference on Intelligent System,* 82-88. 10.1109/BRACIS.2013.22

Gleditsch, N. P. (2020). *Lewis Fry Richardson: His intellectual legacy and influence in the social sciences.* Springer. doi:10.1007/978-3-030-31589-4

Goodfellow, I., Benbio, Y., & Courville, A. (2016). *Deep learning – adaptive computation and machine learning series.* MIT Press.

Google, L. L. C. (1998). *Google Search.* www.google.com

Google, L. L. C. (2016). *API cloud natural language.* Google cloud. https://cloud.google.com/natural-language?hl=pt-br

Halkia, M., Ferri, S., Schiellens, M. K., & Papazoglou, M. (2020). The global conflict risk index: A quantitative tool for policy support on conflict prevention. *Progress in Disaster Science, 6,* 100069. doi:10.1016/j.pdisas.2020.100069

Halsey, T. C., Jensen, M. H., Kadanoff, L. P., Procaccia, I., & Shraiman, B. I. (1987). Fractal measures and their singularities: The characterization of strange sets. *Nuclear Physics B - Proceedings Supplement, 2,* 501–511. doi:10.1016/0920-5632(87)90036-3

Haykin, S. O. (2008). *Neural networks and learning machines.* Pearson.

Hegre, H., Allansson, M., Basedau, M., Colaresi, M., Croicu, M., Fjelde, H., Hoyles, F., Hultman, L., Högbladh, S., Jansen, R., Mouhleb, N., Muhammad, S. A., Nilsson, D., Nygård, H. M., Olafsdottir, G., Petrova, K., Randahl, D., Rød, E. G., Schneider, G., ... Vestby, J. (2019). Views: A political violence early-warning system. *Journal of Peace Research, 56*(2), 155–174. doi:10.1177/0022343319823860

Helle, V., Negus, A., & Nyberg, J. (2018). *Improving armed conflict prediction using machine learning: VIEWS+.* https://pdfs.semanticscholar.org/3008/beffb4496316bb1677253de89eb4b2a695c3.pdf

Hochreiter, S., & Schmidhuber, J. (1997). Long short-term memory. *Neural Computation, 9*(8), 1735–1780. doi:10.1162/neco.1997.9.8.1735 PMID:9377276

Ibañez, M. M., Rosa, R. R., & Guimarães, L. N. (2020). Sentiment analysis applied to analyze society's emotion in two different context of social media data. *Inteligencia Artificial Revista Iberoamericana de Inteligencia Artificial, 23*(66), 66–84. doi:10.4114ubmission/intartif.vol23iss66pp66-84

Ibañez, M. M., Rosa, R. R., & Guimarães, L. N. (2021). *Análise de emoções em mídias sociais utilizando aprendizado de máquina e séries temporais considerando informações de eventos extremos sociais e naturais.* Instituto Nacional de Pesquisas Espaciais - INPE. http://urlib.net/rep/8JMKD3MGP3W34R/44H7S82

Ibañez, M. M., Rosa, R. R., & Guimarães, L. N. (2022). Threat emotion analysis in social media: Considering armed conflicts as social extreme events. In P. Keikhosrokiani & M. Pourya Asl (Eds.), *Handbook of research on opinion mining and text analytics on literary works and social media* (pp. 293–322). IGI Global. doi:10.4018/978-1-7998-9594-7.ch012

Jackson, P., & Mouliner, I. (2002). *Natural language processing for online applications: Textretrieval, extraction and categorization.* John Benjamins B.V. doi:10.1075/nlp.5(1st)

Keikhosrokiani, P., & Asl, M. P. (Eds.). (2022). *Handbook of research on opinion mining and text analytics on literary works and social media.* IGI Global. doi:10.4018/978-1-7998-9594-7

Keylock, C. J. (2017). Multifractal surrogate-data generation algorithm that preserves pointwise hölder regularity structure, with initial applications to turbulence. *Physical Review. E, 95*(3), 032123. Advance online publication. doi:10.1103/PhysRevE.95.032123 PMID:28415176

Lateral Gmb, H. (2019). *NewsBot - Give me 5.* https://getnewsbot.com/

Lim, B., & Zohren, S. (2021). Time-series forecasting with deep learning: A survey. *Philosophical Transactions - Royal Society. Mathematical, Physical, and Engineering Sciences, 379*(2194), 20200209. Advance online publication. doi:10.1098/rsta.2020.0209 PMID:33583273

Mahmud, A., & Mohammed, A. (2021). A survey on deep learning for time-series forecasting. In A. E. Hassanien & A. Darwish (Eds.), *Machine Learning and Big Data Analytics Paradigms: Analysis* (pp. 365–392). Applications and Challenges. doi:10.1007/978-3-030-59338-4_19

Marcus, J. (2020, April 24). *US-Iran war of words raises fresh fears of Gulf clash.* BBC News. https://www.bbc.com/news/world-middle-east-52399283

Meneveau, C., & Sreenivasan, K. R. (1987). Simple multifractal cascade model for fully developed turbulence. *Physical Review Letters, 59*(13), 1424–1427. doi:10.1103/PhysRevLett.59.1424 PMID:10035231

Moyer, J. D., & Kaplan, O. (2020, July 6). Will the Coronavirus fuel conflict projections based on economic and development data show an increased. *Foreign Policy – the Global Magazine of News and Ideas.* https://foreignpolicy.com/2020/07/06/coronavirus-pandemic-fuel-conflict-fragile-states-economy-food-prices/

Muchlinski, D., Siroky, D., He, J., & Kocher, M. (2016). Comparing random forest with logistic regression for predicting class-imbalanced civil war onset data. *Political Analysis, 24*(1), 87–103. doi:10.1093/pan/mpv024

Oliveira, C. A. (1990). *IDEAL - uma interface dialógica em linguagem natural para sistemas especialistas.* São José dos Campos: Instituto Nacional de Pesquisas Espaciais (INPE). http://urlib.net/rep/6qtX3pFwXQZ3r59YCT/GUpqq

Pozzi, F. A., Fersini, E., Messina, E., & Liu, B. (2016). *Sentiment analysis in social networks.* Morgan Kaufmann.

Rangapuram, S. S., Seeger, M. W., Gasthaus, J., Stella, L., Wang, Y., & Januschowski, T. (2018). Deep state space models for time series forecasting. In S. Bengio, H. Wallach, H. Larochelle, K. Grauman, N. Cesa-Bianchi, & R. Garnett (Eds.), *Advances in Neural Information Processing Systems.* Curran Associates, Inc. https://proceedings.neurips.cc/paper/2018/file/5cf68969fb67a a6082363a6d4e6468e2-Paper.pdf

Reuters. (2019). *Reuters news agency: World's largest news agency.* Reuters. https://www.reuters.com/

Reyes-Menendez, A., Saura, J., & Alvarez-Alonso, C. (2018). Understanding #WorldEnvironmentDay user opinions in Twitter: A topic-based sentiment analysis approach. *International Journal of Environmental Research and Public Health, 15*(11), 2537. doi:10.3390/ijerph15112537 PMID:30428520

Richardson, L. F. (1960). *Arms and insecurity: A mathematical study of the causes and origins of war.* The Boxwood Press.

Rosa, R. R., Neelakshi, J., Pinheiro, G. A., Barchi, P. H., & Shiguemori, H. (2019). Modeling social and geopolitical disasters as extreme events: a case study considering the complex dynamics of international armed conflicts. In L. Santos, R. G. Negri, & T. J. Carvalho (Eds.), Towards mathematics, computers and environment: A disasters perspective (pp. 233-254). Springer. doi:10.1007/978-3-030-21205-6_12

Salinas, D., Flunkert, V., & Gasthaus, J. (2018). *DeepAR: Probabilistic forecasting with autoregressive recurrent networks.* Cornell University. doi:10.48550/arXiv.1704.04110

Sornette, D. (2006). Endogenous versus exogenous origins of crises. In S. Albeverio, V. Jentsch, & H. Kantz (Eds.), *Extremes events in nature and society* (pp. 107–131). Springer. doi:10.1007/3-540-28611-X_5

SpaCy. (2019). *Industrial-strength natural language processing.* SpaCy. https://spacy.io/

Tavenard, R., Fouzi, J., Vandewiele, G., Divo, F., Androz, G., Holtz, C., Payne, M., Yurchak, R., Rußwurm, M., Kolar, K., & Woods, E. (2020). Tslearn, a machine learning toolkit for time series data. *Journal of Machine Learning Research, 21*(118), 1–6. https://jmlr.org/papers/v21/20-091.html

The Guardian. (2020). News, sport and opinion from the guardian's US edition. *The Guardian.* https://www.theguardian.com/international

University of Harvard. (2019). *Detrended fluctuation analysis (DFA).* University of Harvard. http://reylab.bidmc.harvard.edu/download/DFA/intro/

UOL. (2017, June 4). *EUA ataca síria com mais de 50 mísseis.* UOL. https://noticias.uol.com.br/ultimas-noticias/ansa/2017/04/06/

Zafarani, R., Abbasi, M. A., & Liu, H. (2014). *Social media mining - an introduction.* Cambridge University Press. doi:10.1017/CBO9781139088510

KEY TERMS AND DEFINITIONS

Data Science: Collection, preparation, and analysis of a great amount of data.

Endogenous Events: Event that generates reaction based only on the domain of the event itself.

Extreme Events: Natural or social events that generate large problems for society.

Interstate Conflict: Conflict that takes place between different countries.

Sentiment Analysis: Analysis to identify emotions in some kind data as text, video, sound, and image.

Social Conflict: Conflict generated by some social situation such as economic, political and health.

Social Medias: Place where public information is made available that can be collected and analyzed to extract some value´s type.

Chapter 12
Artificial Intelligence Techniques to Understand Braille:
A Language for Visually Impaired Individuals

Syed Asif Ali

Department of Artificial Intelligence and Mathematical Sciences, Sindh Madressatul Islam University, Karachi, Pakistan

ABSTRACT

The special-needs individuals have their own literary system called Braille for printing, reading, and writing since 1824 that assist them in easily connecting with each other. Because of the isolated education system, formally called the heterogeneous education system, they faced a lot of problems and challenges from society. Artificial intelligence tools and techniques play a vital role in mitigating communication gap between blind/visually impaired individuals and non-blind people. Thus, this chapter focuses on reviewing artificial intelligence techniques to understand Braille for normal people associated with visual imperative individuals. It is found that natural language processing (NLP) helps in translating native language into Braille. Machine learning and artificial neural network algorithms help in translating by matching the equivalent pattern of Braille. The concept of finite automata is used with natural language processing to recognize and convert the Braille pattern equivalent to their native language pattern and vice versa.

INTRODUCTION

The history of Braille literacy is very old. In 1824, Louis Braille (1809–1852), a French inventor who went blind from an accident when he was three, introduced the braille literacy system of printing and writing for the blind or visually impaired. Individuals who are blind or visually impaired are global

DOI: 10.4018/978-1-6684-6242-3.ch012

members of every society's community, and they communicate with other blind or visually impaired people using braille. As communication is a way of expressing or sharing information by means of speaking or writing in some specific medium, braille is the best way of communicating between blind individuals. Braille is used all over the world as a language for blind or visually impaired individuals to communicate. Globally, there are separate schools for blind or visually impaired individuals where they learn braille. However, they face a few problems and challenges, as do other people who are related to or close to blind or visually impaired individuals. In any nation, people communicate in their own native language, like Urdu, English, etc., which is entirely different from braille literacy which is used by blind or visually impaired individuals of their nation. Therefore, there is a need to introduce a technology-based intelligent system that can translate native languages into their equivalent braille and vice versa. The Artificial Intelligence (AI) based approach of Natural Language Processing (NLP) is the best approach for the process of translating native language into its equivalent braille.

Natural Language Generation is essentially a translator that converts computerised data into native language representation. It mostly involves the planning and realisation of texts and sentences. To understand and analyse human language by mining the data from content using the concepts of syntax, relations, and semantic parts of language, NLP helps in the smooth translation of human languages more accurately and with grammatical correction in the results using finite automata. This is substantially supportive when trying to communicate with someone in another language, like Braille. Therefore, this chapter will review artificial intelligence techniques to understand the Braille Literary.

BACKGROUND

BRAILLE LITERARY

Braille is a tactile literary system used for reading and writing purposes by blind or visually impaired individuals. Braille literacy is the best way to provide accessibility to blind and visually impaired people so that they can stay connected to society and gain access to information or knowledge. Without a doubt, Braille literacy plays a very active role in enhancing the self-confidence of blind or visually impaired individuals. They can read and write on their own, which helps them gain self-esteem as they fully engage in their work independently and become self-exploratory (Rex, E. et al., 1995), (National Institute for the Blind, 2018).

They can enjoy books from the shelf on various topics written in Braille without any assistance; they can enjoy stories, food recipes, and enhance their knowledge about morals, history, politics, etc. Because we live in an age of technology and artificial intelligence, there are many intelligent software programmes available with text-to-voice conversion that help them learn to not only keep up with society's affairs but also connect with international communities. Online intelligence applications enable users to enjoy online shopping, banking, and financial transaction, among other things. They, too, can work as self-employed individuals or as freelancers.

The basic building block of Braille literacy is comprised of six-dot configurations called "cells" that are combined to create words. The dots of braille cells are embossed, or raised, and are read by touch rather than eyesight. Braille is not a different language. Just like the print alphabet, it is a symbolic code used to write various languages, such as English. Braille can also be used for writing mathematics, scientific notation, musical notation, and computer code. The Braille basic building block is in text format. As a normal case study, a blind child who is born blind can easily start learning Braille literacy by the age of five (5). Braille literacy is offered to blind individuals; however, sighted people like special education teachers, researchers, and parents also learn to read and write Braille to guide their blind students, their children, or for research purposes (Rex, E. et al., 1995).

In most countries, the teachers of blind or visually impaired students are sighted people with master's degrees in special education. They are trained teachers of Braille literacy. To maintain the quality of education for blind students, it is very important that the teachers are well-trained in braille literacy before delivering the knowledge to visually impaired students. This is a very unfortunate fact: when blind newborns enter their families, they essentially present numerous challenges for their families and themselves, particularly in less developed countries. Parents of blind children are concerned about their children's future and hesitant to send them to school. Most sensible parents easily accept the challenges associated with their children and begin teaching themselves Braille literacy for the betterment of their children (Wittenstein et al., 1996), (Zabelski, 2009).

In this era of technology and artificial intelligence, research areas are open for researchers to work on intelligent applications and internet of things (IoT)-based systems for the betterment of blind or visually impaired individuals. Many technological challenges for teachers and their parents have already been overcome (Hoskin et al., 2022).

BRAILLE HISTORY

Braille is a system of printing and writing for the blind that was created in 1824 by Louis Braille (1809–1852), a French inventor who went blind from an accident when he was three. Each character in Braille is made up of an arrangement of one-to-six raised points used in 64 possible combinations; see Figures 1 and 2. Braille is read by passing the fingers over the raised patterns. Braille is a series of raised dots that can be read with the fingers by people who are blind or whose eyesight is not sufficient for reading printed material.

Braille symbols are formed within units of space known as Braille cells. A full Braille cell consists of six raised dots arranged in two parallel rows, each having three dots. The dot positions are identified by numbers from one to six. Sixty-four combinations are possible using one or more of these six dots. A single cell can be used to represent an alphabet letter, number, punctuation mark, or even a whole word. The enclosed Braille alphabet and numbered card illustrates what a cell looks like and how each dot is numbered (D'Andrea et al., 1997).

The Braille Literacy is used worldwide. Braille literacy is the only way for the majority of blind and partially sighted people to communicate and coordinate their actions with others.

Users of Braille literacy and others now have previously unimaginable communication freedom thanks to the advancement of information technology. The users of Braille language who communicate and coordinate with other individuals using other languages seem to meet certain obstructions and hindrances, especially when Braille printed on paper is used.

Figure 1. The Braille Cell

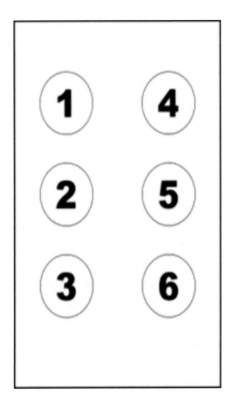

IMPORTANCE OF BRAILLE LITERACY

Terminology reflects social attitudes, legal rights, and so on, and as a result, it evolves over time. The concept of blindness is out of date. Blindness is instead replaced by the concept of "visual impairment", with two sub concepts: "severe visual impairment" and "low vision".

In this text, the concepts "blind and partially sighted" and "blind and visually impaired" are used to describe both groups of people having "severe visual impairment" and "low vision".

Figure 2. Braille Literary pattern

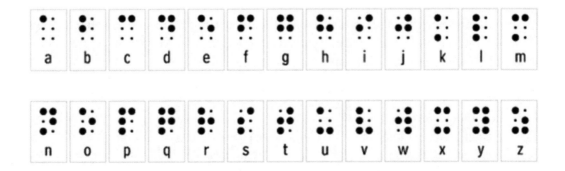

Braille is now regarded as a reading and writing system for people who are not completely blind. As discussed in the previous section, partially sighted people can become good Braille readers if they are motivated and given training.

Braille literacy has its own importance, even in the age of technology and artificial intelligence. Braille is the literacy or language of communication for the blind and visually impaired. Braille is considered a language, but in fact, it is a set of tactile symbols introduced by Louis Braille, as discussed. Braille is now considered a form of language for many languages spoken around the world. It may also be a fact that there are different braille systems for different languages. In fact, there are braille versions of many of the languages spoken today. Pakistani Braille follows the scrip of Urdu as the national language and English as the official language. Unified English Braille (UEB) is adopted by countries of the International Council on English Braille (ICEB), including Nigeria. Chinese are using Braille script of standard Mandarin language used in China. Japanese Braille script follows the Japanese language. Text or literary braille has non-contracted (alphabetic braille) and contracted braille (for saving space) (Clark, 2014).

Braille literacy makes blind and visually impaired individuals confident. Every blind and visually impaired community has its own Braille literacy drive based on their country's spoken or native language. Even some sighted children with severe disturbances in visual perception have affirmed that reading Braille is preferrable to visual reading. Future research and new technology may result in additional groups of Braille readers. Braille literacy helps in reducing the asymmetrical communication patterns between the blind and the non-blind. There is very little data available on Braille literacy; therefore, there is a lack of understanding of the importance of Braille literacy. Using the fundamental skills of Braille literacy—reading and writing—the blind and visually impaired can confidently expressed their feelings, ideas, etc. successfully and without any assistance. Alternate forms of Braille literacy are available as audiobooks and online tutorials, such as IoT based device, but Braille literacy has its own importance and beauty. According to available data, 90% of blind and visually impaired people have reading and writing skills in Braille. Because there is no implementation or use of Braille literacy in workplace, the rate of unemployment among the blind and visually impaired is increasing. Most of the blind and visually impaired attend public school where there are no facilities to assist them in their learning process, which become the reasons they drop out of school (around 60%). So, the rate of literacy in the blind and visually impaired is also decreasing. The teachers at public school do not have Braille literacy qualification, thus, they cannot deliver instructions in Braille.

BRAILLE LITERACY LEARNING, EDUCATION AND EMPLOYMENT

This is evidence that braille literacy is providing assistance in academic achievement and employment for the blind and visually impaired. A person who reads braille can roam independently in the community, as braille is becoming increasingly relevant everywhere. According to the 2008 Convention on the Rights of Persons with Disabilities, over 150 countries have signed and ratified it since then.

The declaration establishes the recognition of people with disabilities to be on equal footing with others around the world. Additionally, society is beginning to recognise the need to promote equality for all citizens within its communities.

To declare equal rights for blind and visually impaired people in public places, tools and aids for all individuals with disabilities are installed. For this reason, the use of braille can be widely observed in public spaces and facilities such as elevators, airplanes, restaurants, bank notes, etc.

Figure 3. Learning, Education & Employment through Braille Literacy

In fact, blind and visually impaired people feel more comfortable and confident with Braille than with today's accessibility tools and devices, which can also be confusing to non-blind people. This is the truth: Braille is a literacy that cannot be completely replaced by digital or other forms of technology (Clark, 2014; Ali et al., 2010).

To make blind and visually impaired individuals productive for society, there is a need to educate them through the learning strategies necessary to accommodate them with suitable employment according to their education level (see Figure 3).

THE WORTH OF BRAILLE LITERACY IN LEARNING AND EDUCATION

As the blind and visually impaired people are a part of every country, they have their education in Braille (based on their mother tongue). So there are some breaches (see Figure 4);

1. The education system is based on three entities: teachers, students, and parents. In normal practice, the teacher of blind and visually impaired people is familiar with both their own native language and braille.
2. However, students (blind and visually impaired people) only use braille for reading and writing.
3. The parents of blind and visually impaired people are only aware of their native language.

The blind and visually impaired people get education in an isolated education environment where they have separate education institutions and a separate language (Braille). This education system is called the "Homogeneous Education System (HoES)" where the students are comprised of blind and visually impaired people that have their own culture (Ali et al., 2010).

Parents of blind and visually impaired children are more involved with their children. They are the primary care providers. They have the capacity for action and a range of potential actions. Their involvement is critical for the wellbeing of special children.

This is the reality: blind and visually impaired individuals are facing day-to-day challenges to meet their needs. However, what makes their role more central is that as these people grow older, challenges will multiply, and these challenges are hard to tackle. All areas of development, from social participation to health, are critical to address. However, it has been observed that many parents, particularly adults, are unaware of their special children needs, which leads to further challenges for these parents in helping and understanding their children.

Some recognised issues are whether parents are familiar with the social needs of children and know about their rights. In addition, other issues include: 1) whether parents are generally aware about their children other needs, 2) whether parents have knowledge about identification and early interventions, 3)

Figure 4. Learning and Education systems in Braille Literacy

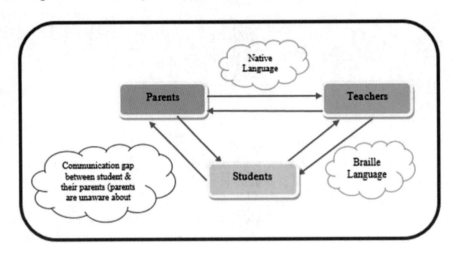

what challenges have to be faced by parents, 4) what do their children needs to learn, and 5) how their children perceive social norms etc.

THE WORTH OF BRAILLE LITERACY IN THE WORKPLACE

The unemployment rate among disabled people is twice the people without disabilities. Despite having desirable skills, they have difficulty finding a job, or at least a work that is adequate for their skills. Many of them have received training, and there are a few other functions where blind people have worked effectively.

Attempts to integrate special people into the workplace are more than just a social obligation. There are many benefits if blind people can assimilate and get a job: they can improve their living standards, their families will grow, and the level of poverty will be reduced.

Unfortunately, despite their qualifications, very few visually impaired and blind people have found suitable employment. Even though there is a number of ways this problem may be solved, one of them is to determine whether they belong to any particular class in their lives like rehabilitation clients, students, or working-age adults losing their vision. They are made conscious and aware of the numerous jobs that are being offered and could be successfully done in the workplace (Ali et al., 2013; O'Mally et al., 2016).

After appropriate training, these individuals can do several jobs as they have a similar range of abilities as normal people, except for vision. Therefore, blind individuals can successfully accommodate themselves in workplace (Soede, M., 1986).

There are many suitable and appropriate jobs for blind or partially sighted people. If they manage to perform well, they can be absorbed into the labour force. They can, for example, be incorporated into the following areas (Malakpa, S. W., 1994): assistant to the manager, clerical assistant, typist, receptionist, computer operator, data entry operator, customer service provider, telephone operator, etc. Besides these, listed below are other employment opportunities that may suit them:

a. They can be assimilated in the field of education as teachers, braille instructors (teachers for visually impaired students), writers, curriculum specialists, librarians, etc.
b. They can be assimilated in the media (TV and radio), as TV or radio broadcasters, or as journalists.
c. They can be assimilated into showbiz as musicians, actors, clergy, professional storytellers, etc.
d. Further, they can also serve as lawyers, inventors, factory workers, repair and service representatives, artisans, social workers, shopkeepers, etc.

There are many barriers to employment for blind people. There is a difference between academic training and practical work blind or visually impaired individuals will face a lot of problems in workplace, similarly to normal people who are sighted. Internship practises should be introduced during their schooling to familiarise them with work environment.

COMMUNICATION PROBLEM

Further, they have a separate cultural communication pattern with their own group called "Braille." This is the biggest barrier encountered in their work environment. If a separate communication medium is provided, the community of this segment of society may experience effective outreach.

In a formal environment, they will be required to communicate with normal people who cannot understand 'Braille'. This causes an important conflict in the conformance of identical brain wave lengths.

UNAPPROACHABLE INFORMATION, EMPLOYMENT AND SELECTION

Due to limited approach to find job information, blind or visually impaired people with good qualifications who are interested in finding a job cannot apply. This is a matter of great concern as it is an obstruction while in search of employment. In addition to this, it is a tedious task for them to obtain the relevant information and materials regarding vacancies. It becomes a vicious circle for them (Lazar et al., 2012; Rumrill Jr et al., 1997).

Most job advertisements and application forms are not available in braille. Moreover, this may be a sign that employment procedures can be discriminatory against them.

Adaptive technology becomes one of the vital tools in enhancing the path to employment, along with orientation and mobility guidance.

ARTIFICIAL INTELLIGENCE TECHNIQUES AND BRAILLE LITERACY, SOLUTION AND RECOMMENDATIONS

Technology has eliminated a number of burdens in the fields of education and employment for the visually impaired or the blind. These individuals who are students can benefit from assistive devices; they can finish their assignments, do research, take examinations, and read books by using talking devices, textbooks on CD or flash drive, Braille textbooks, talking dictionaries, and tape recorders for taking notes.

Blind adults can easily use information and communication technology (ICT) at the workplace. Assistive technology interfaces used in software can make it easier to speak out the content that is already on the screen and increase the content in a word processor for blind and visually impaired individuals. Therefore, they can easily be utilized in a specific email application, web browser, or any other applications in which they are interested. With the help of internet application, blind people and people with visual impairment can connect to social networks. Furthermore, through the use of information and communication technology, blind and visually impaired individuals can access and read official documents via voice applications, and organise and schedule meetings, among other things. Blindness and visual impairment can also be facilitated by providing them with optical character readers (OCR) so they can scan and read text with voice applications or software. They can also get embossed text for their office file records from braille printer (Ali et al., 2016; Bhowmick, et al., 2017; Martinez et al., 2017).

Cell phone is a very common technology for communication via voice command, which allows blind people to use the device as little as possible. Mobile wireless technologies, such as mobile phones and PDAs, are rapidly expanding as a new transfer source for sending and receiving information, content, and voice. The latest and newly developed wireless technologies may allow mobile phones data to be made transferable to computers. Computers can perform their tasks as universally accessible consoles for obtaining data and facilities, in addition for controlling and monitoring different appliances and devices. To sum up, wireless technology may soon become a vital and integral part of the lives of every individual, and without its assistance, the disabled may feel even more neglected and ignored by society in social activities and interaction (Zhang, S., et al, 2007).

During the last few decades, the benefit of new technologies has been gradually and impressively applied to facilitate the blind and visually impaired. This is a fact: education plays a very important or significant role in the development of an individual. Education shapes the life of an individual and changes their ideology. Unfortunately, there is a disparity between the education system of normal people and those with visual impairments. Basically, language is a way of communicating or transforming information and knowledge between people. In different countries, education and knowledge are delivered in their own mother tongue or natural language with proper syntax and semantics (Murthy, 2017; Isayed et al., 2015).

Computer-assisted instructions, artificial intelligence-based education systems, and communication and sensory methods of communication are examples of technologies and their applications. Many of the technologies were originally developed for settings outside of special education, but they have been adapted and used in the education of the blind and visually impaired. To identify relevant technologies in the future, special education is broadening its capabilities for monitoring and encouraging new technology development through different activities.

The potential uses of new technologies for blind and visually impaired education can apply as a methodology to advanced technology like artificial intelligence techniques. Through the use of artificial intelligence, researchers are striving to develop an education system for the blind and visually impaired (hardware and software-based systems) that will impact the way blind individuals communicate and learn in a friendly, homogeneous environment. Several disciplines of artificial intelligence, like neural networks, speech recognition, computer vision, natural language processing (NLP), virtual reality (VR), modelling language (HMM), intelligent computer-aided instruction (CIAI), etc., can be used to make the environment comfortable for the blind and visually impaired.

Blind and visually impaired people are a part of every society, and they interact and communicate with other people. They have their own culture in which blind individuals communicate with other blind individuals. Therefore, the way of communication they employ can be categorised as shown in Table 1.

First, when a blind or visually impaired individual starts communicating, they use their parent's natural or native language, which they learn from their parents. But as they grow, they need literature to

Table 1. Ways of Communication of blinds and visually impaired

Individuals	Communicate/correspondence	Individuals
Blind and visually impaired	Braille ® translate® natural or native language	Normal Persons
Normal Persons	Natural or native language® translate ® Braille	Blind and visually impaired
Blind and visually impaired	Braille ® Braille	Blind and visually impaired

learn more to which they cannot learn verbally. This is a matter of fact; all literature is available in their parental natural or native language, which they cannot read. Therefore, they need the help or assistance from others to provide them with this literature in audio recording form. Braille literacy is the best way for them to learn on their own without any assistance.

In every society, Braille instructors are available to guide and help blind or visually impaired individuals in learning and reading braille literature in early stage; after that, they should be able to learn all information or knowledge in braille literature by themselves. They can even comfortably communicate within their own blind culture through braille literacy. Their braille instructors guide them, but their parents are not able to guide them in braille reading and writing the same way. Similarly, when they start looking for jobs following their education, they will face difficulties in finding suitable jobs because jobs are normally advertised in newspapers—which are mostly written in their native language and which they can see and read. If they can find any opportunity with the assistance of someone, the second issue they will face is the organisation that will possibly not allow employment opportunity. The organisation may assume that because of their vision problem, they will not be as productive as normal sighted individuals. If they are fortunate enough to find suitable accommodations, the third issue they will face is having transportation and arriving to the office on time. However, the main challenges they will encounter are possible discriminatory attitude of their colleagues and lack of facilities at their workplace, which are necessary for them. Now, technology can provide the solution to some of their challenges.

Natural language processing (NLP) is thought to be a branch of artificial intelligence, but it is a part of computer science (CS), artificial intelligence (AI), and human language processing (HLP). It is called "natural language understanding" (NLU) and includes "natural language generation" (NLG) that acts as translation, spell check, automatic summarization, and more. NLP offers the exact answers to users' queries and works very efficiently and accurately with or on large databases (Keikhosrokiani & Asl, 2022).

The modified form of an artificial intelligence-based solution for learning and education systems in braille literacy are mentioned in Figure 5. In this modified learning and education system of Braille literacy, automata theory is used to translate native language into Braille patterns, and similarly, Braille patterns into related native languages. The theory of automata plays a significant role in providing solutions to many problems in natural language processing like speech recognition, spelling correction, information retrieval, etc. Finite state methods are useful in processing natural language, as the modelling of information using rules has many advantages for language modeling. A finite state automaton has a mathematical model that is quite understandable; data can be represented in a compacted form using a finite state automaton, and it allows automatic compilation of system components.

Finite state automata (deterministic and non-deterministic finite automata) provide decisions regarding the acceptance and rejection of a string, while transducers provide some output for a given input. As a result, the two machines are extremely useful in language processing tasks. Finite state automata are

Figure 5. Artificial Intelligence based solution Learning and Education systems in Braille Literacy

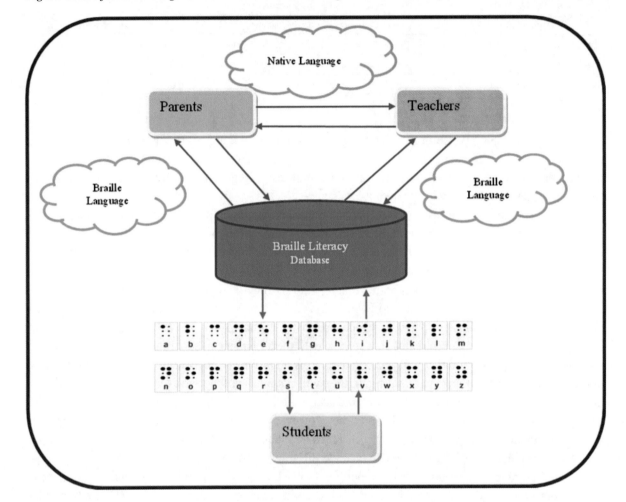

useful in deciding whether a given word belongs to a particular language or not. Similarly, transducers are useful in parsing and generating words from their lexical form.

Natural Language Generation is essentially a translator that converts computerised data into native language representation. It mostly involves the planning and realisation of text and sentences. To understand and analyse human language by mining data through the concepts of syntax, relations, and semantic parts of language using finite automata, NLP aids in producing an accurate and grammatically correct translation of human languages. This is substantially supportive when trying to communicate with someone in another language, like Braille.

AUTOMATA FOR BRAILLE LITERACY PATTERN USING NLP

The concept of regular expression can be used to express patterns or tokens in a language. In automata theory, machines receive regular expressions in stream form (one-by-one) and recognize their validity on the basis of their syntax and semantic analysis before accepting them (Ali et al., 2013).

Figure 6. Braille Alphabets

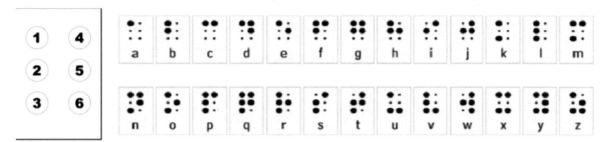

In the Braille literacy pattern, any type of character or a sequence of characters is produced when, at some of the six positions, a dot is raised to form a total of sixty-four possible combinations (including the possible combination in which not even a single dot is raised).

The Braille dots are the base upon which the Braille literacy characters against all the alphabets are formed, so the regular expression of these six dots is as follows:

$$L\,(\text{r.e}) = \{1, 2, 3, 4, 5, 6\} \tag{1}$$

In constructing the regular expression for the Braille literacy pattern, the combinations illustrated in Figure 6 are taken using pattern matching techniques for software development, packet pattern matching for voice patterns, and related technologies. The word tokens of the Braille literacy pattern are mentioned in Table 2.

Braille-to-Text translation ® {Braille ® (Characters ® Words ® Lines ®Paragraphs) ® Text}

$$\text{å} = 1 +12 +14 +145 +15 +124 +1245 +125 +24 +245 +13 +123 +134 +1345 +135 +1234 +12345$$
$$+1345+234 +2345 +136 +1236 +2456 +1346+13456 +1356 \tag{2}$$

The Braille literacy pattern also has the facility of representing capital letters as well as digits. The braille language also includes the number sign and capital letters formed on those six dots.

For writing uppercase alphabets in Braille, a capital sign pattern is used to concatenate with lowercase characters. e.g., if a capital "A" is required, then the capital sign is used, in which dots arise at position six along with the lowercase "a." To get the capital letters in Braille, the capital sign is used in a unique sequence of dots, as shown in Figure 7.

For writing number in Braille pattern, a number sign (left cell) along with lowercase characters (right cell) is used e.g., if one is required then use number sign in which dots arise at position 3456 along with lowercase 'a' (See Figure 8).

Now at this stage, it is also necessary to add the regular expression to match the pattern if any capital letter or number occurs. The capital sign has a regular expression of 6 and the number sign has a regular expression of 2456.

Table 2. Braille literacy pattern with their Code

Alphabets	Braille code	Alphabets	Braille code
A	1	N	1345
B	12	O	135
C	14	P	1234
D	145	Q	12345
E	15	R	1235
F	124	S	234
G	1245	T	2345
H	125	U	136
I	24	V	1236
J	245	W	2456
K	13	X	1346
L	123	Y	13456
M	134	Z	1356

$$L\ (r.e2) = \{6 + 3456\} \tag{3}$$

In addition to this, special characters may also be represented in the Braille literacy (See Figure 9). A language can't be complete without special characters, so Braille literacy has a few special characters to match them.

Its regular expression is:

$$L\ (r.e3) = \{256 + 2 + 3 + 235 + 236 + 36\} \tag{4}$$

Now by combining r.e1, r.e2 and r.e3 from Eq (2), (3) and (4):

Figure 7. Capital Letter in Braille

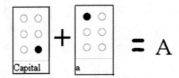

Figure 8. Number in Braille

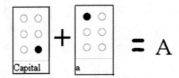

Figure 9. Special Characters in Braille

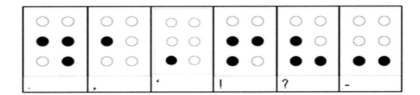

r.e =(1 + 12 + 14 + 145 + 15 + 124 + 1245 + 125 + 24 + 245 + 13 + 123 + 134 + 1345 + 135 + 1234 + 12345 + 1345 + 234 + 2345 + 136 + 1236 + 2456 + 1346 + 13456 + 1356 + 6 + 3456 + 256 + 2 + 3 + 235 + 236 + 36)   (5)

The deterministic finite automata for the above Braille regular expression can be designed as shown in Figure 10 to 12.

Q ® Total Numbers of State(s)

Q={a, b, c, d, e, f, g, h, i, j, k, l, m, n, o, p, q, r, s, t, u, v, w, x, y, z, A, B, C, D, E, F, G, H, I, J, K, L, M

q$_f$ ® Final State(s)

q$_f$={b, c, d, e, f, g, h, i , k, n, o, p, q, r, s, t, u, v, w, x, y, A, B, C, D, E, F, G, H, I, J, K, L, M}
The various transitions are described below:

Figure 10. Automata of Braille

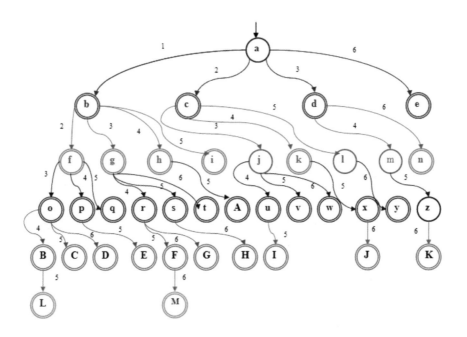

Figure 11. Automata of Braille with Initial state 'a'

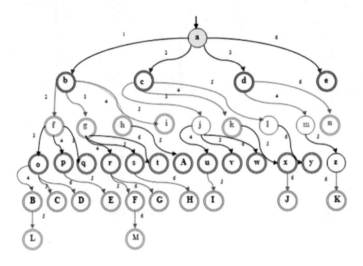

If a character, for instance "a," is taken from the Braille literacy pattern, the transition performed against the following character is shown in Figure 13.

Similarly, if a character, for example "b," is taken from the Braille literacy pattern, then the corresponding transition against the given character is shown in Figure 14.

In the same manner for any other random character for transition, "h" will have the corresponding transition as shown in Figure 15.

By following this, each pattern will be matched through the transaction (Table 3) for the correct character pick.

Figure 12. Automata of Braille with Final states

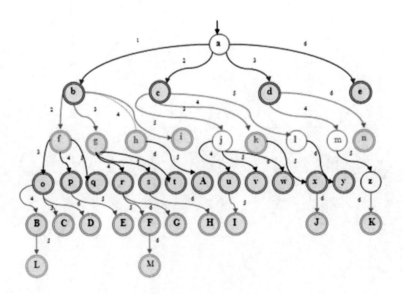

Figure 13. δ(a,1)=b

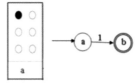

Figure 14. Transition δ (a, 1) =b, δ (b, 2) =f

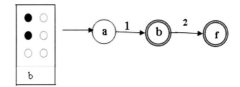

To minimise the above-mentioned finite state, the merging of all equivalent states is automated. This may be defined as shown in Figure 4, 5, and 6.

Braille Finite State Automata can easily be converted into minimum state automata using the minimization algorithm as follows: In table 1, replace similar states with a new state ξ (See Table 4). In transition table replace similar state with π, β (See Table 5). in transition table replace similar states with ζ, χ (See Table 6).

Figure 16 shows the minimized finite automata of braille patterns in which the minimized DFA has only Q=13 states.

After reducing the complexity of the incoming Braille pattern (input) by reducing the deterministic finite automata of the Braille literacy pattern from 39 states to 13 states, Braille has been greatly simplified. In the beginning, there are 64 possible combinations. By reducing the structural complexity of the DFA, it is expected that the minimised DFA will be more efficient with respect to time and space complexity. This minimised finite automaton is used in the braille database proposed in artificial intelligence solutions for learning and education systems in braille literacy (see Figure 5), which works very fast to translate native language into Braille pattern and vice versa. This process provides a way for the parents of blind or visually impaired people to get the translation of braille in their native language.

Figure 15. Transition δ (a, 1) =b, δ (b, 2) =f, δ (f, 5) =q

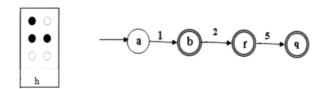

Table 3. Transition Table

δ:Q X I	1	2	3	4	5	6	Q X I	1	2	3	4	5	6
a	B	c	d	⊥	⊥	e	u	⊥	⊥	⊥	⊥	I	⊥
b	⊥	f	g	h	i	⊥	v	⊥	⊥	⊥	⊥	⊥	⊥
c	⊥	⊥	j	k	l	⊥	w	⊥	⊥	⊥	⊥	⊥	⊥
d	⊥	⊥	⊥	m	⊥	n	x	⊥	⊥	⊥	⊥	⊥	J
e	⊥	⊥	⊥	⊥	⊥	⊥	y	⊥	⊥	⊥	⊥	⊥	⊥
f	⊥	⊥	⊥	o	p	q	z	⊥	⊥	⊥	⊥	⊥	K
g	⊥	⊥	⊥	r	s	t	A	⊥	⊥	⊥	⊥	⊥	⊥
h	⊥	⊥	⊥	⊥	A	⊥	B	⊥	⊥	⊥	⊥	L	⊥
i	⊥	⊥	⊥	⊥	⊥	⊥	C	⊥	⊥	⊥	⊥	⊥	⊥
j	⊥	⊥	⊥	u	v	w	D	⊥	⊥	⊥	⊥	⊥	⊥
k	⊥	⊥	⊥	⊥	x	⊥	E	⊥	⊥	⊥	⊥	⊥	⊥
l	⊥	⊥	⊥	⊥	⊥	y	F	⊥	⊥	⊥	⊥	⊥	M
m	⊥	⊥	⊥	⊥	z	⊥	G	⊥	⊥	⊥	⊥	⊥	⊥
n	⊥	⊥	⊥	⊥	⊥	⊥	H	⊥	⊥	⊥	⊥	⊥	⊥
o	⊥	⊥	⊥	B	C	D	I	⊥	⊥	⊥	⊥	⊥	⊥
p	⊥	⊥	⊥	⊥	E	⊥	J	⊥	⊥	⊥	⊥	⊥	⊥
q	⊥	⊥	⊥	⊥	⊥	⊥	K	⊥	⊥	⊥	⊥	⊥	⊥
r	⊥	⊥	⊥	⊥	F	G	L	⊥	⊥	⊥	⊥	⊥	⊥
s	⊥	⊥	⊥	⊥	⊥	H	M	⊥	⊥	⊥	⊥	⊥	⊥
t	⊥	⊥	⊥	⊥	⊥	⊥							

(Where is used for error or null set)

FUTURE RESEARCH DIRECTIONS

Most of the regions still prefer to educate blind or visually impaired individuals in their own literary system in separate institutions specifically established for them. These people are totally reliant on their teachers and fellow students for their educational needs, particularly the braille system. Even after they return from their academic institutions, this reliance persists as a result of segregated educational system. Most parents are only familiar with their own literary system, not braille. Parents or other family members cannot help blind or visually impaired individuals with their schooling by becoming proficient in braille. Natural language processing, machine learning, and pattern matching are examples of artificial intelligence approaches that allow blind and visually impaired people, as well as those who care for them, to communicate. An intelligent system may readily help them at all times—not just for educational purposes, but also in finding appropriate employment and transporting to workplace with their coworkers.

This chapter is an effort at analysing general problems faced by blind and visually impaired individuals because of a specific literary system called braille. This chapter also shares ways to reduce this limitation by using artificial intelligence techniques. Furthermore, there is a lot of improvement to be done for the betterment of the social lives of blind and visually impaired individuals, which is essentially their basic right. Artificial intelligence techniques are useful for providing technical assistance in their education

Table 4. Transition table1 replace similar state with ξ

δ:Q X I	1	2	3	4	5	6
a	b	c	d	⊥	⊥	ξ
b	⊥	f	g	h	ξ	⊥
c	⊥	⊥	j	k	l	⊥
d	⊥	⊥	⊥	m	⊥	ξ
ξ	⊥	⊥	⊥	⊥	⊥	⊥
f	⊥	⊥	⊥	o	p	ξ
g	⊥	⊥	⊥	r	s	ξ
h	⊥	⊥	⊥	⊥	ξ	⊥
j	⊥	⊥	⊥	u	ξ	ξ
k	⊥	⊥	⊥	⊥	x	⊥
l	⊥	⊥	⊥	⊥	⊥	y
m	⊥	⊥	⊥	⊥	z	⊥
o	⊥	⊥	⊥	B	ξ	ξ
p	⊥	⊥	⊥	⊥	ξ	⊥
r	⊥	⊥	⊥	⊥	ξ	ξ
s	⊥	⊥	⊥	⊥	⊥	ξ
u	⊥	⊥	⊥	⊥	ξ	⊥

Let i=n=q=t=v=w=y=z=A=C=D=E=F=G=H=I=J=K=L=M= ξ

and employment. Further applications of artificial intelligence can also be adapted to work on security issues for female with blindness by using intelligent technology-based services to help them protect themselves in society. Parents of blind and visually impaired individuals, as well as other people associated with them, must ensure that the existence and sustainability of blind and visually impaired individuals in society are the collective responsibility of every sector. The role of government is also critical in this regard. Education institutions should be set up in order to meet the educational and vocational needs of blind and visually impaired people with the help of modern technology like assistive technology. Standard

Table 5. Transition table replace similar state with π, β

δ:Q X I	1	2	3	4	5	6
a	b	c	D	⊥	⊥	ξ
b	⊥	f	G	β	ξ	⊥
c	⊥	⊥	j	k	l	⊥
d	⊥	⊥	⊥	m	⊥	ξ
ξ	⊥	⊥	⊥	⊥	⊥	⊥
f	⊥	⊥	⊥	o	β	ξ
g	⊥	⊥	⊥	r	s	ξ
β	⊥	⊥	⊥	⊥	ξ	⊥
j	⊥	⊥	⊥	β	ξ	ξ
k	⊥	⊥	⊥	⊥	π	⊥
l	⊥	⊥	⊥	⊥	⊥	y
m	⊥	⊥	⊥	⊥	π	⊥
o	⊥	⊥	⊥	β	ξ	ξ
r	⊥	⊥	⊥	⊥	ξ	ξ
π	⊥	⊥	⊥	⊥	⊥	ξ

Let h=p=u=B= β , s=x=z=F= π

braille literary should be created by all stakeholder groups and policymakers, with the involvement of parents and non-governmental organisations (NGOs) who work with the blind in particular.

Table 6. Transition table replace similar states with ζ, χ

δ:Q X I	1	2	3	4	5	6
a	b	c	d	⊥	⊥	ξ
b	⊥	f	g	β	ξ	⊥
c	⊥	⊥	ζ	χ	1	⊥
d	⊥	⊥	⊥	χ	⊥	ξ
ξ	⊥	⊥	⊥	⊥	⊥	⊥
f	⊥	⊥	⊥	ζ	β	ξ
g	⊥	⊥	⊥	r	s	ξ
β	⊥	⊥	⊥	⊥	ξ	⊥
ζ	⊥	⊥	⊥	β	ξ	ξ
χ	⊥	⊥	⊥	⊥	π	⊥
1	⊥	⊥	⊥	⊥	⊥	y
r	⊥	⊥	⊥	⊥	ξ	ξ
π	⊥	⊥	⊥	⊥	⊥	ξ

j=o= ζ , k=m=χ

Figure 16. Minimised Finite Automata of Braille Patterns

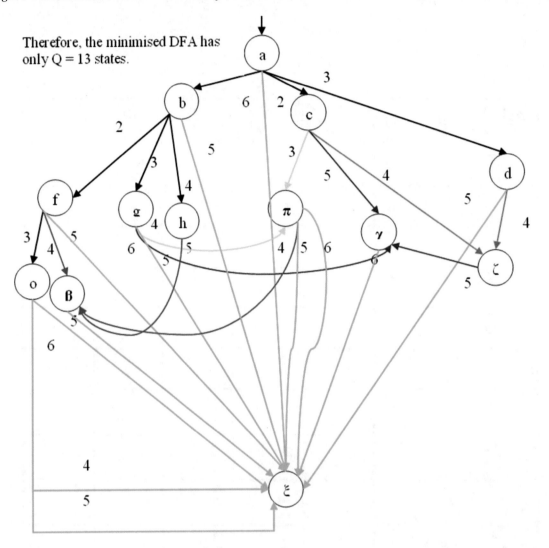

Therefore, the minimised DFA has only Q = 13 states.

CONCLUSION

It is a fact that there are people with special needs in every community, and they require assistance in adjusting to life among regular people. For a family with a special child, however, this is exceedingly challenging. Previously, in order for blind or visually impaired people to exist in society without feeling like a social and financial burden on society and their families, independence is necessary despite the exceeding difficulties to educate and accommodate them at work. Nowadays, it is simpler to educate and accommodate them at work as less-reliant members of society thanks to artificial intelligence technologies. Artificial intelligence technologies can help bridging the communication gap between people who are blind or visually impaired and those who are sighted.

Computer vision algorithms can be used to help people who are blind or visually impaired understand the locations and the distances of things in their surroundings. By understanding speech tones or facial expressions of others around them, those who are blind or visually challenged can understand others' moods and emotions (because they cannot see, but artificial intelligence algorithm can provide help in understanding feelings from others' facial expressions using a tracking system).

Having discussed the advantages of artificial intelligence technologies for blind or visually impaired individuals, the findings of this chapter should be useful to all researchers and educators who work with blind or visually impaired people, as well as to everyone who knows them.

REFERENCES

Ali, S. A., & Ahmed, M. (2013). ICT's impact on HRM: Special peoples endeavors. *International Journal of Inventive Engineering and Sciences*, *1*(6), 46–49. https://www.ijies.org/portfolio-item/f0220051613/

Ali, S. A., & Burney, S. A. (2010). Conversion of heterogeneous education system (HeES) into homogeneous education system (HoES) for ease of disabled persons using information technology. *2010 International Conference On Computer Design and Applications*, V2-298-V2-301. doi: 10.1109/ICCDA.2010.5541470

Ali, S. A., Hussain, S., & Hasan, B. (2016). Context aware computing used for education and communication of people with special needs; Focus on deaf and dumb. *Journal of Information & Communication Technology-JICT*, *10*(2), 56–58. https://www.researchgate.net/publication/317184239_Context_A ware_Computing_Used_For_Education_and_Communication_of_Peopl e_with_Special_Needs_Focus_on_Deaf_and_Dumb

Asif, A. S. (2013). Design of minimal states deterministic finite automaton to recognize braille language pattern using the concept of regular expression. *Australian Journal of Basic and Applied Sciences*, *7*(7), 49–53. http://www.ajbasweb.com/old/ajbas/2013/may/49-53.pdf

Bhowmick, A., & Hazarika, S. M. (2017). An insight into assistive technology for the visually impaired and blind people: State-of-the-art and future trends. *Journal on Multimodal User Interfaces*, *11*(2), 149–172. doi:10.100712193-016-0235-6

Clark, J. (2014). The importance of braille in the 21st century. *Journal of South Pacific Educators in Vision Impairment*, *7*(1), 24–29. https://www.spevi.net/wp-content/uploads/2015/07/JSPEVI-Vol-7-No-1-2014.pdf

D'Andrea, F. M. (1997). *Instructional strategies for braille literacy* (Vol. 1). American Foundation for the Blind.

Hoskin, E. R., Coyne, M. K., White, M. J., Dobri, S. C., Davies, T. C., & Pinder, S. D. (2022). Effectiveness of technology for braille literacy education for children: A systematic review. *Disability and Rehabilitation. Assistive Technology*, 1–11. doi:10.1080/17483107.2022.2070676 PMID:35575120

Isayed, S., & Tahboub, R. (2015). A review of optical Braille recognition. *2015 2ndWorld Symposium on Web Applications and Networking (WSWAN)*, 1-6. doi: 10.1109/WSWAN.2015.7210343

Keikhosrokiani, P., & Asl, M. P. (Eds.). (2022). *Handbook of research on opinion mining and text analytics on literary works and social media*. IGI Global. doi:10.4018/978-1-7998-9594-7

Lazar, J., Olalere, A., & Wentz, B. (2012). Investigating the accessibility and usability of job application web sites for blind users. *Journal of Usability Studies, 7*(2), 68–87.

Malakpa, S. W. (1994). Job placement of blind and visually impaired people with additional disabilities. *RE:view. Rehabilitation and Education for Blindness and Visual Impairment, 26*(2), 69–77.

Martinez, M., Roitberg, A., Koester, D., Stiefelhagen, R., & Schauerte, B. (2017). Using technology developed for autonomous cars to help navigate blind people. *2017 IEEE International Conference on Computer Vision Workshops (ICCVW)*, 1424-1432. 10.1109/ICCVW.2017.169

Murthy, V. V., & Hanumanthappa, M. (2017). Pre-processing the braille image for improving optical braille recognition performance. *International Journal of Advanced Research in Computer Science, 8*(7), 561–564. http://ijarcs.info/index.php/Ijarcs/article/view/4188. doi:10.26483/ijarcs.v8i7.4188

National Institute for the Blind. (2018). *Standard English braille: Grades I and II*. Forgotten Books.

O'Mally, J., & Antonelli, K. (2016). The effect of career mentoring on employment outcomes for college students who are legally blind. *Journal of Visual Impairment & Blindness, 110*(5), 295–307. doi:10.1177/0145482X1611000502

Rex, E., Koenig, A., Wormsley, D. P., & Baker, R. (Eds.). (1995). *Foundations of braille literacy*. American Foundation for the Blind Press.

Rumrill, P. D. Jr, Schuyler, B. R., & Longden, J. C. (1997). Profiles of on-the-job accommodations needed by professional employees who are blind. *Journal of Visual Impairment & Blindness, 91*(1), 66–76. doi:10.1177/0145482X9709100111

Soede, M. (1986). Innovation, braille, information and workplace design. In P. L. Emiliani (Ed.), *Development of Electronic Aids for the Visually Impaired* (pp. 37–43). Springer. doi:10.1007/978-94-009-4281-3_5

Wittenstein, S. H. (1994). Braille literacy: Preservice training and teachers' attitudes. *Journal of Visual Impairment & Blindness, 88*(6), 516–524.

Wittenstein, S. H., & Pardee, M. L. (1996). Teachers' voices: Comments on braille and literacy from the field. *Journal of Visual Impairment & Blindness, 90*(3), 201–209. doi:10.1177/0145482X9609000309

Zabelski, M. (2009). A parent's perspective on the importance of braille for success in life. *Journal of Visual Impairment & Blindness, 103*(5), 261–263. doi:10.1177/0145482X0910300502

Zhang, S., & Yoshino, K. (2007). A braille recognition system by the mobile phone with embedded camera. *Second International Conference on Innovative Computing, Information and Control, ICICIC*, 223–223. doi:10.1109/ICICIC.2007.4

Chapter 13
Text Analytics of Vaccine Myths on Reddit

Sylvia Shiau Ching Wong
School of Computer Sciences, Universiti Sains Malaysia, Malaysia

Jing-Ru Tan
School of Computer Sciences, Universiti Sains Malaysia, Malaysia

Keng Hoon Gan
School of Computer Sciences, Universiti Sains Malaysia, Malaysia

Tien Ping Tan
School of Computer Sciences, Universiti Sains Malaysia, Malaysia

ABSTRACT

Widespread online misinformation that aims to convince vaccine-hesitant populations continues to threaten healthcare systems globally. Assessing features of online content including topics and sentiments against vaccines could help curb the spread of vaccine-related misinformation and allow stakeholders to draft better regulations and public policies. Using a public dataset extracted from Reddit, the authors performed text analytics including sentiment analysis, N-gram, and topic modeling to grasp the sentiments, the most popular phrases (N-grams), and topics of the subreddit. The sentiment analysis results revealed mostly positive sentiments in the subreddit's discussions. The N-gram analysis identified "cause autism" and "MMR cause autism" as the most frequent bigram and trigram. The NMF topic modeling results revealed five topics discussing different aspects of vaccines. These findings implied the significance of the ability to assess public confidence and sentiment from social media platforms to enable effective responses against the proliferation of vaccine misinformation.

INTRODUCTION

The World Health Organization (WHO) has named vaccine hesitancy – the reluctance or refusal to vaccinate despite having access to vaccines – as one of the ten most significant threats to global health in 2019

DOI: 10.4018/978-1-6684-6242-3.ch013

(Ten Threats to Global Health in 2019, 2019). According to the WHO, vaccines have saved 2-3 million of lives globally each year, and it is estimated that a further 1.5 million lives could be saved if global coverage of vaccination improved (Ten Threats to Global Health in 2019, n.d.). Despite the growing body of evidence that proves the efficacy of vaccines – which is particularly evident in the recent contribution of COVID-19 vaccinations toward the disease's subsidence, vaccine hesitancy remains pervasive and threatens to reverse the progresses achieved in combating vaccine-preventable diseases. For instance, measles had seen a 30% increase in cases worldwide in 2019, which was in part due to vaccine hesitancy (Patel et al., 2019). The reasons why some individuals choose not to vaccinate are complex, though the vaccine advisory group to WHO has identified the key reasons underlying this hesitancy, which include complacency, inconvenience in accessing vaccines, and lack of confidence in vaccine safety.

Considering the ongoing COVID-19 pandemic at the time of writing, achieving herd immunity for this disease through vaccination remains a challenging task for many governments and authorities in part due to vaccine hesitancy, which gets worsened by the widespread counteracting false information on various social media platforms. Thus, it remains vital for regulatory bodies to be able to assess features of online contents including text patterns, popular topics, and public sentiments toward crucial issues such as vaccines in order to combat against the spread of misinformation and improve the progress toward achieving a high vaccination rate. In this paper, we employ a series of text analysis methods on public discussions extracted from Reddit's r/VaccineMyths – a subreddit where people discuss about various vaccine-related myths – with the goal of identifying the most popular topics surrounding vaccines and assessing public sentiments toward vaccines in general.

PROBLEM STATEMENT

Social media platforms have contributed to the propagation of vaccine misinformation significantly and subsequently fueled the pervasiveness of vaccine hesitancy, which has become a serious threat to public health. As stated by the WHO, the ongoing COVID-19 outbreak and its response have brought along an info-demic: "an overabundance of information – some accurate and some not – that makes it hard for people to find trustworthy sources and reliable guidance when they need it" (Understanding the Infodemic and Misinformation in the Fight Against COVID-19, 2020). The exponential information growth surrounding vaccines has been accompanied by misinformation and myths, along with manipulation of information with malicious intent. A report by the Centre for Countering Digital Hate (CCDH) had condemned social media giants including Facebook, Twitter, Instagram, and YouTube for allowing anti-vaccine movements to remain active on their platforms and failing to implement policies that were put in place to prevent the propagation of vaccine misinformation (Nogara et al., 2022). As such, the number of followers for anti-vaccine social media pages and advocates has increased by millions particularly after the outbreak of COVID-19. Another study by Johnson (2020) has found that the undecided population in issues of contention surrounding vaccine are more connected to the anti-vaccination voices on Facebook, and predicted that if such situation remains uncontrolled, the anti-vaccination movement could overwhelm pro-vaccination voices on online platforms. If that came to pass, the consequences would be even more detrimental than what is currently being observed for the COVID-19 pandemic. As such, partnerships and collaborations need to be established to develop more effective global resources for fact-checking and misinformation management, knowledge translation, community engagement, and amplification of information. Such efforts require extensive natural language processing (NLP) techniques to dissect massive volumes of unstructured data in order to obtain meaningful and actionable insights.

Aside from the giant social media platforms including Facebook, Twitter, Instagram, and YouTube, Reddit has also been susceptible to promoting misinformation. As the 19th most popular site on the Internet globally with more than 330 million registered users, Reddit is an interesting platform to consider as it allows self-defined communities to establish themselves, which provides an unusual basis for the analysis of online interactions. The feature of "subreddits" allow users to form communities dedicated to a specific topic or theme, which provides more ease for users to connect and reinforce the views of others. As of writing, the rollout of COVID-19 vaccines for the COVID-19 pandemic has led to a spike in the numbers of public discussion about COVID-19 vaccines as well as vaccines in general on various social media platforms, including Reddit. By analyzing the interactions on the subreddit r/VaccineMyths, the derivable insights could potentially help us identify patterns or factors associated with vaccine hesitancy or confidence. On the other hand, by assessing the public sentiment toward vaccine from the interactions on the subreddit, the resulting information could potentially help regulatory bodies and public health policy makers to develop more effective policy implementations, communications, and education strategies to reduce vaccine hesitancy and lessen its impact.

RELATED WORKS

To analyze the sentiments around vaccine on Twitter, Kang et al. (2017) built semantic networks of vaccine-related information from articles shared on Twitter from United States-based users. The networks' topologies and semantic differences were analyzed, and the authors were able to identify the most prominent concepts associated with positive, neutral, and negative vaccine sentiments. For the positive sentiment network, the most salient concepts revolve mostly around 'parents' and the communication of health risks and benefits. On the other hand, the negative sentiment network mostly centered around 'children' and focused on organizational bodies.

In the paper by Luo et al. (2019), an NLP framework with AI-based phrase association mining was developed to assess the opinions on HPV vaccination specifically over a 10-year period from 2008 to 2017 and was able to identify the associations between entities including organizations, geographical locations, events and the negative and positive tweets. The results revealed that organizations such as FDA, CDC and Merck occur in both negative and positive tweets across the 10-year period of the data collected, while the geographical location entities mentioned in both negative and positive tweets fluctuated from year to year due to the events happened that were specific to certain regions at different times.

In another study done on Twitter's data, the authors obtained around 1.2 million public tweets posted between the timeframe of 19th July 2020, to 19th August 2020 to identify the main topics surrounding a potential COVID-19 vaccination (Tasnim et al., 2020). Using Latent Dirichlet Allocation for topic modeling, the authors identified 20 topics and categorized 4,868 tweets based on their sentiments. Out of those tweets, about 27% were identified as having negative sentiments associated with some of the themes identified earlier including 'misinformation', 'vaccine safety and effectiveness', 'conspiracy theories', and 'mistrust of scientists and governments'.

Some of the more recent works include the work by Hussain et al. (2021), where over 300,000 Facebook posts and tweets related to COVID-19 vaccines were analyzed to predict topics of discussion and sentiments using NLP and deep learning-based methods, with findings correlating well with nationwide surveys. In both nations covered by this study, positive sentiments were the majority (58% in United Kingdom and 56% in the United States). Topic modeling revealed public optimism over the development of vaccines, their effectiveness, and trials results as well as concerns over their safety, economic viability, and corporation control.

In another study by Piedrahita-Valdés et al. (2021), a hybrid approach was used to conduct an opinion-mining analysis on around 1.5 million tweets related to vaccine from the period of 1ˢᵗ June 2011 to 30ᵗʰ April 2019. The model categorized 69% of the tweets as neutral, 22% as positive, and 9% as negative, with the neutral tweets showing a decreasing tendency while the positive and negative tweets increasing slowly over time. This study demonstrated the potential of using such models to monitor vaccine-related information that were exchanged or spread on the Internet.

One recent study performed sentiment analysis and topic modeling on COVID-19 vaccine-related textual data collected from 13 Reddit communities from the period of 1ˢᵗ December 2020 to 15ᵗʰ May 2021 (Melton et al., 2021). Polarity analysis suggested mostly positive sentiments from these Reddit communities which exhibit minimal change across the 6-months timeframe of the data collected. The results of topic modeling revealed that the discussions from the 13 communities mainly focused on vaccine side effects with minimal discussions that centered around conspiracy theories.

To assess the efficacy of neural models for text summarization and machine learning in delivering WHO-matched COVID-19 information, Gautam et al. (2021) developed a machine learning application that uses conversational Artificial Intelligence (AI), machine translation, and NLP to encourage the public to perform fact-checking and mitigate the spread of misinformation. Within 45 days of launching and continuous machine learning, the authors observed improved relevance of AI-filtered news content and increased prudence of the integrated AI chatbot, thus proving the usefulness of a machine learning application in mitigating health misinformation.

These authors and developers have demonstrated the significance of NLP's role in not just assessing the public's discussion topics and sentiments but also its potential in influencing these features. Many of these studies also highlighted the need for authorities to devise a better large-scale vaccine communication plan that will better curb the widespread of misinformation and conspiracy theories on social media platforms.

PROPOSED SOLUTION

The following sections will detail the text analysis performed on the subreddit r/VaccineMyths posts using Sentiment Analysis, N-Gram, and Topic Modelling. Prior to the analysis, we performed exploratory data analysis to explore the dataset, followed by text pre-processing to create a more text-analytics-friendly dataset. All text analyses were performed on Jupyter Notebook using Python3.

Dataset Description

The dataset used in this paper was obtained from Kaggle. It contains Reddit posts from the subreddit VaccineMyths and was extracted from https://www.reddit.com/r/VaccineMyths/ using *praw* (The Python Reddit API Wrapper) by Gabriel Preda, the dataset's original author who is a well-known contributor in the Kaggle community. The dataset contains post titles (Title) and comments (Body) of the subreddit,

Table 1. Definition and data types of attributes associated with each title or body

Fields	Description	Data Types
Title	Title of a post; often represents a start of a new topic within a subreddit	Object
Score	The score of the post; in the context of upvotes given by readers	Integer
ID	A unique ID for posts and comments	Object
URL	The web address to the post thread	Object
Commns_num	The number of comments to a post	Integer
Created	The date of creation of the post or comment	Float
Body	The body text of a post or comments responding to a post	Object
Timestamp	Timestamp	Object

which are the two attributes that hold the text that are of interest to us. The details of the attributes of this dataset including their descriptions and data types are detailed in Table 1.

Reddit is a forum that allows users to organize communities and express individual opinions freely if adherence to both the platform's general policies and the specific rules designated by each subreddit's moderators is observed. As a result, it adopts a more lenient restriction on speech as compared to other professional forums, where most of the content obscurement are usually the result of too many downvotes from the Reddit community. Due to its relaxed nature, our dataset's primary text sources – the "title" and "body" attributes – contains a certain amount of vulgar language, slang, and acronyms. More than three-fourth of the instances under the "title" attribute contains only the word "Comment" as the main texts of all these instances were written as comments responding to posts, with the comments recorded under the "body" attribute. This dataset is a running dataset as the author updates the dataset regularly with new content from the subreddit. At the time of writing, the dataset contained a total of 1597 instances of titles and comments with the same eight columns detailed in Table 1. The dataset was loaded using the *read_csv* function in Python's pandas module as a data frame.

Exploratory Data Analysis

Exploratory Data Analysis (EDA) can be understood as a process of performing initial investigations on a dataset with the intention to discover possible trends, outliers, and missing values using summary statistics and graphical visualizations. Before delving into the text corpus, we first investigated the missing values in each of the attribute. Only two of the eight attributes, namely, "url" and "body" contain 71% and 23% of missing values respectively. The number of missing values was expected in the "body" attribute since users on Reddit might start a post with only a title without including any additional text in the post's body text section. A heatmap was created using seaborn package to visualize the missing values for each attribute as shown in Figure 1.

The attributes "id" and "url" were dropped since they do not add value to our analysis. The attribute "created" was dropped as it holds similar information to the "timestamp" attribute. Since "timestamp" was recorded with combination of date and time, the attribute content was converted into months and years, adding two attributes with integers as their data type. For instance, the original entry of "2021-02-27 06:33:45" was converted into year "2021" and month "2", under the two new "year" and "month" attribute. This conversion enabled the data to be presented in a time series format which would come

Figure 1. Heatmap showing the distribution of missing values with black colour representing non-null values and beige colour representing null values

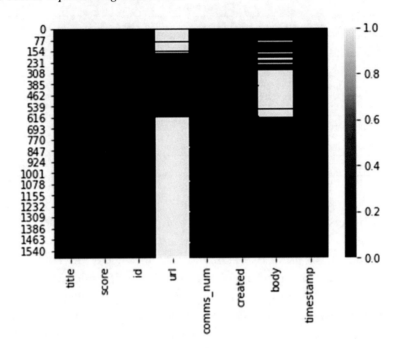

in handy for observation of trends. A sorting was carried out using the attribute "score" to observe the most impactful posts or comments. The content of the top 10 most impactful post, as listed in Figure 2, suggests the presence of an equal distribution of pro-vaccine and anti-vaccine voices in the subreddit.

The final task in this section was to visualize the discussion of vaccine myths over the years in this subreddit. We presented the visualization with the countplot function from the seaborn module. As shown in Figure 3, the time series count plot showed that this subreddit forum was created since 2014 and with the content generated in the year 2019.

Given that COVID-19 was first discovered in December 2019, the months of 2019 (Figure 4) and 2020 (Figure 5) were examined further to investigate if any surge of discussion was present during those months.

The result was slightly surprising given that number of discussions on vaccine myths in this community reached its peak in April of 2019 while a decline is observed during the second half of 2020 when COVID-19 was the most ravaging. This may be explained by the distraction caused by the mass coverage of COVID-19's impact and lethality instead of its vaccine progress during that period.

Text Pre-Processing

In this paper, we performed nine steps of text pre-processing methods to ensure the corpus was text analytics-ready. The steps were separated into two parts of self-defined function using the def function in Python. The first function included text conversion to lower case, removal of special character, hyperlink, newline character, numbers, and elongated empty spaces. We utilized 're' (Regular expression operations) module and 'sub()' function to perform the removal by replacing occurrences of a defined

Figure 2. Top 10 most impactful post sorted by score in descending order

	title	score	comms_num	body	timestamp	year	month
507	I would rage if this was handed to me...	1181	595	NaN	2014-04-02 05:32:42	2014	4
505	From /r/Rage	45	13	NaN	2014-04-02 23:01:49	2014	4
207	Vaccines exposed	39	4	NaN	2020-12-18 05:11:12	2020	12
286	Do not give a platform for anti-vaxxers to pro...	36	5	I am of the mind to report social media groups...	2019-02-12 01:04:08	2019	2
296	Oh no! I got vaccinated!	30	6	\n\n\nAnd I'm completely fine, do some researc...	2018-11-21 20:35:02	2018	11
271	Vaccines have a huge side effect	30	13	Vaccines have a huge side effect, vaccines are...	2019-06-08 11:16:35	2019	6
233	How ironic	29	3	NaN	2020-03-06 11:19:39	2020	3
460	Meet my friend's anti-vax wife	28	1	NaN	2014-04-29 22:47:41	2014	4
503	Typical debate with an anti-vaxer (I'm teal)	27	16	NaN	2014-04-03 13:56:34	2014	4
241	Vaccinate folks.	26	7	NaN	2020-01-09 03:25:37	2020	1

Figure 3. Distribution of count of posts and comments over the years as presented on a histogram

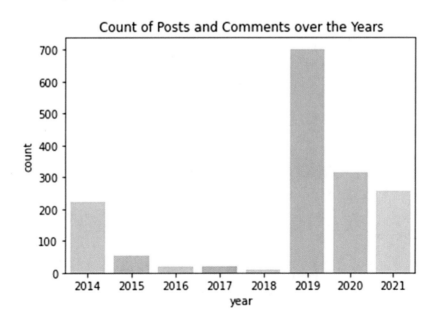

Figure 4. Distribution of posts and comments counts in 2019 on a histogram

Non Verified	
Positive	Negative
Inactive	Active
True Positives	True Negatives
False Positives	False Negatives
Accuracy=(TP+TN)/(TP+TN+FP+FN)	
TN=0	
TP=83	
Total= 108	
Accuracy=	0+83/108 =	83/108	77
Accuracy=	**77.00%**

regular expression with either no value or a blank space (Re — Regular Expression Operations — Python 3.10.8 Documentation, 2022). Newline and elongated empty spaces were replaced with a single space to prevent two words from concatenating with one another. In the second part, we used spaCy, an open-source software library designed for advanced natural language processing, to perform tokenization, lemmatization, and removal of stop words. A package named 'en_core_web_sm' from spaCy module was loaded to perform the aforementioned tasks. This package is an English pipeline trained based on written web text (blogs, news, and comments) which contains vocabulary, syntax, and entities

Figure 5. Distribution of posts and comments counts in 2020 on a histogram

Protected	
Positive	Negative
Inactive	Active
True Positives	True Negatives
False Positives	False Negatives
Accuracy=(TP+TN)/(TP+TN+FP+FN)	
TN=124	
TP=0	
Total= 154	
Accuracy=	124+0/154 =	124/154	0.805
Accuracy= 80.55%

(Trained Models & Pipelines · spaCy Models Documentation, 2022). STOP_WORDS package from spaCy module was also imported and updated with a list of text that was deemed to have no value to be added to the analysis. Examples of those stop words include "vaccine", "vaccination", "vaccinate", and "vaccinated". Since they were expected to be mentioned at a high rate given the domain of our dataset, including these words would interfere the findings of our analysis. Embedded in the second function were functions for the disabling of unwanted components followed by two for loops to generate lemmatized tokens and to remove stop words and non-alphabetic tokens. The data frame was duplicated before applying both pre-processing functions to ensure that we reserve a copy of the data frame with a clean slate for future applications. Both functions were applied only to the content of "title" and "body" attributes in the duplicated data frame.

Sentiment Analysis

Sentiment analysis on text analytics is the utilization of natural language processing to identify, extract, and transform unstructured text and their relevant information into a certain degree of expression polarity that encompasses positive, negative, and neutral sentiment (Keikhosrokiani & Asl, 2022). In our paper, we started the analysis with the generation of word clouds to observe the most common words in the subreddit forum. Prior to that, the corpus was generated using a for loop to iterate through every instance in the "title" attribute and only join the text in the predefined corpus array "corpus_title" if the value contains more than the single word "Comment". This generated a Title corpus that contains titles of posts on the subreddit r/VaccineMyths. Similar for loop was created to generate the corpus, defined as "corpus_body", from the "body" attribute with a filter to skip instances with null values. This generated a Body Corpus that contains the body texts of posts or comments responding to posts on the subreddit r/VaccineMyths. The word clouds were generated on the two aforementioned corpuses using the WordCloud function with stop words parameters setting to the predefined STOP_WORDS variable and maximum number words limited to 200 counts.

Word clouds alone are insufficient for inferring the semantic meanings of the texts involved. Sentiment analysis is performed through analyzing the results generated using the TextBlob module (Tutorial: Quickstart — TextBlob 0.16.0 Documentation, 2022). TextBlob functions via lexicon-based approaches where the "averaging" technique is applied on a word to compute its semantic orientation and intensity (Fahad, 2021). Hence, applying the method on every word and the combination results will yield a semantic orientation and intensity for a sentence. TextBlob computes semantic orientation and intensity by assigning a polarity score that ranges from -1 to 1, with 1 indicating a positive sentiment and -1 indicating a negative sentiment. The library also allows the measure of subjectivity property in a sentence with 1 leaning towards personal opinion and 0 leaning towards factual information. We only performed sentiment analysis on the Body corpus due to the following reasons:

- the relatively shorter average length of the sentences in the Title corpus,
- the rather limited number of usable instances available in the Title corpus as compared to the Body corpus (467 vs. 1223), and
- the overlapping nature of the content in both corpuses, as indicated by the high degree of similarity between their word clouds.

A separate set of text pre-processing function without the removal of special characters was applied onto the original dataset for sentiment analysis. Reason being that TextBlob has the semantic labels to identify emoticon and special characters with of likes of hashtags and alias. Polarity and subjectivity functions were defined using the sentiment property in TextBlob library and applied onto the "Body" attribute of the cleaned dataset. Two columns were created as a result with sentiment, consisting of the words "Positive", "Negative", and "Neutral" as well as subjectivity with numbers ranging from 0 to 1. The results were visualized on two histograms which the context will be examined later in the discussion section. A number of samples from each sentiment type were also generated as evaluation metrics in the next section.

N-Gram Analysis

Since the concept of N-gram largely pertains to the probability of words occurring next in a sequence of words, an N-gram analysis could be used to inform the most probable occurrence of combinations of words for a specific N-sequence. By identifying the bigrams or trigrams with the highest occurrence frequency, it allows us to better grasp the common ideas or contexts that exist within a corpus as compared to interpreting a word cloud that informs only frequencies of single words.

We only performed N-Gram analysis on the Body corpus due to considerations over the average text length, number of available instances, and the overlapping nature between the Title and Body corpus – the same reasons outlined in the previous section.

In this analysis we utilized the CountVectorizer function from the sklearn module. CountVectorizer function creates a matrix of word token count from a corpus of text through tokenization and assigning the total count of appearance to each specific word (sklearn.feature_extraction.text.CountVectorizer, 2022). The "ngram_range" parameters in CountVectorizer allowed us to define the lower and upper boundary of the range of n-values that need to be extracted. A (2,2) parameter value would return bigram from the corpus. A function "most_ngram" was defined with parameter "text" referring to the corpus and "n" indicating the number N-gram to be extracted. The top 10 appearances of bigrams and trigrams were extracted from the "Body" attribute and presented on 2 separate bar plots.

Topic Modelling

Topic Modelling as the name implies, is a probabilistic generative model that apply statistical technique to reveal the underlying semantic structure of a corpus by segregating a large collection of text into separate topics (Kherwa & Bansal, 2018). As presented in (Hong & Davison, 2010), the used of topic modelling has enabled new possibilities and perspective when it comes to text analytics specially in the domain of social media which Reddit falls right into. In our paper, we adopted two different topic modelling techniques, namely Non-Negative Matrix Factorization (NMF) and Gensim's Latent Dirichlet Allocation (LDA). We performed Topic Modelling only on Title corpus due to the fact that comments that populates the Body corpus are often responses to the title of a post, effectively making them share the same topic in a post thread.

NMF decomposes the document-term matrix into two smaller matrices, namely, document-topic matrix and topic-term matrix whereby document is comprised of an order of topics while a topic is comprised of an order of terms. As our model would not be able to text, we converted the titles into numbers using the function TfdfVectorizer from the scikit-learn module (sklearn.feature_extraction.

text.CountVectorizer, 2019). This function creates a term frequency-inverse document frequency (tf-idf) matrix. The formula will assign a weightage to a word depending on its appearance in a document and across the corpus essentially putting more emphasis on significant words that do not appear regularly across man-idocuments (Scott, 2021). We created a tf-idf matrix that left out terms that have a document frequency strictly higher than 95% and lower than 2. The result showed a document-term matrix of 467 titles (documents) and 507 vocabularies. We arbitrarily set the number of topics to be generated to five and fit the scikit-learn NMF model to the Title corpus (sklearn.decomposition.NMF, 2022). This was followed a function to display the list words in each topic and limiting the number of words to the top 10 candidates considering that displaying all 500 vocabularies will not help in understanding the context of each topic. A new column was created to assign each instance with their respective topic number with a range of 0 to 4. Using the function value_counts(normalize=True), we were able to observe the percentage of each topic and display 5 instances each representing their own topics with the highest weightage.

Since NMF does not provides any means to evaluate models with different number of topics, we attempted another technique - Gensim's Latent Dirichlet Allocation (LDA) which provides a convenient measure to do so with Coherence Score. The score is created by flowing topics generated by the model through 4 different pipelines where the topics will be segmented, quantified using probability, assigned a qualitative measurement, and aggregated into a final score (Röder et al., 2015). A separate list of Title corpus was created since the LDAModel functions required a different format from the earlier corpus. The corpus was first generated with five topics using LDAModel function from the Gensim's package and yielded a coherence score of 0.5796. A for loop was created to find highest coherence score by iterating through number of topics from 1 to 10.

EVALUATION CRITERIA

In this section, we attempted to evaluate each of the proposed solution through a mix of empirical and non-empirical approaches. For sentiment and N-gram analysis, we will assess the results based on their relevancy to their semantic orientation and overall context of the subreddit forum. As for topic modelling, the same non-empirical approach will be applied on the NMF technique while coherence score will be the formal evaluation metric for Gensim's LDA technique.

Sentiment Analysis

As stated in the previous section, five random samples of instances were selected from each of the sentiment categories using the *sample()* function. Figures 6, 7, and 8 show the outputs of the samples for each of the sentiment type (Positive, Neutral, and Negative).

Based on the text output as shown above, we observed a reasonable performance of sentiment classification. Even though Positive and Neutral sentiments were not classified as accurate as they should be, they do have three out of five majority of instances labelled correctly. Negative sentiments, on the other hand, matched all five random instances from the random sampling, which is unsurprising since the domain of the forum represented users' uncertainties toward vaccines. An average result is expected since lexicon-based sentiment analysis would not be able to handle slangs, acronyms, and sarcasm widely adopted on social media well as the sentiment is predicted based on pre-defined rules that may be adapted from a completely different domain.

*Figure 6. Five randomly selected **Positive** instances from the Body corpus*

Impressions			
Positive	**Negative**		
Inactive	**Active**		
True Positives	True Negatives		
False Positives	False Negatives		
Accuracy=(TP+TN)/(TP+TN+FP+FN)			
TN=109			
TP=3			
Total= 154			
Accuracy=	109+3/154 =	112/154	0.727
Accuracy=	**72.70%**		

N-Gram Analysis

The top ten phrases generated from our N-gram analysis revealed satisfactory results. Bigrams such as "cause autism", "immune system", and "herd immunity" clearly represented the phrases heavily associated with vaccines, especially in light of the current COVID-19 pandemic. As for trigram, we observed a resemblance of relevancy in the vaccine topic with N-grams like "mmr cause autism", "measle mump rubella", and "public health official".

Topic Modelling

Using the NMF model, we created a statistic summary for the distribution of each topic in the Title corpus as shown in Figure 9. Titles categorized under Topic 4, which is related to Anti-vaccination and Vaccine Myths (with details presented in the discussion section), showed the highest percentage of instances among other topics. This proves that the NMF model preformed with decent level of accuracy since the largest topic we identified is directly related to the domain of our text corpus.

*Figure 7. Five randomly selected **Neutral** instances from the Body corpus*

```
["Probably shouldn't have made a thread without doing so",
 'Cell lines.',
 'Could you explain "mercurate(1-)"?',
 'Ok, I was wrong, apologies, I have now deleted the comments.',
 'Where is your immunology PHD?']
```

Figure 8. Five randomly selected **Negative** *instances from the Body corpus*

```
["Your OP. It's not a myth. Only one vaccine contains it and you can get it wit
hout it. So your OP is pointless flex. ",
 'As of today we have 0 vaccines for SARS AIDS MERS combined And the flu vaccin
e which was developed 70 years ago, changes every year, because the flu virus c
hanges every year, and showed efficacy of 40.25% on average for the past 16 yea
rs And what? 90+ % efficacy from something made in 2 days and tested over 9 mon
ths? And what about the variants? South Africa / Switzerland already rejected A
Z Oxford vaccine because they saw it did not show efficacy against the South Af
rican variant',
 "When people realized that DTP caused brain damage in some cases in the 80s so
me people speculated that this could manifest as autism, but it could have star
ted before that, when Leo Kanner first described autism in 1944, he noted that
one of the autistic children became autistic 1 month after a smallpox vaccine,
while there wasn't evidence that the vaccine caused the autism, he did make a c
onnection",
 "The claim leads to extremely damaging actions. It's a stupid claim, and the b
acklash is exactly how it should be",
 'yes I can answer it, and the answer is that your speculation about my motives
is just wrong']
```

For Gensim's LDA model, the aforementioned Coherence Score was utilized as an evaluation metrics to determine the optimum number of topics to generate. The selection of topic number is an important process for a narrow selection will lead to an overly broad topics while a wide selection tends to generate topics that overlap with one another and could not produce a clear distinction between topics. After performing 10 iterations on the LDA model with different topic numbers, we observed the highest coherence score when the number of topics is set at seven (see Figure 10). The content of the seven topics will be examined in the discussion section.

Figure 9. Percentage distribution of each topic

```
4    0.336188
3    0.269807
0    0.211991
2    0.098501
1    0.083512
Name: topic, dtype: float64
```

Figure 10. Number of topics generated by LDA model and their respective Coherence Scores

```
Num Topics = 1
Coherence Score:  0.5531906845236474
Num Topics = 2
Coherence Score:  0.5632407438295429
Num Topics = 3
Coherence Score:  0.51724679595501333
Num Topics = 4
Coherence Score:  0.5567488211062875
Num Topics = 5
Coherence Score:  0.5795661177892722
Num Topics = 6
Coherence Score:  0.5981313202425306
Num Topics = 7
Coherence Score:  0.6030425258477446
Num Topics = 8
Coherence Score:  0.5914458817243476
Num Topics = 9
Coherence Score:  0.5911395798783515
Num Topics = 10
Coherence Score:  0.5764528990223603
```

ANALYSIS AND DISCUSSIONS OF FINDINGS

In this section, we analyze the results obtained through the proposed solutions in the previous sections. Attempts of discussion about these results in the context of our Problem Statement – identification of patterns or factors associated with vaccine hesitancy or confidence through text analytics on the subreddit r/VaccineMyths – are also included here.

By observing the word clouds generated from the Body (Figure 11) and Title (Figure 12) corpuses, we can identify the most common words being "study", "child", "measle", "autism", "cause", and "time" in both. Since there are many overlaps between the words of highest frequencies in the two corpuses, it adds to the interconnection between the post titles and bodies – which is expected.

Sentiment Analysis

Based on the polarity properties of the sentences in the Body corpus as seen in Figure 13, about half of them are classified as positive, while the other half is split between negative and neutral. This might attribute to the nature of the subreddit, where most of the posts were created from the users' thoughts

Figure 11. Word cloud generated from the Body corpus

Figure 12. Word cloud generated from the Title corpus

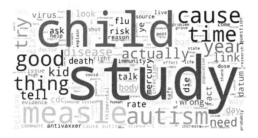

Figure 13. Sentiments extracted from texts in the Body corpus based on polarity values

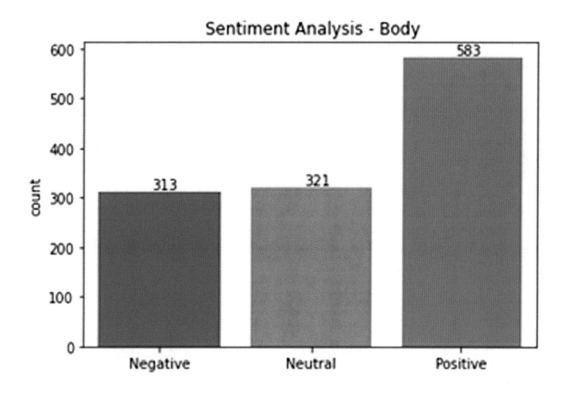

Figure 14. Subjectivities extracted from texts in the Body corpus

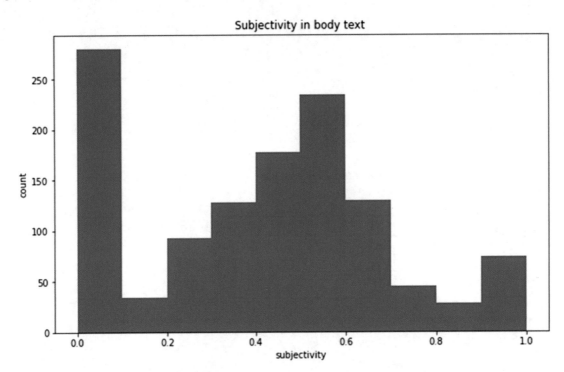

and concerns on vaccines and thus inviting over comments that attempt to answer, explain, or clarify the topics raised. As sentences of clarifying or affirming nature tend to use positive words or sentences to express opinions or facts, this may explain the results we observed.

As discussed in the Evaluation Criteria section, the sentiment analysis results are considered decent at most. One way of improving the results would be to create a dataset with labelled sentiments for each sentence and use it to train and optimize a machine learning classifier. As the classifier learns more of the patterns from the three polarities, it would yield more accurate results when predicting sentiments of new instances.

Textblob indicates the subjectivity of texts using a score range of (0, 1) – the higher the score toward 1, the more personal opinion the sentence contains. In other words, the lower the score toward 0, the more factual information is contained in the sentence. Our results as visualized in Figure 14 shows a slightly right-skewed distribution between the assigned subjectivity scores. This means that slightly more than half of the sentences in the Body corpus were written with inclusion of factual information, which is not surprising due to the nature of this subreddit which exists mainly for topics around vaccines – a scientific topic that requires factual approach.

However, the fact that almost half of the sentences having subjectivity scores higher than 0.5 should not be overlooked as well, as it indicates a rather high percentage of inclusions of personal opinions in an environment specially dedicated to a scientific topic. This might be attributed to the expressions of emotions frequently observed in heated discussions – which is particularly common for widely-discussed topics such as vaccines – between users who are for or against vaccines, including anxiety, anger, frustration, fear, disgust, contempt, or sadness.

Figure 15. Top 10 most frequently occurring bigrams from the Body corpus

	Retweets Received	Likes Received	User Followers	User Following	Impressions	Unnamed: 21
count	386.000000	386.000000	386.000000	386.000000	386.000000	0.0
mean	0.730570	2.839378	2516.904145	1067.401554	1137.849741	NaN
std	1.884991	9.423381	10529.124870	1409.750825	2381.107457	NaN
min	0.000000	0.000000	0.000000	4.000000	0.000000	NaN
25%	0.000000	0.000000	348.000000	379.000000	0.000000	NaN
50%	0.000000	0.000000	796.000000	542.000000	0.000000	NaN
75%	0.000000	1.000000	2922.500000	1123.000000	882.000000	NaN
max	13.000000	98.000000	198675.000000	12476.000000	12033.000000	NaN

N-Gram Analysis

The top ten most frequently occurring bigrams are all either significantly (e.g., "cause autism", "immune system", "herd immunity", "chicken pox", "measle outbreak", "unvaccinated child", "public health", "increase risk") or reasonably (e.g., "year old", "bad faith") related to vaccines, as shown in Figure 15.

The bigram "cause autism" tops the list, which is unsurprising due to it being the most widely used reason for those who opposes vaccines ever since the publishing of the controversial case-study in 1998 by Andrew Wakefield (Sabra et al., 1998). Even though the case-study has since been proven to be fraudulent (Deer, 2011) (Godlee et al., 2011), its impact still continues to be significant even to this day as suggested by our findings. The ninth most common bigram "bad faith" could also be attributed to the low confidence expressed toward vaccines by those who are against them.

Another interesting observation is the bigram "measles outbreak", which is one of the reasons often cited by those who are pro-vaccines as it is most likely written in the context of the global measles resurgence observed between the year 2018 to 2019 (World Health Organization, 2021). As the measles outbreak was largely driven by the immunity gaps present in populations across the globe, it explains the high occurrence of this bigram.

The bigrams "immune system", "herd immunity", "chicken pox", "public health", and "increase risk" are all pertaining to either the general concepts of how vaccines work or diseases with available vaccines (chicken pox). As for the sixth bigram in the list "year old", it most likely refers to the subreddit's members concerns on how an individual's age factors into vaccines in general. The seventh most common bigram, "unvaccinated child" might point to the topics raised by those who are worried about children's vaccine uptake either from a pro-vaccine or an anti-vaccine perspective.

Based on the results for trigram analysis as shown in Figure 16, the trigrams that made it to the top ten list are all significantly related to the common themes we observe around the vaccines topic in the more recent timelines. As much as six of the trigrams from this list ("mmr cause autism", "measles mump rubella", "measle virus sequence", "cross blood brain", "blood brain barrier", and "autism tell cause")

Figure 16. Top 10 most frequently occurring trigrams from the Body corpus

04733	Sat May 30 19:07:26 PDT 2009	NO_QUERY	22	chatting away, said bye to rachie
25442	Tue Jun 16 16:37:29 PDT 2009	NO_QUERY	127	still dont know what to do with my cat when i move
30878	Mon Jun 15 08:07:30 PDT 2009	NO_QUERY	136	Feels bad I have to lock the cats in the room stupid bug spray
00729	Fri Apr 17 21:07:37 PDT 2009	NO_QUERY	338	At beach. Will get about / less than 6 hrs and 45 min of sleep. XD I still miss some people & the Despair Factior
59456	Sun May 31 00:22:21 PDT 2009	NO_QUERY	407	#asylm no coffee lounge for me with misha been queueing since 6 this mornin
54709	Wed Jun 17 15:23:46 PDT 2009	NO_QUERY	427	Blacksheep is this weekend and I'm super excited, I just wish I had money to spend to buy fibery goodness
73456	Fri May 22 03:09:26 PDT 2009	NO_QUERY	431	@ Blue Tits in our wall: stop making those incredible cute sounds, trying to work...
42097	Fri May 22 04:40:32 PDT 2009	NO_QUERY	431	Still working on finishing the K3 chocolate sprinkles. Need to finish those before allowed to eat the Piet piraat sprin
63875	Mon Apr 20 03:36:51 PDT 2009	NO_QUERY	723	No sleep and I tried my hardest to sleep
92729	Fri May 01 23:36:21 PDT 2009	NO_QUERY	723	@Shaantastic its ugly outside tmrw.. raining.. it was like this last yr, we thought it was gonna rain
13464	Sat Jun 06 19:14:14 PDT 2009	NO_QUERY	723	@standfornothing yes finals are 11th, 12th, 15th. and then i have state tests, then i go back to school like 26th.
74390	Sat Jun 06 19:21:27 PDT 2009	NO_QUERY	723	@standfornothing haha thats so early i dont really mind starting in sept, its still like 90 degree weather by sept, so
87230	Sat Jun 06 19:34:39 PDT 2009	NO_QUERY	723	@ZaccariahTwiter well can i at least get it during your presentation? im in the yrbk staff next year and i didnt even g
05521	Sat Jun 20 17:31:38 PDT 2009	NO_QUERY	723	@checkmarks refresh? you better come here cuz the game is gonna be sloow and boring
19822	Sat Jun 20 21:14:13 PDT 2009	NO_QUERY	723	gniteee, stupid coughing
97160	Sun Apr 19 23:27:28 PDT 2009	NO_QUERY	723	@onefullyear yea twitterfox lagged my ff immensly idk why but i def prefer tweetdeck
27646	Thu Jun 18 20:35:23 PDT 2009	NO_QUERY	1071	@loquatmusic gah!! i can't make your beach show. hope you make it down this way again soon!
15136	Mon Jun 15 05:16:03 PDT 2009	NO_QUERY	1389	@brianDdew it gives you a popup msg when you get ready to close the tab and navigate away from their webpage
63214	Wed Jun 03 07:57:35 PDT 2009	NO_QUERY	1732	Unlimited interner started and I'm reaching Mumbai on 7th
73798	Fri Jun 19 10:37:45 PDT 2009	NO_QUERY	1732	No windows #jailbreak till now
38728	Thu May 14 01:31:17 PDT 2009	NO_QUERY	2089	Sup Bomarr, I just spent 2 bucks for you. I was wondering, do you think you can send me that remix you've done for w
15908	Fri Jun 05 17:11:31 PDT 2009	NO_QUERY	2147	ive lost some contacts, dont know why
51627	Sat May 02 05:17:04 PDT 2009	NO_QUERY	2525	@matheuswartjes op dat pad wel
24233	Mon Jun 15 17:39:42 PDT 2009	NO_QUERY	4320	On Myspace, worrying about him!!!
93099	Thu Jun 18 04:13:42 PDT 2009	NO_QUERY	5987	@YaggaYow My vacations are not until november.These five year olds are kicking the hell out of me. I am sooo tired
13886	Tue Jun 02 03:11:16 PDT 2009	NO_QUERY	6000	@JeremyTNell There were 227 other people as well. FTL
21613	Tue Apr 07 02:47:02 PDT 2009	NO_QUERY	6277	@Mirror_Kiss no, i don't have money, i'm very upset too

revolve around the "MMR vaccine causes autism" or "vaccines cause autism" arguments frequently used by those who are anti-vaccines, as explained earlier. In particular, the trigrams "cross blood brain" and "blood brain barrier" are most likely originated from the claims of aluminium "nanoparticles" in vaccines crossing the blood-brain barrier and thus harming brain cells – a claim that remains unconfirmed (Blood-brain Barrier and Vaccines, n.d.).

The third and fifth most common trigrams "public health official" and "health maintenance organization" indicate the common inclusion of health authorities in vaccines-related discussions.

An intriguing observation comes from the sixth trigram in the list, "adverse event report", which most likely refers to The FDA Adverse Event Reporting System (FAERS), which is a database that "contains adverse event reports, medication error reports and product quality complaints resulting in adverse events that were submitted to FDA" (Center for Drug Evaluation and Research, 2018). In our specific context, the VAERS (Vaccine Adverse Event Reporting System) – which is a branch of FAERS – is the most probable source behind the high occurrence of this trigram as VAERS contains records of adverse events associated with vaccines (Center for Biologics Evaluation and Research, 2021). The purpose of VAERS combined with its reputable nature due to it being an official government website inevitably makes it a popular source for those who argue against vaccines.

As for the tenth most common trigram "stick reputable source", it most likely comes as a request from those who are pro-vaccines while responding against those who are anti-vaccines, due to the common citations of irreputable sources containing mostly misinformation from the latter group (Germani & Biller-Andorno, 2021).

Figure 17. Documents with the highest weightage under identified topics 0-4 using NMF

	title	score	comms_num	body	timestamp	year	month	topic
240	cause autism	0	9	wonderful daughter hailey autism autistic doct...	2020-01-11 12:51:59	2020	1	0
135	cast covid volunteer freezer truck driver	6	0	NaN	2021-03-02 02:58:59	2021	3	1
213	measle overview	3	0	NaN	2020-11-25 09:34:22	2020	11	2
293	child	20	24	mom extremely antivax swear let I long live I ...	2019-01-03 06:41:44	2019	1	3
262	I need help debunk	2	1	NaN	2019-08-28 07:40:54	2019	8	4

Topic Modelling

Non-Negative Matrix Factorization (NMF)

Using the NMF model, we obtained the following five topics with their respective top-ten most frequently occurring keywords.

- Topic 0: **autism cause mmr link** court proof owner prove bad **cdc**
- Topic 1: **covid canada** penicillin magnetic la **pfizer** actually **coronavirus prevent available**
- Topic 2: **measle myth outbreak** body **mump** chance polio baby **die** daughter
- Topic 3: child unvaccinated parent reason polio year mmr choose immunity right
- Topic 4: help need antivax debunk antivaxxer anti new discuss podcast vax

By examining the keywords from each identified topic and correlating them to their respective most representative posts (Figure 17), we can deduce the most probable topic titles for Topic 0, 3, and 4. However, these methods did not provide enough context to help us determine the themes of Topic 1 and 2. Therefore, we investigated a random ten sample titles under each of the topics, as listed in Table 2.

By relating the topic keywords to the sample titles, we reinterpreted the keywords from the five identified topics and highlighted the more suggestive ones among them. Next, we postulated the most probable topics for each of them, as detailed in Table 3.

Since the keywords for each identified topics do correlate quite well with their respective representative posts (Figure 17) and at least a few of their sample posts (Table 2), we were able to solidify the most probable themes for each topic that are reasonably well-rounded in Table 3. This proves that the NMF topic model performed reasonably well for this case.

Topic 0 (The Debate on MMR Vaccine and Its Potential Causal Relationship with Autism) covers about 21.1% of the total instances in Title corpus based on the percentage distribution from Figure 9,

Table 2. Sample documents under identified topics 0-4 using NMF, with the more suggestive titles bolded

Topic	Approaches
0	[**'mmr cause autism'**, 'enlarge heart enlarge heart microwave definitely', 'damn hipster', '', **'cdc fda credible source th cdc prove'**, **'irrefutable prufe'**, 'I rant', 'fake news trump sign executive order ban childhood lead story', 'delicious', **'I crazy year old mom campaign lose cause I uk whilst dr wakefield godfather brother I feel biased'**]
1	['ebola prevent treat naturallyso approach completely ignore', **'fact ama american medical association finance pfizer monsanto company manufacture controversial proventobedangerous product insecticide ddt pcb agent orange recombinant bovine somatotropin'**, **'covid actually prevent covid'**, **'vietnam covid nanocovax effective variant university vietnam currently work covid produce nanogen institute medical biological'**, **'official confront challenge public covid new abc newsipsos poll release monday americans plan immediately available eventually signal grow confidence'**, 'approve nursing mother', **'covid canada passport near certainty bioethicist'**, 'parent dose chinese covid pfizer come recently pfizer time gap', 'hand magnetic', **'canada oxfordastrazeneca approval expect week'**]
2	['water vs mercury', **'immunity wear contract measle actually let body immunize naturally immune life'**, **'measle viron live outside body short period time hour close disney world day'**, 'dr dre slightly credible', **'measle urge amid disneyland outbreak'**, 'pretty terribly write blog', 'mercury', 'daughter safe', **'I mump measle baby I mump measle baby I mump measle babychili baby anti vax idiot'**, 'hear myth coronavirus']
3	[**'I encounter parent social circle kid problem range auto immune disorder asd happen month'**, 'disease fine flu shot year stupid glorious human race immune system fragile soon send er cold', 'I choose delay I', 'swine flu immunity confirm', **'parent choose child riskfree'**, 'course run secret cia program track osama bin laden live terrible stretch run depopulation program', **'doctor ashamed submit family terrifying ordeal'**, **'believe I happen child I care study post'**, 'oral polio grow chimpanzee kidney africa prior emergence hivaid administer m certainly culprit disease human', 'inject shit']
4	[**'typical debate antivaxer I teal'**, **'new apparent antivaccine strategy study ignore information disappear magic'**, 'sad everybody dangerous nurse hero', **'dr wakefield obviously strike major nerve research quickly tear apart establishment maliciously parade fraudulent groundbreake finding repeatedly validate replicate study'**, 'I interested discuss aspect documentary argument present note available day free', 'gardasil remove japanese market remove', 'lol', **'antivaccine blogger refute la time whoop cough story monopoly truth'**, **'beware contain deadly chemical dihydrogen monoxide'**, 'fix stupid']

Table 3. Postulated themes for the identified topics 0-4 using NMF

Topic no.	Keywords	Postulated Theme
0	**autism cause mmr link** court proof owner prove bad **cdc**	The Debate on MMR Vaccine and Its Potential Causal Relationship with Autism
1	**covid canada** penicillin magnetic la **pfizer** actually **coronavirus prevent available**	Authorization of and Responses toward Covid-19 Vaccines by Governments and Authorities
2	**measle myth outbreak** body mump chance polio baby **die** daughter	Measles Outbreak and Debate for/against Measles Vaccines
3	**child unvaccinated parent reason** polio year **mmr choose immunity right**	Vaccination Uptake in Children
4	help need **antivax debunk antivaxxer anti** new discuss **podcast vax**	Anti-vaccination and Vaccine Myths

and revolves around the debate concerning the linkage between MMR vaccine and autism. This result correlates with our N-gram analysis as we also found significant representations of text relevant to this topic and confirms the prevalence of this vaccine myth among the users of this subreddit community.

For topic 1 (*Authorization of and Responses toward Covid-19 Vaccines by Governments and Authorities*), the postulation process of this topic was not as direct as the other ones due to its low number of representations in the Title corpus (8.4%). Further investigation into its sample posts later revealed a few titles concerning the news on the efforts from authorities in response to Covid-19 vaccination (see Table 2, Topic 1). This shows the at least some users care about what authorities do in response to the disease and its vaccines, whether they are for or against vaccines in general.

Topic 2 (*Measles Outbreak and Debate for/against Measles Vaccines*) also required deeper investigation in order for us to deduce its theme due to its relatively low coverage of 9.9%. Several instances under topic 2 mentioned the words "measle", "outbreak", and "Disneyland", indicating discussions on the renowned Disneyland measles outbreak in 2014 were carried out on this subreddit (Measles Outbreak — California, 2015).

Vaccination Uptake in Children is the topic derived from identified topic 3, with a relatively high distribution of 27%. Considering the word "child" and "unvaccinated" being the first two keywords under this topic and the mentions of "kid" or "child" in its sample posts, it is evident that users on this subreddit care about children being either vaccinated or unvaccinated.

Based on the percentage distribution of each topic from Figure 9, topic 4 (*Anti-vaccination and Vaccine Myths*) covers most of the post instances from the Title corpus (33.6%). As topic 4's keywords and posts generally surround the themes of anti-vaccinations and vaccine myths, it validates the results of our NMF model further since we are performing text analytics on a subreddit with the title r/VaccineMyths – a domain that is directly relevant.

Gensim's LDA

To further confirm the findings we obtained from NMF's results, we attempted topic modelling again using a different model, Gensim's LDA, to see if we can get topics with overlapping features from the two topic models.

Table 4. Six topics generated using Gensim's LDA model with keywords and their respective weights

Topic no.	Key word 1's weight * "key word 1" + key word 2's weight * "key word 2" + ...
0	0.037*"I" + 0.022*"kid" + 0.019*"government" + 0.016*"post" + 0.015*"link" + 0.015*"prove" + 0.014*"immunity" + 0.013*"actually" + 0.012*"cdc" + 0.012*"reddit"
1	0.023*"inject" + 0.019*"antivax" + 0.017*"court" + 0.015*"myth" + 0.012*"fda" + 0.012*"conspiracy" + 0.012*"fwd" + 0.011*"let" + 0.010*"legally" + 0.009*"country"
2	0.020*"study" + 0.018*"big" + 0.016*"disease" + 0.015*"year" + 0.015*"pharma" + 0.012*"healthy" + 0.010*"wakefield" + 0.010*"dr" + 0.009*"talk" + 0.009*"die"
3	0.035*"parent" + 0.015*"new" + 0.014*"anti" + 0.014*"guy" + 0.013*"time" + 0.012*"lot" + 0.011*"bullshit" + 0.010*"chili" + 0.009*"vax" + 0.009*"fact"
4	0.033*"measle" + 0.021*"cancer" + 0.018*"fuck" + 0.015*"problem" + 0.013*"body" + 0.012*"life" + 0.012*"family" + 0.012*"good" + 0.012*"baby" + 0.011*"tell"
5	0.081*"I" + 0.049*"child" + 0.027*"cause" + 0.025*"flu" + 0.024*"autism" + 0.012*"shot" + 0.012*"day" + 0.010*"work" + 0.010*"right" + 0.010*"spread"
6	0.037*"I" + 0.022*"polio" + 0.020*"immune" + 0.019*"autism" + 0.014*"system" + 0.013*"son" + 0.012*"trust" + 0.010*"run" + 0.010*"admit" + 0.010*"human"

Even though the choice of creating seven topics gave us the highest coherence score (Figure 11), the topics generated using Gensim's LDA model are not as intuitive as the results of NMF's. For instance, the generated keyword lists contain many unhelpful terms that do not suggest straightforward or meaningful context, including the pronouns ("I", "dr", "guy"), adverb ("actually"), adjectives ("big", "new") and a number of common nouns ("fwd", "year", "time", "lot", "day"). Furthermore, unlike NMF's results, it is rather difficult to link the keywords identified for each topic, which are detailed in Table 4.

This observation could be attributed to the fact that Gensim's LDA model is generally more useful for longer texts (Editor, 2021) such as articles, essays, and book extracts due to its usage of word distributions in the topic fitting process. Title lengths on Reddit tend to be considerably short due to its 300-character limit for post titles and could therefore be unsuitable for analytics using this model.

CONCLUSION

NLP-enabled social media analysis provides opportunities of real-time assessment of public confidence and sentiment in important topics such as vaccines, where the derived insights could help stakeholders address the concerns of vaccine hesitancy and develop more effective policies and communication strategies to optimize vaccine uptake of the general public. This proves the significance of NLP analytics approach and its beneficial adoptability by institutions and governments alongside public surveys and other conventional methods of assessing public attitude. By analyzing data specifically from social media platforms, the results could potentially help public health researchers better understand the nature of social media influence on vaccine confidence and hesitancy and develop better strategies to combat the proliferation of misinformation.

Limitations do present in our data, proposed solutions, and findings. For instance, analytics results from Reddit data tend to be less generalizable to regions outside of the Unites States as a large proportion of Redditors are located inside the US. Also, our results might not represent the overall population on Reddit as there are several more communities or subreddits on the platform that are dedicated to different aspects of the vaccines topic. Finally, for sentiment analysis, classification of sentiments could be greatly improved with the availability of labelled historical dataset for machine learning model's prediction training.

REFERENCES

Blood-brain barrier and vaccines. (n.d.). Retrieved February 6, 2022, from https://www.chop.edu/centers-programs/vaccine-education-center/vaccine-safety/blood-brain-barrier-and-vaccines

Center for Biologics Evaluation and Research. (2021, January 27). *Vaccine Adverse Events*. U.S. Food and Drug Administration. Retrieved February 6, 2022, from https://www.fda.gov/vaccines-blood-biologics/report-problem-center-biologics-evaluation-research/vaccine-adverse-events

Center for Drug Evaluation and Research. (2018, June 4). *Questions and Answers on FDA's Adverse Event Reporting System (FAERS)*. U.S. Food and Drug Administration. Retrieved February 6, 2022, from https://www.fda.gov/drugs/surveillance/questions-and-answers-fdas-adverse-event-reporting-system-faers

Deer, B. (2011, January 5). How the case against the MMR vaccine was fixed. *BMJ, 342*(1), c5347–c5347. doi: 1 doi:0.1136/bmj.c5347

Fahad, A. H. (2021, December 30). *Sentiment Analysis — Let TextBlob do all the Work! - Red Buffer*. Medium. Retrieved February 6, 2022, from https://medium.com/red-buffer/sentiment-analysis-let-textblob-do-all-the-work-9927d803d137

Gautam, V., Pal, R., Bandhey, H., Dhingra, L. S., Misra, V., Sharma, H., Jain, C., Bhagat, K., Arushi, A., Patel, L., Agarwal, M., Agrawal, S., Jalan, R., Wadhwa, A., Garg, A., Agrawal, Y., Rana, B., Kumaraguru, P., & Sethi, T. (2021, June 14). A Machine Learning Application for Raising WASH Awareness in the Times of COVID-19 Pandemic. *Research Square*. doi: 1 doi:0.21203/rs.3.rs-562183/v1

Germani, F., & Biller-Andorno, N. (2021, March 3). The anti-vaccination infodemic on social media: A behavioral analysis. *PLoS One, 16*(3), e0247642. doi:10.1371/journal.pone.0247642 PMID:33657152

Godlee, F., Smith, J., & Marcovitch, H. (2011, January 5). Wakefield's article linking MMR vaccine and autism was fraudulent. *BMJ, 342*(1), c7452–c7452. doi: 1 doi:0.1136/bmj.c7452

Hong, L., & Davison, B. D. (2010). Empirical study of topic modeling in Twitter. *Proceedings of the First Workshop on Social Media Analytics - SOMA '10*. 10.1145/1964858.1964870

Hussain, A., Tahir, A., Hussain, Z., Sheikh, Z., Gogate, M., Dashtipour, K., Ali, A., & Sheikh, A. (2021, April 5). Artificial Intelligence–Enabled Analysis of Public Attitudes on Facebook and Twitter Toward COVID-19 Vaccines in the United Kingdom and the United States: Observational Study. *Journal of Medical Internet Research, 23*(4), e26627. doi:10.2196/26627 PMID:33724919

Johnson, N. F. (2020, May 13). *The online competition between pro- and anti-vaccination views*. Nature. Retrieved February 12, 2022, from https://www.nature.com/articles/s41586-020-2281-1?error=cook ies_not_supported&code=d99e8f7c-4c3e-4163-880b-2133c5e79905

Kang, G. J., Ewing-Nelson, S. R., Mackey, L., Schlitt, J. T., Marathe, A., Abbas, K. M., & Swarup, S. (2017, June). Semantic network analysis of vaccine sentiment in online social media. *Vaccine, 35*(29), 3621–3638. doi:10.1016/j.vaccine.2017.05.052 PMID:28554500

Keikhosrokiani, P., & Asl, M. P. (Eds.). (2022). *Handbook of research on opinion mining and text analytics on literary works and social media*. IGI Global. doi:10.4018/978-1-7998-9594-7

Kherwa, P., & Bansal, P. (2018, July 13). Topic Modeling: A Comprehensive Review. *ICST Transactions on Scalable Information Systems*, 159623. doi:10.4108/eai.13-7-2018.159623

Luo, X., Zimet, G., & Shah, S. (2019, July 16). A natural language processing framework to analyse the opinions on HPV vaccination reflected in twitter over 10 years (2008 - 2017). *Human Vaccines & Immunotherapeutics, 15*(7–8), 1496–1504. doi:10.1080/21645515.2019.1627821 PMID:31194609

Measles Outbreak — California, December 2014–February 2015. (2015). Retrieved February 12, 2022, from https://www.cdc.gov/mmwr/preview/mmwrhtml/mm6406a5.htm

Melton, C. A., Olusanya, O. A., Ammar, N., & Shaban-Nejad, A. (2021b, October). Public sentiment analysis and topic modeling regarding COVID-19 vaccines on the Reddit social media platform: A call to action for strengthening vaccine confidence. *Journal of Infection and Public Health, 14*(10), 1505–1512. doi:10.1016/j.jiph.2021.08.010 PMID:34426095

Natural Language Processing: A Guide to NLP Use Cases, Approaches, and Tools. (2021, August 25). AltexSoft. Retrieved February 6, 2022, from https://www.altexsoft.com/blog/natural-language-processing/

Nogara, G., Vishnuprasad, P. S., Cardoso, F., Ayoub, O., Giordano, S., & Luceri, L. (2022, June 26). The Disinformation Dozen: An Exploratory Analysis of Covid-19 Disinformation Proliferation on Twitter. *14th ACM Web Science Conference 2022*. 10.1145/3501247.3531573

Patel, M., Lee, A. D., Clemmons, N. S., Redd, S. B., Poser, S., Blog, D., Zucker, J. R., Leung, J., Link-Gelles, R., Pham, H., Arciuolo, R. J., Rausch-Phung, E., Bankamp, B., Rota, P. A., Weinbaum, C. M., & Gastañaduy, P. A. (2019, October 11). National Update on Measles Cases and Outbreaks— United States, January 1–October 1, 2019. *MMWR. Morbidity and Mortality Weekly Report, 68*(40), 893–896. doi:10.15585/mmwr.mm6840e2 PMID:31600181

Piedrahita-Valdés, H., Piedrahita-Castillo, D., Bermejo-Higuera, J., Guillem-Saiz, P., Bermejo-Higuera, J. R., Guillem-Saiz, J., Sicilia-Montalvo, J. A., & Machío-Regidor, F. (2021, January 7). Vaccine Hesitancy on Social Media: Sentiment Analysis from June 2011 to April 2019. *Vaccines, 9*(1), 28. doi:10.3390/vaccines9010028 PMID:33430428

re — Regular expression operations — Python 3.10.8 documentation. (2022). Retrieved February 20, 2022, from https://docs.python.org/3/library/re.html

Röder, M., Both, A., & Hinneburg, A. (2015, February 2). Exploring the Space of Topic Coherence Measures. *Proceedings of the Eighth ACM International Conference on Web Search and Data Mining.* 10.1145/2684822.2685324

Sabra, A., Bellanti, J. A., & Colón, A. R. (1998, July). Ileal-lymphoid-nodular hyperplasia, non-specific colitis, and pervasive developmental disorder in children. *Lancet, 352*(9123), 234–235. doi:10.1016/S0140-6736(05)77837-5 PMID:9683237

Scott, W. (2021, December 7). *TF-IDF from scratch in python on a real-world dataset.* Medium. Retrieved February 20, 2022, from https://towardsdatascience.com/tf-idf-for-document-ranking-from-scratch-in-python-on-real-world-dataset-796d339a4089

sklearn.decomposition.NMF. (2022). Scikit-learn. Retrieved February 22, 2022, from https://scikit-learn.org/stable/modules/generated/sklearn.decomposition.NMF.html

sklearn.feature_extraction.text.CountVectorizer. (2022). Scikit-learn. Retrieved February 22, 2022, from https://scikit-learn.org/stable/modules/generated/sklearn.feature_extraction.text.CountVectorizer.html

Tasnim, S., Sanjwal, R. K., Trisha, N. F., Rahman, M., Mahmud, S. M. F., Arman, A., Chakraborty, S., & Hossain, M. M. (2020, December 11). COVID-19 vaccination hesitancy, misinformation and conspiracy theories on social media: A content analysis of Twitter data. *SocArXiv.* Advance online publication. doi:10.31235/osf.io/vc9jb

Ten threats to global health in 2019. (2019). Retrieved February 22, 2022, from https://www.who.int/news-room/spotlight/ten-threats-to-global-health-in-2019

Trained Models & Pipelines spaCy Models Documentation. (2022). Trained Models & Pipelines. Retrieved February 3, 2022, from https://spacy.io/models/

Tutorial: Quickstart — TextBlob 0.16.0 documentation. (2022). Retrieved February 3, 2022, from https://textblob.readthedocs.io/en/dev/quickstart.html

Understanding the Infodemic and Misinformation in the fight against COVID-19. (2020). PAHO/WHO | Pan American Health Organization. Retrieved February 12, 2022, from https://www.paho.org/en/documents/understanding-infodemic-and-misinformation-fight-against-covid-19

World Health Organization. (2021, April 7). *Measles outbreaks strategic response plan: 2021–2023: measles outbreak prevention, preparedness, response and recovery.* Retrieved February 16, 2022, from https://apps.who.int/iris/handle/10665/340657

Chapter 14
Analytics of User Behaviors on Twitter Using Machine Learning

Noman Islam
Karachi Institute of Economics and Technology, Pakistan

Muntaha Mehboob
NED University, Pakistan

Rimsha Javed
Mohammad Ali Jinnah University, Pakistan

ABSTRACT

Twitter is a leading social networking site when it comes down to topics such as politics, news, and trends around the globe. Another main reason for people to use Twitter is because they are able to share their emotions and feelings with others and form new relationships and views. With about 330 million users on Twitter (in 2020), it continues to rapidly grow, but at the same time, it is also losing users at a fast pace. In 2019, Twitter had 340 million users, but a year later, it lost 10 million of them. The goal of this chapter is to find the reasons of three questions. The first, to find the reason behind Twitter losing its users. The second, to see how a user changes behavior after usage of Twitter, and third, how a user's behavior changes when expanding his/her social circle on Twitter. For all of these questions, this chapter has designed a data set and executed experiments based on the authors' hypotheses. The results report the accuracies of each of these hypotheses.

INTRODUCTION

Twitter is a well-known social networking service where users can interact while using Tweets. Users can post images, videos, gifs and even plain text and interact with their followers. Twitter was first established by Jack Dorsey, Noah Glass, Evan Williams, and Biz Stone in March 2006 and later, in July, it was launched. By 2012, there were more than a 100 million users posting 340 million Tweets in a day.

DOI: 10.4018/978-1-6684-6242-3.ch014

Twitter handled about 1.6 billion search queries every day in the same year. It was named one of the top ten most visited websites and in 2013 and in 2018, twitter established more than 321 million active users.

There has been a significant volume of research on analyzing twitter trends (Keikhosrokiani & Asl, 2022). For instance, Branz & Brockmann, (2018), by acquiring data through sentiment analysis, then filtering it, analyzing it, and finally, interpreting it. They collected more than 1,000 Tweets using Twitter API j4 java tool. Their aim is to present an outlook for analyzing sentiment of Tweets towards filtering and interpreting the data. Along these lines, this perspective is affirmed by the two examination inquiries from programming (SE) field. The accompanying theories were proposed:

Theory 1: The quantity of good emotions, in Tweets, about games, was differed essentially between the male and female designers. Guys indicated more good sentiments towards sports related themes when contrasted with females.

Theory 2: The measure of estimation communicated in the Tweets differs altogether between engineers from collectivist societies and architects from independent societies, with clients from the previous communicating less slant.

Sentiment Analysis was performed on Tweets utilizing WEKA. It is utilized to choose the sorts of feelings and their force in Tweets. They applied different feelings like outrage, sicken, dread, bliss, pity, and trust. The assessment scores depend on estimation dictionaries.

The assortment of solo channels was extended to separate highlights for slant order, considering focuses, for example, emoticons, words and articulations demonstrating a specific feeling as well as feeling, and hashtags. The methodology is affirmed by applying it to two exploration questions and this affirmed the previous discoveries on social and sex disparity in opinion articulation.

Grant Williams and Mahmoud (2017) introduced an investigation that was pointed toward identifying, arranging, and deciphering the different feelings of various programming clients' Tweets. They move the thought viewing writing computer programs customers' Tweets instead of originators' Tweets. They show that emotions imparted in writing computer programs structures' with, unravel and legitimize their end-customer's reactions. The data was then normally requested using SentiStrength and two comprehensively valuable substance. The managed content are exact all around valuable presumption assessment procedures in recognizing unequivocal conveyed in programming Tweets. The work portrayed affirmation and thought examination assessment feeling in programming Tweets.

Based on other reports and research, the reasons for people leaving Twitter is because people were annoyed with the application, or they forgot about it after making an account, or also that they could get the same information that they might have wanted through other apps, etc. There are other various reasons in different papers, and we will go through them to come to our own conclusion.

The motivation for this work is to analyze users' behaviors on Twitter. The research questions that would be answered here are:

i)   What leads the users to leave Twitter? *(Problem 1)*
ii)   How a user's behavior changes while using Twitter? *(Problem 2)*
iii) How a user's behavior changes while expanding his/her social circle on Twitter? *(Problem 3)*

Rest of the sections of this chapter presents the proposed work. The next section presents the literature review. This is followed by methodology and hypothesis formulation. Then the results are presented. The paper concludes with discussion and future work.

LITERATURE REVIEW

Xia et al. (2014) mined the user's activity on Twitter. They conduct a test on the larger dataset for Twitter and do some investigation about the activity patterns of the user and user's relationship with others. They find that people are prone to use Twitter at night and less on weekends. They proposed a text-dividing function and divided the user's Tweets into four categories such as, Politics, Economy, society, and Art. Discarding all Tweets that are original, only because we cannot get any such useful or prominent flow of information. They compare users' activity time pattern with these four categories. Because of this, they are aware of the time users are active on Twitter. They use some text preprocessing techniques like calculate TF-IDF values and after that, they apply the K-means algorithm to cluster the vectors. They utilize 151,029 Tweets, 32,861 client's very own data and 791,633 connection between clients. Through this they can develop the informal community dependent on the information. Each client is spoken to as a hub in an informal community. The connection between clients is spoken to as coordinated edges in the set. At long last, they find the data stream between various classes.

Martha et al. (2013) revealed the vital properties of the client devotee organization. It incorporates dispersion of degree, availability, following connections strength, and bunching coefficient. They research the force law degree circulation following the client adherent organization. They found Twitter to be a related organization, which implies there is a route from each customer to some other customer. The strength of the associations among customers is appropriated practically uniform on the size of 0.0 to 1.0. From this they understand that the disciple after associations in Twitter are lacking and achieve very few as relatively few as 300,000 organizations in the association.

Ahmed and ElKorany (2015) proposed a structure for associate figure that utilizes the semantic of associations around customers. Various types of client credit are detached and used to assess the tie strength between them. The proposed structure contemplates both brief and circuitous relationship among clients in a tantamount easygoing affiliation. They presented a changed FriendTNS calculation for interface figure for better precision of suspicion. This assessment depicts transitive focus point closeness utilizing close by and in general highlights of the affiliation. They included affiliation factors between clients like Retweets, notice, and replies. They utilize a Twitter dataset. The outcomes demonstrated that in the majority of the cases our calculation performed better and adjacent.

Semertzidis et al. (2013) worked on the user profile bios on Twitter. They have two aims for this research, first, is to understand what users write in their profile, and the second one is to look into possible information of the user to exploit the tasks of the user for predicting the connections between the Twitter users. They study the watchwords that are normal in Twitter profiles and sort them as indicated by the job they play in the client bio. At that point study the relationship between the data in the bio of associated clients. They do some preprocessing techniques on the dataset and find most frequently used words and give them categories such as, occupation, personal information, and interests/Hobbies. They, then, analyzed the repeated keywords and categorized them according to the purpose they serve. They use matches to predict connectivity between Twitter users.

Cunha et al. (2011) focused on the formation and usage of hashtags that help users to categorize and spread information through the internet. With more than 175 million users, hashtags help to categorize and other people to understand what some post is about and what they mean. Hashtags can be used for publicity and promotion. By adding these hashtags, it helps people to create communities who are interested about the same topic. For this research, more than 1.7 billion Tweets were analyzed which were posted in a time frame between July 2006 to August 2009. To better understand the topic of research, different hashtags used for the same reason or purpose for the same topic were looked at and collected. These are known as interchangeable hashtags and they can be condensed as one tag only. 3 topics were selected namely Michael Jackson, whose death was widely reported by many social networks, Swine Flu and Music Monday. One base was built for each of the topics: MJ, SF and MM accordingly. Tweets were filtered into these bases if they contained at least one hashtag or at least a hashtag related to the base topic. Using tables and graphs data was compiled and studied and, in the end, it was revealed that a tag's length matters in whether a hashtag is successful or not. There are other factors along with it as well, but the length is one of the important ones. The objective of (Wadley et al. 2014) was to feature the behavior and mindset of smoking quitters. The narratives were deployed and the changes throughout about which user posted the stories. As of late online media have become part of the antismoking ordnance. Twitter is utilized by associations to advance projects and items for stopping. A few examinations have featured the chances of sharing anecdotes about stopping through web journals and portable applications. To consider the idea of trade in this network, the specialists utilized topical coding techniques. Initial an example outline was set up as the 732 presents made on Stop Smoking. Each measurement was then tried by arranging the example posts into few classifications. The two analysts thought about their arranging and refined the meaning of measurements and classifications until agreement could be reached, in any case the measurement was disposed of. This was rehashed until 7 stable measurements were recognized, each characterizing between 2 to 9 classifications. The tales portray encounters of stopping at all phases of the quit direction.

Taxidou and Fischer (2014) have focused on how information is spread rapidly with the help of online social media platforms. Very quickly, social networks have become a huge part of everyone's life and whether it is a private matter or public matter, every decision is influenced by the information we see online. By studying the trends and rapid spread of information, it can be quite beneficial for politicians, celebrities, news publications and many more. Every bit of information being spread online has some sort of emotion from the person spreading it, whether positive or negative and this, in turn, can lead to others developing a similar opinion to that person or sometimes, even an opposing opinion. Therefore, this topic has become a hot topic for research. The authors have focused on finding influence chains and using that to see how a person can be influenced by something said or tweeted by an "influencer" and then it is further retweeted by millions of people who share that point of view or emotion. Using tables and graphs, the influence chains were followed to see how they form, and it was enough to show how such things make possible the information diffusion. Since, this was only a start, it was minor, but it can be done large-scale as well.

Elbagir and Yang (2018) have used machine learning algorithms for sentiment analysis of Tweets of users. Feature extraction was first performed to create efficient features and later, classifiers named as BernoulliNB, MultinomialNB, LogisticRegression and SGD classifier were trained and tested. BernoulliNB, Logistic Regression and SGD classifier were successful and mostly correct whereas SVC gave the lowest predicting accuracy at half the result meaning 50% results. So, it was concluded that BernoulliNB, SGD classifier and Logistic Regression can be the base for learning techniques in sentiment analysis of Tweets.

Li and Abhari (2017) have talked about how collecting data of users can be a tough process and collecting a user's data and then collecting his/her followers and their data is gonna make it hard as the followers of one user are bound to be similar, in one way or another, to the first user. So, this paper is focused on creating stochastic Tweets to test calculations of recommender frameworks for preparing enormous informational collections. The algorithms require some information of a user to attain a recommendation. Creating the stochastic information will assist with testing the calculations by giving comparable clients. The data collected for this research was 1,000 Tweets of 10 users. The data had to be cleaned by removing any words that are not recognized by the English language. For the most part, the username and Tweet message were the only things that are of interest. The test system for the prescribed framework was made to test the bunching of genuine and counterfeit information. The recommender framework planner needs to test effectiveness of calculations against a lot of information. Taking everything into account, this paper has helped by proposing a technique for creating stochastic Tweets. It follows a Weibull circulation which creates TF-IDF and afterward stochastic words are produced to coordinate clients' Tweets.

Hadgu and Jaschke (2014) have discussed how Twitter is not just a platform for people to socialize but many people can use it as a platform of discussion or sharing some important research with each other. How someone will know if the person on this account a researcher is, or not is what has been told here. The methodology that the creators have utilized for their exploration is by first structure a seed set S of different Twitter accounts that are accepted to be trailed by different analysts. Subsequent to gathering this, an underlying set C of applicants is acquired, and this can be extended by rehashing the cycle a few times. The competitors are thought about against ground-truth information G and the other piece of the information that is left will be N, the clients that are not analysts. Next, the features are identified and extracted for the users. Using this method, a total of 170 Twitter users were found by searching up names for 98 conferences. After studying about whether computer scientists are likely to follow each other, retweet each other or mention each other, the research brought forward a lot of things and allowed us to learn many things by using machine learning.

Tsugawa et al. (2015) have discussed how one can observe someone's activity on social media and decipher whether they are depressed or not. For ground-truth data, the results of a questionnaire form are used to determine degree of depression. The data was collected by making a website and publishing about it on Twitter for users to come and answer the questionnaire form. Some features that were used to predict whether an individual has depression or not is by seeing how many times words have been repeated in their Tweet and how many times, topic of the Tweet, ratio of positivity or negativity in the Tweet, Tweets frequency and many more. This study was successfully done, and it proves that people can detect such things from a user's posts. The accuracy rate was 69% for detecting users with depression. Azzouza et al. (2017) presented a constant usage of framework and gives various conclusions' portrayals through unique realistic representations. They utilize a solo AI procedure, to break down sentiments and distinguish Tweets extremity. Thusly, they could suggest significant watchwords with respect to the primary subject.

Bild et al. (2015) have introduced an underlying portrayal of total client conduct, depicting the conveyances of lifetime commitments correspondence stages, however results vary from earlier investigation, proposing future examination to decide the genuine degree of the similitudes. Retweet diagram examination uncovered underlying contrasts from the supporter's chart that are more reliable with true interpersonal organizations. Clarifying the hidden reasons for the noticed contrasts is an open issue. They uncover that Retweets all the more intently reflect genuine connections and trust.

Abel et al. (2011) explore and present a structure for client recognizes elements (e.g., people, occasions, and items) referenced in Tweets. We break down how methodologies for building hash tag-based, element based, or point based client profiles profit by semantic advancement and investigate the fleeting elements. This outcomes in uncovering how semantic improvement upgrades the assortment and nature of the created client profiles. Further, they perceive how the distinctive client displaying methodologies.

Alp and Oguducu (2017) are tending to how to distinguish effective specialists/powerful clients in Twitter. They additionally give a novel portrayal of clients' effective advantages called center rate. Likewise, consolidate nodal highlights into network includes and present an altered variant of PageRank calculation which productively investigates effective impact of clients. Then again, test results show that spotlight pace of clients on explicit points increment their impact scores and lead to higher data dissemination. They additionally have a circulated figuring climate which empowers them to work with huge informational indexes and show results on Turkish Twitter messages.

In (Mendes et al. 2014), Social Network Sites have filled extensively lately. An approach to look for postings of clients on Twitter was utilized, made out of channels which consolidate designs which might be identified with the utilization of the framework. The outcomes have indicated proof that a few messages posted in these kinds of frameworks are about the framework being used. As a commitment, the creator introduced a few qualities of the messages of the clients of long-range interpersonal communication destinations to encourage the comprehension of its use insight. A device for tallying and gathering postings found for each search led on Twitter was so created for this work. The check of the postings was directed in three stages: the initial step to dispose of unimportant posts, the subsequent one to arrange presents alluded on the utilization of the framework and the third one to look at presents related on utilization of the framework to see how clients compose of the framework being used. In this examination, an approach to gather and characterize postings of clients on Twitter was applied, in light of channels through which join designs identified with the framework being used.

Hana, Akram and Aziz (2014) have discussed various methods that can be used to retrieve Twitter data, Twitter user rankings and network topology. They have also discussed some techniques for information diffusion like hashtag life cycle, network topology and Retweet rate. Using NLP and ML, the writers discuss different approaches for sentiment analysis. Using datasets and analyzing patterns and words among them is a common way to conduct research. In this case, if we were to take a Twitter dataset and use the Tweets of different users to calculate their emotions and sentiments, it could be done by extracting keywords and collecting hashtags. Tweets can range from short messages to images or videos to links. The next step will be to classify the users into categories: network of users within a specific event, network of users within a specific group, etc. Sentiment analysis is done using 2 common techniques: machine learning or natural language processing. Using NLP, one can classify the Tweets as positive, neutral, or negative and sometimes, even mixed. Using ML, by adding various features, it is possible to classify the Tweets and this can also be done to predict, to some extent, who is the winner for presidential elections as one can tell how many users are satisfied with someone and how many are not.

Giovanni Borruto (2015) mines the data through the Tweets posted in the time frames year. Through this investigation they reach some significant determinations about the conduct of Twitter clients. Their examination was done on the Tweets posted between April 2013 and March 2014. These Tweets have been inspected and pre-handled to dispose of uproarious information. At that point, they applied a few examination procedures to acquire some significant outcomes. Information is extricated by means of the Twitter Streaming API v1.1 in the Spritzer rendition, which is openly accessible. Each Tweet is spoken to in JSON design, and contains a ton of data, for example, timestamp of the age, identifier, the Tweet content, IP address, client ID, area organizes, etc. In this paper their investigations are not just of measurable sort, as they concern parts of client's conduct. They zeroed in on Tweet typology, area and language of clients, recurrence of Tweeting, and discovered significant relations between client movement and its season of Twitter enlistment.

Sona and Ezgi (2014) have examined that as indicated by the Global Digital Statistics report, the total populace is around 7.1 billion and among them around 2.5 billion individuals are web clients. From these, there are 1.9 billion clients that are dynamic online media clients. Twitter has around 232 million clients who speak with one another and share their substance as pictures, recordings, music, and so forth. The focal point of this examination is to figure out what elements influence the clients and makes them use Twitter habitually. The exploration model that has been utilized for this investigation is TAM. It is a model that was proposed by Davis in 1989 and the fundamental components of this model are seen convenience and seen helpfulness. Later in 2000, Davis and Venkatesh built up the TAM2 model and added social impact and intellectual cycles. Social impact measures included emotional standard, intentionality, and picture though intellectual cycles. Also, in 2008, TAM3 was proposed by Venkatesh and Bala, which included outside factors to test apparent usability. Some new things that were available in the TAM3 were PC self-viability, impression of outer control, PC uneasiness, PC fun loving nature, seen delight, and target convenience. Another model that has likewise been utilized. It was proposed in 2003. It has eight measurements: execution hope, exertion anticipation, social impact, encouraging conditions, willfulness of utilization, experience, age, and sex.

Social media isn't just used for expressing emotion but also as a platform for sharing opinions on different thoughts (Maruf et al. 2015). They use Twitter and Disqus to review the behavior of an individual through their opinions on different topics. According to the paper, about 42% of people use more than one platform for communication. They analyze 105 people's profiles on Twitter and Disqus. They extracted comments from Disqus and Twitter profiles. It produces the statistics on 70 features of the Tweets in 5 categories. Then they use correlation coefficient on the result. Here they analyze the user's usage in different ways, extracting information on user's behaviors, interested topics on Twitter and disqus. They used Golbeck et.al's correlation coefficient to guess Big5 traits from the LIWC scores, they compare the 105 people's use of these platforms and extract some correlations and contrasts related to the LIWC five personality traits of a user. Through this platform analysis they can predict the user's personality. In this way, one can understand the user more clearly as they will have an idea of their likes, dislikes and thought process.

The investigation of (Pentina et al. 2014) analyzed the thought processes and their consequences. Nations were chosen as a result of contrasts in financial and innovative turn of events, contrasts in the Internet and web-based media entrance, just as likely contrasts in predominant correspondence styles dictated by their social settings. Bragging advanced schooling and education and delegated a developing business sector. Other fascinating discoveries of this examination remember differential wellsprings of individuals' ubiquity for Twitter, estimated by the quantity of devotees. Individuals to share proficient data, tackle issues, and decide (just as more seasoned clients) get a bigger after. While it appears to be that significant substance creation and sharing drive prominence in the two nations, various sorts of substance appear to be significant. The quantity of brands one follows on Twitter likewise is by all accounts driven by various Twitter inspirations in various nations.

Tago and Jin (2018) have focused on user relationships on Twitter and how their Tweets can tell what kind of feelings and sentiments they have. Unlike Facebook, users can follow other users out of interest for their posts or out of friendship or any other reason. They will not need to seek the user's permission for doing this. Many users Tweet about various things and every Tweet has some emotion associated with it. Just like in real life, if someone says something, there is always an emotion behind it, either negative or positive or even neutral. Tweets work in the same way. Users post things and there is an emotion associated with it and usually if a user has only negative emotions and negative Tweets, it will make other users uncomfortable whereas if a user has positive Tweets and emotions, users will likely follow that person. In another study, Kiichi and Qun learned that optimistic users have more social relationships than pessimistic users despite being less active than them. The approach that the authors went by was to divide users into 2 groups: P group meaning positive users and N group meaning negative users. Then, a test is applied on both these groups to see the influence of their emotional behaviors and how it affects their relationships. The data that was collected was collected from Japanese users by a keyword "Ha" as this word is used for any topic, gender, or generation. So, it made things easier to collect many Tweets, whether positive or negative. A total of 574 users were selected who's totaled up to be about 62,729 within a time of one month only.

Khan et al. (2016) investigated about the behavior of Pakistani users and their reactions on Twitter with respect to different aspects. Most frequent users, hash tags, and other Twitter related information have been explored. The researchers perform profile analysis and statistical analysis which can be applied in the fields of marketing, resolving social issues like detection of movement in a society. The researchers used the crawling method in the preparation of the data set from Twitter which is designed based on reasons such as to extract only Tweets content, or date and time. The verified Twitter user accounts are used to gather information regarding their provinces and regions to perform demographic analysis. The statistical analysis is performed to explore significant Twitter features. Similarly found out the top ten influential users and active users. The behavior of Pakistani users is compared with the rest of the world. This analysis can help to understand the people and society. Many techniques have been applied to observe the geological location of users. A novel technique was introduced using map API with respect to position in the user's profile.

Burns and Walker (2018) investigated how Twitter clients drew in individuals utilize web-based media to talk about issues, occasions, or, for this situation, an amusement item. Since this investigation zeroed in on a Netflix program that delivered each of the 13 scenes on the day it debuted, it varied from past examinations that investigated discussion about transmission TV arrangement. Themes examined by clients in unique investigation. This investigation additionally investigated how clients draw in on Twitter about a show managing adolescent self-destruction, a difficult issue for the present youth. Furthermore, in view of the irregular testing constraints on Sysomos, another stage may be utilized to play out the arbitrary determination. Notwithstanding with discussion with each other through answers and Retweets while viewing or in light of a TV program.

Ramakrishnan and Shankar (2015) do the comparative study of each of the existing methods and statistical approaches. Methodologies of the existing systems are categorized as lexicon-based approaches. They collect dataset using OAuth tool for taking the Tweets of Twitter and obtain a dataset. Then Process the data using the classifier techniques and generate the result as Tweets were positive or negative. Firstly, they train the data which have the same meaning and apply the Bag of Words BOW model on it which categorizes the Tweets as positive and negative. Then apply some ML machine learning categories to predict the accuracy and polarity of the Tweets. They use NLP to read the data and compare it with a dictionary of words. The NLP algorithm has put them into a lot of emphasis on finding verbs and subjective. They proposed a system which crawls the Twitter data and obtains the Tweets based on topic and language and then determines the user behavior. Then they conclude by the polarity of the Tweets generated. The solution proposed by them solves the problem of ambiguity and it gives more accurate results. The existing systems do not train their systems based on the factors like user behavior, region, language, popularity, trends, Retweets depicted by RT, formation of opinion based on Tweets in authorized portals. So, these methods are useful in concluding the result which shows the positive, negative, and neutral Tweets generated for a specific topic that is searched for.

In (Sharma et al. 2012), authors plan and assess a novel who-will be who administration for surmising credits that portray singular Twitter clients. They show that their strategy can precisely and completely induce characteristics of millions of Twitter clients, including a dominant part of Twitter's persuasive clients. Their work gives an establishment to building better hunt and proposal administrations on Twitter. They utilized the proposed theme deduction system to build a who-will be who administration for Twitter and indicated that this administration can consequently surmise an exact and thorough arrangement of characteristics for over 1,000,000 Twitter clients, including a large portion of the well-known clients.

In (Mahmud et al. 2016), there are computational models to foresee Twitter clients' demeanor towards a particular brand through their own and social attributes. The creators likewise anticipate their probability of making various moves dependent on their perspectives. To operationalize their examination on clients' mentality and activities, they gathered ground-truth information through studies of Twitter clients. They have led tests utilizing two genuine world datasets to approve the adequacy of mentality and activity expectation structure. Besides, they have incorporated their expectation models to a representation interface to show utilization in client intercession. They performed broad trials utilizing two genuine world datasets to approve the adequacy of our models. For mentality qualities, they noticed blended outcomes. They created factual models to arrange every disposition qualities and activity expectation. Such models utilized a bunch of highlights separated from clients' chronicled Tweets.

In (Hannon et al. 2010), as of late the universe of the web has become more social and all the more ongoing. Facebook and Twitter are maybe the instances of another age of social, continuous web administrations and we accept these kinds of administration give a ripe ground to recommender frameworks research. In this paper the creator centers on one of the critical highlights of the social web, in particular the production of connections between clients. The pursuit and proposal usefulness gave by the Twittomender framework depends on the accessibility of client profiles that mirror the reasonable interests of clients, in any event regarding their Twitter narratives. In this work we will take a gander at some various wellsprings of Tweet data accessible for profiling. For each situation, we have discovered our substance based and communitarian separating profiling ways to deal with be equipped for conveying suggestion records that incorporate a sensibly high level of important clients showing up towards the first spot on these lists. In this paper the creator recommends that Twitter clients can be helpfully displayed by the Tweets and connections of their Twitter social diagrams. They have shown how these profiles can be utilized as the reason for an adherent proposal called Twittomender.

In (Yamamoto et al. 2016), Twitter occasions and patterns in clients' genuine lives in light of the fact that a considerable lot of them present Tweets related on their encounters. Numerous investigations have prevailing with regards to recognizing occasions, for example, quakes and flu pandemics, alongside genuine data from numerous Tweets, by expecting clients as social sensors. Gather numerous Tweets dependent on explicit clients for effective Twitter considers, the creator should know the attributes of clients who are dynamic throughout extensive stretches of time. In this paper, it can unmistakably be seen the qualities of development clients throughout quite a while to deliberately gather numerous particular clients' Tweets. In this paper, the creator dissected expected client status and development dependent on element esteems saw in every client conduct. From the outcomes, unmistakably the adequacy of highlight esteems per dynamic hour to distinguish planned Twitter client development for deliberately gathering numerous Tweets.

Thinking of a person differs according to the time and situation. In this paper, Aditya, and Vasudeva (2012) work on the structured overview of the behavioral analysis in social networks. They compare a user's behavior analysis method with recognition and prediction of the prediction under the two perspectives one is persistent and other one is non persistent. They also discuss various types of datasets that can be used by researchers in social network user behavior analysis. Initially they do the preprocessing about 36344 users of Twitter who Tweet in the month of June and July 2009. More than 150 users out of this Tweet in both months. Tweets are separated into different languages and domains. They do different assumptions for cleansing the data and label the moods using different approaches. They do feature conversion for regression for giving numerical scores ranging from negative to positive. They remove the noise in the Tweets by using different techniques. Language analyzer achieved 90.2% and Domain identifier achieved 93.9%. They define 100 Tweets of users randomly selected to calculate recall (Measure the total number of Tweets posted), precision (measures correct mood labels) and F1-score. Prediction accuracy is low because of the data skewness. They apply different regression algorithms and compare them for prediction. They use Linear, Least Mean Squares (LMS) and Support Vector Machine. There are three categories for defining the moods that are positive, negative, and neutral.

Sinha and Das (2016) work on the structured overview of the behavioral analysis in social networks. They compare a user's behavior analysis method with recognition and prediction of the prediction under the two perspectives one is persistent and other one is non persistent. They also discuss various types of datasets that can be used by researchers in social network user behavior analysis. In Section I of the paper describes the user behavior analysis, characterization, systems, research issues, and recognition prediction methods. In Section II they discuss the basics of user behavior analysis on social networks, Section III describes the characterization of behavior and its different aspects. Section IV and V compares different methods and systems for behavior recognition and prediction and both the methods and systems for analysis presented in the VI section. Section VII tells different datasets for evaluation of the performance of user behavior on social networks. Krishna Das et. al. used some data sets like profile data, posted data to study the social network users' group dynamic in community detection problems. They apply different algorithms and approaches to predict the behavior. The study tells us different activities in the social network platforms, like connections and interactions, traffic activities, positional arrangements of the users in network.

Horng (2101) investigates the information of three interpersonal organization destinations in Taiwan. Three SNS devices are Blogs, Mashups, and Wikis. The three models show the fittingness of using. Google Analytics on examining clients' practices on SNS. They have three destinations which are to distinguish and examine the significant measures and connection among them, locate the basic components in the three organizations, and dependent on factual outcomes give administrative ramifications. Because of some secret explanation, the organization's name was spoken to as A, B and C. It gathered information from the year 2006 to 2009. 15 significant factors are distinguished from these destinations which are accessible on Google Analytics and their information are gathered. In the wake of doing some element designing, applying connections and relapses on the information, it gives the reasonings to a few client's personal conduct standard recognizable pieces of proof. Further separated into the eight cases by various individuals' status and plans of action. They investigated information by measurable methods and proposed the outcomes. Each of the three organizations have distinctive client bases. In this examination, organizations which are wanting to change the plan of action, this contextual analysis causes them a ton. Albeit not plainly uncovered in the information investigation results, the relapse models and relationships appear to furnish a specific level of association with the procedures of organizations.

Khanna et al. (2018) distinguish the client mentality for opinion Analysis. They proposed a SoftMax base demeanor location calculation which recognizes the client's inclination productively. This calculation is assessed on the Twitter Tweets. They proposed the procedure for improving the assumption precision and forecast of the Tweets by client nature recognition. Contingent upon the client demeanor it very well may be characterized into various classes. Here they ordered into three classes which are hopeful, negative, and impartial. Hopeful when individuals keep an eye on is called critical. They can decide the client demeanor by dissecting the Tweets posted by the client and apply a SoftMax relapse calculation to distinguish it. This calculation is assessed on the corpus of Twitter information. The SAD technique will go about as a preprocessing phase of the nostalgic investigation strategies. The demeanor of the client is arranged utilizing SoftMax Regression dependent on the historical backdrop of client Tweets. In this calculation the main stage is distinguishing proof stage, in this client id of the client is taken and saved as a client list then from this rundown, examined the Tweets of the client whether the client has tweeted more than the fifty Tweets. On the off chance that it is in excess of fifty Tweets, they are just considered for disposition recognition. They do some content pre-preparing procedures on Tweets and concentrate the extremity of the Tweets utilizing dictionary dependent on supposition investigation. Contrast each word and the pack of extremity of the Tweets. The Tweets posted by almost 250 clients are brought from Twitter. In all out 250 clients, the base number of Tweets made by the client is 50 and most extreme number of Tweets is roughly 500. At the point when they register the mean supreme scores for various clients, the higher mistake is represented by 25 clients though the normal blunder rate is 0.16087. From this rate, it will in general be exhibited that the assumption for the customer mindset using SoftMax backslide based computations will give extraordinary exactness. At the point when we discover the client, from the Tweet posted.

Rao et al. (2010) have told us that there is a total of about 10 million global users of Twitter as compared to Facebook which has only 6 million users. Most users of Twitter don't like to disclose their personal info that can be useful to decipher their likes, dislikes, interests, opinions, etc. So, instead of using that data, we move towards their Tweets and posts which will give us an idea of what we want to know. Some basic things that some users hide are their gender, age, regional origin, political orientation, dietary preferences, and student status. The first thing that the paper discusses is how to figure out gender of a person on Twitter. Most times you can know through their usernames if they have kept their real names as their usernames. But in most cases, people keep randomized usernames, and it makes it harder to guess their gender. In this case, their Tweets are analyzed and checked for their style of writing and the content they post. As for age, calculating the exact age is quite difficult so instead, users are divided into 2 categories: below 30 and above 30. One more thing that makes it hard to calculate as it keeps changing. Next, a users' regional origin can be told by paying attention to the dialects of the users' Tweets. Finding out the political orientation of the users through their Tweets and hashtags proved fruitful as users may use many hashtags like #ISuportArizona and so on. Afterwards, the dataset was to evaluate the different models and to see if they can correctly predict.

Tsai et al. (2012) have focused on being able to detect social leaders or influencers by their actions and following. They have used a variant of the Apriori algorithm called APPM. Social networks have allowed many people to connect with each other and share information in the form of texts, pictures, videos, games, etc. Due to this, there have been many social communities or social groups that everyone is a part of. And in these communities, social leaders are those whose posts influence others the most. We can detect these leaders by following and observing influence chains and that is what the authors have accomplished in this paper. The approach they have used can be divided into 2 parts: First, there

Table 1. Gap analysis of literature

Paper Title	Topic	Publication	Rank	Year	Page Length	Dataset Filtering	Foreign Language	Language Tool	Evaluation	Dataset	Language Independent	Supervised	Unsupervised	Semi Supervised	Keyword Structure	Emotions/ Reactions/ Behaviour/Mood Detection	Features	Domain
Predicting Attitude and Actions of Twitter Users	Computational Models of two real world data set and analysing the framework of visual analytics system	Conference	A	2016	5	-	-	✓	H	M	-	✓	-	-	-	✓	C, Sen, U	S(Brand)
Do users write about the system in use? An investigation from messages in Natural Language on Twitter	Methodology to search posting of twitter users and evaluation of user's characteristics	Workshop	C	2014	6	RT,S,H,?	F,S,G,P	✓	H	M	-	✓	-	-	Noun, Adjectives, Adverbs	✓	Sen	-
#13ReasonsWhy Twitter Users are Tweeting about a Netflix Show about Teen Suicide	Twitter interactivity about the show, and the communities formed were examined in this study.	Conference	A	2018	5	#,@,RT	-	✓	H	L	-	✓	-	-	-	✓	Sym	S(13reasonswhy)
Recommending Twitter Users to Follow Using Content and Collaborative Filtering Approaches	Modeling of twitter users and evaluating a range of different profiling and recommendation strategies	Conference	B	2010	8	-	-	✓	A	M	-	✓	-	-	-	-	-	-
Who are Growth Users?: Analyzing and Predicting Intended Twitter User Growth	Analyzing intended user status and growth based on feature values observed in each user behavior	Conference	C	2016	8	-	J	✓	H	L	-	-	✓	-	-	✓	R,Rob	S(Growth Type)
An Analysis of Behaviours Data of Twitter users of Pakistan	Analysis/Data Visualization of Tweets in Pakistan	Journal	-	2018	11	RT	-	✓	O	M	-	✓	-	-	-	✓	R	S(User's of Pakistan)
What people talk about when they talk about quitting	Community Behaviour Analysis	Workshop	Australasian	2014	4	-	-	-	H	S	✓	✓	-	-	-	✓	-	S(Smokers)
A cross-national study of Twitter users' motivations and continuance intentions	Demographic/ Exploratory Behaviour Analysis of Twitter Marketing	Journal	-	2014	21	✓	C	✓	H	M	-	✓	-	-	-	✓	-	S(Ukraine and US)
Twitter User Behavior Understanding with Mood Transition Prediction	Statistical analysis and categorizing the data	Workshop	-	2012	4	RT,!,@,?	-	✓	A	L	✓	✓	-	-	-	✓	-	-
Analyzing Factors Affecting Users' Behavior Intention to Use Social Media: Twitter Case	Analyzing structure and wquation modeling of social media users	Journal	-	2014	11	-	-	-	A	M	✓	-	✓	-	-	✓	-	-
A Literature Review on Twitter Data Analysis	Measuring the life cycles of tweets over a period of time	Journal	-	2016	9	-	-	✓	-	-	-	-	-	-	-	-	-	-
Influence Analysis of Emotional Behaviours and User Relationships Based on Twitter Data	Extracting features and documenting the behaviour comparision	Journal	B	2018	11	-	J	-	A	M	✓	-	-	✓	-	✓	Sen	-
Classifying Latent User Attributes in Twitter	Modeling and analyzing latent users of twitter	Workshop	A	2010	8	-	-	-	A	M	✓	-	-	✓	-	-	-	-

continued on following page

Table 1. Continued

Paper Title	Topic	Publication	Rank	Year	Page Length	Dataset Filtering	Foreign Language	Language Tool	Evaluation	Dataset	Language Independent	Supervised	Unsupervised	Semi Supervised	Keyword Structure	Emotions/Reactions/Behaviour/Mood Detection	Features	Domain
Discovering leaders from social network by action cascade	Using influence chains to find social leaders	Journal	A	2014	10	?, #, E, T	-	-	A	L	✓	-	-	✓	-	-	-	S(Posts)
Emotions and Information Diffusion in Social Media—Sentiment of Microblogs and Sharing Behavior	Observing the spread of information by emotionally charged tweets	Journal	A*	2013	32	-	G	✓	A	L	-	-	-	✓	-	✓	Sen	S(Tweets)
Analyzing the Dynamic Evolution of Hashtags on Twitter: A Language-Based Approach	Studying how hashtags can go viral	Workshop	-	2011	8	RT, ?, E, T	-	-	A	L	✓	-	✓	-	Hashtags Formation	-	L	S(Tweets)
Online Analysis of Information Diffusion in Twitter	To track the speed of how fast a single piece of information can spread	Conference	A	2014	6	?	-	-	A	L	✓	-	✓	-	-	✓	-	I
Sentiment Analysis of Twitter Data Using Machine Learning Techniques and Scikit-learn	Seeing how machine learning algorithms can perform sentiment analysis	Conference	C	2018	5	-	-	✓	A	L	-	-	✓	-	N-gram range	✓	L, Sen	I
Human behaviour in different social medias: A casestudy of Twitter and Disqus	A case study Of Twitter users and Analysing their behaviour	Conference	A*	2015	4	-	-	✓	A	M	-	-	✓	-	-	✓	L	S(Disqus)
A Survey on User Behaviour Analysis in Social Networks	Behaviour recognition, chatagorization and prediction	Journal	C	2016	14	-	-	✓	H	L	-	✓	-	-	-	-	-	I
Analysis of Users' Behavior on Web 2.0 Social Network Sites: An Empirical Study	Behavior recognition, detects significant connections between users' behavior.	Conference	B	2010	6	-	-	✓	A	M	-	✓	-	-	-	✓	-	S(Google Analytics)
SoftMax based User Attitude Detection Algorithm for Sentiment Analysis	Identify the user nature	Conference	B	2017	8	@, #, URLs	-	✓	O	M	-	✓	-	-	-	-	R	I
Analysis of tweets in Twitter	Mines the information from tweets and draw meaningfull conclusion about the user behavior	Workshop	-	2015	11	-	-	✓	A	L	-	✓	-	-	-	✓	-	I
Sentiment Analysis of Twitter Data: Based on UserBehavior	Compare different methodologies and approaches for Analysis the tweets	Journal	B	2015	13	-	-	✓	A	M	-	✓	-	-	Noun, Adjectives, Adverbs	-	-	S(Tweets)
Sentiment Analysis of Twitter Data:Towards Filtering, Analyzing and Interpreting Social Network Data	Filtering, Analyzing and Interpreting Social Network Data	Conference	A	2018	4	RT	-	✓	O	M	-	✓	-	-	Noun, Adjectives, Adverbs	✓	-	S(Tweets)
Generating Stochastic Data to Simulate a Twitter User	Making a method to generate data of a user similar to that of a real user	Conference	-	2017	11	-	-	✓	A	S	-	-	-	✓	-	-	-	S(Tweets)
Identifying and Analyzing Researchers on Twitter	Using machine learning to find computer scientists and researchers	Workshop	-	2014	10	-	-	✓	A	L	✓	-	✓	-	-	-	-	S(Users)

continued on following page

Table 1. Continued

Paper Title	Topic	Publication	Rank	Year	Page Length	Dataset Filtering	Foreign Language	Language Tool	Evaluation	Dataset	Language Independent	Supervised	Unsupervised	Semi Supervised	Keyword Structure	Emotions/Reactions/Behaviour/Mood Detection	Features	Domain
Recognizing Depression from Twitter Activity	Using algorithms to check if a user has depression or not	Conference	A	2015	10	-	-	-	A	L	✓	-	-	✓	-	✓	Sen	I
Twitter Sentiment Analysis Using Natural Language Toolkit and VADER Sentiment	Using VADER Analyzer tool for sentiment analysis of tweets	Conference	-	2019	5	-	-	✓	A	M	-	-	-	✓	-	✓	Sen	S(Tweets)
Analyzing the hate and counter speech accounts on Twitter	Using algorithms to classify hate tweets and their counter speech tweets	Workshop	-	2018	11	-	-	-	A	M	✓	-	-	✓	Intensity, User intent, Hate target	✓	-	S(Tweets)
A Real-time Twitter Sentiment Analysis using an unsupervised method	Visual and SemEva analysis using unsupervised techniques	Conference	-	2017	10	E,T,A	-	✓	A	M	-	-	✓	-	Noun, Adjectives, Adverbs	✓	Sem	S(Sentimental Tweets)
Analyzing User Modeling on Twitter for Personalized News Recommendations	Modeling framework and analysing dynamics of different twitter profiles	Conference	B	2011	12	-	-	✓	H	L	-	✓	-	-	-	-	Sem,L	S(Profile based modelling of twitter users)
Influential User Detection on Twitter: Analyzing Effect of Focus Rate	Targeting influential users of twitter using focus rate	Conference	-	2016	8	ST,P	T	✓	H	L	-	✓	-	-	-	-	N	I
Aggregate Characterization of User Behavior in Twitter and Analysis of the Retweet Graph	Real world analysis of retweet and tweet rates	Journal	-	2015	24	-	-	✓	H	L	-	✓	-	-	-	✓	-	I
Inferring Who-is-Who in the Twitter Social Network	Inferring methodology and attributes that categorize individual twitter user	Workshop	A*	2010	6	ST,D	-	✓	A	L	-	✓	-	-	-	-	Sem	I
Mining Users' Activity on Large Twitter Text Data	mine users' text data	Conference	-	2013	5	RT,@	-	✓	O	L	-	-	✓	-	-	-	-	S(Tweets)
How People Describe Themselves on Twitter	study of the user profile bias	Workshop	A	2013	6	-	-	✓	A	L	-	✓	-	-	Noun, Adjectives, Adverbs	✓	-	S(Profiling Bias and relationship Twitter Dataset)
Enhancing Link Prediction in Twitter using Semantic User Attributes	Link Prediction	Conference	-	2015	7	RT, @ ,replies	-	✓	O	L	-	✓	-	-	-	-	-	S(Tweets)
Analyzing, Classifying, and Interpreting Emotions in Software Users' Tweets	Classifying Emotions	Workshop	-	2017	6	T,E	-	✓	A	M	-	✓	-	-	-	✓	-	I
A Study on Twitter User-Follower Network	Properties of user-follower network	Workshop	-	2013	5	-	-	✓	O	M	-	-	✓	-	-	-	-	I

315

Figure 1. P1-followers accuracy

Followers			
Positive	**Negative**		
Inactive	**Active**		
True Positives	True Negatives		
False Positives	False Negatives		
Accuracy=(TP+TN)/(TP+TN+FP+FN)			
TN=101			
TP=2			
Total= 154			
Accuracy=	2+101/154 =	103/154	0.6688311688
Accuracy=	**66.88%**		

is a probabilistic graph propagation model is used. In second part, is using find in a chain. Along the way, there can be data that may be irrelevant to them and that is why they have used APPM to deal with them. This study concludes that this approach to find social leaders, not only accomplished its task but was able to give us insight through various influence chains and paths.

Stieglitz and Xuan (2013) have focused on how emotions and information diffusion correlate with each other. They have used datasets to see how sentimental Tweets can affect different products and brands. The reason the authors have chosen Twitter is because of the popular "retweeting option" which is vastly used to share information. What has been examined in this paper is a Tweet has retweeted and

Figure 2. Likes received accuracy

Likes Recieved			
Positive	**Negative**		
Inactive	**Active**		
True Positives	True Negatives		
False Positives	False Negatives		
Accuracy=(TP+TN)/(TP+TN+FP+FN)			
TN=110			
TP=4			
Total= 154			
Accuracy=	4+110/154 =	114/154	0.7402597403
Accuracy=	**74.02%**		

Figure 3. Retweets received accuracy

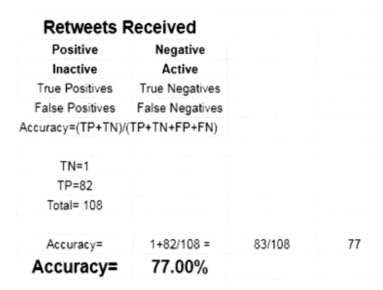

what is the gap between the time of the Tweet and the time of its first Retweet. Companies could use this same strategy and pay attention to Tweets about themselves and promote their items in such a way that would earn them more positive Tweets and Retweets. There were 2 data sets that were used in this paper. The first was for one week spanning. The second was around the state parliament. It covers a pe-

Figure 4. Non-verified accuracy

Non Verified

Positive	Negative
Inactive	Active
True Positives	True Negatives
False Positives	False Negatives
Accuracy=(TP+TN)/(TP+TN+FP+FN)	

TN=0
TP=83
Total= 108

| Accuracy= | 0+83/108 = | 83/108 | 77 |
| **Accuracy=** | **77.00%** | | |

Figure 5. Protected accuracy

Protected				
Positive	**Negative**			
Inactive	**Active**			
True Positives	True Negatives			
False Positives	False Negatives			
Accuracy=(TP+TN)/(TP+TN+FP+FN)				
TN=124				
TP=0				
Total= 154				
Accuracy=	124+0/154 =		124/154	0.805
Accuracy= 80.55%				

riod of about one month in 2011. Furthermore, a Java-based software to gather the data. All such Tweets containing either of the six important German party names, were collected. A total of 100,000 Tweets was obtained from the first data set and 150,000 was obtained from the second data set. The Tweets that seemed redundant with similar usernames or those that were advertising Tweets were excluded. Tweets in languages other than German were also excluded with the help of language detection tools. Finally, from the first data set, they got 64,431 Tweets and from the second data set, they got 104,317 Tweets.

Figure 6. Impressions accuracy

Impressions				
Positive	**Negative**			
Inactive	**Active**			
True Positives	True Negatives			
False Positives	False Negatives			
Accuracy=(TP+TN)/(TP+TN+FP+FN)				
TN=109				
TP=3				
Total= 154				
Accuracy=	109+3/154 =		112/154	0.727
Accuracy= 72.70%				

Figure 7. P1-Classification algorithm

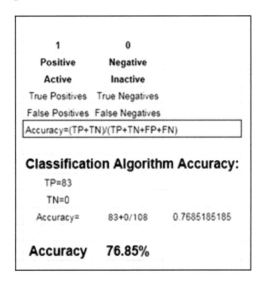

This research was concluded by stating that emotion and sentiment in a Tweet causes the Tweet to become viral quicker. Another thing that they observed was that people try to post most emotional Tweets and this causes many people to relate, to some extent, to their feelings and that is why it is likely to be Retweeted by many people and become viral.

Elbagir and Yang (2019) have used VADER, also known as Valence Aware Dictionary for sEntiment Reasoner, to detect sentiment in Tweets and classify them accordingly. The Tweets of the 2016 election were chosen for this task. Instead of using binary classification this time, a multi-classification model is used here. The methodology can be divided into 3 parts: first part being the collection of data, second being the cleaning of data phase and the third being the usage of VADER analyzer to classify the Tweets. After the first two parts of the methodology being carried out, in the last part, VADER sentiment analyzer was applied to the dataset. It is a rule-based sentiment analyzer tool and a lexicon used for expressing sentiments. The Tweets will be classified as positive, negative, neutral, or compound. The compound value is useful for measuring sentiment in each Tweet. Furthermore, there were five classes decided for the polarity of Tweets. Using charts and tables, the Tweets were classified into the classes. To conclude, VADER analyzer was highly successful for classification of large data.

Mathew et al. (2018) have researched hate Tweets or negative Tweets and how other people counter them. They have performed several lexical, linguistic, and psycholinguistic analysis on the accounts and on the strategy of counter-speech by other users on their negative speech. After the collection of data has been done, hate Tweets were filtered such that those Tweets that had less than 2 replies were cut out. Next, the counter speech was also classified. After applying the algorithms and getting everything done with, the result was that they could see that many people adopt different ways for counter speech against hate Tweets. This research can prove helpful for removing and eliminating hate speeches from different platforms. Table 1 provides the gap analysis of the literature. The next section presents the methodology and formulation of hypothesis.

Figure 8. P2-Classification algorithm

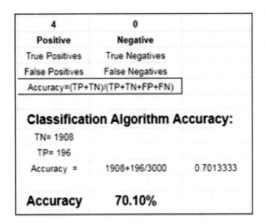

METHODOLOGY AND HYPOTHESIS FORMULATION

The first question that we need to answer is, 'What leads users to leave Twitter?' What we have to consider firstly is that we, as humans, can tell whether a Tweet is negative, positive, or neutral, but a computer has no way to tell whether a Tweet is negative, positive, or neutral. Since our dataset is comparatively small so we will perform sentiment analysis on the Tweets manually. We do not need to make an algorithm or a method for computer to perform sentiment analysis. We can do it by making a list of words/bag of words of negative words in the English language, and then compare Tweets against those words, and categorize them accordingly.

Now, after being done with the categorizing, we move on to the next step which is to collect all the Tweets of certain users and to see how many of them are negative and how many are positive. If a certain user has already left Twitter and majority of his/her Tweets are positive with some of them being negative, then it does not do much to help our case. But before we can do this, we need to confirm if the user has left Twitter or not. How we can do that is by checking if a certain user has not tweeted anything or liked or even Retweeted something within a span of 6 months then it is a sufficient reason to believe that the user is inactive.

Figure 9. Friends accuracy

Friends:
TP= 549
TN=43
Accuracy= 549+43/ 917
592/917 = 0.6455
Accuracy=64.55%

Figure 10. P3-Followers accuracy

Followers:

TP= 687

TN=9

Accuracy= 687+9/ 917

696/917 =0.7589

Accuracy=75.89%

Furthermore, while designing the algorithm consistency is the key that needs to be considered. Accuracy needs to be compared with different other techniques while implementing the algorithm in a systematic way. The major goal while designing this algorithm would be accuracy which has to hit at least 60%. The factors that will improve the performance of the algorithm will be included further. The base of algorithm design would be the performance of supervised, unsupervised, and semi supervised data from the gap table. There will be a need to extract the best of all the columns that are involved in the gap table and analyze them thoroughly before designing the algorithm.

We extracted the following features and worked on them and calculated their accuracies: Followers, Following, Likes received, Impressions, Verified or Non- Verified, Protected or un-protected, Account creation date and time, Posted date, Posted time and Retweets received. For the dates and times, we converted them into numbers and then calculated average of each column separately and compared it with individual values of that column to determine true positive and true negative values. After determining these values, we used a formula to calculate accuracy of every feature and discarded those that had accuracies below 60%.

<u>Hypothesis #1 (Followers)</u>

Followers are the users who are able to see and engage with your Tweets. The hypothesis that we have taken here is that if the value is less than the average of followers, then user is active and if it is greater than average, user is inactive. Figure 1 shows the results.

Figure 11. P3-Classification algorithm

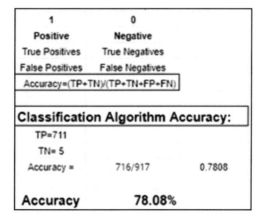

Figure 12. Problem 1-dataset

Tweet Id	Tweet URL	Tweet Pos	Tweet Con	Tweet Typ	Client	Retweets F	Likes Rece	Tweet Loc:	Tweet Lan	User Id	Name	Username	User Bio	Verified o	Profile
"1167429	https://tw	30-08-19	Pets	Tweet	Twitter Ad	0	4	Brussels	English	"1017044	Animalhe:	animalhe:	Animalhe:	Non-Verifi	https://)
"1167375	https://tw	30-08-19	Another s;	Tweet	Twitter Wr	0	5	Pill, Bristc	English	"1909812	Penny Bro	PennyBrol	We help p	Non-Verifi	https://)
"1167237	https://tw	30-08-19	What a gr	ReTweet	Twitter for	0	0	Ohio, USA	English	"7162853	Lord Byro:	lordbyron	It's	Non-Verifi	https://)
"1167236	https://tw	30-08-19	What a gr	ReTweet	Twitter for	0	0		English	"8246837	Lisa Count	CountessE	I am	Non-Verifi	https://)
"1167228	https://tw	30-08-19	What a gr	ReTweet	TweetDeck	0	0	Cincinnat	English	"1610220	Local 12/\	Local12	Local 12 i:	Verified	https://)
"1167228	https://tw	30-08-19	What a gr	Tweet	Twitter for	3	17	WKRC TV	English	"1272139	Liz Bonis	lbonis1	Health an	Verified	https://)
"1167163	https://tw	29-08-19	Will you t	ReTweet	Twitter for	0	0	Scottsdale	English	"4065492	paul knap	luapppanl	16.2 (and	Non-Verifi	https://)
"1167109	https://tw	29-08-19	Will you t	ReTweet	Twitter for	0	0		English	"7135756	Alin	AG_EM33	DO &	Non-Verifi	https://)
"1167071	https://tw	29-08-19	Will you t	ReTweet	Twitter for	0	0	Columbus	English	"2214581	Andy Little	andyglittl	EM DOC @	Non-Verifi	https://)
"1167069	https://tw	29-08-19	Will you t	ReTweet	Twitter for	0	0		English	"4416645	Tanner Gr	MOX13	Emergenc	Non-Verifi	https://)
"1167062	https://tw	29-08-19	Will you t	ReTweet	Twitter for	0	0	Columbus	English	"2418217	Drew Kaln	dkalnow	EM Physic	Non-Verifi	https://)
"1167061	https://tw	29-08-19	Will you t	Twitter Wr		6	19	DK Diner,	English	"7075829	EMOverEa	EMOverEa	Tackling r	Non-Verifi	https://)
"1166892	https://tw	29-08-19	Ya€™all â	Tweet	Twitter for	0	27	Minneapo	English	"3171175	Andrea W	AndreaWc	She/her/h	Non-Verifi	https://)
"1166860	https://tw	28-08-19	@Medtror	ReTweet	Twitter Wr	0	0	Life zig za|	English	"2804510	â,›Î¼Ê'â,"ì	RealZiggyl	Cure Duch	Non-Verifi	https://)
"1166742	https://tw	28-08-19	@Medtror	Reply	Twitter Wr	1	1	San Franc	English	"3285827	Laura Holi	HolmesHa	Writer, mc	Non-Verifi	https://)
"1166686	https://tw	28-08-19	Zoonosen	ReTweet	Twitter for	0	0	sÄ¼dlich c	German	"6609286	Papa Pinh	Pinhead6	74er Jahr;	Non-Verifi	https://)
"1166678	https://tw	28-08-19	Zoonosen	ReTweet	Twitter Wr	0	0	Breuberg,	German	"3020265	Thomas W	VetDocVid	Nutztierha	Non-Verifi	https://)
"1166660	https://tw	28-08-19	Zoonosen	Tweet	Twitter Wr	2	7	Bonn, Deu	German	"1093427	BfTiergesi	BfTGermai	Der	Non-Verifi	https://)
"1166580	https://tw	28-08-19	!Czy	Tweet	Twitter for	0	1	Warszawa	Polish	"8324898	POLPROW	POLPROW	Oficjalny	Non-Verifi	https://)
"1166434	https://tw	27-08-19	Thank	ReTweet	Twitter for	0	0	Connectic	English	"2952636	ricki	ricki_iffer	â€œl am t	Non-Verifi	https://)
"1166409	https://tw	27-08-19	Thank	ReTweet	Twitter Wr	0	0	Manhatta	English	"3149379	The Muse:	museumol	The Muse:	Non-Verifi	https://)
"1166395	https://tw	27-08-19	Thank	Tweet	Twitter Wr	2	3		English	"5811766	Catherine	CHBlades	Senior Vic	Non-Verifi	https://)
"1166381	https://tw	27-08-19	For nearly	ReTweet	Twitter Wr	0	0	Bristol	English	"2446798	Alison Bei	AlisonBev	Director €	Non-Verifi	https://)
"1166239	https://tw	27-08-19	For our	Tweet	Twitter Wr	0	1	Brussels,	English	"1344630	Roxane FE	roxanefell	A true beli	Non-Verifi	https://)
"1166237	https://tw	27-08-19	A study	ReTweet	Twitter Wr	0	0	Brussels,	English	"1344630	Roxane FE	roxanefell	A true beli	Non-Verifi	https://)

Hypothesis #2 (Likes Received)

The likes received are the number of people that have liked your Tweet(s). The hypothesis that we have taken here is that if the value is less than the average of likes received, then user is active and if it is greater than average, user is inactive. Figure 2 shows the result.

Hypothesis #3 (Retweets Received)

Figure 13. Data head

	Tweet Id	Tweet URL	Tweet Posted Time (UTC)	Tweet Content	Tweet Type	Client	Retweets Received	Likes Received	Tweet Location	Tweet Language	
0	"1167429261210218497"	https://twitter.com/animalhealthEU/status/1167...	30-08-19 13:30	Pets change our lives & become a part of o...	Tweet	Twitter Ads Composer	0	4	Brussels	English	
1	"1167375334670557185"	https://twitter.com/PennyBrohnUK/status/116737...	30-08-19 9:55	Another spot of our #morethanmedicine bus in #...	Tweet	Twitter Web App	0	5	Pill, Bristol	English	
2	"1167237977615097861"	https://twitter.com/lordbyronaf/status/1167237...	30-08-19 0:49	What a great team â¦@HealthSourceOHâ© â¦@Lo...	ReTweet	Twitter for Android	0	0	Ohio, USA	English	
3	"1167236897078480898"	https://twitter.com/CountessDavis/status/11672...	30-08-19 0:45	What a great team â¦@HealthSourceOHâ© â¦@Lo...	ReTweet	Twitter for Android	0	0	NaN	English	"824
4	"1167228378191204353"	https://twitter.com/Local12/status/11672283781...	30-08-19 0:11	What a great team â¦@HealthSourceOHâ© â¦@Lo...	ReTweet	TweetDeck	0	0	Cincinnati, OH	English	

Figure 14. P1-data shape

$$(386, \ 23)$$

Retweets received are the number of people who have shared your Tweet on their timeline. The hypothesis that we have taken here is that if the value is less than the average of Retweets received, then user is active and if it is greater than average, user is inactive. Figure 3 shows the results.

Hypothesis #4 (Non-Verified)

Usually, we see a blue tick next to celebrity's accounts. This blue tick ensures that your account is verified ad an authentic person who has a huge followers base. Non- verified is just an account that is normal and the opposite of verified. The hypothesis that we have taken here is that if the value is less than the average of non-verified, then user is active and if it is greater than average, user is inactive. The results are shown in Figure 4.

Hypothesis #5 (Protected)

Protected Tweets are the Tweets made by a private account. They are called protected Tweets because only selected people can view them. The hypothesis that we have taken here is that if the value is less than the average of protected, then user is active and if it is greater than average, user is inactive. The results are shown in Figure 5.

Hypothesis #6 (Impressions)

Figure 6 shows the result of this hypothesis. Impressions is the number of times someone has seen your Tweet. It counts views, regardless of them being your follower or not. The hypothesis that we have

Figure 15. P1-Statistical values of dataset

	Retweets Received	Likes Received	User Followers	User Following	Impressions	Unnamed: 21
count	386.000000	386.000000	386.000000	386.000000	386.000000	0.0
mean	0.730570	2.839378	2516.904145	1067.401554	1137.849741	NaN
std	1.884991	9.423381	10529.124870	1409.750825	2381.107457	NaN
min	0.000000	0.000000	0.000000	4.000000	0.000000	NaN
25%	0.000000	0.000000	348.000000	379.000000	0.000000	NaN
50%	0.000000	0.000000	796.000000	542.000000	0.000000	NaN
75%	0.000000	1.000000	2922.500000	1123.000000	882.000000	NaN
max	13.000000	98.000000	198675.000000	12476.000000	12033.000000	NaN

Figure 16. Problem 2 datasetHere is the data head of our dataset and we have printed it out here to give an idea what our data looks like

04733	Sat May 30 19:07:26 PDT 2009	NO_QUERY	22	chatting away, said bye to rachie
25442	Tue Jun 16 16:37:29 PDT 2009	NO_QUERY	127	still dont know what to do with my cat when i move
30878	Mon Jun 15 08:07:30 PDT 2009	NO_QUERY	136	Feels bad I have to lock the cats in the room stupid bug spray
00729	Fri Apr 17 21:07:37 PDT 2009	NO_QUERY	338	At beach. Will get about / less than 6 hrs and 45 min of sleep. XD I still miss some people & the Despair Factior
59456	Sun May 31 00:22:21 PDT 2009	NO_QUERY	407	#asylm no coffee lounge for me with misha been queueing since 6 this mornin
54709	Wed Jun 17 15:23:46 PDT 2009	NO_QUERY	427	Blacksheep is this weekend and I'm super excited, I just wish I had money to spend to buy fibery goodness
73456	Fri May 22 03:09:26 PDT 2009	NO_QUERY	431	@ Blue Tits in our wall: stop making those incredible cute sounds, trying to work...
42097	Fri May 22 04:40:32 PDT 2009	NO_QUERY	431	Still working on finishing the K3 chocolate sprinkles. Need to finish those before allowed to eat the Piet piraat sprin
63875	Mon Apr 20 03:36:51 PDT 2009	NO_QUERY	723	No sleep and I tried my hardest to sleep
92729	Fri May 01 23:36:21 PDT 2009	NO_QUERY	723	@Shaantastic its ugly outside tmrw.. raining.. it was like this last yr, we thought it was gonna rain
13464	Sat Jun 06 19:14:14 PDT 2009	NO_QUERY	723	@standfornothing yes finals are 11th, 12th, 15th. and then i have state tests, then i go back to school like 26th.
74390	Sat Jun 06 19:21:27 PDT 2009	NO_QUERY	723	@standfornothing haha thats so early i dont really mind starting in sept, its still like 90 degree weather by sept, so
87230	Sat Jun 06 19:34:39 PDT 2009	NO_QUERY	723	@ZaccariahTwiter well can i at least get it during your presentation? im in the yrbk staff next year and i didnt even ge
05521	Sat Jun 20 17:31:38 PDT 2009	NO_QUERY	723	@checkmarks refresh? you better come here cuz the game is gonna be sloow and boring
19822	Sat Jun 20 21:14:13 PDT 2009	NO_QUERY	723	gniteee, stupid coughing
97160	Sun Apr 19 23:27:28 PDT 2009	NO_QUERY	723	@onefullyear yea twitterfox lagged my ff immensly idk why but i def prefer tweetdeck
27646	Thu Jun 18 20:35:23 PDT 2009	NO_QUERY	1071	@loquatmusic gah!! i can't make your beach show. hope you make it down this way again soon!
15136	Mon Jun 15 05:16:03 PDT 2009	NO_QUERY	1389	@brianDdew it gives you a popup msg when you get ready to close the tab and navigate away from their webpage
63214	Wed Jun 03 07:57:35 PDT 2009	NO_QUERY	1732	Unlimited interner started and I'm reaching Mumbai on 7th
73798	Fri Jun 19 10:37:45 PDT 2009	NO_QUERY	1732	No windows #jailbreak till now
38728	Thu May 14 01:31:17 PDT 2009	NO_QUERY	2089	Sup Bomarr, I just spent 2 bucks for you. I was wondering, do you think you can send me that remix you've done for w
15908	Fri Jun 05 17:11:31 PDT 2009	NO_QUERY	2147	ive lost some contacts, dont know why
51627	Sat May 02 05:17:04 PDT 2009	NO_QUERY	2525	@matheuswartjes op dat pad wel
24233	Mon Jun 15 17:39:42 PDT 2009	NO_QUERY	4320	On Myspace, worrying about him!!!
93099	Thu Jun 18 04:13:42 PDT 2009	NO_QUERY	5987	@YaggaYow My vacations are not until november.These five year olds are kicking the hell out of me. I am sooo tired
13886	Tue Jun 02 03:11:16 PDT 2009	NO_QUERY	6000	@JeremyTNell There were 227 other people as well. FTL
21613	Tue Apr 07 02:47:02 PDT 2009	NO_QUERY	6277	@Mirror_Kiss no, i don't have money, i'm very upset too

taken here is that if the value is less than the average of impressions, then user is active and if it is greater than average, user is inactive.

For the classification algorithm, we have worked on 108 users as we were getting some redundancy in the data and the values and so, we have omitted that data. Firstly, we have converted all the values in the column to binary to be able to work on them easily. That way, it was easier to calculate y which is the sum of how many features a user has satisfied. For example, if a user has all the six features marked as 1, then the value of y will be 6 for that user. Next, we have seen if y is greater than, less than or equal to 4. If y is greater than 4, then user is active, other it is inactive. Lastly, just like how we had calculated accuracy for each of the features, we have calculated accuracy of this as well. The results are shown in Figure 7.

The second question that we had to answer is, "How a user's behavior changes while using Twitter?" To do this, we will need to observe user's behavior, sentiments and activity. For our hypothesis and experimentation, we have taken the Days, Time and Sentiment columns. Separating the date and time, we have manually looked over the data and predicted the sentiment of the user based on our hypothesis.

Next, we have made frequency tables for different days of the week. In this table, we have written down the number of rows and what their sentiment is according to time for each day of the week. The reason for making the frequency tables was because the dataset was quite difficult to understand and base hypothesis on, so we collected all these details to help us form a hypothesis so we can continue.

Our hypothesis is that the users have negative Tweets and sentiments from Monday to Saturday for the whole 24 hours. And on Sunday, they have positive Tweets and sentiments because it is the weekend. For positive sentiments, we have labeled it 4 and for negative, we have labeled it 0.

We have taken 3,000 users and we have compared the predicted sentiments with the grounded sentiments and gotten values for True Negative (TN) and True Positive (TP). The formula for the classifica-

Figure 17. P2-Data headHere is the shape of the data which shows that there 1,599,999 rows and 6 columns as shown in Figure 18

	0	1467810369	Mon Apr 06 22:19:45 PDT 2009	NO_QUERY	_TheSpecialOne_	@switchfoot http://twitpic.com/2y1zl - Awww, that's a bummer. You shoulda got David of Third Day to do it
0	0	1467810672	Mon Apr 06 22:19:49 PDT 2009	NO_QUERY	scotthamilton	is upset that he can't update his Facebook
1	0	1467810917	Mon Apr 06 22:19:53 PDT 2009	NO_QUERY	mattycus	@Kenichan I dived many times for the ball. I.
2	0	1467811184	Mon Apr 06 22:19:57 PDT 2009	NO_QUERY	ElleCTF	my whole body feels itchy and like its o
3	0	1467811193	Mon Apr 06 22:19:57 PDT 2009	NO_QUERY	Karoli	@nationwideclass no, it's not behaving at
4	0	1467811372	Mon Apr 06 22:20:00 PDT 2009	NO_QUERY	joy_wolf	@Kwesidei not the whole

Figure 18. P2-Data shape

```
Total Rows in Dataset (1599999, 6)
```

tion algorithm where we substituted the values for TP and TN is (TP + TN) / (TP + TN + FP + FN). The accuracy that we got is 70.10%. We have calculated them like this that if original and predicted

Figure 19. P2-Statistical values of dataset

	target	tweet id
count	1.599999e+06	1.599999e+06
mean	2.000001e+00	1.998818e+09
std	2.000001e+00	1.935757e+08
min	0.000000e+00	1.467811e+09
25%	0.000000e+00	1.956916e+09
50%	4.000000e+00	2.002102e+09
75%	4.000000e+00	2.177059e+09
max	4.000000e+00	2.329206e+09

Figure 20. Total rows and columns of dataset

```
Total Rows in Dataset (1599999, 6)
```

Figure 21. Total count of positive and negative rows of dataset

```
4    800000
0    799999
Name: target, dtype: int64
```

Figure 22. Frequency table for Monday

Frequency Detail for Monday		
time	rows	sentiment
9 AM to 11 59 AM	28	0
12 PM to 5 59 PM	103	0
6 PM to 11 59 PM	16	4
6 PM to 11 59 PM	86	0
12 AM to 8 59 AM	96	4
12 AM to 8 59 AM	149	0
Total	478	

Figure 23. Frequency table for Tuesday

Frequency Detail for Tuesday		
time	rows	sentiment
9 AM to 11 59 AM	33	0
12 PM to 5 59 PM	65	0
6 PM to 11 59 PM	12	4
6 PM to 11 59 PM	69	0
12 AM to 8 59 AM	36	4
12 AM to 8 59 AM	138	0
Total	353	

sentiments are both 0, then it will be TN. If original and predicted sentiments are both 4, then it will be TP. Te results are shown in Figure 8.

The last question that answered was, "How a user's behavior changes while expanding his/her social circle on Twitter?". In order to form a hypothesis, we will need to observe the behavior and social statistics

Figure 24. Frequency table for Wednesday

Frequency Detail for Wednesday		
time	rows	sentiment
9 AM to 11 59 AM	14	0
12 PM to 5 59 PM	28	0
6 PM to 11 59 PM	7	4
6 PM to 11 59 PM	51	0
12 AM to 8 59 AM	2	4
12 AM to 8 59 AM	88	0
Total	190	

Figure 25. Frequency table for Thursday

Frequency Detail for Thursday

time	rows	sentiment
9 AM to 11 59 AM	3	4
9 AM to 11 59 AM	26	0
12 PM to 5 59 PM	32	0
6 PM to 11 59 PM	34	4
6 PM to 11 59 PM	56	0
12 AM to 8 59 AM	28	4
12 AM to 8 59 AM	134	0
Total	313	

Figure 26. Frequency table for Friday

Frequency Detail for Friday

time	rows	sentiment
9 AM to 11 59 AM	37	0
12 PM to 5 59 PM	96	0
6 PM to 11 59 PM	15	4
6 PM to 11 59 PM	100	0
12 AM to 8 59 AM	96	4
12 AM to 8 59 AM	103	0
Total	447	

of the user on his/her Twitter account. We have manually looked over the data and labeled the sentiment of the user based on our hypothesis. We also have to keep in mind that if an account is private, then we cannot view, comment or Retweet their Tweet unless we are in their friend list. Whereas, If the account is public, then retweeting, viewing and commenting on their Tweets is possible by anyone.

We extracted and worked on two features to form hypothesis and calculate their accuracies: Friends and Followers.

Hypothesis #1 (Friends)

Figure 27. Frequency table for Saturday

Frequency Detail for Saturday

time	rows	sentiment
9 AM to 11 59 AM	129+	4
9 AM to 11 59 AM	56	0
12 PM to 5 59 PM	19	4
12 PM to 5 59 PM	130	0
6 PM to 11 59 PM	49	4
6 PM to 11 59 PM	120	0
12 AM to 8 59 AM	52	4
12 AM to 8 59 AM	166	0
Total	601	

Figure 28. Frequency table for Sunday

Frequency Detail for Sunday		
time	rows	sentiment
9 AM to 11 59 AM	76	0
9 AM to 11 59 AM	40	4
12 PM to 5 59 PM	69	0
12 PM to 5 59 PM	5	4
6 PM to 11 59 PM	68	0
6 PM to 11 59 PM	33	4
12 AM to 8 59 AM	209	0
12 AM to 8 59 AM	118	4
Total	**618**	

Fig 9 shows the result of first hypothesis. Friends on Twitter are the people you follow using your account. They don't necessarily have to follow you back. The hypothesis that we have taken here is that if the value is above average of followers, then there is a negative effect on the user and if it is lesser than average, there is positive effect on the user.

Hypothesis #2 (Followers)

Followers are the people that follow your account. You don't necessarily have to follow them back. The hypothesis that we have taken here is that if the value is above average of followers, then there is a negative effect on the user and if it is lesser than average, there is positive effect on the user. Figure 10 shows the results.

We have taken a Y variable that represents every user. We have added all the values in the column of average for every user and written it down in Y. And as such, for every user, the value differs. Then we have made another column and there we have marked 0 if value of Y < 1 and if Y >= 1, it is 1. Next, we attached the sentiment column next to this. And then we compared the value of Y with the sentiment

Figure 29. Problem 3 datasetHere is the data head of our dataset

	user_location	user_description	user_created	user_followers	user_friends	user_favourites	user_verified	date	text	hashtags	source	
ANAWAT	Delhi,India	Live EVS Operator/Coordina	4/2/09 5:06 PM	147	127	205	FALSE	11/11/20 11:49 PM	Time to change the Bubble	['IPL2020', 'ISL2	Twitter for iPhone	
	Bhopal, India	Bhopali	11/10/16 5:09 AM	113	699	1412	FALSE	11/11/20 11:33 PM	Why is #2020Fixing	['2020Fixing']	Twitter for Androi	
don	Carrickfergus, North	Buns are good but puns an	4/3/13 3:03 PM	27	57	41	FALSE	11/11/20 11:04 PM	@ICC And still	['rajasthanroy|	Twitter for Androi	
atel	Montreal Canada	Student at Concordia	7/4/13 4:24 PM	131	1525	10343	FALSE	11/11/20 11:00 PM	I still remember the bus parade after	@m	Twitter Web App	
rds		We are a cricketing blog hi	9/2/16 7:14 PM	551	189	160	FALSE	11/11/20 10:39 PM	#IPL2020	['IPL2020']	Twitter Web App	
rds		We are a cricketing blog hi	9/2/16 7:14 PM	551	189	160	FALSE	11/11/20 10:27 PM	#IPL2020	['IPL2020', 'MI',	Twitter Web App	
r	Bhopal	Being Fake Is A New Trend.	10/3/17 6:11 AM	33	224	159	FALSE	11/11/20 10:14 PM	After #IPL2020 Please	['IPL2020', 'god	Twitter Web App	
Man	United States	I'm here to answer your	10/3/09 6:52 PM	450	1059	1527	FALSE	11/11/20 10:02 PM	Just when all 8 teams looked closely com		Twitter for Androi	
icket		For all the latest cricket up	3/2/11 6:21 PM	113208	819	269	TRUE	11/11/20 10:00 PM	if they are not at the top, they are ven		Buffer	
	#Cricket	A Big Fan of World's Mc	7/21/15 6:35 PM	467	38	3524	FALSE	11/11/20 9:49 PM	The man behind all this i.e	['IPL2020']	Twitter for iPhone	
Cricket	Sky Sports	The official Twitter feed of	5/5/11 2:38 PM	644605	486	458	TRUE	11/11/20 9:39 PM	IPL Cricket Show	['MumbaiIndi	Twitter Media Stu	
n M. Rai	Qatar	believes that the job of de	12/19/09 10:06 AM	1616	2027	25085	FALSE	11/11/20 9:19 PM	Congratulations Rohit Sha	['MumbaiIndi	Twitter for Androi	
ora	depression mein	maa believer	11/11/20 7:29 PM	0	23	0	FALSE	11/11/20 9:19 PM	#IPL2020 khatam hua he	['IPL2020', 'cor	Twitter for Androi	
nita Verma	Dubai, United Arab	Mechanical Engineer / HVA	12/18/17 11:58 AM	12	300	8554	FALSE	11/11/20 9:15 PM	#IPL2020 playing11	['IPL2020', 'MI',	Twitter for iPhone	
nan	United Kingdom	WaLK On wiTh HoPE in yOU	9/20/10 12:21 PM	25	22	521	FALSE	11/11/20 9:13 PM	@MahelaJay Noticed t	['IPL2020']	Twitter for iPhone	
	India	Follow https://t.co/RBTHZ	3/4/09 4:20 PM	12983	380	325	TRUE	11/11/20 9:10 PM	#INDvsAUS #AUSvsIND #cric	['INDvsAUS', 'A	TweetDeck	
ports & Ente	London, England	Talent Management	10/17/18 10:52 AM	161	521	652	FALSE	11/11/20 9:00 PM	Who agrees with @KP24	['ipl2020']	Twitter for iPhone	
Cricket	Sky Sports	The official Twitter feed of	5/5/11 2:38 PM	644605	486	458	TRUE	11/11/20 8:59 PM	Jos Buttler prefers opening	['RR', 'IPL2020']	Twitter for Advert	
sters		Scout Div 6A	6/2/20 10:15 AM	243	3122	101	FALSE	11/11/20 8:57 PM	IPL 2020: How five time champions Mumbi		Twitter for iPhone	
ar Betting	Global	EXCLUSIVE One on One Coa	2/20/18 5:18 AM	1114	924	12845	FALSE	11/11/20 8:57 PM	Back Win Bets		Twitter Web App	
	Seattle, WA, USA	Cricmetric is a website dev	3/30/11 3:39 AM	1121	70	459	FALSE	11/11/20 8:53 PM	The best all rounders of	['IPL2020']	Twitter for Androi	
			12/27/19 10:23 AM	146	0	10	FALSE	11/11/20 8:43 PM	Top 40 batsmen and	['IPL2020', 'Cric	Twitter Web App	
Cricket	Sky Sports	The official Twitter feed of	5/5/11 2:38 PM	644605	486	458	TRUE	11/11/20 8:41 PM	@nassercricket picked a	['IPL2020']	Twitter for Advert	
Men		All your cricket news in one	9/7/19 7:27 AM	706	570	8034	FALSE	11/11/20 8:40 PM	If you thought the Altroz wi	['IPL2020', 'The	Twitter for Androi	
	Kingston, Jamaica	CEEN TV, Caribbean Enterta	11/7/11 4:29 PM	1424	1575	1178	FALSE	11/11/20 8:40 PM	Do you think the WI		eClincher	
			12/28/19 11:45 PM	24	13	592	FALSE	11/11/20 8:38 PM	No congratulations for	['RohithSharm	Twitter for Androi	
gh	Pune, India		10/31/20 12:23 PM	2	43	41	FALSE	11/11/20 8:30 PM	Congratulations @mipaltan @ImRo45 you		Twitter for Androi	
Pundits	Stockholm	Two Scandinavian cricket	7/30/20 7:20 PM	143	254	687	FALSE	11/11/20 8:22 PM	@magnet_GIRLz @gaurav_sundar You are		Twitter for iPhone	

Figure 30. P3-Data headHere

user_name	user_location	user_description	user_created	user_followers	user_friends	user_favourites	user_verified	date	text	hashtags	source
GAURAV DHANAWAT Â'Â â¸Â©âÂ'Â â¸Â¹	Delhi, India	Live EVS Operator/Coordinator | EX Ten Sports ...	4/2/09 5:06 PM	147	127	205	False	11/11/20 11:49 PM	Time to change the Bubble from #IPL2020 to #IS...	['IPL2020', 'ISL2020']	Twitter for iPhone
:'Â â¸Â©âÂ'Â â¸Â¹Â'Â â¸Â©âÂ'Â â¸Â¹ Â ÂªÂ©Â Â..	Bhopal, India	Â'Â â¸'âÂ'Â â¸™Â‡™%BhopalâÂ'Â ÉªÂ½in Â'Â â¸'â..	11/10/16 5:09 AM	113	699	1412	False	11/11/20 11:33 PM	Why is #2020Fixing trending?? \n \n I think rc...	['2020Fixing']	Twitter for Android
Steven Gordon	Carrickfergus, Northern Irelan..	Buns are good but puns are better. best served..	4/3/13 3:03 PM	27	57	41	False	11/11/20 11:04 PM	@ICC And still #rajasthanroyals finished last ..	['rajasthanroyals', 'JofraArcher', 'RR', 'jofr...	Twitter for Android
Bhumish Patel	Montreal, Canada	Student at Concordia University, Montreal, CA\..	7/4/13 4:24 PM	131	1525	10343	False	11/11/20 11:00 PM	I still remember the bus parade after @mipalta..	NaN	Twitter Web App
cricket22yards	NaN	We are a cricketing blog highly focusing on th..	9/2/16 7:14 PM	551	189	160	False	11/11/20 10:39 PM	#IPL2020 \n \n STATS: Most runs, fastest 6th..	['IPL2020']	Twitter Web App

Figure 31. P3-Data shape

Total Rows in Dataset (3000, 13)

Figure 32. P3-Statistical values of dataset

	user_followers	user_friends	user_favourites
count	3.000000e+03	3000.000000	3000.000000
mean	1.873837e+05	598.494000	9153.431333
std	1.006589e+06	1978.106372	24022.675870
min	0.000000e+00	0.000000	0.000000
25%	3.800000e+01	73.000000	145.000000
50%	2.690000e+02	260.000000	871.000000
75%	3.572000e+03	623.250000	6313.750000
max	1.321838e+07	62638.000000	282022.000000

Figure 33. Info about columns of dataset

```
<class 'pandas.core.frame.DataFrame'>
RangeIndex: 3000 entries, 0 to 2999
Data columns (total 13 columns):
 #   Column            Non-Null Count   Dtype
---  ------            --------------   -----
 0   user_name         3000 non-null    object
 1   user_location     2174 non-null    object
 2   user_description  2725 non-null    object
 3   user_created      3000 non-null    object
 4   user_followers    3000 non-null    int64
 5   user_friends      3000 non-null    int64
 6   user_favourites   3000 non-null    int64
 7   user_verified     3000 non-null    bool
 8   date              3000 non-null    object
 9   text              3000 non-null    object
 10  hashtags          2299 non-null    object
 11  source            3000 non-null    object
 12  is_retweet        3000 non-null    bool
dtypes: bool(2), int64(3), object(8)
memory usage: 263.8+ KB
```

and if both values are 1, then it labeled as TP and if both are 0, then it is TN. This is how we calculated TP and TN and then we got the following values as shown in figure and used the formula (TP + TN) / (TP + TN + FP + FN) to calculate accuracy. It is to be noted that 1 represents positive value or positive sentiment and 0 means negative value or negative sentiment. Above average value is marked 0 and below average is marked 1. Figure 11 shows the results.

EXPERIMENTAL RESULTS AND DISCUSSION

Problem 1

Our dataset has 22 columns: Tweet ID, Tweet URL, Tweet posted time, Tweet content, Tweet type, Client, Retweets received, Likes received, Tweet location, Tweet language, User ID, Name, Username, User bio, Verified or non-verified, Profile URL, Protected or non-protected, User followers, User following, User account creation date time, Impressions and User status. We have then added one more column named Label where we have performed sentiment analysis and labeled the Tweets as positive, negative, or neutral. There is a total of 154 users and 386 rows in the dataset. The dataset is shown in Figure 12. The first few rows are shown in Figure 13.

Here is the data head of our dataset and we have printed it out here to give an idea what our data looks like in Figure 13. The shape of the data is 386 rows and 23 columns as shown in Figure 14.

Here are the statistical values of our data set shown in Figure 15.

The accuracy of our experiments for our hypothesis came out to be 76.85%. It shows us that our hypothesis about people with more likes, Retweets and impressions on Twitter are more prone to leave Twitter because they are not getting any human interaction from them. Humans, being social creatures, want to interact with someone and when that condition isn't fulfilled, they are less likely to stick around. Whereas people with less like, Retweets and impressions are more likely to stay active on Twitter because they have set some milestones and they want to achieve them.

The reason, that we deduced, from our experiments conducted was that users with more followers, likes and Retweets are likely to think that since they have already achieved certain milestones, what more can they be offered? Simply put, they lose their motivation to do better and so, they become inactive because they feel like they have already achieved something. Whereas users with less followers, likes and Retweets are motivated to do better to get more followers and likes, etc. So, they are mostly active as they want to get some achievements. This is a psychological fact of the human mind. When they are not getting the results they want, they are more motivated to achieve them but if they have been getting those results repeatedly, the value of those achievements falls in their mind or they don't remain achievements at all for them.

Another assumption for a user with a great following to be inactive is that the user feels like he/she is not getting the same amount of energy as he/she wants from his/her followers. He/She feels like his/her followers are just blankly liking his/her Tweets but not giving him/her the feedback, he/she wants. Just like when a person is holding a conversation with someone and expects the other person to respond to him/her, the user feels like he/she is the only one doing the talking but not receiving a response in return. At most, a like or a Retweet or even a comment, but only sometimes. It feels like the followers are not really understanding or connecting with him/her like he/she wanted them to and so, eventually, he/she becomes inactive. He/She feels like he/she is using up his/her time and energy but not getting the same back. Whereas a person with small following tries to have more interaction with his/her followers and the followers do the same and so, they can connect, and this makes the user feel like they are making friends and want to be on Twitter more. His/Her small platform becomes his/her personal place for talking and connecting with many different people.

Problem 2

The dataset has a total of 1,599,999 rows and 6 columns. The columns are Target, Tweet IDs, Date and Time, Flag, User and Text. Since, the dataset is very large, we only took 3,000 rows for our experiments. Figure 16 shows the dataset while Figure 17 shows first few rows of the data.

Here are the statistical values of our data set as shown in Figure 19.

Here is the number of columns and rows of our data set shown in Figure 20.

Here is the total number of positive and negative rows in our data set (Figure 21). Positive is represented by 4 and negative is represented by 0.

Here are the frequency tables for all the days of the week according to the timings and the sentiments shown in Figure 22-28. These figures show the sentiments on various days of the week and timings.

The accuracy that we achieved after our experiments is 70.10%. This accuracy tells us that our hypothesis about people having negative Tweets from Monday to Saturday due to having work, studies, and personal stuff to keep them busy and having positive Tweets on Sunday because it is their day off and they can relax and vent out their frustrations, is correct for the most part.

The reason that we deduced from our experiments is that since most people are busy during the week, they are unhappy and post negative Tweets. They are either busy with their jobs or their studies or even their basic errands. They rarely find time to relax and so, they are frustrated and tired and let out their emotions on Twitter. But on Sunday, they can relax and go do stuff like partying and meeting friends and even clubbing in some cases and therefore, they have positive Tweets on that day. Even on a Saturday, some people go to their office and others might be at home completing their work and studies and running their basic errands. Thus, on Sundays, they can unwind and relax completely however they want, whether it is by staying at home or going out to party.

Problem 3

Our dataset originally too big to be opened completely in an Excel file. We were only able to access 572,985 rows and not more than that. And even that was too much for us to work on, so we extracted the information of 1,500 users and performed cleaning of the data. After cleaning, we were left with 917 users. And after this, we have completed our experiments and hypothesis-forming based on these users. Figure 29 shows the dataset and Figure 30 shows first few rows of the dataset. P3-Data headHere (Figure 30) is the shape of the data which shows that there 3,000 rows and 13 columns that we have used and worked on as shown in Figure 31.

Here are the statistical values of our data set as shown in Figure 32.

Here is the information of all the columns of the data set (Figure 33). This includes user name, location, creation, friends, favourites, hashtags, text and other information.

The accuracy that we achieved after our experiments is 78.08%. This accuracy tells us that our hypothesis about a bigger social circle having a negative effect on people is true. That means that people with a smaller social circle are more likely to be happy, positive and content.

The reason for such a hypothesis being true is because having a lot of people in your social circle means pleasing and appealing to each and every one to keep them happy and content and this can be quite stressful to the person. On the other hand, a smaller social circle means being comfortable with your company and even when there are differences, there is not much to do to appeal to them and it is manageable.

CONCLUSION AND FUTURE WORK

Coming to the conclusion, this research paper is very much unlike other studies as we have observed. Through our literature review, we came to find out that the questions we had set out to answer were not a common topic of research. In summary, this paper has explored the reason for why most users join Twitter and later, become inactive and eventually, leave Twitter altogether. It has also delved into why and how users behaviors change when they start using Twitter and how a user's behavior changes when his/her social circle on Twitter expands or shrinks. Most of our results revolved around the basis of psychology. A person losing interest in something after achieving some of the goals is basic human psychology. Similarly, a person developing negative habits and feelings because of having a bigger social circle is also a human psychology. These reasons led us to realize that this research can be used, in the future, for psychological studies related to social media as well.

The future work of the first question that we have solved can be used for developing strategies to prevent a user from leaving Twitter or any other social media site. Our algorithms, experimentations and research work can be adapted to fit any other social media according to their datasets and requirements. It can also be used for psychological studies relating to the field of social media and technology.

The future prospects of the second question can be explored even further by using a bigger dataset to see how far the possibilities go and how many variations we can get with the results. Since we were in a hurry and had to meet a deadline, it wasn't possible to do that for us, but it is easily a great topic for more research, if delved into.

The future possibilities for the third question can be, once again, related to psychology of human interaction with people and social media. How a person is affected when in a bigger social circle and how they are affected when in a smaller social circle. Moreover, since we could not access most of the dataset and as we also had a time limit, we could not do more with more features. But this research can be expanded using a bigger dataset with more features to see more possibilities and ranges of effects and answers.

REFERENCES

Abel, F., Gao, Q., Houben, G. J., & Tao, K. (2011). Analyzing user modeling on Twitter for personalized news recommendations. *Lecture Notes in Computer Science*, *6787*, 1–12. doi:10.1007/978-3-642-22362-4_1

Ahmed, C., & Elkorany, A. (2015). Enhancing link prediction in Twitter using Semantic User Attributes. *2015 IEEE/ACM International Conference on Advances in Social Networks Analysis and Mining*, 1155-1161. 10.1145/2808797.2810056

Akar, E., & Mardikyan, S. (2014). Analyzing factors affecting users' behavior intention to use social media: Twitter case. *International Journal of Business and Social Science*, *5*(11), 85–95.

Alp, Z. Z., & Öğüdücü, Ş. G. (2011). Influential user detection on Twitter: Analyzing effect of focus rate. *2016 IEEE/ACM International Conference on Advances in Social Networks Analysis and Mining*, 1321-1328. doi: 10.1109/ASONAM.2016.7752407

Anber, H., Salah, A., & Ahmed, A. E. (2016). A literature review on Twitter data analysis. *International Journal of Computer and Electrical Engineering*, *8*(3), 241–249. doi:10.17706/IJCEE.2016.8.3.241-249

Azzouza, N., Akli-Astouati, K., Oussalah, A., & Bachir, S. A. (2017). A real-time Twitter sentiment analysis using an unsupervised method. *WIMS '17: Proceedings of the 7th International Conference on Web Intelligence, Mining and Semantics*, 1-10. 10.1145/3102254.3102282

Bild, D. R., Liu, Y., Dick, R. P., Mao, Z. M., & Wallach, D. S. (2015). Aggregate characterization of user behavior in Twitter and analysis of the retweet graph. *ACM Transactions on Internet Technology*, *15*(1), 1–24. doi:10.1145/2700060

Borruto, G. (2015). Analysis of tweets in Twitter. *Webology, 12*(1), 1-11. https://www.researchgate.net/publication/285611048_Analysis_ of_tweets_in_Twitter

Branz, L., & Brockmann, P. (2018). Sentiment analysis of Twitter data: Towards filtering, analyzing and interpreting social network data. *The 12th ACM International Conference.* doi: 10.1145/3210284.3219769

Burns, K. S., & Walker, K. (2018). #13ReasonsWhy Twitter users are tweeting about a Netflix show about teen suicide. *The 9th International Conference.* doi: 10.1145/3217804.3217925

Cunha, E., Magno, G., Comarela, G., Almeida, V., Goncalves, M. A., & Benevenuto, F. (2011). Analyzing the dynamic evolution of hashtags on Twitter: A language-based approach. *ACL Workshop on Language in Social Media*, 58-65. https://www.researchgate.net/publication/262214644_Analyzing _the_dynamic_evolution_of_hashtags_on_Twitter_a_language-bas ed_approach

Elbagir, S., & Yang, J. (2018). Sentiment analysis of Twitter data using machine learning techniques and scikit-learn. *ACAI 2018: Proceedings of the 2018 International Conference on Algorithms, Computing and Artificial Intelligence*, 1-5. 10.1145/3302425.3302492

Elbagir, S., & Yang, J. (2019). Twitter sentiment analysis using natural language toolkit and VADER sentiment. *Proceedings of the International MultiConference of Engineers and Computer Scientists*, 1-5. https://www.iaeng.org/publication/IMECS2019/IMECS2019_pp12-1 6.pdf

Hadgu, A. T., & Jaschke, R. (2014). Identifying and analyzing researchers on Twitter. *WebSci '14: Proceedings of the 2014 ACM conference on Web science*, 23-32. 10.1145/2615569.2615676

Hannon, J., Bennet, M., & Smyth, B. (2010). Recommending Twitter users to follow using content and collaborative filtering approaches. *RecSys '10: Proceedings of the fourth ACM conference on Recommender systems*, 199-206. 10.1145/1864708.1864746

Horng, S. (2010). Analysis of users' behavior on web 2.0 social network sites: An empirical study. *Seventh International Conference on Information Technology: New Generations*, 454-459. 10.1109/ ITNG.2010.248

Keikhosrokiani, P., & Asl, M. P. (Eds.). (2022). *Handbook of research on opinion mining and text analytics on literary works and social media.* IGI Global. doi:10.4018/978-1-7998-9594-7

Khan, R., Khan, H. U., Faisal, M. S., Iqbal, K., & Malik, M. S. I. (2016). An analysis of Khanna, B., Moses, S., & Nirmala, M. (2018). SoftMax based user attitude detection algorithm for sentimental analysis. *Procedia Computer Science*, *125*, 313–320. doi:10.1016/j.procs.2017.12.042

Li, J., & Abhari, A. (2017). Generating stochastic data to stimulate a Twitter user. *CNS '17: Proceedings of the 20th Communications & Networking Symposium*, 1-11. https://dl.acm.org/doi/10.5555/3107979.3107989

Mahmud, J., Fei, G., Xu, A., Pal, A., & Zhou, M. (2016). Predicting attitude and actions of Twitter users. *The 21st International Conference*, 1-5. doi: 10.1145/2856767.2856800

Martha, V., Zhao, W., & Xu, X. (2013). A study on Twitter user-follower network. *2013 IEEE/ACM International Conference on Advances in Social Networks Analysis and Mining*, 1405-1409. doi: 10.1145/2492517.2500298

Maruf, H. A., Meshkat, N., Ali, M. E., & Mahmud, J. (2015). Human behavior in different social medias: A case of Twitter and Disqus. *2015 IEEE/ACM International Conference on Advances in Social Networks Analysis and Mining*, 270-273. doi: 10.1145/2808797.2809395

Mathew, B., Kumar, N., Ravina, Goyal, P., & Mukherjee, A. (2018). *Analyzing the hate and counter speech accounts on Twitter*. doi: 1 doi:0.48550/arXiv.1812.02712

Mendes, M. S., Furtado, E. S., & DeCastro, M. F. (2014). Do users write about the system in use?: An investigation from messages in natural language on Twitter. *EATIS '14: Proceedings of the 7th Euro American Conference on Telematics and Information Systems*, 1-6. 10.1145/2590651.2590654

Mogadala, A., & Varma, V. (2012). Twitter user behavior understanding with mood transition prediction. *Proceedings of the 2012 workshop on Data-driven user behavioral modelling and mining from social media*, 31- 34. 10.1145/2390131.2390145

Pentina, I., Basmanova, O., & Zhang, L. (2014). A cross-national study of Twitter users' motivations and continuance intentions. *Journal of Marketing Communications*, 22(1), 1–20. doi:10.1080/135272 66.2013.841273

Ramakrishnan, U., Shankar, R., & Krishna, G. (2015). Sentiment analysis of Twitter data: Based on user-behavior. *International Journal of Applied Engineering Research*, 10(7), 16291–16301. https://www.researchgate.net/publication/284920488_Sentiment_analysis_of_twitter_data_Based_on_user-behavior

Rao, D., Yarowsky, D., Shreevats, A., & Gupta, M. (2010). Classifying latent user attributes in Twitter. *SMUC '10: Proceedings of the 2nd international workshop on Search and mining user-generated contents*, 37-44. 10.1145/1871985.1871993

Semertzidis, K., Pitoura, E., & Tsaparas, P. (2013). How people describe themselves on Twitter. *DB-Social '13: Proceedings of the ACM SIGMOD Workshop on Databases and Social Networks*, 25-30. 10.1145/2484702.2484708

Sharma, N. K., Ghosh, S., Benevenuto, F., Ganguly, N., & Gummadi, K. P. (2012). Inferring who-is-who in the Twitter social network. *Computer Communication Review*, 42(4), 533–538. doi:10.1145/2377677.2377782

Sinha, S. K., & Das, K. (2016). A survey on user behavior analysis in social networks. *International Journal of Computer Science and Information Security*, 14(11), 895–908.

Stieglitz, S., & Dang-Xuan, L. (2013). Emotions and information diffusion in social media – sentiment of microblogs and sharing behavior. *Journal of Management Information Systems*, 29(4), 217–248. doi:10.2753/MIS0742-1222290408

Tago, K., & Jin, Q. (2018). Influence Analysis of emotional Behaviors and user relationships based on Twitter data. *Tsinghua Science and Technology*, 23(1), 104–113. doi:10.26599/TST.2018.9010012

Taxidou, I., & Fischer, P. M. (2014). Online analysis of information diffusion in Twitter. *WWW '14 Companion: Proceedings of the 23rd International Conference on World Wide Web*, 1313-1316. 10.1145/2567948.2580050

Tsai, M., Tzeng, C., Lin, Z., & Chen, A. L. P. (2012). Discovering leaders from social network by action cascade. *SNS '12: Proceedings of the Fifth Workshop on Social Network Systems*, 1-10. 10.1145/2181176.2181188

Tsugawa, S., Kikuchi, Y., Kishino, F., Nakajima, K., Itoh, Y., & Ohsaki, H. (2015). Recognizing depression from Twitter activity. *CHI '15: Proceedings of the 33rd Annual ACM Conference on Human Factors in Computing Systems*, 3187–3196. 10.1145/2702123.2702280

Twitter users of Pakistan. (n.d.). *International Journal of Computer Science and Information Security, 14*(8), 855-864. https://www.researchgate.net/publication/325396654_An_Analysis_of_Twitter_users_of_Pakistan

Wadley, G., Smith, W., Ploderer, B., Pearce, J., Webber, S., Whooley, M., & Borland, R. (2014). What people talk about when they talk about quitting. *OzCHI '14: Proceedings of the 26th Australian Computer-Human Interaction Conference on Designing Futures: The Future of Design*, 388-391. 10.1145/2686612.2686671

Williams, G., & Mahmoud, A. (2017). Analyzing, classifying, and interpreting emotions in software users' tweets. *2017 IEEE/ACM 2nd International Workshop on Emotion Awareness in Software Engineering*, 2-7. doi: 10.1109/SEmotion.2017.1

Xia, R., Jia, Y., Han, Y., & Li, H. (2013). Mining users' activity on large Twitter text data. *ICIMCS '13: Proceedings of the Fifth International Conference on Internet Multimedia Computing and Service*, 214-218. 10.1145/2499788.2499809

Yamamoto, S., Wakabayashi, K., Kando, N., & Satoh, T. (2016). Who are growth users?: Analyzing and predicting intended Twitter user growth. *WAS '16: Proceedings of the 18th International Conference on Information Integration and Web-based Applications and Services*, 64-71. 10.1145/3011141.3011145

ADDITIONAL READING

Islam, N., Khan, A. R., Ahmed, U., Jaffer, A., & Akhtar, S. (2022). Course Recommendation, Exploratory Data Analysis And Visualizations of Massive Open Online Courses (MOOCS). *Journal of Independent Studies and Research Computing, 20*(1), 72–85. doi:10.31645/JISRC.22.20.1.9

Islam, N., Rizvi, S. S. A., & Anzar, M. (2021, November). Analyzing the quality of responses of Pakistani software developers over stack overflow. In *2021 4th International Conference on Computing & Information Sciences (ICCIS)* (pp. 1-6). IEEE. 10.1109/ICCIS54243.2021.9676399

KEY TERMS AND DEFINITIONS

Accuracy: The ratio of the number of the outputs correctly predicted by the algorithm to the total number of predictions

Classification: A type of supervised learning algorithm in which algorithm predicts the output as discrete class labels.

False Negative: The number of observations in which the actual output is true and the output predicted by algorithm is false.

False Positive: The number of observations in which the actual output is false and the output predicted by algorithm is true.

Machine Learning: The process of training a machine based on a set of data that provides a mapping from input to output.

Supervised Learning: One of the types of machine learning algorithm that trains that data based on both input and output.

True Negative: The number of observations in which the both the actual output and the output predicted by algorithm is false.

True Positive: The number of observations in which both the actual output and the output predicted by algorithm is true.

Unsupervised Learning: A type of the machine learning algorithm in which only the input of the algorithm is considered such as for clustering or dimensionality reduction.

Compilation of References

Abadah, M. S. K., Keikhosrokiani, P., & Zhao, X. (2023). Analytics of Public Reactions to the COVID-19 Vaccine on Twitter Using Sentiment Analysis and Topic Modelling. In D. Valle-Cruz, N. Plata-Cesar, & J. L. González-Ruíz (Eds.), *Handbook of Research on Applied Artificial Intelligence and Robotics for Government Processes* (pp. 156–188). IGI Global. doi:10.4018/978-1-6684-5624-8.ch008

Abbas. (2016). *Machine Learning and Mental Health*. Academic Press.

Abel, F., Gao, Q., Houben, G. J., & Tao, K. (2011). Analyzing user modeling on Twitter for personalized news recommendations. *Lecture Notes in Computer Science, 6787*, 1–12. doi:10.1007/978-3-642-22362-4_1

Abouzeid, R. (2018). *No turning back: Life, loss, and hope in wartime Syria*. WW Norton & Company.

Abramowitz, A. I. (2015). The new American electorate. American Gridlock. *The Sources, Character, and Impact of Political Polarization, 19*, 408–446.

Abramowitz, A., & McCoy, J. (2019). United States: Racial resentment, negative partisanship, and polarization in Trump's America. *The Annals of the American Academy of Political and Social Science, 681*(1), 137–156. doi:10.1177/0002716218811309

Ahmad, H., Nasir, F., Faisal, C. M. N., & Ahmad, S. (2022). Depression Detection in Online Social Media Users Using Natural Language Processing Techniques. In P. Keikhosrokiani & M. Pourya Asl (Eds.), *Handbook of Research on Opinion Mining and Text Analytics on Literary Works and Social Media* (pp. 323–347). IGI Global. doi:10.4018/978-1-7998-9594-7.ch013

Ahmed, C., & Elkorany, A. (2015). Enhancing link prediction in Twitter using Semantic User Attributes. *2015 IEEE/ACM International Conference on Advances in Social Networks Analysis and Mining*, 1155-1161. 10.1145/2808797.2810056

Ahmed, Q. (2008). *In the land of invisible women: A female doctor's journey in the Saudi Kingdom* (1st ed.). Sourcebooks, Inc.

Akar, E., & Mardikyan, S. (2014). Analyzing factors affecting users' behavior intention to use social media: Twitter case. *International Journal of Business and Social Science, 5*(11), 85–95.

Akhtar, M. S., Ekbal, A., & Cambria, E. (2020). How intense are you? predicting intensities of emotions and sentiments using stacked ensemble. *IEEE Computational Intelligence Magazine, 15*(1), 64–75. doi:10.1109/MCI.2019.2954667

Al Mamun, M. H., Keikhosrokiani, P., Asl, M. P., Anuar, N. A. N., Hadi, N. H. A., & Humida, T. (2022). Sentiment Analysis of the Harry Potter Series Using a Lexicon-Based Approach. In P. Keikhosrokiani & M. Pourya Asl (Eds.), *Handbook of Research on Opinion Mining and Text Analytics on Literary Works and Social Media* (pp. 263–291). IGI Global. doi:10.4018/978-1-7998-9594-7.ch011

Alaei, A. R., Becken, S., & Stantic, B. (2019). Sentiment Analysis in Tourism: Capitalizing on Big Data. *Journal of Travel Research*, *58*(2), 175–191. doi:10.1177/0047287517747753

Alanazi, F., & Jones, A. (2015). The value of metadata in digital forensics. *2015 European Intelligence and Security Informatics Conference*. 10.1109/EISIC.2015.26

Ali, S. A., & Burney, S. A. (2010). Conversion of heterogeneous education system (HeES) into homogeneous education system (HoES) for ease of disabled persons using information technology. *2010 International Conference On Computer Design and Applications*, V2-298-V2-301. doi: 10.1109/ICCDA.2010.5541470

Ali, A. H. (2006). *The caged virgin: An emancipation proclamation for women and Islam*. Simon and Schuster.

Ali, A. H. (2008). *Infidel*. Simon and Schuster.

Ali, A. H. (2011). *Nomad: From Islam to America: A personal journey through the clash of civilizations*. Simon and Schuster.

Ali, S. A., & Ahmed, M. (2013). ICT's impact on HRM: Special peoples endeavors. *International Journal of Inventive Engineering and Sciences*, *1*(6), 46–49. https://www.ijies.org/portfolio-item/f0220051613/

Ali, S. A., Hussain, S., & Hasan, B. (2016). Context aware computing used for education and communication of people with special needs; Focus on deaf and dumb. *Journal of Information & Communication Technology-JICT*, *10*(2), 56–58. https://www.researchgate.net/publication/317184239_Context_Aware_Computing_Used_For_Education_and_Communication_of_Peopl e_with_Special_Needs_Focus_on_Deaf_and_Dumb

Alomari, K. M., ElSherif, H. M., & Shaalan, K. (2017). Arabic tweets sentimental analysis using machine learning. *Advances in Artificial Intelligence: From Theory to Practice*, 602–610. doi: 1 doi:0.1007/978-3-319-60042-0_66

Alp, Z. Z., & Öğüdücü, Ş. G. (2011). Influential user detection on Twitter: Analyzing effect of focus rate. *2016 IEEE/ACM International Conference on Advances in Social Networks Analysis and Mining*, 1321-1328. doi: 10.1109/ASONAM.2016.7752407

Al-Sharif, M. (2017). *Daring to drive: A Saudi woman's awakening* (1st ed.). Simon and Schuster.

Anandarajan, M., Hill, C., & Nolan, T. (2019). *Practical text analytics*. Advances in Analytics and Data Science. doi:10.1007/978-3-319-95663-3

Anber, H., Salah, A., & Ahmed, A. E. (2016). A literature review on Twitter data analysis. *International Journal of Computer and Electrical Engineering*, *8*(3), 241–249. doi:10.17706/IJCEE.2016.8.3.241-249

Anderson, D. R., Sweeney, D. J., Williams, T. A., Camm, J. D., & Cochran, J. J. (2016). *Statistics for Business & Economics*. Cengage Learning.

Andreevskaia, A., & Bergler, S. (2007). CLaC and CLaC-NB: Knowledge-based and corpus-based approaches to sentiment tagging. *Proceedings of the Fourth International Workshop on Semantic Evaluations (SemEval-2007)*.

Anishchenkova, V. (2014). *Autobiographical identities in contemporary Arab culture*. Edinburgh University Press.

Ansari, M. Z., Aziz, M. B., Siddiqui, M. O., Mehra, H., & Singh, K. P. (2020). Analysis of political sentiment orientations on twitter. *Procedia Computer Science*, *167*, 1821–1828. doi:10.1016/j.procs.2020.03.201

Anuar, N. A. N. B., & Asl, M. P. (2021). Gender and Sexual Identity in Arundhati Roy's The Ministry of Utmost Happiness: A Cixousian Analysis of Hijra's Resistance and Remaking of the Self. *Pertanika Journal of Social Science & Humanities*, *29*(4), 2335–2352. Advance online publication. doi:10.47836/pjssh.29.4.13

Anuar, N. A. N., & Asl, M. P. (2022). Gender, Resistance, and Identity: Women's Rewriting of the Self in Chitra Banerjee Divakaruni's Before We Visit the Goddess. *Pertanika Journal of Social Science & Humanities, 30*(3). Advance online publication. doi:10.47836/pjssh.30.3.15

Anuar, N. A. N., & Asl, M. P. (2022). Rewriting of Gender and Sexuality in Tanwi Nandini Islam's Bright Lines: A Cixousian Approach. In M. Pourya Asl (Ed.), *Gender, Place, and Identity of South Asian Women* (pp. 131–151). IGI Global. doi:10.4018/978-1-6684-3626-4.ch007

Aoki, N. (2020). An experimental study of public trust in AI chatbots in the public sector. *Government Information Quarterly, 37*(4), 101490. doi:10.1016/j.giq.2020.101490

Appel, O., Chiclana, F., Carter, J., & Fujita, H. (2016). A hybrid approach to sentiment analysis. *2016 IEEE Congress on Evolutionary Computation (CEC)*, 4950-4957. 10.1109/CEC.2016.7744425

Arafa, M., & Armstrong, C. (2016). Facebook to Mobilize, Twitter to Coordinate Protests, and YouTube to Tell the World": New Media, Cyberactivism, and the Arab Spring. *Journal of Global Initiatives: Policy, Pedagogy, Perspective, 10*(1), 6.

Arciniegas, Y. (2020). *Trump vs. Biden: las promesas de los candidatos en cinco temas cruciales.* France 24. https://www.france24.com/es/ee-uu-y-canadá/20201030-eeuu-propuestas-campaña-trump-biden-pandemia-salud-economia

Ashour, R. (2014). *The woman from Tantoura: A Palestinian novel* (1st ed.). Oxford University Press.

Asif, A. S. (2013). Design of minimal states deterministic finite automaton to recognize braille language pattern using the concept of regular expression. *Australian Journal of Basic and Applied Sciences, 7*(7), 49–53. http://www.ajbasweb.com/old/ajbas/2013/may/49-53.pdf

Asl, M. P. (2018). Practices of counter-conduct as a mode of resistance in Middle East women's life writings. *3L: Language, Linguistics, Literature®, 24*(2), 195-205. doi:10.17576/3L-2018-2402-15

Asl, M. P. (2019). Foucauldian rituals of justice and conduct in Zainab Salbi's Between Two Worlds. *Journal of Contemporary Iraq & the Arab World, 13*(2–3), 227–242. doi:10.1386/jciaw_00010_1

Asl, M. P. (2020). Spaces of change: Arab women's reconfigurations of selfhood through heterotopias in Manal al-Sharif's Daring to Drive. *KEMANUSIAAN the Asian Journal of Humanities, 27*(2), 123–143. doi:10.21315/kajh2020.27.2.7

Asl, M. P. (2018). Fabrication of a desired truth: The oblivion of a Naxalite woman in Jhumpa Lahiri's The Lowland. *Asian Ethnicity, 19*(3), 383–401. doi:10.1080/14631369.2018.1429892

Asl, M. P. (2019). Foucauldian rituals of justice and conduct in Zainab Salbi's Between Two Worlds. *Journal of Contemporary Iraq & the Arab World, 13*(2-3), 227–242. doi:10.1386/jciaw_00010_1

Asl, M. P. (2020). Micro-Physics of discipline: Spaces of the self in Middle Eastern women life writings. *International Journal of Arabic-English Studies, 20*(2). Advance online publication. doi:10.33806/ijaes2000.20.2.12

Asl, M. P. (Ed.). (2022). *Gender, Place, and Identity of South Asian Women.* IGI Global. doi:10.4018/978-1-6684-3626-4

Asongu, S. A., Orim, S.-M. I., & Nting, R. T. (2019). Terrorism and social media: Global evidence. *Journal of Global Information Technology Management, 22*(3), 208–228. doi:10.1080/1097198X.2019.1642023

Asri, M. A. Z. B. M., Keikhosrokiani, P., & Asl, M. P. (2022). Opinion Mining Using Topic Modeling: A Case Study of Firoozeh Dumas's Funny in Farsi in Goodreads. Advances on Intelligent Informatics and Computing. doi:10.1007/978-3-030-98741-1_19

Asri, M. A. Z. B. M., Keikhosrokiani, P., & Asl, M. P. (2022a). Opinion Mining Using Topic Modeling: A Case Study of Firoozeh Dumas's Funny in Farsi in Goodreads. In F. Saeed, F. Mohammed, & F. Ghaleb (Eds.), *Advances on Intelligent Informatics and Computing* (pp. 219–230). Springer International Publishing. doi:10.1007/978-3-030-98741-1_19

ATF. (2022, September 8). *Criminal profilers.* https://www.atf.gov/careers/criminal-profilers

Azzouza, N., Akli-Astouati, K., Oussalah, A., & Bachir, S. A. (2017). A real-time Twitter sentiment analysis using an unsupervised method. *WIMS '17: Proceedings of the 7th International Conference on Web Intelligence, Mining and Semantics,* 1-10. 10.1145/3102254.3102282

Bagheri, H., & Islam, M. J. (2017). *Sentiment analysis of twitter data.* arXiv preprint arXiv:1711.10377. doi: 1 doi:0.48550/arXiv.1711.10377

Bailey, L., Harinam, V., & Ariel, B. (2020). Victims, offenders and victim-offender overlaps of Knife Crime: A Social network analysis approach using Police Records. *PLoS One, 15*(12), e0242621. Advance online publication. doi:10.1371/journal.pone.0242621 PMID:33306696

Bakshi, R. K., Kaur, N., Kaur, R., & Kaur, G. (2016). Opinion mining and sentiment analysis. *2016 3rd International Conference on Computing for Sustainable Global Development (INDIACom).*

Bao, W., Yue, J., & Rao, Y. (2017). A deep learning framework for financial time series using stacked autoencoders and long-short term memory. *PLoS One, 12*(7), e0180944. doi:10.1371/journal.pone.0180944 PMID:28708865

Barakat, I. (2016). *Balcony on the moon: Coming of age in Palestine.* Farrar, Straus and Giroux (BYR).

Barron-Estrada, M. L., Zatarain-Cabada, R., & Oramas-Bustillos, R. (2019). Emotion Recognition for Education using Sentiment Analysis. *Research in Computing Science, 148*(5), 71–80. doi:10.13053/rcs-148-5-8

Basrawi, F. (2009). *Brownies and kalashnikovs: A Saudi moman's memoir of American Arabia and wartime Beirut.* South Street Press Reading.

Becker-Asano, C., & Wachsmuth, I. (2010). Affective computing with primary and secondary emotions in a virtual human. *Autonomous Agents and Multi-Agent Systems, 20*(1), 32–49. doi:10.100710458-009-9094-9

Bell, J. (2005, February 23). *Transporters, replicators and phasing FAQ.* Star Trek. https://www.calormen.com/Star_Trek/FAQs/transport-faq.htm

Bhowmick, A., & Hazarika, S. M. (2017). An insight into assistive technology for the visually impaired and blind people: State-of-the-art and future trends. *Journal on Multimodal User Interfaces, 11*(2), 149–172. doi:10.100712193-016-0235-6

Bhutto, F. (2016). *The shadow of the crescent moon.* Penguin Books.

Biggs, J. (2011, September 21). *Is printing a gun the same as buying a gun?* Tech Crunch. https://techcrunch.com/2011/09/20/is-printing-a-gun-the-same-as-buying-a-gun/

Bild, D. R., Liu, Y., Dick, R. P., Mao, Z. M., & Wallach, D. S. (2015). Aggregate characterization of user behavior in Twitter and analysis of the retweet graph. *ACM Transactions on Internet Technology, 15*(1), 1–24. doi:10.1145/2700060

Bin Laden, N., bin Laden, O., & Sasson, J. (2009). Growing up Bin Laden: Osama's wife and son take us inside their secret world (1st ed.). St. Martin's Press.

Bird, S., Klein, E., & Loper, E. (2009). *Natural language processing with python: Analysing text with the natural language toolkit.* O'Reilly Media.

Blood-brain barrier and vaccines. (n.d.). Retrieved February 6, 2022, from https://www.chop.edu/centers-programs/vaccine-education-center/vaccine-safety/blood-brain-barrier-and-vaccines

Bonn, U. (2019). *Venema P-Model algorithm.* https://www2.meteo.uni-bonn.de/staff/venema/themes/surrogates/

Borruto, G. (2015). Analysis of tweets in Twitter. *Webology, 12*(1), 1-11. https://www.researchgate.net/publication/285611048_Analysis_of_tweets_in_Twitter

Branz, L., & Brockmann, P. (2018). Sentiment analysis of Twitter data: Towards filtering, analyzing and interpreting social network data. *The 12th ACM International Conference.* doi: 10.1145/3210284.3219769

Brownlee, J. (2017, May 24). *A Gentle introduction to long short-term memory networks by the experts.* Machine Learning Mastery. https://machinelearningmastery.com/gentle-introduction-long-short-term-memory-networks-experts/

Buchholz, F., & Spafford, E. (2004). On the role of file system metadata in digital forensics. *Digital Investigation, 1*(4), 298–309. doi:10.1016/j.diin.2004.10.002

Buneman, P. (1997). Semistructured data. In *PODS'97: Proceedings of the 16th ACM SIGACTSIGMOD-SIGART Symposium on Principles of Database Systems.* ACM Press. 10.1145/263661.263675

Burns, K. S., & Walker, K. (2018). #13ReasonsWhy Twitter users are tweeting about a Netflix show about teen suicide. *The 9th International Conference.* doi: 10.1145/3217804.3217925

Calvo, R. A., D'Mello, S., Gratch, J. M., & Kappas, A. (2015). *The Oxford handbook of affective computing.* Oxford Library of Psychology. doi:10.1093/oxfordhb/9780199942237.001.0001

Cambria, E., Das, D., Bandyopadhyay, S., & Feraco, A. (2017). Affective computing and sentiment analysis. In *A practical guide to sentiment analysis* (pp. 1–10). Springer. doi:10.1007/978-3-319-55394-8_1

Cambria, E., Li, Y., Xing, F. Z., Poria, S., & Kwok, K. (2020). SenticNet 6: Ensemble application of symbolic and sub-symbolic AI for sentiment analysis. *Proceedings of the 29th ACM International Conference on Information & Knowledge Management,* 105–114. 10.1145/3340531.3412003

Campion, A., Hernandez, M.-G., Jankin, S. M., & Esteve, M. (2020). Managing Artificial Intelligence Deployment in the Public Sector. *Computer, 53*(10), 28–37. doi:10.1109/MC.2020.2995644

Caprolu, M., Sadighian, A., & Di Pietro, R. (2022). *Characterizing the 2022 Russo-Ukrainian conflict through the lenses of aspect-based sentiment analysis: Dataset, methodology, and preliminary findings.* doi:10.48550/arXiv.2208.04903

Ceci, F., Gonçalves, A. L., & Webe, R. (2016). A model for sentiment analysis based on ontology and cases. *IEEE Latin America Transactions, 14*(11), 4560–4566. doi:10.1109/TLA.2016.7795829

Cederman, L., & Weidmann, N. (2017). Predicting armed conflict: Time to adjust our expectations? *Science, 355*(6324), 474–476. doi:10.1126cience.aal4483 PMID:28154047

Center for Biologics Evaluation and Research. (2021, January 27). *Vaccine Adverse Events.* U.S. Food and Drug Administration. Retrieved February 6, 2022, from https://www.fda.gov/vaccines-blood-biologics/report-problem-center-biologics-evaluation-research/vaccine-adverse-events

Center for Drug Evaluation and Research. (2018, June 4). *Questions and Answers on FDA's Adverse Event Reporting System (FAERS)*. U.S. Food and Drug Administration. Retrieved February 6, 2022, from https://www.fda.gov/drugs/surveillance/questions-and-answers -fdas-adverse-event-reporting-system-faers

Chatterjee, A., Gupta, U., Chinnakotla, M. K., Srikanth, R., Galley, M., & Agrawal, P. (2019). Understanding emotions in text using deep learning and big data. *Computers in Human Behavior*, *93*, 309–317. doi:10.1016/j.chb.2018.12.029

Chauhan, P., Sharma, N., & Sikka, G. (2020). The emergence of social media data and sentiment analysis in election prediction. *Journal of Ambient Intelligence and Humanized Computing*, 1–27.

Choi, Y., & Joo, S. (2020). Identifying facets of reader-generated online reviews of children's books based on a textual analysis approach. *The Library Quarterly*, *90*(3), 349–363. doi:10.1086/708962

Chollet, F. (2015). *Keras: The Python deep learning library*. Keras. https://keras.io/

Chowdhary, K. R. (2020). Natural Language Processing. In K. R. Chowdhary (Ed.), *Fundamentals of Artificial Intelligence* (pp. 603–649). Springer India. doi:10.1007/978-81-322-3972-7_19

Christie, J. (2015, September 8). *Are these the dumbest thieves ever?* Dailymail. https://www.dailymail.co.uk/news/article-3248275/Are-dumbest -thieves-Cocky-bank-robbing-couple-arrested-posing-Facebook- photos-thousands-dollars-cash-stole.html

Chu, K. E., Keikhosrokiani, P., & Asl, M. P. (2022). A Topic Modeling and Sentiment Analysis Model for Detection and Visualization of Themes in Literary Texts. *Pertanika Journal of Science & Technology*, *30*(4), 2535–2561. doi:10.47836/ pjst.30.4.14

Chung, W., & Zeng, D. (2020). Dissecting emotion and user influence in social media communities: An interaction modeling approach. *Information & Management*, *57*(1), 103108. doi:10.1016/j.im.2018.09.008

Clark, J. (2014). The importance of braille in the 21st century. *Journal of South Pacific Educators in Vision Impairment*, *7*(1), 24–29. https://www.spevi.net/wp-content/uploads/2015/07/JSPEVI-Vol- 7-No-1-2014.pdf

Clauset, A. (2018). Trends and fluctuations in the severity of interstate wars. *Science Advances*, *4*(2), 1–10. doi:10.1126ciadv. aao3580 PMID:29507877

CNN. (2020). *CNN - breaking news, latest news and videos*. CNN. https://edition.cnn.com

Colombini, C., & Colella, A. (2011). Digital profiling: A computer forensics approach. In *International Conference on Availability, Reliability, and Security* (pp. 330-343). Springer.

Cortis, K., & Davis, B. (2021). Over a decade of social opinion mining: A systematic review. *Artificial Intelligence Review*, *54*(7), 4873–4965. doi:10.100710462-021-10030-2 PMID:34188346

Criado, J. I., Sandoval-Almazan, R., Valle-Cruz, D., & Ruvalcaba-Gómez, E. A. (2021). Chief information officers' perceptions about artificial intelligence. *First Monday*.

Cuadrado, J. C., & Gómez-Navarro, D. P. (2011). *Un modelo lingüístico-semántico basado en emociones para la clasificación de textos según su polaridad e intensidad*. [Doctoral Thesis]. Complutense University of Madrid. http://nil.fdi.ucm.es/sites/default/files/Thesis_Jorge_Carri llo_De_Albornoz.pdf

Cunha, E., Magno, G., Comarela, G., Almeida, V., Goncalves, M. A., & Benevenuto, F. (2011). Analyzing the dynamic evolution of hashtags on Twitter: A language-based approach. *ACL Workshop on Language in Social Media*, 58-65. https://www.researchgate.net/publication/262214644_Analyzing_the_dynamic_evolution_of_hashtags_on_Twitter_a_language-based_approach

D'Andrea, F. M. (1997). *Instructional strategies for braille literacy* (Vol. 1). American Foundation for the Blind.

Dagamsheh, A. M., & Downing, D. (2016). *Neoliberal Economy: Violence of Economic Deregulation in Mohsin Hamid's Moth Smoke*. Retrieved 9 20, 2022, from https://journals.ju.edu.jo/dirasathum/article/view/14174

Dang, S., & Ahmad, P. H. (2014). Text mining: Techniques and its application. *International Journal of Engineering & Technology Innovations*, *1*(4), 22–25.

Daniel, L. (2017). *Cell Phone Location Evidence for Legal Professionals: Understanding Cell Phone Location Evidence from the Warrant to the Courtroom*. Academic Press.

Dean, G., & Bell, P. (2012). The dark side of social media: Review of online terrorism. *Pakistan Journal of Criminology*, *3*(4), 191–210.

Deer, B. (2011, January 5). How the case against the MMR vaccine was fixed. *BMJ, 342*(1), c5347–c5347. doi: 1 doi:0.1136/bmj.c5347

Deerwester, S., Dumais, S. T., Furnas, G. W., Landauer, T. K., & Harshman, R. (1990). Indexing by latent semantic analysis. *Journal of the American Society for Information Science, 41*(6), 391-407.

Dejevsky, M. (2017, June 21). As Syria's war enters its endgame, the risk of a US-Russia conflict escalates. *The Guardian*. https://www.theguardian.com/commentisfree/2017/jun/21/syria-war-endgame-us-russia-conflict-washington-moscow-accidental-war

Demidova, L. A. (2021). Two-stage hybrid data classifiers based on svm and knn algorithms. *Symmetry*, *13*(4), 615. Advance online publication. doi:10.3390ym13040615

Department of Peace and Conflict Research at Uppsala University. (1980). *Uppsala Conflict Data*. Uppsala Conflict Data Program – UCDP. https://ucdp.uu.se/

Desouza, K. C., Dawson, G. S., & Chenok, D. (2020). Designing, developing, and deploying artificial intelligence systems: Lessons from and for the public sector. *Business Horizons*, *63*(2), 205–213. doi:10.1016/j.bushor.2019.11.004

Devi, D. N., Kumar, C. K., & Prasad, S. (2016). A feature based approach for sentiment analysis by using support vector machine. *2016 IEEE 6th International Conference on Advanced Computing (IACC)*, 3-8. doi: 10.1109/IACC.2016.11

Devika, M. D., Sunitha, C., & Ganesh, A. (2016). Sentiment Analysis: A Comparative Study on Different Approaches. *Procedia Computer Science*, *87*, 44–49. doi:10.1016/j.procs.2016.05.124

Dhaoui, C., Webster, C. M., & Tan, L. P. (2017). Social media sentiment analysis: Lexicon versus machine learning. *Journal of Consumer Marketing*, *34*(6), 480–488. doi:10.1108/JCM-03-2017-2141

Dover, R. (2020). SOCMINT: A shifting balance of opportunity. *Intelligence and National Security*, *35*(2), 216–232. doi:10.1080/02684527.2019.1694132

Druckman, J. N., & Levendusky, M. S. (2019). What do we measure when we measure affective polarization? *Public Opinion Quarterly*, *83*(1), 114–122. doi:10.1093/poq/nfz003

Dsouza, D. D., Deepika, D. P. N., Machado, E. J., & Adesh, N. D. (2019). Sentimental analysis of student feedback using machine learning techniques. *International Journal of Recent Technology and Engineering (IJRTE), 8*(1S4), 986-991.

Dwivedi, O., & Lau, L. (2014). *Indian Writing in English and the Global Literary Market.* Springer. doi:10.1057/9781137437716

El Badry, H. (2014). Rain Over Baghdad: An Egyptian Novel (1st ed.). The American University in Cairo Press.

El Kaliouby, R., & Colman, C. (2020). *Girl decoded: A scientist's quest to reclaim our humanity by bringing emotional intelligence to technology.* Currency.

Elbagir, S., & Yang, J. (2019). Twitter sentiment analysis using natural language toolkit and VADER sentiment. *Proceedings of the International MultiConference of Engineers and Computer Scientists,* 1-5. https://www.iaeng.org/publication/IMECS2019/IMECS2019_pp12-16.pdf

Elbagir, S., & Yang, J. (2018). Sentiment analysis of Twitter data using machine learning techniques and scikit-learn. *ACAI 2018: Proceedings of the 2018 International Conference on Algorithms, Computing and Artificial Intelligence,* 1-5. 10.1145/3302425.3302492

El-Din, D. M. (2016). Enhancement bag-of-words model for solving the challenges of sentiment analysis. *International Journal of Advanced Computer Science and Applications, 7*(1), 244–252. doi:10.14569/IJACSA.2016.070134

Ellis, F. (2013). Insatiable Desire. *Philosophy (London, England), 88*(02), 243–265. doi:10.1017/S0031819113000041

Ellison, N. B., Vitak, J., Steinfield, C., Gray, R., & Lampe, C. (2011). Negotiating privacy concerns and social capital needs in a social media environment. In *Privacy online* (pp. 19–32). Springer. doi:10.1007/978-3-642-21521-6_3

Emmert-Strib, F., Yang, Z., Feng, H., Tripathi, S., & Dehmer, M. (2018). An introductory review of deep learning for prediction models with big data. *Frontiers in Artificial Intelligence - Deep Learning in Computational Social Science, 27,* 16-32. doi:10.3389/frai.2020.00004

Fabre, C. (2016). 1. Ideological Tropes of Contemporary Addiction Narratives. In *Challenging Addiction in Canadian Literature and Classrooms* (pp. 25–49). University of Toronto Press. doi:10.3138/9781442624443-004

Fahad, A. H. (2021, December 30). *Sentiment Analysis — Let TextBlob do all the Work! - Red Buffer.* Medium. Retrieved February 6, 2022, from https://medium.com/red-buffer/sentiment-analysis-let-textblob-do-all-the-work-9927d803d137

Fasha, E. F. B. K., Keikhosrokiani, P., & Asl, M. P. (2022). Opinion Mining Using Sentiment Analysis: A Case Study of Readers' Response on Long Litt Woon's The Way Through the Woods in Goodreads. Advances on Intelligent Informatics and Computing. doi:10.1007/978-3-030-98741-1_20

Fasha, E. F. B. K., Keikhosrokiani, P., & Asl, M. P. (2022a). Opinion Mining Using Sentiment Analysis: A Case Study of Readers' Response on Long Litt Woon's The Way Through the Woods in Goodreads. In F. Saeed, F. Mohammed, & F. Ghaleb (Eds.), *Advances on Intelligent Informatics and Computing* (pp. 231–242). Springer International Publishing. doi:10.1007/978-3-030-98741-1_20

Fauzi, M. A. (2019). Word2Vec model for sentiment analysis of product reviews in Indonesian language. *Iranian Journal of Electrical and Computer Engineering, 9*(1), 525–530. doi:10.11591/ijece.v9i1.pp525-530

Floreano, D., & Mattiussi, C. (2008). *Bio-inspired artificial intelligence: theories, methods, and technologies.* MIT Press.

Floridi, L. (2016). Faultless responsibility: On the nature and allocation of moral responsibility for distributed moral actions. *Philosophical Transactions - Royal Society. Mathematical, Physical, and Engineering Sciences, 374*(2083), 20160112. doi:10.1098/rsta.2016.0112 PMID:28336791

Fox, A. M., Novak, K. J., Van Camp, T., & James, C. (2021). Predicting violent victimization using social network analysis from Police Data. *Violence and Victims, 36*(3), 436–454. doi:10.1891/VV-D-19-00037 PMID:34103416

Gaba, V., & Verma, V. (2022). Sentiment Analysis of Twitter Data Using Machine Learning Approaches. *Communications in Computer and Information Science, 1572 CCIS*, 140–152. doi: 1 doi:0.1007/978-3-031-05767-0_12

Galtung, J. (1990). Cultural Violence. *Journal of Peace Research, 27*(3), 291–305. doi:10.1177/0022343390027003005

García-Contreras, R., Muñoz-Chávez, J. P., Valle-Cruz, D., & López-Chau, A. (2022). Teleworker Experiences in #COVID-19: Insights Through Sentiment Analysis in Social Media. In P. Keikhosrokiani & M. Pourya Asl (Eds.), *Handbook of Research on Opinion Mining and Text Analytics on Literary Works and Social Media* (pp. 388–412). IGI Global. doi:10.4018/978-1-7998-9594-7.ch016

García-Ortega, R. H., García-Sánchez, P., & Merelo-Guervós, J. J. (2020). StarTroper, a film trope rating optimizer using machine learning and evolutionary algorithms. *Expert Systems: International Journal of Knowledge Engineering and Neural Networks, 6*(37), 1–15. doi:10.1111/exsy.12525

Gautam, V., Pal, R., Bandhey, H., Dhingra, L. S., Misra, V., Sharma, H., Jain, C., Bhagat, K., Arushi, A., Patel, L., Agarwal, M., Agrawal, S., Jalan, R., Wadhwa, A., Garg, A., Agrawal, Y., Rana, B., Kumaraguru, P., & Sethi, T. (2021, June 14). A Machine Learning Application for Raising WASH Awareness in the Times of COVID-19 Pandemic. *Research Square*. doi: 1 doi:0.21203/rs.3.rs-562183/v1

Germani, F., & Biller-Andorno, N. (2021, March 3). The anti-vaccination infodemic on social media: A behavioral analysis. *PLoS One, 16*(3), e0247642. doi:10.1371/journal.pone.0247642 PMID:33657152

Gershowitz, A. M. (2015). The post-riley search warrant: Search protocols and particularity in cell phone searches. SSRN *Electronic Journal*. doi:10.2139/ssrn.2634473

Giusti, R., & Batista, G. E. (2013). An empirical comparison of dissimilarity measures for time series classification. *Brazilian Conference on Intelligent System*, 82-88. 10.1109/BRACIS.2013.22

Gkotsis, G., Oellrich, A., Velupillai, S., Liakata, M., Hubbard, T. J. P., Dobson, R. J. B., & Dutta, R. (2017). Characterisation of mental health conditions in social media using Informed Deep Learning. *Scientific Reports, 7*(1), 1–11. doi:10.1038rep45141 PMID:28327593

Glassman, M., & Kang, M. J. (2012). Intelligence in the internet age: The emergence and evolution of Open Source Intelligence (OSINT). *Computers in Human Behavior, 28*(2), 673–682. doi:10.1016/j.chb.2011.11.014

Gleditsch, N. P. (2020). *Lewis Fry Richardson: His intellectual legacy and influence in the social sciences*. Springer. doi:10.1007/978-3-030-31589-4

Godlee, F., Smith, J., & Marcovitch, H. (2011, January 5). Wakefield's article linking MMR vaccine and autism was fraudulent. *BMJ, 342*(1), c7452–c7452. doi: 1 doi:0.1136/bmj.c7452

Golley, N. A.-H. (2007). *Arab women's lives retold: Exploring identity through writing*. Syracuse University Press.

Goodfellow, I., Benbio, Y., & Courville, A. (2016). *Deep learning – adaptive computation and machine learning series*. MIT Press.

Google, L. L. C. (1998). *Google Search*. www.google.com

Google, L. L. C. (2016). *API cloud natural language.* Google cloud. https://cloud.google.com/natural-language?hl=pt-br

Gray, G., & Benning, B. (2019). Crowdsourcing criminology: Social Media and citizen policing in missing person cases. *SAGE Open, 9*(4), 215824401989370. doi:10.1177/2158244019893700

Greenwald, G., & MacAskill, E. (2013). *NSA Prism program taps into user data of Apple, Google and others.* https://www.pulitzer.org/files/2014/public-service/guardianus/02guardianus2014.pdf

Greenwald, G., MacAskill, E., Poitras, L., Ackerman, S., & Rushe, D. (2013, September 8). Revealed: How Microsoft handed the NSA access to encrypted *messages. The Guardian.* http://shorturl.at/ajmR8

Guo, F., Li, F., Lv, W., Liu, L., & Duffy, V. G. (2020). Bibliometric Analysis of Affective Computing Researches during 1999~2018. *International Journal of Human-Computer Interaction, 36*(9), 801–814. doi:10.1080/10447318.2019.1688985

Gupta, R. K., & Yang, Y. (2018). Crystalfeel at semeval-2018 task 1: Understanding and detecting emotion intensity using affective lexicons. *Proceedings of the 12th International Workshop on Semantic Evaluation.*

Hadgu, A. T., & Jaschke, R. (2014). Identifying and analyzing researchers on Twitter. *WebSci '14: Proceedings of the 2014 ACM conference on Web science*, 23-32. 10.1145/2615569.2615676

Hadi, N. H. A., & Asl, M. P. (2022). The Real, the Imaginary, and the Symbolic: A Lacanian Reading of Ramita Navai's City of Lies. *GEMA Online® Journal of Language Studies, 22*(1), 145–158. doi: 1 doi:0.17576/gema-2022-2201-08

Hakak, N. M., Mohd, M., Kirmani, M., & Mohd, M. (2017). Emotion analysis: A survey. *2017 International Conference on Computer, Communications and Electronics (Comptelix).*

Halkia, M., Ferri, S., Schiellens, M. K., & Papazoglou, M. (2020). The global conflict risk index: A quantitative tool for policy support on conflict prevention. *Progress in Disaster Science, 6*, 100069. doi:10.1016/j.pdisas.2020.100069

Halsey, T. C., Jensen, M. H., Kadanoff, L. P., Procaccia, I., & Shraiman, B. I. (1987). Fractal measures and their singularities: The characterization of strange sets. *Nuclear Physics B - Proceedings Supplement, 2*, 501–511. doi:10.1016/0920-5632(87)90036-3

Hamid, M., & Veyret, P. (2022). "The glint of catastrophe": An Interview with Mohsin Hamid. *Angles. New Perspectives on the Anglophone World*, (14). doi:10.4000/angles.5349

Hand, L. C., & Ching, B. D. (2020). Maintaining neutrality: A sentiment analysis of police agency Facebook pages before and after a fatal officer-involved shooting of a citizen. *Government Information Quarterly, 37*(1), 101420. doi:10.1016/j.giq.2019.101420

Hannon, J., Bennet, M., & Smyth, B. (2010). Recommending Twitter users to follow using content and collaborative filtering approaches. *RecSys '10: Proceedings of the fourth ACM conference on Recommender systems*, 199-206. 10.1145/1864708.1864746

Haque, T. U., Saber, N. N., & Shah, F. M. (2018). Sentiment analysis on large scale Amazon product reviews. *2018 IEEE international conference on innovative research and development (ICIRD)*, 1-6. doi: 1. doi:0.1109/ICIRD.2018.8376299

Harel, T. O., Jameson, J. K., & Maoz, I. (2020). The normalization of hatred: Identity, affective polarization, and dehumanization on Facebook in the context of intractable political conflict. *Social Media+ Society, 6*(2).

Harvey, C. (2020). *Insatiable: Why everything is not enough.* Philosophy in the Contemporary.

Hasan, A., Moin, S., Karim, A., & Shamshirband, S. (2018). Machine learning-based sentiment analysis for twitter accounts. *Mathematical and Computational Applications, 23*(1), 11. doi:10.3390/mca23010011

Haykin, S. O. (2008). *Neural networks and learning machines*. Pearson.

Hegre, H., Allansson, M., Basedau, M., Colaresi, M., Croicu, M., Fjelde, H., Hoyles, F., Hultman, L., Högbladh, S., Jansen, R., Mouhleb, N., Muhammad, S. A., Nilsson, D., Nygård, H. M., Olafsdottir, G., Petrova, K., Randahl, D., Rød, E. G., Schneider, G., ... Vestby, J. (2019). Views: A political violence early-warning system. *Journal of Peace Research, 56*(2), 155–174. doi:10.1177/0022343319823860

Heidegger, M. (1977). *The question concerning technology and other essays* (W. Lovitt, Trans.). Garland Publishing. (Original work published 1954)

Helle, V., Negus, A., & Nyberg, J. (2018). *Improving armed conflict predic-tion using machine learning: VIEWS+*. https://pdfs.semanticscholar.org/3008/beffb4496316bb1677253de89eb4b2a695c3.pdf

Hernandez, E., Anduiza, E., & Rico, G. (2021). Affective polarization and the salience of elections. *Electoral Studies, 69*, 102203. doi:10.1016/j.electstud.2020.102203

Hilborg, P. H., & Nygaard, E. B. (2015). *Viability of sentiment analysis in business*. The Copenhagen Business School. Retrieved from http://studenttheses. cbs. dk…

Hobolt, S. B., Leeper, T. J., & Tilley, J. (2021). Divided by the vote: Affective polarization in the wake of the Brexit referendum. *British Journal of Political Science, 51*(4), 1476–1493. doi:10.1017/S0007123420000125

Hochreiter, S., & Schmidhuber, J. (1997). Long Short-Term Memory. *Neural Computation, 9*(8), 1735–1780. doi:10.1162/neco.1997.9.8.1735 PMID:9377276

Hofmann, T. (1999). Probabilistic latent semantic indexing. *Proceedings of the 22nd Annual International ACM SIGIR Conference on Research and Development in Information Retrieval*.

Hofmann, T. (2001). Unsupervised Learning by Probabilistic Latent Semantic Analysis. *Machine Learning, 42*(1), 177–196. doi:10.1023/A:1007617005950

Hogenboom, A., Heerschop, B., Frasincar, F., Kaymak, U., & de Jong, F. (2014). Multi-lingual support for lexicon-based sentiment analysis guided by semantics. *Decision Support Systems, 62*, 43–53. doi:10.1016/j.dss.2014.03.004

Hollow, M. (2013). *Confronting a new era of duplication? 3D printing, replicating technology and the search for au-thenticity in George O. Smith's Venus Equilateral Series*. SSRN Electronic Journal. doi:10.2139srn.2333496

Hong, L., & Davison, B. D. (2010). Empirical study of topic modeling in Twitter. *Proceedings of the First Workshop on Social Media Analytics - SOMA '10*. 10.1145/1964858.1964870

Horng, S. (2010). Analysis of users' behavior on web 2.0 social network sites: An empirical study. *Seventh International Conference on Information Technology: New Generations*, 454-459. 10.1109/ITNG.2010.248

Hoskin, E. R., Coyne, M. K., White, M. J., Dobri, S. C., Davies, T. C., & Pinder, S. D. (2022). Effectiveness of technol-ogy for braille literacy education for children: A systematic review. *Disability and Rehabilitation. Assistive Technology*, 1–11. doi:10.1080/17483107.2022.2070676 PMID:35575120

Hosseini, K. (2003). *The kite runner*. Penguin.

Hosseini, K. (2009). *A thousand splendid suns*. Bloomsbury Publishing.

Hribar, G., Podbregar, I., & Ivanuša, T. (2014). OSINT: A "grey zone"? *International Journal of Intelligence and Coun-terIntelligence, 27*(3), 529–549. doi:10.1080/08850607.2014.900295

Hudson, A. (2014, June 24). *Nestle plans to create a 'Star Trek-like food replicator'*. BBC News. https://www.bbc.co.uk/news/newsbeat-27996163

Hu, M., & Liu, B. (2004). *Mining opinion features in customer reviews*. American Association for Artificial Intelligence.

Hussain, A., Tahir, A., Hussain, Z., Sheikh, Z., Gogate, M., Dashtipour, K., Ali, A., & Sheikh, A. (2021, April 5). Artificial Intelligence–Enabled Analysis of Public Attitudes on Facebook and Twitter Toward COVID-19 Vaccines in the United Kingdom and the United States: Observational Study. *Journal of Medical Internet Research, 23*(4), e26627. doi:10.2196/26627 PMID:33724919

Hutto, C., & Gilbert, E. (2014). Vader: A parsimonious rule-based model for sentiment analysis of social media text. *Proceedings of the International AAAI Conference on Web and Social Media.*

Hu, X., & Liu, H. (2012). Text analytics in social media. In *Mining text data* (pp. 385–414). Springer. doi:10.1007/978-1-4614-3223-4_12

Ibañez, M. M., Rosa, R. R., & Guimarães, L. N. (2021). *Análise de emoções em mídias sociais utilizando aprendizado de máquina e séries temporais considerando informações de eventos extremos sociais e naturais*. Instituto Nacional de Pesquisas Espaciais - INPE. http://urlib.net/rep/8JMKD3MGP3W34R/44H7S82

Ibañez, M. M., Rosa, R. R., & Guimarães, L. N. (2020). Sentiment analysis applied to analyze society's emotion in two different context of social media data. *Inteligencia Artificial Revista Iberoamericana de Inteligencia Artificial, 23*(66), 66–84. doi:10.4114ubmission/intartif.vol23iss66pp66-84

Ibañez, M. M., Rosa, R. R., & Guimarães, L. N. F. (2022). Threat Emotion Analysis in Social Media: Considering Armed Conflicts as Social Extreme Events. In P. Keikhosrokiani & M. Pourya Asl (Eds.), *Handbook of Research on Opinion Mining and Text Analytics on Literary Works and Social Media* (pp. 293–322). IGI Global. doi:10.4018/978-1-7998-9594-7.ch012

Imperial College London. (2014, May 18). *Scientists discover how to turn light into matter after 80 years quest*. Phys.org. https://phys.org/news/2014-05-scientists-year-quest.html

Ince, J., Rojas, F., & Davis, C. A. (2017). The social media response to Black Lives Matter: How Twitter users interact with Black Lives Matter through hashtag use. *Ethnic and Racial Studies, 40*(11), 1814–1830. doi:10.1080/01419870.2017.1334931

Ingole, P., Bhoir, S., & Vidhate, A. V. (2018). Hybrid Model for Text Classification. *Proceedings of the 2nd International Conference on Electronics, Communication and Aerospace Technology, ICECA 2018, Iceca,* 7–15. doi: 10.1109/ICECA.2018.8474738

Innes, C. M. (2021). Thinking about bad taste in a funny way. In D. K. Johnson & M. R. Berry (Eds.), *Exploring the Orville: Essays on Seth MacFarlane's space adventure* (p. 245). McFarland & Company.

Isayed, S., & Tahboub, R. (2015). A review of optical Braille recognition. *2015 2nd World Symposium on Web Applications and Networking (WSWAN),* 1-6. doi: 10.1109/WSWAN.2015.7210343

Islam, T. (2019). Yoga-veganism: Correlation mining of twitter health data. *8th KDD Workshop on Issues of Sentiment Discovery and Opinion Mining (WISDOM).* doi:10.1609/icwsm.v8i1.14550

Iyengar, S., Lelkes, Y., Levendusky, M., Malhotra, N., & Westwood, S. J. (2019). The origins and consequences of affective polarization in the United States. *Annual Review of Political Science, 22*(1), 129–146. doi:10.1146/annurev-polisci-051117-073034

Iyengar, S., Sood, G., & Lelkes, Y. (2012). Affect, not ideologya social identity perspective on polarization. *Public Opinion Quarterly*, *76*(3), 405–431. doi:10.1093/poq/nfs038

Jackson, P., & Mouliner, I. (2002). *Natural language processing for online applications: Textretrieval, extraction and categorization*. John Benjamins B.V. doi:10.1075/nlp.5(1st)

Jacobs, A. M. (2019). Sentiment Analysis for Words and Fiction Characters From the Perspective of Computational (Neuro-)Poetics. *Frontiers in Robotics and AI*, *6*. Advance online publication. doi:10.3389/frobt.2019.00053

Jafery, N. N., Keikhosrokiani, P., & Asl, M. P. (2022). Text analytics model to identify the connection between theme and sentiment in literary works: A case study of Iraqi life writings. In P. Keikhosrokiani & M. P. Asl (Eds.), *Handbook of research on opinion mining and text analytics on literary works and social media* (pp. 173–190). IGI Global. doi:10.4018/978-1-7998-9594-7.ch008

Jagdale, R. S., Shirsat, V. S., & Deshmukh, S. N. (2016). Sentiment analysis of events from Twitter using open source tool. *IJCSMC*, *5*(4), 475–485.

Jain, P., Gyanchandani, M., & Khare, N. (2016). Big data privacy: A technological perspective and review. *Journal of Big Data*, *3*(1), 1–25. doi:10.118640537-016-0059-y

Jamal, N., Xianqiao, C., & Aldabbas, H. (2019). Deep learning-based sentimental analysis for large-scale imbalanced twitter data. *Future Internet*, *11*(9), 190. doi:10.3390/fi11090190

Jeanis, M. N. (2020). Missing Persons and Runaway Youth: The Role of Social Media as an Alert System and Crime Control Tool. In *Science Informed Policing* (pp. 181–193). Springer. doi:10.1007/978-3-030-41287-6_9

Jinjri, W. M., Keikhosrokiani, P., & Abdullah, N. L. (2021). Machine Learning Algorithms for The Classification of Cardiovascular Disease-A Comparative Study. *2021 International Conference on Information Technology (ICIT)*. doi:10.1109/ICIT52682.2021.9491677

John, S. A., & Keikhosrokiani, P. (2022). COVID-19 fake news analytics from social media using topic modeling and clustering. In P. Keikhosrokiani (Ed.), Big Data Analytics for Healthcare (pp. 221–232). Academic Press. doi:10.1016/B978-0-323-91907-4.00003-0

John, S. A., & Keikhosrokiani, P. (2022). COVID-19 fake news analytics from social media using topic modeling and clustering. In P. Keikhosrokiani (Ed.), *Big Data Analytics for Healthcare* (pp. 221–232). Academic Press. doi:10.1016/B978-0-323-91907-4.00003-0

Johnson, J. A., & Reitzel, J. D. (2011, September 8). *Social network analysis in an operational environment: Defining the utility of a network approach for crime analysis using the Richmond City Police Department as a case study*. Researchgate. http://shorturl.at/dIKRU

Johnson, N. F. (2020, May 13). *The online competition between pro- and anti-vaccination views*. Nature. Retrieved February 12, 2022, from https://www.nature.com/articles/s41586-020-2281-1?error=cookies_not_supported&code=d99e8f7c-4c3e-4163-880b-2133c5e79905

Jordan, M. I., & Mitchell, T. M. (2015). Machine learning: Trends, perspectives, and prospects. *Science*, *349*(6245), 255–260. doi:10.1126cience.aaa8415 PMID:26185243

Joshi, V. C., & Vekariya, V. M. (2017). An approach to sentiment analysis on Gujarati tweets. *Advances in Computational Sciences and Technology*, *10*(5), 1487–1493.

Jungherr, A., Jürgens, P., & Schoen, H. (2012). Why the pirate party won the german election of 2009 or the trouble with predictions: A response to tumasjan, a., sprenger, to, sander, pg, & welpe, im "predicting elections with twitter: What 140 characters reveal about political sentiment." *Social Science Computer Review, 30*(2), 229–234. doi:10.1177/0894439311404119

Kang, G. J., Ewing-Nelson, S. R., Mackey, L., Schlitt, J. T., Marathe, A., Abbas, K. M., & Swarup, S. (2017, June). Semantic network analysis of vaccine sentiment in online social media. *Vaccine, 35*(29), 3621–3638. doi:10.1016/j.vaccine.2017.05.052 PMID:28554500

Keikhosrokiani, P. (Ed.). (2022a). *Big Data Analytics for Healthcare: Datasets, Techniques, Life Cycles, Management, and Applications.* Elsevier Science. doi:10.1016/C2021-0-00369-2

Keikhosrokiani, P. (Ed.). (2022b). *Handbook of Research on Consumer Behavior Change and Data Analytics in the Socio-Digital Era.* IGI Global. doi:10.4018/978-1-6684-4168-8

Keikhosrokiani, P., & Asl, M. P. (Eds.). (2022). *Handbook of research on opinion mining and text analytics on literary works and social media.* IGI Global. doi:10.4018/978-1-7998-9594-7

Keikhosrokiani, P., & Kamaruddin, N. S. A. B. (2022). IoT-Based In-Hospital-In-Home Heart Disease Remote Monitoring System with Machine Learning Features for Decision Making. In S. Mishra, A. González-Briones, A. K. Bhoi, P. K. Mallick, & J. M. Corchado (Eds.), *Connected e-Health: Integrated IoT and Cloud Computing* (pp. 349–369). Springer International Publishing. doi:10.1007/978-3-030-97929-4_16

Kelion, L. (2013, September 8). *Q&A: NSA's Prism internet surveillance scheme.* BBC. https://www.bbc.com/news/technology-23051248

Kerr, J., Panagopoulos, C., & van der Linden, S. (2021). Political polarization on COVID-19 pandemic response in the United States. *Personality and Individual Differences, 179,* 110892. doi:10.1016/j.paid.2021.110892 PMID:34866723

Keshavarz, H., & Abadeh, M. S. (2017). ALGA: Adaptive lexicon learning using genetic algorithm for sentiment analysis of microblogs. *Knowledge-Based Systems, 122,* 1–16. doi:10.1016/j.knosys.2017.01.028

Keylock, C. J. (2017). Multifractal surrogate-data generation algorithm that preserves pointwise hölder regularity structure, with initial applications to turbulence. *Physical Review. E, 95*(3), 032123. Advance online publication. doi:10.1103/PhysRevE.95.032123 PMID:28415176

Keyvanpour, M., Karimi Zandian, Z., & Heidarypanah, M. (2020). OMLML: A helpful opinion mining method based on lexicon and machine learning in social networks. *Social Network Analysis and Mining, 10*(1), 10. Advance online publication. doi:10.100713278-019-0622-6

Khalifa, S. M., Marie, M. I., & El-Defrawi, M. M. (2022). Aspects Detection Model for Users' Reviews Using Machine Learning Techniques. *Journal of Theoretical and Applied Information Technology, 100*(19), 5776–5786.

Khan, D. (2018). *Born with wings: The Spiritual Journey of a modern muslim woman.* Random House.

Khan, F. H., Bashir, S., & Qamar, U. (2014). TOM: Twitter opinion mining framework using hybrid classification scheme. *Decision Support Systems, 57,* 245–257. doi:10.1016/j.dss.2013.09.004

Khan, R., Khan, H. U., Faisal, M. S., Iqbal, K., & Malik, M. S. I. (2016). An analysis of Khanna, B., Moses, S., & Nirmala, M. (2018). SoftMax based user attitude detection algorithm for sentimental analysis. *Procedia Computer Science, 125,* 313–320. doi:10.1016/j.procs.2017.12.042

Khan, S. K. (2021). 'Anxious Citizens of the Attention Economy': In Conversation with Mohsin Hamid. *Wasafiri, 36*(1), 14–19. doi:10.1080/02690055.2021.1838796

Kherwa, P., & Bansal, P. (2020). Topic modeling: a comprehensive review. *EAI Endorsed Transactions on Scalable Information Systems, 7*(24).

Kherwa, P., & Bansal, P. (2020). Topic modeling: A comprehensive review. *EAI Endorsed Transactions on Scalable Information Systems, 7*(24).

Kherwa, P., & Bansal, P. (2018, July 13). Topic Modeling: A Comprehensive Review. *ICST Transactions on Scalable Information Systems*, 159623. doi:10.4108/eai.13-7-2018.159623

Kim, J., Lee, J., Park, E., & Han, J. (2020). A deep learning model for detecting mental illness from user content on social media. *Scientific Reports, 10*(1), 1–6. doi:10.103841598-020-68764-y PMID:32678250

Kim, J., Seo, J., Lee, M., & Seok, J. (2019). Stock price prediction through the sentimental analysis of news articles. *2019 Eleventh International Conference on Ubiquitous and Future Networks (ICUFN)*, 700-702. 10.1109/ICUFN.2019.8806182

Kiritchenko, S., Zhu, X., & Mohammad, S. M. (2014). Sentiment analysis of short informal texts. *Journal of Artificial Intelligence Research, 50*, 723–762. doi:10.1613/jair.4272

Knoke, D., & Yang, S. (2019). *Social network analysis*. SAGE Publications.

Kosovski, J. R., & Douglas, C. S. (2011). Everybody hurts: Addiction, drama, and the family in the reality television show Intervention. *Substance Use & Misuse, 7*(46), 852–858. doi:10.3109/10826084.2011.570610 PMID:21599500

Krishnaveni, K. S., Pai, R. R., & Iyer, V. (2017). Faculty rating system based on student feedbacks using sentimental analysis. *2017 International Conference on Advances in Computing, Communications and Informatics (ICACCI)*, 1648-1653. 10.1109/ICACCI.2017.8126079

Küçük, D., & Arıcı, N. (2022). Sentiment Analysis and Stance Detection in Turkish Tweets About COVID-19 Vaccination. In P. Keikhosrokiani & M. Pourya Asl (Eds.), *Handbook of Research on Opinion Mining and Text Analytics on Literary Works and Social Media* (pp. 371–387). IGI Global. doi:10.4018/978-1-7998-9594-7.ch015

Kumar, S. A., Vijayalakshmi, M., Divya, T., & Subramanya, K. (2019). Computational Intelligence for Data Analytics. In *Recent Advances in Computational Intelligence* (pp. 27–43). Springer. doi:10.1007/978-3-030-12500-4_2

Kurdi, T. (2018). *The boy on the beach: My family's escape from Syria and our hope for a new home*. Simon and Schuster.

Landis, G. A. (1998). The Fermi paradox: An approach based on percolation theory. *JBIS. Journal of the British Interplanetary Society, 5*(51), 163–166.

Lateral Gmb, H. (2019). *NewsBot - Give me 5*. https://getnewsbot.com/

Laxmiprasad, P. (2020). Diasporic literature—An overview. *Journal of English Language and Literature, 7*(3), 98–106. doi:10.33329/joell.7.3.20.98

Lazar, J., Olalere, A., & Wentz, B. (2012). Investigating the accessibility and usability of job application web sites for blind users. *Journal of Usability Studies, 7*(2), 68–87.

Lelkes, Y. (2021). Policy over party: Comparing the effects of candidate ideology and party on affective polarization. *Political Science Research and Methods, 9*(1), 189–196. doi:10.1017/psrm.2019.18

Levinson-Waldman, R. (2022, September 8). *School social media monitoring won't stop the next mass shooting*. Brenna Center. https://www.brennancenter.org/our-work/analysis-opinion/school-social-media-monitoring-wont-stop-next-mass-shooting

Li, J., & Abhari, A. (2017). Generating stochastic data to stimulate a Twitter user. *CNS '17: Proceedings of the 20th Communications & Networking Symposium*, 1-11. https://dl.acm.org/doi/10.5555/3107979.3107989

Lim, C. (2022, September 8). *Police have arrested 62-year-old Frank James, the Brooklyn Subway shooting suspect*. MSN. https://www.msn.com/en-us/news/crime/police-have-arrested-62-year-old-frank-james-the-brooklyn-subway-shooting-suspect/a r-AAWbTfB?ocid=BingNewsSearch

Lim, B., & Zohren, S. (2021). Time-series forecasting with deep learning: A survey. *Philosophical Transactions - Royal Society. Mathematical, Physical, and Engineering Sciences, 379*(2194), 20200209. Advance online publication. doi:10.1098/rsta.2020.0209 PMID:33583273

Li, N., & Wu, D. D. (2010). Using text mining and sentiment analysis for online forums hotspot detection and forecast. *Decision Support Systems, 48*(2), 354–368. doi:10.1016/j.dss.2009.09.003

Lissauer, G. (2014). *The Tropes of Fantasy Fiction*. McFarland.

Liu, B. (2012). Sentiment analysis and opinion mining. *Synthesis Lectures on Human Language Technologies, 5*(1), 1-167. doi: 1 doi:0.1007/978-3-031-02145-9

Liu, B. (2012). Sentiment analysis and opinion mining. *Synthesis Lectures on Human Language Technologies, 5*(1), 1–167. https://www.cs.uic.edu/~liub/FBS/liub-SA-and-OM-book.pdf

Liu, H. (2017). *Sentiment analysis of citations using word2vec*. doi: 1 doi:0.48550/arXiv.1704.00177

Liu, C. (2015). *The Dark Forest* (K. Liu & J. Martinsen, Trans.). Tor Books. (Original work published 2008)

Li, Z., Fan, Y., Jiang, B., Lei, T., & Liu, W. (2019). A survey on sentiment analysis and opinion mining for social multimedia. *Multimedia Tools and Applications, 78*(6), 6939–6967. doi:10.100711042-018-6445-z

Lodin, H., & Balani, P. (2017). Rich Semantic Sentiment Analysis using Lexicon Based Approach *ICTACT JOURNAL ON. Soft Computing, 07*(04), 1486–1491.

Lombardi, M., Rosenblum, T., & Burato, A. (2015, September 8). *From SOCMINT to digital humint: Re-frame the use of social media within the intelligence cycle*. Academia. http://shorturl.at/fqtz2

López-Chau, A., Valle-Cruz, D., & Sandoval-Almazán, R. (2020). Sentiment Analysis of Twitter Data Through Machine Learning Techniques. In Software Engineering in the Era of Cloud Computing (pp. 185–209). Springer. doi:10.1007/978-3-030-33624-0_8

López-Chau, A., Valle-Cruz, D., & Sandoval-Almazán, R. (2021). Sentiment Analysis in Crisis Situations for Better Connected Government: Case of Mexico Earthquake in 2017. In Web 2.0 and Cloud Technologies for Implementing Connected Government (pp. 162–181). IGI Global. doi: 10.4018/978-1-6684-6303-1.ch006

Luo, X., Zimet, G., & Shah, S. (2019, July 16). A natural language processing framework to analyse the opinions on HPV vaccination reflected in twitter over 10 years (2008 - 2017). *Human Vaccines & Immunotherapeutics, 15*(7–8), 1496–1504. doi:10.1080/21645515.2019.1627821 PMID:31194609

Madiou, M. S.-E. (2021). The Truth Will Out: Mohsin Hamid Speaks His Name in The Reluctant Fundamentalist. *Arab Studies Quarterly, 43*(4), 304–319. doi:10.13169/arabstudquar.43.4.0304

Mahmud, J., Fei, G., Xu, A., Pal, A., & Zhou, M. (2016). Predicting attitude and actions of Twitter users. *The 21st International Conference*, 1-5. doi: 10.1145/2856767.2856800

Mahmud, A., & Mohammed, A. (2021). A survey on deep learning for time-series forecasting. In A. E. Hassanien & A. Darwish (Eds.), *Machine Learning and Big Data Analytics Paradigms: Analysis* (pp. 365–392). Applications and Challenges. doi:10.1007/978-3-030-59338-4_19

Malakpa, S. W. (1994). Job placement of blind and visually impaired people with additional disabilities. *RE:view. Rehabilitation and Education for Blindness and Visual Impairment, 26*(2), 69–77.

Malik, E. F., Keikhosrokiani, P., & Asl, M. P. (2021, 4-5 July 2021). Text mining life cycle for a spatial reading of Viet Thanh Nguyen's *The Refugees* (2017). *2021 International Congress of Advanced Technology and Engineering (ICOTEN).* doi:10.1109/ICOTEN52080.2021.9493520

Malik, E. F., Keikhosrokiani, P., & Asl, M. P. (2021, July 4-5). Text Mining Life Cycle for a Spatial Reading of Viet Thanh Nguyen's *The Refugees* (2017). *2021 International Congress of Advanced Technology and Engineering (ICOTEN).* doi:10.1109/ICOTEN52080.2021.9493520

Mantelero, A., & Vaciago, G. (2015). Data protection in a big data society. Ideas for a future regulation. *Digital Investigation, 15,* 104–109. doi:10.1016/j.diin.2015.09.006

Marcus, J. (2020, April 24). *US-Iran war of words raises fresh fears of Gulf clash.* BBC News. https://www.bbc.com/news/world-middle-east-52399283

Martha, V., Zhao, W., & Xu, X. (2013). A study on Twitter user-follower network. *2013 IEEE/ACM International Conference on Advances in Social Networks Analysis and Mining,* 1405-1409. doi: 10.1145/2492517.2500298

Martinez, M., Roitberg, A., Koester, D., Stiefelhagen, R., & Schauerte, B. (2017). Using technology developed for autonomous cars to help navigate blind people. *2017 IEEE International Conference on Computer Vision Workshops (ICCVW),* 1424-1432. 10.1109/ICCVW.2017.169

Maruf, H. A., Meshkat, N., Ali, M. E., & Mahmud, J. (2015). Human behavior in different social medias: A case of Twitter and Disqus. *2015 IEEE/ACM International Conference on Advances in Social Networks Analysis and Mining,* 270-273. doi: 10.1145/2808797.2809395

Marx, K. (1967). Capital, Vols. I—III. International Publishers.

Marx, K. (1967). *Value, Price, and Profit.* International Publishers.

Mathew, B., Kumar, N., Ravina, Goyal, P., & Mukherjee, A. (2018). *Analyzing the hate and counter speech accounts on Twitter.* doi: 1 doi:0.48550/arXiv.1812.02712

Measles Outbreak — California, December 2014–February 2015. (2015). Retrieved February 12, 2022, from https://www.cdc.gov/mmwr/preview/mmwrhtml/mm6406a5.htm

Melton, C. A., Olusanya, O. A., Ammar, N., & Shaban-Nejad, A. (2021b, October). Public sentiment analysis and topic modeling regarding COVID-19 vaccines on the Reddit social media platform: A call to action for strengthening vaccine confidence. *Journal of Infection and Public Health, 14*(10), 1505–1512. doi:10.1016/j.jiph.2021.08.010 PMID:34426095

Mendes, M. S., Furtado, E. S., & DeCastro, M. F. (2014). Do users write about the system in use?: An investigation from messages in natural language on Twitter. *EATIS '14: Proceedings of the 7th Euro American Conference on Telematics and Information Systems,* 1-6. 10.1145/2590651.2590654

Meneveau, C., & Sreenivasan, K. R. (1987). Simple multifractal cascade model for fully developed turbulence. *Physical Review Letters, 59*(13), 1424–1427. doi:10.1103/PhysRevLett.59.1424 PMID:10035231

Mikhail, D. (2018). *The beekeeper: Rescuing the stolen women of Iraq* (1st ed.). New Directions Publishing.

Mogadala, A., & Varma, V. (2012). Twitter user behavior understanding with mood transition prediction. *Proceedings of the 2012 workshop on Data-driven user behavioral modelling and mining from social media*, 31-34. 10.1145/2390131.2390145

Moyer, J. D., & Kaplan, O. (2020, July 6). Will the Coronavirus fuel conflict projections based on economic and development data show an increased. *Foreign Policy – the Global Magazine of News and Ideas*. https://foreignpolicy.com/2020/07/06/coronavirus-pandemic-fuel-conflict-fragile-states-economy-food-prices/

Muchlinski, D., Siroky, D., He, J., & Kocher, M. (2016). Comparing random forest with logistic regression for predicting class-imbalanced civil war onset data. *Political Analysis*, *24*(1), 87–103. doi:10.1093/pan/mpv024

Muller, D. A. (2000). Criminal profiling: Real science or just wishful thinking? *Homicide Studies*, *4*(3), 234–264. doi:10.1177/1088767900004003003

Munn, L. (2021). More than a mob: Parler as preparatory media for the US Capitol storming. *First Monday*. Advance online publication. doi:10.5210/fm.v26i3.11574

Murad, N., & Krajeski, J. (2017). *The last girl: My story of captivity, and my fight against the Islamic State*. Tim Duggan Books.

Murarka, A., Radhakrishnan, B., & Ravichandran, S. (2020). *Detection and Classification of mental illnesses on social media using RoBERTa*. Academic Press.

Murthy, V. V., & Hanumanthappa, M. (2017). Pre-processing the braille image for improving optical braille recognition performance. *International Journal of Advanced Research in Computer Science*, *8*(7), 561–564. http://ijarcs.info/index.php/Ijarcs/article/view/4188. doi:10.26483/ijarcs.v8i7.4188

Mustafa, N., & Lamb, C. (2016). *Nujeen: One girl's incredible journey from war-torn Syria in a wheelchair*. Harper Wave.

Mutanga, M. B., & Abayomi, A. (2022). Tweeting on COVID-19 pandemic in South Africa: LDA-based topic modelling approach. *African Journal of Science, Technology, Innovation and Development*, *14*(1), 163–172. doi:10.1080/20421338.2020.1817262

Nafisi, A. (2010). *Things I've been silent about: Memories of a prodigal daughter*. Random House Incorporated.

Nahar, L., Sultana, Z., Iqbal, N., & Chowdhury, A. (2019). Sentiment Analysis and Emotion Extraction: A Review of Research Paradigm. *2019 1st International Conference on Advances in Science, Engineering and Robotics Technology (ICASERT)*.

Naing, C. H., Zhao, X., Gan, K. H., & Samsudin, N.-H. (2022). What Is Love?: Text Analytics on Romance Literature From the Perspective of Authors. In P. Keikhosrokiani & M. Pourya Asl (Eds.), *Handbook of Research on Opinion Mining and Text Analytics on Literary Works and Social Media* (pp. 148–172). IGI Global., doi:10.4018/978-1-7998-9594-7.ch007

Naresh, A., & Venkata Krishna, P. (2021). An efficient approach for sentiment analysis using machine learning algorithm. *Evolutionary Intelligence*, *14*(2), 725–731. doi:10.100712065-020-00429-1

National Institute for the Blind. (2018). *Standard English braille: Grades I and II*. Forgotten Books.

Natural Language Processing: A Guide to NLP Use Cases, Approaches, and Tools. (2021, August 25). AltexSoft. Retrieved February 6, 2022, from https://www.altexsoft.com/blog/natural-language-processing/

Nawaz, Z. (2016). *Laughing all the way to the mosque: The misadventures of a Muslim woman*. Virago.

Naydan, L. M. (2016). Beyond economic globalization in Mohsin Hamid's How to Get Filthy Rich in Rising Asia: The false promise of self-help and possibilities through reading with a creative mind. *Journal of Commonwealth Literature*, *53*(1), 92–108. doi:10.1177/0021989416632565

Noga-Hartmann, E., & Kotzinos, D. (2022). Assessing Together the Trends in Newspaper Topics and User Opinions: A Co-Evolutionary Approach. In P. Keikhosrokiani & M. Pourya Asl (Eds.), *Handbook of Research on Opinion Mining and Text Analytics on Literary Works and Social Media* (pp. 348–370). IGI Global. doi:10.4018/978-1-7998-9594-7.ch014

Nogara, G., Vishnuprasad, P. S., Cardoso, F., Ayoub, O., Giordano, S., & Luceri, L. (2022, June 26). The Disinformation Dozen: An Exploratory Analysis of Covid-19 Disinformation Proliferation on Twitter. *14th ACM Web Science Conference 2022*. 10.1145/3501247.3531573

Nordbrandt, M. (2021). Affective polarization in the digital age: Testing the direction of the relationship between social media and users' feelings for out-group parties. *New Media & Society*.

O'Mally, J., & Antonelli, K. (2016). The effect of career mentoring on employment outcomes for college students who are legally blind. *Journal of Visual Impairment & Blindness*, *110*(5), 295–307. doi:10.1177/0145482X1611000502

Obagbinoko, C. O. (2018). State Response to Violent Conflicts: An Assessment of the Nigerian State and the Indigenous People of Biafra (Ipob) Separationist Movement. *AfSol*, *2*, 157.

Olah, C. (2015). Understanding LSTM Networks. *Colah's blog*. http://colah.github.io/posts/2015-08-Understanding-LSTMs/

Oliveira, C. A. (1990). *IDEAL - uma interface dialógica em linguagem natural para sistemas especialistas*. São José dos Campos: Instituto Nacional de Pesquisas Espaciais (INPE). http://urlib.net/rep/6qtX3pFwXQZ3r59YCT/GUpqq

Omand, D., Bartlett, J., & Miller, C. (2012). Introducing social media intelligence (SOCMINT). *Intelligence and National Security*, *27*(6), 801–823. doi:10.1080/02684527.2012.716965

Omar, I. (2020). *This is what America looks like: My Journey from refugee to congresswoman*. C. Hurst (Publishers) Limited.

Oramas Bustillos, R., Zatarain Cabada, R., Barrón Estrada, M. L., & Hernández Pérez, Y. (2019). Opinion mining and emotion recognition in an intelligent learning environment. *Computer Applications in Engineering Education*, *27*(1), 90–101. doi:10.1002/cae.22059

Ostrowski, D. A. (2015). Using latent Dirichlet allocation for topic modelling in twitter. *Proceedings of the 2015 IEEE 9th International Conference on Semantic Computing (IEEE ICSC 2015)*.

Oyebode, O., Alqahtani, F., & Orji, R. (2020). Using Machine Learning and Thematic Analysis Methods to Evaluate Mental Health Apps Based on User Reviews. *IEEE Access: Practical Innovations, Open Solutions*, *8*, 111141–111158. doi:10.1109/ACCESS.2020.3002176

Pang, B., & Lee, L. (2004). *A sentimental education: Sentiment analysis using subjectivity summarization based on minimum cuts*. doi:10.48550/arXiv.cs/0409058

Pang, B., Lee, L., & Vaithyanathan, S. (2002). *Thumbs up? Sentiment classification using machine learning techniques*. doi:10.48550/arXiv.cs/0205070

Paremeswaran, P. p., Keikhosrokiani, P., & Asl, M. P. (2022). Opinion Mining of Readers' Responses to Literary Prize Nominees on Twitter: A Case Study of Public Reaction to the Booker Prize (2018–2020). Advances on Intelligent Informatics and Computing. doi:10.1007/978-3-030-98741-1_21

Pascale, A. (2017, September 4). *Interview: Seth MacFarlane talks mission of 'The Orville' and defends Star Trek: TNG's replicators.* TrekMovie.com. https://trekmovie.com/2017/09/04/interview-seth-macfarlane-t alks-mission-of-the-orville-and-defends-star-trek-tngs-repli cators/

Passini, S. (2012). The Facebook and Twitter revolutions: Active participation in the 21st century. *Human Affairs*, *22*(3), 301–312. doi:10.247813374-012-0025-0

Patel, M., Lee, A. D., Clemmons, N. S., Redd, S. B., Poser, S., Blog, D., Zucker, J. R., Leung, J., Link-Gelles, R., Pham, H., Arciuolo, R. J., Rausch-Phung, E., Bankamp, B., Rota, P. A., Weinbaum, C. M., & Gastañaduy, P. A. (2019, October 11). National Update on Measles Cases and Outbreaks— United States, January 1–October 1, 2019. *MMWR. Morbidity and Mortality Weekly Report*, *68*(40), 893–896. doi:10.15585/mmwr.mm6840e2 PMID:31600181

Pentina, I., Basmanova, O., & Zhang, L. (2014). A cross-national study of Twitter users' motivations and continuance intentions. *Journal of Marketing Communications*, *22*(1), 1–20. doi:10.1080/13527266.2013.841273

Perfect, M. (2019). 'Black holes in the fabric of the nation': Refugees in Mohsin Hamid's Exit West. *Journal for Cultural Research*, *23*(2), 187–201. doi:10.1080/14797585.2019.1665896

Perner, C. (2010). Tracing the Fundamentalist in Mohsin Hamid's Moth Smoke and The Reluctant Fundamentalist. *Ariel-a Review of International English Literature*, *41*(3), 23-31. Retrieved 9 20, 2022, from https://questia.com/library/journal/1g1-266467176/tracing-th e-fundamentalist-in-mohsin-hamid-s-moth

Picard, R. W. (2000). *Affective computing*. MIT Press. doi:10.7551/mitpress/1140.001.0001

Picard, R. W. (2003). Affective computing: Challenges. *International Journal of Human-Computer Studies*, *59*(1–2), 55–64. doi:10.1016/S1071-5819(03)00052-1

Piedrahita-Valdés, H., Piedrahita-Castillo, D., Bermejo-Higuera, J., Guillem-Saiz, P., Bermejo-Higuera, J. R., Guillem-Saiz, J., Sicilia-Montalvo, J. A., & Machío-Regidor, F. (2021, January 7). Vaccine Hesitancy on Social Media: Sentiment Analysis from June 2011 to April 2019. *Vaccines*, *9*(1), 28. doi:10.3390/vaccines9010028 PMID:33430428

Pike, O. J., Mackenroth, F., Hill, E. G., & Rose, S. J. (2014). A photon–photon collider in a vacuum hohlraum. *Nature Photonics*, *8*(6), 434–436. doi:10.1038/nphoton.2014.95

Poria, S., Cambria, E., Bajpai, R., & Hussain, A. (2017). A review of affective computing: From unimodal analysis to multimodal fusion. *Information Fusion*, *37*, 98–125. doi:10.1016/j.inffus.2017.02.003

Pourgharib, B., & Asl, M. P. (2022). Cultural Translation, Hybrid Identity, and Third Space in Jhumpa Lahiri's Interpreter of Maladies. *Pertanika Journal of Social Science & Humanities*, *30*(4). Advance online publication. doi:10.47836/pjssh.30.4.10

Pourgharib, B., Hamkhiyal, S., & Asl, M. P. (2022). A Non-Orientalist Representation of Pakistan in Contemporary Western Travelogues. *GEMA Online Journal of Language Studies*, *22*(3), 103–118. doi:10.17576/gema-2022-2203-06

Pourya Asl, M. (Ed.). (2023). *Urban poetics and politics in contemporary South Asia and the Middle East.* IGI Global. doi:10.4018/978-1-6684-6650-6

Pozzi, F. A., Fersini, E., Messina, E., & Liu, B. (2016). *Sentiment analysis in social networks.* Morgan Kaufmann.

Prabhu, A., Guhathakurta, D., Subramanian, M., Reddy, M., Sehgal, S., Karandikar, T., Gulati, A., Arora, U., Shah, R. R., Kumaraguru, P., & Associates. (2021). *Capitol (Pat) riots: A comparative study of Twitter and Parler.* ArXiv Preprint ArXiv:2101.06914.

Probst, E. (2010). *Exploring hedonistic consumption from an identity perspective: an interpretative study.* [Doctoral dissertation, Nottingham Trent University]. IRep. https://irep.ntu.ac.uk/id/eprint/207

Ramakrishnan, U., Shankar, R., & Krishna, G. (2015). Sentiment analysis of Twitter data: Based on user-behavior. *International Journal of Applied Engineering Research, 10*(7), 16291–16301. https://www.researchgate.net/publication/284920488_Sentiment _analysis_of_twitter_data_Based_on_user-behavior

Rameshbhai, C. J., & Paulose, J. (2019). Opinion mining on newspaper headlines using SVM and NLP. *Iranian Journal of Electrical and Computer Engineering, 9*(3), 2152–2163. doi:10.11591/ijece.v9i3.pp2152-2163

Rangapuram, S. S., Seeger, M. W., Gasthaus, J., Stella, L., Wang, Y., & Januschowski, T. (2018). Deep state space models for time series forecasting. In S. Bengio, H. Wallach, H. Larochelle, K. Grauman, N. Cesa-Bianchi, & R. Garnett (Eds.), *Advances in Neural Information Processing Systems.* Curran Associates, Inc. https://proceedings.neurips.cc/paper/2018/file/5cf68969fb67a a6082363a6d4e6468e2-Paper.pdf

Rao, D., Yarowsky, D., Shreevats, A., & Gupta, M. (2010). Classifying latent user attributes in Twitter. *SMUC '10: Proceedings of the 2nd international workshop on Search and mining user-generated contents,* 37-44. 10.1145/1871985.1871993

Ravichandran, B. D., & Keikhosrokiani, P. (2022). Classification of Covid-19 misinformation on social media based on neuro-fuzzy and neural network: A systematic review. *Neural Computing & Applications.* Advance online publication. doi:10.100700521-022-07797-y PMID:36159189

Ravi, K., & Ravi, V. (2015). A survey on opinion mining and sentiment analysis: Tasks, approaches and applications. *Knowledge-Based Systems, 89,* 14–46. doi:10.1016/j.knosys.2015.06.015

re — Regular expression operations — Python 3.10.8 documentation. (2022). Retrieved February 20, 2022, from https:// docs.python.org/3/library/re.html

Redacción. (2021). *Asalto al Capitolio: las pistas sobre cómo el ataque no fue tan espontáneo (y las sospechas de que hubo ayuda desde dentro).* BBC News Mundo. https://www.bbc.com/mundo/noticias-internacional-55671725

Rehman, S. (2016). Threading my prayer rug: One woman's journey from Pakistani Muslim to American Muslim. Audible Studios on Brilliance Audio.

Reuters. (2019). *Reuters news agency: World's largest news agency.* Reuters. https://www.reuters.com/

Rex, E., Koenig, A., Wormsley, D. P., & Baker, R. (Eds.). (1995). *Foundations of braille literacy.* American Foundation for the Blind Press.

Reyes-Menendez, A., Saura, J., & Alvarez-Alonso, C. (2018). Understanding #WorldEnvironmentDay user opinions in Twitter: A topic-based sentiment analysis approach. *International Journal of Environmental Research and Public Health, 15*(11), 2537. doi:10.3390/ijerph15112537 PMID:30428520

Rezaeinia, S. M., Rahmani, R., Ghodsi, A., & Veisi, H. (2019). Sentiment analysis based on improved pre-trained word embeddings. *Expert Systems with Applications, 117,* 139–147. doi:10.1016/j.eswa.2018.08.044

Richardson, L. F. (1960). *Arms and insecurity: A mathematical study of the causes and origins of war.* The Boxwood Press.

Rigano, C. (2021, September 8). *Using artificial intelligence to address criminal justice needs.* Office of Justice Programs. https://www.ojp.gov/pdffiles1/nij/252038.pdf

Röder, M., Both, A., & Hinneburg, A. (2015, February 2). Exploring the Space of Topic Coherence Measures. *Proceedings of the Eighth ACM International Conference on Web Search and Data Mining.* 10.1145/2684822.2685324

Rogers, M. (2003). The role of criminal profiling in the computer forensics process. *Computers & Security*, *22*(4), 292–298. doi:10.1016/S0167-4048(03)00405-X

Rogowski, J. C., & Sutherland, J. L. (2016). How ideology fuels affective polarization. *Political Behavior*, *38*(2), 485–508. doi:10.100711109-015-9323-7

Rosa, R. R., Neelakshi, J., Pinheiro, G. A., Barchi, P. H., & Shiguemori, H. (2019). Modeling social and geopolitical disasters as extreme events: a case study considering the complex dynamics of international armed conflicts. In L. Santos, R. G. Negri, & T. J. Carvalho (Eds.), Towards mathematics, computers and environment: A disasters perspective (pp. 233-254). Springer. doi:10.1007/978-3-030-21205-6_12

Rosenbach, M., Poitras, L., & Stark, H. (2013). How the NSA accesses smartphone data. *Spiegel Online, 9.*

Rosli, N. H. B., & Keikhosrokiani, P. (2022). Big medical data mining system (BigMed) for the detection and classification of COVID-19 misinformation. In P. Keikhosrokiani (Ed.), *Big Data Analytics for Healthcare* (pp. 233–244). Academic Press. doi:10.1016/B978-0-323-91907-4.00014-5

Ross, J. (2009). *IraqiGirl: Diary of a teenage girl in Iraq.* Haymarket Books.

Rumrill, P. D. Jr, Schuyler, B. R., & Longden, J. C. (1997). Profiles of on-the-job accommodations needed by professional employees who are blind. *Journal of Visual Impairment & Blindness*, *91*(1), 66–76. doi:10.1177/0145482X9709100111

Rutland, M. (2016, August 10). *NASA's 3D food printer will make pizza at amusement parks.* Vice. https://www.vice.com/en/article/aekjnb/nasas-3dfood-printer-will-make-pizza-at-amusement-parks

Ryan, M. L. (2009). Cheap plot tricks, plot holes, and narrative design. *Narrative*, *1*(17), 56–75.

Sabra, A., Bellanti, J. A., & Colón, A. R. (1998, July). Ileal-lymphoid-nodular hyperplasia, non-specific colitis, and pervasive developmental disorder in children. *Lancet*, *352*(9123), 234–235. doi:10.1016/S0140-6736(05)77837-5 PMID:9683237

Saif, H., He, Y., Fernandez, M., & Alani, H. (2016). Contextual semantics for sentiment analysis of Twitter. *Information Processing & Management*, *52*(1), 5–19. doi:10.1016/j.ipm.2015.01.005

Sailunaz, K., & Alhajj, R. (2019). Emotion and sentiment analysis from Twitter text. *Journal of Computational Science*, *36*, 101003. doi:10.1016/j.jocs.2019.05.009

Salbi, Z., & Becklund, L. (2006). *Between two worlds: Escape from tyranny: Growing up in the shadow of Saddam.* Penguin.

Salinas, D., Flunkert, V., & Gasthaus, J. (2018). *DeepAR: Probabilistic forecasting with autoregressive recurrent networks.* Cornell University. doi:10.48550/arXiv.1704.04110

Salman, A. (2019). *The wrong end of the table: A mostly comic memoir of a muslim Arab American woman just trying to fit in.* Skyhorse.

Sandoval-Almazan, R., & Valle-Cruz, D. (2020). Sentiment Analysis of Facebook Users Reacting to Political Campaign Posts. *Digital Government: Research and Practice*, *1*(2), 1–13. doi:10.1145/3382735

Santos, O. C. (2016). Emotions and personality in adaptive e-learning systems: an affective computing perspective. In *Emotions and personality in personalized services* (pp. 263–285). Springer. doi:10.1007/978-3-319-31413-6_13

Sapiński, T., Kamińska, D., Pelikant, A., & Anbarjafari, G. (2019). Emotion Recognition from Skeletal Movements. *Entropy (Basel, Switzerland)*, *21*(7), 646. doi:10.3390/e21070646 PMID:33267360

Sari, S., & Kalender, M. (2021). Sentiment Analysis and Opinion Mining Using Deep Learning for the Reviews on Google Play. *Lecture Notes in Networks and Systems, 183*(July), 126–137. doi:10.1007/978-3-030-66840-2_10

Sasson, J. (1992). *Princess: A true story of life behind the veil in Saudi* (1st ed.). Windsor-Brooke Books.

Sasson, J. (2003). *Mayada, daughter of Iraq* (1st ed.). Dutton Adult.

Sasson, J. (2010). *For the love of a son: One Afghan woman's quest for her stolen child*. Liza Dawson Associates.

Sasson, J. (2012). *American chick in Saudi Arabia*. Liza Dawson Associates.

Sasson, J. (2013). *Yasmeena's choice: A true story of war, rape, courage and survival*. LDA.

Sassoon, J. (2016). *Anatomy of authoritarianism in the Arab republics*. Cambridge University Press. doi:10.1017/CBO9781107337893

Savva, N., Scarinzi, A., & Bianchi-Berthouze, N. (2012). Continuous Recognition of Player's Affective Body Expression as Dynamic Quality of Aesthetic Experience. *IEEE Transactions on Computational Intelligence and AI in Games, 4*(3), 199–212. doi:10.1109/TCIAIG.2012.2202663

Schmidhuber, J. (2015). Deep learning in neural networks: An overview. *Neural Networks, 61*, 85–117. doi:10.1016/j.neunet.2014.09.003 PMID:25462637

Scott, W. (2021, December 7). *TF-IDF from scratch in python on a real-world dataset*. Medium. Retrieved February 20, 2022, from https://towardsdatascience.com/tf-idf-for-document-ranking-from-scratch-in-python-on-real-world-dataset-796d339a4089

Scott, J. (1988). Social network analysis. *Sociology, 22*(1), 109–127. doi:10.1177/0038038588022001007

Selvin, S., Vinayakumar, R., Gopalakrishnan, E. A., Menon, V. K., & Soman, K. P. (2017). Stock price prediction using LSTM, RNN and CNN-sliding window model. *2017 International Conference on Advances in Computing, Communications and Informatics (ICACCI)*.

Semertzidis, K., Pitoura, E., & Tsaparas, P. (2013). How people describe themselves on Twitter. *DBSocial '13: Proceedings of the ACM SIGMOD Workshop on Databases and Social Networks*, 25-30. 10.1145/2484702.2484708

Seubold, G. (1986). *Heideggers Analyse der neuzeitlichen Technik*. Alber.

Severyn, A., & Moschitti, A. (2015, August). Twitter sentiment analysis with deep convolutional neural networks. *SIGIR '15: Proceedings of the 38th International ACM SIGIR Conference on Research and Development in Information Retrieval*, 959–962. 10.1145/2766462.2767830

Shabaz, M., & Kumar, A. (2018). AS: A novel sentimental analysis approach. *International Journal of Engineering and Technology, 7*(2.27), 46-49. https://doi/org/1 doi:0.14419/ijet.v7i2.27.11679

Shafak, E. (2015). *The gaze*. Penguin Books

Shafak, E. (2017). *Three daughters of eve*. Bloomsbury Publishing USA.

Sharma, A., & Ghose, U. (2020). Sentimental analysis of twitter data with respect to general elections in India. *Procedia Computer Science, 173*, 325–334. doi:10.1016/j.procs.2020.06.038

Sharma, N. K., Ghosh, S., Benevenuto, F., Ganguly, N., & Gummadi, K. P. (2012). Inferring who-is-who in the Twitter social network. *Computer Communication Review, 42*(4), 533–538. doi:10.1145/2377677.2377782

Shears, L. A., & Shears, R. (2009). Betrayed: A terrifying true story of a young woman dragged back to Iraq (1st ed.). Academic Press.

Shen, F., Xia, C., & Skoric, M. (2020). Examining the roles of social media and alternative media in social movement participation: A study of Hong Kong's Umbrella Movement. *Telematics and Informatics*, *47*, 101303. doi:10.1016/j.tele.2019.101303

Shirbhate, A. G., & Deshmukh, S. N. (2016). *Feature Extraction for Sentiment Classification on Twitter Data*. Academic Press.

Shrestha, H., Dhasarathan, C., Munisamy, S., & Jayavel, A. (2020). Natural Language Processing Based Sentimental Analysis of Hindi (SAH) Script an Optimization Approach. *International Journal of Speech Technology*, *23*(4), 757–766. doi:10.100710772-020-09730-x

Siami-Namini, S., Tavakoli, N., & Namin, A. S. (2018). A Comparison of ARIMA and LSTM in Forecasting Time Series. *2018 17th IEEE International Conference on Machine Learning and Applications (ICMLA)*.

Sinha, S. K., & Das, K. (2016). A survey on user behavior analysis in social networks. *International Journal of Computer Science and Information Security*, *14*(11), 895–908.

Sisk, D. (1975). Simulation: Learning by doing revisited. *Gifted Child Quarterly*, *19*(2), 175–180. doi:10.1177/001698627501900225

sklearn.decomposition.NMF. (2022). Scikit-learn. Retrieved February 22, 2022, from https://scikit-learn.org/stable/modules/generated/sklearn.decomposition.NMF.html

sklearn.feature_extraction.text.CountVectorizer. (2022). Scikit-learn. Retrieved February 22, 2022, from https://scikit-learn.org/stable/modules/generated/sklearn.feature_extraction.text.CountVectorizer.html

Smith, M., Szongott, C., Henne, B., & von Voigt, G. (2012). Big Data Privacy Issues in public social media. *2012 6th IEEE International Conference on Digital Ecosystems and Technologies (DEST)*. 10.1109/DEST.2012.6227909

Smith, G. O. (1975). *Venus Equilateral: Volume One*. Futura Publications Ltd.

Snook, B., Eastwood, J., Gendreau, P., Goggin, C., & Cullen, R. M. (2007). Taking stock of criminal profiling. *Criminal Justice and Behavior*, *34*(4), 437–453. doi:10.1177/0093854806296925

Soares, C. (2003). Corporate versus individual moral responsibility. *Journal of Business Ethics*, *2*(46), 143–150. doi:10.1023/A:1025061632660

Soede, M. (1986). Innovation, braille, information and workplace design. In P. L. Emiliani (Ed.), *Development of Electronic Aids for the Visually Impaired* (pp. 37–43). Springer. doi:10.1007/978-94-009-4281-3_5

Sofian, N. B., Keikhosrokiani, P., & Asl, M. P. (2022). Opinion mining and text analytics of reader reviews of Yoko Ogawa's The Housekeeper and the Professor in Goodreads. In P. Keikhosrokiani & M. Pourya Asl (Eds.), *Handbook of Research on Opinion Mining and Text Analytics on Literary Works and Social Media* (pp. 240–262). IGI Global. doi:10.4018/978-1-7998-9594-7.ch010

Sornette, D. (2006). Endogenous versus exogenous origins of crises. In S. Albeverio, V. Jentsch, & H. Kantz (Eds.), *Extremes events in nature and society* (pp. 107–131). Springer. doi:10.1007/3-540-28611-X_5

SpaCy. (2019). *Industrial-strength natural language processing*. SpaCy. https://spacy.io/

Srividya, M., Mohanavalli, S., & Bhalaji, N. (2018). Behavioral Modeling for Mental Health using Machine Learning Algorithms. *Journal of Medical Systems*, *42*(5), 88. Advance online publication. doi:10.100710916-018-0934-5 PMID:29610979

Stieglitz, S., & Dang-Xuan, L. (2013). Emotions and information diffusion in social media – sentiment of microblogs and sharing behavior. *Journal of Management Information Systems*, *29*(4), 217–248. doi:10.2753/MIS0742-1222290408

Suhendra, N. H. B., Keikhosrokiani, P., Asl, M. P., & Zhao, X. (2022). Opinion mining and text analytics of literary reader responses: A case study of reader responses to KL Noir volumes in Goodreads using sentiment analysis and topic. In P. Keikhosrokiani & M. Pourya Asl (Eds.), *Handbook of Research on Opinion Mining and Text Analytics on Literary Works and Social Media* (pp. 191–239). IGI Global. doi:10.4018/978-1-7998-9594-7.ch009

Sultan, W. (2011). *A god who hates: The courageous woman who inflamed the muslim world speaks out against the evils of Islam*. St. Martin's Press.

Suryawati, E., Munandar, D., Riswantini, D., Abka, A. F., & Arisal, A. (2018). POS-Tagging for informal language (study in Indonesian tweets). *Journal of Physics: Conference Series*, *971*(1), 012055. doi:10.1088/1742-6596/971/1/012055

Tago, K., & Jin, Q. (2018). Influence Analysis of emotional Behaviors and user relationships based on Twitter data. *Tsinghua Science and Technology*, *23*(1), 104–113. doi:10.26599/TST.2018.9010012

Talebi, S. (2011). *Ghosts of revolution: Rekindled memories of imprisonment in Iran* (1st ed.). Stanford University Press. doi:10.1515/9780804775816

Tally, R. T. Jr. (2017). *The Routledge handbook of literature and space*. Taylor & Francis. doi:10.4324/9781315745978

Tariq, S., Akhtar, N., Afzal, H., Khalid, S., Mufti, M. R., Hussain, S., Habib, A., & Ahmad, G. (2019). A Novel Co-Training-Based Approach for the Classification of Mental Illnesses Using Social Media Posts. *IEEE Access: Practical Innovations, Open Solutions*, *7*, 166165–166172. doi:10.1109/ACCESS.2019.2953087

Tasnim, S., Sanjwal, R. K., Trisha, N. F., Rahman, M., Mahmud, S. M. F., Arman, A., Chakraborty, S., & Hossain, M. M. (2020, December 11). COVID-19 vaccination hesitancy, misinformation and conspiracy theories on social media: A content analysis of Twitter data. *SocArXiv*. Advance online publication. doi:10.31235/osf.io/vc9jb

Tavenard, R., Fouzi, J., Vandewiele, G., Divo, F., Androz, G., Holtz, C., Payne, M., Yurchak, R., Rußwurm, M., Kolar, K., & Woods, E. (2020). Tslearn, a machine learning toolkit for time series data. *Journal of Machine Learning Research*, *21*(118), 1–6. https://jmlr.org/papers/v21/20-091.html

Taxidou, I., & Fischer, P. M. (2014). Online analysis of information diffusion in Twitter. *WWW '14 Companion: Proceedings of the 23rd International Conference on World Wide Web*, 1313-1316. 10.1145/2567948.2580050

Ten threats to global health in 2019. (2019). Retrieved February 22, 2022, from https://www.who.int/news-room/spotlight/ten-threats-to-global-health-in-2019

Teoh Yi Zhe, I., & Keikhosrokiani, P. (2021). Knowledge workers mental workload prediction using optimised ELANFIS. *Applied Intelligence*, *51*(4), 2406–2430. doi:10.100710489-020-01928-5

Terán, L., & Mancera, J. (2019). Dynamic profiles using sentiment analysis and twitter data for voting advice applications. *Government Information Quarterly*, *36*(3), 520–535. doi:10.1016/j.giq.2019.03.003

The Guardian. (2020). News, sport and opinion from the guardian's US edition. *The Guardian*. https://www.theguardian.com/international

Thomas, M., & Latha, C. A. (2020). Sentimental analysis of transliterated text in Malayalam using recurrent neural networks. *Journal of Ambient Intelligence and Humanized Computing, 12*(6), 6773–6780. doi:10.100712652-020-02305-3

Tickell, A. (2007). *Arundhati Roy's the god of small things: A Routledge study guide* (1st ed.). Routledge. doi:10.4324/9780203004593

Tickell, A. (2016). *South-Asian Fiction in English: Contemporary Transformations.* Springer. doi:10.1057/978-1-137-40354-4

Tickell, A. (2020). Postcolonial Fiction and the Question of Influence: Arundhati Roy, The God of Small Things and Rumer Godden. *Postcolonial Text, 15*(1), 1–20.

Topal, K., & Ozsoyoglu, G. (2016). Movie review analysis: Emotion analysis of IMDb movie reviews. *2016 IEEE/ACM International Conference on Advances in Social Networks Analysis and Mining (ASONAM),* 1170-1176. 10.1109/ASONAM.2016.7752387

Torkkola, K. (2004). Discriminative features for textdocument classification. *Formal Pattern Analysis &Applications, 6*(4), 301–308. doi:10.100710044-003-0196-8

Törnberg, P., Andersson, C., Lindgren, K., & Banisch, S. (2021). Modeling the emergence of affective polarization in the social media society. *PLoS One, 16*(10), e0258259. doi:10.1371/journal.pone.0258259 PMID:34634056

Trained Models & Pipelines spaCy Models Documentation. (2022). Trained Models & Pipelines. Retrieved February 3, 2022, from https://spacy.io/models/

Tripathy, A., Agrawal, A., & Rath, S. K. (2016). Classification of sentiment reviews using n-gram machine learning approach. *Expert Systems with Applications, 57,* 117–126. doi:10.1016/j.eswa.2016.03.028

Trupthi, M., Pabboju, S., & Narasimha, G. (2017). Sentiment analysis on twitter using streaming API. *2017 IEEE 7th International Advance Computing Conference (IACC).*

Tsai, M., Tzeng, C., Lin, Z., & Chen, A. L. P. (2012). Discovering leaders from social network by action cascade. *SNS '12: Proceedings of the Fifth Workshop on Social Network Systems,* 1-10. 10.1145/2181176.2181188

Tsapatsoulis, N., & Djouvas, C. (2019). Opinion mining from social media short texts: Does collective intelligence beat deep learning? *Frontiers in Robotics and AI, 6*(JAN), 1–14. doi:10.3389/frobt.2018.00138 PMID:33501016

Tsugawa, S., Kikuchi, Y., Kishino, F., Nakajima, K., Itoh, Y., & Ohsaki, H. (2015). Recognizing depression from Twitter activity. *CHI '15: Proceedings of the 33rd Annual ACM Conference on Human Factors in Computing Systems,* 3187–3196. 10.1145/2702123.2702280

Tu, C., & Brown, S. (2020). Character mediation of plot structure: Toward an embodied model of narrative. *Frontiers of Narrative Studies, 6*(1), 77–112. doi:10.1515/fns-2020-0007

Tuomo, K., Niko, M., Erkki, S., & Jari, T. (2008). Comparison of Dimension Reduction Methods for Automated Essay Grading. *Journal of Educational Technology & Society, 11*(3), 275–288. https://www.jstor.org/stable/jeductechsoci.11.3.275

Turing, I. B. A. (1950). Computing machinery and intelligence-AM Turing. *Mind, 59*(236), 433–460. doi:10.1093/mind/LIX.236.433

Tutorial: Quickstart — TextBlob 0.16.0 documentation. (2022). Retrieved February 3, 2022, from https://textblob.readthedocs.io/en/dev/quickstart.html

Twitter users of Pakistan. (n.d.). *International Journal of Computer Science and Information Security, 14*(8), 855-864. https://www.researchgate.net/publication/325396654_An_Analysis_of_Twitter_users_of_Pakistan

Understanding the Infodemic and Misinformation in the fight against COVID-19. (2020). PAHO/WHO | Pan American Health Organization. Retrieved February 12, 2022, from https://www.paho.org/en/documents/understanding-infodemic-and-misinformation-fight-against-covid-19

University of Harvard. (2019). *Detrended fluctuation analysis (DFA)*. University of Harvard. http://reylab.bidmc.harvard.edu/download/DFA/intro/

UOL. (2017, June 4). *EUA ataca síria com mais de 50 mísseis*. UOL. https://noticias.uol.com.br/ultimas-noticias/ansa/2017/04/06/

US Department of Justice. (2020, September 8). *Legal considerations when gathering online cyber threat intelligence and purchasing data from illicit sources*. DOJ. https://www.justice.gov/criminal-ccips/page/file/1252341/download

Valle-Cruz, D., Fernandez-Cortez, V., López-Chau, A., & Sandoval-Almazan, R. (2020). *Does Twitter affect Stock Market Decisions? Financial Sentiment Analysis in Pandemic Seasons: A Comparative Study of H1N1 and COVID-19*. Academic Press.

Valle-Cruz, D., Lopez-Chau, A., & Sandoval-Almazan, R. (2021). How much do Twitter posts affect voters? Analysis of the multi-emotional charge with affective computing in political campaigns. *DG. O2021: The 22nd Annual International Conference on Digital Government Research*, 1–14.

Valle-Cruz, D., Criado, J. I., Sandoval-Almazán, R., & Ruvalcaba-Gomez, E. A. (2020). Assessing the public policy-cycle framework in the age of artificial intelligence: From agenda-setting to policy evaluation. *Government Information Quarterly, 37*(4), 101509. doi:10.1016/j.giq.2020.101509

Valle-Cruz, D., López-Chau, A., & Sandoval-Almazán, R. (2020). Impression analysis of trending topics in Twitter with classification algorithms. *Proceedings of the 13th International Conference on Theory and Practice of Electronic Governance*, 430–441. 10.1145/3428502.3428570

Valle-Cruz, D., López-Chau, A., & Sandoval-Almazán, R. (2022). Review on the Application of Lexicon-Based Political Sentiment Analysis in Social Media. In P. Keikhosrokiani & M. Pourya Asl (Eds.), *Handbook of Research on Opinion Mining and Text Analytics on Literary Works and Social Media* (pp. 1–21). IGI Global., doi:10.4018/978-1-7998-9594-7.ch001

Van Vugt, G. (2016). The killer idea: How some gunslinging anarchists held freedom of speech at Gunpoint. In B. V. D. Berg, S. V. D. Hof & E. Kosta. (Eds.), 3D Printing: Information Technology and Law Series (pp. 117-134). Asser Press. doi: 1 doi:0.1007/978-94-6265-096-1_7

Vayansky, I., & Kumar, S. A. P. (2020). A review of topic modeling methods. *Information Systems, 94*, 101582. doi:10.1016/j.is.2020.101582

Vincent, D. (2019). *Hong Kong protesters turn to Uber and Pokemon*. BBC News, Hong Kong. Https://Www. Bbc. Com/News/Technology-49280726

Vinciarelli, A., & Mohammadi, G. (2014). A survey of personality computing. *IEEE Transactions on Affective Computing, 5*(3), 273–291. doi:10.1109/TAFFC.2014.2330816

Volavka, J. (1999). The Neurobiology of Violence. *The Journal of Neuropsychiatry and Clinical Neurosciences, 11*(3), 307–314. doi:10.1176/jnp.11.3.307 PMID:10440006

Wadley, G., Smith, W., Ploderer, B., Pearce, J., Webber, S., Whooley, M., & Borland, R. (2014). What people talk about when they talk about quitting. *OzCHI '14: Proceedings of the 26th Australian Computer-Human Interaction Conference on Designing Futures: The Future of Design*, 388-391. 10.1145/2686612.2686671

Wagner, M. (2021). Affective polarization in multiparty systems. *Electoral Studies, 69*, 102199. doi:10.1016/j.electstud.2020.102199

Wan, C. H., Lee, L. H., Rajkumar, R., & Isa, D. (2012). A hybrid text classification approach with low dependency on parameter by integrating K-nearest neighbor and support vector machine. *Expert Systems with Applications, 39*(15), 11880–11888. doi:10.1016/j.eswa.2012.02.068

Wang, M.-H. (2020). Positioning and Categorizing Mass Media Using Reaction Emojis on Facebook. *The Computer Journal*.

Wang, Z., Ho, S.-B., & Cambria, E. (2020). A review of emotion sensing: Categorization models and algorithms. *Multimedia Tools and Applications, 79*(47-48), 1–30. doi:10.100711042-019-08328-z

Wasserman, S., & Faust, K. (2019). *Social network analysis: Methods and applications*. Cambridge University Press.

Weber, H. (2022, September 8). *How the NSA and FBI made Facebook the perfect mass surveillance tool*. https://venturebeat.com/business/how-the-nsa-fbi-made-facebook-the-perfect-mass-surveillance-tool/

Webster, S. W., & Abramowitz, A. I. (2017). The ideological foundations of affective polarization in the US electorate. *American Politics Research, 45*(4), 621–647. doi:10.1177/1532673X17703132

Wei, D., Wang, B., Lin, G., Liu, D., Dong, Z., Liu, H., & Liu, Y. (2017). Research on Unstructured Text Data Mining and Fault Classification Based on RNN-LSTM with Malfunction Inspection Report. *Energies, 10*(3), 406. doi:10.3390/en10030406

White, M. (2017). Framing travel and terrorism: Allegory in The Reluctant Fundamentalist. *Journal of Commonwealth Literature, 54*(3), 444–459. doi:10.1177/0021989417738125

Williams, G., & Mahmoud, A. (2017). Analyzing, classifying, and interpreting emotions in software users' tweets. *2017 IEEE/ACM 2nd International Workshop on Emotion Awareness in Software Engineering*, 2-7. doi:10.1109/SEmotion.2017.1

Wirtz, B. W., Weyerer, J. C., & Geyer, C. (2019). Artificial intelligence and the public sector—Applications and challenges. *International Journal of Public Administration, 42*(7), 596–615. doi:10.1080/01900692.2018.1498103

Wittenstein, S. H. (1994). Braille literacy: Preservice training and teachers' attitudes. *Journal of Visual Impairment & Blindness, 88*(6), 516–524.

Wittenstein, S. H., & Pardee, M. L. (1996). Teachers' voices: Comments on braille and literacy from the field. *Journal of Visual Impairment & Blindness, 90*(3), 201–209. doi:10.1177/0145482X9609000309

World Health Organization. (2021, April 7). *Measles outbreaks strategic response plan: 2021–2023: measles outbreak prevention, preparedness, response and recovery*. Retrieved February 16, 2022, from https://apps.who.int/iris/handle/10665/340657

Xia, R., Jia, Y., Han, Y., & Li, H. (2013). Mining users' activity on large Twitter text data. *ICIMCS '13: Proceedings of the Fifth International Conference on Internet Multimedia Computing and Service*, 214-218. 10.1145/2499788.2499809

Yamamoto, S., Wakabayashi, K., Kando, N., & Satoh, T. (2016). Who are growth users?: Analyzing and predicting intended Twitter user growth. *WAS '16: Proceedings of the 18th International Conference on Information Integration and Web-based Applications and Services*, 64-71. 10.1145/3011141.3011145

Yarchi, M., Baden, C., & Kligler-Vilenchik, N. (2021). Political polarization on the digital sphere: A cross-platform, over-time analysis of interactional, positional, and affective polarization on social media. *Political Communication*, 38(1–2), 98–139. doi:10.1080/10584609.2020.1785067

Yazbek, S. (2012). *A woman in the crossfire: Diaries of the Syrian revolution*. Haus Publishing. doi:10.2307/j.ctt1zxsm7p

Ye, Q., Zhang, Z., & Law, R. (2009). Sentiment classification of online reviews to travel destinations by supervised machine learning approaches. *Expert Systems with Applications*, 36(3, Part 2), 6527–6535. doi:10.1016/j.eswa.2008.07.035

Ying, S. Y., Keikhosrokiani, P., & Asl, M. P. (2022). Opinion Mining on Viet Thanh Nguyen's The Sympathizer Using Topic Modelling and Sentiment Analysis. *Journal of Information Technology Management, 14*, 163-183. doi: 10.22059/jitm.2022.84895

Ying, S. Y., Keikhosrokiani, P., & Pourya Asl, M. (2022). Opinion mining on Viet Thanh Nguyen's The Sympathizer using topic modelling and sentiment analysis. *Journal of Information Technology Management, 14*, 163–183. doi:10.22059/jitm.2022.84895

Yousaf, A., Umer, M., Sadiq, S., Ullah, S., Mirjalili, S., Rupapara, V., & Nappi, M. (2021). Emotion Recognition by Textual Tweets Classification Using Voting Classifier (LR-SGD). *IEEE Access: Practical Innovations, Open Solutions*, 9, 6286–6295. doi:10.1109/ACCESS.2020.3047831

Yu, S. (2013). Behavioral Evidence Analysis on Facebook: A Test of cyber-profiling. *Defendologija*, 16(33), 19–30. doi:10.5570/dfnd.en.1333.02

Yu, S. (2015). *Human trafficking and the internet. In Combating Human Trafficking: A multidisciplinary approach*. CRC Press.

Yu, S. (2020a). Predicting the writer's gender based on electronic discourse. *International Journal of Cyber Research and Education*, 2(1), 17–31. doi:10.4018/IJCRE.2020010102

Yu, S. (2020b). *The art of criminal investigation*. Kindle Publishing.

Yu, S. (2021). Cyber profiling in criminal investigation. In *Encyclopedia of Information Science and Technology* (5th ed., pp. 333–343). IGI Global. doi:10.4018/978-1-7998-3479-3.ch024

Zabelski, M. (2009). A parent's perspective on the importance of braille for success in life. *Journal of Visual Impairment & Blindness*, 103(5), 261–263. doi:10.1177/0145482X0910300502

Zafarani, R., Abbasi, M. A., & Liu, H. (2014). *Social media mining - an introduction*. Cambridge University Press. doi:10.1017/CBO9781139088510

Zhang, S., & Yoshino, K. (2007). A braille recognition system by the mobile phone with embedded camera. *Second International Conference on Innovative Computing, Information and Control, ICICIC*, 223–223. doi:10.1109/ICICIC.2007.4

Zou, H., Tang, X., Xie, B., & Liu, B. (2015). Sentiment classification using machine learning techniques with syntax features. *2015 International Conference on Computational Science and Computational Intelligence (CSCI)*, 175-179. 10.1109/CSCI.2015.44

Zucco, C., Calabrese, B., Agapito, G., Guzzi, P. H., & Cannataro, M. (2020). Sentiment analysis for mining texts and social networks data: Methods and tools. *Wiley Interdisciplinary Reviews. Data Mining and Knowledge Discovery*, *10*(3), e1333. doi:10.1002/widm.1333

About the Contributors

Pantea Keikhosrokiani received the Bachelor of Science degree in electrical and electronics engineering, the master's degree in information technology from the School of Computer Sciences, Universiti Sains Malaysia (USM), Malaysia, and the Ph.D. degree in service system engineering, information system. She was a Teaching Fellow with the National Advanced IPv6 Centre of Excellence (Nav6), USM, where she is currently a Senior Lecturer with the School of Computer Sciences. Her recent books are published by Elsevier and IGI Global. She is Professional Technologist with the Malaysia Board of Technologist (MBOT). Her research interests include information systems, business intelligence, health and behavioral analytics, opinion mining, and technopreneurship.

Moussa Pourya Asl is a Senior Lecturer in literary studies at Universiti Sains Malaysia, where he also obtained his PhD (English Literature) from School of Humanities. His primary research area is in diasporic literature and gender and cultural studies, and he has published several articles in the above-mentioned areas in Women's Studies, Gender, Place & Culture, Asian Ethnicity, American Studies in Scandinavia, Cogent: Arts & Humanities, Gema Online, and 3L.

* * *

Syed Asif Ali, BSc, MS (Computer Science), MIBM (Industrial & Business Mathematics) M.Sc. (Organic Chemistry), PhD (Artificial Intelligence), is an educator, author, and researcher in artificial intelligence. He is currently working as Professor at the Department of Artificial Intelligence, Sindh Madressatul Islam University, Karachi, Pakistan, a public sector university. He has a non-conventional and diverse academic background. He has a Master of Science in Computer Science, a Master of Industrial and Business Mathematics, a Master of Science in Organic Chemistry, and a PhD in Artificial Intelligence. In 2012, he was appointed as the first Professor at the Faculty of Information Sindh Madressatul Islam University, Karachi, Pakistan. Professor Ali has more than two decades of experience in professional teaching and research. He is the inaugural Dean of the Faculty of Information Technology for the period of six years (2015-2018 & 2018-2021). In 2018, he established the Department of Artificial Intelligence & Mathematical Sciences. Over the past 25 years, Professor Ali has dedicated his life to understanding how artificial intelligence can be used to enhance the lives of Special Need People (SNP) and make them capable of decision-making. His research interests include Artificial Intelligence, software engineering, ICT for Special Needs Persons (SNP), cognitive science, educational technology, educational psychology, and digital social networks. His literary work, computer software, entitled "Use of Information and Communication Technology (ICT)/Computer Science for Special People'', Sindh, Karachi, Pakistan was registered patent/copyright in the year 1998 by the Intellectual Property Organization (IPO) of Pakistan. (Registration Number: 35297) and received two awards for this achievement. He provides overarching leadership in academic policy development and implementation. He has been associated with various international and national higher academic boards of different universities and organisations. Since 2022, he has served as a convener for research committees. He is the author of "Information and Communication Technology for Special Education: Application of Artificial Intelligence Techniques, Theory of Automata, and Special Education Software Development" and "Computer Graphics: A Practical Approach for Beginners. "published in Germany Professor Ali has supervised more than 400 projects, MS theses, and PhD MS students. His recent research projects are "Artificial Intelligent Approach for Down Syndrome Individuals", "Improve the Growth of Prawn, Shrimp, and Lobsters in Artificial Environments" and "Improving Agriculture using AI".

Anupama Angadi is working as Associate Professor in the Information Technology department, at Anil Neerukonda Institute of Technology(ANITS), Bheemunipatnam, Visakhapatnam. She was awarded Ph.D. in 2016 from Adikavi nannaya university, Rajahmundry, and M.Tech from GITAM in 2009. She has 14 years of teaching experience. Her research areas of interest are Deep learning, Big Data Analytics, and Social Network Analysis. She is a certified faculty from Wipro to train the students in java based technologies. She has completed 20+ Moocs courses from Coursera, NPTEL, Big Data University, etc.

Nur Ain Nasuha Anuar is pursuing her master degree in English Literature at School of Humanities, Universiti Sains Malaysia.

Kah Em Chu received her Master of Science (Data Science & Analytics) from the School of Computer Sciences, Universiti Sains Malaysia (USM), Malaysia.

Abdikadir Hussein Elmi received the Master of Science (Data Science & Analytics) from the School of Computer Sciences, Universiti Sains Malaysia (USM), Malaysia.

Annuur Farahhim received the master's degree in data science and analytics from School of Computer Sciences, Universiti Sains Malaysia.

Satya Keerthi Gorriparti currently working as an Associate Professor, CSE, Gayatri Vidya Parishad College of Engineering(A), Visakhapatnam. He received Ph.D from Andhra University and M.Tech from GITAM. He has 13+ years of experience in teaching. His areas of interests are Recommender systems, Social Network Analysis, BigData Analytics. He is certified as Educator for leading Android Educator program. He got certifications in online courses offered by NPTEL and Coursera. He published 20+ research papers in Journals and conferences.

Keng Hoon Gan is a senior lecturer in School of Computer Sciences, Universiti Sains Malaysia. She received her Ph. D. degree from Universiti of Malaya (UM) in 2013. She is currently the Cluster Head of Data to Knowledge cluster at the School of Computer Sciences. She was the Program Manager of Research Ecosystem and Innovation at the School of Computer Sciences from 2019-2021. Her domains of specialization include information retrieval, structured retrieval, structured document representation and query optimization. She has initiated a research platform SIIR (Semantics in Information Retrieval

@ ir.cs.usm.my) which is a research initiative related to semantically enhanced information retrieval, and its related applications.

Lamartine Nogueira Frutuoso Guimarães earned his Ph.D. in Nuclear Engineering from The University of Tennessee, Knoxville, TN in 1992. He has been a Researcher at the Institute for Advanced Studies since 1984. He has been a full researcher since 1992, and has served as head of the Nuclear Energy Division from 2005 to 2021. Also has been a professor at the graduate level of Applied Computing at the National Institute for Space Research in Applied Artificial Intelligence since 1998, teaching the disciplines of Artificial Intelligence and Intelligent Control Theory. Additionally, is a professor at the graduate level of Space Science and Technology at the Aeronautical Institute of Technology in Space Propulsion and Hypersonics, having as research line Nuclear Propulsion, since 2012, teaching the disciplines Nuclear Power Generation in Space and Nuclear Systems. He is also a full professor at Universidade Paulista since 2015. He teaches courses of Computer Science, Computer Engineering, Systems Analysis and Development, Artificial Intelligence, Mathematics for Computing, Computable Systems, and Basic Physics. He worked for 9 years at Faculdade de Tecnologia São Francisco in the Control and Automation Engineering course. He worked for 2 years at the IBTA College in the Decision Making course. He worked for 13 years at Universidade Braz Cubas, in basic physics, numerical calculus, transport phenomena, advanced calculus, linear algebra, analytic geometry and artificial intelligence. He received 2 awards and/or honors. He received the Santos Dumont Medal of Merit, in 2009. Between 1994 and 2008 he coordinated 6 research projects. Currently, he coordinates 4 scientific projects. He works in the area of Nuclear Engineering, with emphasis on Dynamic Simulation of Systems and Processes. In his "Lattes" curriculum the most frequent terms in the contextualization of scientific, technological and artistic-cultural production are: nuclear technology applied to space, numerical simulation, liquid metal cooled reactor, nuclear microreactor technology, fast reactor, applied nuclear technology and AI in aerospace and nuclear applications (fuzzy logic, genetic algorithms, neural networks, deep learning, big data, data mining, computer vision, defense analysis using threat emotion analysis in social medias and their combinations). Since 2008, he is the manager and was the creator of the TERRA - Advanced Fast Reactor Technology project, which aims to research the key technologies of advanced high-temperature fast microreactors, planned to be used in space nuclear propulsion. His main current interest is in the application of nuclear technology in space exploration, such as: space nuclear propulsion, nuclear reactors as a power source for facilities, satellites and space vehicles, Radioisotope Thermoelectric Generators and IA applications in space and defense.

Marilyn Minicucci Ibañez received her PhD in Applied Computing at the National Institute for Space Research in the area of Machine Learning, with emphasis in sentiment analysis. Master in Applied Computing, with emphasis in image analysis, from the National Institute for Space Research and Bachelor in Computer Science from the Federal University of Itajubá. Moreover, has already worked as a substitute teacher in basic, technical, and technological education at the Federal Institute of São Paulo. She has also worked in the area of software analysis, development, and testing in companies.

Noman Islam, did PhD in Computer Science from National University of Computer and Emerging Sciences, Karachi. Then, he completed a PostDoc in Information Technology from University of Kuala Lumpur, Malaysia. He is currently working as a Professor at Karachi Institute of Economics and

Technology, Karachi. His research interests are deep learning, cloud computing, and wireless and ad hoc networks.

Nurul Najiha Jafery has finished her master's degree in Master of Science (Data Science& Analytic) from School of Computer Sciences, Universiti Sains Malaysia. Currently, she is perusing her PhD at the Centre for Electrical Engineering Studies, Universiti Teknologi Mara (UiTM).

Rimsha Javed received her Bachelors of Science in Computer Science degree from Mohammad Ali Jinnah University (MAJU) in 2020. She is pursuing a Master's degree in Computer Science at Mohammad Ali Jinnah University (MAJU). Currently, she has been engaged at Mohammad Ali Jinnah University (MAJU) as a faculty member of Computer Science for the last 2 years. Her areas of research include data mining, machine learning, natural language processing, and social media analysis.

Chun Keat Kng received Master of Science (Data Science & Analytics) from School of Computer Sciences, Universiti Sains Malaysia (USM).

Asdrúbal López-Chau, Ph.D. in Computer Science, Master in Computer Engineering, and M.S. in Communications and Electronics Engineering for National Polytechnic Institute (IPN). He is currently an Associate Professor at the Autonomous University of the State of Mexico (UAEM). His research interests include machine learning, data mining, computer vision and embedded systems. His scientific production includes more than 12 articles with impact factor and more than 8 book chapters in international publishers. He is a reviewer of articles in JCR journals and has participated in several research projects in Mexico. He is a member of the Mexican National Council of Science and Technology – CONACyT.

Patruni Muralidhara Rao obtained the degree of B. Tech (Computer Science and Engineering), JNTUK, Kakinada, India, in 2012. He obtained the degree of M. Tech (Software Engineering), JNTUH, Hyderabad, India, in 2014. He is currently working as Assistant Professor in School of Computer Science and Engineering at Vellore Institute of Technology, Vellore. He is an active member of IEEE and IAENG professional bodies. His research interests include wireless sensor networks and networks security. His research interests include Network Security, Intelligent Secure systems, and Machine Learning. He has good publication record in well reputed journals, conferences and books.

Reinaldo Roberto Rosa was technician in Electronics and Telecommunications (ITJ-1982). Graduated in Physics and Astronomy at the Federal University of Rio de Janeiro (1988), MS (1991) and PhD (1995) in Astrophysics and Space Science from INPE with research conducted at the University of Maryland, USA (SW-CNPq scholarship) from Nov 1993 to Nov 1995. He did post-doctoral research in Computational Space Physics at Nagoya University (1997) under FAPESP sponsorship. Created the Nucleus for Simulation and Analysis of Complex Systems in the Laboratory of Computation and Applied Mathematics (LABAC) at INPE as a FAPESP young researcher fellow in an emerging center (1998-2002). He is a full time S&T civil servant at LABAC-INPE-MCTIC, hired in 2002, 40 hours regime, where he works as a professor of the Post-Graduation Course in Applied Computing (CAP). He was Coordinator of PG of CAP (2003-2004/2012-2013). Former Secretary General of SBMAC (2003-2005). He is a Council

Member of the Pan-American Association of Interdisciplinary Computational Sciences. He is Deputy Head of LABAC-INPE. Chair of COSPAR (2012/2014/2016).He has experience in Space Science and Technology, with emphasis on Applied Computing, working mainly on the following topics: statistical physics of nonlinear processes, computational physics for simulation and signal analysis, Big Data and Artificial Intelligence Technologies. In the last eight years he has been dedicated to computational space physics, with focus on Data Science and HPC. He works in R&D with a predominantly interdisciplinary profile having published about 90 articles in international journals and 02 books. Collaborates on projects with institutional partnerships in Brazil and abroad, with emphasis on applied computing (machine learning and neurocomputing with pyCUDA and R) to space physics and environmental physics. He is Principal Investigator (PI) of FAPESP Thematic Project (Case No. 14/11156-4). He is a member of the advisory committee for evaluation of FAPESP's PIPE Program.

Rodrigo Sandoval-Almazan is Associate Professor of Social and Political Sciences Faculty of the Autonomous University of the State of Mexico (UAEM) based in Toluca, México. He has been professor of the Graduate School of Public Administration (EGAP) and Business Administration (EGADE) of the Institute of Technology and Superior Studies of Monterrey (ITESM), Campus Estado de Mexico. He is a member of the National Researchers System Level 2. He has authored or coauthored more than 30 research papers and the book Building Digital Government Strategies (2017). In 2013 he won the 2nd Latin American Award for Public Administration (INAP). Dr. Sandoval Almazan is a member of Mexican Academy of Science and some editorial boards of e-government journals such as Government Information Quarterly, IJPADA. His research interests include e-government metrics, public innovation, information technology organizations, social media in government, and open government.

Pedada Saraswathi obtained the degree of B. Tech (Computer Science and Engineering), JNTUK, Kakinada, India, in 2014. She obtained the degree of M. Tech (Computer Science and Engineering), JNTUK, Kakinada, India, in 2016. Currently, She is working as Assistant Professor in the Computer Science and Engineering department, GITAM Institute of Technology, GITAM University, Visakhapatnam, India. She is currently pursuing doctoral studies at GITAM University, Visakhapatnam, India. Her research interests include wireless sensor networks and networks security. Recently, she has published around five articles in SCIE and Scopus indexed journals and published more than five book chapters in Elsevier Academic Press.

Sylvia Shiau Ching Wong was a Data Science postgraduate student at Universiti Sains Malaysia (USM). She received her Master of Science (Data Science & Analytics) from the School of Computer Sciences of USM in 2022.

Jing-Ru Tan was a Data Science postgraduate student at Universiti Sains Malaysia (USM). He received his Master of Science (Data Science & Analytics) from the School of Computer Sciences of USM in 2022. Past Business and Data Analyst with Fitbit in San Francisco, USA. Currently a Lean Deployment Executive with ViTrox Sdn. Bhd.

Tien-Ping Tan received his PhD in 2008 from Université Joseph Fourier, France. He is currently a senior lecturer in School of Computer Sciences, Universiti Sains Malaysia. Dr. Tan's research interests are automatic speech recognition, machine translation, and natural language processing.

David Valle-Cruz, Ph.D., is an Assistant Professor at the Universidad Autónoma del Estado de México. He is a member of the National Research System and the i-Lab México. David is a Computer Engineer and a Computer Scientist; he holds a Ph.D. in Economics and Management. He has been a visiting researcher at the Center for Technology in Government (CTG), SUNY Albany, NY, and at the Computer Science and Multi-AgentSystems Laboratory of CINVESTAV, Guadalajara, Mexico. His articles have been published in leading journals, including Government Information Quarterly, Cognitive Computation, First Monday, Information Polity, and the International Journal of PublicSector Management (among others). His research interests are related to Applied Artificial Intelligence, Data Science, and Emerging Technologies.

Szde Yu is an associate professor with the School of Criminal Justice at Wichita State University. His research interests include criminology, computer forensics, and cyber security. His specialization areas include intelligence analysis, digital investigation, cyber profiling, and elite data machine learning (as opposed to big data).

Ally Zlatar holds a BFA in Visual Art & Art History from Queen's University & an MLitt Curatorial Practice and Contemporary Art from the Glasgow School of Art. Her Doctorate of Creative Arts is with the University of Southern Queensland focusing on embodied experiences of eating disorders in contemporary art. Zlatar is a Lecturer at the University of Glasgow (Anderson College, GIC). She has taught at KICL London, and University of Essex (UEIC).

Index

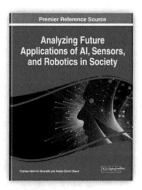

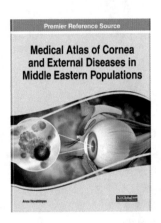
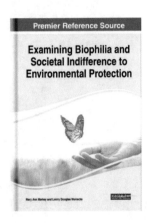
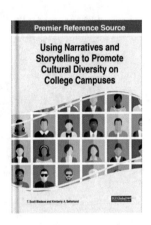

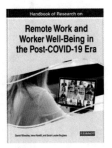

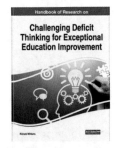